Business Cycles

AND

National Income

EXPANDED EDITION

Business Cycles AND *National Income*

EXPANDED EDITION

ALVIN H. HANSEN

LUCIUS N. LITTAUER PROFESSOR OF POLITICAL ECONOMY, EMERITUS, HARVARD UNIVERSITY

With a revised bibliography by

RICHARD V. CLEMENCE

WELLESLEY COLLEGE

W · W · NORTON & COMPANY · INC · *New York*

Library of Congress Catalog Card No. 63-21708

Published simultaneously in the Dominion of Canada by George J. McLeod Limited, Toronto

PRINTED IN THE UNITED STATES OF AMERICA
FOR THE PUBLISHERS BY THE VAIL-BALLOU PRESS, INC.

1 2 3 4 5 6 7 8 9

TO

Lois, Eric, *and* Randall

Preface to the Expanded Edition

This edition (1964) of *Business Cycles and National Income* includes the whole of the 1951 edition (Parts I–IV) in unaltered form and adds five new chapters (Part V). This new material presents a survey and analysis of the four recessions and recoveries which we have witnessed in the American economy in the period 1948–1963.

The first two recoveries were buoyant; the second two anemic. The first two cyclical upswings carried the economy close to the full-employment ceiling; the last two lacked "steam," leaving the economy, even at the "peak" levels, considerably below the country's growth potential.

One of the two full-fledged recoveries came in the Truman Administration; the other in the first Eisenhower Administration. One of the two weak recoveries came in the second Eisenhower term, and one in the Kennedy Administration. But the Kennedy recovery has turned out to be a long recovery though well below full employment levels.

Public policy was not the main factor. Spontaneous forces, rather than deliberate policy, account for the high level employment and rapid growth in the first two recoveries. These automatic, expansionist forces exhausted themselves and remained at a low ebb throughout the period of the last two cycles. So long as the expansionist forces dominated, unemployment averaged over the entire period of the first two cycles only 4 per cent of the labor force. Once these forces subsided, however, the unemployment rate rose to an average of 6 per cent in the two-cycle period 1957–1963.

Now we are about to witness, we hope, an exciting new venture. At the moment when this Preface is being written, we do not yet know what Congress may or may not do. A bill is being pressed by the Administration in Congress designed to forestall the recession which past business cycle experience tells us may be imminent early in 1964. The bill if passed would make a major cut in individual and corporate income taxes, amounting to about $10 billion per year—this cut to be implemented in two installments, the first to be effective in January 1964 and the second one year later.

If the bill finally passes the Congress and is signed by the President, it will be the first time, as far as I know, that the U.S. Government has carried through a program *in advance,* designed to *prevent* the next recession. We are familiar with programs designed to halt a recession that has already reached serious proportions. But never before have we undertaken an anti-recession program while recovery was still on the way.

It could be an interesting spectacle to observe how it might all come out. The tax cut might indeed do the trick so far as 1964 and 1965 go. But it is likely to take much more than this to conquer, once and for all, the age-long recurring periodic recessions.

What are the probable limits within which the tax cut may prove to be effective? This problem is analyzed in the new Chapter 35. And what further policies will be necessary to keep full "steam" up (over the longer-term trend) in the economic boiler?

Part V contains also a theoretical chapter (36) on economic growth and a practical policy chapter (37) on inflation and balance of payments, together with a discussion of the relations of these two currently burning problems to the business cycle.

It appears evident, based to be sure on limited experience, that the postwar business cycle swings have become more moderate. Credit for this would probably be given by most students of the cycle to the built-in stabilizers. Rapid growth trends, especially in Western Europe, have profoundly influenced the pattern of postwar cycles. In the United States, however, there is a tendency on the part of business forecasters to relate cycle movements to the previous peak rather than to the potential growth trend.

November, 1963 Alvin H. Hansen

Preface

The twentieth century has been filled with cataclysmic upheavals—two destructive world wars and a world-shaking depression. Institutions—economic, social, and political—which seemed fixed and enduring have been undergoing drastic transformation. The rapid flow of events is carrying all modern societies over dangerous waters into new and uncertain terrain. Pioneering in the social frontiers of the twentieth century is more hazardous than was the adventure into the geographic frontiers of the nineteenth century. In addition to the difficult problem of welding the modern social order into a cohesive and workable structure, there is the overwhelming task of establishing a peaceful and neighborly world order in which a humane and enlightened civilization can again grow and flourish.

In the interwar years we had abundant unused economic and social resources, but we did not have the wisdom to apply them to our many urgent needs. Out of the experiences of the depression we were just beginning—though still in the kindergarten stage—to apply new, and still unproved, business-cycle policies. Then came the Second World War with its wartime ravages, its postwar shortages, and the fearful postwar cold war. We are now so busy in attempting to strengthen this war-shattered world that we have not the resources to do many of the things we had hoped to accomplish on a more adequate scale.

This book is intended as a modest contribution to a better understanding of the current theory and historical development of macro-economics—that branch of economic analysis which deals with the general level of output and income in the economic system as a whole. It deals with the business cycle, the national income, the modern theory of employment, and the evolution of economic thinking on these problems.

Part I presents the historical development of fluctuations in the United States. Monthly, quarterly, and annual data are presented on general cyclical movements, and charts are shown for each major cycle from 1865 to the present. This method of presentation enables the reader, it is hoped, to compare and contrast one cycle with another, and to see in a general way the unique characteristics of each. Among the differences which are disclosed between major cycles are the presence or absence of minor recessions during the general upswing phase, the varying length of the upswing, the time required for recovery, and the sweep and speed of the upswing movement.

Each major cycle is also set off against the background of the longer building cycles. Similarly, several major cycles are projected against the background of the grand cycle of railroad construction culminating in the 1880's, and in this connection the growth and decline of dominant industries in relation to cyclical fluctuations is discussed.

Consideration is given to the unique development of each major cycle against the background of long-run secular movements. The implications of these trends, in terms of technological and monetary factors, for cyclical fluctuations are discussed. Finally a number of charts disclose the relation of different categories of investment outlays to the general business cycle.

Part II is devoted to the modern theory of income and employment and its relation to the theory of cyclical fluctuations. Special emphasis is given to the analytical tools developed by Wicksell, Aftalion, and Keynes. It begins with an analysis of the gross national product and its component parts, together with a comprehensive exposition of the four accounts in the nation's economic budget. There follow several chapters dealing with the theory of investment determination, the consumption function, the multiplier, the interrelations between the multiplier and the accelerator, and finally the role of government outlays, together with the effects of different methods of financing, on the income flow. Numerous charts and diagrams are used to show the interrelationships involved in modern income analysis.

Parts I and II are intended to give the reader a realistic and concrete picture of the nature of the business cycle and to illuminate the causes of these fluctuations by the aid of the modern theory of income determination.

Part III provides a survey of the historical development of business-cycle theories.[1] This is a task that very much needs to be done. Keynesian economics did indeed represent in some respects a revolution in economic thinking. Yet it had its deep roots in a long development of macro-economic thinking. Keynesian economics is sometimes viewed as a sharp break with the past. Part III reveals that this is not the case. The roots of the Keynesian consumption analysis (the consumption function and the multiplier) go back to the early nineteenth century, notably to Lord Lauderdale and Malthus. Yet the gap between Keynes and his predecessors is very great, and it is in this area that Keynes made his most brilliant and significant contribution. Much less generally recognized is the vast importance of the Continental development of the theory of investment demand and the role of investment in income formation—the work of Wicksell, Tugan-Baranowsky, Spiethoff, Schumpeter, and Cassel—a development largely overlooked by English-speaking economists until it became incorporated as a basic cornerstone of the Keynesian theory. Even now the connection between the Keynesian theory and Continental thinking is not widely appreciated. Yet Keynesian economics is the logical outgrowth of the Continental development. A knowledge of the business-cycle theories as they emerged on the Continent in the fifteen-year period 1898–1913 is vitally important for any broad understanding of Keynesian economics.[2]

Part III, it is hoped, will help to disclose the essential continuity of macro-economic thinking. Monetary economics dealing with the general level of prices, business-cycle theory dealing with fluctuations in aggregate output and employment, and finally

[1] The most authoritative work on cycle theory is the internationally famous volume by Professor G. Haberler, *Prosperity and Depression,* League of Nations, 3rd ed., 1941.

[2] In this connection see the survey of the Continental theoretical development given in Chapter IV of Alvin H. Hansen, *Business-Cycle Theory* (Ginn and Company), published in 1927.

the more inclusive modern theory of income determination—all these fall in the area of macro-economics.

Econometric contributions to business-cycle analysis (Tinbergen, Frisch, Samuelson, Hicks, etc.) are considered in connection with the theory of income determination in Part II; and also in Chapters 21, 22, and 23 of Part III. Basic to many of these formulations is the brilliant theoretical work of Aftalion, whose analysis forms the starting point for leading econometric models. In this connection, I am particularly happy to include an authoritative and brilliant chapter on "Econometrics in Business-Cycle Analysis" (Chapter 22) by Dr. Richard M. Goodwin, Assistant Professor of Economics, Harvard University.

With respect to the development of theory, the method applied is to put the spotlight on some twenty-five to thirty prominent economists who have either made important contributions to our subject or at least have aroused fruitful controversy. Thus the works of individual thinkers are made to stand out as landmarks on the way. But individuals are grouped with kindred spirits. Thus the attack is made not by individuals alone but by battalions.

Part IV deals with business-cycle policy. Comparison is made between policies dominant in the twenties and modern cycle policy. Detailed consideration is given to the President's Economic Reports and to various current proposals, including pronouncements on cycle policy by widely representative groups of outstanding economists. An appraisal is made of past efforts (and failures) at forecasting, and current attempts to find "anticipators," or at least early recognition of where the economy stands in the cycle movement. Finally, a chapter is devoted to international aspects of business-cycle policy.

I wish again, as on former occasions, to express appreciation for facilities made available by the Graduate School of Public Administration of Harvard University, and for stimulating discussions with graduate students and colleagues in the Department of Economics. I am especially indebted to Miss Helen Poland for faithful assistance in the preparation of this volume.

Alvin H. Hansen

Cambridge, Mass.

Contents

Part III. Business-Cycle Theory

Part IV. Business Cycles and Public Policy

Part V. Prosperity and Recession since the Second World War

List of Charts

PART ONE

The Nature of Business Cycles

1 · *Some Preliminary Concepts*

Growth and Upheaval

At the halfway point in the twentieth century, two characteristics of the American economy stand out in bold relief. One is the impressive demonstration of the growth in productive capacity. The physical output of goods and services, in round numbers, was nearly sixfold greater in 1950 than in 1900, and on a per capita basis it was over three times greater. The American economy had become an industrial giant. Its performance in the Second World War amazed the entire world.

The second striking fact about our economy is the titanic upheavals through which it has passed in this fateful half-century. The national income has been carried up and down, and up again, in massive tidal waves from $30 billion in 1910 to $87 billion in 1929; then down to $40 billion in 1933, and up to $225 billion in 1948. Wholesale prices, climbing from an index of 65 in 1911 to 155 in 1920, tumbled down to 65 in 1932, only to top the former yearly peak at 165 in 1948. Employment has surged from 36 million in 1911 to 48 million in 1929; back to 39 million in 1932 and up to 61 million in 1948. To describe movements of such magnitude by such terms as "oscillations" or "cycles" seems to be an understatement. In the twentieth century the "cycle" has indeed been swamped by colossal upheavals. The older and more colorful terminology may perhaps appear more appropriate—boom and slump, inflation and deflation, crisis and stagnation, upsurge and collapse. In the kind of world we have lived in, one almost hesitates to write a book about business *cycles.*

The Cycle and Structural Balance

The suggestion is frequently encountered nowadays that the business cycle reveals a pathological condition in the economy which can readily be cured if certain structural adjustments are made. If a wage-price balance is found, if labor-management relations are improved, if the tax structure is reformed, et cetera, the economy will be in a sufficiently healthy state, it is said, to resist any tendency to fluctuate violently. This is, however, a dangerous illusion. Structural balance in the economy is indeed important for the healthy functioning of the economy. But the tendency to fluctuate is not a pathological disease. It is an inherent characteristic of the private enterprise, market economy. To stabilize it requires something more than structural adjustments; it requires a deliberate and positive anti-cyclical program.

Definition of the Cycle

Wesley Mitchell, in his *Business Cycles: The Problem and Its Setting* (1927) defined business cycles as a fluctuation in aggregate economic activity. The most all-inclusive manifestation of aggregate economic activity is the real income, or output, of a nation. Closely related thereto is the volume of employment. As output and employment fluctuate, prices will in varying degree change in response to changes in aggregate demand and in marginal costs. Changes in output and prices together reflect changes in the total money value of all goods and services produced. The business cycle consists, then, of fluctuations in: (1) employment, (2) aggregate output, (3) prices, and (4) money value of the national product. Since the last item—money value of the national product—is a composite of the second and third items—output and prices—we suggest the following definition: the business cycle is a fluctuation in (1) employment, (2) output, and (3) prices (both consumer and wholesale prices).

Cyclically, these three move more or less in consonance, particularly employment and output. In the recovery from deep depression, output and employment may rise rapidly with little increase in prices. Toward the end of the boom output and employment may rise very little, while prices may rise more rapidly.

The cyclical fluctuations (monthly data) of industrial produc-

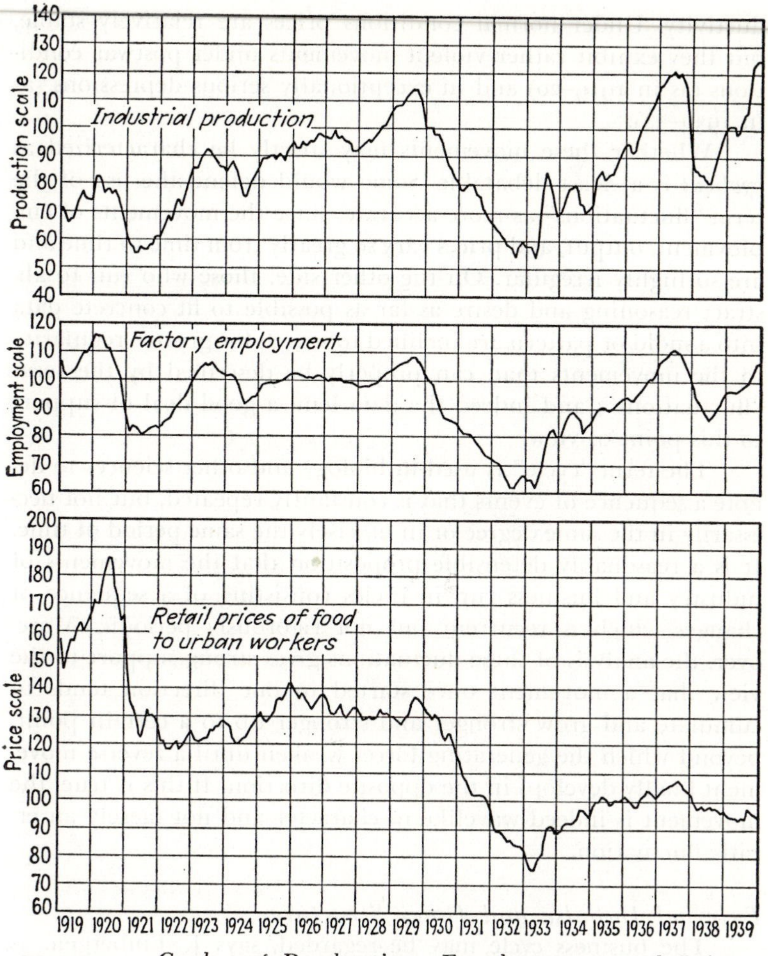

FIGURE 1. *Cycles of Production, Employment, and Prices*

Source: (a) Production: Federal Reserve Board
(b) Employment: Bureau of Labor Statistics
(c) Prices: Bureau of Labor Statistics

tion, employment, and retail food prices are presented in Figure 1. Very similar are the short-run fluctuations of output and employment. From decade to decade, however, production rises more than employment, owing to long-run increases in per worker productivity. Under normal conditions prices are relatively stable, but they exhibit rather violent movements under postwar conditions (as in 1919–20) and in exceptionally serious depressions (as in 1930–34).

Whether these movements may strictly be characterized as *cyclical* is at least debatable. Some would defend the use of the term "fluctuations" as more accurate, since the movements of employment, output, and prices vary so greatly from time to time and are so highly irregular. On the other side, those who run to abstract reasoning and desire as far as possible to fit concrete data into a mold or pattern are inclined to search for greater regularity in the movements than can properly be described by the term "fluctuations"; and indeed the data lend a good deal of support to this point of view.

The term "cycle" is used in biology and other sciences to denote a sequence of events that is constantly repeated, but not necessarily in the same degree or in precisely the same period of time. It is a reasonably defensible proposition that the movements of industry and business run in cycles consisting of a sequence of changes which is recurrent but not rigorously periodic. Moreover, the analysis of these fluctuations gives strong support to the view that a movement once started in one direction tends to cumulate and grow stronger and stronger up to a certain point, beyond which the generating forces weaken until a reverse movement finally develops in the opposite direction. If this is true, the movement is indeed wavelike in character and not merely an erratic fluctuation.

External Impulse and Inner Structure

The business cycle may be regarded, says J. Tinbergen, as the interplay between erratic shocks and an economic system able to perform cyclical adjustment movements to such shocks.[1]

A similar conception is expressed by Ragnar Frisch.[2] Impulses from outside operate upon the economy, causing it to move in a

---

1 J. Tinbergen, review of Burns and Mitchell, *Measuring Business Cycles,* in *Erasmus,* 1947, pp. 627–630.

2 Ragnar Frisch, *Noen Trekk av Konjunkturlaeren,* Forlagt av H. Aschehang & Co. (W. Nygaard), Oslo, 1947, pp. 72–73.

wavelike manner, just as an external shock will set a pendulum swinging.[3] But it is the "inner structure of the swinging system" which determines the length of the wave movement. The oscillations of the system may have a high degree of regularity, even though the impulses which set it going are quite irregular in their behavior.

A. C. Pigou, in his *Industrial Fluctuations*,[4] presents a similar view of the cycle. For any industrial wave movement we may expect to find some initiating impulse. Such an initiating impulse, when it comes into play, operates upon a certain complex of economic conditions. Given the impulse, these conditions will determine the nature of the effect produced, and they are, in this sense, causes of industrial fluctuations.

Phases of the Cycle

Among various conceptions of the cycle—in terms of a succession of phases, one phase leading into another—two will be singled out here for brief comment.

Burns and Mitchell [5] regard the *peaks* and *troughs* as the critical mark-off points in the cycle. From this standpoint the greater part of the cycle can be divided into two main parts: (a) the *expansion* phase, extending from trough to peak, and (b) the *contraction* phase, extending from peak to trough. There are, moreover, the lower and upper turning points, of relatively short duration. At the lower turning point, *revival* is happily hatched and grows rapidly into the long expansion phase. At the upper turning point, *recession* grips the economy, and soon develops into the contraction phase. Thus the cycle is regarded as consisting of four closely interrelated phases: (1) revival, (2) expansion, (3) recession, and (4) contraction.

Schumpeter, on the other hand, believes that the critical mark-off points are to be found, not in the peaks and troughs of

---

[3] An analogy of this type was first suggested by Wicksell. See Ragnar Frisch in *Economic Essays in Honour of Gustav Cassel*, George Allen and Unwin, Ltd., London, 1933, p. 198.

[4] A. C. Pigou, *Industrial Fluctuations*, Macmillan & Co., Ltd., London, 1927, pp. 7–9.

[5] Arthur F. Burns and Wesley C. Mitchell, *Measuring Business Cycles*, National Bureau of Economic Research, New York, 1946.

the cycle, but at or near the points of inflection. These he designates as "neighborhoods of equilibrium." The Schumpeterian model may be graphed as in Figure 2.

A, B, and C are the points of inflection, around which cluster the areas or "neighborhoods" of equilibrium. The farther the economy moves up (or down) away from the neighborhood of equilibrium, the stronger become the forces which stop the cumulative upward (or downward) movement and pull it back toward the area of equilibrium. In the portion of the cycle extending

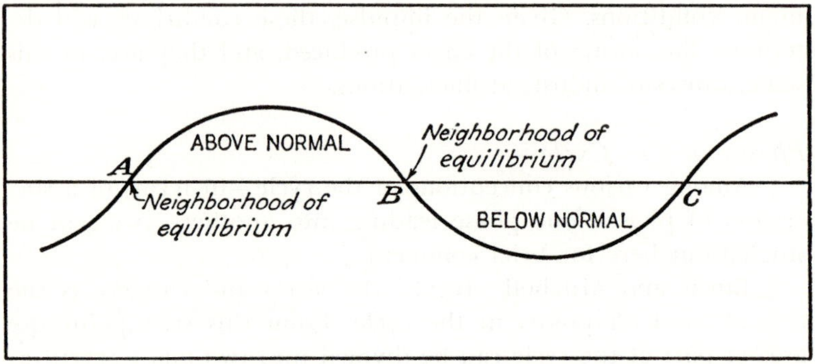

FIGURE 2. *Schumpeter's Neighborhoods of Equilibrium*

from A to B, economic activity is running above normal, and this period may be regarded as the "good" years; in the period extending from B to C, economic activity is running below normal, and this phase may be regarded as the "bad" years.

Schumpeter's analysis involves the *four-phase cycle:* (1) prosperity, (2) recession, (3) depression, (4) recovery.[6]

The "upper" half of the four-phase cycle is divided into two parts: (a) prosperity, and (b) recession. In the "prosperity" phase,

---

[6] As a first approximation, Schumpeter suggests a two-phase cycle consisting simply of (a) prosperity and (b) recession. In the prosperity phase the system, under the impulse of entrepreneurial activity, draws away from the neighborhood of equilibrium. In the recession phase (a period of adaptation which necessarily follows from prosperity) the system draws toward another equilibrium position. In the two-phase cycle the system does not fall below normal; expansion occurs when equilibrium has been reached following directly after the recession phase.

employment will continue to increase, but at a slackening rate, until the peak of the cycle is reached. In the "recession" phase, employment will decrease at an accelerating rate until the point of inflection is reached. From here on the cycle moves into the "lower" half of the four-phase cycle, and this also may be divided into two phases: (a) depression, and (b) recovery. During the "depression" phase, employment will go on decreasing, but at a gradually decreasing rate, until the trough of the cycle is reached. During the "recovery" phase employment will increase at an increasing rate up to the point of inflection.[7] The four-phase cycle model may be graphed as in Figure 3.

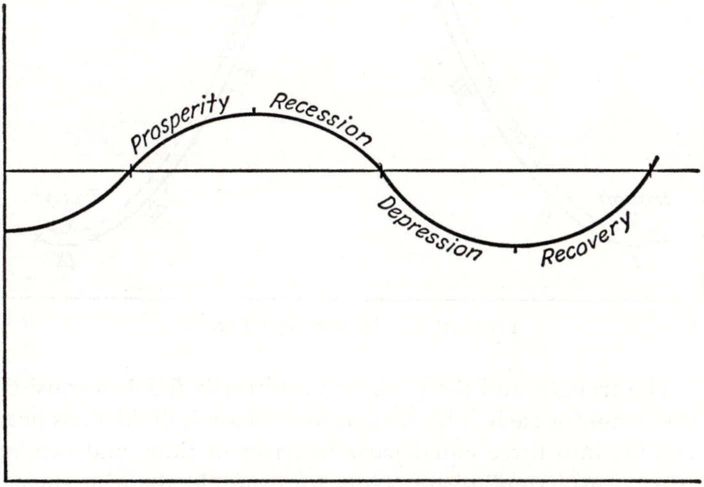

FIGURE 3. *Schumpeter's Four-Phase Cycle*

For Burns and Mitchell, the turning points are regarded as more meaningful than Schumpeter's cumulative processes which oscillate around the neighborhoods of equilibrium. In *Measuring Business Cycles,* they divide each complete cycle from trough to trough inclusive into nine stages. The trough, from which the cycle starts, is designated by the Roman numeral I, the trough in which the cycle is terminated is designated by IX, and the peak by

[7] J. A. Schumpeter, *Business Cycles,* McGraw-Hill Book Co., New York, 1939, Vol. I, pp. 207–209.

V. The "expansion" phase is divided into three stages, designated by II, III, and IV; and the "contraction" phase is similarly divided into three stages, designated by the numerals VI, VII, and VIII. This model may be graphed as in Figure 4.

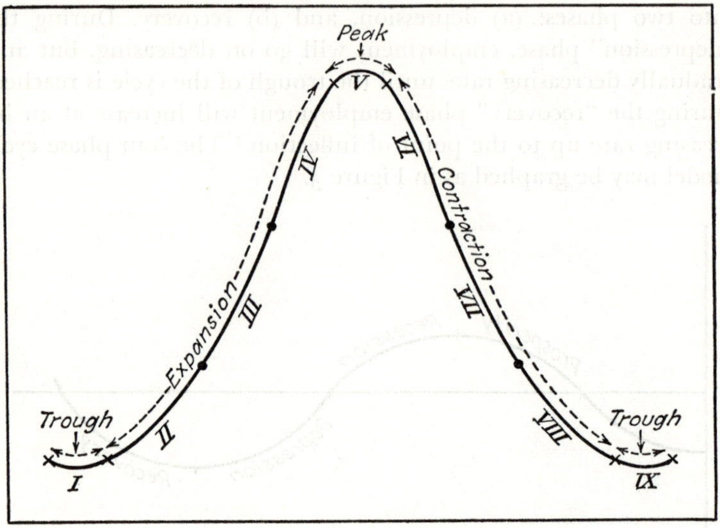

FIGURE 4. *Reference Dates*

The troughs and the peaks are arbitrarily fixed as consisting of three months each. The "expansion" phase is divided, as nearly as can be, into three equal parts in terms of time, and similarly for the "contraction" phase. Thus, for example, the nine stages in the 1904–08 cycle are set out as follows:

TABLE I

Stage	*Number of Months*	*Period*
I	3	July–Sept. 1904
II	11	Sept. 1904–July 1905
III	10	Aug. 1905–May 1906
IV	11	June 1906–April 1907
V	3	April–June 1907

TABLE I (*continued*)

Stage	*Number of Months*	*Period*
VI	4	June–Sept. 1907
VII	4	Oct. 1907–Jan. 1908
VIII	4	Feb.–May 1908
IX	3	May–July 1908

Burns and Mitchell first seek to discover the troughs and peaks of general economic activity. Then the interval studied is marked off into periods of general business expansion and contraction, as indicated for the 1904–08 cycle above, and similarly for each other cycle. After fixing definite dates for the troughs and peaks of successive business cycles, a study is made of the behavior of each particular statistical series (for example, pig iron production) within the cycles of general economic behavior.

Reference and Specific Cycles

Each particular time series—bond yields, clearings, stock prices, shares traded, freight car orders, and many others—is fitted into the nine stages of the general business cycle. This makes the "reference cycle" for each series. The average figure for freight car orders, for example, for the entire reference cycle is expressed as 100, and the figures for each of the nine stages are reduced to percentages of this average. A typical reference cycle for each series can then easily be computed by averaging the index numbers for each of the nine stages over several successive cycles.

In addition, each particular series is analyzed into "specific" cycles marked off by the troughs and peaks of that particular series. Each such cycle is divided into nine stages. Again, the successive specific cycles for each series are averaged into a "typical" specific cycle.

These relationships are illustrated in Figure 5, where a specific cycle (an average of 18 cycles of stock prices) is plotted against a reference cycle (an average of 19 cycles).

The low and high points of the reference cycle of any particular series may not correspond to the reference date troughs and peaks of the general business cycle. By comparing the typical or average *reference* cycles of various particular series with the

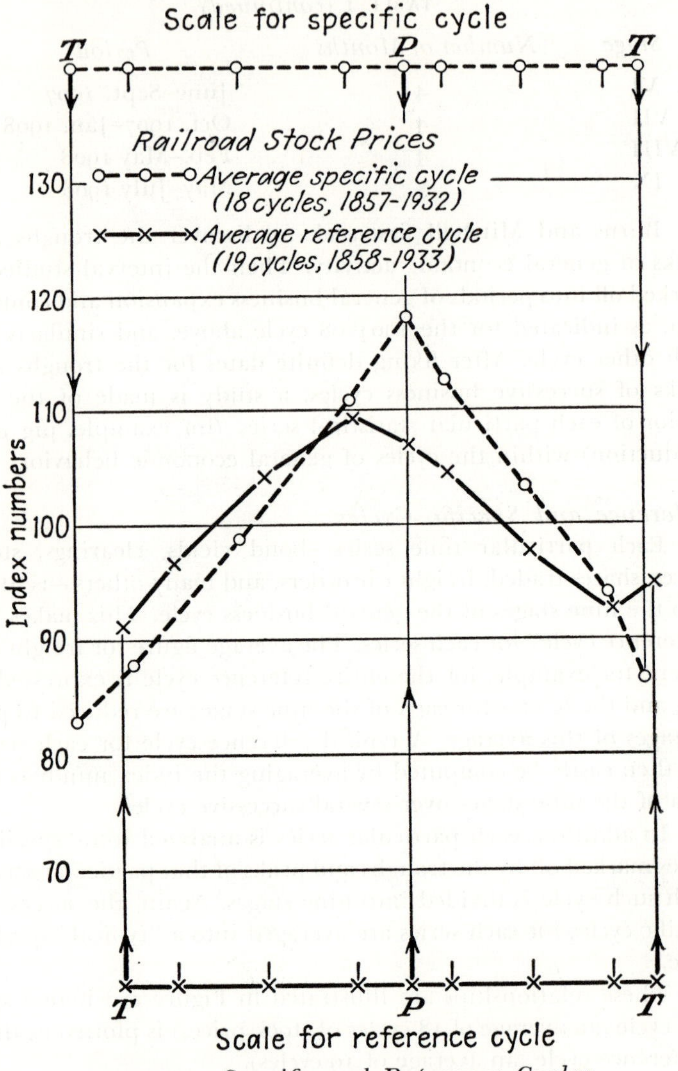

FIGURE 5. *Specific and Reference Cycles*

Data from Burns and Mitchell, *Measuring Business Cycles,* National Bureau of Economic Research, 1946, pp. 378–379.

specific cycles, leads and lags, timing and amplitude, can be studied; and this type of analysis is emphasized by Burns and Mitchell. Similarly, comparison may be made between specific cycles.

In Figure 6 the reference cycles of (a) pig iron production and (b) railroad bond yields are plotted on the nine reference dates of the general business cycle extending from August, 1904, to June, 1908 (with peak in May, 1907). The reference cycle for pig iron production reached its high point in Stage VI and low point in Stage VIII; and for railroad bond yields the low point was reached in Stage II and the high point in Stage VII. Thus pig iron led the general business cycle at the lower turning point, but lagged behind at the upper turning point.

The analysis of leads and lags is doubtless of value for the study of oscillations. Some students of business cycles have, however, questioned the validity of multi-cycle averages, which purport to disclose the "typical" cyclical behavior over many cycles of any particular series. They hold that by compressing the data into the rigid mold of nine stages in each cycle, and then averaging these figures over several cycles which in fact may be widely different, an artificial picture is given of the diverse movements of economic activity. For example, Burns and Mitchell treat the war expansion of 1914–18 in the same manner as any other period of expansion. Likewise, the terrific world depression of 1929–33 is averaged in with other periods of contraction, despite the fundamentally different character of this particular depression.[8]

Of great importance is the study of leads and lags in order to discover "indicators" of the cyclical turning points. In 1938, Mitchell and Burns published *Statistical Indicators of Revivals,*[9] and this study was elaborated by Geoffrey H. Moore in his *Statistical Indicators of Cyclical Revivals and Recessions.*[10] If it is found that certain series (for example, new orders for durable goods) usually lead at both turning points, this fact may prove of value in predicting reversals or at least in recognizing reversals more

[8] See Lloyd Metzler's review of Burns and Mitchell's "Measuring Business Cycles" in *Social Research,* September, 1947, pp. 370–377.

[9] Bulletin 69, National Bureau of Economic Research.

[10] Occasional Paper 31, National Bureau of Economic Research.

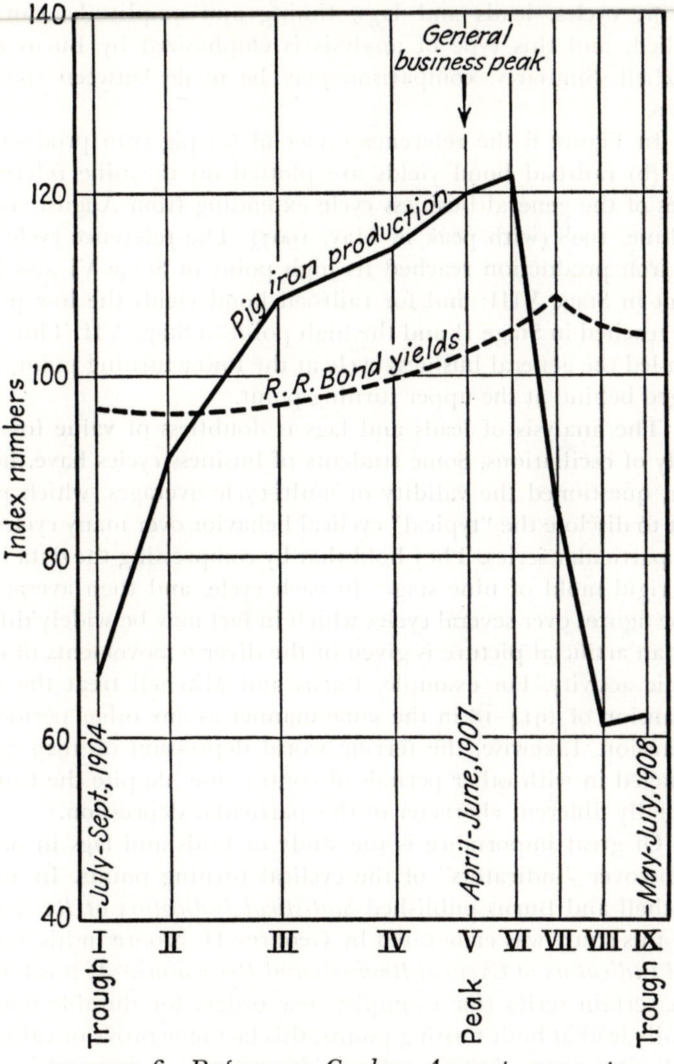

FIGURE 6. *Reference Cycles: August, 1904, to June, 1908*

Data from Burns and Mitchell, *Measuring Business Cycles*, National Bureau of Economic Research, 1946, pp. 530, 533.

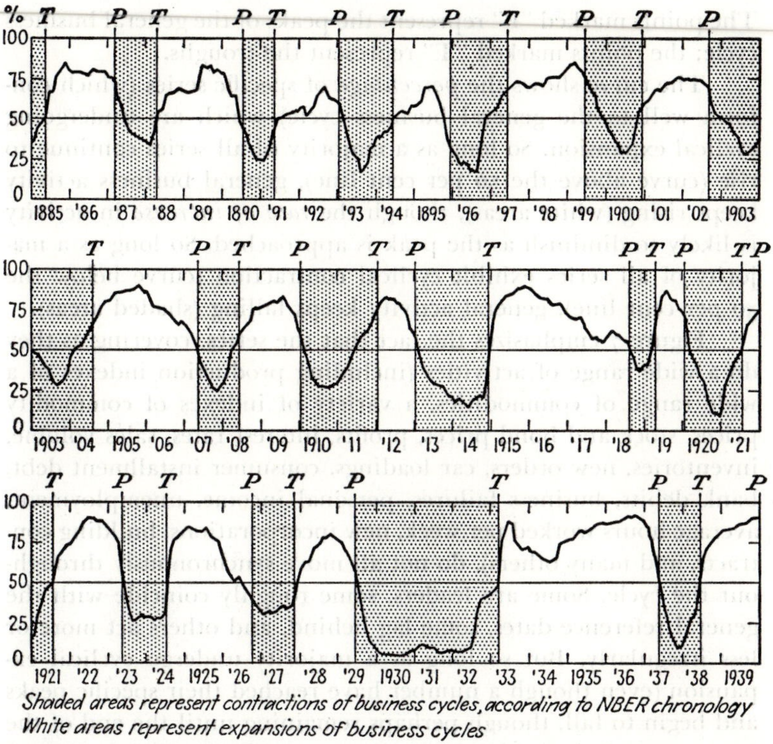

FIGURE 7. *Cyclical Expansion and Contraction. (The curve shows the* percentage *of economic time series undergoing cyclical expansion. The T's and P's indicate troughs and peaks respectively in the general business cycle.)*

This chart is reproduced by permission of the National Bureau of Economic Research from *New Facts on Business Cycles*, 30th Annual Report, by Arthur F. Burns.

promptly. In Chapter 30 of this book a brief analysis will be made of the work of the National Bureau of Economic Research, and that of other investigators, on this problem.

A comprehensive view of the reference dates for the general business cycles, according to the chronology of the National Bureau of Economic Research, is presented in Figure 7. The white areas represent periods of expansion of general business activity; the shaded areas represent periods of general business contraction.

The points marked "P" represent the peaks of the general business cycle; the points marked "T" represent the troughs.

The curve shows the *percentage* of specific series (which conform well to the general business cycle) which are undergoing cyclical expansion. So long as a majority of all series continue to rise (curve above the 50 per cent line), general business activity keeps rising (white areas), though the *rate of increase* in activity is likely to diminish as the peak is approached. So long as a majority of all series exhibit cyclical contraction (curve below the 50 per cent line), general activity keeps falling (shaded areas).

Figure 7 emphasizes the fact that the series, covering as they do a wide range of activities (including production indexes of a wide range of commodities, a variety of indexes of commodity prices, stock and bond prices, profits, interest rates, sales volume, inventories, new orders, car loadings, consumer installment debt, bank debits, business failures, personal income, unemployment, average hours worked per week, new incorporations, building contracts, and many others), do not all move synchronously throughout the cycle. Some are leaders, some roughly coincide with the general reference dates, some lag behind, and others act more or less irregularly. But so long as a majority undergo cyclical expansion (even though a number have reached their specific peaks and begin to fall, though perhaps remaining until the end of the boom at a relatively high level), the economy as a whole will tend to experience general expansion.

2 · *Major and Minor Cycles*

Fluctuations in the Rate of Investment

The upward and downward movements which together make business cycles are commonly believed to be mainly associated with fluctuations in the volume of real investment. We distinguish between real investment and financial investment. When one purchases a share in a corporate enterprise, a bond, a mortgage, or title to a house already built, one is making a *financial* investment. When one, however, invests in the construction of new capital goods—a house or a factory or a machine—one is making a *real* investment. Financial investment involves the transfer of ownership of income-yielding claims—equities, corporate securities, and government securities. Real investment involves *capital formation*—net additions to the total stock of capital goods of all kinds.

We have noted the view that the upswing and downswing movements of income, output, and employment are mainly characterized by fluctuations in the rate of real investment. Fluctuations in income, output, and employment involve, of course, more than fluctuations in real investment alone. Consumption also rises and falls with the cycle movement, but less violently *proportionately* than the rise and fall of real investment. Moreover, consumption rises or falls, in large part, in response to movements in real investment, though to some extent—particularly with respect to consumers' durable goods, such as automobiles—the movements are of a more or less independent or autonomous character.

We distinguish real investment from consumption in a more or less arbitrary manner, though following conventional terminology. By real investment we mean the purchase of capital goods. These include: (1) producers' goods, comprising (a) industrial, public utility, and commercial *plant* and *equipment,* and (b) *inventories* of stocks of goods in process or held for future sale; (2) residential building; and (3) public works, such as public buildings, roads, and public improvement projects of all kinds. Under consumption we include the purchases of (a) durable consumers' goods, such as automobiles and household equipment, (b) semidurable consumers' goods, such as clothing, (c) nondurable consumers' goods, such as food and the like, and (d) personal services.

The most general, all-inclusive statement of the essential character of cyclical movements is that they consist in an increase or decline, as the case may be, in the purchase of real investment goods and of durable consumers' goods as defined above. But these fluctuations induce a rise and fall of general consumption expenditures, and so income rises and falls by a magnified amount. While the role of durable consumers' goods plays an increasingly important part, it is nevertheless true that the causes of business fluctuations are to be found mainly in the factors which bring about a rise and fall in the rate of real investment. This analysis will be developed with the necessary qualifications in subsequent chapters.

Major and Minor Cycles

Quite commonly, particularly in the United States, the term "business cycle" is applied with reference not only to what is called the *major* cycle but also to the *minor* cycle. And the term "depression" is often applied to both minor recessions and major depressions. In Europe, when a "business cycle" or "trade cycle" is spoken of, reference is usually made to what we call the major cycle.

Special attention will be given in this chapter to the major cycle. But it is not possible in doing so to overlook the fact that, particularly in the expansion phase of the major cycle, there often occur, especially in American experience, one or two (sometimes more) interruptions to the upswing movement. As we shall see below, from 1865 to 1938 we have had seven major cycles. Later we shall give special attention to the war and postwar upheaval, 1939–50. But our account begins with the interval between the Civil War and the Second World War. In this period, one major upswing was interrupted by one minor recession, three upswings were interrupted by two minor recessions, and one by three minor recessions, while two upswings swept through the whole expansion phase without any significant interruption. Only one major downswing was interrupted by a minor recovery. Thus in this 73-year period there were altogether 18 cycles in the United States—7 major cycles and 11 minor cycles.[1]

Apart from outlays on consumers' durables (which we shall consider later) the cycle upswing can be characterized essentially as an expansion in the rate of real investment. For the purpose currently in hand, it is useful to classify real investment into the two categories suggested above: (a) *fixed capital,* including plant, equipment, and residential construction; and (b) *inventories* of stocks of goods and raw materials, semifinished and finished.

When an upsurge in real investment occurs, it is not unusual for the spurt in inventory accumulation to run ahead of the normal requirements indicated by the rising tide. When this is the case, sooner or later a temporary saturation in inventory accumulation develops, leading to an inventory recession. Not infrequently the minor setbacks experienced in the major upswings may be characterized as inventory recessions. But sometimes other situations may initiate or aggravate these minor recessions. Thus, for example, at the beginning of a major upswing, large investment in special cost-reducing machinery may have been made, and after a time a temporary saturation may have been reached, leading to a short recession. If, however, a general condition of buoyancy prevails, the economy will soon start upward again with a further burst of real investment in fixed plant and residential building despite the temporary setback. Sometimes special situations are responsible for minor recessions, such as critical international developments, labor disturbances, or even special factors

[1] Burns and Mitchell, in *Measuring Business Cycles,* similarly find 18 cycles from 1867 to 1938.

having to do with major industries, such as the Ford shutdown in 1927. Apart from these special circumstances, one can regularly look for *inventory* movements to play an important role in the minor cycle.

While major expansions often suffer one or two temporary setbacks before the major peak is reached, very rarely, as we have noted, is the downswing of the major cycle interrupted by a temporary revival. One notable exception was the short recovery which occurred in 1895 in the midst of the major depression extending from 1893 to 1897. The brief recovery was, however, swamped by the powerful adverse factors at work, and so the economy fell back, after a weak spurt, into a deep depression. This is, it seems, the only case, since the Civil War at any rate, of a temporary upturn sufficiently pronounced to make a noticeable impact upon the annual data in the downswing phase of the major cycle.

As already noted, in the majority of cases prolonged periods of expansion have been interrupted by minor depressions or setbacks. A continuous upswing extending without interruption beyond a period of about four years has rarely occurred, and generally the period of uninterrupted upswing is somewhat shorter. From this we may conclude that a major upswing represents typically a discontinuous, jerky spurt in the rate of real investment. An upsurge of real investment proceeds in the usual case by fits and starts. In particular, as we have noted, it is difficult in the upswing period, when demand and prices are rising, to hold inventory accumulation to an appropriate pace. The fluctuation in inventory investment appears to be the leading cause of the minor cycle.

The major cycles, from trough to trough, vary in length from a minimum of six years to a maximum of thirteen years. If we include all the minor peaks and depressions as well as the major ones, the eighteen cycles thus defined from 1865 to 1938 range in length, from trough to trough, from a minimum of two years to a maximum of nine years. Three years is the model figure, and thirteen of the eighteen cycles fall within the range of three to five years.

The Heavy Industries

Fluctuations of *output* in manufacturing reflect the business cycle pretty accurately. With respect to agricultural prosperity and depression, on the other hand, it is basically fluctuations in agricultural *prices* that are relevant. The movements of agricultural prices, in turn, are largely determined by the fluctuations in the aggregate demand of urban communities for agricultural products. Thus the prices of agricultural products correlate very closely with the purchasing power of urban workers, and this depends basically upon the volume of employment. In the short run (i.e., within the limits of any one business cycle) the employment of urban workers fluctuates very closely with industrial or manufacturing output. Accordingly, fluctuations in the output of manufacturing industries reflect fairly accurately the ebb and flow of prosperity or depression for both the industrial and the agricultural population. These together may be regarded as the primary producing groups.

Account must of course also be taken of the ancillary workers employed in trade, finance, transportation, communications, and the service industries. Most of these workers are largely engaged in activities relating to the sale and transportation of goods and commodities arising from manufacture or agricultural production. This is of course less true of the service industries and some other branches of economic activity. Nevertheless, the economic prosperity of all of these groups is heavily conditioned by the fortunes of manufactures and of agriculture.

Thus it appears that the business cycle is peculiarly a manifestation of the industrial segment of the economy from which prosperity, or depression, is redistributed to other groups in the highly interrelated modern society. More than that, it is particularly one segment of the economy, namely the heavy goods industries, that is peculiarly susceptible to violent cyclical fluctuations. We have noted above the view that the essential characteristic of the business cycle is the fluctuation in the rate of real investment. And real investment means the manufacture of machinery and all kinds of business equipment, together with the manufacture of a vast range of materials and finished products entering into residential, commercial, and industrial structures. A great expansion in the rate of real investment necessarily entails a large increase in the output of that segment of the manufacturing industry which produces durable commodities—iron and steel, lumber, metals and metal products other than iron and steel, railway and transportation equipment, and the like.

Pig iron production, being basic to the manufacture of durable goods, can be used as a means to give a quick, general survey of business-cycle fluctuations. Moreover, pig iron production is also a good index of the tremendous growth of modern industry. Figure 8 shows both the *growth* and the *oscillations* of pig iron production (based on quarterly data) in the United States from 1877 to 1938.

Spiethoff, Cassel,[2] and other distinguished cycle theorists have placed great emphasis upon the role of pig iron production in the modern economy. More broadly, the data on the output of *durable* manufactured products can be regarded as a dependable index of the business cycle, and as means of marking off the troughs and the peaks.

Fortunately, at long last, we have the exhaustive and painstaking research of Edwin Frickey on production in the United States from 1860 to 1914.[3] And from 1919 on, we have the production figures of the Federal Reserve Board. The intervening period can be filled in by using the data provided by Solomon Fabricant.[4] Both the Frickey and the F.R.B. data provide a breakdown of manufacturing production into durable and nondurable goods. Thus we have a nearly continuous index of durable manufactures from 1860 down to the present.

Seven Major Cycles

On the basis of the fluctuations in the output of durable goods, seven major booms and depressions stand out in bold relief. The dates for the peaks and the troughs, together with the percentage decline in output, are given in Table II.

---

[2] See Chapter 16 in this book.

[3] Edwin Frickey, *Production in the United States, 1860–1914,* Harvard University Press, Cambridge, 1947.

[4] Solomon Fabricant, *The Output of Manufacturing Industries, 1899–1937,* National Bureau of Economic Research, New York, 1940.

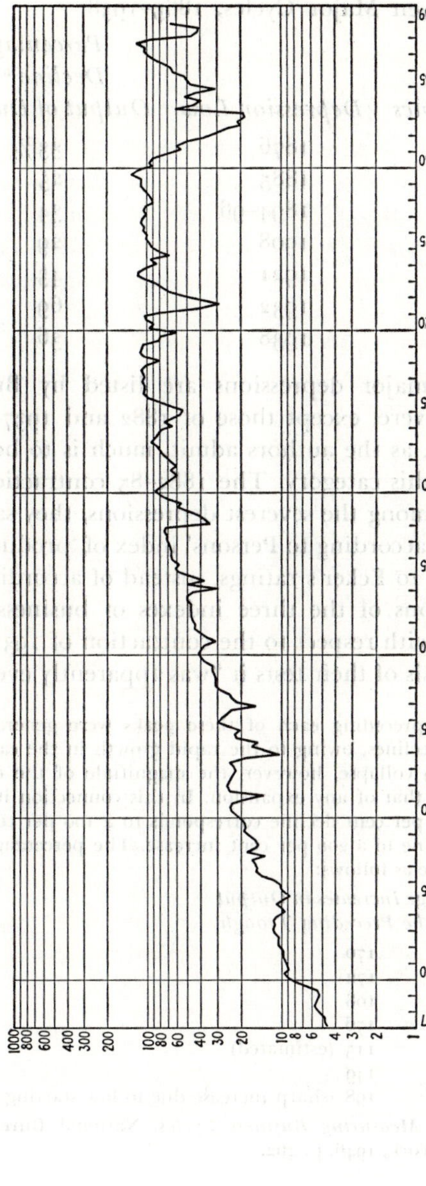

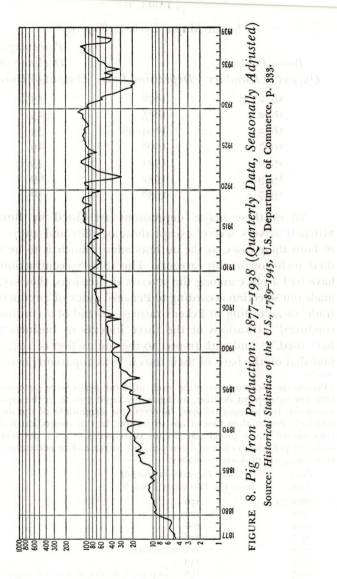

FIGURE 8. *Pig Iron Production: 1877–1938 (Quarterly Data, Seasonally Adjusted)*

Source: *Historical Statistics of the U.S., 1789–1945*, U.S. Department of Commerce, p. 333.

TABLE II

Seven Major Cycles, 1865–1938

Boom Peak in Output of Durables	*Depression Low*	*Percentage Decline[5] in Output of Durables*
1872–73	1876	33%
1882	1885	25
1892	1894–96	34
1907	1908	29
1920	1921	43
1929	1932	69
1937	1938	36

All of these major depressions are listed by Burns and Mitchell as very severe, except those of 1882 and 1937—though in both these cases, as the authors admit, much is to be said for their inclusion in this category. The 1882–85 contraction would have had a place among the severest depressions, they say, "if we made our selection according to Persons' index of 'production and trade' or according to Ecker's ratings, instead of according to the combined indications of the three indexes of business that we have used." [6] And with respect to the contraction of 1937–38 they find that on the basis of their tests it "was apparently even severer

[5] Percentage increases preceding each of these peaks were generally greater than the subsequent declines, owing to the rapid growth in the capital goods industries. In the 1929 collapse, however, the magnitude of the decline was relatively greater than that of any expansion. In this connection it should be remembered that a 50 per cent decline corresponds to a 100 per cent increase and a 67 per cent decline to a 200 per cent increase. The percentage increases from trough to peak are as follows:

Peak Year	*Percentage Increases in Output from the Preceding Trough*
1872–73	170
1882	172
1892	108
1907	176
1920	115 (estimated)
1929	149
1937	198 (sharp increase due to low starting point)

[6] Burns and Mitchell, *Measuring Business Cycles,* National Bureau of Economic Research, New York, 1946, p. 462.

than that of 1920–21; so that once again we get one severe depression following upon another." [7] On the basis of their own analysis, therefore, it is difficult to see why these two depressions should be excluded from the list of serious contractions.

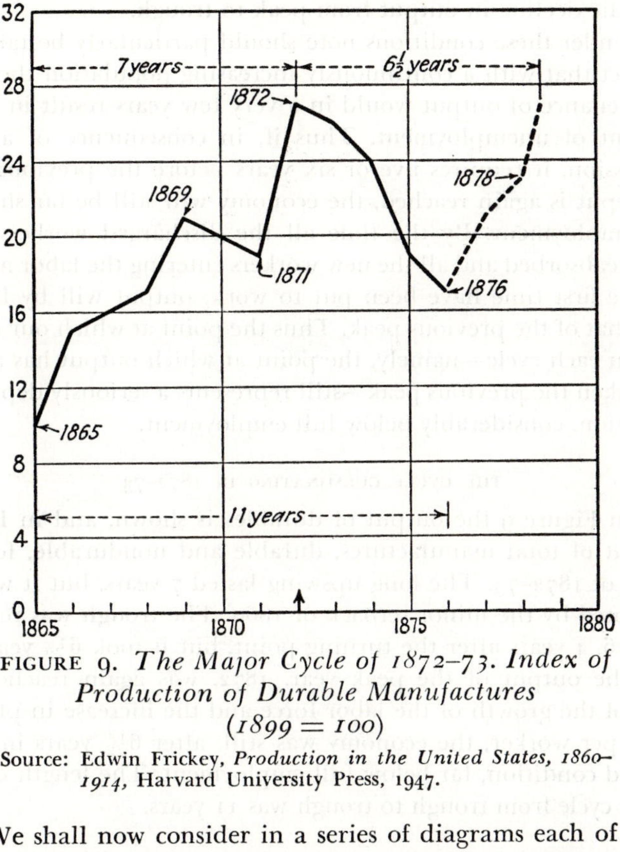

FIGURE 9. *The Major Cycle of 1872–73. Index of Production of Durable Manufactures (1899 = 100)*

Source: Edwin Frickey, *Production in the United States, 1860–1914,* Harvard University Press, 1947.

We shall now consider in a series of diagrams each of these major cycles. In each case we present the data on output for the full upswing, the downswing, and also the interval following the depression low in which production remains below the peak previously reached. The data are presented uncorrected for secular trend so as to reveal the long-run upsurge of an economy dis-

7 *Ibid.*, pp. 462–464.

playing a rapid rate of growth in terms both of increase in the labor force and of technical progress. The trend of output rises rapidly by reason of the increase in the number of workers and also because of increasing productivity per worker. Thus the increase in output from trough to peak is regularly far greater than the decline in output from peak to trough.

Under these conditions note should particularly be taken of the fact that with a continuously increasing population the mere maintenance of output would in a very few years result in a vast amount of unemployment. Thus if, in consequence of a deep depression, it requires five or six years before the previous peak in output is again reached, the economy will still be far short of full employment. By the time all the discharged workers have been reabsorbed and all the new workers entering the labor market for the first time have been put to work, output will by far exceed that of the previous peak. Thus the point at which our charts stop in each cycle—namely, the point at which output has at last overtaken the previous peak—still represents a seriously depressed condition, considerably below full employment.

THE CYCLE CULMINATING IN 1872–73

In Figure 9 the output of durables is shown, and in Figure 10 that of total manufactures, durable and nondurable, for the boom of 1872–73. The long upswing lasted 7 years, but it was interrupted by the minor setback of 1869. The trough was reached in 1876, 4 years after the turning point, but it took 6½ years before the output of the peak year, 1872, was again reached. In view of the growth of the labor force and the increase in productivity per worker, the economy was still, after 6½ years in a depressed condition, far below full employment. The length of this major cycle from trough to trough was 11 years.

THE CYCLE CULMINATING IN 1882

Significantly different is the general shape of the major cycle of 1882 (see Figure 11). The long upswing of 6 years (as vigorous as that of 1872) was uninterrupted by any minor recession. The downswing was shorter, reaching the trough in 3 years, while the

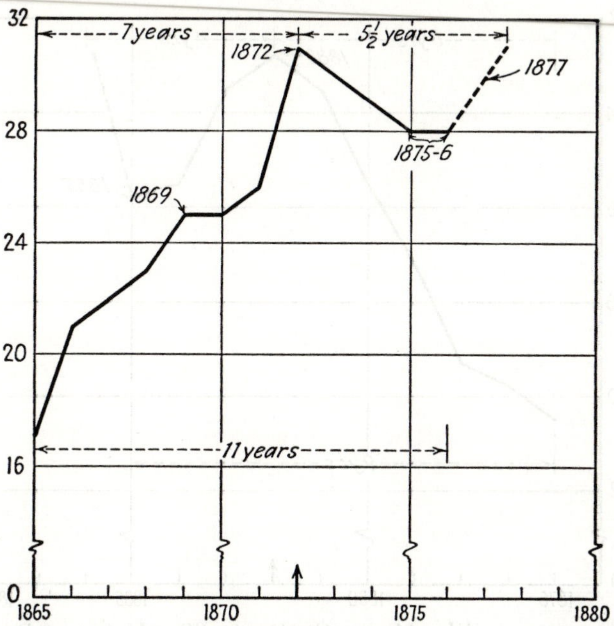

FIGURE 10. *The Major Cycle of 1872–73. Index of Production of Manufactures: Durables and Non-durables (1899 = 100)*

Source: Edwin Frickey, *Production in the United States, 1860–1914*, Harvard University Press, 1947.

output recovered the level of the peak year 1882 after only 4 years of depression. The length of this cycle from trough to trough was 9 years.

THE CYCLE CULMINATING IN 1892

The major cycle of 1892 (Figure 12) presents a very interesting picture, radically different from those of 1872–73 and 1882. The increase in output from trough to peak was significantly less, percentagewise, than in the two earlier cycles. The upswing was interrupted by two minor recessions. The decline in output was very severe, equaling, percentagewise, the drastic cut in production following 1872–73. It required 5½ years before the output

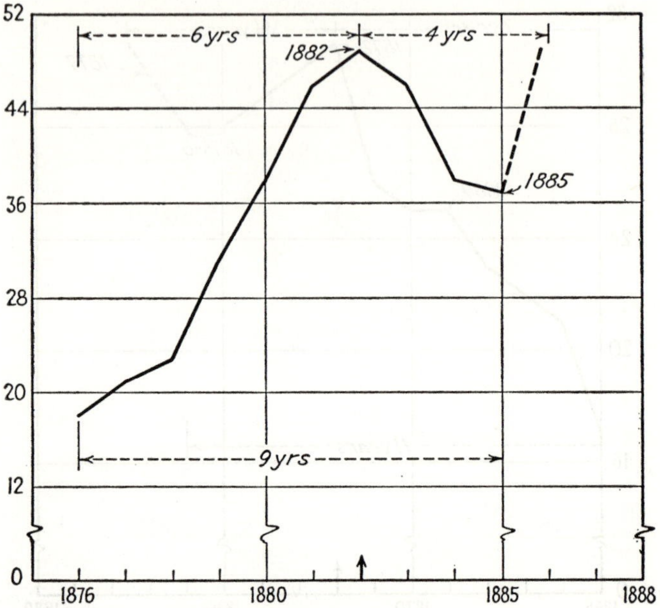

FIGURE 11. *The Major Cycle of 1882. Index of Production of Durable Manufactures (1899 = 100)*

Source: Edwin Frickey, *Production in the United States, 1860–1914,* Harvard University Press, 1947.

of 1892 was again reached, only one year short of the 1872–73 slump. But the 1892 depression discloses a marked difference from that of 1872–73 in that it was interrupted by the short but incomplete recovery of 1895. The length of the cycle from trough to trough (1896) was 11 years.

An examination of the diagrams for these three major cycles makes it quite clear that any effort to compress all cycles into a common pattern or mold is a highly artificial procedure.

THE CYCLE CULMINATING IN 1907

The expansion phase of the 1907 cycle (Figure 13 and Figure 14) was quite as vigorous as those of 1872–73 and 1882. But the 1907 upswing, like that of 1892, was interrupted by two minor

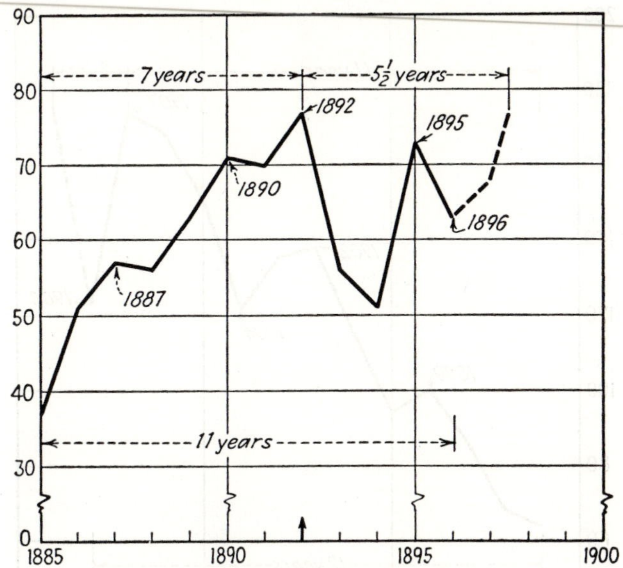

FIGURE 12. *The Major Cycle of 1892. Index of Production of Durable Manufactures (1899 = 100)*

Source: Edwin Frickey, *Production in the United States, 1860–1914,* Harvard University Press, 1947.

recessions, the last of which was of considerable magnitude. The contraction after 1907 was very sharp but was compressed within a relatively short interval. The magnitude of the decline was, however, less severe than that of 1872–73 or that of 1892. And the recovery came much faster. After only 2 years the 1907 level of output was again reached. The length of the cycle from trough to trough, owing to the long upswing, was 12 years. Again marked differences are disclosed between this and each of the three earlier cycles.

THE CYCLE CULMINATING IN 1920

We come now to the 1920 cycle. As would be expected, this cycle discloses quite unusual features by reason of the distortion

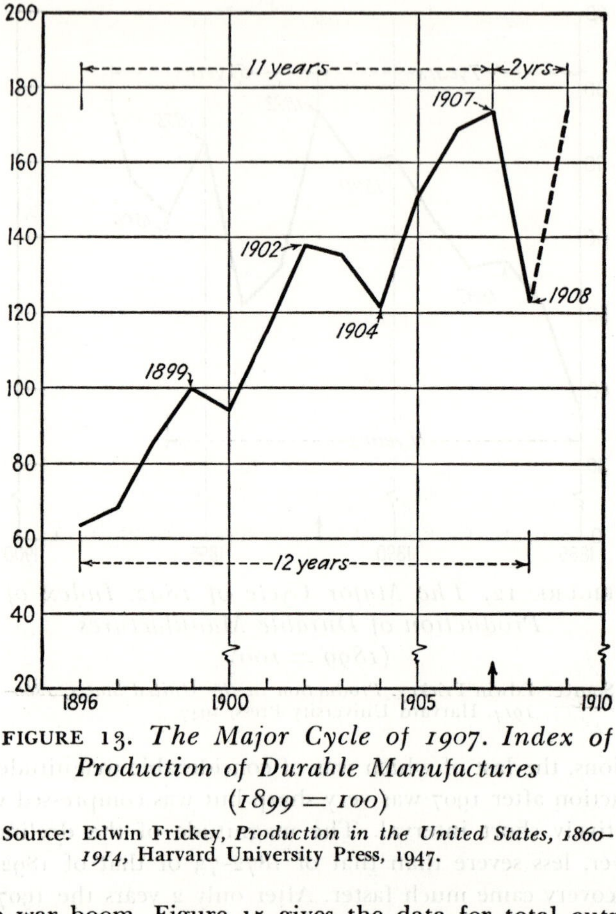

FIGURE 13. *The Major Cycle of 1907. Index of Production of Durable Manufactures (1899 = 100)*

Source: Edwin Frickey, *Production in the United States, 1860–1914,* Harvard University Press, 1947.

of the war boom. Figure 15 gives the data for total output of manufactures.[8] Here we have two minor peaks, 1910 and 1913, followed by the vast upsurge culminating in the war boom, and ending (with a minor setback after 1918) in the postwar peacetime peak of 1920. The decline in output was extraordinarily

[8] A diagram of the index of production of durables (estimated for the missing period, 1915–1918, from Solomon Fabricant's *Output of Manufacturing Industries, 1899–1937,* National Bureau of Economic Research, New York, 1940) discloses a picture in general similar to that for total manufactures, but with sharper fluctuations.

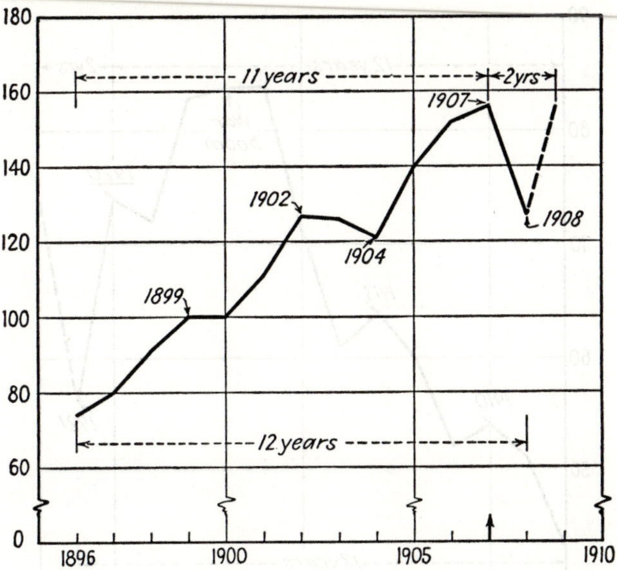

FIGURE 14. *The Major Cycle of 1907. Index of Production of Manufactures: Durables and Non-durables (1899 = 100)*

Source: Edwin Frickey, *Production in the United States, 1860–1914,* Harvard University Press, 1947.

severe, especially in the case of durables (see Tables II, p. 24), falling nearly to the absolute level of 1908. But there was a quick comeback, as in the 1907 cycle. The length of the cycle from trough to trough was 13 years, the longest of all the major cycles.

The extraordinary length of this cycle is doubtless due to the impact of the war. Housing and other capital investment projects had to be postponed because of the war, and so the boom was extended far beyond any normal peacetime period of high activity. Indeed, the war-created backlog of pent-up demand, especially in housing, was far from being satisfied even by 1920. The sharp but relatively short depression of 1921 was mainly, as we shall see later, due to an overaccumulation of inventories and a drastic decline in exports. But the basis for a strong recovery was present, partly by reason of the housing shortage and partly

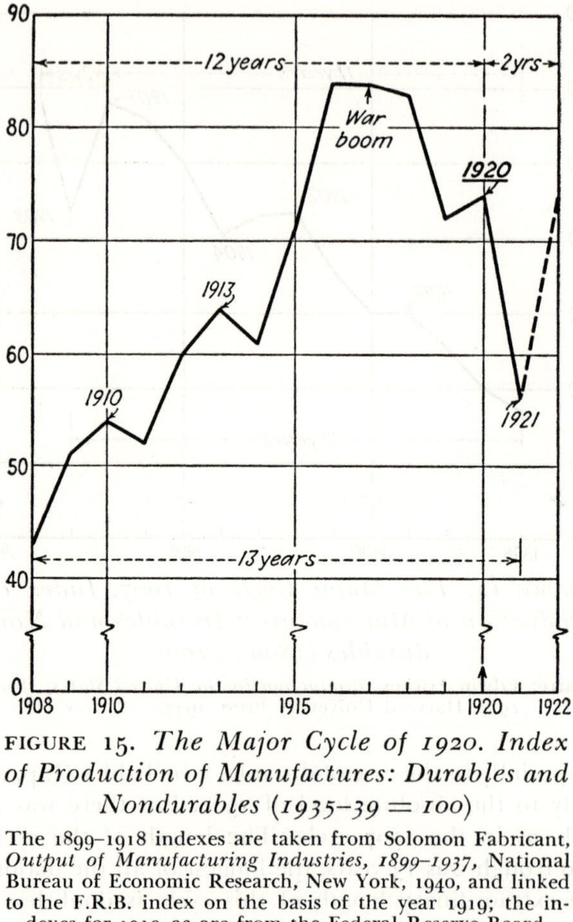

FIGURE 15. *The Major Cycle of 1920. Index of Production of Manufactures: Durables and Nondurables (1935–39 = 100)*

The 1899–1918 indexes are taken from Solomon Fabricant, *Output of Manufacturing Industries, 1899–1937,* National Bureau of Economic Research, New York, 1940, and linked to the F.R.B. index on the basis of the year 1919; the indexes for 1919–23 are from the Federal Reserve Board.

by reason of the emergence of a goodly number of new industries whose youthful growth, already begun, had been interrupted by the war.

Thus, in view of the impact of the war and the technological developments which were rapidly gaining strength, it is no cause for wonderment that the major cycle culminating in 1920 was of quite exceptional length from trough to trough.

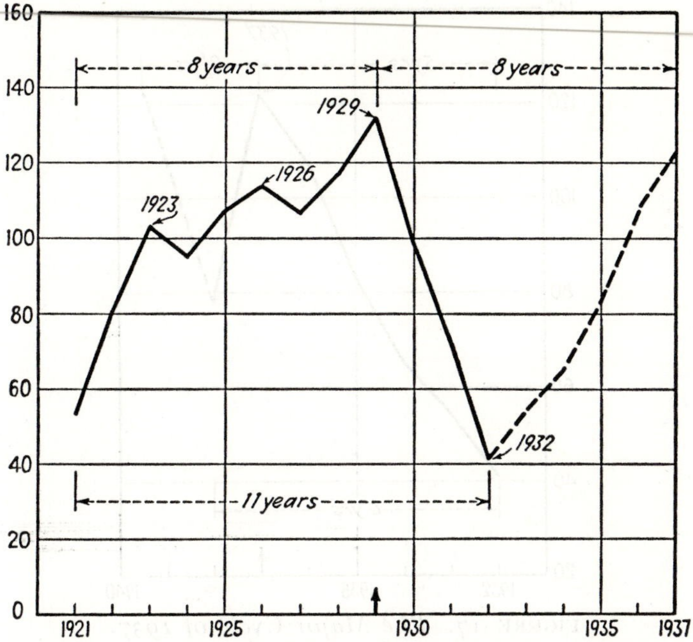

FIGURE 16. *The Major Cycle of 1929. Index of Production of Durable Manufactures (1935–39 = 100)*

Source: Federal Reserve Board, *Index of Production of Durable Manufactures.*

THE CYCLE CULMINATING IN 1929

This brings us to the great boom of the nineteen-twenties. While the expansion culminating in 1929 was more buoyant, the output curve for this cycle (Figure 16) is in many respects similar to that for the 1892 cycle. Indeed, if one blots out of the picture the peculiar brief recovery of 1895, the two curves (from 1885 to 1896, and from 1921 to 1932) bear a striking resemblance to each other. The upswing phases are very similar both in the magnitude of the expansion and in the duration of the period of high activity. Both upswings were interrupted by two minor recessions. In the 1929 upsurge, the first spurt was stronger; in the 1892 boom, the second spurt was the more vigorous. In gen-

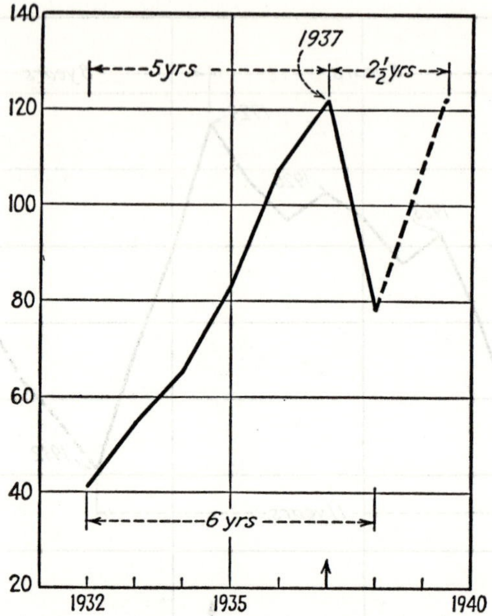

FIGURE 17. *The Major Cycle of 1937. Index of Production of Durable Manufactures (1935–39 = 100)*

Source: Federal Reserve Board, *Index of Production of Durable Manufactures.*

eral the contour is the same, and the length of the two cycles from trough to trough was in each case 11 years.

The contraction was, however, sharper and more prolonged in the 1929 crash, and it took a wholly unprecedented length of time—eight years—to recover the output level of the previous peak.

THE CYCLE CULMINATING IN 1937

For total manufactures, the absolute level of output of 1937 exceeded that of 1929, but for durables the 1929 level was not quite reached. And no sooner was the earlier output peak reached than a new major depression (beginning 1937) set in. Nothing of this sort had ever occurred before. Always in the past, each

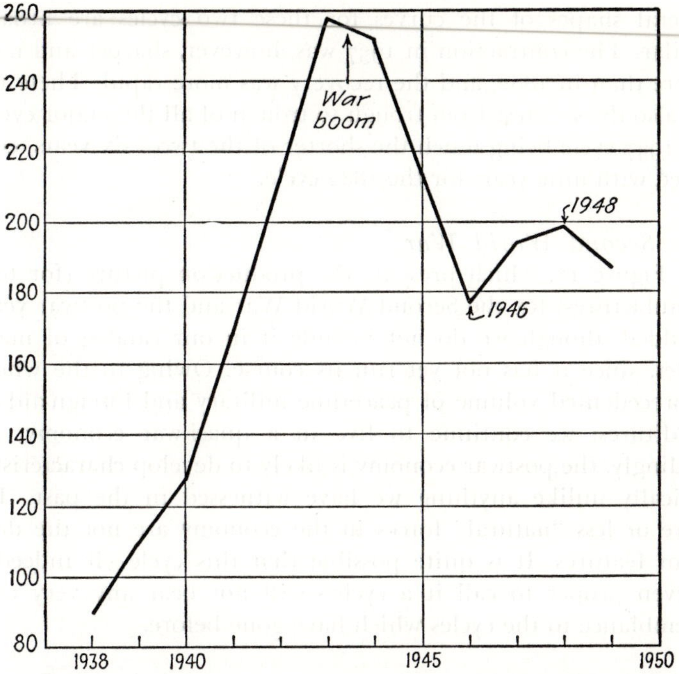

FIGURE 18. *The Boom of the Second World War. Index of Production of Manufactures: Durables and Nondurables (1935–39 = 100)*

Source: Federal Reserve Board, *Index of Total Manufactures.*

successive major peak of output had by far exceeded the previous peak. Here, then, was something utterly at variance with all past experience with respect to major cycles.

It is accordingly not possible to regard the 1937 cycle (Figure 17) as strictly of the same general character as the other major cycles. But there are important differences between all of them, and there appears to be no good reason for excluding the 1937 cycle altogether from our classification. The upswing, as far as annual data are concerned, continued on through to 1937 with great steadiness and with a high annual percentage rate of increase without any significant interruption for five years. In this respect the upswing of 1937 resembles that of 1882. Indeed, the general shapes of the curves for these two cycles are broadly similar. The contraction in 1937 was, however, sharper and more severe than in 1882, and the recovery was more rapid. These two are also the shortest from trough to trough of all the major cycles, the 1937 cycle being much the shorter of the two—six years, compared with nine years for the 1882 cycle.

The Second World War

Figure 18, which presents the production picture (for total manufactures) for the Second World War and the postwar years, is added, though we do not include it in our catalog of major cycles, since it has not yet run its course. Owing to the wholly unprecedented volume of peacetime military and foreign-aid expenditures, we continue to live in a quasi-war economy. Accordingly, the postwar economy is likely to develop characteristics radically unlike anything we have witnessed in the past. The more or less "natural" forces in the economy are not the dominant features. It is quite possible that this cycle—if indeed it is even proper to call it a cycle—will not bear any very close resemblance to the cycles which have gone before.

1908 to 1948

Finally, to assist the reader in getting a broad perspective of the development of the economy, both in terms of the cyclical *fluctuations* of economic activity and also of the *trend* of its capacity to turn out industrial products, we present Figure 19. Here is a picture of the upward sweep of total industrial production (manufactures, both durable and nondurable, together with mineral products) during the last forty years. Three major depressions fall in this forty-year interval, those beginning in 1920, 1929, and 1937; but notably that beginning in 1929. There were, moreover, also a number of minor recessions—beginning in 1910, 1913, 1918, 1923, and 1926—during the first half of the period; but none are visible (from annual production data) in the last half of the period.

The curved dotted line connecting the production points at 1915, 1929, and 1941 represents a *constant percentage* rate of increase of production.[9] The 1948 production level falls slightly below this line. A curved line drawn through 1909, 1920, and 1948 gives a similar compound rate of increase of 3½ per cent per annum. It thus appears that industrial production, measured by comparable high performance years, has shown no sign of

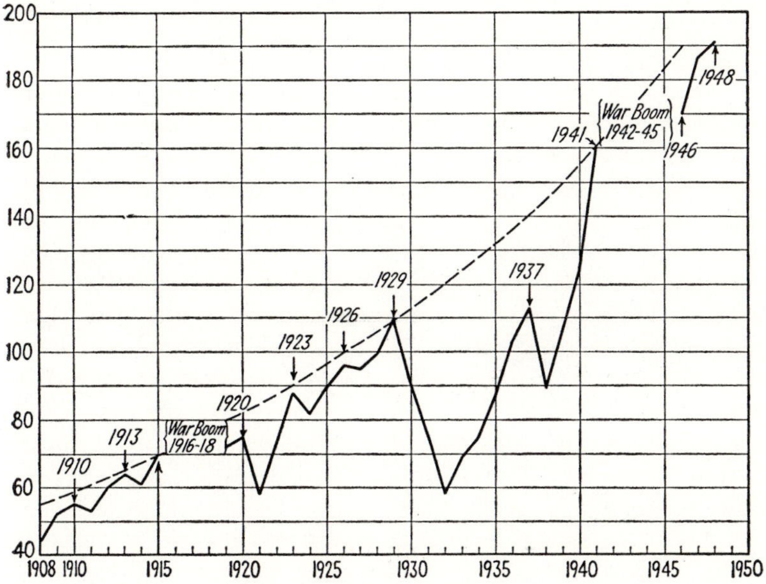

FIGURE 19. *Industrial Production (1935–39 = 100)*
Source: Federal Reserve Board.

slackening off during the past forty years. The production *potential* of the American economy, as revealed in its best years, has continued down to the present to grow at substantially a constant percentage rate. Output in the best years has in fact doubled every twenty years.

The record of course shows that the economy has, over much of the period, fallen far short of its potential capacity. Thus even in the prosperous twenties output fell below the optimum rate

[9] This can easily be verified by drawing the data on a semi-logarithmic chart. On such a scale a straight line represents a constant percentage rate of increase.

of growth as established by the benchmarks of 1915, 1929, and 1941. Most of the prosperous years of the twenties did, however, reach the output level set by the high, but slightly lower, benchmarks of 1909, 1920, and 1948.

3 · *The Building Cycle*

In Chapter 2 we noted seven major and eleven minor cycles of business activity from 1865 to 1938—a total of eighteen cycles. The peaks of the major cycles came in 1872–73, 1882, 1892, 1907, 1920, 1929, and 1937. The minor cycles usually represent interruptions in the long upswing phase of the major cycle. Occasionally, however, no significant interruptions occur; in the upswings of 1882 and 1937, particularly, no minor peaks appear before the major peak is reached.

The Role of Building Construction

We have noted that some major depressions have been more severe than others. There are, of course, many factors which alter the course of the development of the major cycle and influence the intensity and violence of both the upswing and the downswing. One of the most important of these factors, strangely enough, has been neglected, in large measure, in the analysis of business cycles. And this factor, as we shall see later, is peculiarly important for an understanding of the Great Depression of the nineteen-thirties.

The factor to which we refer is the fluctuation in building construction. Building follows, in large measure, a wavelike movement which is much longer than that of the major business cycle. Notable studies of building construction, both residential and non-residential, have been made by Riggleman, Newman, Wenzlick, and Long.[1] Riggleman's study extends over a century, from 1830 to 1934, and covers three cities in the earlier period and sixty-five cities in the latter period. Long's study covers the period from 1864 to 1934 and includes twenty-nine cities. Newman's study is for seventeen cities and covers the period 1879 to 1934. Wenzlick's study of the volume of new building in the United States is for 1875 to 1936. All of these studies relate either directly or indirectly to volume, or to the value of building corrected for price changes.

From these studies it appears, according to experience in the United States, that building construction over the last hundred years has followed a fairly regular cyclical pattern. The Riggleman study reveals six building cycles from 1830 to 1934, with an average duration of 17.3 years. The studies of Long and Riggleman reveal four cycles from 1864 to 1934, with an average duration of 17.5 years. All four studies cover the last three cycles and reveal for this period an average duration of about 18 years. The period from 1900 to 1934 gives two cycles of an average duration of 17 years. Thus, it appears that the building cycle averages between 17 and 18 years in length with a range from 16 to 20 years.[2]

In our analysis of major business cycles in Chapter 2 we noted wide variations in the amplitude, period, and general contour of the various major cycles. These differences can be partly accounted for by the position of each major cycle in the longer building cycle. When the downturn of a major cycle coincides with the slump in building, the ensuing depression is likely to be severe and prolonged. If, however, the major-cycle downturn comes when the building cycle is on the upgrade, the depression is likely to be shorter and less severe.

---

1 See G. F. Warren and F. A. Pearson, *World Prices and Building Industry*, John Wiley and Sons, 1937; J. R. Riggleman, "Building Cycles in the U.S., 1875–1922," *Journal of the American Statistical Association*, 1933; W. H. Newman, *The Building Industry and Business Cycles*, University of Chicago Press, 1935; R. Wenzlick, "Preliminary Study of National Cycles of Real Estate Activity," *The Real Estate Analyst*, October, 1936, p. 622; C. D. Long, Jr., *Building Cycles and the Theory of Investment*, Princeton University Press, 1940.

2 See Walter Isard, "Transport Development and Building Cycles," *Quarterly Journal of Economics*, November, 1942; "A Neglected Cycle: The Transport-Building Cycle," *The Review of Economic Statistics*, November, 1942.

The periods of the four building cycles from 1864 to 1934 are as follows:

TABLE III

	Low	*High*	*Low*
Cycle 1	1864	1871	1878–80
Cycle 2	1878–80	1890–92	1900
Cycle 3	1900	1909	1918
Cycle 4	1918	1925	1934

The Three Severe Depressions

The major business depressions which coincided with a sharp curtailment in building construction followed the high peaks of 1872–73, 1892, and 1929. It will be noticed that each one of these major-cycle depressions was of unusual severity and duration. Indeed, these three are *super-depressions* and constitute a class by themselves. From their relation to the building cycle (apart from other factors), this is precisely what we would expect. If temporary saturation in other forms of real investment coincides with temporary saturation in investment in building construction, it is reasonable to suppose that the total decline in real investment will be far greater than would otherwise be the case. Moreover, since it takes longer to overcome the temporary saturation in building construction—indicated by the average length of the downswing in the building cycle, namely eight to nine years—it is not hard to see that recovery of general investment activity is made more difficult so long as building construction, which has always been an enormously important industry in American life, is still ebbing away or scraping along on a comparatively low level.

Thus if a major-cycle peak coincides roughly with the peak of the building cycle, its expansion phase is likely to be exceptionally buoyant and prolonged, as was the case in the booms preceding 1872–73, 1892, and 1929. And the depression phase, striking just when building is falling rapidly into a deep slump, is likely to be severe and prolonged.

The Four Less Severe Major Cycles

In contrast consider the 1882, 1907, 1920, and 1937 major cycles. In all four cases, the upswing phase developed just as the building cycle had begun to move out of low ebb and was starting on the upgrade. And it is a notable fact that in each of these cases the following business depressions, while sufficiently severe to be characterized as major, were relatively short in duration. This also conforms to what one would expect. If the depression of a major business cycle occurs at a time when building construction is well started on the upgrade, it is reasonable to suppose that the decline in general business activity will be fairly quickly reversed. The moment forces making for revival reappear, they will be powerfully strengthened by the upsurge of building activity.

Thus a prolonged slump in building played a significant role in the three severest and longest depressions in our history—the depressions following the peaks of 1872–73, 1892, and 1929. On the other hand, the beginning phase of a rising tide of building construction helped to cut short the depressions following 1882, 1907, 1920, and 1937. There were, of course, other important contributing factors, of widely different character in each case, making for wide diversity in these seven major business cycles.

The First World War

Of the four building cycles from 1864 to 1934, one only—that extending from 1900 to 1918—failed to produce an exceptionally deep and prolonged depression. This building cycle, in its later phase, was profoundly influenced by the events of the First World War. Construction had begun to turn down after 1909 and again after 1912, but the war boom, while the United States was still at peace, pushed building activity to new high levels in 1915 and 1916. The American entry into the war brought a sharp curtailment of building construction, which reached the low point in 1918. This curtailment coincided with the war boom. Thus our third building cycle, being dominated in its later phase by the impact of the war, has no relevance for the problem of the peacetime impact of the building cycle upon the ordinary business cycle.

The First Building Cycle

The interrelations of the seven major business cycles with the four building cycles (from 1864 to 1934) can be envisaged more clearly by studying the accompanying charts. In the various building-cycle curves, the points are indicated which correspond to the major business-cycle peaks.

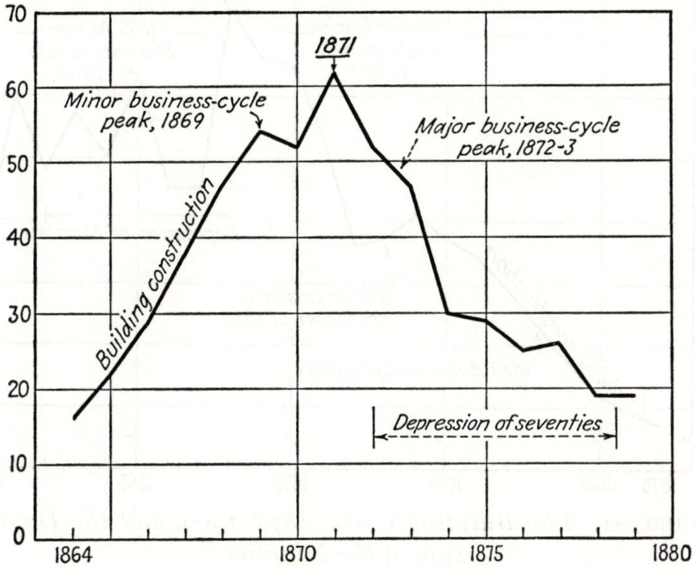

FIGURE 20. *The Building Cycle, 1864–80, and the Great Depression of the Seventies*

Source: Clarence D. Long, Jr., *Building Cycles and the Theory of Investment*, Princeton University Press, 1940. Indexes of aggregate building volume, 1920–30 = 100.

Figure 20 (Building Cycle, 1864–80) may usefully be compared with Figure 9 (Major Business Cycle, 1865–76). In this case, and this alone, the two are nearly coterminous. The building cycle reached the peak in 1871, one to two years ahead of the business cycle, and the contraction phase continued on to 1878–80,[3] or about two to three years longer than the contraction of business activity, which reached its low in 1876–77. As we have seen, the

[3] Long puts the low in 1880, but Newman, Riggleman, and Wenzlick in 1878.

economy, owing to the factor of growth, continues to be seriously depressed for a considerable period, often years, after the trough is reached. Business recovery was, however, really on the way to prosperity by 1880, and that year marked the turning point for building construction.

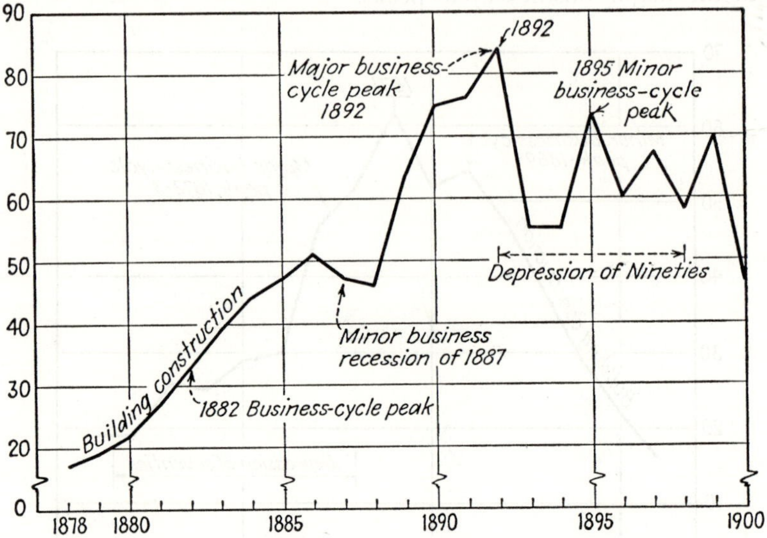

FIGURE 21. *The Building Cycle, 1878–1900, and the Depression of the Nineties*

Source: William H. Newman, *The Building Industry and Business Cycles,* The University of Chicago Press, 1935. Permits index, seasonally adjusted (1920–30 = 100) and corrected for price changes by building-costs index (1913 = 100).

The Second Building Cycle

Figure 21 (Building Cycle, 1878–1900) covers the span of two major business cycles with peaks in 1882 and 1892. Building construction continued on upward (though the level of building was comparatively low) despite the depression following 1882. This fact goes far to explain the relative mildness of this major depression.[4] From 1885 to 1896, the two curves—building and

[4] It will be recalled that Burns and Mitchell do not include the 1882 depression among the major depressions.

business cycles—look a good deal alike. There is a dip in the upswing of building connected with the minor business recession following 1887. But the building and business cycles reach their high peak simultaneously in 1892, and both display mild recoveries in 1895. Both drop in 1896 and rise in 1897. Thereafter, building oscillates up and down, reaching its low point in 1900, while business has, in the meantime, already moved up a substantial notch in the great expansion culminating in 1907.

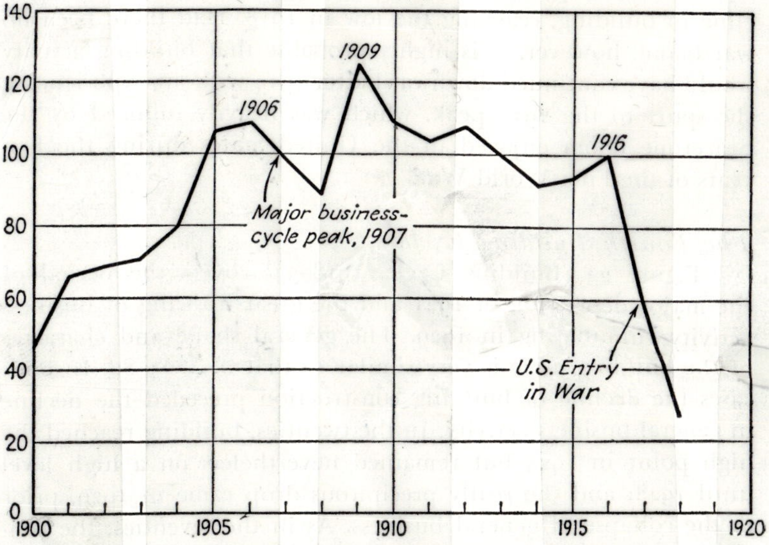

FIGURE 22. *The Building Cycle, 1900–18, and the Depression of 1907*

Source: William H. Newman, *The Building Industry and Business Cycles,* The University of Chicago Press, 1935. Permits index, seasonally adjusted (1920–30 = 100) and corrected for price changes by building-costs index (1913 = 100).

The Third Building Cycle

Figure 22 (Building Cycle, 1900–18) covers the span of the 1907 business boom and on through the First World War boom. First there was a strong upsurge in building construction, with a setback coinciding with the 1908 depression. But building construction declined only moderately, and it quickly resumed its upward trend, which culminated in 1909. No doubt the buoyancy of building construction contributed greatly toward stopping the sharp decline in business activity in 1908 and rapidly turned the tide into a quick recovery in 1909. Thereafter building correlated more or less with business activity, leading the way down in the minor recessions of 1911 and 1914, and moving up with business to 1916. With the entry of the United States into the war, building construction was necessarily sharply curtailed to make room for the expansion of military output. Hence the sharp decline in building, reaching the low in 1918. Had there been no war boom, however, it is highly probable that building activity would have continued downward after 1914 without experiencing the spurt to the 1916 peak, which was heavily induced by the peacetime boom enjoyed in the United States during the first years of the First World War.

The Fourth Building Cycle

Figure 23 (Building Cycle, 1918–34) covers the period of the major depression of 1921 and the great upswing of business activity culminating in 1929. The general shape and character of the building cycle is very similar to that of 1864–80. In both cases the decline of building construction preceded the decline in general business activity. In the twenties, building reached the high point in 1925 but remained nevertheless on a high level until 1928; and the really precipitous drop came in 1929, prior to the collapse of general business. As in the seventies, the contraction of building activity was catastrophic and contributed greatly toward the severity and duration of the Great Depression.

It is reasonable to suppose that the most important single explanation for the speed of the recovery from the 1921 depression was the phenomenal upturn in building construction which began in 1921 and which rose to an unprecedented crest in 1925 and remained at an extraordinarily high level until 1928. No explanation of the boom of the twenties or the severity and duration of the depression of the thirties is adequate which leaves out of account the great expansion and contraction in building activity. Probably at no time in our history had we reached as complete a temporary saturation in building construction, including apartment houses, residences, office buildings, and other commercial structures, as was the case in the late twenties. Under these circumstances it was to be expected that it would take a long time to work through this period of oversaturation.

It is thus apparent that it is not possible to give an adequate analysis of the major cycles of business activity without taking

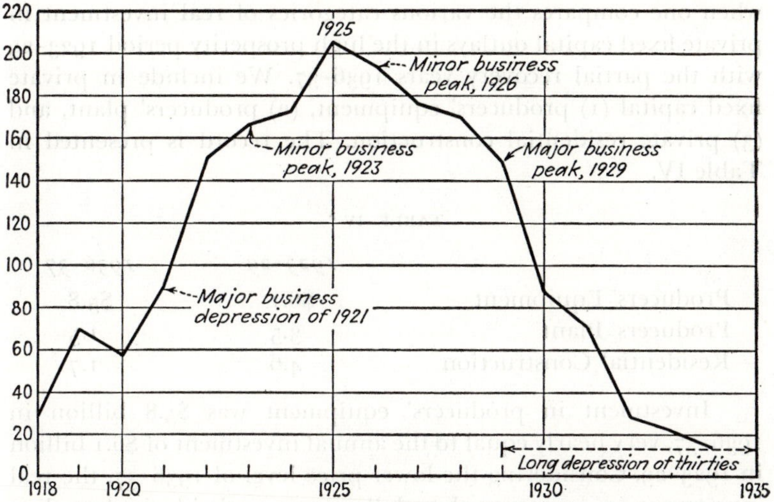

FIGURE 23. *The Building Cycle, 1918–34, and the Great Depression of the Thirties*

Source: William H. Newman, *The Building Industry and Business Cycles,* The University of Chicago Press, 1935. Permits index, seasonally adjusted (1920–30 = 100) and corrected for price changes by building-costs index (1913 = 100).

into account the impact on those cycles of the longer cycle of building construction. Various factors cause one major business cycle to differ from another, and in this respect the building cycle plays a significant role.

The Great Depression

With respect to the Great Depression of the thirties, it is worthy of note that the constructional boom of the twenties was the greatest in our history and that the precipitate drop in building, notably after 1928 (the decline began slowly to set in after 1925), exceeded that of any earlier period. Thus in the long swings of building construction we are able to see against the background of earlier American experience a part of the explanation of the severity of the Great Depression starting in 1929.

The role of the construction cycle in the boom of the twenties and the depressed conditions of the thirties is strikingly revealed when one compares the various categories of real investment in private fixed capital outlays in the high prosperity period 1923–29 with the partial recovery years 1936–37. We include in private fixed capital (1) producers' equipment, (2) producers' plant, and (3) private residential construction. The record is presented in Table IV.

TABLE IV [5]

	1923–29	*1936–37*
Producers' Equipment	$6.1	$5.8
Producers' Plant	3.5	1.5
Residential Construction	4.6	1.7

Investment in producers' equipment was $5.8 billion in 1936–37, very nearly equal to the annual investment of $6.1 billion in 1923–29. Considering the lower price level of 1936–37, the real investment in constant-value dollars was probably higher than that of 1923–29. The failure to achieve full recovery in the thirties was not due (at least not to any appreciable extent) to inadequate expenditures on new producers' equipment.

The next two categories of private investment reveal clearly where the deficiency lay. Investment in producers' plant amounted to only $1.5 billion in 1936–37, compared with $3.5 billion in 1923–29. Plant investment was down by $2.0 billion per year. Residential construction averaged $1.7 billion in 1936–37, compared with $4.6 billion in 1923–29. The shortage here amounts to the large figure of $2.9 billion per annum. Together private plant investment and residential construction ran annually $4.9 billion below the 1923–29 level. It is in this area that one must look

[5] See *Federal Reserve Bulletin,* September, 1945, p. 873.

for a large part of the explanation of the incomplete recovery of the thirties. Moreover, considering the growth in the labor force and the increase in man-hour productivity, investment would have had to rise considerably *above* the 1923–29 level in order to produce full employment.

The building cycle is a cycle of construction of *buildings,* not of constructional activity in general, which includes also road, railroad, and similar non-building constructional work. The construction of business plant, however, consists largely of building structures. Thus the figures in Table IV for plant and residential construction relate mainly to the building cycle. And according to our experience with the building cycle since the Civil War, we should expect a relatively weak recovery in residential and plant construction in the first upswing of business activity following the intense constructional boom of the twenties. Looking still farther forward, we could have expected, even though there had been no Second World War, that the major upswing of the forties would have made a more favorable record than that made in the thirties.

The categories of construction in which the highest saturation was reached in the twenties were also those most depressed in the thirties. Office buildings and housing are examples. The same situation is found with respect to railroad plant. In this field we find that expenditures rose progressively (with a very slight recession in 1925 and 1927–28) to the peak of the boom, and even continued (despite the growing encroachment of trucks) into the depression, reaching the highest point in 1930. Similarly, investment in electric power plant, after a moderate decline from the 1924 peak, rose again in 1929 and even in 1930. Despite a sharp decline in electric power output in 1930, plant capacity was greatly increased. Installed capacity of plant and equipment remained far in excess of current output requirements for several years. Not until a relatively high electric power production was attained in 1936 and 1937 was capacity sufficiently utilized to justify further large capital outlays. Thus the thirties offer a conspicuous illustration of the prolonged saturation which follows a high constructional boom involving, in large part, building structures. The long building cycle was a highly important factor both in the boom leading up to 1929 and also in the deep and prolonged depression of the thirties.

The Problem of the Building Cycle

The question may be raised why building construction should have a cycle of its own, different in length from that of the major business cycle. Neither has an exact periodicity, but the building cycle clearly averages a longer span than the cycle of business activity. It might be well to point out that building is not the only field of economic activity which reveals a periodicity which varies from that of the major cycle. Thus, for example, we know that there is a short cycle in textile production of about two years' duration which fits neither the minor cycle nor the major business cycle; that there is a cycle of hog production of about three to four years; and indeed a cycle of greater or shorter duration in the production of several of the more important domestic animals.

The corn-hog cycle, for example, has been explained by the interrelation of the price of corn and the price of hogs. When there is a large production of corn, and feed prices are low, farmers find that it is desirable to produce more hogs, but it takes some time to make the decision and some time to raise the new pig crop. Thus, after an interval, an excessively large supply of hogs appears on the market, causing a low price of hogs in relation to the price of corn. Thereupon, the farmers conclude that it is better to sell the corn in the market and raise fewer hogs. Again it takes some time to make the decision and to adjust the pig crop to the new price situation, and after a lag a relative shortage appears in the hog production, causing a high price of hogs in relation to the price of corn. Thus, in the lagged reaction of producers to the market situation one finds the explanation of the hog production cycle.

In somewhat similar fashion one may advance a tentative explanation of the seventeen- or eighteen-year cycle of building construction. We shall apply the argument particularly with respect to residential building, though the same analysis holds to a degree for other kinds of construction. Let us suppose that residential building has for a period been depressed and that, increasingly, rented space is becoming scarce. Rents thus rise. But it takes some time before the building industry is sufficiently convinced of the permanence of the higher rents to be stimulated to activity. Moreover, the building industry by its very nature cannot suddenly be set going on a large scale. In a period of building depression many contractors, particularly the smaller ones, have gone into other industrial activities, and the same is true of the skilled workmen. It follows that it takes a considerable period of time to recruit a sufficient number of new entrepreneurs and skilled workmen to develop construction on a large scale. Once expansion is under way, constructional activity continues as long as the rents appear favorable. Plans and structures are in process which cannot be completed for many months, and sometimes even years, after it appears that the rent situation, owing to the increasing surplus of available houses, is becoming less favorable. Thus, the adjustment of the supply of houses to the demand for houses takes place with a considerable lag, and this, it appears, accounts in part for the cyclical movement in residential building.

The fluctuation in rents, resulting from the failure of quick adjustment of available housing space to the number of families seeking accommodations, is the major cause of the fluctuation in residential construction. There are, however, other factors which have a bearing on the building cycle, including fluctuations in the cost of building, availability of investment funds, changes in national income, changes in the rate of urban population growth, and general pessimism or optimism with respect to the long-run factors.[6]

Some of these factors are themselves affected by the building cycle, and are therefore in part caused by, as well as causes of, the building-cycle movement. Thus, as building construction increases, the cost of building is advanced by reason of activity in the industry. And the ever-mounting cost is itself a factor caus-

---

[6] Cf. J. Tinbergen, *Statistical Testing of Business Cycle Theories, A Method and Its Application to Investment Activity,* League of Nations, 1939; C. F. Roos, *Dynamic Economics,* The Principia Press, Inc., 1934; J. B. D. Derksen, "Long Cycles in Residential Building: An Explanation," *Econometrica,* April, 1940; see also the extended bibliography cited in C. D. Long, Jr., *Building Cycles and the Theory of Investment,* Princeton University Press, 1940, pp. 9–10.

ing a reduction in building operations. Much the same may be said about the availability of real estate investment funds. Moreover, while changes in the national income are affected by the building cycle, on the other side these changes often act in a manner to reinforce and accelerate the upswing or the downswing of constructional activity.

Yet while all these factors play, more or less, a role, it appears that the dominant factor is the relation of the supply of houses offered for rent to the demand for houses. When vacancies begin to rise above the normal rate, rents begin to decline, and this is the signal to begin to curtail construction. Thus in the twenties, vacancies rose from 2 per cent in 1922 to 6½ per cent in 1928, and rents began to fall in 1925.[7] In this year also residential construction *began* to decline, yet remained relatively high until 1928. But rents continued to decline, and after 1928 there occurred a precipitous decline in construction.

---

[7] See Bureau of Labor Statistics, *Handbook of Labor Statistics,* 1941, Vol. I; Bulletin 699; and *Monthly Labor Review.*

4 · *Secular Trends and Business Cycles*

We have presented in Chapters 2 and 3 a general picture of the seven major business cycles from 1865 to 1938 and of some significant differences between them. In part these differences relate to the presence or absence of minor recessions, since in some major cycles the period of expansion is interrupted by one or more minor recessions. Other differences lie in the relation of the various major cycles in point of timing to the long building cycle. In this chapter we shall consider how far the differences in the duration and magnitude of the expansion and contraction phases of the various major cycles may be associated with secular trends (particularly rising and falling price trends) and the underlying factors involved.

Secular Price Trends

While the production data on business cycles presented in our diagrams do not antedate the Civil War,[1] we have figures on price movements from the formation of the federal union. There was a long upswing in prices from 1788 to 1814, a downswing from 1814 to 1843, an upswing until 1872–73 (with a "greenback" inflationary wartime peak in 1865), a downswing from 1872–73 to

[1] There are, of course, indexes of business fluctuations, such as the Cleveland Trust Index, covering the pre-Civil War period, but satisfactory data on production are lacking.

1897, an upswing from 1897 to 1920, and a downswing from 1920 to 1933.

In the literature there is much discussion of the relation of these long-run price movements to the business cycle. Some economists have held the view that these price trends must be regarded as important factors affecting the business cycle; others regard these price trends as *effects* of fundamental underlying factors operating upon business activity (and so upon the business cycle) and causing economic developments which, among other things, manifest themselves in rising or falling prices.

If the underlying conditions are such that a succession of major-cycle expansions are exceptionally vigorous, these buoyant conditions are likely to be manifested in a rising price trend. If, however, a number of business cycles happen to occur in a period in which the expansionist factors are relatively weak, the resulting condition of quasi stagnation is likely to manifest itself in a sagging price level. From this point of view the price level is regarded as the *result* of fundamental conditions underlying the state of business activity. Long-run price movements are held to be *indicators* registering the impact of the deeper factors which cause the periods of buoyancy or stagnation, as the case may be. Price trends are considered to be the statistical thermometers, so to speak, registering the fact of prolonged buoyancy or chronically hard times.

Monetary Factors

Economists who emphasize the role of changes in the quantity of money (and particularly in the nineteenth century the changes in the supply of monetary gold) have taken a different view of economic developments. They have sought to find the causal explanation of periods of buoyancy or stagnation in the secular movements of prices. For them gold and monetary movements account for the long swings of prices, and these in turn are thought to affect the cycle of business activity. Rising prices are regarded as having a buoyant effect on the economy, tending to produce pronounced booms and mild depressions; and falling prices are looked upon as having a depressant effect on industry with a consequent tendency toward stagnation.

Long Upswing of Prices

The strong business expansion culminating in the boom of 1872–73 coincided with the last phase of the long world-wide upswing in prices extending from 1843 to 1872–73. This whole period is usually regarded as one of general buoyancy, though suffering setbacks, more or less severe, in 1847, 1857, and 1869 (1866 in England and 1869 in the United States). Was this buoyancy (if indeed we may so characterize the period) the *cause* or the *effect* of the rising price trend?

Long Downswing of Prices

Also the literature displays a common belief that the period of falling prices from 1872–73 to 1897 was one of preponderantly hard times. This period included the severe depressions of the seventies and the nineties, together with the moderately sharp depression of the early eighties. In contrast, the period of rising prices, after 1897 to the First World War, has generally been regarded as a golden age of prosperity.

The period of falling prices from 1872–73 to 1897 was one of serious financial distress for the farm population, from which arose widespread disturbing social and political movements calling for drastic monetary reforms and other institutional changes intended to cure or alleviate the condition. Much of the political turbulence of the period can be explained in terms of the increasing weight of debt in view of falling prices. The differential effect of falling prices on debtors and creditors tended to create serious inequities which resulted in disturbing social and political upheavals. Professor John R. Commons has indeed called the price level the "backbone" of American social and political history. This period of long-run falling prices appears also to have been associated with widespread unemployment and labor unrest. Indeed, many relevant facts concerning the peculiar characteristics of this period are to be found in social and labor history.[2]

---

[2] See John R. Commons, *Documentary History of American Industrial Society*, A. H. Clark Co., 1910–11; and also John R. Commons, *et al.*, *History of Labor in the United States*, The Macmillan Company, 1918.

The Long-Wave Hypothesis

Many writers, including Spiethoff, Schumpeter, Mitchell and Thorp, Kondratieff, Woytinski, Ciriacy-Wantrup, and others [3] have pointed out that the past economic experience of the Western world discloses prolonged periods of relatively buoyant times, extending far beyond the boundaries of the major business cycle, and similarly prolonged periods of more or less chronic hard times, within which, however, the swings of the business cycle occur. In the long periods of buoyancy or good times it has been noted that the expansion phase of the business cycle was vigorous and often reached high levels of activity, while the depression phase of the cycle tended to be relatively brief in duration and appeared comparatively easy to overcome. The long periods of preponderantly good times were apparently periods in which there was present a strong undercurrent of buoyancy, a powerful upsurge in investment activity, interrupted, to be sure, at fairly regular intervals by more or less serious depressions. In the long periods of chronic hard times, on the contrary, it appears that depressions were often deep and prolonged, while recoveries were weak and anemic and often failed to reach a level of reasonably full activity.

Attention should be called to the fact that with respect to real income it is not appropriate to speak of these prolonged periods as "upswing" and "downswing" periods. Even in the so-called long periods of hard times of the seventies and nineties the *trend* of per capita output and real income continued to rise, though possibly (about this we are not certain) at a somewhat retarded rate of increase. But these periods did at any rate reveal falling prices and falling interest rates, the latter indicating a condition of capital saturation.

---

[3] See J. A. Schumpeter, *Business Cycles,* McGraw-Hill, 1939; A. Spiethoff, "Krisen," *Handwörterbuch der Staatswissenschaften,* 4th ed., 1923; N. D. Kondratieff, "Die Langen Wellen der Konjunktur," *Archiv für Sozialwissenschaft und Sozialpolitik,* December, 1926 (translated in abridged form in *Review of Economic Statistics,* November, 1935); W. C. Mitchell, *Business Cycles, the Problem and Its Setting,* National Bureau of Economic Research, 1927, pp. 441–442; S. von Ciriacy-Wantrup, *Agrarkrisen und Stockungsspannen,* Paul Parey, 1936; and Alvin H. Hansen, *Economic Stabilization in an Unbalanced World,* Harcourt, Brace, and Co., 1932, Chapter VI.

Many economists would indeed contend that price and interest-rate movements alone are involved in these long-period movements. The "hard times" are, it is said, merely a price phenomenon, not an output phenomenon. Statisticians point out that, as far as their data go, production trends fail to disclose any convincing evidence of long-run periods of buoyancy and hard times. And, it is said, if cost-reducing improvements are going on, declining prices are only a sign of increasing per capita productivity. From this point of view falling prices are regarded as merely an index of rapid progress. This optimistic interpretation, however, scarcely agrees with the opinions of the generations of businessmen, farmers, and working people who lived in the quarter-century of falling prices from 1873 to 1897.

Some writers have systematized these long-period movements (more or less coterminous with rising and falling prices) into a theory of "long waves." With respect to this matter we must take at least an agnostic position, if indeed not a highly skeptical one. All that we can be sure of is that we have in fact experienced long-run secular price movements which have had associated with them contrasting economic conditions: farm distress and unemployment in falling price periods; farm prosperity and a buoyant investment and labor market in rising price periods. These relationships appear to be sufficiently pronounced to justify singling out periods of secular price movements into special categories for study and analysis with respect to the behavior patterns of business cycles. *Price trends* we have indeed had, but not necessarily long-run *cumulative movements* which can properly be referred to as "long cycles" or "long waves." [4]

Burns and Mitchell find some evidence to support the view that the secular movements of prices affect the duration of the expansion and contraction of the business cycle. "Allowing as

[4] Professor Edwin Frickey (in *Production in the United States, 1860–1914*, Harvard University Press, 1947), whose exhaustive research has contributed so much to our knowledge of economic progress since the Civil War, is agnostic with respect to the long-wave thesis. Yet he repeatedly says that his data are at least not inconsistent with the so-called "long-wave" hypothesis. See also the critical discussion of these views and the analysis of empirical data by W. W. Rostow in *British Economy of the Nineteenth Century*, Oxford University Press, 1948. See also W. B. Smith and A. H. Cole, *Fluctuations in American Business, 1790–1860*, Harvard University Press, 1935.

best we can for the interrelation of business cycles in our four countries,[5] we judge that the evidence in hand supports the common opinion that there is a real relation between the direction of the trend in wholesale prices and business-cycle contractions: the contractions tend to be long or short according as the trend of prices is falling or rising, and this relation seems to hold for the duration of contractions relatively to full cycles as well as for their absolute duration."[6] They add the warning, however, that the "relation between the duration of price trends and the relative duration of business-cycle phases is heavily overlaid by other factors."

In his *Business Cycles, the Problem and Its Setting*[7] Mitchell found that the ratio of the duration of prosperity to the duration of depression was 2.7 to 1 in rising price periods, while it was only 0.85 to 1 in falling price periods in the United States. "These results are so uniform and so striking," he said, "as to leave little doubt that the secular trend of the wholesale price level is a factor of great moment in determining the characteristics of business cycles."

If we exclude the earlier periods, for which business-cycle data are highly unsatisfactory, and restrict ourselves to the period following the Civil War, we obtain some interesting conclusions, based on data relating to the production of durable manufactures. In the downswing of prices from 1872–73 to 1897 we have three major contractions in business activity, for which the average period of contraction was four years.[8] In the upswing of prices from 1897 to 1920 we have but one major business contraction, for which the period of decline was only one year.

If we, more or less arbitrarily, measure the full length of the depression period from the beginning of the decline to that point at which output again equals the previous peak (see Chapter 1) we get the following results: The average length of the depression

---

5 United States, Great Britain, Germany, and France.

6 Burns and Mitchell, *Measuring Business Cycles*, National Bureau of Economic Research, 1946, p. 438.

7 P. 411.

8 Or 3.3 years, if one takes 1894 instead of 1896 as the trough for the 1892 contraction.

period, so defined, was 5.3 years in the 1873–97 downward price trend period, while it was only 2 years in the period of rising price trend from 1897 to 1920. The comparison is, of course, based on a very slim foundation, since there is only one major depression in the rising price period.

It should be noted, moreover, that if we include the minor recessions both in the period of falling price trend and in the period of rising price trend, the results still point impressively to the conclusion that falling price trends are associated with long periods of business-cycle contraction, while in rising price trends the periods of contraction are relatively brief. The data are as follows: for falling price trends, the average period of contraction for all recessions (major and minor) is 2.5 years; for the rising price trend it is 1.3 years.

Next consider the expansion phase of the business cycle. In the falling price trend from 1872–73 to 1897 we have two periods of major expansion (minor recessions disregarded) averaging 6.5 years in length. In the rising price trend from 1897 to 1920 also we have two major expansions, and these averaged 11.5 years in length. The period of expansion was much longer in the period of rising price trend. But if we include the minor recessions in our calculations, the falling price trend period included four periods of expansion averaging 3.25 years in length, while the rising price trend included seven expansions averaging 3.3 years in length. On this basis there is no difference between rising and falling price trends.

Theories of Secular Trends

Four major explanations have been offered for the secular trends of prices and the associated buoyant business conditions. One runs in terms of innovations and technological developments, exploitation of new resources, and the opening of new territory. This explanation has been advanced notably by Wicksell, Spiethoff, and Schumpeter. A second runs in terms of government expenditures for war. This explanation has been advanced prominently by Ciriacy-Wantrup and has also been noted by Kondratieff and Wicksell. A third, running in terms of gold and monetary developments, has been advanced by Cassel, Warren and Pearson, Woytinski, and others. A fourth runs in terms of developments in the field of agriculture.

TECHNOLOGY AND SECULAR TRENDS

According to the first theory, the eras of buoyancy are periods in which the development of technology, innovations, and the discovery of new resources provide a favorable underlying basis for the growth of real investment. In such periods, it is said, the pace of technological progress is accelerated far beyond what may be expected from the usual run of multitudinous inventions, each of relatively small significance. In the long periods of buoyant expansion, quite revolutionary new techniques are introduced which profoundly change the character of the whole economy. They furnish the underlying basis for a vast growth in the stock of capital goods, for an upsurge of real investment. In the succeeding period of prolonged hard times and falling prices, these exceptional technological developments are damped down or run out. The great investment opportunities exploited in the preceding period of buoyant expansion are now largely exhausted. General technological improvements of a less profound character are, to be sure, continually going on, gradually raising the productivity of labor and increasing the real income. Indeed, the great technological advances and the vast real investments completed by the end of the long period of buoyant expansion become the foundation upon which an advancing real income is projected into the succeeding period of falling prices. The rise in real income experienced in this period is in part a function of higher productivity achieved by reason of the technical advance of the period of buoyant expansion.

Schumpeter, with his emphasis on the role of innovations, explains the prolonged buoyant expansion resulting in the rising price trend from 1788 to 1815 by the emergence of the Industrial Revolution. The long period of hard times with the concomitant falling price trend (1815–43) is regarded as the result of readjustments and adaptations which inevitably had to be made once the new structure of productive technique had become more or less firmly incorporated into the economic system.

The second period of buoyant good times, with its rising price trend from 1843 to 1873, he explains by the admittedly new revolutionary technique which, perhaps more than anything else, has profoundly altered the character of modern industrial civilization—namely, the railroad. There can be no question that the development of the railroad opened up vast real investment outlets throughout the Western world, and that this gave a continuous upward push to the economy, making every burst of investment associated with the major business cycle a pronounced and strong one, and tending to weaken the forces making for depression. In the last part of the nineteenth century (1873–97), however, there came a sharp decline in the rate of growth of the railroad industry. The third period of buoyancy, from 1897 to 1920, Professor Schumpeter explains by the emergence of the electrical, chemical, and automotive industries.

The Swedish economist Wicksell, in his famous Chapter XI in *Interest and Prices,*[9] emphasized fundamentally the same technological factors which are heavily relied upon in Schumpeter's explanation. Wicksell quotes Jevons' remark that it was just in the period from 1782 to 1815 that "the very foundations of our home industries were being energetically laid." [10] Similarly Wicksell characterizes the period 1851–73 as one "distinguished, not only by a general progressive movement in industry, but in particular by the freezing of enormous quantities of liquid capital as a result of the completion of the west European railway system." [11] In the period which followed, however, investment opportunities, he thought, were less favorable. "Railway building, though it was continued on an enormous scale, took place mainly in countries outside Europe, or in its more remote regions. In short, there was a considerable lack of really profitable openings for the additions to liquid capital which arose out of the savings of almost all classes of the community." [12]

In the United States, railroad construction reached its peak in the mid-eighties (1882 and 1887 being the all-time high years).

9 K. Wicksell, *Geldzins und Güterpreise,* J. Fischer, Jena, 1898; English translation, *Interest and Prices,* Macmillan and Co., Ltd., 1936.

10 *Ibid.,* p. 171.

11 *Ibid.,* p. 174.

12 *Ibid.,* p. 175.

Thereafter the powerful impulse stemming from this giant industry rapidly ebbed away. Railroad construction proceeded by fits and starts, and for several decades these undulations dominated the cycles of business activity and powerfully influenced the volume of capital formation.

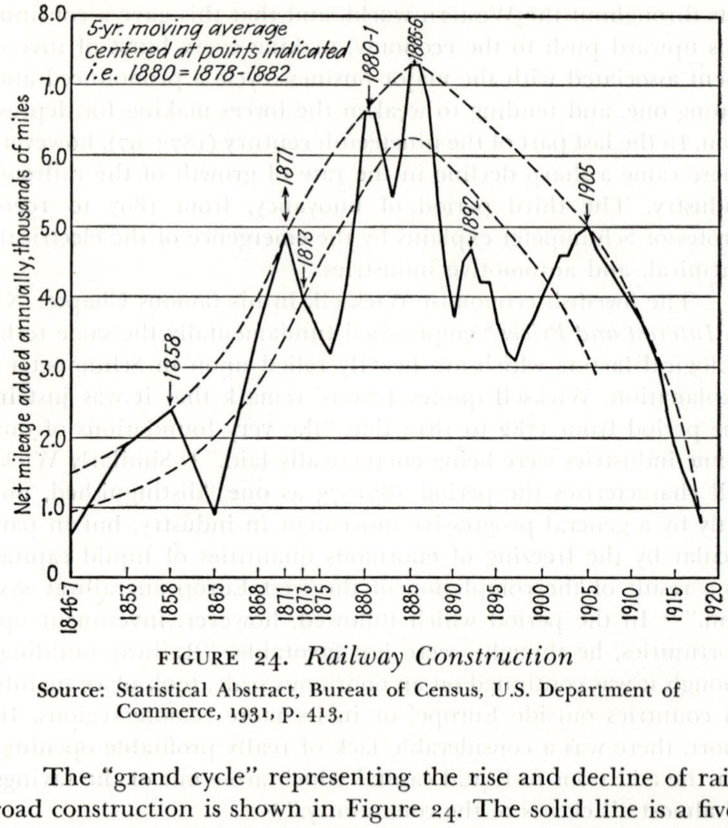

FIGURE 24. *Railway Construction*

Source: Statistical Abstract, Bureau of Census, U.S. Department of Commerce, 1931, p. 413.

The "grand cycle" representing the rise and decline of railroad construction is shown in Figure 24. The solid line is a five-year moving average of railroad mileage constructed from 1846–47 to 1918.

The growth of an industry from infancy to maturity often proceeds at first at an accelerating rate up to the point of inflection. Thereafter the *rate* of growth begins to slow down. Finally the peak is reached, after which the volume of activity flattens out or may even recede into an absolute decline. Occasionally, however, the rate of growth (trend line) may be virtually constant right up to the peak. These two types of growth are illustrated in Figure 25.

The data on new mileage added (Fig. 24) strongly resembles the second type (Fig. 25)—namely a constant rate of growth (trend line) clear up to the peak, though there is also the suggestion of an *accelerating* rate of growth in the first phase of

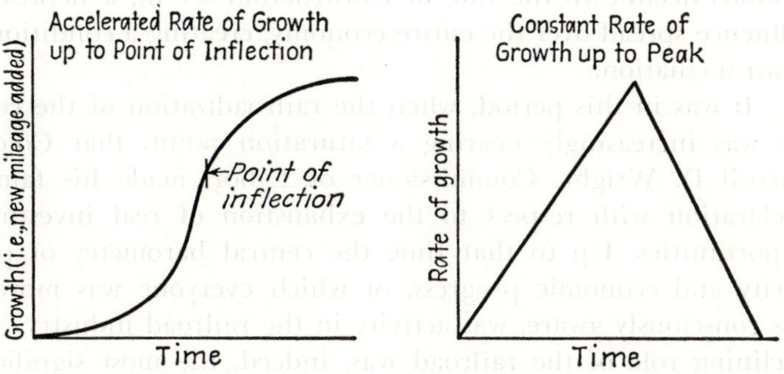

FIGURE 25. *Types of Growth and Decline*

expansion up to around 1871–73. So long as the rate of growth continues without slackening, all the basic underlying industries, such as iron and steel and the equipment-producing industries, will need to continue to expand their production facilities. But once the *rate* of growth slows down, even if there is no actual decline in new construction, further expansion in the basic industries is no longer required. If an actual decline in new mileage occurs (as did in fact happen after the mid-eighties) the underlying industries will find themselves possessed of excess capacity unless, indeed, the growth of other industries takes up the slack. Net investment requires continued growth; net investment ceases whenever replacement and maintenance of facilities already built is all that is required. We shall have much more to say later in this volume about the relation of growth to net investment.

The chart showing the fluctuations in new mileage added (Fig. 24) discloses intermittent surges of growth followed by precipitous declines, each new wave of railroad construction rising higher and higher until the peak level was reached in the mid-eighties. It was the fact of continued growth in new mileage, proceeding though it did by fits and starts, which opened vast outlets for investment in a host of related industries. These surges of railroad construction dominated the cycles of business activity for several decades. And finally after the mid-eighties, when a precipitous decline in the rate of construction set in, a depressant influence spread over the entire economy, creating a condition of quasi stagnation.

It was in this period, when the railroadization of the country was increasingly nearing a saturation point, that Colonel Carroll D. Wright, Commissioner of Labor, made his famous declaration with respect to the exhaustion of real investment opportunities. Up to that time the central barometer of prosperity and economic progress, of which everyone was more or less consciously aware, was activity in the railroad industry. The declining role of the railroad was, indeed, the most significant single fact for this period, and it offers the most convincing explanation for the chronic hard times which characterized the period, particularly the decade of the nineties. Colonel Wright's analysis has, especially in recent years, attracted widespread attention and received much comment. Some, in view of the tremendous expansion ushered in by the electrification and motorization beginning at the end of the century, have been disposed to criticize his analysis as shortsighted. But others regard his observations as the most penetrating and valid analysis of the economic difficulties of his own generation. The investment saturation to which he called attention was evidenced by the continued difficulties which confronted not only the United States, but also the countries of western Europe, for more than a decade after he had made his lucid exposition of the deep, underlying, real factors in the situation. While others were stressing superficial aspects, Colonel Wright placed his finger upon the really significant cause of the world-wide experience of widespread unemployment and hard times.[13] Wicksell's analysis, twelve years later, ran, as we have seen, along similar lines.

WARS AND "LONG WAVES"

The view that the periods of prolonged good times ("Aufschwungsspannen") and bad times ("Stockungsspannen")[14] have been caused by wars has been most effectively presented by Ciriacy-Wantrup.[15] According to this analysis, the long periods of good times are basically caused by the vast governmental expenditures relating to preparation for war and the war itself, while on the other hand the periods of chronic hard times are caused by the difficult readjustments incident to the sharp curtailment of war expenditures.

The best case for this thesis can probably be made with respect to the first "long wave." During the long period of the Napoleonic Wars, the vast government expenditures which they entailed gave a stimulus to economic expansion and hastened the changes in the economic system ushered in by the Industrial Revolution. There can be no doubt that the impact of these wars played a very considerable role. Similarly, the sharp curtailment of expenditures, together with the necessary readjustments to a peacetime basis after the whole of western Europe had for a quarter of a century adjusted itself to war conditions, goes far to explain the difficulties of the long period of chronic hard times from 1815 to the middle forties.

With respect to the second so-called "long wave" the argument for this hypothesis is much less valid. It is true that in the "Aufschwungsspanne" (1843–73) there occurred a number of important wars at various intervals, including the Crimean War, the American Civil War, the Danish-Prussian and Austro-Prussian wars of the sixties, and the Franco-Prussian War of 1871. But

---

13 See U.S. Commissioner of Labor, *First Annual Report,* Government Printing Office, 1886, dealing with industrial depressions.

14 These terms are used by Spiethoff to describe long periods of "expansion" and "stagnation." See his article "Krisen," in *Handwörterbuch der Staatswissenschaften,* 4th Ed., Vol. VI.

15 S. von Ciriacy-Wantrup, *Agrarkrisen und Stockungsspannen,* Paul Parey, 1936.

these wars affected the economy less than the Napoleonic Wars had done in the first long upswing.

For the "Aufschwungsspanne" of the third cycle also, the case for the war thesis seems relatively weak. Reliance would have to be placed upon the expansion of armament expenditures, since the First World War did not come until the very end of the long period of good times. At all events, there is much force in the contention that the difficulties confronting the countries of western Europe from 1920 to 1929 were indeed in large measure related to the aftermath of the First World War. The years following the Second World War presented quite different problems, in view of the "cold war" which eventually led to the Korean crisis of 1950.

On balance, it may perhaps be said that, in the "upswing" phase of the first so-called "long wave," wars occupied a position of major importance, perhaps equal to that of the innovations introduced by the Industrial Revolution. Each reinforced the other, and it is difficult to disentangle the relative potency of each factor. For the second "Aufschwungsspanne" it appears reasonable to conclude that the major factor was the railroadization of the world and that wars played a relatively smaller role, with respect to both the good times and the ensuing period of chronic hard times which followed. For the third period the most reasonable conclusion appears to be that the electrification and motorization of the Western world played by far the dominant role, reinforced toward the end of the period by preparation for the First World War; and that for the succeeding period of economic difficulties, readjustments flowing from the war played an important role, though it may well be that the adaptation of the economic structure to the innovational developments of the preceding period was of equal importance.

GOLD AND SECULAR PRICE TRENDS

Those who have stressed price factors in the so-called long waves have tended to lay great emphasis upon the *effective* supply of monetary gold, a function, on the one hand, of the annual net additions to the gold stock from gold production and, on the other hand, of the increasing volume of trade. Those, like Cassel, who have stressed this analysis have usually limited their discussion to the period from the mid-nineteenth century to 1913. Cassel calculated the effective gold supply by correcting the monetary gold stock by an index of an estimated rising trend of the physical volume of trade assumed to increase at a compound rate of 3 per cent per annum. He found that the *effective* gold supply rose during the period from around 1850 to the early seventies, fell from the early seventies to the middle nineties, and rose again to 1913. This movement correlates closely with the general movement of commodity prices and also with the dates usually assigned for the second so-called "long wave" and the first half of the third. According to this type of analysis, the price movements are caused by the gold movements.

Gold production is clearly more or less a result of accidental discoveries and the development of new mining and refining techniques. While these developments may themselves, to a certain extent, be related to changes in the profitableness of producing gold, they are certainly, in some measure, independent or autonomous. Nevertheless, it is quite clear that the fluctuation of gold production is, in part, related to the changes in the general commodity price level which alter the costs of gold production and therefore (since the monetary price of gold is fixed by law) the profitableness of producing gold.[16] From this standpoint, gold production may be looked upon as a result of price movements, and not a cause.

The farther prices fall, the lower are the costs of gold production. The ratio of cost of gold production to the fixed monetary price of gold thus becomes increasingly favorable in a period of falling prices, so that eventually a point is reached at which the production of gold begins to rise.[17] In the period of high prices (1853 to 1881) gold production was discouraged, and this influence continued until prices fell below "normal." But when prices had fallen below normal, the cost of gold production was low in relation to the fixed monetary price of gold. This caused an upturn of gold production, and this trend continued so long as prices re-

16 The increase in the monetary price of gold in terms of most currencies in recent years has stimulated gold production.

17 See Warren and Pearson, *Gold and Prices,* John Wiley & Sons, Inc., New York, 1935, p. 132.

mained below normal. Prices reached bottom in the nineties but remained below the trend line from about 1881 to 1913. Thus the stimulus to gold production continued throughout the period of relatively low prices.

The interrelations between prices and gold production are disclosed in Figure 26. At the bottom of the diagram is a curve of

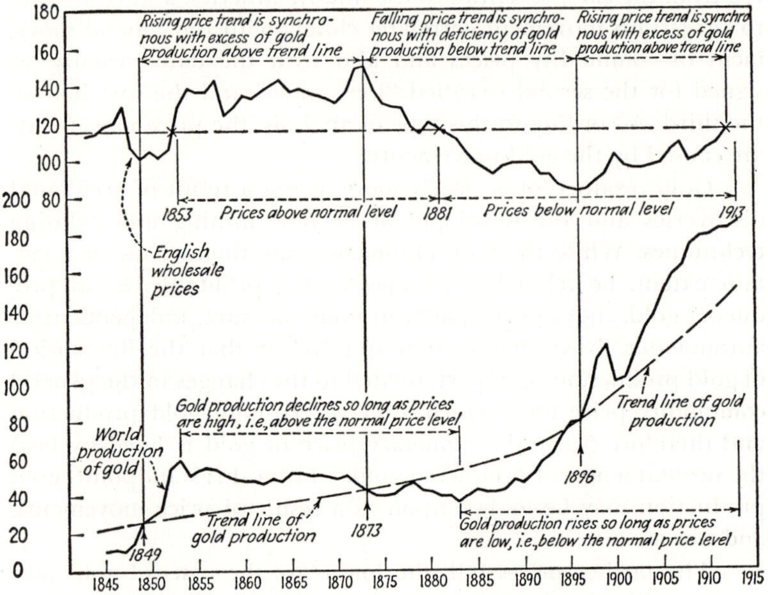

FIGURE 26. *Gold Production and Prices*

Source: *Gold and Prices,* by George F. Warren and Frank E. Pearson, John Wiley and Sons, 1935, pp. 92–93, 121.

world gold production from 1845 to 1913, together with a trend line representing the long-run rate of growth of gold production. When gold production exceeds the trend line, gold stocks are being added to at a rate exceeding the normal growth of gold stocks. Thus from 1849 to 1873 the gold stock was growing at a rate exceeding normal. It is Cassel's view that this explains why prices were rising in this period (see the curve at the top of the diagram). Similarly, from 1873 to 1896 gold production ran below the normal trend line. In Cassel's view, gold stocks were accumulating at a slower than normal rate and so prices were falling (see curve at top).

Looking at the matter quite the other way around, it is equally logical to argue that it was the movement of prices (determined, for example, by the buoyancy or stagnation of real investment) which caused the fluctuations in gold production. Thus the price level was above "normal" (see top curve) from 1853 to 1881; and as long as prices (and costs) were abnormally high, gold production was discouraged. In consequence (see lower curve) gold production sagged slowly from 1853 to 1884. Similarly, prices were running below "normal" (see top curve) from 1881 to 1913; and as long as prices (and costs) were abnormally low, gold production was stimulated. Accordingly (see lower curve) gold production continued to rise from 1883 to 1913. From this point of view, then, the trends of gold production are to be explained by price movements, not the other way around. The gold production curve leads the price curve roughly by a quarter cycle, and this gives the superficial impression that the price movement is caused by the gold movement. Actually the causal relation, as explained above, could run the other way.

Evidently it is possible to find in the interrelation between gold production and prices an illustration of econometric models based on the lagged response of supply to demand. In this case "supply" refers to the *stock* of gold. When prices are high (i.e., above normal), the current production of gold is discouraged and so falls progressively until, after a lag, the stock of gold is being added to at less than the normal rate. If the stock of gold is growing at less than the normal rate of the aggregate output of goods, this means that the *effective* gold supply (i.e., gold stock in relation to aggregate output) is falling. Aggregate output of goods, in other words, is outrunning the gold supply, and so prices tend to fall. But low prices in turn lead to an increase in the current production of gold, and so eventually the stock of gold will grow at a rate in excess of the normal rate. This means that the supply (stock) of gold is outrunning the aggregate output of goods, and so prices tend to rise. Low prices cause increased current production of gold; increased production *after a lag* causes the gold stock to grow in excess of the rate of the aggregate output of goods; this leads to high prices, which in turn curtails current gold production, resulting, after a lag, in a fall in the ratio of gold stock to industrial production—and so on indefinitely. Thus, if we accept this analysis, we have here an illustration of a self-perpetuating endogenous cycle.[18]

While it is not possible at this point to go into any extended discussion of the theory of money and prices,[19] it may be said that the trend of monetary thinking is in the direction of laying less stress than formerly upon the purely monetary factors and still less stress upon gold. It is clear that the more credit instruments are developed, the farther modern money is removed from gold. The development of deposit currency, and also the development of central banking, permit a high degree of variation between the volume of money (including deposits) and the gold supply. There is no longer any close connection between them.

The trend of modern monetary thinking runs in the direction of emphasizing the factors which influence fluctuations in total money income rather than factors influencing the constituent elements in the total volume of money payments, namely, M, the amount of money (including demand deposits), and V, the velocity of turnover. If the prevailing forces tend to cause a rise in the money income, the possibilities under modern conditions of increasing the quantity of money regardless of the gold base, or of utilizing any given quantity of money more efficiently through changes in turnover or velocity, are so great that it may, on a broad basis, safely be said that there are no serious limits, from the point of view of the money supply, to movements of money income. We must look for other factors, notably those affecting the prospective marginal rate of return on investment, rather than limitation or superabundance of the money supply, to explain secular movements of income and prices.

Thus, if technological developments and innovations tend to favor a rapid expansion in real investment, money incomes may be expected to rise, and the money supply and its utilization (MV)

---

18 See the discussion of econometric lagged models in Chapters 21 and 22 of this book.

19 See Alvin H. Hansen, *Monetary Theory and Fiscal Policy,* McGraw-Hill Book Company, New York, 1949.

may be expected to be adjusted to these conditions. If, on the other hand, the underlying technological developments are unfavorable to a rapid expansion of real investment, money income will fail to keep pace with output and the secular trend of prices will be downward. Here again the money supply (M) and its utilization (V) are thought to adjust themselves to the demands of the underlying real factors. Still more obvious is the fact that, in periods of vast war expenditures, governments, through radical readjustments in the monetary system such as the abandonment of the gold standard, adapt the money situation to their own demands. Monetary expenditures in wartime have never encountered any limits in terms of the money supply. Such limits as have been imposed run mainly in terms of direct price controls and of governmental policies with respect to the methods employed for obtaining revenues, whether by taxation or by borrowing.

In line with Wicksell's ideas, the trend of modern thinking points to the conclusion that gold and monetary factors play a subsidiary role and that the main causes of the long periods of upswing and downswing of prices must be sought in technological and innovational factors and, at times, to a greater or less degree, in the fiscal policies of governments hitherto related mainly to the conduct of war.

AGRICULTURE AND SECULAR TRENDS [20]

During most of the nineteenth century, agriculture still played a dominant role in economic life. And even now, in the highly industrialized part of the world, the movements of agricultural prices are of the highest significance. Thus food shortages greatly increased inflationary pressures following the Second World War, and the emergence of agricultural surpluses (the first signs of which appeared in January, 1948) more than any other single factor helped to conquer the world-wide inflation.

Agriculture the world over suffered from prolonged depression from 1873 to 1896. Then came a long period of agricultural prosperity, from 1896 to 1920. After 1920, agriculture was again afflicted with secular difficulties.

[20] See Tinbergen and Polak, *The Dynamics of Business Cycles,* University of Chicago Press, 1950, Chapter 12.

In the period 1873–96, the vast expansion of the great West, the flooding of world markets with agricultural products from the new world, made possible by the development of railroad and ocean transportation, adversely affected the older agricultural areas.

On the other hand, in the period 1896 to 1920, two factors caused the world demand to outrun agricultural productive capacity. The first was the rapidly increasing world population; the second was the First World War. This growing demand called forth increased output at rising marginal cost. Agricultural prices rose far more rapidly than commodity prices in general. Farm lands advanced rapidly in value. It was an era of prolonged agricultural prosperity.

Again from 1920 to 1939 we had agricultural hard times. The expansion incident to the First World War stimulated the opening up of grain-producing areas, and this development was greatly facilitated by agricultural mechanization. When Europe came back into full production after the war, the world was left with agricultural overcapacity. The "terms of trade" between agriculture and industry seriously deteriorated.

The Thirties and Earlier Long Depressions

According to the technological and innovational thesis, the electrification and motorization of the American economy dominated the period from the late nineties to 1929. From this standpoint this epoch may be compared to the earlier period of rapid expansion in railroadization from around 1845 to 1875. Both of these innovations caused a profound structural change in economic life and institutions. Both related mainly to speed of communication and transportation. Both opened up enormous opportunities for real investment, not only directly but indirectly. Thus in the latter period investment was made not only in automobile factories and in roads, but also in a vast network of underlying and supplementary industries, including glass, rubber, steel, cement, electrical appliances, petroleum, and the like.

These epochs are clear illustrations of the profound impact of the rise of quite new techniques which give birth to a range of new industries and lead to the expansion and development of old ones into new lines. Both epochs represent a period of rapid growth and expansion.

But all new developments finally reach the stage of maturity. Thus, new railroad mileage experienced a rapidly rising trend from the middle forties of the nineteenth century to the decade of the seventies, and thereafter flattened out—with, however, a major spurt in the middle eighties—and eventually, in the nineties, sharply declined. Similarly, the production of automobiles and the construction of roads experienced a rapid growth into the decade of the twenties of this century. But this rate of growth could obviously not be continued indefinitely. Automobile production gradually reached an asymptotic level after 1923, and the curve of the construction of roads similarly flattened out toward the end of the twenties and thereafter declined.

In the long sweep of technological and innovational developments the decade of the thirties was, therefore, in many respects not unlike the fourth quarter of the nineteenth century, with its deep depressions of the seventies and the nineties. Thus against the background of earlier experience the decade of the thirties is more understandable.

The period of railroad expansion served to promote vigorous booms and to cut short temporary lapses into depression. But gradually the railroad reached maturity, and eventually it ceased to grow. The mere slowing down in the *rate* of growth caused an absolute decline in the volume of new investment required in the plant and equipment of subsidiary industries, such as iron and steel, which manufactured the materials that went into railroad construction. Those who point to the high level of new railroad construction which continued on into the eighties miss the point. It is not enough that new railroad construction should continue at the high level reached. New construction must *continue to rise at a constant rate* if new investment in the underlying, subsidiary industries is to be maintained at the pace set. Thus the mere slowing down in the *rate of increase* in new railroad construction was already beginning to have a damping effect on the economy long before there was an actual decline in the volume of new construction. This is the important lesson which we learn from the principle of derived demand. Finally came the *absolute* decline in railroad construction in the decade of the nineties; and this was a significant factor in that depressed decade.

But now a new era of buoyancy superseded the railroad era—the era of electricity and motorcars. The three decades 1900–1929 witnessed the rise of four new giant industries.[21] Streetcars led the way in the nineties and reached the investment peak ($2.5 billions) in the decade 1900–1909. Capital outlays on telephones increased rapidly after 1900 and doubled in each of the two succeeding decades, rising to $2.5 billions in the twenties. Electric power investment first assumed large proportions in the decade 1900–1909 ($1.7 billions), increased 50 per cent in the following decade, and leaped forward with a capital expenditure of $8.1 billions in the twenties. Automobile production rose from only 4,000 units in 1900 to 187,000 units in 1910, to 1,000,000 in 1915, to 2,200,000 in 1920, to 4,400,000 in 1925, and to 5,600,000 in 1929. Garages, repair shops, and service stations multiplied throughout the country. Thus the rise in the automobile industry not only induced the construction of gigantic production plants, largely concentrated in a single industrial area, but also opened opportunities for thousands of small business units located in all sections of the country roughly in proportion to the consuming population. Major subsidiary industries were created or expanded on the tide of the vast purchasing power of the automobile industry, including such giants as petroleum, rubber, glass plate, and steel. Finally, outlays on public roads, largely induced by the rise of the automobile, reached the figure of $9.9 billions in the decade 1920–29.[22]

Thus an era of buoyant prosperity was generated by the growth of four great industries: street railways, telephone, electric power, and automobile industries (including petroleum, rubber, and glass plate, largely accessory to the automobile). Also important, but nevertheless dwarfed by the four giants, were the movie, chemical, and electrical equipment industries.

Just as the railroad expansion came to an end, so also did the buoyant era of 1900–29. Street railway development was largely completed in the first decade, telephone and automobile ex-

21 I am indebted to John Wilson, formerly instructor in economics at Harvard University, for the use of data in his unpublished manuscript.

22 From *Temporary National Economic Committee Hearings,* Part 1, p. 232.

pansion in the third decade. Of the four, electric power had the largest remaining prospects for further growth. But taking all these industries together, the spectacular era of expansion was over by 1930. Thus conditions in the decade of the thirties resembled those in the nineties.

In the Great Depression of the thirties there occurred for the first time in American history a drastic decline in the absolute rate of population growth. Every previous depression had been buoyed up by the capital requirements associated with an ever larger increment of population. The decade of the nineteen-thirties enjoyed no such stimulus.

In the decade of the nineteen-forties, however, there was a strong resurgence of population growth, and this in part accounts for the high level of capital requirements in the years following the Second World War. The accumulated backlog of capital needs which confronted the economy after 1945 was in some measure greater by reason of the large growth in population in the decade of the forties. By the same token the decade of the thirties suffered from a dearth of investment opportunities, partly by reason of the drastic decline in the rate of growth.

Here again, as in the case of the growth of railroad mileage, discussed above, the full impact can be understood only in terms of the acceleration principle. If the capital capacity of the heavy industries has been built up to a point adequate to take care of railroad replacement *plus* new mileage, excess capacity in these basic industries will appear whenever the *rate of growth* of mileage declines. The same holds true if the basic industries have developed a capacity adequate to take care of a given rate of population growth. Any decline in that rate will tend to have a depressional effect upon the volume of investment. After the economy has become adjusted to a rate of growth of around 16 or 17 million per decade, a decline in the rate of growth to less than 9 million could not fail to chill the outlook for investment. On the other hand, as we have just noted, the remarkable and unexpected spurt of population in the decade of the forties has raised expectations with respect to profitable investment outlets. Whether this postwar increase in population is based on fundamental factors which have altered the specific fertility rates, or whether it is merely a reflection of temporary factors stemming from the war, is not yet clear.

A large growth in population is favorable to investment and therefore to income generation and employment. This is the Keynesian view of population growth. But a population may become so large in relation to natural resources and food supply that real wages tend to fall, or at least to fall below the optimum level. This is the Malthusian view of population growth.[23]

As far as general economic expansion is concerned, it must always be remembered that throughout the era of modern industrialization there were three strands to the process—namely, technological innovations, the development of new territory, and the growth of population. Each has reinforced the others, but at times, when one or another has slackened, one of the other factors has taken an exceptional spurt, as was, for example, the case with respect to technology in the period of electrification and motorization of the American economy.[24]

---

23 The following table gives the decennial increase in population in the United States during the last five decades. There was a moderate decline in the second decade, 1910–19, but any unfavorable investment effects of this decline were swallowed up in the advancing tide of wartime prosperity. Thus the decade of the thirties was the first peacetime decade to suffer a significant absolute decline in the rate of population growth.

Decade	*Increase*
1900–09	16,000,000
1910–19	13,700,000
1920–29	17,000,000
1930–39	8,900,000
1940–49	18,000,000

24 For a fuller discussion of the problems of extensive and intensive investment, see Alvin H. Hansen, *Fiscal Policy and Business Cycles,* W. W. Norton and Company, Inc., 1941, Chapters I and XVII; and also the reply to George Terborgh's *The Bogey of Economic Maturity* in Alvin H. Hansen, *Economic Policy and Full Employment,* McGraw-Hill Book Company, 1947, Appendix B.

5 · *Investment in the Business Cycle*

In previous chapters we have repeatedly referred to the role of capital investment and consumers' durables in the business cycle. In this chapter we shall consider this matter factually, especially the fluctuations in the outlays on different categories of capital or investment goods in the different phases of the business cycle. The theoretical analysis will be reserved for Parts Two and Three.

Investment Categories

It may be well to remind the reader again of what we mean by investment. We do *not* mean "financial" investment—the purchase of a mortgage, bond, or share of stock in a corporation. By investment we mean *real* investment—in other words, the purchase of new capital goods. This includes (a) producers' plant, (b) producers' equipment, (c) residential structures, (d) net additions to inventory stocks held by business firms in the form of raw materials and semifinished and finished products, and (e) net foreign investment.

Investment in producers' plant includes outlays on all kinds of construction, not only buildings but also railroad and other public utility construction. (The building cycle involves a part, but *only* a part, of the total outlays included in the construction investment category.) Producers' equipment includes machinery and all kinds of equipment in commercial, financial, and industrial establishments.

Outlays made on producers' plant and equipment together make up the real investment in *producers' fixed capital.* Thus we could reclassify total private investment into (a) producers' fixed capital, (b) inventory stocks, (c) residential construction, and (d) net foreign investment.

Consumers' Durables

Outlays on durable consumers' goods (automobiles, household equipment, and the like) are sometimes included under "investment." Consumers' durables bear a resemblance to producers' equipment in several important respects. They require an investment of funds during the interval in which they are used. Moreover, since they have a durability which is not rigorously fixed, it is possible to postpone the purchase of a new unit, if necessary, beyond the normal period of use. Further, durable consumers' goods, like producers' equipment, are subject to obsolescence in the event that new inventions are introduced. Finally, since they are durable, some part of the available flow of loanable funds may be channeled into the financing of their sale, ownership in such goods being thereby divided, as in the case of fixed capital, into equities and debt obligations.

In all these respects, durable consumers' goods resemble producers' equipment, and, indeed, investment goods in general; and, from a strictly logical standpoint, they might well be included (as indeed they often are) in the investment category. This procedure requires, however, the calculation of an imputed "rent" from these goods, which "rent" becomes then a part of consumers' expenditures precisely as is done with respect to housing. On these lines, the purchase of an automobile would then be an investment outlay, and the imputed rental value during each year of its life would constitute the "consumption" item for automobiles. It is, however, common practice—for example in the Commerce Department figures on total expenditures on goods and services—to count the purchase of the automobile itself as a consumption expenditure, just as we count the purchase of a fur coat as a consumption expenditure. For some purposes, however, it may be preferable to include outlays on consumers' durables as a part of investment.

Consumption

Consumption expenditures, as the term is commonly used, include outlays on (a) consumers' durables, (b) semidurable goods, such as clothing, (c) nondurables, such as food, and (d) services (such as amusement, recreation, medical, legal, professional, and personal services, motion pictures, hotel services, private education, house rents, etc.)

The Role of Investment

We now turn to an examination of investment outlays divided into various categories and their relation to the business cycle. The role of building construction as a whole we have already examined in some detail in the chapter on building cycles.

The major business cycle consists essentially of fluctuations in investment outlays of all kinds. The central core of this investment activity has to do with total fixed capital, including producers' durable equipment, producers' plant, and residential construction. But there enter also in every case, though with varying degrees of intensity, fluctuations in outlays on inventories and net foreign investment.

FIXED CAPITAL

Figures 27 and 28 relate the fluctuations of investment in total fixed capital (producers' plant and equipment, and residential construction) to fluctuations in gross national product [1] for (a) the period 1919–33 and (b) the period 1929–41. Note how the outlays on fixed capital establish the essential character and pattern of the fluctuations of general business activity (as revealed in the gross national product) for each of the two periods. It should be noted that the scales are adjusted so as to make the amplitude of

---

1 This means the money value of all "final" goods and services produced each year, not counting "intermediate" products such as the leather used in the production of shoes. Leather is an "intermediate" product; shoes are a "final" product. The concept "gross national product" will be discussed more fully in Chapter 6.

the two curves approximately the same. The gross national product, in fact, fluctuated from $55 billion to about $100 billion in the period 1919–33, while total fixed capital outlays fluctuated from $3 billion to around $16 billion. Percentagewise total fixed capital outlays fluctuated far more violently. Much the same relationship between these two variables will be observed for the period 1929–41 as disclosed in Figure 28.

These two charts together present a general picture of the cyclical movements from 1919 to 1941. Later in our analysis (see Chapters 9 and 10) we shall show that fixed capital outlays play a highly dynamic role in the rise and fall of economic activity and so in the rise and fall of the value of goods and services produced (gross national product). The two charts (Figs. 27 and 28) reveal that the fluctuations in the aggregate value of output correspond very closely to the fluctuations in fixed capital outlays. The causal relationship, as we shall see later, runs both ways. In part, the rise and fall in gross national product induces a rise and decline in fixed capital outlays; and in part, independent or autonomous increases and decreases in fixed capital outlays raise and lower the volume of employment and purchasing power and thereby exert a rapidly spreading influence upon the economy as a whole.

Total fixed capital outlays include, as we have seen, (a) producers' plant and equipment and (b) residential construction. Let us now exclude residential construction and concentrate upon that part of fixed capital outlays made by business—namely, producers' plant and equipment. Of especial significance are the fluctuations in outlays on plant and equipment in relation to fluctuations in business outlays on inventories. Consider, for example, Figure 29, which compares these fluctuations from 1919 to 1933, and Figure 30, which gives the movements of these variables from 1929 to 1941.

Particularly interesting is Figure 29. The period from 1921 to 1933 covers a major cycle with a great upsurge in 1929, but checked in its general upward sweep at two intervals, 1923 and 1926. This is clearly disclosed in the curve showing the outlays in producers' plant and equipment. In both instances the drag on the general expansion is comparatively slight. Outlays on plant and equip-

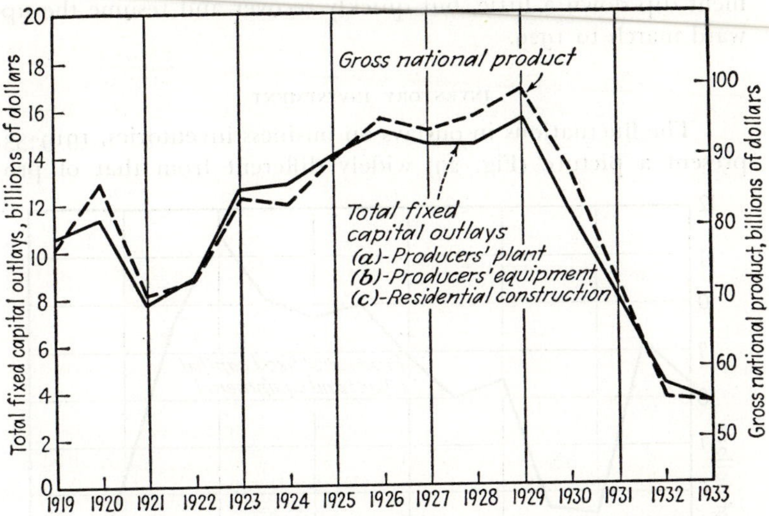

FIGURE 27. *Gross National Product and Fixed Capital Outlays, 1919–33*

Source: *Federal Reserve Bulletin*, September, 1945, p. 873. Senate Document Print No. 4, 79th Congress, 1st Session.

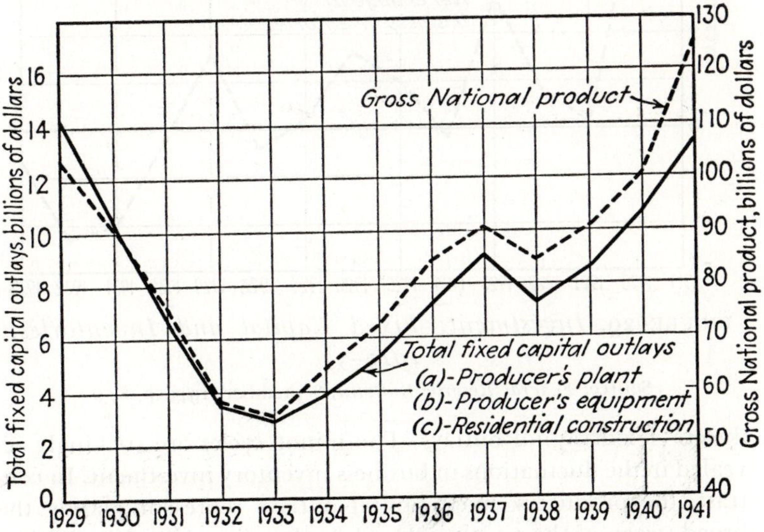

FIGURE 28. *Gross National Product and Fixed Capital Outlays, 1929–41*

Source: *Economic Report of the President*, January, 1950.

ment dip down a little, but quickly recover and resume the upward march to 1929.

INVENTORY INVESTMENT

The fluctuations in outlays on business inventories, 1919–33, present a picture (Fig. 29) widely different from that of pro-

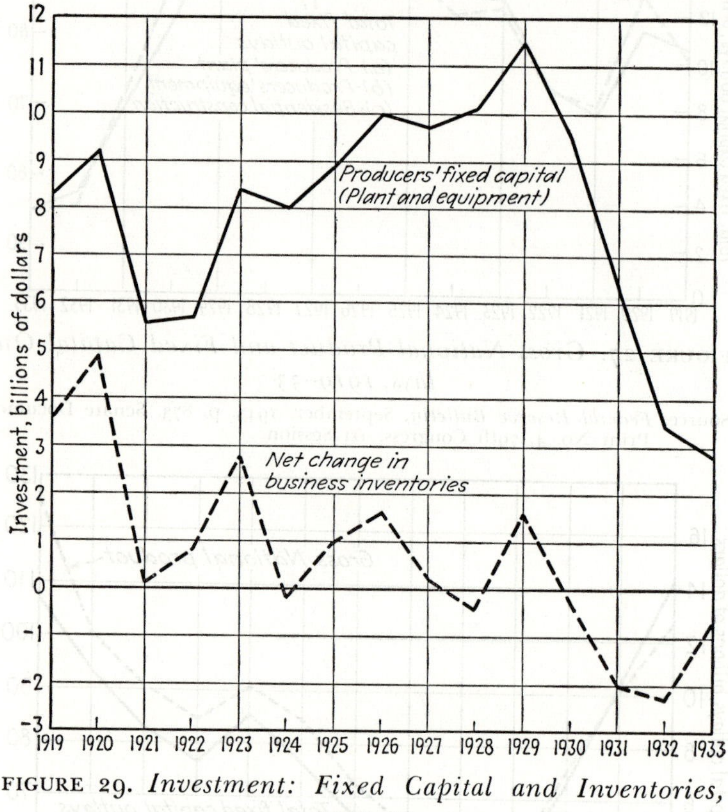

FIGURE 29. *Investment: Fixed Capital and Inventories, 1919–33*

Source: *Federal Reserve Bulletin*, September, 1945, p. 873.

ducers' fixed capital outlays. The minor cycles are strikingly revealed in the fluctuations in business inventory investment. In contrast, the producers' fixed capital outlays represent mainly the broad sweep of the major cycle, while the minor dips in 1924 and

1927 reflect the relatively mild response of fixed capital outlays to the dramatic changes in inventory investment. Though checked in the general expansionist sweep by the rather violent fluctuations in inventories, producers' fixed capital outlays remain high

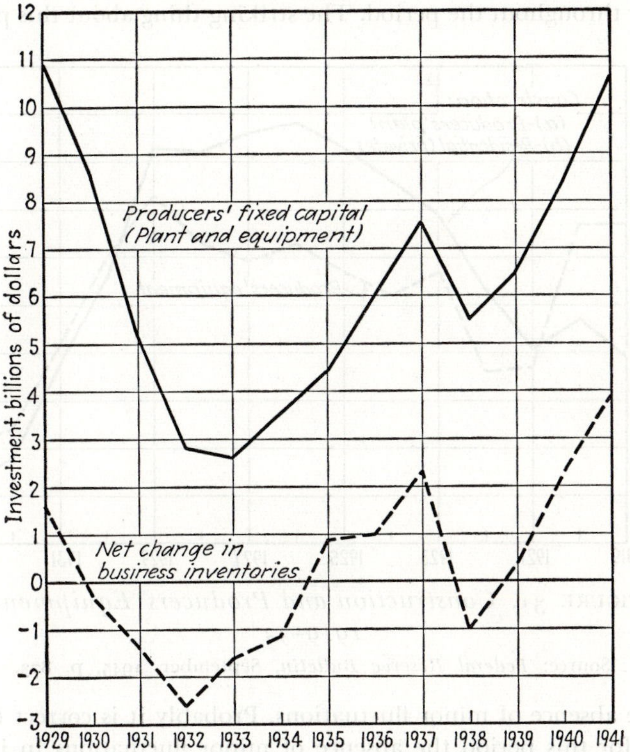

FIGURE 30. *Investment: Fixed Capital and Inventories, 1929–41*

Source: *Economic Report of the President,* January, 1950.

and continue their upward course until 1929. Thereafter, however, the sharp recession in inventory holdings reinforces the heavy decline in producers' fixed capital outlays. Together they initiate the drastic decline in total business activity in the Great Depression.

In Figure 30 the picture (1929–41) is considerably different. There are no minor cycles, only the downswing from 1929 to 1932, the major cycle of 1932 to 1938, and the subsequent upswing to the high prewar year of 1941. Here the fluctuations in producers' fixed capital outlays and in business inventories reinforce each other throughout the period. The striking thing about this period

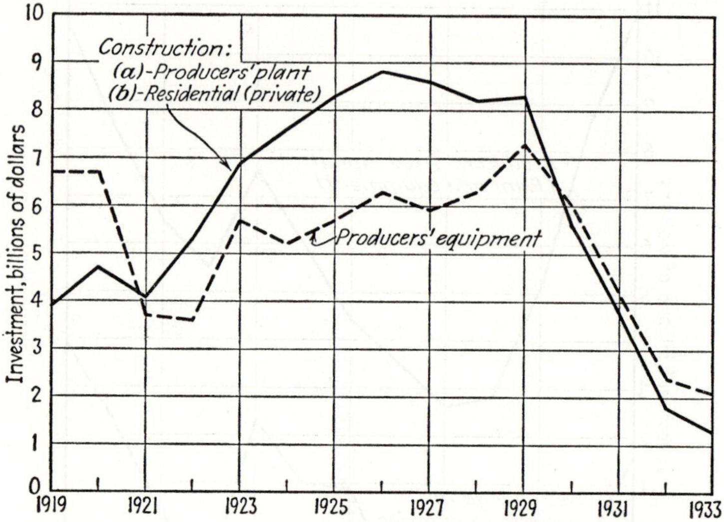

FIGURE 31. *Construction and Producers' Equipment, 1919–33*

Source: *Federal Reserve Bulletin*, September, 1945, p. 873.

is the absence of minor fluctuations. Probably it is correct to say that for this period the absence of minor fluctuations in inventories explains the absence of minor cycles for business activity as a whole.

PRODUCERS' EQUIPMENT

In Figure 31 we present the relation of total construction (producers' plant and residential construction) to outlays on producers' equipment for the period 1919–33. Outlays on producers' equipment declined drastically from 1920 to 1921, but construction, which was already at a low ebb because of the war, declined very little. Outlays on equipment continued to decline in 1922, but construction forged ahead, preparing the way for the great expansion of the twenties. Indeed, for the entire boom of the twenties, it was first and foremost *construction* which constituted the firm foundation of this buoyant decade. The outlays on producers' equipment ran at a relatively moderate level from 1923 to

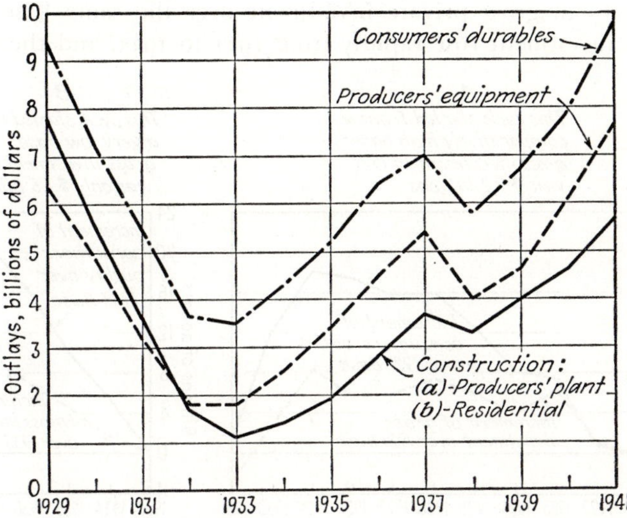

FIGURE 32. *Construction, Producers' Equipment, and Consumers' Durables, 1929–41*

Source: *Economic Report of the President,* January, 1950.

1927, but advanced sharply to the 1929 peak just as construction was beginning to recede. This, together with the inventory advance of 1929 (see Fig. 29), carried the economy up to the high peak of 1929 despite the sagging tendency of construction.

In contrast (Fig. 32) the outlays on producers' equipment played a dominant role in the period of expansion from 1933 to 1941. Construction, however, lagged behind, and this accounts in large part for the relatively depressed thirties. The fluctuations in the outlays on consumers' durables paralleled at every point in this period the fluctuations in outlays on producers' equipment.

Together these two variables produced the main support for the expansion culminating in the high peacetime level of 1941.

Consumption and Investment

Let us now take a still more general view. Consider (Fig. 33) the increases in total consumer expenditures over the level of 1921 (the initial trough of the 1929 cycle) compared with the increases in gross private investment over the same base year. Gross investment rose rapidly from 1921 to 1923, and thereafter

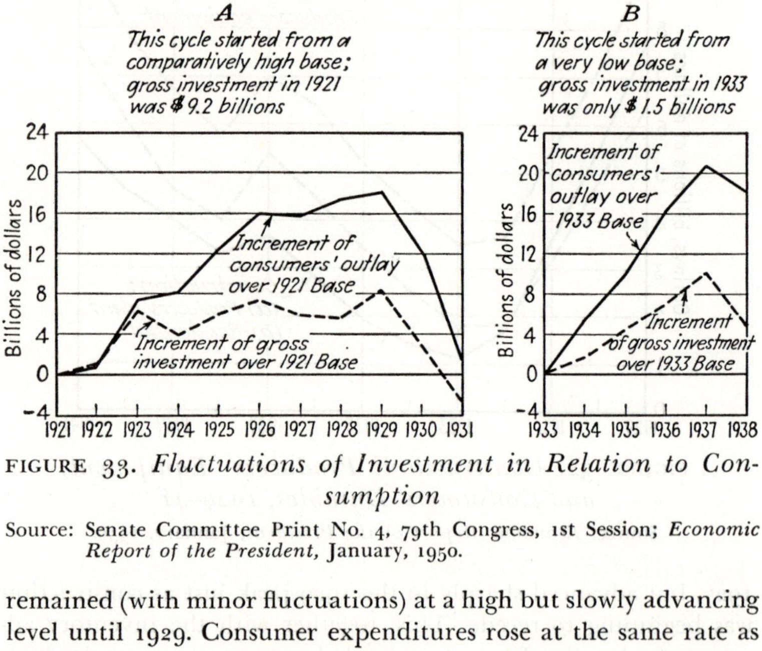

FIGURE 33. *Fluctuations of Investment in Relation to Consumption*

Source: Senate Committee Print No. 4, 79th Congress, 1st Session; *Economic Report of the President,* January, 1950.

remained (with minor fluctuations) at a high but slowly advancing level until 1929. Consumer expenditures rose at the same rate as gross investment outlays for two years, but thereafter continued to climb until a fairly stable high plateau was reached in 1926, with, however, some further (relatively small) expansion in 1928 and 1929. From 1926 to 1929 consumption outlays rose (above the level of 1921) more than twice as much as did gross investment. Thus if we regard the investment outlays as the dynamic factor mainly responsible for the boom, we see that investment raised income, gradually and with a lag, by a magnified amount via the large induced rise in consumer expenditures. Since consumption finally rose by more than double the investment, income as a whole rose by a multiple of more than three. As employment in the heavy (investment) industries rose to high levels, this in turn induced an expansion of consumption expenditures not only by the newly employed workers in the capital goods industries but also by the additional workers employed in related industries (including consumption goods industries), which experienced an uplift by reason of the general expansion.

The second section (B) of Figure 33, depicting the period 1933–38, presents a broadly similar picture. Some important differences may, however, be noted. First attention should be called to the fact that the level of both gross investment outlays and consumption outlays was exceptionally low in the trough year, 1933, compared with the 1921 trough. The increase of both investment and consumption above the 1933 level from 1933 to 1937 was indeed spectacular, but both started from an abnormally low level. The rate of advance was unusually rapid, but the level reached by 1937 was nevertheless abnormally low because of the depth from which the upward movement started. As we have seen in an earlier chapter, this was the first major cycle in which the recovery did not rise to a level surpassing that of the previous peak.

Another difference to be noted is that in the 1933–37 expansion, government outlays to consumers played a significant role. Accordingly, consumer outlays in the early years of the 1937 expansion advanced, relative to gross investment, more rapidly than in the 1929 expansion. Throughout the period of the expansion, consumption outlays rose (over the 1933 level) by about twice the increase in investment outlays.

Government Outlays and Investment

During the First World War, and especially in the Second World War, government outlays largely determined the gross national product of the entire economy. Government outlays also played an important part in the expansion from 1933 to 1937, reinforced, however (unlike the war years), by gross private investment. Throughout the expansion of the twenties, private investment was the controlling factor.

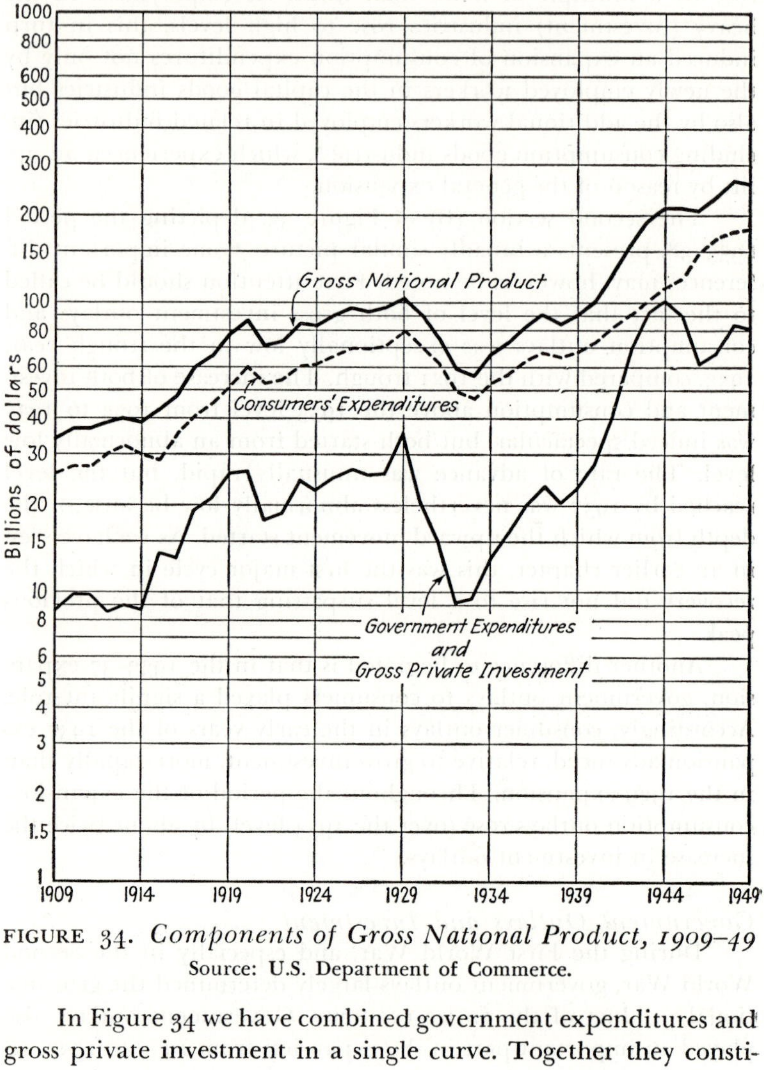

FIGURE 34. *Components of Gross National Product, 1909–49*
Source: U.S. Department of Commerce.

In Figure 34 we have combined government expenditures and gross private investment in a single curve. Together they constitute the spark plug for the economy as a whole. When gross private investment and government expenditures rise to high levels, the effect is to raise income by a magnified amount, since the prosperity these expenditures engender induces a rise in consumption expenditures. The stimulating effect of governmental expenditures is conspicuously evident in the war experience. During the boom twenties, on the other hand, the stimulating effect of large private investment outlays was the dominating feature.

Gross National Product

The top curve in Figure 34 represents gross national product. The gross national product is the sum of the other two components represented in the chart: (1) consumers' expenditures and (2) government expenditures plus gross private investment. The chart is drawn on a semilogarithmic scale, so that the steepness of the curve displays the *percentage* changes. Percentagewise the fluctuations in the "government expenditure plus gross private investment" curve are much greater than those of consumers' expenditures, though *absolutely* the changes in the latter are usually greater in peacetime periods. In the peak of the Second World War, 1944, government expenditures plus gross private investment (the latter was insignificant in 1944) nearly equaled consumers' expenditures. But this was unprecedented. In the First World War they reached together only half the level of consumers' outlays. Altogether Figure 34 gives us an impressive picture of the sweeping fluctuations in the economy from 1909 to 1948, together with the main components of the total national product for this period.

PART TWO

The Theory of Income and Employment

6 · *The National Income*

One of the most important achievements of economics in the twentieth century is the development of concepts and data relating to the national income. "National income" can be interpreted in various ways, and there are at least five different variants which we shall need to distinguish.

The development of this concept, together with the statistical data relating thereto, has awakened a public interest in the national economy. As a nation we have become aware of the importance and role of the major components of the national income, and we study their movements and interrelations with a view to determining whether the current situation is balanced and sound or whether it is likely to lead to inflationary or deflationary strains and stresses.

Business executives, large and small, labor and agricultural leaders, members of Congress, administrative heads of the various divisions of the federal government, local officials, and informed individuals generally, all use national income concepts and data. Publicists and commentators, whether in the press or on the radio, find it difficult to discuss current economic developments without relating events to the central barometer, the national income. The concept of the "national income" has become an essential tool for thought and action with respect to economic affairs in the modern world.

But it is a complicated and difficult concept, much misused and often misunderstood. We shall attempt in this chapter to cut through the technicalities and complexities, and to present a straightforward account which we hope may be useful to the student and to the general reader. Through the process of education, we shall gradually become more competent, as a nation, in our handling of these useful but complex tools for intelligent thought and action.

National Income Variants

We said above that the "national income" is a broad concept of which there are at least five variants. They are as follows:

1. Gross national product
2. Net national product
3. National income at factor cost
4. Personal income
5. Disposable income

GROSS NATIONAL PRODUCT

The most inclusive concept of all these is "gross national product," or in more extended form "gross national product at market prices." By "gross national product" we mean the money value of all the final goods and services produced in any given period, usually a month, a quarter, or a year.

In the phrase "final goods and services" used above, the word "final" is important. The gross national product does not include *all* the goods produced. Many goods are *intermediate* products—products which enter as raw materials, or semifinished materials, into the final goods produced and whose cost is a part of the cost of the final goods. Thus a suit of clothes is a final product, and we include it in the gross national product; but we do not also include the cloth of which the suit was made or the wool from which the cloth was made. Similarly, we do not include the coal used to produce electricity, heat, or light in the textile-manufacturing plant. All these myriad forms of intermediate products are excluded.

Many textile products are, of course, sold directly to consumers and are not made into suits or other articles of apparel before reaching the consumer. Such textiles are *final* products.

Similarly, coal is not only used in a factory; it is also sold to households for direct consumer use. Such coal is a *final* product.

The vast productive process of the nation as a whole consists of a long succession of operations through which materials pass from the raw to the finished state, including the transfer of the product from the final manufacturer to the wholesaler, the retailer, and ultimately the consumer. Let us suppose that we can view this vast interrelated production process from the vantage point of a reviewing stand before which the final goods move continuously in a vast parade. From this reviewing stand we check off all the final products which pass by during a month, or a year, or whatever period we choose in which to measure the sum of goods and services produced. But we count only the *final* products as they ultimately emerge from a long production process. We do not cast our eyes over the long assembly line and count also the various products which emerge at different stages in the process, but which are rapidly transformed into the final or end products.

The total volume of purchases and sales of all kinds made in the market in any one year exceeds by ten to twelve times the volume of final goods and services produced. In the process of production there is a vast "churning around" of raw materials and semifinished products. The same raw material passes through many forms and is sold again and again before it finally reaches, in finished form, the ultimate consumer. But no product which enters into the making of a *final* product is included in the gross national income; only the final product is included in the category.

NET NATIONAL PRODUCT

Now what we have said about final goods and services applies not only to the gross national product but also, with one exception, to the net national product. In computing the net national product a further deduction is made for the "consumption" (the wearing out) of machinery and of other capital goods. In the gross national product, despite the deduction of raw materials and semifinished goods, there remains some double counting, since no allowance is made for the wastage or consumption of capital goods such as producers' plant and machinery.

In other words, while the gross national product includes, in addition to final consumers' goods and services, *all* the new capital goods produced in the period in question without any deduction for the capital goods consumed in the process, the net national product includes only the *final consumers'* goods and services plus the *net additions to capital goods,* account having been taken of capital consumption. Thus, while in the year 1947 the gross national product was $231.6 billion, the capital consumption amounted to $13.3 billion. Accordingly, the net national product was only $218.3 billion.

NATIONAL INCOME AT FACTOR COST

We now come to national income at factor cost,[1] usually called simply "national income," though this nomenclature is probably unfortunate, since all five concepts represent a kind of national income. National income at factor cost differs from net national product only because, in most modern countries, some part of the national product is supplied by government without *direct* taxation. If there were no indirect taxes—excises, sales taxes, tariff duties, and the like—net national product and national income (so-called) would be identical.

That this is so becomes quite clear if we compare two hypothetical situations which differ only in the type of tax levied. Let us suppose first that the net national product, in a certain country, is $100 billion, of which $90 billion is privately produced goods and services, while $10 billion is government-provided goods and services. A sale of $90 billion of goods and services is made by private business, and included in these prices are $10 billion of sales taxes. After paying these indirect taxes to the government, the business concerns pay out all the remaining $80 billion in the form of wages, salaries, dividends, rents, and interest. For simplicity we assume that no business concern retains any undistributed profits. The $10 billion in sales taxes transferred to the government is paid out in wages and salaries to government em-

---

1 As used in the Commerce Department figures, the term "national income" in fact means "national income at factor cost."

ployees who produce the "free" goods and services (schools, etc.) supplied by the government to the community.

Thus all the "factors of production" employed in private industry receive, we assume, \$80 billion of income, and those employed by government receive \$10 billion. The total income received by all factors (privately and publicly employed) is then \$90 billion, and all this we assume, is spent to buy the goods and services privately produced. Accordingly business concerns receive a total of \$90 billion for the privately produced goods and services, enough to cover the sales taxes of \$10 billion and in addition to pay all privately employed factors \$80 billion.

We may now sum up the situation as presented in Table V.

TABLE V

National income (i.e., income at factor cost) equals:	
1. Income received by privately employed factors	\$80 billion
2. Income received by publicly employed factors	\$10 billion
Total	\$90 billion
Net national product equals:	
1. Value of privately produced goods and services [2]	\$90 billion
2. Value of publicly produced goods and services	\$10 billion
Total	\$100 billion

But now let us suppose that the sales taxes are abolished. The government must now raise its funds in some other way, let us say by means of a personal income tax. If the sales taxes are abolished, one of two things may happen. First, business concerns, no longer being required to collect sales taxes, may sell their goods and services at lower prices, in fact, for \$10 billion less than before. Prices being lower, the employed factors can now afford to pay \$10 billion income taxes without lowering their standard of living. Under these circumstances the data are altered as presented in Table VI.

[2] Money value of goods at market prices, including the sales tax.

TABLE VI

National income (i.e., income at factor cost) equals:		
1. Income received by privately employed factors		$80 billion
2. Income received by publicly employed factors		$10 billion
	Total	$90 billion
Net national product equals:		
1. Value of privately produced goods and services		$80 billion
2. Value of publicly produced goods and services		$10 billion
	Total	$90 billion

Thus the abolition of the sales tax would, in the circumstances described above, lessen the money value of privately produced goods to $80 billion, which is also the amount paid out by business to the employed factors (including dividends and salaries of executives). The total national income ($90 billion) received by *all* the employed factors (both privately and publicly employed) would now be allocated as follows: $80 billion spent on privately produced goods and services and $10 billion (income taxes) for publicly provided goods and services. There being no indirect taxes, net national product equals national income (i.e., income at factor cost).

The other possible result of abolishing the sales tax is that business concerns, being no longer obligated to collect sales taxes for the government, would, rather than lower prices by the amount of the erstwhile sales taxes, attempt to continue to charge the prices formerly received, which included the sales tax. So long as they are able to do this, they will be making large undistributed profits. However, under these conditions competition among employers, together with the pressure of trade unions, is likely to raise wages, salaries, and dividend payments. It is thus not unreasonable to suppose that, under these circumstances, the income received by the employed factors would eventually rise by the full amount of the abolished sales taxes. We thus have the situation as in Table VII.

TABLE VII

National income (i.e., income at factor cost) equals:	
1. Income received by privately employed factors	$90 billion
2. Income received by publicly employed factors	$10 billion
Total	$100 billion
Net national product equals:	
1. Value of privately produced goods and services	$90 billion
2. Value of publicly produced goods and services	$10 billion
Total	$100 billion

Again we observe that, with the sales taxes abolished, net national product equals national income (i.e., income at factor cost). For a society using no indirect taxes, national income (at factor cost) and net national product would be identical.[3]

PERSONAL INCOME

We now come to the fourth concept, personal income. In a sense personal income is likely to be regarded by the public as of primary significance, since it is the money income *payments* made to all individuals in the community. It differs from national income at factor cost in several respects. First, the income earned by the employed factors may not all be paid out; and second, some of the income paid out to individuals may not be paid for services performed in the process of production.

Both these matters require further elucidation. Consider the first point mentioned above. The stockholders of a corporation,

[3] Some minor discrepancies between the two might still remain. If publicly provided goods and services are sold by government enterprise at a profit, the value of publicly provided goods and services will then exceed the cost (income paid to employed factors). Thus the net national product would exceed the national income (at factor cost) by the current surplus of government enterprises. Again, if government subsidies are paid to private business concerns in order, for example, to help them to sell below factor cost, it follows that the value of privately produced goods and services at market prices will be less than factor cost by the amount of the subsidy. Accordingly, the net national product will be less than national income at factor cost by the amount of such subsidies.

being the ultimate owners, are the legal claimants to the income of the corporation. But if a country has a corporate income tax, the corporation must first pay this tax before any profits are distributed in dividends. This part of the income is therefore never paid out. Yet, since these profits belong to the stockholders, the corporate tax may be regarded as paid *for* the stockholders, even though they will again be taxed on that part of the profits actually distributed in dividends. At all events, whatever rationalizations we may wish to make about corporation income taxes, the fact is that there is a difference between the income earned by the stockholders and the income paid to them in dividends.

After the corporate income tax is paid, the remaining part of the profits could all be distributed in dividends. But in fact they may not be. A part may be retained by the corporations to provide for expansion or security. Thus the income *earned* by stockholders may exceed the income *paid out* to stockholders by two amounts: (1) corporate income taxes, and (2) undistributed corporate profits.

Consider now the second point mentioned—that some part of the income paid out to individuals may not be earned by them as producers and may thus not be included in national income (income at factor cost). Such "unearned" payments (unearned in the sense that they are not direct payments for services rendered) are called "transfer payments." Illustrations of transfer payments are: (1) social security benefits paid to aged or unemployed persons, (2) veterans' benefits, and (3) interest payments on the public debt. Thus personal income includes: (1) payments to individuals for the production of goods and services (factor cost payments) and (2) transfer payments.

One offsetting deduction must, however, be made. Social security contributions are deducted before wage payments are made. Income paid out to individuals is therefore reduced by the amount of these contributions. If in fact these contributions happen to offset exactly the social security benefits received, then *net* transfer payments with respect to this type of benefits would be zero.

To sum up: Starting from national income (at factor cost) we deduct corporate income taxes, undistributed profits, and contributions for social security. Then we add to this figure transfer payments and interest on the public debt. The net result is personal income, or income paid out to individuals.

DISPOSABLE INCOME

Finally we consider the concept disposable income. This is a quite simple matter. It means personal income minus personal taxes—i.e., all *direct* taxes paid by individuals, whether federal, state, or local. Personal taxes include income taxes, death and gift taxes, motor vehicle and drivers' licenses, poll taxes, etc. They do not, of course, include indirect taxes such as sales taxes, excises, tariff duties, or residential property taxes.

COMPARISON OF INCOME CONCEPTS

In order to get a comprehensive view of this rather complex matter, we present below the actual figures for these five different concepts of national income for the year 1947, together with the derivation of each. We compare these five concepts by pairing them off as in Table VIII.

TABLE VIII

Gross National Product and Net National Product for 1947
(*in billions*)

Gross National Product	\$231.6
Less Capital Consumption Allowances	13.3
Net National Product	\$218.3

Net National Product and National Income (at Factor Cost)
(*in billions*)

Net National Product	\$218.3
Plus subsidies, and minus current surplus of government enterprises	(−0.1)
Less indirect business taxes	18.5
Less business transfer payments [4] (including consumer bad debts, unrecovered	

[4] These losses and gifts enter into the national product at market prices, but are not a part of the income received by the employed factors, i.e., national income (at factor cost). As transfer payments they constitute a part of income *paid out* to individuals.

TABLE VIII (*continued*)

thefts, cash prizes, and corporate gifts to non-profit organizations)	0.6
Less statistical discrepancy	(−3.4)
National Income (at Factor Cost)	$202.5

National Income (at Factor Cost) and Personal Income

(*in billions*)

National Income (at Factor Cost)	$202.5
Less: Undistributed Corporate Profits [5]	6.1
Corporate Profits Tax	11.7
Contributions for Social Security	5.6
Plus: Net Interest Paid by Government	4.4
Government Transfer Payments	11.1
Business Transfer Payments	0.6
Personal Income	$195.2

Personal Income and Disposable Income

Personal Income	$195.2
Less Personal Taxes	21.6
Disposable Income	$173.6

In order to fix attention firmly on the more important features distinguishing the various concepts of national income, we present below a brief summary statement emphasizing the salient features. This more general survey can be stated as in Table IX.

TABLE IX

(*in billions*)

1. Gross National Product		$231.6
Less Capital Consumption Allowances		13.3
2. Net National Product		218.3
Less Indirect Taxes, etc.		15.8
3. National Income (at Factor Cost)		202.5
Less: Undistributed Profits	6.1	
Corporate Taxes	11.7	23.4
Social Security Contributions	5.6	
Plus: Transfer Payments		16.1

[5] After correction for inventory valuation.

4. Personal Income	\$195.2
Less Personal Taxes	21.6
5. Disposable Income	173.6
Less Personal Saving	8.8
Leaving for Private Consumption Expenditures	\$164.8

A thorough mastery of these five concepts of national income is highly important for the student of business cycles and current economic developments. Indeed, without a precise knowledge of these various income concepts it is not possible to follow intelligently the data published monthly by various governmental divisions, such as that contained in the *Survey of Current Business,* the *Federal Reserve Bulletin,* the *Treasury Bulletin,* the *Monthly Labor Review,* the *Social Security Bulletin,* or the Economic Reports of the President.

Disposal of Income

We are now prepared to take a comprehensive view of the gross national product from two very fundamental standpoints: (1) what disposal is made of income received from the total production process, and (2) on what categories of goods and services these funds are spent.

From the first standpoint, we may say that the disposal of receipts from the gross national product can be divided into three categories:

1. Disposal of income for *consumption expenditures.*
2. Disposal of income for *tax payments.*
3. Disposal of income for *savings.*

Let GNP stand for gross national product, C for consumption, T for taxes, and S′ for gross savings. We can thus summarize the categories into which the gross national product is divided from the standpoint of disposal of income as follows: $GNP = C + T + S'$.

Expenditure of Income

From the second standpoint we may say that income is expended for the goods and services of which the gross national product is composed, as follows:

1. Consumption disposal sums are expended on consumption expeditures.

2. Tax and savings sums are expended on government projects and services and on gross investment.

Let G stand for government outlays and I′ for gross investment. Then $GNP = C + G + I'$.

Taxes Plus Savings Equal Government Outlays Plus Investment

These equations are, of course, mere identities or truisms. That part of GNP which is not spent on private consumption must necessarily either be saved or paid out in taxes. And again that part of GNP which is not consumption outlays must be government outlays or investment outlays on capital goods. Thus $T + S' = G + I'$.

To illustrate these concepts let us take the data (Table X) for the year 1944—a good year for our purpose, since it happens to be free from complications which are likely to divert attention from the main issues.

TABLE X

(in billions)

A. Gross Savings Items for the Year 1944:	
1. Capital Consumption Allowances	\$11.9
2. Undistributed Corporate Profits (corrected for inventory valuation adjustment)	5.8
3. Personal Saving	34.2
Gross Savings	\$51.9
B. Taxes for 1944:	
1. Indirect Business Taxes	\$14.0
2. Corporate Profits Tax	13.5
3. Personal Taxes	18.9
Total Taxes	\$46.4
C. Gross Savings plus Taxes, $S' + T$	\$98.3

Government purchases of goods and services for 1944 were \$96.5 billion, while gross investment was only \$4.3 billion. Accordingly, $G + I' = \$100.8$ billion. The slight discrepancy between $(G + I')$ on the one hand and $(S' + T)$ on the other is accounted for mainly by statistical discrepancies.

We have omitted on the tax side the social security taxes (\$5.2 billion); and on the side of government expeditures we have omitted transfer payments (\$5.8 billion). Transfer payments in 1944 consisted mainly of social security benefits and interest on the federal debt. Transfer payments are not made for the purchase of goods and services, and so are excluded from gross national product. Accordingly, the government receipts collected to pay for these transfer payments must also be excluded. It happens that for 1944 social security taxes approximately covered the transfer payments, and so we have deducted these revenues from total taxes as an offset to the excluded transfer payments. For postwar years these items would not balance each other off. As a general proposition applicable to all years, it is necessary to deduct from government cash receipts an amount equal to the excluded transfer payment expenditures. When this is done, taxes (thus adjusted) plus gross savings will equal government outlays (thus adjusted) plus gross investment.

In the year 1944 most of the savings of individuals and of business were loaned to the government to finance the deficit created by the vast war expenditures. Hardly any of the savings went into investment, since private outlays for construction and producers' equipment were held to a minimum. In prosperous peacetime years, however, savings are employed mainly to finance private capital outlays. But we are here on the threshold of a difficult problem, which will be considered in detail in Chapter 12.

7 · *The Nation's Economic Budget*

The nation's economic budget represents a new development in national accounting. It is a tool of economic analysis highly important for aggregative economics. It is a product of the development of Keynesian economic thinking, and represents one of the major contributions of economics, not only toward an understanding of the manner in which the economy functions, but especially toward the development of practical economic policy. It is no longer possible for any President of the United States to consider the "state of the nation," or to present the budget of the federal government, or indeed to weigh the impact of any governmental policy upon the economy of the country as a whole, without coming to grips with the nation's economic budget.

In fact, following the passage of the Employment Act of 1946, the President is required by law not merely to present to the Congress each year the traditional state of the nation message and the budget message; he must now present at the opening of each regular session of Congress an economic report which, under the terms of the Employment Act, must contain an analysis of the current and prospective levels of employment and purchasing power, a review of the economic conditions and governmental policies affecting employment, and finally a program of the federal government for carrying out the declared policy of maximum employment, production, and purchasing power which underlies the act. In effect this means, as indeed the Economic Reports of the President to date exemplify, an analysis of the nation's economic budget, together with a program to maximize employment and real income.

The Economic Budget vs. the Treasury Budget

What, then, is the nation's economic budget? To begin with, it is not the same thing as the budget of the United States. The latter is set forth in the President's annual budget message, and it contains summary and detailed tables dealing with governmental expenditures and receipts. The nation's economic budget, on the other hand, deals with the expenditures and receipts of four groups whose accounts make up the aggregate expenditures and income of the nation as a whole. Thus the nation's economic budget is in reality a composite of four budgets: (a) the budget of expenditures and receipts of consumers, (b) the budget of expenditures and receipts of business, (c) the budget of expenditures and receipts on international account, and (d) the budget of expenditures and receipts of government (federal, state, and local).

The Cash Budget vs. the Conventional Budget

First a caution must be registered in order to avoid a serious misconception. The government budget (item "d" above), which constitutes a part of the nation's economic budget, is *not* the conventional budget of the United States. The latter is a statement of *recorded expenditures* (as voted by Congress) on one side of the balance sheet, and of *recorded receipts* on the other. But neither the appropriations nor the recorded receipts are necessarily on a current cash basis. For instance, terminal-leave bonds may be issued to veterans, and these are counted as budgetary expenditures in the conventional budget, even though they may not be redeemed in cash until years later. The government sector of the nation's economic budget is, however, on a *current cash basis.* No expenditure is entered for any given year which is not made in cash in that year.

Similarly on the receipts side of the ledger, the conventional budget includes among recorded receipts, items which in fact do not represent cash paid by the public to the government. For example, in the conventional budget deduction is made from federal employees' salaries for retirement funds, and such deductions are entered as recorded receipts. Actually no cash is paid by the employees to the Federal Treasury. In the government sector of the nation's economic budget only cash actually received is counted on the receipts side of the balance sheet. Thus while the conventional budget is on an accrual basis, the government's account in the nation's economic budget is on a current cash basis.

Again, the conventional budget contains a considerable amount of double counting, since it includes intragovernmental transactions, such as transfers from the Treasury's general fund to Social Security trust accounts. Thus all funds received from social security taxes are appropriated to trust funds, and so are entered both as expenditures and as receipts. So entered, these receipts and expenditures are always in balance. If, however, the social security taxes in fact exceed the social security benefits paid out to individuals, the cash received from the public will exceed the cash paid out to the public. So far as the conventional budget is concerned, the social security receipts and expenditures are always in balance; from the "cash budget" standpoint, the cash received from the public and paid out to the public may not be in balance. If the social security taxes are in excess of the benefits paid out, the "cash budget" will run a surplus even though the conventional budget is in balance.

The Consumers' Account

We are now prepared to consider the four accounts in the nation's economic budget. We begin with the consumers' account.

The consumers' account consists on the one hand of a statement of "receipts," so called—namely, the disposable income (personal income minus personal taxes) of all individuals—and, on the other, of a statement of "expenditures" for consumption. The excess of disposable income over consumption expenditures is personal saving. Such savings may be used directly to buy a new house (a capital goods expenditure); they may be invested by a farmer or an independent business proprietor in farm or business equipment; or they may be loaned to business concerns or to the government. The savings of individuals represent the excess of "receipts" over "expenditures."

The Business Account

The business account is a more formidable affair, less easily understood, and more likely to be misinterpreted. "Receipts" in the business account does not refer to the total volume of sales made by business. It refers only to (a) the undistributed profits of corporations, and (b) the "capital consumption" allowances of all business units, whether incorporated or unincorporated (i.e., capital consumption allowances representing additions to reserves available for replacement of worn-out or obsolete capital). The first item (undistributed profits) represents "net" savings made by corporations; the second item represents "replacement" savings made by all business units. Together they represent gross business savings.[1] Thus "receipts" in the business account means the funds retained and reserved (from the year's current operations) for capital replacement and for expansion and security.

Similarly, the "expenditures" item in the business account does not refer to all the various costs incurred in the operation of the business. "Expenditures," as here used, means only the purchases made by business concerns as *final* buyers—that is to say, as buyers of goods which are intended for business use. Now that, quite naturally, means capital goods of some sort. Accordingly, "expenditures" in the business account means business outlays for (a) new producers' plant, (b) producers' equipment, (c) net additions to inventories, and (d) residential construction.

The last item comes, perhaps, as something of a surprise, since houses are something quite different from the capital goods used by business concerns, such as business structures, equipment, and inventories. However, much of the residential property (apartment houses, multiple-family structures, and even single-family houses) is indeed owned and operated as a business venture. And even the resident-owner may be regarded as a small capitalist who leases the property to himself. Housing represents a major

1 Gross business savings do not include the "net" savings of proprietors of unincorporated enterprises of all kinds, since these are a part of the savings of individuals.

part of capital formation, and the outlays made for new residential structures are therefore counted as a part of the "expenditures" in the business account of the nation's economic budget.

The expenditures for new producers' plant, producers' equipment, net additions to inventories, and new residential construction, together constitute gross private domestic investment. And these are likely, except in severe depression years, to exceed the gross business savings. This means that business typically supplements its own savings by tapping the savings of individuals through the sale of common and preferred stock, bonds, and mortgages.

The International Account

Next we come to the international account. This represents the net change in our financial position as a nation (whether as creditor or debtor) in relation to the rest of the world. Changes in our financial position, vis-à-vis other countries, are of sufficient importance to justify separating these items out and placing them in a special account. This helps toward clarity of thinking with respect to our nation's economic budget. The international account is, however, not strictly comparable in all respects to the other three accounts. Clearly the international account refers to our position as a nation (including both the citizens and the government itself) with respect to the rest of the world. It involves dealings of individuals, corporations, and the government itself with other nations. We must, however, be careful not to engage in double counting. The operations included in the international account are *over and above* those already accounted for in the budgets of consumers, business, and government.

In the international account "expenditures" represents a net foreign investment, and this is offset by a "deficit" as a bookkeeping balancing item. This simply means that if we supplied foreigners with more goods and services than we received from them, the excess represents a "goods and services" deficit in our dealings with the rest of the world. Looked at another way, these excess goods transferred abroad represent investments made by us in other countries against which we acquired claims.

"Receipts," on the other hand, means a net reduction in our

foreign investment (repayment of debt owed to us from the rest of the world). If it happened that we had no net accumulated foreign investment, the emergence of "receipts" in our international account would then represent a debt owing to foreigners—in other words, a net investment by foreign countries in the United States. These "receipts" are represented on the opposite side of the ledger in the international account as an "excess."

Thus a country which is acquiring claims abroad (net foreign investment) will have an "expenditures" item balanced by a so-called "deficit" in its international account, while a country which is losing foreign assets (or increasing its foreign debts) will have a "receipts" item, balanced by a so-called "excess."

Net foreign investment in the international account in the nation's economic budget should not be confused with the net export surplus. Net foreign investment consists only of items which add to this country's net claims abroad. Governmental *grants* from this country to foreign nations and *gifts* made by individuals to foreigners are not a part of net foreign investment, though they enter into the net export surplus. In 1948, for example, net foreign investment fell drastically, owing in large part to the fact that a much larger proportion of the government's foreign aid took the form of grants rather than loans. Loans, whether governmental or private, are counted as a part of net foreign investment; grants and gifts, whether governmental or private, are not.

The Government Account

Finally we come to the government account (federal, state, and local combined). This account consists of cash receipts from the public on the one side and cash payments to the public on the other, together with an "excess of receipts" (+) or "excess of payments" (—) as the balancing item.

"Receipts" are cash receipts from the public, not including funds obtained from borrowing. These receipts are taxes of all kinds plus some miscellaneous receipts from the sale of surplus property, etc. "Expenditures" means all cash payments to the public, including salaries and wages to government personnel, pensions and social benefit payments, loans and subsidies, interest on debt, refund of taxes, and payments to business for the purchases of goods and services. Government trust funds and government-owned corporations are included in this account as a part of government in its relation to the public.

And now we come to an important adjustment that must be made in the government account in order to fit it into the nation's economic budget. The nation's economic budget is concerned, in the final analysis, with expenditures for goods and services produced and with the receipts flowing from this productive process. A part, however, of the government's expenditures is not made for goods and services, but is merely a *transfer* payment. Expenditures such as old-age or veterans' benefit payments, etc., do not constitute a draft on the nation's productive resources; they are not payments for goods and services currently produced. They are simply transfers of income, like gifts. They are made on general grounds of social welfare, not as payments for production.

Accordingly it is necessary to deduct all transfer payments from the total of government expenditures in order to arrive at the expenditures made for goods and services. A corresponding deduction must be made from the "receipts" side of the government account. If no transfer payments were made, government receipts required to cover cash payments could be much lower. Transfer payments are deducted, since they are not related to the production process, and therefore the corresponding cash receipts must also be eliminated. Thus there remain (after these adjustments are made) only those cash receipts and cash payments [2] to the public which relate to the *production* of goods and services.

The Nation's Economic Budget

In Table XI is presented the nation's economic budget, including its four component parts for the year 1948.

[2] Some other minor adjustments are sometimes made in summing up the total figures from the four accounts in the nation's economic budget as presented in the President's Economic Report. These grow, for example, out of discrepancies such as the fact that corporate taxes are reckoned on a liability, rather than on a cash, basis, while the government's receipts and expenditures are on a cash basis.

TABLE XI

Nation's Economic Budget, 1948

(in billions of dollars)

Economic Group	Receipts	Expenditures	Excess of receipts (+) or deficit (−)
I. *Consumers*			
1. Disposable income relating to current production	175.9		
2. Government transfers to individuals	14.9		
3. Disposable personal income	190.8		
4. Expenditure for goods and services		178.8	
5. Personal savings (+)			+12.0
II. *Business*			
1. Retained business earnings	26.8		
2. Gross private domestic investment		45.0	
3. Excess of investment over receipts			−18.2
III. *International*			
1. Government loan transfers	1.3		
2. Net foreign investment		1.9	
3. Excess of expenditures			−0.6
IV. *Government (Federal, State, and Local)*			
1. Taxes	59.9		
2. Purchases of goods and services		36.7	

TABLE XI (*continued*)

Nation's Economic Budget, 1948
(*in billions of dollars*)

Economic Group	Receipts	Expenditures	Excess of receipts (+) or deficit (−)
3. Government transfers		16.0	
4. Cash payments to public, (2) + (3)		52.7	
5. Excess of receipts			+7.2
Adjustments			
1. Government transfers (deducted to arrive at gross national product)	−16.0	−16.0	
2. Statistical discrepancy	−0.4		−0.4
Total: Gross National Product	262.4	262.4	0

8 · *Saving and Investment*

In our analysis of the "national income" concepts in Chapter 6 we encountered the equation $I' + G = S' + T$, in which I' is gross investment, G is government expenditures for goods and services (i.e., government expenditures corrected for transfer payments), S' is gross private saving, and T is cash receipts other than from borrowing (after adjustment for receipts needed to finance transfer payments).

In this chapter we shall analyze gross private saving, S', and gross investment, I', in some detail.

Gross Private Saving

We begin with gross saving. This includes capital consumption allowances (depreciation charges, etc., as noted in Chapter 6), corporate saving, and personal saving.

Corporate saving is a concept presenting difficult accounting and statistical problems. As used in the Commerce Department figures, corporate saving is estimated by making an adjustment of the reported corporate profits for inventory valuation. When prices are rising, inventories purchased at low prices cost less than current replacements. When inventory costs are calculated on the basis of *original* cost (known as the "first-in, first-out" or FIFO method) profits will for this very reason be high in periods of rising prices. If inventory costs are calculated on the basis of *replacement* cost (known as "last-in, first-out," or LIFO method) such profits disappear. When this latter method is not used by corporations in reporting their profits, the Commerce Department, in its estimates of the gross national income and its component parts, makes an inventory valuation adjustment in order to obtain a truer picture of corporate profits. For most years the inventory valuation adjustment is small; for some years it is considerable. In periods of falling prices, profits tend to be "understated" and the inventory valuation adjustment is positive, thereby raising the corrected profits figures above the uncorrected values; in periods of rising prices, profits tend to be "overstated," and so the inventory valuation adjustment is negative, thereby reducing the corrected profits figures below the declared values.

Table XII gives the figures for gross business savings (capital consumption allowances plus undistributed corporate profits, corrected for inventory valuation), together with the components from which the corrected profits figures are derived, from 1929 to 1950.[1]

The other major component of gross private saving (besides gross business saving) is personal saving—the net savings of individual proprietors and of consumers. These (with unavoidable statistical discrepancies in the figures) are given in Table XIII.

It will be noted that except for the war years 1942–45, gross business saving has regularly exceeded personal saving by a good deal (see Table XIII). But this is due to the large "capital consumption" component of business saving. In the war years, however, personal saving far outstripped gross business saving. Ordinarily net corporate saving (compare Tables XII and XIII) is considerably less than personal saving, except in highly prosperous peacetime years such as 1929 and 1948–50, when they were approximately equal.

Gross Investment

Next we consider gross investment and its component parts, which include: (1) new construction, (2) producers' durable equipment, (3) change in business inventories, and (4) net foreign investment. The first three components constitute what is known

---

1 For the statistical discrepancy in gross business saving between Table XII and Table XIII, see *Survey of Current Business,* July, 1950, p. 10.

TABLE XII

Gross Business Saving (*in billions*)

Year	*Gross Business Saving*	*Capital Consumption Allowances (Depreciation Charges, etc.)*	*Undistributed Corporate Profits*[2] *Adjusted for Inventory Valuation (Net Corporate Saving)*	*Undistributed Corporate Profits (Before Adjustment)*	*Inventory Valuation Adjustment*
1929	$11.9	$ 8.8	$ 3.1	$ 2.6	$0.5
1930	8.9	8.7	0.2	−3.0	3.3
1931	5.3	8.3	−3.0	−5.4	2.4
1932	2.7	7.7	−5.0	−6.0	1.0
1933	2.6	7.2	−4.6	−2.4	−2.1
1934	5.0	7.2	−2.2	−1.6	−0.6
1935	6.6	7.4	−0.8	−0.6	−0.2
1936	6.7	7.7	−1.0	−0.3	−0.7
1937	8.0	8.0	0.0	0.0	0.0
1938	8.1	8.0	0.1	−0.9	1.0
1939	8.6	8.1	0.5	1.2	−0.7
1940	10.7	8.4	2.3	2.4	−0.1
1941	11.6	9.3	2.3	4.9	−2.6
1942	13.9	10.0	3.9	5.1	−1.2
1943	16.1	10.7	5.4	6.1	−0.8
1944	17.8	11.9	5.9	6.1	−0.3
1945	15.6	12.4	3.2	3.4	−0.6
1946	15.1	12.2	2.9	8.1	−5.2
1947	21.0	14.8	6.2	12.0	−5.8
1948	28.8	17.4	11.4	13.4	−2.0
1949	30.2	18.8	11.4	9.2	−2.2
1950 (1st half)	28.5	19.9	8.6	10.2	−1.6

[2] After deduction of corporate profits tax.

TABLE XIII

Gross Private Saving and Its Components
(in billions)

Year	*Gross Private Saving*	*Gross Business Saving*	*Personal Saving*
1929	$15.5	$11.8	$ 3.7
1930	11.2	8.3	2.9
1931	8.4	6.6	1.8
1932	2.8	4.2	−1.4
1933	2.7	3.9	−1.2
1934	5.6	5.8	−0.2
1935	7.9	6.1	1.8
1936	13.3	9.7	3.6
1937	10.8	6.9	3.9
1938	8.9	7.9	1.0
1939	12.7	10.0	2.7
1940	16.0	12.3	3.7
1941	23.0	13.2	9.8
1942	41.8	16.2	25.6
1943	47.4	17.2	30.2
1944	57.0	21.6	35.4
1945	48.5	20.5	28.0
1946	28.7	16.7	12.0
1947	25.3	21.4	3.9
1948	36.8	25.9	10.9
1949	36.9	28.3	8.6
1950 (1st half)	41.2	28.5	12.7

as gross private domestic investment. By far the largest components are construction and producers' equipment. (See data for 1929–50 as given in Table XIV.)

Gross investment rises and falls sharply in boom and depression. In the war boom, however, wartime controls sharply suppressed capital outlays in order to make room for military expenditures. As soon as the war was over, gross investment rose to exceptionally high peacetime levels.

TABLE XIV

Gross Investment and Its Components, 1929–50
(in billions)

Year	*Gross Investment*	*New Construction*	*Producers' Durable Equipment*	*Change in Business Inventories*	*Net Foreign Investment*
1929	$16.6	$ 7.8	$ 6.2	$ 1.6	$ 0.8
1930	10.9	5.6	4.8	−0.3	0.7
1931	5.6	3.6	3.1	−1.4	0.2
1932	1.1	1.7	1.8	−2.6	0.2
1933	1.5	1.1	1.8	−1.6	0.2
1934	3.2	1.4	2.4	−1.1	0.4
1935	6.0	1.9	3.3	0.9	−0.1
1936	8.2	2.8	4.3	1.0	−0.1
1937	11.5	3.7	5.2	2.3	0.1
1938	7.4	3.3	3.8	−1.0	1.1
1939	10.8	4.9	4.4	0.4	0.9
1940	15.4	5.6	5.8	2.3	1.5
1941	19.4	6.8	7.3	3.9	1.1
1942	10.7	4.0	4.6	2.1	−0.2
1943	3.5	2.5	4.0	−0.9	−2.2
1944	5.6	2.8	5.3	−0.8	−2.1
1945	9.3	3.9	7.0	−0.7	−1.4
1946	33.3	10.3	12.0	6.1	4.6
1947	39.1	13.9	16.5	−0.8	8.9
1948	45.0	17.7	19.0	5.5	1.9
1949	33.4	17.3	18.4	−3.7	0.4
1950 (1st half)	43.9	20.7	20.1	1.6	−2.0

$S' + T = I' + G$

From the analysis of gross national product (Chapter 6) we have already learned that $S' + T = I' + G$. Now any excess of government outlays (G) over cash receipts (T) we may call "loan expenditures,"[3] which we shall designate as "L." Thus G −

[3] This refers to *governmental* loan expenditures.

T = L. Transferring the T in the first equation above, we get $S' = I' + (G - T)$, or $S' = I' + L$; gross private saving, then, equals gross investment plus loan expenditures.

$S' = I' + L$

Throughout most of the period 1929–50, government outlays for goods and services (G) exceeded cash receipts (T); in other words, loan expenditures (L) were positive. In some years, however (1929, 1937, 1946–48), $T > G$, and L was a negative quantity. These data are presented in Table XV.

TABLE XV

Gross Investment, Loan Expenditures, and Gross Private Saving
(*in billions*)

Year	*Gross Investment* I′	*Loan Expenditures* L	*Gross Private Saving*[4] I′ + L, or S′
1929	$16.6	$−1.1	$15.5
1930	10.9	0.3	11.2
1931	5.6	2.8	8.4
1932	1.1	1.7	2.8
1933	1.5	1.3	2.7
1934	3.2	2.4	5.6
1935	6.0	1.8	7.8
1936	8.2	2.9	11.1
1937	11.5	−0.7	10.8
1938	7.4	1.5	8.9
1939	10.8	1.9	12.7
1940	15.4	0.5	16.0
1941	19.4	3.5	23.0
1942	10.7	31.1	41.8
1943	3.5	43.9	47.4
1944	5.6	51.4	57.0
1945	9.3	39.2	48.5

[4] Statistical discrepancies are lumped in this column; hence the figures here given must be regarded as only approximately correct.

Year	*Gross Investment* I′	*Loan Expenditures* L	*Gross Private Saving*[4] I′ + L, or S′
1946	33.3	−4.6	28.7
1947	39.1	−13.8	25.3
1948	45.0	−8.2	36.8
1949	33.4	3.4	36.9
1950 (1st half)	40.2	1.0	41.2

9 · *The Determinants of Investment*

The Role of Private Investment

In consequence of the development of business-cycle theory during the last half-century, from Wicksell (1898),[1] Tugan-Baranowsky (1901),[2] and Spiethoff (1902)[3] to Keynes' *Treatise* (1930) and *General Theory* (1936), it is now generally understood that investment is a highly dynamic component of the national income. When a major change in the rate of investment occurs, a turn in the cycle can be expected. It is a commonplace matter for business analysts and investment counselors to keep a close eye on prospective changes in any of the component parts of gross investment. What is happening to new construction, to expenditures on producers' equipment, to inventory accumulation, and to net foreign investment throws light on how business activity, employment, and income are likely to unfold.

But investment does not tell the whole story. Consumers' durables play a significant role. And more and more, particularly

---

1 K. Wicksell, *Geldzins und Güterpreise*, J. Fischer, Jena, 1898; English translation, *Interest and Prices*, Macmillan and Co., Ltd., 1936. For a full analysis of these contributions to business-cycle theory, see Chapters 16 and 17 of this book.

2 The Russian edition of Tugan-Baranowsky's book was published in 1894, but the first German edition appeared in 1901, and the French edition, *Les Crises Industrielles en Angleterre*, in 1913.

3 See Spiethoff's notable article in *Jahrbuch für Gesetzgebung des Deutschen Reichs*, 1902.

since the Great Depression and especially since the Second World War, changes in government expenditures, and in taxes, claim attention almost equally with changes in the level of gross investment. Thus it is to private investment and to government outlays that one must look in the main for an explanation of changes in employment and income. And when these fluctuate, income (as we shall see in detail later) will fluctuate by a magnified amount.

Gross vs. Net Investment

In this chapter we shall examine the factors which determine both the *fluctuations* and the *level* of investment. If we are interested in analyzing fluctuations in the gross national product, *gross* investment is the relevant datum. If it is net national product that concerns us, the relevant factor is *net* investment. Gross and net investment fluctuate very nearly (in the short run) by the same *absolute* amounts, since the difference between them is capital consumption, and this changes very little from one year to the next when corrected for price movements. Over time, of course, capital consumption grows as the stock of capital gets larger. How stable capital consumption is normally, is evident from 1929 to 1946 in Table XII. Fluctuations in gross and net investment are in the short run fairly similar. Accordingly, if one is interested primarily in the short-run changes in investment it is often unimportant which one chooses to use—the gross or the net investment figures.

The Value of Capital Goods

The volume of investment will be high if the *value* of new capital goods is high in relation to the *cost* of capital goods. When this is the case, as it is in all boom periods, the inducement to invest will be strong.

Now the value of a new capital good depends, for one thing, upon what one expects to get out of it—in other words, what *earnings* it is expected to yield. A capital good, in value terms, consists of a "series of prospective returns" [4] obtained from the

[4] Keynes, *General Theory of Employment, Interest and Money,* Harcourt, Brace and Company, 1936, p. 135.

sale of its output after deducting such expenses as wages, cost of materials used, etc. A series of annual returns can be expected so long as the capital good remains in active use—in the case of a machine, from three to ten years, more or less. The returns for the first year we may designate as R_1, for the second year R_2, etc. The series of annual returns on a house, for example, is the expected net rentals (after deducting from gross rentals the taxes, maintenance, upkeep, etc.).

If the sum of such a series equaled only the replacement cost, it would obviously not pay to invest in the new capital good. In this case the expected annual returns would just equal the capital consumption itself, and there would be no profit, no *rate of return over cost* on the capital invested. Had this money instead been loaned out on the capital market, it would at least have earned the prevailing rate of interest. Unless the sum of the series of returns on the capital good can be expected to exceed the replacement cost by an amount at least sufficient to pay a rate of return on the capital invested equal to the rate of interest that can be obtained for loanable funds in the money market, it would clearly not be worth while to purchase such a capital good. The series of returns from the capital goods must at least cover: (1) depreciation charges (replacement cost) and (2) the interest charges on invested capital. Normally the sum of the series of returns would have to exceed this amount in order to provide a strong inducement to invest.

The Marginal Efficiency of Investment

The series of prospective annual returns we shall call the *prospective yield* of the capital good. The *rate* of return on the capital sum laid out [5] to purchase an additional unit of capital goods we shall call the *marginal efficiency of investment.* The marginal efficiency of investment is a *ratio,* a percentage. The series of annual returns (or yields) referred to above are *absolute amounts.* It is important, therefore, to distinguish clearly between (1) the prospective yield of a capital good (the series of expected

[5] Irving Fisher called this the "rate of return over cost." See Chapter 17 in this book.

annual returns) and (2) the marginal efficiency of investment (the *rate* of return over cost), which we shall designate as "r."

In order to ascertain the marginal efficiency of investment, r, it is necessary to know two things: (1) the series of expected annual returns, and (2) the cost[6] of the capital good. If the sum of the series of annual future yields or returns exceeds the cost of the capital good, we know that *some* rate will be earned on the invested capital. What that rate will be can easily be ascertained from the following formula, in which C is the cost of the capital good, $R_1, R_2, \ldots\ldots R_n$ is the series of expected annual returns, and r is the marginal efficiency of investment:

$$C = \frac{R_1}{(1+r)} + \frac{R_2}{(1+r)^2} \cdots\cdots\cdots\cdots \frac{R_n}{(1+r)^n}$$

This equation simply says that there is some rate of discount (namely, r) which if applied to the series of annual returns will make the present value of these discounted future annual returns equal to the cost of the capital good. Or, putting it the other way around, the sum of money invested in the capital good (namely, C) will earn a rate equal to r when the series of expected annual returns is equal to $R_1, R_2, \ldots\ldots R_n$. Thus the marginal efficiency rate is simply the net percentage rate earned on the invested capital, say 8 or 10 per cent.

If the marginal efficiency of investment, r, is greater than the rate of interest, i, that can be obtained by lending funds in the capital market, it will pay to purchase the capital good. This means in effect that the *value* of the capital good exceeds its *cost.* The *value* of a capital good, V, is equal to the sum of the series of expected returns, discounted back to the present at the prevailing rate of interest on loanable funds. The equation is as follows:

$$V = \frac{R_1}{(1+i)} + \frac{R_2}{(1+i)^2} \cdots\cdots\cdots \frac{R_n}{(1+i)^n}$$

Whenever $r > i$, then $V > C$ in the same proportion. The inducement to invest will be strong to the degree that the *value*

6 Keynes said "the supply price" or "replacement cost" of the capital asset. See *General Theory,* p. 135.

of a capital good exceeds its *cost*—which amounts to the same thing as saying that the marginal efficiency of investment exceeds the rate of interest.

Now the series of expected future returns (R_1, R_2, ... R_n), at a given level of technique, will be large or small according to how much investment has already taken place. We know from the law of diminishing productivity that each successive increment of investment will yield lower and lower returns. As more and more investment is made, the entire series $R_1 + R_2 + \ldots\ldots R_n$ will fall. Accordingly, the marginal efficiency of investment, r, will also fall as investment proceeds. Moreover, under the stimulus of the boom, it is also likely that the *cost* of the capital good will rise. Thus the marginal efficiency of investment, r, will fall for two reasons, first because the expected annual future returns will decline as more and more investment is made, and second because the cost of the capital good is rising. As more and more apartment houses, for example, are built, the series of expected returns will fall, and the cost will rise, until finally the marginal efficiency of investment, r, is pushed down to the level of the prevailing rate of interest, i. At this point investment will cease and the constructional boom will be over.

True, for a time an excess of optimism may maintain a high level of investment. Expectations engendered in the over-confidence of a rising tide of business activity may overcome, for a while, cooler and sounder calculations. Waves of optimism may carry investment far beyond the requirements set by the increase of population and by changes in the level of technique. So long as highly favorable yields are *expected,* investment will continue. But mere optimism can only prolong an investment boom; it cannot for long maintain a level of investment that greatly exceeds the long-run requirements of growth and progress. Eventually the hard facts underlying the law of diminishing productivity will prevail.

We must not forget that the marginal efficiency of investment, r, is in fact based on the expectations of businessmen, and is therefore subject to violent changes in business sentiment. Given a certain state of optimism, however, more and more investment will progressively lower the marginal efficiency of investment. We can therefore speak of a *schedule* of marginal efficiency of investment. This is illustrated in Table XVI, which shows that the larger the investment the lower is the marginal efficiency of investment.

TABLE XVI

Schedules of Marginal Efficiency of Investment

Marginal Efficiency of Investment	*Volume of Investment*	
(r)	*Curve A*	*Curve B*
16	100	300
13	200	400
9	300	500
4	400	600

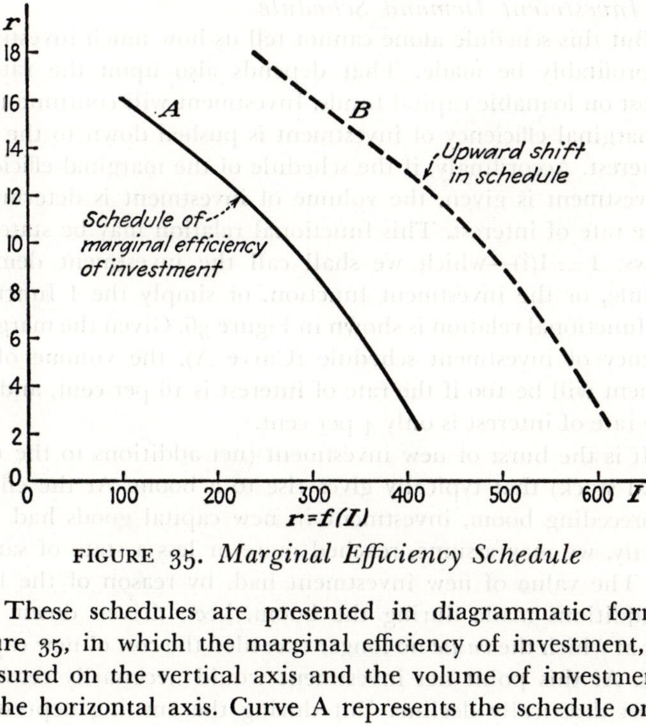

FIGURE 35. *Marginal Efficiency Schedule*

These schedules are presented in diagrammatic form in Figure 35, in which the marginal efficiency of investment, r, is measured on the vertical axis and the volume of investment, I, on the horizontal axis. Curve A represents the schedule on the basis of a certain given state of optimism and prevailing level of technique. Curve B represents an upward *shift* in the schedule. This shift may be quite justified, as is the case when marked improvements in technology or increases in population open up new profitable investment outlets. But it may also be due merely to a purely psychological change in expectations. Similarly, once the turning point has come, there may occur a rapid downward shift in the schedule, owing to a decline in optimistic expectations.

The schedule of marginal efficiency of investment (Curve A, for example) shows what the marginal efficiency would be at any given volume of investment. The larger the volume of investment, I, the lower the marginal efficiency rate, r. Thus the marginal efficiency of investment is a function of the volume of investment; $r = f(I)$.

The Investment Demand Schedule

But this schedule alone cannot tell us how much investment can profitably be made. That depends also upon the rate of interest on loanable capital funds. Investment will continue until the marginal efficiency of investment is pushed down to the rate of interest. Accordingly, if the schedule of the marginal efficiency of investment is given, the volume of investment is determined by the rate of interest. This functional relation may be stated as follows: $I = I(i)$—which we shall call the investment demand schedule, or the investment function, or simply the I function. This functional relation is shown in Figure 36. Given the marginal efficiency of investment schedule (Curve A), the volume of investment will be 100 if the rate of interest is 16 per cent, and 400 if the rate of interest is only 4 per cent.

It is the burst of new investment (net additions to the total capital stock) that typically gives rise to a boom. At the end of the preceding boom, investment in new capital goods had temporarily, we may assume, reached more or less a state of saturation. The value of new investment had, by reason of the large net additions made during the boom, been driven down to a point at which the *value* no longer exceeded the *cost* of new capital goods. At this point net investment would necessarily cease, or at least drastically decline. But during the ensuing depression, growth factors (increases in population and improvements in technique) will be constantly at work. Thus there will accumulate, year by year, additional capital requirements that need to be filled. These new requirements will continue to accumulate throughout the depression and during the following boom. Eventually these new investments will be made; and when they are completed, the stage is set for the next slump.

The marginal efficiency of investment, r, will diminish as more and more investment is made in the boom period. This fol-

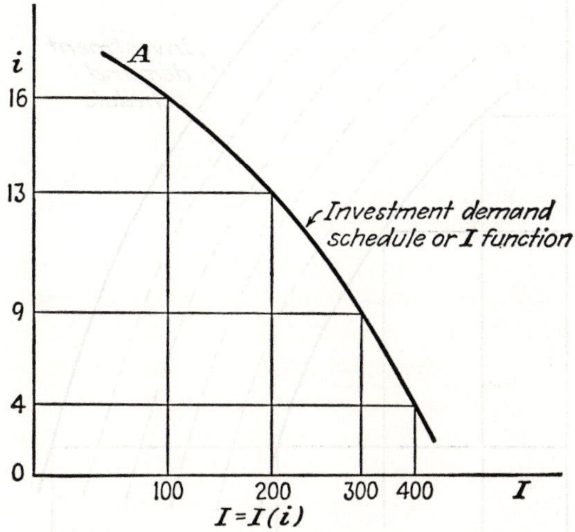

FIGURE 36. *Investment Demand Schedule*

lows partly because the prospective annual yields will decline, and partly because costs will rise. Accordingly, as more and more equipment is installed, the marginal efficiency of investment, r, will progressively fall toward the rate of interest, i. Thus eventually all the investment opportunities created by growth (increases in population and changes in technique) will become exhausted. All this is represented diagrammatically in Figure 37.

Consider first Curve A. So long as investment is restricted to OD, the marginal efficiency rate will be r_1, far in excess of the rate of interest, i_0. When eventually OF investment is made (assuming no change in technique and no growth in population), the marginal efficiency rate will have fallen to r_3, the same level as the rate of interest, i_0. Here no further investment will be made until growth factors have again opened new investment outlets, causing a shift of the curve upward and to the right.

When it is said that investment will proceed until the marginal efficiency rate, r, is pushed down to the interest rate level,

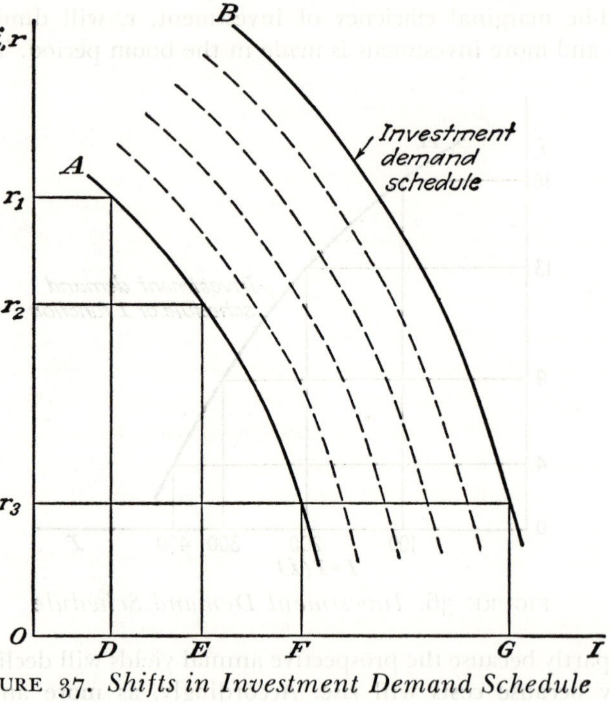

FIGURE 37. *Shifts in Investment Demand Schedule*

i, it must be understood that the rate, r, is net of risk. Since usually a generous allowance has to be made for risk factors, the *gross* rate of return will be much larger. Deducting for risk, investment will tend to be pushed to the point at which the *net* marginal efficiency of investment (allowance being made for risk) will approach the rate of interest currently paid for loanable funds in the capital markets.

Investment in Boom Years

The more the outlets for investment have been filled, the less profitable are the remaining ones. Let us assume that the volume of investment OF (Fig. 37) is made over a period of, say, three boom years, OD being invested in the first year, DE in the second, and EF in the third. At the end of three years all investment opportunities, we assume, have been fully exploited. A state of investment saturation has thus temporarily been reached. The marginal efficiency rate on new investment has been pushed down to the rate of interest on loanable capital funds. Beyond that point it is not profitable to invest.

When the investment opportunities have thus been fully exhausted, a drastic decline in investment occurs. The result is a serious depression. Something like this happened in 1929. Gross investment fell off from $16.6 billion in 1929 to $1.1 billion in 1932.

Technology and Growth

But soon growth factors will again open up new investment opportunities. Advances in technology, cost-reducing machinery, the development of new products and new industries, the discovery of new natural resources, the growth of population, will soon open the way for further new investment. These developments are going on all the while, even in the midst of a great depression. But for many months, and often for some years, relatively little investment may be made despite the potential backlog of new investment opportunities which is accumulating. This failure of investment may be due partly to the fact that investment in many lines was perhaps overdone during the preceding boom. This was true, for example, of office buildings in the 1929 boom. In part, a prolonged failure of investment to recover may be due to an excess of pessimism, engendered by the depression itself. It may require a large accumulation of "combustible material" (investment outlets) before the pile catches fire; in other words, it may take a long time before entrepreneurs acquire sufficient confidence in the future and that renewed spirit of enterprise which is required to undertake large new ventures.

In the diagram the dotted lines represent the new *potential* investment opportunities which advances in technology and growth of population are opening up. But for a time they may lie dormant. Eventually, as new investment begins to take hold, the stage of revival is reached and a new investment boom is on the way.

The continued progress of technology and growth of population widen the boundaries of new investment, and this is represented in the diagram by the shift (Fig. 37) of the investment demand function up, and to the right, from Curve A to Curve B. Let us assume that Curve B represents the investment boundaries reached in the second boom. Thus, all told, the volume of investment which is available for exploitation in the second boom is FG. To achieve this volume of investment may require two, three, or four years, and when it is completed the second boom will be over. Investment saturation will again have been reached. The stage is thus set for another collapse.

While the investment boom is going on, the investment demand function is constantly being pushed to the right by the continued progress of technology and the growth of population. But once the boom is on, the rate of investment is likely to be more rapid than the rate of growth requirements. If the rate of investment proceeded, during the boom, at the same pace as the long-run rate of growth and technical progress, the marginal efficiency rate would not fall. In this event, the movement *down* the schedule would always be offset by a shift in the schedule sufficiently rapid to maintain a constant marginal efficiency rate. In fact, however, it is the typical characteristic of the boom that the rate of investment proceeds feverishly, so that investment outstrips the rate of technical progress. Accordingly, despite the continued upward shift of the schedule, the movement *down* the schedule progressively pushes the marginal efficiency of investment down toward the minimum (the current rate of interest on loanable capital funds) below which further investment is not profitable. Thus the boom "dies a natural death." The accumulated outlets for investment have been exhausted.[7]

[7] This is a first approximation. In later chapters we shall consider far more complicated situations involving the multiplier and the accelerator.

Lowering the Rate of Interest

One further matter demands consideration. Let us assume that there are no changes in technology and no growth in population—in other words, no growth factors causing a shift in the investment demand schedule to the right. Could we not nevertheless open up investment opportunities by means of a monetary policy designed to lower the rate of interest?

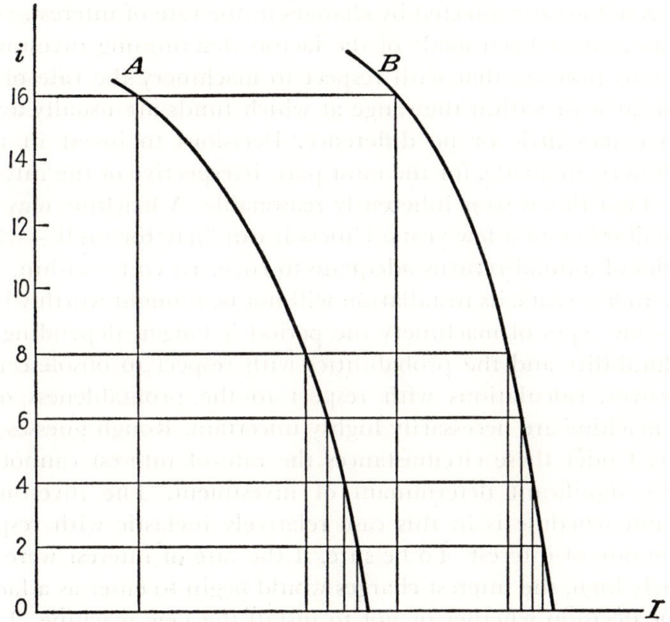

FIGURE 38. *Elasticity of Investment Demand Schedules*

Assume an investment demand schedule such as Curve A in Figure 38. It will be noted that the curve is fairly elastic with respect to the rate of interest at high interest rate levels, and is fairly inelastic within a rather wide range of interest rates at the lower levels. This indicates that, within a considerable range of interest rates, of, say, from 2 to 8 per cent, a lower rate of interest will not stimulate much new investment. Higher interest rates, however, of from 8 to 16 per cent (and above), will rapidly choke off investment.

Put in concrete terms, this means that by and large investment can be stimulated in a wide range of capital goods by lowering the rates of interest down to a certain level. Below this level, however, lower rates of interest will induce relatively little investment.

Investment in machinery, and producers' equipment in general, is not greatly affected by changes in the rate of interest. Such studies as have been made of the factors determining investment decisions indicate that with respect to machinery the rate of interest (at least within the range at which funds are usually available) makes little or no difference. Decisions to invest in new machinery are made, for the most part, irrespective of the interest rate. That this is so is inherently reasonable. A machine may become obsolete in a few years. Unless it can "pay for itself"—yield a series of annual returns adequate to cover its cost—within, say, three to five years, its installation will not be thought worth while. For some types of machinery the period is longer, depending on its durability and the probabilities with respect to obsolescence. Moreover, calculations with respect to the profitableness of a new machine are necessarily highly uncertain. Rough guesses are made. Under these circumstances the rate of interest cannot be a very significant determinant of investment. The investment demand schedule is in this case relatively inelastic with respect to the rate of interest. To be sure, if the rate of interest were extremely high, the interest charges would begin to enter as a factor in the decision whether or not to install the new machine. Thus beyond a certain interest rate level (in Figure 38, say above 8 per cent) the high cost of borrowing does become a deterrent to investment. In other words, investment, at this upper interest rate range, may become, in a considerable measure, interest-elastic.

On the other hand, investment in residential property and in business structures is likely to be affected by the rate of interest at all interest rate levels, high or low. Capital goods of this sort have typically a long life, are highly durable, and are not usually subject to a high rate of obsolescence.

In the diagram, the demand for all forms of investment goods combined is assumed to be interest-elastic above the rate of 8 per cent, while below this level the total demand for investment goods becomes relatively inelastic. This is due to the fact that the investment demand for some kinds of capital goods (notably machinery) cannot be stimulated much by lower rates of interest. If we assume that *half* of the total of all capital goods falls in the "interest-inelastic investment demand" category below the 8 per cent interest rate level, while the other half remains fairly interest-elastic at all interest rates, we should then have curves somewhat like those in Figure 38. That portion of any curve *below* the 8 per cent level would have an interest-elasticity approximately one-half as great as the portion *above* the 8 per cent level.

Of the three broad categories of private domestic investment (construction, producers' equipment, and business inventories) much of construction is probably fairly interest-elastic at all interest rate levels, while investment in producers' equipment and in business inventories is largely interest-inelastic except for very high rates of interest. Now in the period from 1919 to 1941, of the three categories of domestic investment enumerated above, construction was about 50 per cent of the total. It is therefore not unreasonable to assume that the *total* domestic investment demand schedule has an elasticity somewhat like that depicted in Figure 38. The choice of the rate of 8 per cent as the dividing line, below which a further fall in the rate of interest is not regarded as an effective stimulant to investment in producers' equipment and business inventory, is of course somewhat arbitrary; but it is likely to be somewhere in that area—for some types of investment a good deal higher, and for others lower.

If the curves in Figure 38 do in a general way indicate the interest-elasticity of the investment demand schedule, it is pertinent to remark that it is especially the lower part of any curve which is of practical significance, since, except in very backward areas, interest rates are typically in the lower interest-rate range. This means that in industrially advanced countries, which enjoy a relatively low rate of interest, the investment demand schedule (despite the relatively high interest-elasticity of investment demand for many kinds of construction) tends to be fairly interest-inelastic. This is a matter of great significance with respect to practical policy. It means that it is not possible to induce any very large investment (except in construction) by pushing interest rates down to levels even lower than those already prevailing. Monetary policy cannot, therefore, be regarded as of leading importance as a means to increase total investment. In terms of the diagram in Figure 38, only limited results can be achieved, for example, by moving down on the investment curve A (via lowering the rate of interest). One must await a shift in the curve upward or to the right to Schedule B. And such an upward shift depends basically upon the growth factors—advances in technology and increase in population. But as we shall see in Part IV, much can also be accomplished by deliberate investment in public improvement projects—regional resource development, urban redevelopment, etc. Public resource developments such as those in the Tennessee Valley, the Columbia River Basin, and elsewhere, have opened the way for much private investment which otherwise could not have been profitable.

From what has been said above, it should not be thought that interest rate policy is unimportant. In underdeveloped countries, a vast amount of investment is held back merely because the rate of interest is too high. In such countries it is highly essential to develop savings institutions, improve credit and banking facilities, and in every way enlarge the stream of financial investment funds. And even in advanced industrial countries, whose investment demand schedule is in a comparatively low interest-rate range, the maintenance of a low rate of interest is desirable. Only by means of a low rate of interest can a country take *maximum* advantage of the existing level of technique. Unless the rate of interest is reduced to the lowest feasible level, some considerable volume of investment (particularly in housing) *will* be deterred. In addition, a low rate of interest promotes a more equitable distribution of income. This is true because under these circumstances relatively more of the national income goes into wages, salaries, and profits, and less into the payment of interest to the owners of past accumulations of wealth. The active elements (entrepreneurs and workers) get more; the passive elements (fixed-income groups) get relatively less.

If it were true that the investment demand schedule is highly interest-elastic, then vast investment opportunities could be opened up merely by lowering the rate of interest, and there would be almost endless possibilities for the investment of virtually any given volume of current savings. In advanced industrial countries this does not appear to be true. After a great war, indeed, nearly all countries are capital-hungry. But it is astonishing how rapidly the necessary capital requirements can be rebuilt. After the Second World War, a tremendous volume of investment in new capital facilities had already been made by 1950. The Marshall Plan was directed primarily at rebuilding the production capacity of western Europe. In view of the ensuing high level of investment, it appears not unlikely, unless we are destined for another full-scale war, that excess capacity in many lines will become evident in a few years. It is remarkable how rapidly advanced industrial countries can make good the ravages of war and again become relatively satiated with capital goods. If the investment demand schedule were highly interest-elastic, capital satiation would not be reached so quickly after a great destructive war.

Taking a historical view, it is evident that the vast outlets for capital investment during the last hundred years in the United States were due fundamentally to two things: (1) the remarkable advances in technology (the railroad, the electrical and automotive industries) and (2) the increase in population. Growth factors account for our vast accumulation of capital goods in the form of residential structures, plant, and equipment. Without these growth factors we should have comparatively little more capital today than a hundred years ago. It was the continuous upward *shift* in the investment demand schedule, induced by population growth and technical progress, which opened the flood gates of the prodigious volume of capital formation which the past century has witnessed.

This development was facilitated, and the movement was given larger proportions than would otherwise have been possible, by all those factors—savings and banking institutions—which served to provide adequate investment funds at (taking a very long-run view of the whole past century) downward-trending interest rates. Had it not been for this development with respect to the supply side of investment funds, capital formation would quickly have been choked by rapidly rising interest rates. Every shift to the right of the investment demand schedule brought with it a more than compensating shift of the supply schedule of loanable funds, thereby making possible continued investment at secularly falling rates of interest. While all this is true, it nevertheless remains a fact that the increasing supply of investment funds *by itself alone* could not have opened large investment outlets. And the reason is that the investment demand schedule is not highly interest-elastic. It was the continued *shift* of the investment demand schedule upward and to the right (because of technological advances and population growth) which opened the door to the vast capital formation of the past century. And it was this growth in our accumulated stock of capital goods which provided the basis for every period of prosperity.

Investment and Expectations

Investment in new capital goods over a large section of the economy is based on solid business experience extending over many years, and is related largely to the expected trend of sales volume. Growth in sales in turn depends upon the growth in the nation's real income, and this depends upon increases in per capita productivity (technological advances) and population growth. Investment of this sort is typically the result of cautious calculations and is based upon the expectation that past trends are likely to continue into the future. If this turns out not to be the case, adjustments in the investment program can usually be made before any large excess capacity has been added. In a broad range of consumer goods industries, fairly dependable calculations can be made with respect to the probable rate that can be earned on new investment.

But then there are the "frontiers" of the economy—the daring, adventurous areas. These relate particularly to innovations, often quite revolutionary in character. These developments have to do with new methods of production; they may involve new and untried products, the popular acceptance of which is quite unknown. Large-scale projects may be undertaken relating to changes in the location of industry, population shifts, etc., which are highly uncertain in their consequences and the extent to which they will develop. Some projects may involve vast capital investments which could not possibly pay out except over a great many years, during which all sorts of things could happen. A considerable segment of capital formation in a dynamic society is necessarily highly speculative. The risks are very great.

The Promoter

Here the promoter plays an important role. It is his task to initiate the project, to arouse interest in it, and to induce people to risk investment of large or small sums in the hope of unusual gains. Often thousands of people are induced to participate. The promoter may himself risk very little. Often he comes out with a handsome return for his enterprising organizational work, even though the investors lose all or nearly all the funds poured into the venture. Often the original investors are squeezed out through a process of bankruptcy, and the new owners acquire the property at bargain rates.

On occasion, what seemed to be the foolish venture of an irresponsible promoter may turn out after some years to be a thoroughly sound enterprise. In the wildly speculative boom of the twenties, office buildings and apartment houses were built which were not even fully completed when the Great Depression came. Some stood idle, or largely so, for many years—a monument, apparently, to frenzied and foolhardy finance. But after more than a decade came the Second World War, and then the postwar prosperity with the housing and office-space shortages. The folly of one period served to relieve dire need in a subsequent decade. Many an industry which seemed to have an excess capacity in the thirties, later rued the day when it had failed, in a period of slack employment, to enlarge its productive facilities.

Volatile Expectations

In many categories of business, investment cannot be based upon clearly calculated margins between the prospective rate of return on invested capital (the marginal efficiency of investment) and the rate of interest on loanable funds. Investment must often be made on a daring hunch which may or may not work out. Much investment is the result of waves of optimism produced by boom conditions. It cannot be justified on the basis of close and cautious calculations. Yet investment *is* based on expectations. The investment demand schedule toward the end of a boom may look silly in the cold aftermath when bitter realities must be faced. But the investment demand schedule is nonetheless a market reality. It does not show what in fact the rate of return on new investment *will* turn out to be; it shows what it is *expected* to be.

Accordingly, the investment demand schedule may shift far to the right, purely by reason of extravagant expectations. And when it is at last realized (at first by a few leaders, more far-seeing and penetrating than the herd of followers) that current expectations are unduly optimistic, mass optimism may rapidly develop into mass pessimism. This means a sudden and drastic fall (shift to the left) of the marginal efficiency schedule. Investment thus collapses, not because of a movement *down* the schedule, but because of a rapid downward *shift* in the schedule.

It is scarcely possible to discuss investment without having in mind two kinds of schedules of the marginal efficiency of investment—the one based on highly volatile expectations, the other (in some sense) on cooler and more realistic calculations. Yet it is in fact the former that determines what investment will be made. Decisions are made on the basis of expectations in the minds of entrepreneurs. Booms are in large measure a product of social psychology.

Keynes has something of this sort in mind when he speaks of investment being made in "conditions which are unstable and cannot endure, because it is prompted by expectations which are destined to disappointment." He then goes on to speak of investments which "in fact yield, say, 2 per cent," but which were made on the optimistic "expectation of a yield of, say, 6 per cent." [8]

It is possible that Wicksell, when he spoke of the "natural real rate" or the "expected yield on the newly created capital" [9] had in mind a rate that could really be earned, based on expectations, to be sure, but in some sense on realistic and rational calcu-

[8] *General Theory of Employment, Interest and Money,* Harcourt, Brace and Company, New York, 1936, p. 321.

[9] Knut Wicksell, *Lectures on Political Economy,* Vol. II, *Money,* The Macmillan Company, New York, 1935, p. 193; also *Interest and Prices,* Macmillan & Co., Ltd., London, 1936, Chapter 8.

lations. Keynes' marginal efficiency of capital, on the other hand, is the rate expected in the rosy atmosphere of boom psychology, or in the equally abnormal pessimism of the slump. Both the Wicksellian and Keynesian concepts have validity. Ocean waves may ride high and low, but they fluctuate around the basic level of the sea. The volatile investment demand schedule may shift violently up and down, swayed by the waves of optimism and pessimism. But there are certain solid facts underneath: (1) a population (slowly changing in size) with basic standard wants, the bulk of which change relatively slowly, and (2) a technique of production, which for the greater part of the economy is in the short run relatively fixed. With these data given, the increasing accumulation of capital goods, as more and more investment is made in the boom period, inevitably results in diminishing marginal returns. The construction of office buildings and apartment houses proceeded in the twenties to a point at which an excess of vacancies appeared. At long last it began to be realized that the expected annual returns or yields on additional increments of capital goods could not be realized. Optimistic expectations were then supplanted by pessimistic expectations.

Thus the volatile investment demand schedule, based on expectations, will shift back and forth from boom to depression. But the point around which these volatile fluctuations oscillate is the volume of capital requirements determined basically by the conditions of population growth and changes in technology. The law of diminishing marginal yields finally limits the volume of capital which can profitably be employed. Thus real factors underlie the volatile swings in expectations which in the short run determine the investment demand schedule.

Value Schedules and Marginal Efficiency Schedules

The analysis which we have presented runs in terms of a schedule of the marginal efficiency of capital at varying amounts of investment. Given this schedule, the volume of investment will be determined by the rate of interest. Now the determinants of investment could equally well be put in terms of a schedule showing the *value* of new capital goods assuming different amounts of investment. Thus the value of new houses will tend to be high if the volume of new investment (new houses being built) is low; and the value will tend to decline if the volume of new investment (the number of new houses built) is greatly increased. Given the schedule of declining *values* as investment increases, the volume of investment will be determined by the *cost* of capital goods.

The value of a new capital good depends, as we have seen, upon (a) the series of expected returns and (b) the rate of interest at which these returns are discounted back to the present. Accordingly the schedule showing the value of different quantities of new investment will shift upward (or to the right) if the rate of interest falls; and correspondingly will shift downward (or to the left) when the rate of interest rises. Shifts in the schedule will also occur if the expected returns rise or fall.

Now the amount of investment which will be made depends upon the cost of new investment in relation to the schedule of the values of the successive increments of new investment. In the first phase of expansion in the cycle, the schedule is likely to move up (or to the right) both because the rate of interest is still falling and because expectations with respect to returns are rising. As we move into the high boom, the rising rate of interest will tend to shift the schedule downward (or to the left), and this will eventually be reinforced by less favorable expectations with respect to anticipated returns. At the same time, the cost of new capital goods will tend to rise. Thus all three factors (rate of interest, expectations, and cost) combine to reduce the volume of investment. The investment boom therefore comes to an end in consequence of the combined effect of all these unfavorable factors.

Precisely the same developments can be stated in terms of the schedule of the marginal efficiency of investment. Rising expectations with respect to future returns on capital goods will tend to shift the schedule to the right, falling expectations to the left. A rise in the cost of new capital goods will shift the schedule to the left; a fall in cost will shift the schedule to the right. In the first stage of the expansion the schedule will shift upward because of favorable expectations. As the high boom is approached, the rising cost of new capital goods will shift the schedule to the left, and this movement will sooner or later be reinforced by a fall in expectations with respect to anticipated returns. In the meantime the rate of interest will tend to rise; and this, combined with the downward shift in the marginal efficiency schedule, will cause a sharp curtailment in the volume of investment.

Figure 39 is designed to illustrate these tendencies. The figure shows both a set of "value" schedules and a set of "marginal efficiency" schedules. On the "value" schedule diagram, Schedule I_1 represents the condition in the first phase of the expansion. The cost of new investment goods (say new houses) is C_1, and so

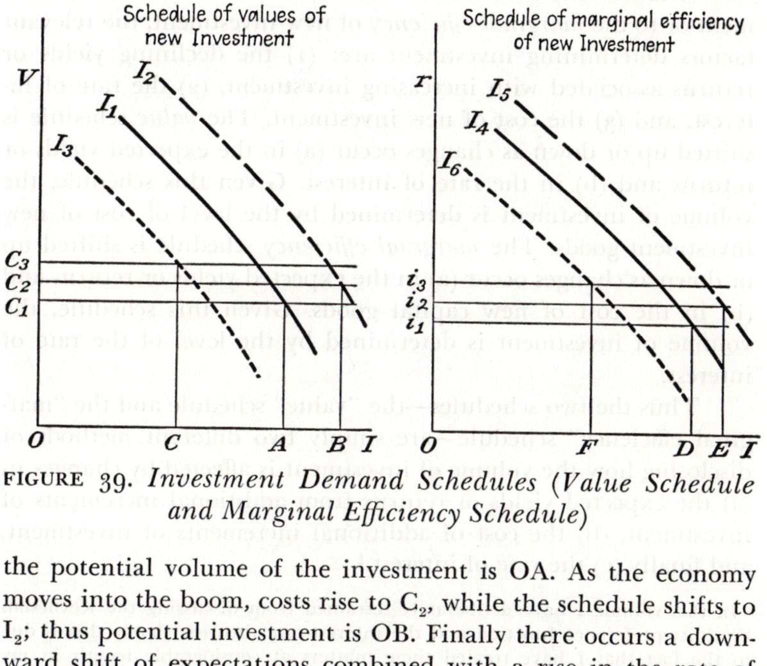

FIGURE 39. *Investment Demand Schedules (Value Schedule and Marginal Efficiency Schedule)*

the potential volume of the investment is OA. As the economy moves into the boom, costs rise to C_2, while the schedule shifts to I_2; thus potential investment is OB. Finally there occurs a downward shift of expectations combined with a rise in the rate of interest, and these together cause a shift in the schedule to I_3. At the same time the cost of new capital goods rises to C_3. Accordingly the potential investment falls to OC.

With respect to the marginal efficiency schedule, as the boom progresses, the schedule is shifted upward from I_4 to I_5 in consequence of improved expectations with respect to the yields or returns on new investment. As the peak of the boom is approached, the cost of new capital goods rises; and this causes a downward shift in the schedule, since the higher the cost, the lower is the marginal efficiency of investment. The downward shift in the schedule will at this point be reinforced by the fall in expectations with respect to yields or returns; and so the schedule shifts back to I_6. At the same time the rising rate of interest adversely affects the volume of investment. With the rate of interest at i_3 and the marginal efficiency schedule at I_6, the potential investment will fall to OF.

Whether one relates investment to the *value* of new investment or to the *marginal efficiency* of new investment, the relevant factors determining investment are: (1) the declining yields or returns associated with increasing investment, (2) the rate of interest, and (3) the cost of new investment. The *value* schedule is shifted up or down as changes occur (a) in the expected yields or returns and (b) in the rate of interest. Given this schedule, the volume of investment is determined by the level of cost of new investment goods. The *marginal efficiency* schedule is shifted up or down as changes occur (a) in the expected yields or returns and (b) in the cost of new capital goods. Given this schedule, the volume of investment is determined by the level of the rate of interest.

Thus the two schedules—the "value" schedule and the "marginal efficiency" schedule—are simply two different methods of disclosing how the volume of investment is affected by changes in (a) the expected yields or returns from additional increments of investment, (b) the cost of additional increments of investment, and finally (c) the rate of interest.[1]

---

1 In this volume I have deliberately refrained from discussing the Keynesian liquidity-preference function and the interest-rate theories. Partly this is due to the fact that I have treated these matters at considerable length in my *Monetary Theory and Fiscal Policy* (McGraw-Hill, 1941) and did not wish to repeat here; and partly, I feel that an extensive discussion of these topics would in effect involve the inclusion of the field of money and banking in a textbook on business cycles, and this I wished to avoid.

10 · *The Consumption Function and the Multiplier*

Consumption and Income

In the preceding chapter we analyzed the determinants of investment. Investment, as we have already noted, is a highly dynamic component of national income, and acts as a barometer in forecasting the turns of the cycle. If investment rises to high levels, income and employment rise also, but by a magnified amount. The expansion of output and employment in the capital goods industries increases the incomes of wage and salaried workers and stockholders in these industries. And this increase in income and spending power raises the demand for consumption goods. And so employment and income in turn rise also in these industries. Thus the initial increase in investment has an expanding effect upon the whole economy, causing income to rise by some multiple of the increment of investment.

To what extent income will rise as a result of a given increase in investment—this is the question to which we shall address ourselves in this chapter. The question can only be answered by an analysis of the behavior pattern of consumers.

The Consumption-Income Schedule

As consumers' incomes rise, they will spend more on consumers' goods. And they will also save more. Are there more or less stable patterns of behavior which determine how they will divide their spending and saving as income rises and falls? Does the ratio between spending and saving change when incomes move from low to high or from high to low levels?

To put it another way, what is the ratio of spending (i.e., consumption expenditure) to income at different income levels? A schedule showing the amounts spent on consumers' goods at different income magnitudes we shall call the consumption-income schedule. Whenever any two variables—for example, consumption and income—are in some systematic and dependable way related to each other (i.e., when, as one varies, the other changes in some dependable manner) we have what is known as a "function." We say that there is a *functional relation* between the two. If variable A is determined by variable B, we call A the dependent variable and B the independent variable. We may then say that A is a function of B; in other words, whenever B changes, A will change also in some dependable manner. "Dependable manner" does not necessarily mean, however, that at all levels of B, any change in B will cause the same proportionate change in A. It does, however, mean that the relation of A to B is not haphazard, accidental, or wholly unpredictable. A schedule or curve showing the relation of A to B at different levels of B will disclose how A varies in relation to B at all values of B. If A is a function of B, then A will change, when B changes, in some fairly dependable manner. In diagrammatic form, what this manner is will be disclosed by the *shape* of the curve relating these two variables. The curve may or may not be linear, but whatever the *shape,* it may nonetheless be stable.

Statistics cannot disclose which of two variables is the dependent one and which the independent one. That must be ascertained on grounds of general reasoning—that is, by theoretical analysis. Now it is reasonable to suppose that consumer expenditures are *mainly* determined by the level of current income, or perhaps by the income earned in the recent past. But if income suddenly changes, and especially if the new income is not likely to last for long, consumption will probably not change much. On the other hand, if the new income remains at the same level for a considerable period, consumption standards will adjust to the new level, and consumption will rise. When we speak of the "consumption function" (the schedule showing the relation of consumption to income) we assume short-run lags away. The consumption shown in the consumption-income schedule is the consumption expenditure which would be made at each income level, assuming that income to prevail over a reasonably long period of time. The consumption function is, in other words, a schedule showing how much will be spent on consumers' goods at various *sustained* levels of income. It is a schedule showing the more or less dependable behavior pattern of the community with respect to consumer spending at different levels of income.

With respect to the familiar price-demand schedule, it is assumed that other factors remain unaltered—the prices of competing goods, the tastes and relative preferences of consumers, etc. An upward shift in the demand curve, for example, represents a fundamental change in the preferences for different types of commodities, or the emergence of more desirable or cheaper substitutes. The demand curve or schedule represents the relation of one variable to another in a "period" within which all other variables are assumed to be constant. Such hypothetical schedules are highly abstract in that they seek to isolate, from the multitude of factors which are constantly changing in a highly dynamic world, the *one* variable (or at most a few) which is regarded as a significant determinant of the other variable. Such schedules, however abstract, are nevertheless useful for analysis, especially if the variables selected are overwhelmingly important and if other factors change rather slowly. Every effort should be made, however, to take account of all the significant variables and to correct as far as possible for changes tending to disturb the functional relation in question. Econometricians are indeed at work, more and more, on just such problems.

The consumption function, and indeed any functional relation in economics, is of course a heroic abstraction. Everything in economic life depends upon everything else. But this statement, while true, is not very meaningful. Economic analysis performs the function of isolating certain highly important variables and showing what are the *main* determinants of the events of economic life. When it is said that demand is determined by price, what is meant is not that price alone determines demand, but that price is a main determinant of demand. And in the schedule showing the precise influence of changes in price upon demand, all other factors are assumed to be constant, or else disturbing influences have, by statistical methods, been eliminated. In this manner it is possible to concentrate on a single important determinant of demand, namely the price of the commodity in question. Thus, for short, we say that the demand for wheat is determined by the price of wheat, though in fact we know quite well that it is also determined by the price of oats, corn, etc.[1]

Types of Consumption Schedules

Two types of schedules can be drawn up showing the relation of consumption to income: (1) the family-budget consumption schedule and (2) a schedule based on time series. The former is derived from studies of family budgets; the latter, on national income statistics such as those discussed in Chapter 6. The former is a snapshot picture at one single interval of time—the period in which the budget studies were made. It discloses a range of family incomes from low to high, and shows how much is spent on consumption at different levels of family income. The latter is based on time series showing different levels of national income and consumption expenditures year by year over an entire business cycle or several cycles. It discloses a range of national incomes over many years and shows how much was spent on consumers' goods at each of these income levels.

THE FAMILY-BUDGET SCHEDULE

Let us first consider the family-budget schedule, or "family consumption function." In Figure 40 we show the data on family incomes and consumption based on a sample study of urban families in sixty-two cities scattered throughout the United States and covering the full twelve months of 1941.[2] Family income,

1 In equation form we could write this as follows, in which p_1 is the price of wheat, p_2 is the price of oats, and p_3 is the price of corn, and D the demand for wheat:

$$D = \Psi (p_1, p_2, p_3, \text{etc.})$$

2 *Family Spending and Saving in Wartime*, Bulletin No. 822, Bureau of Labor Statistics, U.S. Department of Labor, pp. 194–195.

ranging from an average of $367 for the lowest income class to an average of $14,933 for the highest income class included in this study, is measured on the horizontal scale, and consumption expenditures on the vertical. The area below Curve A represents

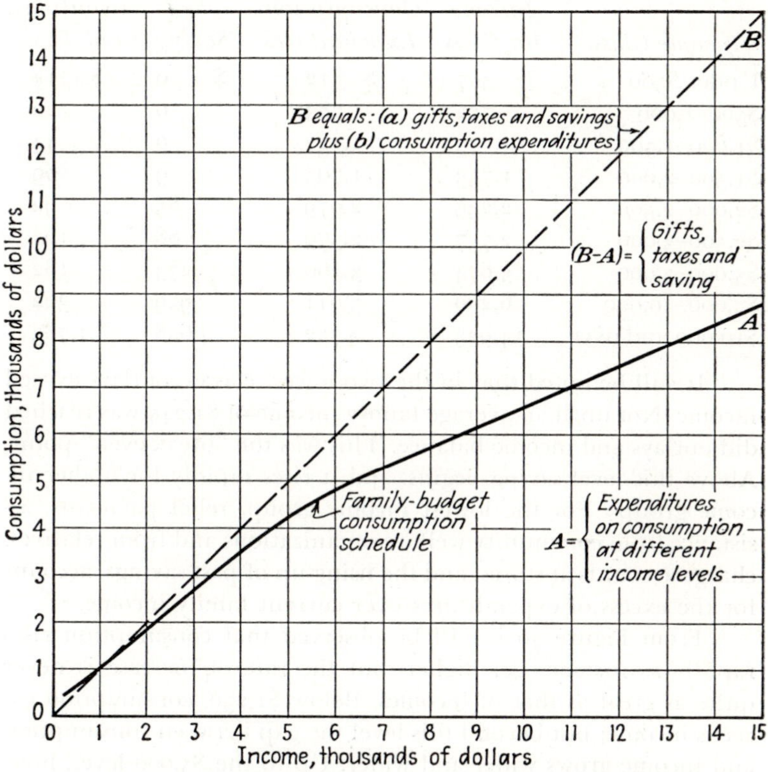

FIGURE 40. *Family-Budget Consumption Schedule*

Source: *Family Spending and Saving in Wartime,* Bulletin No. 822, United States Department of Labor, Bureau of Labor Statistics, p. 197.

consumption, and the area between Curve A and Curve B represents that part of income in excess of consumption expenditures. This part was put into savings, or was used to make gifts and contributions of various kinds and to make tax payments. The figures are given in Table XVII.

TABLE XVII

Family Incomes and Income Disposal in the United States for Twelve-Month Period, 1941

Income Class	*Average Income for Class*	*Consumption Expenditures*	*Saving*	*Gifts, Contributions, and Taxes*
Under $500	$ 367	$ 512	$ 0	$ 13
$500–1,000	752	783	0	26
$1,000–1,500	1,245	1,222	0	44
$1,500–2,000	1,753	1,705	9	69
$2,000–2,500	2,239	2,079	85	92
$2,500–3,000	2,737	2,579	88	104
$3,000–5,000	3,674	3,260	273	182
$5,000–10,000	6,290	5,011	929	362
$10,000 and over	14,933	8,752	4,658	1,783

It will be noted that in the two lowest classes, outlays exceed income. Not until an average family income of $1,245 was reached did outlays and income balance. This was the "break-even" point. Above this level saving begins, and it rises rapidly for higher income groups. For the lowest income group, relief payments, assistance from community welfare organizations and from relatives, charge accounts at stores, and the using up of past savings, account for the excess of expenditures over current family income.

From Figure 40 it will be observed that consumption rises rapidly as incomes get higher, but the rate of increase is never quite as great as that of incomes. Below $1,250, consumption exceeds income; but beyond this level the gap between consumption and income grows wider and wider. Up to the $5,000 level, however, the consumption line is fairly steep; that is, consumption rises nearly as rapidly as income. Beyond the $5,000 level, the gap between consumption and income rapidly becomes very great. In general we conclude that as income rises, consumption also increases, but not as much as income.

THE TIME-SERIES SCHEDULE

We turn now to the time-series schedule, or the "cyclical consumption function" based on national income data extending over a number of years. Here we are concerned with the question of how total consumption for the entire country changes when the total national income changes from low levels to high levels, as is the case during the span of the upswing in a major business cycle. With respect to the various phases of the business cycle we are concerned with the cyclical consumption-income pattern, the cyclical changes in total consumption relative to national income. The assumption is that from one phase of the business cycle to another one can detect a pattern in the changing relationship of consumption to income. It is believed that this cyclical pattern of consumption with respect to income is of fundamental importance.

The volume of consumption is determined not merely by the size of the income, but also, in part, by the particular stage in the cycle at which this income is received. We are here dealing with relatively short-run changes. As income rises in the prosperity phase of the cycle, consumption expenditures may not at once rise to that normal relation of consumption to income which would prevail if income remained for a considerable time at this new level. There is likely to occur a consumption-expenditure lag. We may thus distinguish between the "cyclical" consumption-income pattern and the "pure" consumption function. The latter gives the normal relation of consumption to income with no time lag. There appears to be some evidence that a consumer-expenditure lag does occur, especially at the upper and lower turning points of the cycle.

Consider first the "pure" consumption function with no time lag. Here it is assumed that at each income level consumption holds the *normal* relation to income. In other words, consumption, at each income level, is assumed to stand at the level it would reach if income remained at that volume long enough so that consumers could have time to adjust their expenditures according to their normal propensity to consume. Consumption therefore corresponds, at each income level, to the normal behavior pattern of the community.

The "pure" consumption function cannot be represented by a schedule of the raw time series of consumption and income as found in the data of any business cycle. For one thing, the raw data are likely to be vitiated by price changes. While money income doubled, real income, owing to price increases, might remain unchanged. If the time series data over a cycle reflected only changes in prices there is no good reason (if there were no time lags in price and wage movements) to suppose that consumption should change in relation to money income. If, however, there were a *real* increase in income it could be expected that consumption would rise by a smaller amount as income increased. Similarly if the rise in national income were merely due to an increase in population, with no change in per capita real income, there is no good reason for expecting a change in the ratio of consumption to income. A 10 per cent rise in population would not mean a 10 per cent rise in per capita real income. The ratio of consumption to income could be expected to change only if per capita real income increased. For these reasons, corrections for price and population changes must be made in order to arrive at the "pure" consumption function.

The consumption function is a "reversible analytical relationship" and not simply a "historical description of past happenings."[3] Thus the raw data do not reveal the true cyclical consumption-income pattern. Spurious elements are present, including price and population changes, and time lags.

Average vs. Marginal Propensity to Consume

Figure 41 presents diagrammatically a pure consumption function, without time lags, and corrected for price and population changes. The figure is drawn purely for illustrative purposes. In this figure two schedules (functions) are shown. Schedule A is a straight line drawn at a 45° angle from the horizontal base line. A country with a consumption function such as Schedule A would spend *all* its income on consumers' goods at all income levels. This means that, at any income level, the ratio of total consumption to total income is always unity, or $\frac{C}{Y} = 1$. In other words, the "*average* propensity to consume," represented by $\frac{C}{Y}$, is unity. Moreover, in the case of Schedule A, for any increment of income, $\triangle Y$, there will always be a correspondingly large incre-

[3] See Paul A. Samuelson (Appendix to Chapter XI) in Alvin H. Hansen, *Fiscal Policy and Business Cycles,* W. W. Norton & Company, Inc., 1941.

ment of consumption, ΔC. In other words, the "*marginal* propensity to consume" (i.e., $\frac{\Delta C}{\Delta Y}$) will also in this case be unity at all income levels.

In the case of Schedule B the case is very different. Here, for every increment of income, consumption increases by only two-

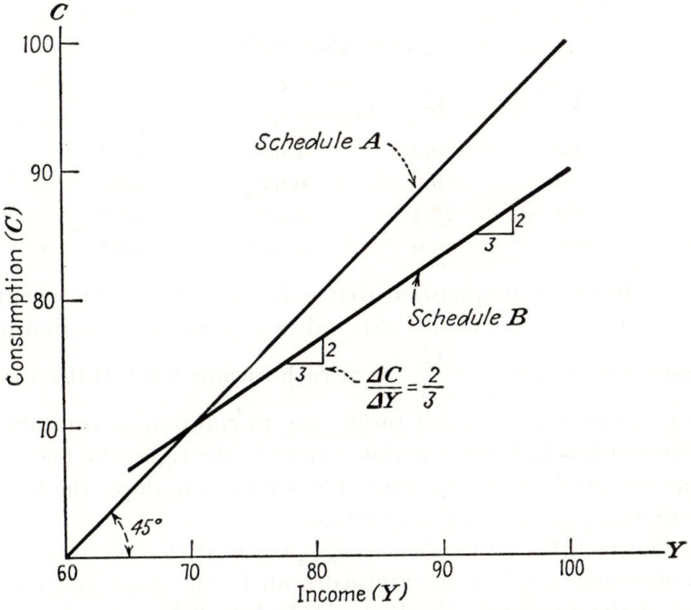

FIGURE 41. *Consumption Function*

thirds this amount. This is true since the slope of the curve is such that for three units of increase in income, consumption rises by two units. Thus $\frac{\Delta C}{\Delta Y} = \frac{2}{3}$, as indicated in the triangle on the diagram. And since Schedule B is a straight line, the marginal propensity to consume, $\frac{\Delta C}{\Delta Y}$, is always ⅔ at all income levels. If, however, the curve sloped off to the right (i.e., flattened out toward the top of the chart), the marginal propensity to consume would get smaller and smaller at higher levels of income.

But while the *marginal* propensity to consume is constant (namely, ⅔) at all income levels in the case of Schedule B, the *average* propensity to consume, $\frac{C}{Y}$, changes at every income level. At the income 70, $\frac{C}{Y} = 1$; below this level it is greater than 1; and above this level, less than 1. These data are given in Table XVIII.

TABLE XVIII (*Schedule B*)

Y	C	$\frac{C}{Y}$	$\frac{\Delta C}{\Delta Y}$
70	70.0	1.000	0.67
80	76.6	0.955	0.67
90	83.3	0.925	0.67
100	90.0	0.900	0.67

It should be emphasized that it is the *slope* of the schedule (at various income levels) which indicates what the marginal propensity to consume, $\frac{\Delta C}{\Delta Y}$, is at each income level. If the schedule is linear, the marginal propensity to consume is constant at all income levels. If the schedule curves to the right, the marginal propensity falls as income rises. The steeper the slope, the higher the marginal propensity to consume.

On the other hand, the *average* propensity to consume at different income levels is determined both by the *slope* and by the *level* of the schedule. The higher Schedule B lies in relation to the 45° line (Fig. 41), the higher $\frac{C}{Y}$, the average propensity to consume, will be at all income levels. If the slope of the schedule is relatively flat, the average propensity to consume, $\frac{C}{Y}$, will fall rapidly as income rises; if the schedule is relatively steep (approaching the 45° line), $\frac{C}{Y}$ will fall very slowly as income rises.

Fluctuations over Time

Figures 40 and 41 show the functional relation of consumption to income at different income levels. Income is measured on the horizontal scale and consumption on the vertical scale, and the curve (or schedule) relates the two variables. Let us next consider the *movement* of consumption and income *over time,* from the depression phase of the cycle to the peak of the boom. Figure 42 represents a historical development of consumption in relation to income. In this case *time* is measured on the horizontal scale, and both consumption and income are measured on the vertical scale. Both income and consumption expenditures are assumed to

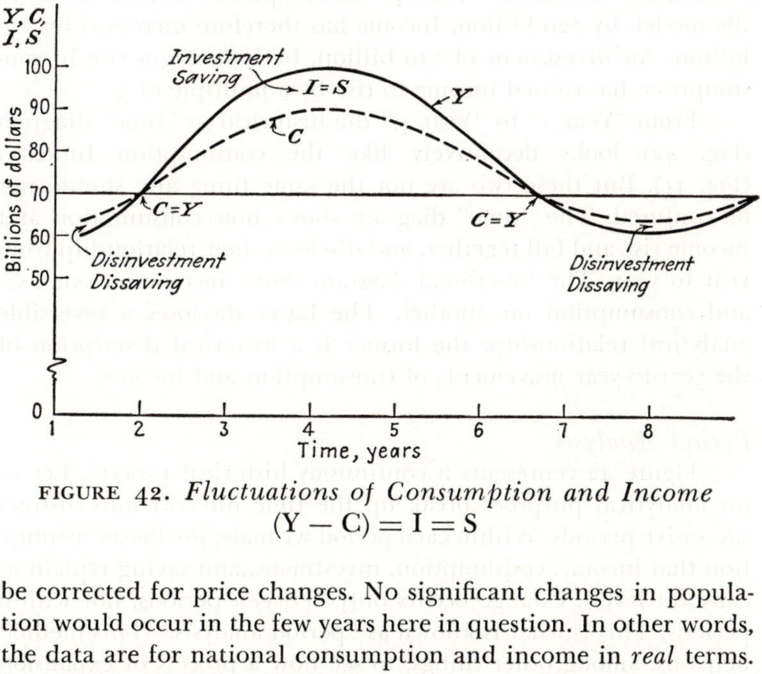

FIGURE 42. *Fluctuations of Consumption and Income*

$$(Y - C) = I = S$$

be corrected for price changes. No significant changes in population would occur in the few years here in question. In other words, the data are for national consumption and income in *real* terms. But time lags are retained, since these may be important in the historical process of income formation.

In Figure 42, prior to "Year 2" it will be noted that consumption, C, exceeds income, Y. This means that the community is consuming more than its current production, the excess being drawn from stocks of goods and from using up capital goods which are not being fully replaced. The difference between consumption and income is thus represented by dissaving or disinvestment. Beyond

"Year 2" income rises above consumption, the difference being from one point of view investment, and from another, saving.

In this simplified model, income equals investment plus consumption ($Y = I + C$). But saving is that part of income which is not spent on consumers' goods. Hence $Y - C = S$. Therefore $S = I$ if all terms apply to the *same* period of time.

At "Year 2" income and consumption are equal, and investment is therefore zero. As investment rises from this point to around \$10 billion, in "Year 4," consumption rises, according to the model, by \$20 billion. Income has therefore increased by \$30 billion. An investment of \$10 billion, by inducing a rise in consumption, has caused income to rise by a multiple of 3.

From "Year 1" to "Year 4," the historical or "time" diagram (Fig. 42) looks deceptively like the consumption function (Fig. 41). But these two are not the same thing and should not be confused. The "time" diagram shows how consumption and income rise and fall together, and discloses their relationship from year to year. The functional diagram shows income on one axis and consumption on another. The latter discloses a reversible analytical relationship; the former is a historical description of the year-to-year movements of consumption and income.

Period Analysis

Figure 42 represents a continuous historical process. Let us for analytical purposes break up the time interval into distinct successive periods. Within each period we make the heroic assumption that income, consumption, investment, and saving remain at constant levels. Change occurs only *between* periods, not within periods. This is what is known as "period analysis." This method helps us, among other things, to see how a process of expansion and contraction works itself out from period to period, and especially the role played by time lags.

Though period analysis presupposes a discontinuous leap from one period to the next, it is particularly valuable as a pedagogical device, since it views the process of change in a manner which appeals to common sense. We are accustomed to a world of frictions and lags, and we do not easily think of a process of change as a continuous movement without time lag. It appeals to common sense to compare the condition in one period with that in the next period.

Now, having broken our time interval into discrete periods, let us assume a consumer-expenditure lag of one period. Indeed, we may wish to define the length of a period in terms of the expenditure lag. If changes in consumption tend to lag behind changes in income by an interval of one month, we may choose to call a "period" one month. We may designate these periods by subscripts 1, 2, 3, etc.

If we assume a consumer-expenditure lag of one period, then consumption in the current period will depend upon income in the preceding period. In other words, current consumption C_1 is regarded as a function of prior income Y_0, or $C_1 = \Phi(Y_0)$. Current saving S_1 is then defined as the difference between prior income Y_0 and current consumption C_1. Thus $S_1 = Y_0 - C_1$. But current income Y_1 must necessarily equal current consumption expenditures C_1 plus current investment expenditures I_1; therefore $Y_1 = I_1 + C_1$. On these terms, viewing the problems in successive periods of time, I_1 will equal S_1 only if $Y_1 = Y_0$. But if current income, Y_1, exceeds prior income Y_0, then $I_1 > S_1$. From all this it should be clear that $Y_1 = Y_0 + (I_1 - S_1)$, or current income Y_1 will exceed prior income Y_0 by the amount that current investment I_1 exceeds current saving S_1.[4]

In terms of period analysis, saving and investment may be unequal. On the other hand, if *all* categories (Y, C, I, and S) are defined so as to apply to the *same* point of time, then saving and investment must necessarily always be equal since, on these terms, both are simply the difference between income and consumption.

In Figure 43 we present the process of income formation in terms of period analysis. The model, for convenience of presentation, is somewhat arbitrary in several respects. First, we assume a sudden injection of a large flow of investment; and we assume further that precisely this amount of investment then continues unabated over a considerable number of succeeding periods; second, we assume a constant marginal propensity to consume of ⅔; and finally, we assume a definitive consumption lag of one "period."

Let us say that income in Period 0 was already at $70 billion

[4] See Appendix of this book on the Robertsonian and Swedish systems of period analysis.

and that in this period consumption was equal to income, there being no investment and no saving. This we shall call the "basic consumption" level or break-even point. Now in Period 1, invest-

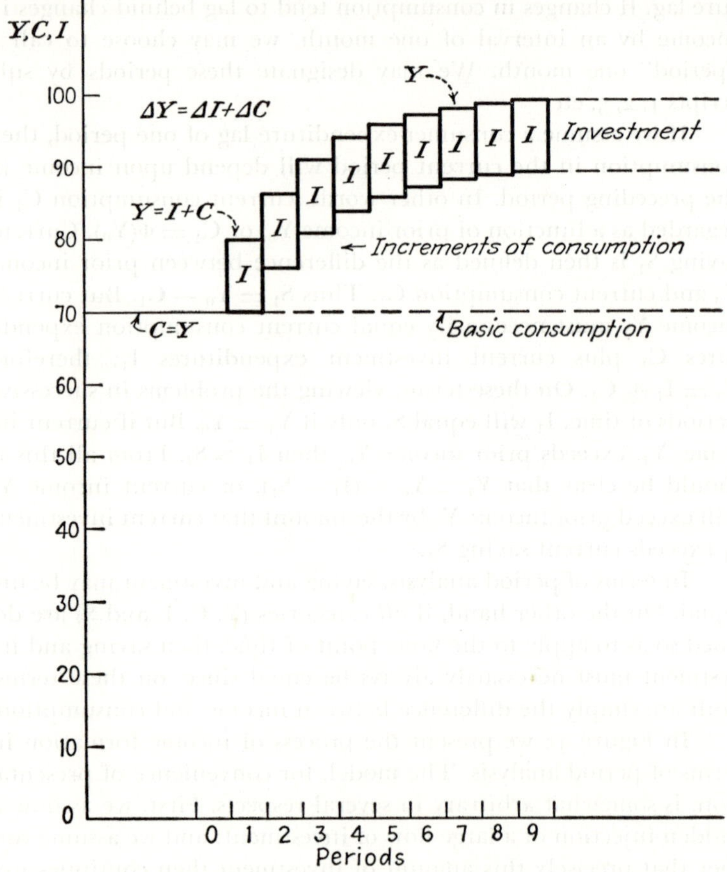

FIGURE 43. *Period Analysis:* $\Delta Y = \Delta I + \Delta C$

ment suddenly rises to $10 billion and remains at this level for a considerable time. Consumption will now rise, but by a lagging adjustment, since the consumption of one period is always a function of the income of the preceding period. The *increase* of consumption in any one period is always equal to ⅔ of the *increase* in income in the preceding period. This process will continue until consumption has "caught up," or in other words has reached a normal relation to income. Table XIX, from which Figure 43 is derived, shows these relationships and lagged adjustments.

TABLE XIX

Period	Y (I + C)	I	*Increment of C over Preceding Period*	*Total C (Basic C plus Increment)*
Period 0	70	0	0	70
Period 1	80	10	0	70
Period 2	86.67	10	6.67	76.67
Period 3	91.11	10	4.44	81.11
Period 4	94.07	10	2.96	84.07
Period 5	96.04	10	1.97	86.04
Period 6	97.36	10	1.32	87.36
Period 7	98.24	10	.88	88.24
Period 8	98.82	10	.58	88.82
Period 9	99.20	10	.38	89.20
Asymptote	100.00	10	.00	90.00

Figure 43 shows how (given a marginal propensity to consume of ⅔ and a consumer-expenditure lag of one period) $10 billion of investment will gradually raise income by $30 billion in view of the induced increase in consumption of $20 billion. If there were no time lag in consumer expenditure, if consumption instantly adjusted itself currently to income changes, then income would already have risen by Period 1 from $70 billion to $100 billion. Assuming a time lag in consumer expenditure, the process of income expansion is spread over several periods.

The Multiplier

A little experimentation will disclose the fact that the higher the marginal propensity to consume, the greater the multiplier by which income will be raised. Let us designate the multiplier by k. Then $k\Delta I = \Delta Y$. As we have suggested above, k varies with the marginal propensity to consume, $\frac{\Delta C}{\Delta Y}$. From Figure 43, it is seen that when $\frac{\Delta C}{\Delta Y} = \frac{2}{3}$, then the multiplier is 3. If the marginal propensity to consume were $\frac{1}{2}$, the multiplier would be 2. Thus $k = \frac{1}{1 - \frac{\Delta C}{\Delta Y}}$.

Two Definitions of Saving

We noted above two definitions of saving. One is the commonsense definition in terms of which it is conceived that income earned in one period is disposed of in the next succeeding period. This seems quite natural. There are two ways in which one can dispose of one's income: one can save it or one can spend it. Hence $Y_0 = S_1 + C_1$, or $S_1 = Y_0 - C_1$.[5]

According to the second definition (the Keynesian definition, which is adopted by national-income statisticians), saving is that part of *current* income which is currently not spent. Therefore $Y_1 = S_1 + C_1$.

Let us now see how these two definitions of saving apply to the situations depicted in Figure 44. To explain this it will not be necessary to go through all the stages, and we shall concentrate on only the first three or four periods. We have blown the diagram up to a much larger size than that of Figure 43 in order to indicate more clearly the relevant changes from period to period.

According to the Robertsonian definition, S_1 (Period 1) is zero, since $S_1 = Y_0 - C_1$. This means that the whole of the new investment I_1 must be financed from new bank credit or from borrowing idle balances. In Period 2, however, $S_2 = Y_1 - C_2 = \$3.3$; in Period 3, $S_3 = Y_2 - C_3 = \$5.6$; and in Period 4, $S_4 = Y_3 - C_4 = \$7.0$. Thus progressively as income rises, saving out of the rising income received in the preceding period grows larger and larger and eventually, beyond Period 9, when ultimately the asymptote is reached, saving equals \$10 billion, corresponding to the volume of investment. As saving increases, period by period, less and less new bank credit or idle balances are needed. Eventually, when I = S (Robertsonian definition) a new equilibrium

[5] This is the so-called Robertsonian definition of saving. See D. H. Robertson, *Essays in Monetary Theory*, P. S. King & Son, Ltd., London, 1940.

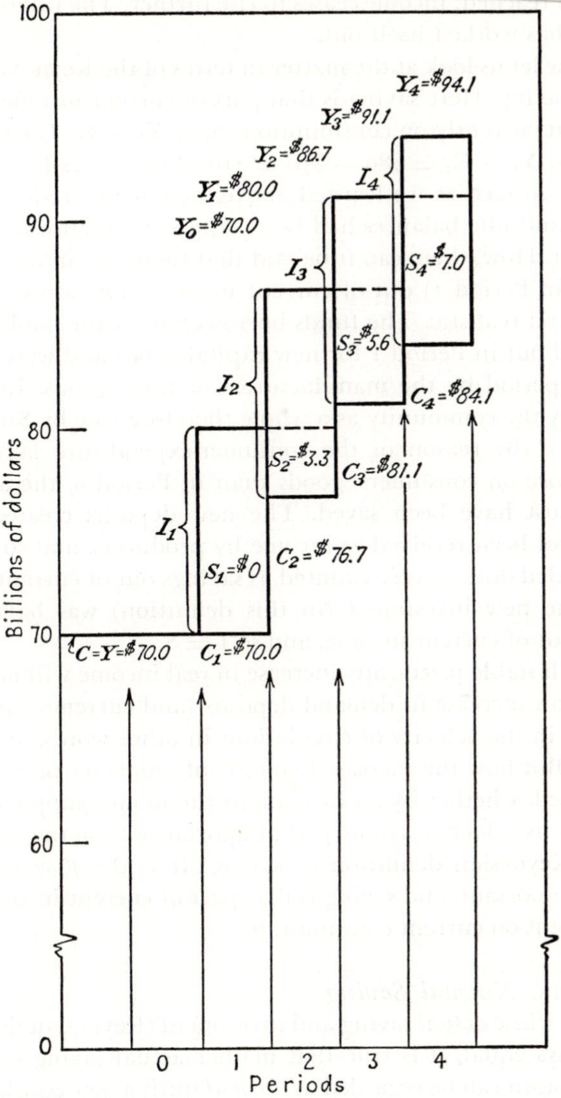

FIGURE 44. *Period Analysis: Investment and Saving*

has been reached; income ceases to rise further. The full multiplier process has worked itself out.

Now let us look at the matter in terms of the Keynesian definition of saving. Here saving is that part of current income which is not spent currently on consumption: $S_1 = Y_1 - C_1$. Consider now Period 1. $Y_1 - C_1 = \$80 - \$70 = \$10$. Thus, $S_1 = I_1$.

But in fact, as we learned above, new bank credit had been created and idle balances had been tapped to finance the new investment. How, then, can it be said that there was in fact any new saving (in Period 1) out of current income? The answer is quite simple and realistic. The funds borrowed from the banks were in fact paid out in Period 1 for new capital goods and were received in that period by the manufacturers of these goods. Income received by the community as a whole therefore rose by $10 billion, and since (by reason of the consumer-expenditure lag) no one spent more on consumers' goods than in Period 0, the added income must have been saved. The new deposits created by the banks had been received as income by producers, and somewhere these added dollars were counted as savings out of current income. Thus the new investment (in this definition) was balanced by saving out of current income, and so $I = S$.

With stable prices, any increase in real income will necessarily involve an increase in demand deposits (and currency) and/or an increase in the velocity of circulation; in other words, an increase in MV. But how the increased volume of monetary payments will be effected, whether by an increase in the money supply or an increase in its velocity, is of no great importance from the standpoint of the Keynesian definition of saving. It is the *flow of income* that is important, and saving is that part of current income which is not spent on current consumption.

Actual vs. Normal Saving

But while *actual* saving and investment (Keynesian definition) are always equal, it is true that neither actual saving nor actual consumption can be regarded as *normal* until a new equilibrium is finally reached at which $I = S$ in the Robertsonian sense. This is due to the expenditure lag. So long as consumption has not caught up with income, the amount saved (and conversely the amount consumed) is not the *desired* amount. Thus while actual saving and investment are always equal in the Keynesian sense, desired saving may not be equal to the actual saving. When the actual saving also becomes the amount that people desire to save out of current income, the expenditure lag will have worked its way through, and consumption will have caught up with income. When actual saving equals desired saving, we may then say that $S = I$ in an *equilibrium* sense and not merely as an identity. Only when the full multiplier process has worked itself out are saving and investment equal in an equilibrium sense.

Saving and investment would, however, not merely be equal, but also equal at all times in an equilibrium sense if the multiplier process were instantaneous, or in other words if there were no consumer-expenditure lag. In the pure consumption function (Fig. 41, Schedule B) it is assumed that there is no expenditure lag. The multiplier is regarded as instantaneous—that is, it is assumed that consumption always adjusts itself at once to changes in current income. This is the pure or logical theory of the multiplier. Whether in fact there is an expenditure lag (as Keynes himself believed there was, though he thought it to be short) is not important for the *theory* of the consumption function or of the multiplier. The pure consumption function shows what is the *normal* relation of consumption to income after accounting for the expenditure lag. It is analagous to the "short-run normal supply curve." If demand suddenly shifts upward and to the right, the supply curve may become, for a time, price-inelastic. But gradually supply will adjust itself and assume a normal relationship to price. So also with consumption and saving in relation to income. Because of the expenditure lag a sudden change in income will throw actual consumption and actual saving out of line with their normal relationships to income. Only as this normal relationship is restored will actual consumption and actual saving also be the desired consumption and the desired saving.[6]

---

[6] See Alvin H. Hansen, *Monetary Theory and Fiscal Policy,* McGraw-Hill Book Co., 1949, Appendix B: "A Note on Savings and Investment."

Secular Shift of Consumption Function

In a period of high prosperity, consumption will progressively adjust itself to the new high level of income. The community is achieving living standards higher than any previously reached. Having once become accustomed to this standard, strong resistance is offered to a decline in consumption, if depression drives income down. Thus as income falls, consumption declines also, but at a rate proportionately less than that of income. As a first approximation one might assume that as income rises and falls, consumption will rise and fall in direct proportion to changes in income. But this is not true. The lower the income, the harder it is "to make both ends meet," or in other words the harder it is to maintain what has come to be regarded as a more or less minimum standard. As income falls, consumption is partly sustained by cutting down on current saving, so that the *ratio* of saving to income declines. The decline in this ratio is caused by the fall of current income below the previously achieved high income level. We may therefore say that the ratio of saving to income is a function of the current income in relation to the highest income previously reached.[7]

Thus in the equation $\frac{S}{Y} = F\left(\frac{Y_t}{Y_A}\right)$, S is saving, Y is income, Y_t is current income, and Y_A is the highest income previously achieved to which the country has become accustomed.

Figure 45A presents the movements of Y_t, from which one can readily derive the movements of $\frac{Y_t}{Y_A}$. From t_0 to t_1 the fraction $\frac{Y_t}{Y_A}$ gets smaller, and so $\frac{S}{Y}$, which is a function of $\frac{Y_t}{Y_A}$, will fall. From t_1 to t_2, $\frac{Y_t}{Y_A}$ is rising, and so the ratio $\frac{S}{Y}$ will rise. From t_2 to t_3, Y_A rises step by step, lagged one period behind Y_t, until it reaches a new high at Y_{A_2}. In other words, from t_2 to t_3, $\frac{Y_t}{Y_A}$ is virtually unity. From t_2 to t_3, the ratio $\frac{S}{Y}$ remains constant. This

[7] See James S. Duesenberry, Chapter III in *Income, Employment and Public Policy*, W. W. Norton & Co., 1948, and *Income, Saving, and the Theory of Consumer Behavior*, Harvard University Press (1949), Chapter V, and pp. 114–116.

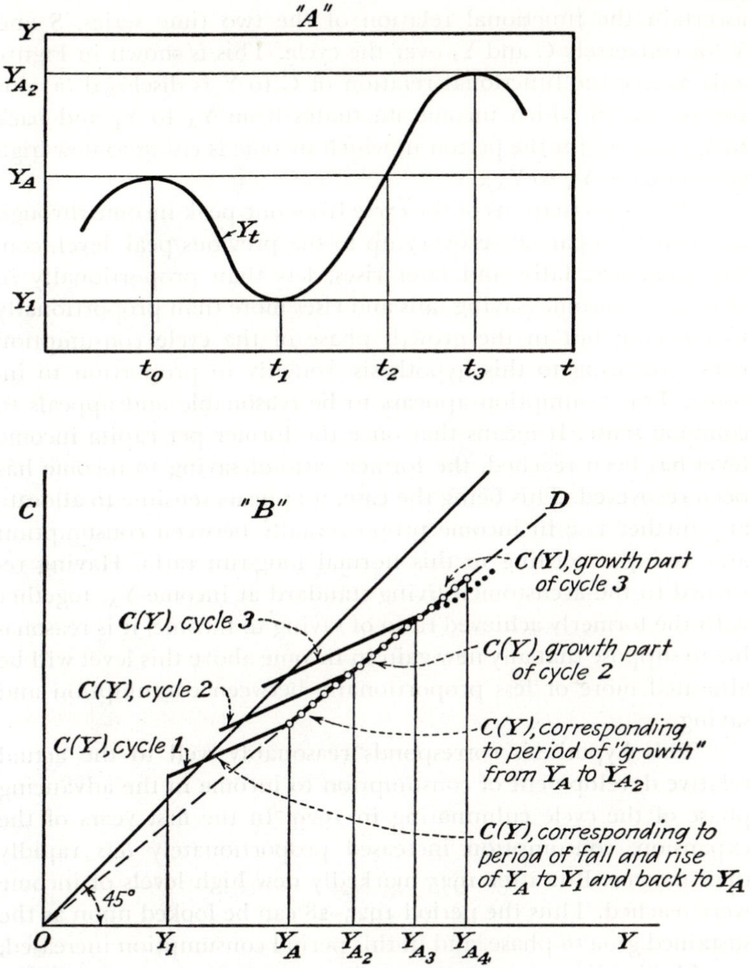

FIGURE 45. *Secular and Cyclical Consumption Functions*

means that as income rises, consumption rises proportionally, though *absolutely* not as much as income.

Taking the data given by the historical movements of $\frac{S}{Y}$ over the various phases of the cycle, as revealed in Figure 45A, and assuming *ceteris paribus* conditions throughout the period, we can ascertain the functional relation of the two time series, S and Y (or conversely C and Y) over the cycle. This is shown in Figure 45B, where the functional relation of C to Y is disclosed (a) for the period in which income fluctuates from Y_A to Y_1 and back to Y_A, and (b) for the period in which income is rising to new high ground from Y_A to Y_{A2}.

In the fluctuations of the cycle from one peak income through depression to partial recovery up to the previous peak level, consumption first falls, and later rises, less than proportionally in relation to income (saving falls and rises more than proportionally to income); but in the growth phase of the cycle consumption rises, according to this hypothesis, roughly in proportion to income. This assumption appears to be reasonable and appeals to common sense. It means that once the former per capita income level has been reached, the former ratio of saving to income has been recovered. This being the case, it appears sensible to allocate any further rise in income proportionally between consumption and saving according to this normal long-run ratio. Having returned to the accustomed living standard at income Y_A, together with the formerly achieved ratio of saving to income, it is reasonable to suppose that any new gain in income above this level will be allocated more or less proportionally between consumption and saving.

This hypothesis corresponds reasonably well to the actual relative development of consumption to income in the advancing phase of the cycle culminating in 1929. In the first years of the expansion, consumption increased proportionately *less* rapidly than income. But after 1925 markedly new high levels of income were reached. Thus the period 1925–28 can be looked upon as the sustained *growth* phase, and in this period consumption increased, roughly, in direct proportion to income. A further spurt in income occurred in 1929, but consumption lagged. Had this new high level been maintained, an upward adjustment of consumption could have been expected in the following year.

This experience suggests that if the growth phase is steady and maintained, consumption will rise more or less in direct proportion to increases in income. If, however, the growth phase should develop by rapid leaps, consumption will increase less than proportionally, or along the dotted path of the C(Y) curve in Cycle 3 (Fig. 45B). Such rapid leaps in income cannot continue, however, for as soon as full employment is reached increases in real income will slow down; then consumption will adjust itself to the new living standard corresponding to the steeper growth curve OD.

If this hypothesis is valid (and it corresponds reasonably well to statistical facts in peacetime years), then, in the growth phase of the cycle, consumption will rise more or less in direct proportion to the increase in income; in the oscillatory phase of the cycle, however—that is, the period from the previous peak output to the point of subsequent recovery to this output level—consumption will fluctuate less violently than income. This means that in the growth phase, the consumption function is a linear curve with its point of origin at O, so that the *average* and the *marginal* propensity to consume are equal. In the oscillatory phase of the cycle, however, the consumption function has a slope such that the curve intersects the 45° line; i.e., the *average* propensity to consume falls as income rises, while the *marginal* propensity (assuming a linear function) is constant. Thus, if this hypothesis is correct, the marginal propensity to consume is lower in the oscillatory phase of the cycle than in the growth phase.

This hypothesis offers a satisfactory explanation for the secular stability of the consumption function, and also for the observed slope of the consumption function in the oscillation phase of the cycle. It integrates the cyclical and the secular behavior of the consumption function. It explains (a) the fact that consumption fluctuates percentagewise less violently than income over the greater part of the cycle, and (b) the fact that secularly, consumption appears to rise more or less in direct proportion to income.

With respect to the secular upward drift of the consumption function from cycle to cycle, note should be made of the fact that this is essentially a formulation in modern terminology of a conception long held by economists relating to the progressive rise in living standards as real incomes increase. For example, in 1932 I discussed this problem [8] in very much the manner of modern writers—namely, in terms of everyone's tendency to make his consumption standard correspond to his position on the Lorenz income-distribution curve.[9] Among other things, relating to trends during the preceding century I said: "Real wages have tripled and quadrupled, yet the lower fringe of workers finds it as difficult as ever to escape destitution. . . . Every increase in real wages brought a corresponding increase in the requirements necessary for what was considered ordinary decency in a civilized country. . . . Higher real wages for the unskilled have not materially eased the difficulty of making both ends meet. Bowley and Stamp have shown that over long-run periods the percentage differential between different economic groups has not materially changed. As incomes rose all around, the whole manner of living changed. It was just as difficult as ever for the unskilled to keep up with the procession. . . . Every assimilated group strives to live somewhat like other people. Each level feels the pull of the standards of those just a step higher in the social scale. The lower the income, the more difficult it is to set aside any surplus above what is absolutely necessary in order to live according to minimum current standards."

The tendency of consumption to rise secularly in relation to increases in income should not be regarded as in any sense unalterable. All relations between economic variables are subject to change over time as institutions change. For example, the emergence of life insurance, especially during its period of rapid growth (when total premium payments greatly exceeded benefit payments), must have had a considerable influence on the secular

---

[8] Alvin H. Hansen, *Economic Stabilization in an Unbalanced World,* Harcourt, Brace & Co., 1932, pp. 373–374.

[9] Cf. James S. Duesenberry, *Income, Saving, and the Theory of Consumer Behavior,* with respect to the upward secular drift in the cyclical consumption function. See also F. Modigliani, "Fluctuations in the Saving-Income Ratio—a Problem in Economic Forecasting," *Studies in Income and Wealth,* Vol. II, National Bureau of Economic Research; and Dorothy Brady and Rose D. Friedman, "Savings and Income Distribution," *Studies in Income and Wealth,* Vol. 10, National Bureau of Economic Research.

consumption function.[10] Other structural changes may have operated in the opposite direction.

It is quite possible that the hypothesis here discussed—which emphasizes the *growth* in income as the primary factor responsible for the secular rise in consumption—needs to be supplemented by the thesis that the secular upward shift can in part be explained by the emergence of new products and new ways of living incident to the passage of time in a continuously dynamic society. It is, however, plausible to suppose that, in the absence of a *growth* in income, new products are to a degree more likely to supplant old products than to cut into saving.[11]

It should, moreover, be noted that the Duesenberry hypothesis applies specifically to the behavior of consumers, or, in other words, to the relation of consumption to "disposable" income. Nevertheless, this principle is not altogether inapplicable to the behavior of consumption in relation to the national income. With respect to the latter, we are concerned not merely with the saving of individuals but also with corporate saving. And there can be little doubt that corporations also behave, more or less, in accordance with the Duesenberry principle. As income declines, corporations are reluctant to cut dividends; and therefore retained earnings (corporate savings) fall off sharply as national income declines. When income rises again, in the next recovery, they are equally reluctant to raise dividends, at least until the former level of corporate profits has been restored. Once income has returned to the previously attained high, corporations will be under pressure from stockholders to raise dividends, since corporate profits may now have moved into new high levels. The effect would be a tendency for corporate savings to behave according to the Duesenberry principle—that is, during the growth phase

---

10 For a discussion of the role of life insurance, mortgage financing, etc., on the consumption function, see Alvin H. Hansen, *Fiscal Policy and Business Cycles,* W. W. Norton & Company, Inc., 1941, pp. 238–242.

11 For a further discussion of the secular upward shift of the consumption function, see Alvin H. Hansen, *Fiscal Policy and Business Cycles,* pp. 231–234, and *Economic Policy and Full Employment,* McGraw-Hill Book Company, 1947, pp. 162–164; also Paul Samuelson, in Chapter II, *Post-War Economic Problems,* McGraw-Hill Book Company, 1943, edited by Seymour Harris.

corporate savings would tend to rise *in proportion* to the rise in income. But this is perhaps an overstatement. In fact, dividend increases lag behind the increase in profits, and so corporate savings tend to rise (even in the growth phase of the cycle) more than proportionally in relation to corporate profits. In addition, corporate profits may rise more than proportionally in relation to national income throughout the whole of the expansion phase of the cycle, including the growth phase. Thus the behavior of corporate profits and corporate saving may modify considerably the application of the Duesenberry principle to the relation of consumption to *national* income.

11 · *The Multiplier and the Acceleration Coefficient*

The Multiplier Process

The investment multiplier has to do with the *magnified* effect of an increment of investment upon the level of income. $k\triangle I = \triangle Y$. An increase of investment raises incomes in the capital goods industries, and this induces an increase of consumption expenditures. Thus an increment of investment induces an increase in consumption. The two increments together equal the increase in income, $\triangle I + \triangle C = \triangle Y$. But the cumulative effect of an increase in investment may be more far-reaching. The induced rise in income may in turn induce a further rise in investment. This latter effect is known as the principle of derived demand or the acceleration principle.

Before considering this principle in detail, it may be well to clear up a possible misunderstanding. While the investment multiplier has to do with the magnified effect of an increment of investment upon income, it is not true that the multiplier process operates only through investment increases. An upward shift of the consumption function (i.e., a general increase in the propensity to consume) will raise income by a magnified amount, precisely in the same manner as in the case of an increase in investment. This can best be made clear by reference to diagrams A and B in Figure 46.

Diagram A in Figure 46 shows the magnified effect on income from adding a certain volume of investment to the consumption schedule. We assume for simplicity that this amount of investment is the same at all income levels.

In Diagram A the addition of a relatively small volume of investment to the CC consumption schedule (the volume being measured by the margin between the CC line and the C + I line) raises income by MN, an amount much larger than the increase in investment.

In Diagram B is shown the magnified effect of an upward shift in the consumption function, with no increase in invest-

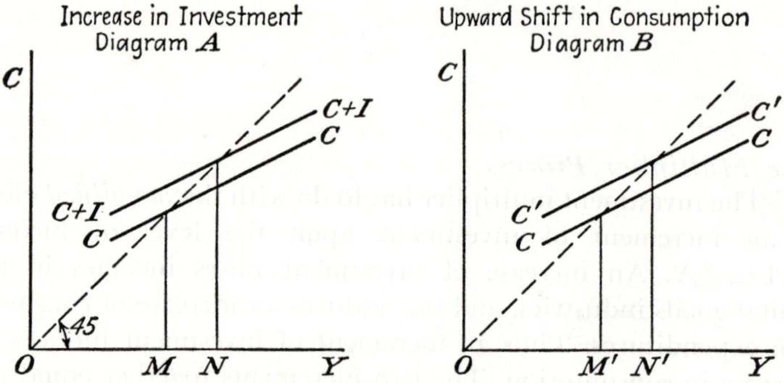

FIGURE 46. *The Multiplier Effect*

ment. An upward shift of the consumption function from the CC line to the C′C′ line raises income by M′N′, an amount equal to MN in Diagram A. Thus the multiplier process operates equally potently whether income is raised in the first instance by an increase in investment or by an increase in consumption.

Just as an increase in investment raises income in the capital goods industries and this in turn increases the spending on consumer goods, so also an increase in consumption will raise incomes in the consumption goods industries, and this will similarly lead to an increase in consumer expenditures and so raise income by an amount greater than the initial increase in spending. How large the secondary effect will be depends upon the *slope* of the consumption function—in other words, upon the marginal propensity to consume. The *slope* tells us how powerful the multiplier is.

But why will not any initial increase in expenditure (whether for investment or consumption) spread and spread, expanding income and spending indefinitely? The initial increase in spending raises income, and this causes further spending. Why does not the process go on and on endlessly?

The answer is found in the slope of the consumption function. The slope tells us how much of the net addition to income is *saved* and how much is *spent.* If it were *all* spent and *none* saved, the cumulative process would indeed go on and on. If the marginal propensity to consume is $\frac{3}{4}$, the process will continue until income has grown by four times the initial expenditure. If the marginal propensity to consume is $\frac{2}{3}$, income will rise by a threefold amount, and so on. The multiplier process is limited by the fact that part of each net addition to income is saved. The multiplier is the *reciprocal* of the marginal propensity to save; the higher the propensity to save, the lower the multiplier.

The Interaction of the Multiplier and the Accelerator

So much to clear away possible misconceptions. But now the cumulative process may (at least in the short run) go beyond the limits set by the multiplier. This is due to the interaction of the *multiplier* and the *accelerator.* First an autonomous increase in investment occurs. This raises income by a magnified amount according to the value of the multiplier. *This increase in income may, however, induce a further increase in investment.* The multiple by which investment is increased for each dollar of increase in income is called the *acceleration coefficient,* or simply the *accelerator.*

Now this *induced* increase in investment will start the multiplier process all over again. Here we encounter a supercumulative process based on the interaction of the multiplier and the accelerator. The *full* magnified effect of the initial increase in investment we may call the *leverage* effect. If we designate the combined multiplier-accelerator leverage (the "super-multiplier") by k^*, then the full leverage effect from period to period is $k^* \Delta I = \Delta Y$.

TABLE XX

Interaction of Multiplier and Accelerator [2]

(*in billions*)

Period	(1) *Autonomous Investment* (deviation from base period)	(2) *Induced Consumption* [3] (deviation from base period)	(3) *Induced Investment* [4] (deviation from base period)	(4)=(1)+(2)+(3) *Total Deviation of Income* (from base period)
Base period	$ 0.0	$ 0.0	$ 0.0	$ 0.0
Period 1	10.0	0.0	0.0	10.0
Period 2	10.0	6.7	13.4	30.1
Period 3	10.0	20.0	26.6	56.6
Period 4	10.0	37.8	35.6	83.4
Period 5	10.0	55.6	35.6	101.2
Period 6	10.0	67.5	23.8	101.3
Period 7	10.0	67.6	(−0.2)	77.4
Period 8	10.0	51.6	(−10.0)	51.6
Period 9	10.0	34.4	(−10.0)	34.4
Period 10	10.0	22.9	(−10.0)	22.9
Period 11	10.0	15.2	(−10.0)	15.2
Period 12	10.0	10.1	(−10.0)	10.1
Period 13	10.0	6.7	(−6.8)	9.9
Period 14	10.0	6.6	0.2	16.8

[2,3,4] See footnotes on opposite page.

Here also the cumulative process (including the accelerator) encounters limits. We noted above that the multiplier process would result in continuous expansion if the marginal propensity to consume were unity. In fact, however, a positive marginal propensity to save stops the process. But when the accelerator is combined with the multiplier, an explosive, continuing expansion *may* result if the acceleration coefficient is very high and is combined with a high marginal propensity to consume [1] (i.e., a high multiplier). In this case an explosive expansion will occur until the ceiling of full utilization of labor or capital facilities is reached. At this point output will flatten out, and so (via the accelerator) induced investment will decline.

In order to see how a cycle might unfold, let us, for purposes of illustration, assume that there is no limitation of productive

---

[1] The limiting values for the marginal propensity to consume and the acceleration coefficient which will produce the explosive effect are discussed fully in Alvin H. Hansen, *Fiscal Policy and Business Cycles,* W. W. Norton & Company, Inc., 1941, Chapter XII, based on the brilliant article by Paul Samuelson, "Interactions Between the Multiplier and the Principle of Acceleration," *Review of Economic Statistics,* May, 1939.

[2] The marginal propensity to consume is ⅔ and the accelerator is 2.

[3] The figures in this column increase for each period by ⅔ the *increment* of income in the *preceding* period. This procedure follows from the assumptions (1) that the marginal propensity to consume is ⅔, and (2) that changes in consumption lag one period behind changes in income. Thus ⅔ of $10.0 (the increment of income in Period 1) is $6.70 (the first induced increase of consumption; ⅔ of $30.1 (the increment of income in Period 2 over the base year) is $20.0, etc.

[4] The figures in this column in each period are twice the difference between the induced consumption of that period and that of the preceding period. Thus the induced investment of Period 3, for example, is twice $13.30 (the induced consumption of Period 3 minus the induced consumption of Period 2). This procedure follows from the assumption that every increase in consumption induces (via the acceleration principle) an increase in investment equal to twice the increase in consumption.

It is assumed that disinvestment (capital consumption) cannot exceed $10.0 per annum. Thus, with the drastic fall in consumption from Period 7 to Period 8, though excess capacity develops on a grand scale, it is not possible to get rid of this excess capacity, since it takes time for the capital stock to be used up. Thus induced investment cannot fall below (—10.0). Offsetting this capital wastage, we assume a continuing autonomous investment of $10.0 per annum. Despite the excess capacity, this assumption is not unreasonable, since cost-reducing improvements may well justify this volume of autonomous investment. Thus, taking account of the autonomous investment and maximum capital consumption, net investment on the basis of these assumptions could not fall below zero in any one year.

resources. No limiting ceiling would then be reached. Assume an initial basic income of $100 billion, to which is now added a volume of autonomous investment (continuously maintained)

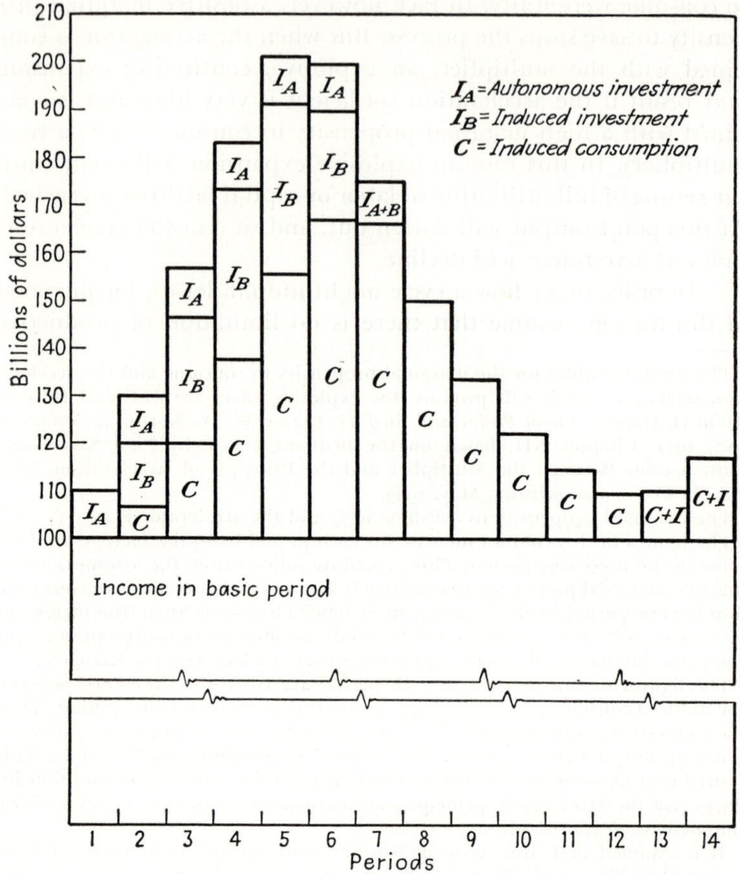

FIGURE 47. *Autonomous Investment, Induced Consumption, and Induced Investment*

of $10 billion. Assume a marginal propensity to consume of ⅔, and an acceleration coefficient of 2. Then the deviation of consumption, of induced investment, and of income from the base period for a succession of periods is given in columns 2, 3, and

4 in Table XX. These data are presented in diagrammatic form in Figure 47.

Quite possibly values for the multiplier and the accelerator lower than those assumed in Table XX could be regarded as realistic. Again, for purposes of illustration let us assume a marginal propensity to consume of ½ and an accelerator of 2. The

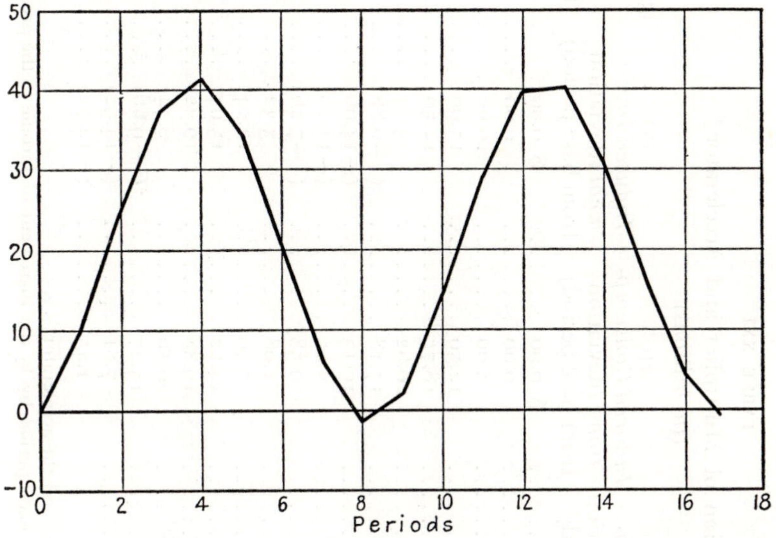

FIGURE 48. *Multiplier-Accelerator Interaction (A Recurring Cycle)*

result is a quite moderate recurring cycle which repeats itself indefinitely. The data are given in Table XXI and in diagrammatic form in Figure 48.

Why the Cumulative Process Ends

A careful study of these data, as disclosed in tabular and chart form, will show that the rise in income is progressively slowed down by the fact that a large part of each increment of income is not spent in the succeeding period. This fact eventually brings about a decline in the volume of induced investment, and when this decline exceeds the increase in induced consumption

TABLE XXI

Interaction of Multiplier and Accelerator [5]

(in billions)

Period	(1) *Autonomous Investment* (deviation from base period)	(2) *Induced Consumption* [6] (deviation from base period)	(3) *Induced Investment* (deviation from base period)	(4)=(1)+(2)+(3) *Total Deviation of Income* (from base period)
Base period	$ 0.0	$ 0.00	$ 0.00	$ 0.00
Period 1	10.0	0.00	0.00	10.00
Period 2	10.0	5.00	10.00	25.00
Period 3	10.0	12.50	15.00	37.50
Period 4	10.0	18.75	12.50	41.25
Period 5	10.0	20.62	3.74	34.36
Period 6	10.0	17.18	(−6.88)	20.30
Period 7	10.0	10.15	(−14.06)	6.09
Period 8	10.0	3.05	(−14.20)	(−1.15)
Period 9	10.0	(−0.58)	(−7.26)	2.16
Period 10	10.0	1.08	3.32	14.40
Period 11	10.0	7.20	12.24	29.44
Period 12	10.0	14.72	15.04	39.76
Period 13	10.0	19.88	10.32	40.20
Period 14	10.0	20.10	0.44	30.54
Period 15	10.0	15.27	(−9.66)	15.61
Period 16	10.0	7.81	(−14.92)	2.89
Period 17	10.0	1.45	(−12.72)	(−1.27)

[5] The marginal propensity to consume is ½ and the accelerator is 2.

[6] The figures in this column increase for each period by ½ the increment of income in the preceding period.

a decline in income sets in. Thus it is the marginal propensity to save which calls a halt to the expansion process even when the expansion is intensified by the process of *acceleration* on top of the *multiplier* process.

All this would be true even if the autonomous investment continued at a uniform rate. But this is highly improbable beyond a few years. Owing to the diminishing marginal efficiency of capital, autonomous investment tends progressively to exhaust itself unless the movement down the schedule is fully offset by an upward shift in the schedule owing to changes in technique and population growth. A continued process of investment tends to "kill itself off" because every net addition to the capital stock drives the marginal efficiency of capital lower and lower until further investment is no longer profitable.

Thus there are two reasons (apart from the induced decline when the full employment ceiling is reached) why the cumulative process of expansion comes to an end: (1) the marginal propensity to save would call a halt to the expansion even if the autonomous investment were maintained, and (2) the autonomous volume of investment runs out by reason of the declining slope of the marginal efficiency of investment schedule.

The Principle of Derived Demand

The acceleration principle is sometimes, as we have noted, referred to as the principle of derived demand. This suggests that it has to do with induced changes in the demand for capital goods, such changes being derived from fluctuations in final demand. The principle of derived demand is, in short, a statement of the effect of changes in the demand for final products or utilities upon the rate of net investment. Now the connection between final demand and net investment operates through the fact that, as final demand fluctuates, the stock of capital goods required to satisfy that demand must also fluctuate more or less in direct proportion to changes in final demand. But *net additions* to the *stock* of capital goods is precisely what is meant by *net investment*. Accordingly, if we assume that a given fluctuation in final demand will require a corresponding fluctuation in the stock of capital goods, we can then *derive* from the changes in the stock of capital goods the fluctuations in net investment.

The necessary relation between final demand and the stock of capital goods required to satisfy that demand induces changes in net investment. This can be illustrated with respect to (1) fixed capital goods, (2) inventories, and (3) consumers' durable goods. The stock of capital goods must grow if the demand for the final product grows; the stock of inventories will also fluctuate more or less in proportion to sales volume; and the stock of consumers' durable goods (motorcars, for example) must necessarily grow if the demand for transportation (as a final utility) increases, since an increase in the demand for this utility can be satisfied only by an increase in the stock of motorcars.

The Derived Demand for Fixed Capital

First consider an increase in the stock of fixed capital goods induced by a substantial rise in the demand for the final product. Something of this sort occurs in the case of the growth of every new industry. Assume a growth in the stock of fixed capital (induced by a growth in final demand) as shown in Figure 49. Given this growth in fixed capital stock, what path will net investment take? This is shown in the diagram. The peak of net investment (i.e., net *additions* to the stock of capital) is reached at the point of inflection in the growth of the *stock* from the lower level to the higher level. All growth from one level to another must proceed along the path of an S-shaped curve. At first the increments of growth are small; gradually they become larger and larger; and finally, as growth begins to taper off, the increments get smaller and smaller until growth ceases altogether. These *increments* of growth, in the case of capital accumulation, are precisely what we call "net investment."

Figure 49 represents only a process of growth from one level to a higher level. But suppose the movements of final demand (requiring a corresponding change in the stock of capital goods) should oscillate up and down. We may then assume first a growth of the stock of capital goods and then a decline in the stock; in other words, first net additions to the stock (net investment) and later disinvestment when final demand slumps. Disinvestment

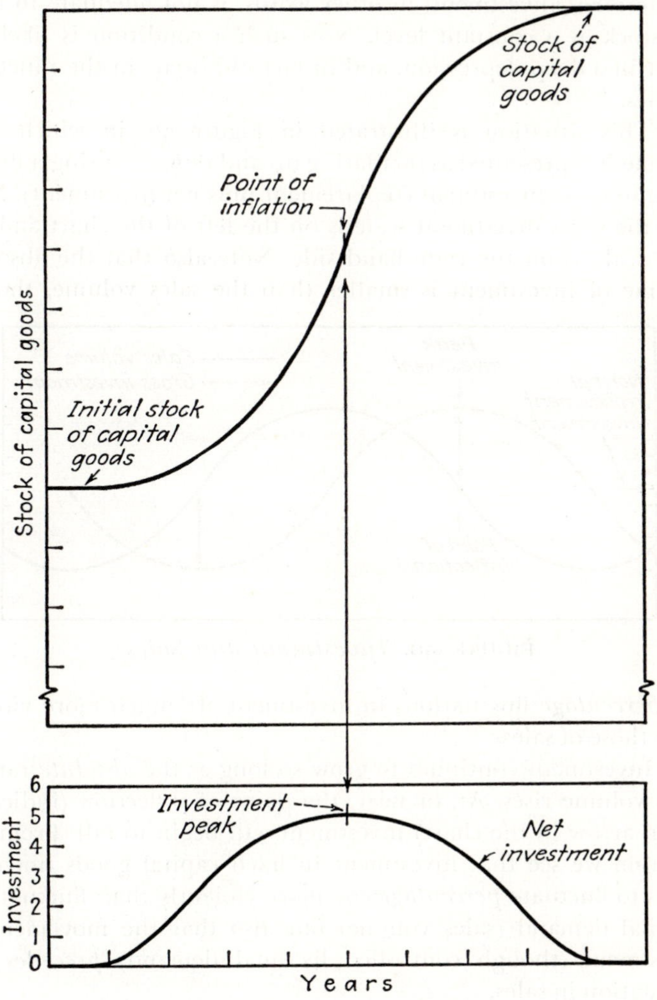

FIGURE 49. *Stock of Capital Goods and Net Investment*

means that the stock of capital goods is not being maintained; *replacement* investment, in other words, is not adequate to hold the stock at a constant level. Now such a condition is likely to occur in a deep depression, and in fact did occur in the nineteen-thirties.

This situation is illustrated in Figure 50, in which sales volume is represented as oscillating up and down, causing a fluctuation in gross investment (replacement plus net investment). Note that the gross investment scale is on the left of the chart and the sales scale is on the right-hand side. Note also that the absolute volume of investment is smaller than the sales volume, though

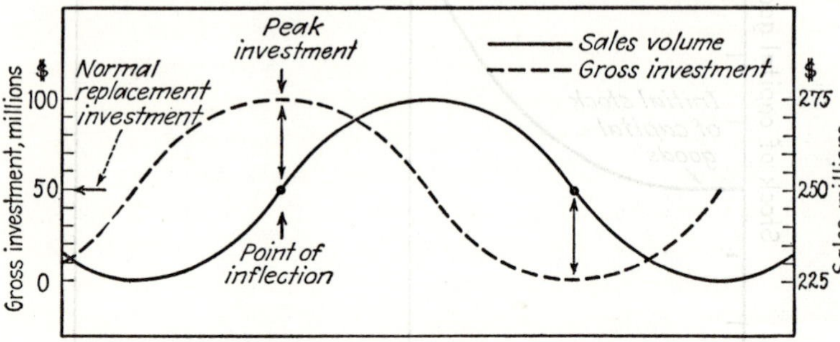

FIGURE 50. *Investment and Sales*

the *percentage* fluctuations in investment are much more violent than those of sales.

Investment continues to grow so long as the *absolute* rate of sales volume rises. At, or near, the point of inflection (indicated by an arrow in the chart) investment will begin to fall. From the diagram we see that investment in fixed capital goods not only tends to fluctuate *percentagewise* more violently than fluctuations in final demand (sales volume) but also that the movement of investment (though controlled by final demand) *precedes* the fluctuation in sales.

With respect to fixed capital goods, the induced fluctuation in net investment is likely to be more violent, percentagewise, than the fluctuation in final demand. The basic reason underlying this fact is that such goods are *durable,* having a more or less extended "life" during which they are only gradually worn out. It follows from this fact that if we have a considerable stock of fixed plant and equipment with a uniform age distribution, only a small part of the total will be replaced by new plant and equipment each year, say 10 per cent. The ratio of the value of the total stock of fixed capital to annual replacement investment outlays is then ten to one. In other words, if the fixed plant and equipment in a certain manufacturing industry is $500 million, an annual investment of $50 million will be sufficient to maintain the capacity required to produce annually, say, $250 million of manufactured products. On this assumption it requires $500 million of fixed capital plant to produce annually $250 million of manufactured goods.

Suppose now there occurred a 10 per cent increase in the total purchases of manufactured products. This would require, then, a 10 per cent increase in fixed capital from $500 million to $550 million. But since the normal replacement investment is $50 million, total investment (replacement plus net) would now rise to $100 million, an increase in investment of 100 per cent. Accordingly a 10 per cent increase in sales (physical volume) would cause a 100 per cent increase in the investment outlays on plant and equipment. Thus small fluctuations in final demand may cause violent fluctuations in the outlays on capital goods.

How violent these fluctuations in total investment will be depends upon the ratio of the stock of capital goods to annual replacement investment. This ratio depends upon the durability of the capital goods. If they are highly durable, replacement investment will be low in relation to the capital stock. The smaller the replacement investment relative to the capital stock, the more violent will be the fluctuations in gross investment springing from relatively small changes in final demand. Thus if replacement investment is normally only 2 per cent of the total capital stock, a mere two per cent increase in final demand would cause a 100 per cent increase in total investment.

The illustration given above provides a highly simplified account of the acceleration principle. In reality the relation between increases in final demand and investment in fixed capital goods is much more complicated. Often the age distribution of equipment is far from uniform, owing to the bunching of investment in high boom periods. Following an intense boom, a high percentage of the equipment may be new, and for a long time replacement investment may be very low. At a later date replacement investment will rise. Moreover, the "life" of equipment and plant is not rigidly fixed; the interval of time within which old equipment can be used varies rather widely according to varying circumstances. Finally, total gross investment is likely to be influenced not only by fluctuations in the sales of the particular firm in question but also by optimism and pessimism engendered by the state of business activity itself. With respect to net investment, sales volume may expand greatly without inducing much net investment if the sales expansion starts from a condition of large excess capacity.

Net investment is likely to be tied rather closely to fluctuations in the increments of sales volume if the industry has no unused capacity of fixed plant and equipment. Replacement investment is more or less closely related to the total stock of fixed capital, and this in turn is more or less closely tied to growth and fluctuations in sales volume. Now net investment tends, as we have noted, to be directly related to increments in final demand, though by no means rigidly. But replacement investment may continue to grow (as the total stock of capital goods grows) after the *increments* of net investment have begun to decline, as indeed will be the case at the point of inflection in the growth of the total sales volume. The growth in replacement investment might therefore, for a time, more than offset the decline in net investment. Thus *total* investment might continue to grow beyond the point of inflection.[7]

The Derived Demand for Inventories

The acceleration principle is also applicable to investment in inventories. Inventory stocks, like fixed capital, are related to sales volume. In general, it will be desired to hold inventory *stocks* in some fairly constant relation to sales. Thus inventory stocks, as a first approximation, may be assumed to fluctuate along with sales, the two reaching high and low points together. In point

[7] See the discussion between Ragnar Frisch and J. M. Clark in *The Journal of Political Economy,* October and December, 1931, and April and October, 1932.

of fact there are special considerations (inventory output lags, etc., which we shall consider in Chapter 22), why the relation is actually not so direct. For our purposes here, however, we may disregard the empirical data with respect to time lags (and the explanations offered) and concentrate on the *pure* principles of the acceleration relationships. Assuming as a first approximation that inventory stocks fluctuate with sales, then investment in inventories will necessarily begin to decline at the point when the growth in sales volume (and stocks) begins to slow down—i.e., at the point of inflection.

The relation between fluctuations in inventory *stocks* (controlled by sales volume) and *net investment* (and disinvestment) in inventories is shown in Figure 51. Inventory stocks continue to rise as long as net investment is above the zero line, but rise most rapidly (the point of inflection) when net investment is highest. Inventory stocks fall to lower and lower levels as long as net investment in inventories is negative (i.e., disinvestment of inventories).

With respect to fluctuations in inventory stocks and in sales volume, it is important to note the ever-widening magnitude of the fluctuation in *output* the farther the productive process is removed from the final consumer. When the sales volume of the final product increases, retailers desire to hold larger stocks, and so they buy more from wholesalers than they sell. Similarly wholesalers endeavor to increase their inventories, and so they in turn buy more from the manufacturers of the finished product than they sell to retailers. In like manner the manufacturers of the finished product now wish to add to their inventories of semifinished materials, and so they buy more from the producers of semifinished goods than they sell to the wholesalers. Finally, the producers of semifinished goods also wish, with expanding sales, to add to their inventories of raw materials, and so they buy more from the producers of raw materials than they sell to the producers of semifinished goods. Thus as one moves farther and farther back, in the long chain of production, the fluctuations in output get greater and greater, since each succeeding stage is not only *selling* a larger volume but is also *adding* to its own holdings of inventory stocks. Small fluctuations in final consumers' demand produce wider fluctuations in the output of manufactured goods, still wider fluctuations in the output of semifinished products, and finally even wider fluctuations in the output of raw materials. All this is due to the tendency to "stock up" in an

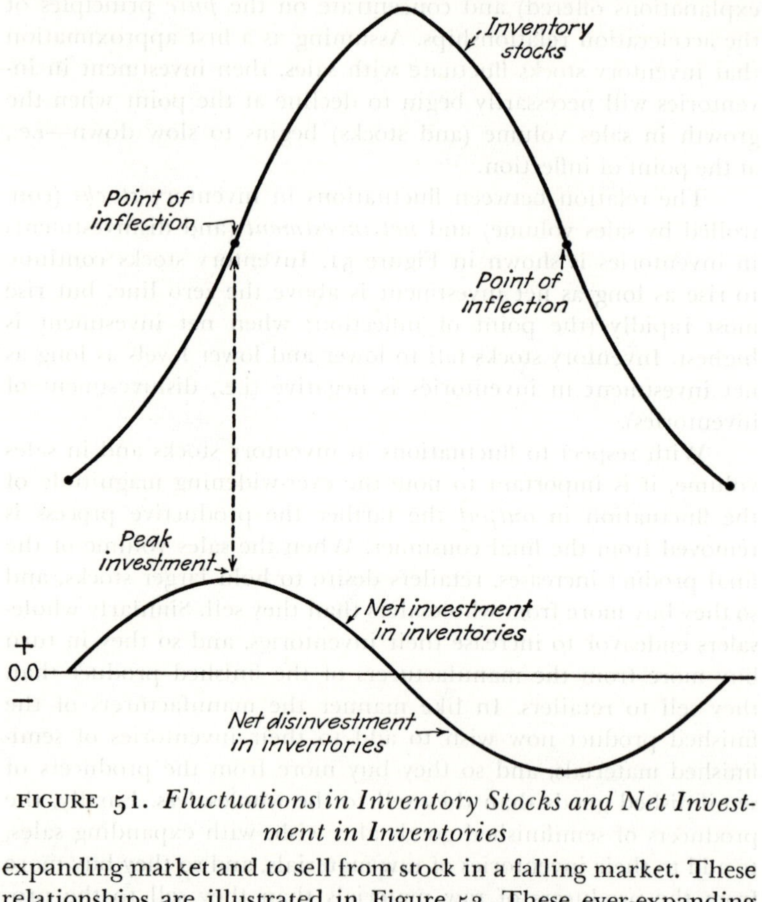

FIGURE 51. *Fluctuations in Inventory Stocks and Net Investment in Inventories*

expanding market and to sell from stock in a falling market. These relationships are illustrated in Figure 52. These ever-expanding fluctuations in output, as one moves back to prior stages in production, grow out of fluctuations in inventory stocks. The fluctuations in *net investment* in inventories are in turn a derivative of the fluctuation in the stock of inventories, and this is related (after a time lag) to changes in sales volume.

The Derived Demand for Consumers' Durables

We have noted the application of the acceleration principle (derived demand) in the cases of fixed capital and inventories. We now consider its application with respect to a durable consumers' good such as automobiles. The utility of automobile transportation cannot be satisfied except by "investing" in a consumers' capital good, namely, a motorcar. When the demand for the utility of automobile transportation rises in the country as a whole, a larger *stock* of motorcars is required. The stock of automobiles will therefore vary more or less closely with the growth and fluctuations in the total demand for auto transportation utilities. And the stock of automobiles can increase only when the *net investment*[8] in automobiles is positive. "Net investment" in automobiles means net additions to the stock (i.e., total number of cars purchased minus "replacement purchases"). "Total annual purchases" may be regarded as "gross annual investment" (here measured in physical quantities) in automobiles.

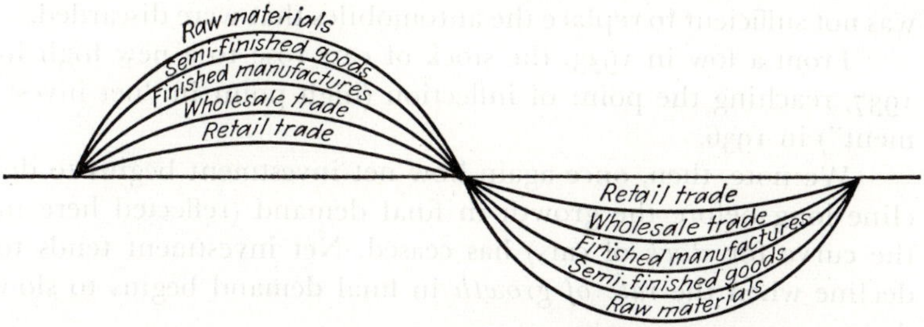

FIGURE 52. *Inventory Accumulation at Different Stages in the Production Process*

THE AUTOMOBILE

The growth and fluctuations in the total stock of cars reflect the growth and fluctuations in the final demand for automobile transportation. So long as the *rate* of growth is rising (i.e., up to the point of inflection) the annual net investment in automo-

[8] "Net investment" (measured in physical quantities) refers here to investment by consumer purchasers; it does *not* refer to business investment in the automobile industry.

biles (net purchases) will rise, as will be noted in Figure 53. This point was reached in 1923. Thereafter, while the total stock continued to rise until 1929, the growth was at a slower rate. Therefore "net investment" (as shown in the lower dotted line) began to fall after 1923. And when the stock actually declined (after 1929) the "net investment" curve fell below zero (1930–33). In other words, there was disinvestment in motorcars. Later, a slight disinvestment recurred in 1938. In these years annual production was not sufficient to replace the automobiles that were discarded.

From a low in 1933, the stock of cars rose to a new high in 1937, reaching the point of inflection (high point in "net investment") in 1936.

We note, then, once again how net investment begins to decline long before the growth in final demand (reflected here in the curve for *stock* of cars) has ceased. Net investment tends to decline when the *rate of growth* in final demand begins to slow down.

One final point with respect to Figure 53. Up to 1923, production went mainly into net additions to the stock of cars and very little into replacements. After 1923 "replacement" production grew rapidly, while net additions to stock ("net investment") declined. Indeed, beginning with 1926 "replacement" production exceeded (in most years by a wide margin) net additions. Replacement demand fluctuated more or less in direct correlation with the growth and fluctuations in the total stock (which in turn was related to the growth and fluctuations in final demand). Net demand (net investment) fluctuated with *increments* in the volume of final demand.

The growth of the automobile industry as revealed in Figure 53 had, however, a far greater significance than any so far indicated. To see its far-flung ramifications over the whole economy, especially with respect to the nation-wide investment in capital goods, we must consider all the basic underlying industries. Investment of plant and equipment in all the industries feeding into the automobile industry had to expand *up to the point of inflection* in the growth of the stock of motorcars. From 1923 on, net additions to the stock of cars declined; and while "replacement" production of cars was still growing, this no more than offset (the only significant exception being 1929) the decline in the "net" production of cars. Total production in 1940 about equaled that of 1923. Accordingly no significant growth in the

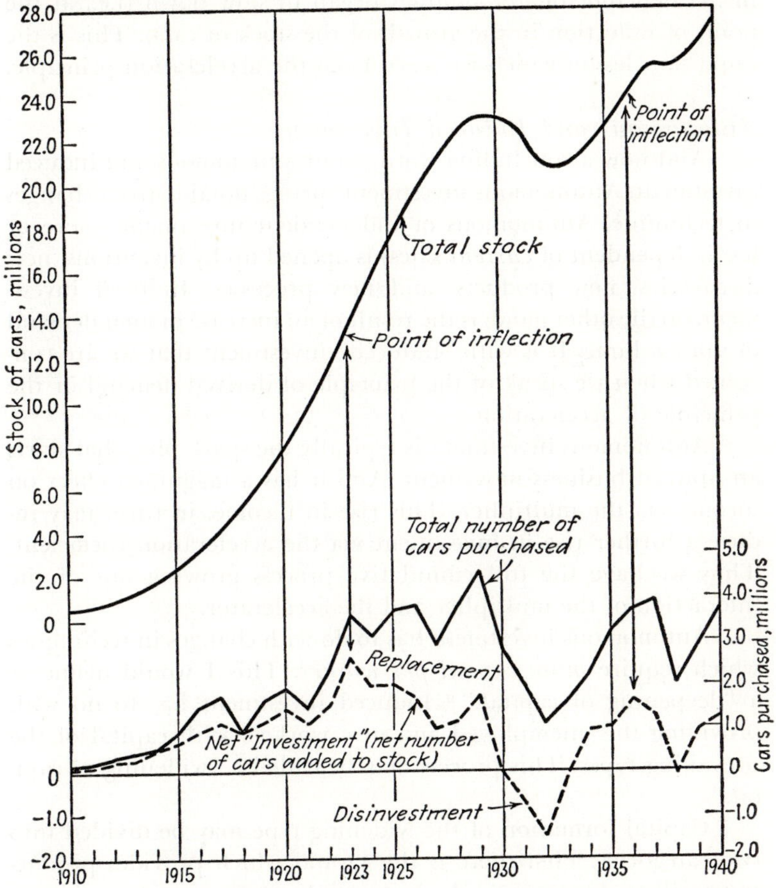

FIGURE 53. *Total Stock of Automobiles and Net and Replacement Purchases, 1910–40*

plant and equipment of the underlying or supplementary industries was required, by and large, after 1923.

Thus, when a new industry develops, the stimulus to investment to which it gives rise ceases long before the final consumer demand for its product has ceased to grow. In the case of automobiles, the growth in final demand is reflected in the *stock* of motorcars. The stimulus to investment ceased when the *rate* of growth in the demand for *automobiles* began to slow down (i.e., at the point of inflection in the growth of the stock of cars). This is the important lesson which we learn from the acceleration principle.

Autonomous and Induced Investment

And now a concluding word about autonomous and induced investment. Autonomous investment springs notably from changes in technique. Autonomous or independent investment (more or less independent of *current* sales) is opened up by inventions, new discoveries, new products, and new processes. Induced investment, on the other hand, is the result of an increase in final demand or sales volume. It is with "induced" investment that we are concerned when we speak of the principle of derived demand or the principle of acceleration.

Autonomous investment is typically the spark plug that starts an upward business movement. And it has a magnified effect on income via the multiplier. This rise in income, in turn, may induce a further rise in investment via the acceleration coefficient. Thus we have the full cumulative process growing out of the interaction of the multiplier and the accelerator.

Autonomous investment has to do with changes in techniques which require *more capital per worker*. This I would define as a "deepening of capital." [9] Induced investment has to do with providing the unemployed and new workers with capital of the prevailing types. This process may be called a "widening of capital."

Capital formation of the widening type may be divided into two categories: First there is the capital which provides productive facilities for workers thrown out of employment by a depression. This is basically replacement investment of the widening variety. Second, net investment (also of the widening type) is required to supply the new laborers just coming on the market with

[9] In earlier writing I have used "deepening of capital" (following Hawtrey) to mean more capital per unit of output. But I have since concluded that "deepening of capital" is a peculiarly convenient phrase with which to describe the process of supplying each *worker* with more capital.

capital, together with the workers displaced by improved machinery. Thus the "widening process" runs partly in terms of replacement investment and partly in terms of net investment.

"Deepening of capital" (autonomous net investment) is due to changes in technique. "Widening of capital" (induced investment) is associated with (a) population growth (net investment) and (b) replacement investment. Net investment relates to growth factors, whether of the deepening sort (changes in technique) or of the widening sort (growth of population). Replacement investment has nothing to do with growth, but merely with the main-

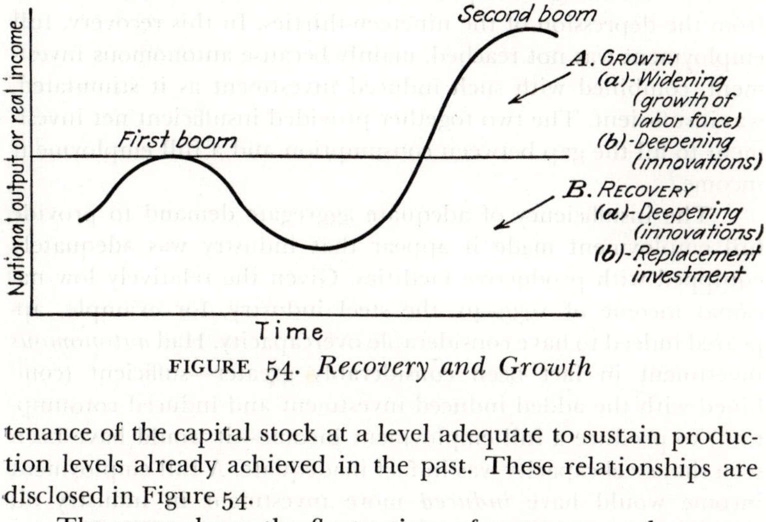

FIGURE 54. *Recovery and Growth*

tenance of the capital stock at a level adequate to sustain production levels already achieved in the past. These relationships are disclosed in Figure 54.

The curve shows the fluctuations of output over the course of the cycle from one boom to the next. If full employment is reached, output will rise in the second boom far above that of the first boom. This is due to the two factors of growth: (a) changes in technique and (b) growth of the labor force. Both of these growth factors require capital formation. The first relates to the deepening process, the second to the widening process. In addition, the stock of capital, to the extent that it has been allowed to deteriorate during the depression, will need to be rebuilt before the "depression idle" can be reabsorbed into industry.

Apart from government intervention, it is not possible to

reach full employment (say in the second boom) unless the autonomous factors (technique) are sufficiently strong to cause an adequately large volume of net investment so that, taking account of the multiplier and the accelerator, output will be pushed up to the full employment ceiling. Thus (via the multiplier and the accelerator) income will rise by a magnified amount until the full growth potential has been realized. Only if the combined deepening and widening process is sufficient, only if the interaction of the multiplier and the accelerator is adequate, will full employment be reached.

Now the full growth potential was not reached in the recovery from the depression of the nineteen-thirties. In this recovery, full employment was not reached, mainly because autonomous investment, combined with such induced investment as it stimulated, was insufficient. The two together provided insufficient net investment to fill the gap between consumption and a full employment income.

The insufficiency of adequate aggregate demand to provide full employment made it appear that industry was adequately equipped with productive facilities. Given the relatively low national income of 1939–40, the steel industry, for example, appeared indeed to have considerable overcapacity. Had *autonomous* investment in fact been considerably greater—sufficient (combined with the added induced investment and induced consumption) to produce a full employment income—it would have been seen that steel capacity was in fact inadequate. A full employment income would have *induced* more investment in industry all around. Thus if the autonomous investment is relatively weak (taking account also of the multiplier), the widening process of capital formation is not likely to occur on an adequate scale. Expansion will not be sufficient to absorb the growing labor force. And the economy, while having overcapacity at depressed income levels, will find itself with undercapacity in many key industries if later (as under the impetus of war) full employment is produced.

Autonomous investment raised income in 1936–39 (operating through the multiplier and accelerator) just enough to equal the 1929 output level. But the growth in the labor force, together with improved production techniques, required a much larger output to provide full employment. Had a more adequate fiscal program or a larger volume of autonomous investment raised income to higher levels, this increase in income would have induced more private investment. The "widening process" of capital formation in the thirties was inadequate precisely because the deepening process was inadequate. Finally, the war expenditures gave the economy the upsurge required to match its growth potential.

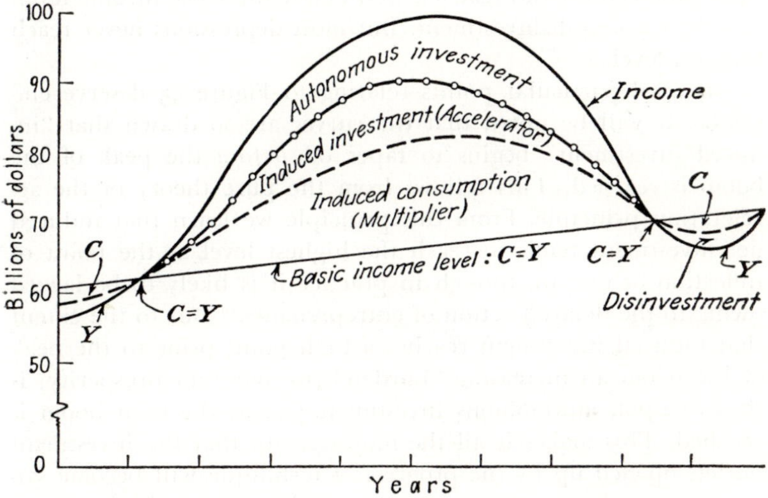

FIGURE 55. *The Precarious Nature of the Boom*

A full employment boom, once achieved, rests precariously on a high volume of autonomous and induced investment. When the autonomous investment fades away, income falls not only by the amount of the autonomous investment but also by the falling away of the induced consumption and the induced investment (the multiplier and accelerator now operate in reverse).

The precarious nature of every boom is illustrated in Figure 55. The entire boom depends fundamentally upon the vitality of autonomous investment. It is autonomous investment that raises income to boom proportions by a magnified amount (via induced consumption and induced investment). And when the autonomous investment drops out, down go also the induced consumption and the induced investment. Finally, when income has fallen to the basic level, the cumulative downward movement automatically comes quickly to a halt. For if income is driven so low that consumption exceeds income, stocks are being used up and capital goods are being exhausted. This situation will stimulate replacement investment until income is driven up to the basic level at which disinvestment will cease. Thus there is a "natural bottom," so to speak, to every depression. The depression of the early nineteen-thirties reached well below the basic income level, thereby causing disinvestment. But most depressions never reach that low level.

Several particular points relating to Figure 55 deserve emphasis. It will be noted that the curves are so drawn that "induced investment" begins to taper off *before* the peak of the boom is reached. This follows from the pure theory of the acceleration principle. From this principle we learn that induced net investment tends to reach the highest level at the point of inflection of output, though in practice it is likely to be lagged owing to the delayed action of entrepreneurs.[10] But to the extent that induced investment reaches a high point prior to the peak of the boom an increasing "burden" (to maintain prosperity) is thrown upon autonomous investment just as the high boom is reached. This makes it all the more certain that the investment outlets opened up by the progress of technique will become saturated after a few years of large-scale investment. Under these circumstances the boom will rapidly exhaust itself. Thus it is that every boom rests precariously on a level of investment which cannot for long be maintained.

---

10 For a full discussion of this lag, see Chapter 22 in this book.

12 · *Government Outlays, Investment, and Consumption*

In the last three chapters we have considered the determinants of investment, the consumption schedule, and the interaction of the multiplier and the acceleration coefficient. In these chapters we have purposely left government outlays out of our account of income determination. We have been dealing with a theoretical society in which private investment and private consumption outlays together determine the whole of the national income. This is, of course, an incomplete analysis, for increasingly, in all modern societies, government outlays play a highly important role in income formation.

Government outlays and autonomous private investment are the most important dynamic factors in the process of expansion or contraction in national income. In particular, government loan expenditures are in some respects closely analogous, in their effect on income, to private investment. Government loan expenditures, no less than private investment, serve as "offsets to saving." The role played by government tax-financed outlays in the determination of income is more complex, and this we shall also discuss in some detail in this chapter.

The Private Enterprise Model

In the simplified model of a purely private-enterprise society, in which private investment and private consumption occupy the entire field, the equation for income determination, stated in the simplest terms, is as follows:

$$Y = I + C(Y),$$

in which I is the volume of private investment and C(Y) is the consumption function. The equation states the following: Given the consumption function C(Y), the level of income will be determined by the volume of investment. Thus in Figure 56, if the

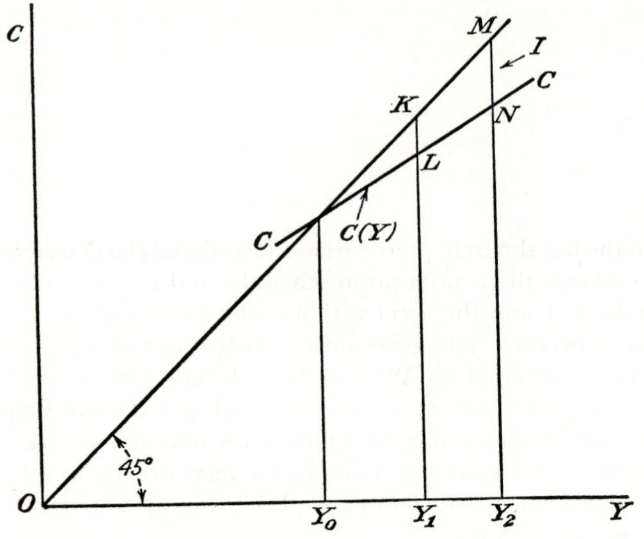

FIGURE 56. $Y = I + C(Y)$

volume of investment is MN, income will be OY_2; if the volume of investment is KL, income will be OY_1.

Here investment is regarded as wholly autonomous, independent of income. The induced effects of short-run changes in income upon investment (the acceleration principle) are left out of account. And if we are concerned with the longer-run equilibrium position of Y, this procedure may be permissible. If autonomous investment is given ($I = \bar{I}$), then income will tend (assuming certain values of the multiplier and the accelerator) to settle down at a certain level, and the effect of changes in income upon investment will vanish.[1] The induced effects will, under these conditions, disappear. At all events, a *maintained* level of income affects only replacement investment, and has no effect on net investment. In other words, once the *stock* of capital goods has been built up to a point commensurate with any given volume of aggregate demand, no further *net additions* to the stock of capital are necessary. The higher the level of income, the higher replacement investment will be; but net investment (barring the factors—changes in technique and growth of population—making for *autonomous* investment) will be zero whatever the level of income. It is in these terms that one has to interpret the equation $Y = I + C(Y)$. In the short run, however, changes in the income level will induce changes in net investment. This is the lesson of the acceleration principle. Over the short run, when the acceleration effect is included, "I" stands for both autonomous and induced investment.

Government Outlays and Private Investment

But now we must introduce government outlays. Among many possible methods of presentation we shall choose two equations, which state in different ways the impact of government fiscal operations (spending, borrowing, and taxing) upon the level of income.

In the first equation, we segregate out the government *loan* expenditures, L, and combine these with private investment outlays, I. Loan-financed expenditures may be regarded algebraically as either positive or negative. When positive, loan expenditures represent a government deficit; when negative, a government surplus. The equation, then, is as follows: $Y = (I + L) + T(Y) + C(Y)$. $(I + L)$ is private investment plus the government deficit (or minus the government surplus). $T(Y)$ is the schedule of tax receipts at different income levels; we may call this schedule the "tax schedule" or "tax function." $C(Y)$ is the consumption function. These relations are presented in diagrammatic form in Figure 57.

[1] See Alvin H. Hansen, *Fiscal Policy and Business Cycles,* W. W. Norton & Company, Inc., 1941, Chapter XII, especially pp. 283–288.

It will be noted that the area between the CC line and the C + T line represents the widening "belt" of tax revenues T(Y) as income rises. As income rises, tax revenues will tend to rise more rapidly, proportionately, than income, even though tax rates remain fixed. This is due to the fact that, with a progressive system of income taxes, more and more incomes move up into the higher tax brackets as the national income rises.

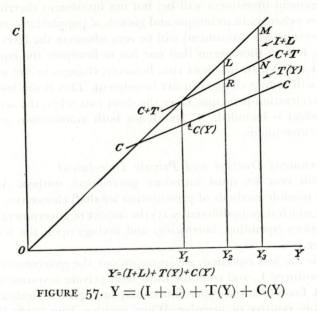

FIGURE 57. $Y = (I + L) + T(Y) + C(Y)$

In Figure 57 it will be noted that if I + L (private investment plus government loan expenditures) is zero, income Y will be equal to OY_1. If I + L rises to LR, then income will rise to OY_2. If I + L rises to MN, income will rise to OY_3.

The second and probably more meaningful method of stating the role of government in income determination is the following equation: $Y = I + G + C(Y)$.

In this case all government outlays on goods and services, no matter how financed, are combined with private investment outlays to represent the dynamic, active variable in income formation. Consumption is again regarded as dependent upon income, and so I and G together, given the consumption schedule C(Y), determine the level of income. These relationships are shown in Figure 58. If (I + G) is equal to FE, the consumption function being CC, income will be OY_1. If (I + G) rises to MN, then income will rise to OY_2.

It will be recalled from Chapter VI that I + G = S + T,[2] in which I is net investment, S is net saving, G is government out-

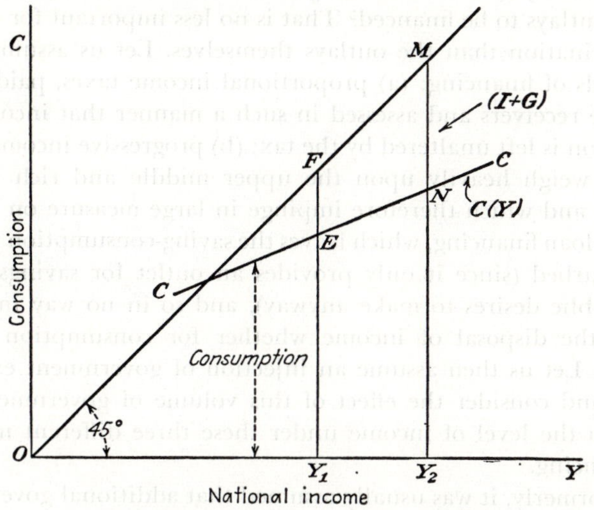

FIGURE 58. $Y = (I + \bar{G}) + C(Y)$

lays on goods and services, and T is tax revenues after deducting the revenues collected to pay for transfer payments.

Now (S + T) is that part of income, at any income level, which is not consumed. And consumption is fixed by the consumption schedule, C(Y). This schedule represents the behavior pattern of the community as affected by the prevailing customs and social institutions and by the economic environment, including the distribution of income and the tax structure. The tax schedule T(Y) is rigorously fixed by the character of the tax structure; and what this is will greatly influence C(Y). An increase in

[2] In Chapter 6 the gross concepts were used. Thus (I′ + G) = (S′ + T), I′ and S′ standing for gross investment and gross saving respectively.

tax rates will encroach upon consumption or saving in varying degree, depending upon the character of the taxes imposed.

Three Methods of Financing Government Outlays

Let us imagine first a society in which there are no government expenditures and no taxes. In this case we assume the consumption and saving schedules to be as depicted in Figure 56. Next we inject a volume of government outlays. But how are these outlays to be financed? That is no less important for income determination than the outlays themselves. Let us assume three methods of financing: (a) proportional income taxes, paid by all income receivers and assessed in such a manner that income distribution is left unaltered by the tax; (b) progressive income taxes, which weigh heavily upon the upper middle and rich income classes, and which therefore impinge in large measure on saving; and (c) loan financing, which leaves the saving-consumption pattern undisturbed (since it only provides an outlet for savings which the public desires to make anyway), and so in no way impinges upon the disposal of income whether for consumption or for saving. Let us then assume an injection of government expenditures and consider the effect of this volume of government outlays on the level of income under these three different methods of financing.

Formerly, it was usually assumed that additional government expenditures financed by taxes having no income-redistributional effects would not raise the level of income at all. This view has in recent years been challenged by a number of writers,[3] and by now it is generally agreed that expenditures thus financed do have an expansionist effect.

As a first approximation we may consider the problem in a rather commonsense manner. Suppose a society is operating on a fairly stable but relatively low income level. All income paid out to the factors of production is continuously put back into

[3] See Alvin H. Hansen and Harvey S. Perloff in *State and Local Finance in the National Economy,* W. W. Norton & Company, Inc., 1944, pp. 244–246; also T. Haavelmo and others in *Econometrica,* October, 1945, and April, 1946. See also Paul Samuelson (Chapter VI, Part I) and Robert Bishop (Chapter V, Part III) in *Income, Employment, and Public Policy,* W. W. Norton & Company, Inc., 1948.

the income stream. Thus the income level is constantly being maintained. But there are unemployed workers. Let us now suppose that a new business is set up which pays out new income to its workers and stockholders, and these in turn pour the income thus received right back into the income stream. They, so to speak, buy back their own products. Of course, in reality they buy from other industries who in turn buy their products. But it is at any rate the *additional* income paid out to the new industry which augments the entire income stream sufficiently to absorb the new additional products.

Assume now that there are still a number of unemployed persons. Imagine that the government sets up public projects and community services and pays out additional income to employees, etc., who supply the new services. This additional income *added* to the income stream will be equal to the sums paid in taxes for the services performed. The additional income is more or less diffused over the entire population, since the public is now relieved of the burden of supporting the unemployed.

The owner of the new business, referred to above, taps (by charging a price for his product) the enlarged income stream to pay for his operating costs. The government similarly taps (by the imposition of taxes) the enlarged income stream to pay for its operating costs. In both cases the additional income poured into the income stream, when taken back (via prices or taxes, as the case may be) is just sufficient to pay for the continuing costs of operating the new business, or the new government service, *without encroaching* upon the previously existing purchasing power of the community.

When government outlays are increased, and when these outlays are financed by taxes which leave income distribution unaltered, the same aggregate income after taxes will be available for consumption as before. Private disposable income will remain constant after the tax-financed outlays have been superimposed. In general, everyone's income will be increased, more or less proportionally, as total expenditures rise, and everyone will contribute, more or less proportionally, to the increased tax burden.

Consider how such a development will affect the *consumption function* defined as a schedule of consumption in relation to national income. The *function* will shift downward. Nevertheless the same absolute amount as before will be spent on private consumption because total national income will have gone up by the amount of the new government outlays, and in real terms by the amount of the government-provided services. After deducting for taxes, disposable income will be left unchanged, and therefore private consumption will remain at its former level.

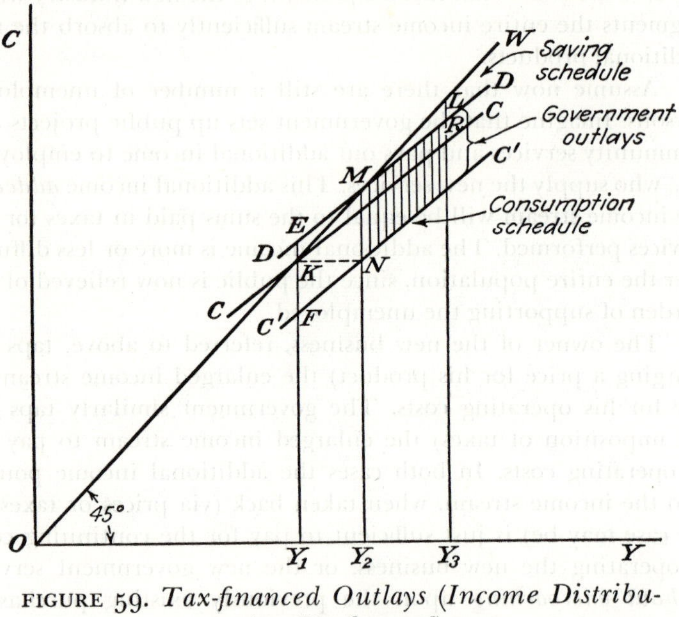

FIGURE 59. *Tax-financed Outlays (Income Distribution Unchanged)*

A more precise and definitive statement is as follows: At income Y_1 (Figure 59), government outlays equal to EF are introduced. Taxes equal to EF are simultaneously imposed. These taxes, we assume, leave the distribution of income unaffected. Accordingly, it is reasonable to suppose that the amount EF taken from the taxpayers will suppress private *consumption,* not by EF but only by KF. This is true because each unit of income taken away in taxes will reduce consumption by a ratio corresponding to the marginal propensity to consume based on the schedule of consumption in relation to national income. In other words, the ratio $\frac{KF}{EF}$ is equal to the community's marginal propensity to consume, $\frac{\Delta C}{\Delta Y}$. The *private* consumption schedule will now be pushed down to C′C′. If the government outlays had been loan-financed (no taxes being imposed), aggregate demand would have risen by EF over and above the formerly prevailing level of private consumption. Being tax-financed, however, the aggregate demand schedule (government tax-financed outlays plus private consumption) will rise only to DD. Accordingly, income will move up from Y_1 to Y_2.

The aggregate demand schedule has been raised from CC to DD, in consequence of the tax-financed government outlays. If we denote the new government outlays (tax-financed) as "T," and the *ratio* of curtailed consumption to T as "a" (i.e., "a" $= \frac{KF}{EF}$ in Figure 59), then demand will rise *in the first period* by T(1 — a); or, in terms of Figure 59, by KE. In other words, the aggregate demand schedule will be shifted upward from CC to DD by an amount equal to T(1 — a). But this means that aggregate demand (DD) exceeds aggregate cost (OW), and so income and employment will rise until the aggregate demand curve (DD) crosses the aggregate supply price (OW) at income Y_2. The taxpayers (the private consumers), having a marginal propensity to consume of less than 1, reduce their expenditures by "aT" dollars when T dollars (or EF in Figure 59) are taxed away.[4] But the government spends the whole T dollars, and so the aggregate demand schedule will rise to DD.[5]

Now it happens in the case under consideration that "a" is

---

[4] See G. Haberler, "Multiplier Effects of a Balanced Budget: Some Monetary Implications of Mr. Haavelmo's Paper," *Econometrica,* April, 1946, p. 149.

We assume no redistribution of income, or more generally that the marginal propensity to consume is the same for the payers of added taxes and for the recipients of added income. The conclusion then is that the new public expenditure paid from taxes has an income-generating effect with a multiplier equal to one. But if there results a redistribution of income there will be additional (positive or negative) effects. See Haavelmo, *op. cit.*

[5] For a comprehensive discussion see Paul Samuelson (pp. 140–143) and Robert Bishop (pp. 331–335) in *Income, Employment and Public Policy,* W. W. Norton & Company, Inc., 1948.

equal to the community's marginal propensity to consume. In *this special case,* the new tax-financed outlays will raise national income by an amount equal to the outlays so financed. The initial increment of demand (after the outlays have been made and the taxes collected) is T(1 — a), or KE (Figure 59). But this will lead to an expansion of income equal to T(1 — a) times "k," the multiplier. Since in this special case "a" $= \frac{\Delta C}{\Delta Y}$, it follows that $k = \left(\frac{1}{1 - a}\right)$. Therefore, $T(1 - a)k = T$. This means that income will rise by the amount of the new tax-financed outlays. Once the multiplier process has worked itself out, the level of private consumption expenditures, Y_2N, will be equal to Y_1K, the old consumption level. But this is true only in the special case in which "a" $= \frac{\Delta C}{\Delta Y}$.

Assume now an increase in private investment equal to LR. Income will now rise to Y_3. This increase is much larger than the new increment of investment in view of the relatively steep slope of the consumption function. Income has risen not only by the increase in investment, but also by the induced increase in consumption as explained in Chapter 10.

Let us now consider the second financing method. We assume that the given increase in government outlays is financed by a progressive income tax. A progressive income tax is likely to impinge relatively lightly on consumption and heavily on saving. Accordingly, the private consumption function will be depressed by an amount less than that shown in Figure 59.

Thus in Figure 60 an increase in government outlays MN, financed by a progressive income tax, is shown to raise income from Y_1 to Y_2, an amount considerably in excess of the increase in government outlays. The tax is shown to depress the consumption function from the line CC to the line C′C′. But the *combined* effect of the outlays MN *and* the tax, while depressing the private consumption function, has the effect of raising the aggregate demand function to DD. The large increase in income from Y_1 to Y_2 will raise private consumption from Y_1K to Y_2N. At the same time the new tax has the effect of encroaching upon the saving schedule by the amount shown in the area between the line CC and the line DD.

Also in this case, once the multiplier process has worked itself out, income will have risen by an amount equal to T(1 — a)k. But this greatly exceeds T, since "a" (namely $\frac{FK}{FE}$) is here much smaller than in Figure 59. T(1 — a) is accordingly larger in Figure 60 than in Figure 59; but the multiplier, k, is unchanged.[6] In Figure 60, "a" is much smaller than the marginal propensity to consume. Hence, in this case, income will rise by more than T.

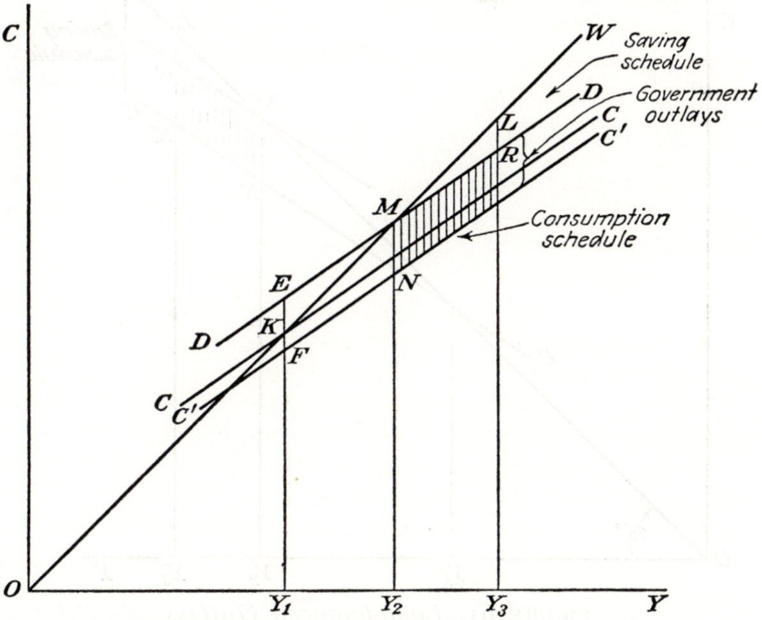

FIGURE 60. *Tax-financed Outlays (Progressive Taxes; Redistribution of Income)*

Assume now an increase in investment equal to LR. In view of the slope of the consumption function such a volume of investment will raise income by a magnified amount from Y_2 to Y_3. The slope of the consumption function determines the multiplier, as explained in Chapter 10.

[6] The multiplier, k, is here determined by the schedule relating consumption to national income, not to disposable income, as also in Figure 59.

Finally, we come to the third case, in which the new government outlays are financed by borrowing. Here the effect is shown in Figure 61. In this case the consumption function is not depressed by any new taxes. Accordingly, the new government outlays MN raise income from Y_1 to Y_2—in other words, by the full multiplier process. If now (on top of the government outlays) private investment LR is injected into the income stream, income

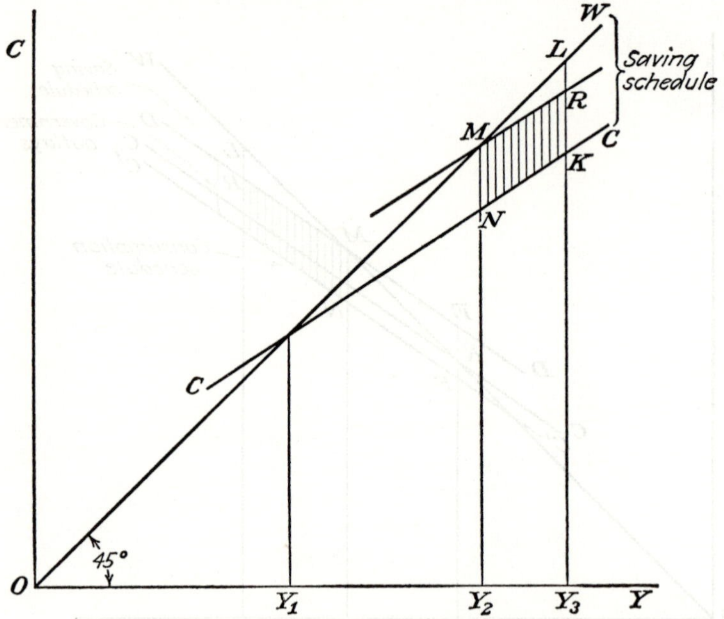

FIGURE 61. *Loan-financed Outlays*

will be raised to Y_3, again by the full multiplier process. Consumption will rise from Y_2N to Y_3K, induced by the increment of investment LR; government outlays remain at RK (MN) and continue to be financed by borrowing. At income Y_3, LK (saving) is offset by LR (private investment) and by RK (government loan expenditure).

A rather rigid theoretical apparatus, such as that explained above, though based on rigorous assumptions, is nonetheless highly useful as a means of understanding economic developments. In actual life, however, there are always many disturbing factors which modify the conclusions reached on the basis of pure theoretical analysis. Thus theory, important as it is, must be supplemented by judgment, practical experience, and broad historical knowledge.

PART THREE

Business-Cycle Theory

13 · *General Survey of Earlier Concepts*

Gustav Cassel, in his *Theory of Social Economy* (1923), begins his study of business cycles with the statement that an inquiry of this kind, "which is to be valid for the whole of Western Europe, cannot, in general, go back farther than the beginning of the seventies." [1] Only since then, he suggests, have the older types of economic structures for the most part been replaced by the modern economy with its large use of fixed capital in manufacturing and transport. From the seventies onward, certain older forms of crises appear to have been largely overcome; and there has emerged instead the modern type of cycle, that of fluctuations in the output of fixed capital goods, with all the special characteristic features of a capitalistic economy.

The character of economic fluctuations has indeed changed with changes in the methods of production and in the institutions of society. Nevertheless, we will do well to remember that depressions of trade and the economic distress associated therewith are almost as old as human history. Moreover, each age has tried in its own way (and sometimes by methods not altogether unlike those of today) to remedy these conditions.

---

[1] From the translation by S. L. Barron (from the fifth German edition), published by Harcourt, Brace and Company (1932). The first German edition was published in 1918, and the first English translation in 1923.

Colonial Depressions

Consider the following passage from *Paul Revere and the World He Lived In,* by Esther Forbes,[2] as illustrative of depressions in colonial times:

"A bank failed for £170,000. Mr. Savage fell in a fatal 'apoplectick fit' in his lawyer's office. . . .

"The merchants were going down like a house of playing cards. . . . Shipwrights, sailors, and sailmakers might suffer first, but tailors and peruke-makers, button-molders or soapboilers, silversmiths or braziers, all followed. Rents and mortgages could not be paid. The clergy began to find more copper and less silver in the alms basins. Farmers drove mutton to town, could get no decent price, and, angrily, drove them home again.

"Only one-fifth of the usual number of ships cleared that year from Boston for the West Indies. Not only was the artificial wartime prosperity over, but the merchants could not pay the duties now demanded of them. They experimented in short runs along the coast or kept their ships laid up, as one after another 'shut up.' "

Other examples of colonial hard times may be found in Lester's *Monetary Experiments:* [3]

"The business depression in Pennsylvania became worse in 1722 and 1723. In August 1722 James Logan, a Philadelphia merchant and chief representative of the Penn interest in the province, wrote:

> 'Our trade is sunk and very little of any thing to be done.
>
> 'I have received about ⅓ of the pay by Discount, but not one farthing in Money and the rest will be long out for the Trade of this place is exceedingly sunk. . . .'

"In November, Logan wrote:

> 'I must acquaint thee that this Country Since it was a Province has never been under such low Circumstances for want of Trade and Money as at present So that Lands will sell for Scarce any thing but a very

---

2 Houghton Mifflin Company, 1942, p. 99.

3 Richard A. Lester, *Monetary Experiments,* Princeton University Press, 1939.

long Trust, and in Jersey they are yet more dull than here.'

"In December 1722, the Governor wrote his superiors in England:

'I am to acquaint your Lordships that the people of this place are just now in a very great Ferment on Account that for some time past their usual Trade has stagnated for want of a sufficient currency of cash amongst themselves whereby to Exchange the produce of their Labour according to their accustomed Maner of Bussiness;

'The Farmer brings his provision to Market but there is no Money to give for it, The ship Builder & Carpenter starve for want of Employment, and we sensibly feel that our usual Export decreases Apace, The Interest on Money is high, and usurer grinds the Face of The poor so that Law suits multiply, our Gaols are full, and we are justly apprehensive of falling into debt, which we have Happily avoided Hitherto.' "

Lester's book is replete with complaints about recurring depressions of trade in Pennsylvania, New York, New Jersey, Delaware, and Maryland. In 1733 the Governor of Maryland reported to the British Board of Trade that the "Trade of the Province [had been] of late years greatly decay'd." In 1734 the Governor of New York reported to the New York Assembly that he had been studying the causes of the decay of trade, hoping to find a remedy that would "give life to the expiring hopes of your ship carpenters and other tradesmen." [4] Again in 1737 and 1738 the Governor of New York complained about the "declining Trade" and the "decay of ship building, Navigation and Trade." [5]

The phrases commonly used to describe depressed conditions were "Decay of Trade and Credit," "languishing Trade," the "general Damp given to Trade," "melancholy Decay of Credit," the "sinking of Trade," etc.[6]

[4] *Ibid.*, pp. 66–69, 102–103.

[5] *Ibid.*

[6] The following picturesque description of a depression appeared in the *Pennsylvania Gazette* for February 18, 1728: "Money here seems very scarce. Trade has been long in a deep consumption, her nerves relax'd, her Spirits

"Overtrading" later became a common explanation of "commercial crises" or "commercial and financial crises"—phrases which came into common use. Doubtless a main source of this kind of thinking derives from Adam Smith, who described the phenomenon of "overtrading" in the following manner:

"When the profits of trade happen to be greater than ordinary, over-trading becomes a general error both among great and small dealers. They do not always send more money abroad than usual, but they buy upon credit both at home and abroad an unusual quantity of goods, which they send to some distant market in hopes that the returns will come in before the demand for payment. The demand comes before the returns, and they have nothing at hand with which they can either purchase money or give solid security for borrowing." [7]

Commercial Crises

The term "commercial crisis" is peculiarly descriptive of the recurrent upheavals which characterized the last half of the eighteenth century and the first half of the nineteenth, especially in England. It was an age in which there occurred a vast extension of commerce over a wide trading area. It was the era of the "merchant-capitalist." The great leaders of enterprise were traders or merchants; it was not yet the day of the great industrialist.

For the period referred to above, commercial crises have been noted beginning in the years 1753, 1763, 1773, 1783, 1793, 1797, 1810, 1815, 1825, 1837, 1847, 1857. But the notion of regularity of occurrence (periodicity) and even the use of the term "crisis" came relatively late. Henry Thornton, in his testimony (House of Commons Committee, 1797) and in his book *An Enquiry into the Effects of the Paper Credit of Great Britain* (1802), does not use the term "crisis." He refers to "great commercial distress," to proposals for "relieving the existing distress," and especially to the "commercial difficulties in 1793." Ricardo (1817) speaks of "revulsions in trade." Neither Lauderdale (1804) nor Malthus (1820) used the

languid, her Joints have grown so feeble, that she has had of late so terrible a Fall that she now lies bleeding in a very deplorable condition. 'Tis said several eminent Physicians have prescribed to restore her to her pristine health, but in vain." (Lester, *op. cit.*, p. 95.)

[7] Adam Smith, *Wealth of Nations*, Modern Library edition, p. 406.

term "crisis," though both were concerned with the problem of depression and inadequate aggregate demand. Sismondi (1819) did, however, refer to the "commercial crisis" which England had just experienced.

Mathew Carey on Banks and Crises

In 1816 Mathew Carey, father of the first prominent American economist, published a little volume entitled *Essays on Banking.* Two of these essays deal with practical policy relating to trade depression. In the introduction he says: "On the revival of trade and commerce, after the close of the late war, our merchants and traders fell into a most serious error. A general spirit of overtrading spread itself through the community. Importations and sales were carried to an extent far beyond the regular consumption of the country."

He goes on to explain that the banks, "which might and ought to have checked this spirit, fostered and extended it. They discounted so freely, that it might be truly said, the scripture rule, 'ask and ye shall have,' was in full operation."

But in September, the "banks abruptly changed their system. They adopted one diametrically opposite. They diminished their loans rapidly and violently.

"Consternation became general. Enterprise and industry were paralized."

At last, though late, the bankers reversed their policies and "generally increased their discounts. The result was precisely the same as in England in 1793. The very resolution to extend their discounts raised murdered Confidence from the grave, and revived her once more. The career of bankruptcy was arrested. And the commercial world now appears in a convalescent state. But it will require a long period, to recover the vigour, and tone, and elasticity which were destroyed by the depleting system so long pursued." [8]

"Had the banks in the first epoch, restrained their discounts within somewhat narrower limits, the spirit of speculation would not have been fostered or encouraged to the length it proceeded. Prices in that case would not have risen so high. And further—the

[8] Mathew Carey, *Essays on Banking,* published by the author, Philadelphia, 1816, pp. iii–vii.

banks would not have found it necessary in the second epoch to have made the heavy reductions of discounts to which they had recourse. . . . And thus trade, commerce, industry, and prosperity would have maintained *'the even tenor of their way,'* without any of those violent ebbs and flows, those rapid elevations and precipitous descents, which are so destructive to happiness, to independence and to morals." [9]

Early Conceptions of a Cycle Movement

Willard Phillips, an American author and editor, in his *Manual of Political Economy* (1828), used not only the term "crisis," but also suggests a wavelike movement in business in this statement: "And since business will have its floods and ebbs, and the spirit of enterprise and production must be checked, for a time, the more promptly an approaching crisis can be seen and provided against, as far as practicable, the less the community will suffer." [10] In 1833 an English journalist, John Wade (*History of the Middle and Working Classes*), used both the term "commercial cycle" and the phrase "periods of prosperity and depression." [11] He says that the commercial cycle is ordinarily completed in five or seven years. Alternate periods of prosperity and depression had been experienced, he suggests, during the preceding seventy years.

In 1837, Samuel Jones Loyd (afterwards Lord Overstone) gave this description of the cycle: "The history of what we are in the habit of calling 'the state of trade' is an instructive lesson. We find it subject to various conditions which are periodically returning; it revolves apparently in an established cycle. First we find it in a state of quiescence—next, improvement—growing confidence—prosperity—excitement—overtrading—convulsion—pressure—stagnation—distress—ending again in quiescence." [12]

---

[9] *Ibid.*, p. 32.

[10] See Harry E. Miller, "Earlier Theories of Crisis in the United States," *Quarterly Journal of Economics*, February, 1924, p. 306.

[11] Quoted in Wesley Mitchell, *Business Cycles: The Problem and Its Setting*, National Bureau of Economic Research, 1927, p. 10.

[12] Samuel Jones Loyd, *Reflections Suggested by a Perusal of Mr. J. Horsley Palmer's Pamphlet on the Causes and Consequences of Pressure on the Money Market*, London, 1837.

Albert Gallatin (1841) said: "All active, enterprising, commercial countries are necessarily subject to commercial crises. A series of prosperous years almost necessarily produce overtrading. These revolutions will be more frequent and greater in proportion to the spirit of enterprise and to the extension or abuse of credit." [13]

The Periodicity of Crises

By 1848 both the use of the term "commercial crises" and also the concept of the periodicity of these crises appear to have come more or less into general use. Marx and Engels in the *Communist Manifesto* (1848) made the following statement:

"It is enough to mention the commercial crises that by their periodical return put on its trial, each time more threateningly, the existence of the entire bourgeois society. In these crises a great part not only of the existing products, but also of the previously created productive forces, are periodically destroyed. . . . And how does the bourgeoisie get over these crises? On the one hand by enforced destruction of a mass of productive forces; on the other, by a conquest of new markets, and by the more thorough exploitation of the old ones."

John Stuart Mill, in his *Principles of Political Economy* (1848), refers to "commercial crises," and to the "almost periodical recurrence of these fits of speculation." He notes the "frequent recurrence during the last half century of the painful series of phenomena called a commercial crisis." Nor does he limit his discussion to crises alone. "There are," he says, "two states of the markets: one which may be termed the quiescent state, the other the expectant, or speculative, state. The first is that in which there is nothing tending to engender in any considerable portion of the mercantile public a desire to extend their operations. . . . But there is another state of the markets, strikingly contrasted with the preceding . . . namely, when an impression prevails, whether well founded or groundless, that the supply of one or more great articles of commerce is likely to fall short of the ordinary consumption. . . . Effects of the same kind may be produced by anything which, exciting more than usual hopes of profit, gives in-

[13] Albert Gallatin, *Writings* (Adams edition), Vol. III, p. 385.

creased briskness to business. . . . This is a state of business which, when pushed to an extreme length, brings on the revulsion called a commercial crisis." Later he speaks of the "excessive contraction which succeeds to an undue expansion." There is a good deal in his discussion which suggests in one way or another the concept of a cycle.

William Langton, in a paper presented in the *Transactions of the Manchester Statistical Society* (December, 1857), not only speaks of periodicity but also regards the economic disturbances as having a wavelike movement. He says: "These disturbances are the accompaniment of another wave which appears to have a *decennial period,* and in the generation of which moral [i.e., psychological] causes have no doubt an important part. The prompting cause of these convulsive movements appears to lie in the inordinate use of credit." [14]

Juglar's Three-Phase Cycle

In 1860 Clément Juglar published his *Des Crises commerciales et de leur retour périodique en France, en Angleterre et aux États-Unis.* The very title of the book refers to the periodicity of commercial crises. Moreover, he used the term "cycle" and developed the concept of a succession of phases in economic fluctuations, in particular the three periods of prosperity, crisis, and liquidation, which he regarded as always following one another in the same order. In his analysis of these periods he made extensive use of statistical materials dealing with the interrelations between bank reserves, interest rates, commercial loans, and commodity prices.

Juglar's book is the first large-scale work devoted exclusively to commercial crises. The second edition (1899) [15] contains 556 pages. Part I, divided into nineteen chapters, is devoted to the theory of commercial crises, Part II to the history of crises (including 1676, 1708, 1714, 1720, 1745, 1763, 1772, 1783, 1793, 1797, 1802, 1810, 1815, 1818, 1825, 1832, 1836–39, 1847, 1857, 1864, 1873, 1882), and Part III to the influence of crises upon the economy.

---

14 Palgrave's *Dictionary of Political Economy,* Vol. I, p. 466.

15 Clément Juglar, *Des Crises commerciales,* Librairie Guillaumin et Cie., Paris, 1889.

Juglar divides the cycle into three periods: (1) prosperity, (2) crisis, (3) liquidation. In particular, he emphasizes the influence of bank credit on the development of crises. He analyzes price movements in the various phases of the cycle, and the role played by the rate of interest. The ideas contained in the book are cast in terms of the mid-nineteenth-century view that crises are predominantly a monetary, banking, and financial phenomenon. The role of investment in fixed capital is not yet recognized.

Jevons on Periodicity of Crises

W. S. Jevons, in a communication to the British Association (Cambridge) in 1862 on the study of periodic fluctuations, said: "There is a periodic tendency to commercial distress and difficulty during the months [October and November]. It is when great irregular fluctuations aggravate this distress, as in the years 1836–39, 1847, 1857, that disastrous breaches of commercial credit occur." In a paper (1866) in the *Journal of the Statistical Society of London* on "The Frequent Pressure in the Money Market" he stated that these "great irregular fluctuations" arise from "deficient or excessive harvests, from sudden changes of supply or demand in any of our great staple articles, from periods of excessive investment or speculation, from wars and political disturbances, or other fortuitous occurrences which we cannot calculate upon, and allow for." Later on he developed the theory that "great vintage years" recur every ten or eleven years, and "it seems probable that commercial crises are connected with a periodic variation of weather affecting all parts of the earth, and probably arising from increased waves of heat received from the sun at average intervals of ten years and a fraction." [16]

Jevons, while concerned with real factors,[17] in particular good harvests, did not overlook business psychology. In his *Investigations in Currency and Finance* (p. 184) he says: "Periodic collapses are really mental in their nature, depending upon variations of

16 W. S. Jevons, *Investigations in Currency and Finance,* Macmillan and Co., Ltd., London, 1884; also Palgrave's *Dictionary of Political Economy,* Vol. I, p. 467.

17 Jevons noted that a characteristic of boom periods is the proportion of invested capital which is "devoted to permanent and remote investment." *Op. cit.,* p. 28.

despondency, hopefulness, excitement, disappointment and panic. But it seems very probable that the moods of the commercial mind, while constituting the principal part of the phenomena, may be controlled by outward events, especially the condition of the harvests."

Credit Cycles and the Role of Confidence

In December, 1867, John Mills (not to be confused with John Stuart Mill) presented a paper before the Manchester Statistical Society on credit cycles and commercial panics.[18] He spoke of the "occult forces which swell or diminish the volume of transactions through a procession of years," and stated categorically that it is an "unquestionable fact that almost every ten years there occurs a vast and sudden increase of demand in the loan market followed by a great revulsion and a temporary destruction of credit." The periodicity of commercial crises he regarded as an established fact. During each of the decades interposed between the great commercial crises, "commercial credit runs through the mutations of a life, having its infancy, growth to maturity, diseased overgrowth, and death by collapse."

Mills divided the credit cycle into four phases: declining trade, increasing trade, overexcited trade, and crisis. He advanced the view that the life history of the credit cycle was governed by "moral causes"—i.e., psychological causes—asserting that "the malady of commercial crises is not, in essence, a matter of the purse but of the mind." The cause of the crisis, he believed, lies not so much in the character or abuse of economic institutions, but rather in psychological aberrations of business judgment. Favorable conditions breed optimism, optimism breeds recklessness, and recklessness breeds stagnation. And trade recovers from depression only when men's spirits recover.[19]

In 1879 Alfred Marshall wrote a little book (jointly with his

[18] John Mills, "Credit Cycles and the Origin of Commercial Panics," *Transactions of the Manchester Statistical Society,* 1867.

[19] Transactions of the Manchester Statistical Society, December 11, 1867. See also Palgrave's *Dictionary of Political Economy,* Vol. I, p. 476, and Wesley Mitchell, *Business Cycles: The Problem and Its Setting,* National Bureau of Economic Research, 1930, pp. 9, 11, 378, and 384.

wife) entitled *Economics of Industry*. In this volume two chapters are devoted largely to the problem of crises and commercial depressions. The paragraphs most relevant to the problem are repeated in his *Principles of Economics* (1890). Lord Overstone's famous description of the cycle is quoted. Marshall regards the crisis as related to reckless inflations of credit. The depression which follows is regarded as a state of commercial disorganization. "The chief cause of the evil is a want of confidence."

Henry George's Progress and Poverty

In the same year (1879) that Marshall published his *Economics of Industry,* there appeared a book which was destined to outsell all other books on economics—Henry George's *Progress and Poverty*. In the introductory chapter, George listed the current theories designed to explain depressions: "Upon high economic authority we have been told that the prevailing depression is due to over-consumption; upon equally high authority, that it is due to over-production; while the wastes of war, the extension of railroads, the attempts of workmen to keep up wages, the demonetization of silver, the issues of paper money, the increase in labor-saving machinery, the opening of shorter avenues to trade, etc., are separately pointed out as the cause, by writers of reputation." [20]

"I propose," he continued, "in the following pages to attempt to solve by the methods of political economy the great problem I have outlined. I propose to seek the law which associates poverty with progress, and increases want with advancing wealth; and I believe that in the explanation of this paradox we shall find the explanation of those recurring seasons of industrial and commercial paralysis which, viewed independently of their relations to more general phenomena, seem so inexplicable." [21] The cause, as Henry George saw it, was speculation in land; and the remedy, the taxation of land rent.

---

[20] Henry George, *Progress and Poverty,* Twenty-fifth Anniversary Edition, Garden City Publishing Company, 1926, pp. 10–11.
[21] *Ibid.,* p. 12.

Colonel Wright's Report

In 1886 the United States Commissioner of Labor issued his First Annual Report dealing with industrial depressions. This report (496 pages) comprises the most comprehensive survey made up to that time of the various explanations and theories of crises and industrial depressions. The report is convincing evidence that while the orthodox economists in general paid relatively scant attention to the problem, a vast literature, much of it superficial and amateurish, had developed in response to the intense interest of the general public in a burning public issue.

Colonel Carroll D. Wright, the Commissioner of Labor, who issued the report, disclosed a penetrating insight into the changing character of modern industry. Unsatisfied with the explanations which stressed the uncertainties of the market, the speculative excesses, the abuse of bank credit, and the ebb and flow of business confidence, he stressed the real factors relating to investment opportunities. He was impressed with the great role played by the growth of the railroad in the expansion of modern industry. His report came just at the end of the great era of railroad expansion. Adequate investment opportunities were temporarily lacking. The great age of electrification and motorization was still to come. In the meantime, all the advanced industrial nations were suffering from stagnation and depression. Colonel Wright was concerned about the volume of investment. Today it is a widely accepted thesis that fluctuations in the volume of investment are the central characteristic of the business cycle.

Wright begins his book with the following significant statement:

"The depressions with which the present generation is familiar belong to the age of invention and of organized industry. Whether these depressions are necessary concomitants of present industrial conditions may be a mooted question, but it is certain that they came with such conditions. . . . History is full of accounts of crises of various descriptions, resulting from various causes. Back of the age of rapid transportation, stagnation in any industrial sense might result from various natural causes, such as floods, famines, earthquakes, or from great political catastrophes, or from long and expensive and exhausting wars, but not through the causes which are potent in producing modern depressions; but the regularity and contemporaneity which characterize commercial, financial, and industrial disturbances belong to modern history, and are not seen in the past."[22]

"The first work, then, is to classify the crises and depressions of the past fifty years for the great producing countries of the world, and to determine how far such crises have been contemporaneous, how far like causes have produced like results, to determine the nature of the present industrial depression. . . . The Bureau has addressed itself to this work without the conceit of expecting to evolve any economic law relative to the cause or causes of depressions, or to lay down in any dogmatic way any positive remedial solution of such depressions."[23]

The book includes a vast amount of factual material, some theoretical discussion, and a survey of remedies. The table of contents is instructive:

Chapter I. Modern Industrial Depressions

Great Britain: 1837, 1847, 1857, 1866, 1873, and 1884; France: 1837, 1856–7, 1866–7, 1873–8, and 1882–6; Belgium: 1837, 1848, 1864, 1873, 1882; Germany: 1837, 1847–8, 1855–6, 1873–9, 1882–6; United States: 1837, 1847, 1857, 1867, 1873–8, 1882–6

Chapter II. Industrial Depression in the United States, 1882–6

The Extent of the Depression; Alleged Causes of the Present Depression—Falling Prices, Machinery and Over-Production, The Variation in the Cost of Production, The Variation in the Rates of Wages, Speculative Railroad Building, Crippled Consuming Power or Under-Consumption, Tariff Inequalities, Miscellaneous

Chapter III. The Manufacturing Nations Considered as a Group in Relation to the Present Depression

Chapter IV. Suggested Remedies for Depressions

The Restriction of Land Grants to Corporations; The Restriction of Immigration; The Enactment of Laws to Stop Speculation; The Establishment of Boards of Arbitration to Settle Industrial Difficulties; The Contraction of Credit;

---

22 *The First Annual Report of the Commissioner of Labor,* 1886, p. 11.

23 *Ibid.*, p. 15

Chapter IV (*continued*)

A Sound Currency; Commercial and Mercantile Conditions; The Distribution of Products; Profit-Sharing; The Organization of Workmen; of Employers

Chapter V. Summary

Contemporaneousness and Severity of Depressions; Causes; Remedies

Appendix A. Occupations, with Number and Wages of Employees by Industries

Appendix B. Earnings and Expenses of Wage Receivers in Europe

Appendix C. Synopsis of Labor Legislation in the United States

Wright regarded the depression of 1882–86 as unique in its character compared with earlier depressions in the respect that it had not been attended with any financial crisis or panic. It had to do, he believed, peculiarly with *modern industry,* not primarily with commercial or financial crises. The "family of nations," he declared, "given to mechanical production have reached an epoch in their existence." In England, France, and Belgium there had been completed a vast construction of railroads, canals, harbors, warehouses, water and gas works, tramways, etc. "In the United States the mileage of new railroads constructed has been out of all proportion to the increase of products to be carried. . . . This full supply of economic tools to meet the wants of nearly all branches of commerce and industry is the most important factor in the present industrial depression."

The 1895 Parliamentary Report

In England, throughout the nineteenth century, various parliamentary select committees received a vast amount of testimony and made significant reports on crises and depressions. The earlier ones were called Reports on Commercial Distress, as for example that of 1847–48; in the eighties there was a Report on Trade Depression, and in 1895 the Report on Distress from Want of Employment.

The last-mentioned report is distinguished for the testimony of Sir Hubert Llewellyn Smith, Commissioner of Labour in charge of the Labour Department of the Board of Trade. From a thorough analysis of the statistics of unemployment in different trades and industries, he had discovered the highly significant fact that industries may be divided into (a) stable industries and (b) fluctuating industries. In the latter he placed shipbuilding, machine making and allied industries, building trades and mining, the trades which Walter Bagehot called the "instrumental trades." These industries reveal a "cycle of fluctuations." "We have," said he, "what I call cyclical fluctuations; that is to say fluctuations of a period which extends over a number of years." These periods "correspond with what we sometimes call periods of inflation and depression of trade." The range of fluctuation in the total volume of production is "probably very small; but even these slight changes are sufficient to throw into violent oscillation the trades connected with the manufacture of the instruments of production." For the country as a whole Sir Hubert thought that these "cyclical oscillations" were the most serious causes of unemployment.

The question was asked whether "the recurrency of cyclical trade depressions is now shorter than it used to be." Answer: "We have lately had experience of one or two shorter cycles."

Another question: "As regards the cycles that you speak of can you give us any information as to the general causes which lead to these cycles of want of employment?" Answer: "I could only say that they are connected with the general movement of trade depression and inflation, and the recurrence of commercial panics." They are "often all over the world. They move very fast. But as to the ultimate causes I am not prepared to give an opinion."

The Emergence of Modern Business-Cycle Theory

By 1890, the date of the publication of Alfred Marshall's great work, a high level of scientific achievement had been reached in the study of the economics of the firm, and of general economic theory relating to value and distribution. No comparable body of scientific work had been done on business cycles and the problem of economic depressions. Apart from the work of Juglar (which suffers from the restricted view of the problem current in the mid-nineteenth century) the work on depressions and cycles had been peripheral and tangential.

At the close of the nineteenth century, however, two great books appeared that were destined to start a new epoch in business-cycle theory and research. I refer to the great works of Wicksell and Tugan-Baranowsky. Wicksell's *Interest and Prices* appeared in a German edition in 1898; Tugan-Baranowsky's *The Industrial Crises in England* appeared in the first Russian edition in 1894, in a German edition in 1901, and in a French edition in 1913.

Wicksell was not directly concerned with depression and cycles, but his analysis was the starting point for the modern theory relating to saving and investment. The first modern scientific work devoted entirely to industrial cycles, as Spiethoff rightly said, was that by Tugan-Baranowsky. This work appeared at the turn of the century, and it stands out as a milestone separating the old from the new.

The history of economic thought reveals again and again a lag in the development of theory behind the march of events. In the eighteenth and early nineteenth centuries, the great fortunes were made in trade and commerce, and it was here that the spirit of enterprise found an outlet for talent and for the investment of capital funds. With the continued progress of inventions, and the ever-expanding development of machinery involving large-scale investment in fixed capital, a profound change had gradually occurred in the fundamental forces which controlled the ebb and flow of economic activity. Theories based on the uncertainty of the market, on speculation in commodities, on "overtrading," on the excesses of bank credit, on the psychology of traders and merchants, did indeed fit reasonably well the early "mercantile" or commercial phase of modern capitalism. But as the nineteenth century wore on, "captains of industry," men who made their fortunes in great industrial enterprises, came to the fore. Investment of fixed capital in railroads, in industrial plant and equipment, in construction, became the main outlet for funds seeking a profitable return. Thus the forces lying behind the business cycle, at long last, were sought in the area of *saving and investment*.

Tugan-Baranowsky boldly set forth the view that the "industrial cycle," as he called it, relates in particular to the "periodic creation of new fixed capital." His analysis came like a fresh ocean breeze. He placed his finger upon the essential characteristic of the cycle—the fluctuation in the rate of investment. This analysis marks an important turning point in business-cycle theory.

Yet as one looks back on the then current annals of business which recorded the commercial crises and depressions of the late eighteenth and early nineteenth centuries, one sees already, in varying degree, some glimmering of the importance of the rate of investment even in this early period. Thus in the crisis of 1793, while stress was laid in the annals of the time on the overstimulated spirit of mercantile enterprise, note was also made of the rate of investment in machinery and land navigation.

In the crisis of 1810 the decline of export trade, especially to South America, played a leading role. It was indeed a commercial crisis. Even more was this true with respect to the crisis of 1815. Vast stocks of goods had been manufactured and assembled ready for shipment in anticipation of heavy exports to the continent of Europe after the fall of Napoleon. But the capacity of the Continent to purchase goods had been greatly overrated. Thus the speculative boom in exports collapsed. This crisis was par excellence a "commercial crisis."

The crisis of 1825 was more complex, indicating not only the growth of commerce, but also the spread of the new era of industrialization. There was extravagant speculation not only in the shares of commercial and insurance companies, but also in those of mining companies, in land development schemes, and in canals. More than thirty acts were brought forward in the House of Commons to give effect to these far-flung undertakings and speculative projects.

But it was the crisis of 1847 which first marked in an impressive way the new role of fixed capital investment in the fluctuations of business activity. "In 1847 speculation was chiefly directed to the development of railways and other improvements at home." There was a "sudden immensely increased outlay of capital on fixed investments"; then an even more sudden and sharp stop was put to this outlay.[24]

[24] Palgrave's *Dictionary of Political Economy*, Vol. I, p. 459.

In this brief survey of early concepts we have noted the changing terminology—"languishing trade," "commercial crises," "periodic crises," "credit cycle," "industrial depression," and finally "investment cycle." These terms reflect the changing character of the economy, a growing understanding of the essential nature of the oscillations of economic life, and finally of the part which growth plays, and especially the role of capital formation and the process of saving and investment. It is particularly these latter ideas, as we shall see, which came to the fore in the development of business-cycle theory in the twentieth century.

14 · *Aggregate Demand:*
LAUDERDALE · MALTHUS · HOBSON

LORD LAUDERDALE (1759–1839)

In 1804 Lord Lauderdale wrote a book (*An Inquiry into the Nature and Origin of Public Wealth*) which is of exceptional interest for us today, not only in its general relation to the theory of depressions, but also because it deals in a realistic fashion with policy problems which are currently of the greatest importance, notably (1) the management of the public debt, and (2) the distribution of income. These matters are discussed in every Economic Report of the President, where they are related (as also with Lauderdale) to the problem of maintaining high and stable levels of employment. In 1818, at a time when Great Britain and the other European countries were much concerned about the post-Napoleonic trade depression, a second edition of Lauderdale's book was published without any substantive change in the argument.

The Propensity to Save and Capital Formation

Since much of the book is concerned with the problem of management of the public debt, it is perhaps not strange that Lauderdale is much interested to point out the "fallacy of composition" commonly encountered in economic argument. In the matter of fiscal policy it is particularly important to see that what is true for the individual is not necessarily true for the group, and conversely, that what is true for the group is not necessarily true for the individual. No one before or since has more effectively explained this truth than Lauderdale. But his teaching was almost wholly neglected by the classical economists. "The sum total of the riches of those who form the community is," he tells us, "often regarded as necessarily conveying an accurate statement of the wealth of a nation." He then quotes Adam Smith as saying: "For the capital of a society, which is the same thing with that of all the individuals who compose it, can be increased only in the same manner." [1] This Lauderdale vigorously denied, and on grounds fundamentally the same as those later advanced by Keynes. An increased propensity to save may well have the effect of reducing, not increasing, the total volume of capital accumulation.

Management of the Public Debt

The British public debt had grown from only £664,000 at the time of the Glorious Revolution (1688) to £556,000,000 in 1804. Then as now, because of the vast increase in the public debt, there was much discussion about debt management. Lauderdale related the management of the public debt to the problem of adequate aggregate demand. Mismanagement of the debt could easily, in his judgment, cause a serious deficiency in demand, and thus lead to depression and unemployment.

Early in the history of the public debt (Lauderdale cites 1717, 1727, and again 1789, 1792), sinking funds [2] were established into which surplus tax funds were to be poured with a view to buying up and retiring outstanding debt. At the time Lauderdale was writing (1804) it was planned that the whole national debt was to be extinguished in forty-five years.

---

[1] Lord Lauderdale, *An Inquiry into the Nature and Origin of Public Wealth and into the Means and Causes of Its Increase.* I have used the second edition, published in 1819 by Archibald Constable & Co., Edinburgh.

[2] The principle of the sinking fund was as follows: A certain sum, say 1 per cent, for example, of the public debt, was to be appropriated and set aside for the purchase of outstanding debt. These bonds were not to be retired but were to be held in the fund continuing to draw interest. Thus the fund would grow partly from the amount of the sum appropriated and partly from the interest earned. Another way of doing the same thing would be to retire the bonds when purchased and add to the amount appropriated for debt retirement the amount saved in interest charges.

Danger of Too Rapid Retirement

Lauderdale undertook to analyze the possible economic consequences if this policy should be carried out.[3] He took the position that the withdrawal of such vast sums per year, from expenditure on "goods and manufactures" which would otherwise have been made, would ruin the country. Capital accumulation he indeed favored, but he was opposed to the "forced parsimony" which so rapid a retirement of the public debt would entail. He opposed the design to abstract from "expenditure in consumable commodities" so vast a sum and forcibly converting it into capital.

Lauderdale cites the experience of former peacetime years when some debt retirement had been made—1714 to 1739, and 1786 to 1793. He says that by 1733 the sinking fund had "grown to a great maturity . . . and was become almost a terror to all the individual proprietors of the public debt. The high state of credit, the low rate of interest of money, and the advanced price of all public stocks and funds above par, made the great monied companies, and all their proprietors, apprehend nothing more than being obliged to receive their principal too fast; and it *became almost the universal consent of mankind, that a million a-year was as much as the creditors of the public could bear to receive* in discharge of part of their principal."[4] Indeed even David Hume, Lauderdale goes on to relate, plainly shows that he was aware of that circumstance, by stating that "in times of peace and security, when alone it is possible to pay debt, the monied interest are averse to receive partial payments, which they know not how to dispose of to advantage."[5] Another authority (Mr. Chalmers) is cited as saying that the effects of the sinking fund operations in retiring public debt were such in the year 1738 that "the great contest among the public creditors at that fortunate epoch, was not so much who should be paid his capital, as who should be suffered

[3] In the foreword to the second edition, he says that "the greatest advocates for the system of forced parsimony by legislative authority, in the shape of a sinking fund, now agree to the necessity of limiting the extent to which it ought to be carried."

[4] Lauderdale, *Inquiry into the Nature and Origin of Public Wealth*, pp. 249–250.

[5] *Ibid.*, pp. 251–252.

to remain the creditors of the state." [6] The bondholders who were paid did not know what to do with the money.[7]

The experience was very much the same, he alleged, in the debt retirement period 1786–93. Yet during these years, one would have imagined, says Lauderdale, "that so many opportunities must have occurred of employing capital in new channels" that the accumulating funds obtained from debt repayment could easily have been absorbed in "new adventures." [8] He gives a table showing the number of parliamentary bills relating to investment projects—roads and bridges, canals and harbors, drainage and enclosures, paving and other parochial improvements (all told, 750 acts relating to these projects were passed in 1785–92). He refers to the increased export trade, increased shipping tonnage, the "extension of machinery in every branch of manufacture and the capital required in these projects." [9] Yet despite these highly favorable investment opportunities (culminating in the crisis of 1793) the accumulating funds were confronted with inadequate new investment outlets. The effect was to bid up the price of outstanding issues. "Stocks rose from 74 to 96." [10] Again the bondholders were not too happy to be paid off. Debt retirement, Lauderdale thought, was proceeding too rapidly even though at that time only £1 million was being set aside annually for accumulation.

In the meantime new legislation had been passed, and at the time Lauderdale was writing (1804) the law contemplated, on the return of peace, "an accumulating fund of more than £6 million *per annum*. Six millions must, therefore, be withdrawn from the acquisition of commodities, the growth and manufacture of the country, and forcibly converted into capital; a situation which will require much attention from those who have the management of the country at the time. It is an experiment hitherto un-

[6] *Ibid.*, p. 252.

[7] After 1730, "though there existed the name of a sinking fund, and though sums were from time to time employed to purchase up portions of the public debt, the plan of a regular forced accumulation, by the authority of government, with a view to public benefit, was, for many years, relinquished in practice. The system was, however, again revived in 1786." (Lauderdale, *op. cit.*, p. 229).

[8] *Ibid.*, p. 254.

[9] *Ibid.*, p. 255.

[10] *Ibid.*

tried. . . . The accumulating fund now provided by law, is nearly six times greater than any of which we have had experience during peace. Indeed, it amounts, in one year, to a sum almost equal to all that was accumulated betwixt the year 1717 and the year 1732; which reduced the value of capital from 6 to 3 *per cent;* for in this last year, 3 *per cents* were at one hundred and one." [11]

Curtailment of Consumption

Under these circumstances, Lauderdale continued, "those who have the management of the Public Treasury on the return of peace, must be careful, on the one hand, lest, from the abstraction of demand to the amount of six millions, the price of commodities be reduced to such a degree as to discourage reproduction; they must be cautious not to mistake, for the effects of abundance, that which in reality may be only the effect of failure of demand." [12]

"We already know, that the value of capital may be reduced from 6 to 3 *per cent* by forced accumulation; and it is impossible to say how low it may be brought by the continued progress of accumulation, which increases the quantity of capital; whilst, far from increasing, (by the effect it has of abstracting revenue from expenditure in consumable commodities, and consequently of abridging consumption,) it inevitably diminishes the demand for it." [13]

The demand for capital, Lauderdale pointed out, depends upon the demand for consumers' goods. "Nothing but a confusion of ideas concerning the nature of the profit of capital could give birth to the fancy, or induce any one to cherish the opinion, that capital might be increased to an unlimited degree; for the moment the profit of capital is regarded as arising from its supplanting or performing labour, it is at once evident, that, as the means of consuming must, at all times, limit the quantity of labour that can be employed in preparing things for consumption, so it must limit the amount of capital that can be used in cooperating with the hands of man, for the purpose of

[11] *Ibid.*, pp. 258–259.
[12] *Ibid.*, p. 260.
[13] *Ibid.*, pp. 261–262.

performing labour; and that, in proportion as forced parsimony abstracts from the funds that would be allotted to acquire consumable commodities, the demand for labour, whether performed by the hand of man, or by capital, must be diminished."[14]

It is hardly possible to suppose, he said, that there could have existed any new channels of so employing capital at a moment when there was forcibly created a diminution of demand for commodities. Under such circumstances, far from its being reasonable to suppose that there could have existed any opportunity of employing an additional quantity of capital, instead so great a diminution of demand must have thrown out of employment some of that capital which was already usefully engaged in the production and transportation of those commodities for which there was no longer any demand.[15]

Savings Going to Waste

In summing up, Lauderdale said, "What is affirmed, and what we have attempted to establish by argument, is *1st,* That the old maxim, 'a penny saved is a penny gained,' is not applicable to public wealth; *2d,* That a nation, in the circumstances and situation of the British empire, cannot, with impunity, either forcibly abstract a sum so large as has been proposed, from expenditure in consumable goods of its produce and manufacture, or forcibly accumulate capital with such rapidity. For no nation, without injury to the progress of its wealth, can thus rapidly increase its capital, at the expence of abstracting annually so large a sum from expenditure in consumable commodities."[16]

"In truth, though Parliament has formally announced, by an act of the legislature, the extinction of the national debt in forty-five years; or in other words, the design of abstracting from expenditure in consumable commodities, and forcibly converting into capital, within that period, a sum amounting nearly to five hundred millions," that act, he says, must be reconsidered, for nothing is more apparent than the impossibility, without the ruin of the country, of abstracting from expenditure, in its goods and

---

14 *Ibid.*, pp. 262–263.
15 *Ibid.*, pp. 247–248.
16 *Ibid.*, pp. 263–264.

manufactures, a revenue so large, ranging from about £5,600,000 to upwards of £20,000,000 per annum over the forty-five-year period.[17]

Forced Parsimony

The conversion of an economy from peace to war entails a profound shift in the direction of demand—"a mischief in itself nowise trifling, as recent experience has taught the merchants of this country." [18] Very different, however, is the effect if the government, instead of spending the tax money, forcibly converts the revenue into capital as proposed in the peacetime debt retirement program. War taxation and war expenditures *change* the currents of demand; but debt retirement *abstracts* a portion of demand from commodities which the public would otherwise have purchased, and there is no offsetting expenditure "to counteract the full effects of this forced parsimony; for it would have been difficult to persuade the proprietors of stock, from whom such extensive purchases would have been made by the Commissioners of the Sinking Fund, all at once to spend . . . that which habit had taught them to regard as capital." [19]

Debt Retirement and the Multiplier in Reverse

Lauderdale argued, moreover, that the effect of any given diminution of demand, say £10 million withdrawn from consumable commodities via the debt retirement program, would be "much more formidable than what is here represented," because the diminution occasioned by a "failure of demand, must be always much greater than the value of the demand abstracted." [20] Lauderdale had, in a vague way, as was true of many early economists, a conception of the multiplier principle. The consequences, he explains, of a sudden curtailment in the consumption of certain articles (meat, wines, etc.) "will not terminate there," for, the producers of those articles having "less to bestow on their different enjoyments, the demand for other commodities must be by this

17 *Ibid.*, pp. 264–265.
18 *Ibid.*, p. 241.
19 *Ibid.*, p. 242.
20 *Ibid.*, p. 246.

means diminished, and that, in every case, to a greater degree than the amount of the sum which represents the demand abstracted. . . . It is on this principle, that a great and sudden alteration of demand for any commodity or class of commodities, has been always found to produce a fatal diminution of individual riches. . . ." [21]

The Proportionality of Factors

Lauderdale had, as we have seen, a fairly clear conception (though not stated in precise or technical terms) of the schedule of the diminishing marginal productivity of capital. Capital, in combination with labor, was productive. But one soon reaches diminishing productivity when the capital factor is increased. That a farmer's capital (such as draft animals or machines) is "very beneficial is undoubted; it supplants a portion of labour, which must otherwise be executed with his hands, and may even execute a portion of labour beyond the reach of his personal exertions to accomplish. If, therefore, he is not possessed of a sufficiency of those animals, instruments, and machines, which form his capital, it will be in the highest degree advantageous that he should augment the exertions of his industry [22] for the purpose of procuring them." [23]

Thus Lauderdale emphasized the productivity of capital. But he did not lose sight of proportionality in the combination of the factors of production. A community may suffer by the "creation of a quantity of capital more than is required." And this condition

[21] *Ibid.*, p. 88.

[22] Lauderdale was correct in saying that one can add *both* to his capital *and* to his income ("wealth" was the term he used) only by increasing his production. "Parsimony," he argued, "does not augment opulence; it only changes the direction in which the labour of the country is exerted." Here, however, it must be admitted that his presentation is not altogether a happy one. At times he seems to deny (and Malthus criticized him for this) that saving does play a role in the process of capital formation. Nevertheless, what he was trying to say was quite right. He was trying to say (to put it in modern language) that the way to overcome depression is not to curtail consumption but rather to increase income. Malthus, while criticizing the *manner* in which Lauderdale put it, nevertheless said substantially the same thing. See Malthus, *Principles of Political Economy*, p. 314.

[23] Lauderdale, *op. cit.*, p. 204.

will be made still worse if the expenditure on consumable commodities is cut.[24]

Enterprise and Thrift

Just as the "mercantile system of political economy has justly been deemed objectionable because it regarded money as wealth," so that system is equally objectionable which "exclusively considers capital[25] as wealth" and is wholly indifferent to the "diminution in the production of consumable commodities, which parsimony must inevitably create."[26]

For Lauderdale, as later with Keynes, it is enterprise, not mere thrift, that makes a country grow in real income and prosperity. Saving—Lauderdale calls it "capital accumulation"—is highly important when there are adequate investment outlets, but "forced parsimony" when outlets are wanting reduces demand and discourages enterprise.

Compare Lauderdale with the following from Keynes: "It has been usual to think of the accumulated wealth of the world as having been painfully built up out of that voluntary abstinence of individuals from the immediate enjoyment of consumption which we call Thrift. But it should be obvious that mere abstinence is not enough by itself to build cities or drain fens. . . . It is enterprise which builds and improves the world's possessions. . . . Not only may thrift exist without enterprise, but as soon as thrift gets ahead of enterprise, it positively discourages the recovery of enterprise and sets up a vicious circle by its adverse effect on profits. If Enterprise is afoot, wealth accumulates whatever may be happening to Thrift; and if Enterprise is asleep, wealth decays whatever Thrift may be doing."[27]

Invention and Technology as Determinants of Investment

Capital (ships, canals, roads, machines, warehouses, etc.), says Lauderdale, must at all times have its limits, beyond which it can-

---

24 *Ibid.*, p. 215.
25 The term "capital" here means "investable funds," not real capital goods.
26 Lauderdale, *op. cit.*, pp. 217–218.
27 J. M. Keynes, *Treatise on Money*, Harcourt, Brace and Company, 1930, Volume II, pp. 148–149.

not be increased to advantage. "In every state of society, a certain quantity of capital, proportional to the existing state of knowledge of mankind, may be usefully and profitably employed in supplanting and performing labour. . . . Man's invention, in the means of supplanting labour, may give scope, in the progress of society, for the employment of an increased quantity; but there must be at all times, a point determined by the existing state of knowledge in the art of supplanting labour with capital, beyond which capital cannot profitably be increased, and beyond which it will not naturally increase," because when it exceeds that point, its value "must in consequence diminish in such a manner, as effectually to check its augmentation." [28]

Here, evidently, is a quite clear conception of the role of invention and technique in opening up outlets for capital formation. Lauderdale was concerned with both the *deepening* of capital (autonomous investment as determined by the "existing state of knowledge in the act of supplanting and performing labour with capital") and the widening of capital (induced investment). Room could be made for capital accumulation both by the progress of technology and by the growth of consumption. A wide distribution of income among the people generally would be favorable to a high level of consumption, and this in turn would create an outlet (induced investment) for capital accumulation.

Income Distribution and the Consumption Function

Lauderdale refers to Great Britain and the United States as countries enjoying a wide distribution of income, resulting in a high level of consumption, which in turn encourages enterprise and outlets for the use of capital. "This nation [Great Britain]," he says, "is at present the greatest commercial country in the world. There is hardly any people, in any climate, with whom our merchants have not dealings; and if we examine the cargoes that are made up to suit the demands of different nations, we shall uniformly observe, that it is the distribution of property, in each country, that dictates the nature and quality of the goods that are sent to it.[29]

---

[28] Lauderdale, *op. cit.*, pp. 224–225.
[29] *Ibid.*, pp. 318–319.

"In the United States of America . . . property is more equally divided than perhaps in any other country. Almost every man possesses not only the means of procuring the mere necessaries of life, but his wealth is such as to extend his demands to some articles of comfort in clothing, furniture, and habitation; and there is hardly such a thing as a princely or overgrown fortune." Accordingly, the goods sent to the American market are all comparatively low-priced, things calculated to secure comfort, not to attract admiration.[30]

"In general, however, it may be observed, that great inequality of fortune, by impoverishing the lower orders, has everywhere been the principal impediment to the increase of public wealth. We know from experience, that no country of equal extent ever enjoyed so much wealth as what is diffused over this island. We have a right, therefore, to conclude, that the distribution of property has been more favourable to the growth of wealth in this than in any other country. In the beginning of the seventeenth century, Lord Bacon, accounting for the advantages obtained by the English in their wars with France, ascribes them chiefly to the superior ease and opulence enjoyed by the common people." [31]

"Thus the distribution of wealth not only regulates and decides the channels in which the industry of every country is embarked, and, of course, the articles in the production of which it excels; but a proper distribution of wealth insures the increase of opulence, by sustaining a regular progressive demand in the home market, and still more effectually, by affording to those whose habits are likely to create a desire of supplanting labour, the power of executing it." [32]

Thus Lauderdale concludes that the "direction which labour in every country takes, and of course the channels of industry in which it excels,—nay, the extent to which the exertions of its industry, and even its population, can be pushed, depend upon the distribution of its wealth." [33]

---

30 *Ibid.*, pp. 319–320.
31 *Ibid.*, pp. 344–345.
32 *Ibid.*, pp. 348–350.
33 *Ibid.*, p. 364. By the phrase "distribution of wealth," Lauderdale really means the distribution of income.

Fiscal Policy and Aggregate Demand

Lauderdale may be regarded as the first able exponent of the role of fiscal policy as a means of promoting aggregate demand. He is concerned with the effect of a tax surplus upon consumption expenditures and fears a too rapid retirement of the public debt. The funds pumped out of the income stream via taxation are poured back to the bondholders via debt retirement. Consumption is thereby curtailed at the moment that investment-seeking funds are accumulating in the hands of the paid-off bondholders. In modern terminology, the consumption function is pushed down to a lower level. Given this reduced consumption function, investment outlets may well turn out to be insufficient to provide adequate aggregate demand. Great inequality in income distribution would mean a still lower consumption function, and would reduce effective demand still more. Management of the public debt—taxation and borrowing—should not, in his view, follow some preconceived rule with respect to debt retirement in forty-five years or any other period. Instead these matters should be decided in terms of what is required in order to maintain adequate effective demand. Similarly, an important consideration in determining the most desirable distribution of income should be, he thought, its influence on effective demand.

As we shall see later, Lauderdale is clearer-headed on these points than Malthus. He deserves a much larger place in the history of the development of the theory of effective demand and fiscal policy than he has hitherto been accorded. Moreover, he is also far clearer than Malthus with respect to the analysis of the demand for capital. He understands amazingly well (much better than Malthus) the role of technology as a determinant of the outlets for capital investment.

In short, we have in Lauderdale the elements, however imperfectly stated, of two of the Keynesian determinants of income and employment: (1) the consumption function, and (2) the schedule of the marginal efficiency of capital. We have, moreover, a fairly good analysis of how fiscal policy affects the former, and how changes in technique affect the latter.

THOMAS ROBERT MALTHUS (1766–1834)

The *Principles of Political Economy* by Thomas Robert Malthus was published in 1820. It contained, in the concluding chapter, VII, an analysis of the problem of inadequate "effectual" demand. The discussion is pointed toward the depressed conditions following the Napoleonic Wars, and there is a final section on the distress of the laboring classes since 1815. A second edition, which he had been working on before his death in 1834, was published in 1836. Here Chapter VII was left substantially as before but was made Chapter I of Book II, under the title "The Progress of Wealth." The references below are to the second edition.[34]

Malthus and Lauderdale

In this part of his work Malthus attacked fundamentally the same problems which had been so ably discussed by Lord Lauderdale; but one gets the impression that inadequate credit was given to his predecessor. The only mention made of Lauderdale is a criticism which, though in a manner justified, might better have been directed toward a defect in exposition rather than a point of substance. Indeed, with respect to the matter in question (namely, saving out of increased income versus increased saving out of the same income) Malthus says precisely the same thing that Lauderdale was trying to say.

In some respects Malthus is more thoroughgoing than Lauderdale; in others he is less sure-footed. Saving and consumption are, as he sees it, deeply rooted in established patterns of behavior and in fundamental institutional arrangements. This discussion is far superior to Lauderdale's. What is missing in both writers is the clear concept of a *schedule* relating saving (or consumption) to income. Had they been able to develop this important tool of analysis, everything would have fallen into place. The same difficulty confronted the early nineteenth-century economists with respect to demand and supply in relation to price; the schedule

[34] T. R. Malthus, *Principles of Political Economy,* William Pickering, London, 1836. (Reprinted by the International Economic Circle, Tokyo, in collaboration with The London School of Economics and Political Science, University of London, 1936.)

concept was missing. Nevertheless, on what we should now call the consumption function, Malthus has some penetrating things to say.

Inadequate Demand and the Saving Process

Malthus did not have the concept of a "cycle" of trade or employment.[35] He was concerned with a *condition*—that of inadequate demand and unemployment. The problem of inadequate demand is related to the process of saving. Inadequate demand could not in any fundamental way arise in a society which consumed all its income. Such a society might indeed, in a money and exchange economy, experience short-run oscillations. This kind of problem Malthus was not concerned with. It was this sort of thing, as we shall see, that interested Mill and Marshall, and that underlay their views of recurring commercial crises. But Malthus was interested in something deeper: inadequate demand growing out of behavior patterns with respect to saving in relation to the capital requirements of the society.

Malthus apparently believed (if we may state it in modern terminology) that the demand schedule for capital is highly interest-inelastic; or in other words that the schedule of the marginal efficiency of capital falls rapidly with each additional increment of investment. But this element in the analysis has to be inferred in large measure from his general argument. He seems to believe that capital, in any given state of technique, could very quickly become redundant. In this he followed Lauderdale. With respect to the consumption function (as we should now put it) Malthus was more thoroughgoing than Lauderdale; with respect to the investment demand schedule, its slope, and the factors causing it to shift upward, Lauderdale's discussion, while inadequate, was nevertheless clearer and sharper than that of Malthus.

[35] He does refer to that "general briskness of demand which is sometimes so very sensibly felt throughout the whole country, and is so strikingly contrasted with the feeling which gives rise to the expression of trade being universally dead." (*Principles of Political Economy*, p. 394.) The problem for him is the *condition* of prosperity or of depression, not a sequence of phases in a cyclical movement.

The Possibility of a General Glut

A leading point of controversy between Malthus and David Ricardo related to the possibility of there being a general glut. This Malthus rightly reduced to the problem of a society's propensity to save on the one hand, and its capital requirements on the other. Ricardo maintained as a general position, said Malthus, that capital cannot be redundant, yet he was obliged to make what seemed to Malthus a fatal concession: "If every man were to forego the use of luxuries and be intent only on accumulation . . . there might undoubtedly be an universal glut." [36]

Here, however, Ricardo gave in a little too easily. A high propensity to save does not by itself alone prove that total effective demand will be inadequate. The investment demand schedule *could* be such that the outlet for capital formation matched the propensity to save. In this case there would be no glut. Two matters must be assessed: on the one side the capital requirements; on the other the propensity to save.

Malthus comes closer to the problem when he charges Jean Baptiste Say, James Mill, and David Ricardo with a very serious error, namely, that of "supposing that accumulation ensures demand." They argued themselves into believing that the process of saving is merely a way of spending money on the goods consumed by the laborers employed to make the capital goods. This is not true. The process of saving does indeed mean forgoing the purchase of consumers' goods which the laborers employed in the capital goods industries can then purchase; everything goes well, so long as machines and other capital goods are wanted, or so long as saving finds investment outlets. *But the act of saving does not ensure that capital goods are wanted.* "Accumulation" does not "ensure demand." What is needed to provide an effective answer to Say, James Mill, and Ricardo, is an analysis of the factors underlying the investment demand schedule. But this is the weak link in Malthus' argument.

Malthus is at his best in analyzing the propensity to save; but he does not adequately analyze what determines capital requirements or investment outlets. He has no adequate conception of the role of *autonomous* investment (the role of technology).

---

[36] D. Ricardo, *Principles of Political Economy,* 1817, Chapter 21.

For him additional capital is needed *when consumption is increased* (i.e., induced investment). Thus it appears to him quite certain that an "inordinate passion for accumulation must inevitably lead to a supply of commodities beyond what the structure and habits of such a society will permit to be profitably consumed." [37] This sentence contains a number of weasel words, such as "inordinate" and "profitably." One cannot know whether the passion to accumulate is "inordinate" or not until an analysis has been made of the capital requirements of the society, autonomous and induced.

The Propensity to Save

This, I repeat, is the weak part in Malthus. The "propensity to save" concept is better formulated. Such phrases as "the structure and habits" of the society and the "passion for accumulation" are highly significant. They imply that the act of saving is deeply rooted in the behavior pattern of the community. The desire to save is one thing; investment outlets for saving are another thing. The determinants of saving are to be found in the structure and habits of a society. But Malthus offers no satisfactory analysis of the investment demand schedule.

Malthus does, indeed, at points, hint vaguely at the schedule of diminishing productivity of capital, as for instance in the following: "But if the conversion of revenue [i.e., "income"] into capital beyond a certain point must, by diminishing effectual demand for produce, throw the laboring classes out of employment, it is obvious that the adoption of parsimonious habits beyond a certain point, may be accompanied by the most distressing effects." [38] The phrase "beyond a certain point," used here with respect to both capital requirements and saving, seeks obviously to relate the propensity to save to the volume of investment outlets. But what determines this point? When accumulation, he says, goes "beyond what is wanted in order to supply the effectual demand for produce, a part of it would very soon lose both its use and its value." There is here no specific recogni-

---

37 Malthus, *op. cit.*, p. 325.

38 *Ibid.*, p. 326.

tion of autonomous investment outlets opened up by changes in technique—namely, the deepening process, or the employment of more capital per worker. Instead the demand for capital is tied closely and directly to changes in the "demand for produce." For Malthus, outlets for capital formation appear to be limited pretty much to induced investment.

A high propensity to save per se does not prove that effective demand will not be adequate to provide full employment. Investment outlets must also be considered. What is indeed true is that a fall in the propensity to consume will decrease aggregate demand if technology and other exogenous factors remain unchanged. A fall in the consumption function will induce a decline in investment.

Now this was precisely what was taking place after the Napoleonic Wars. Government expenditures declined drastically. Private consumer spending did not rise adequately to take its place. Thus the aggregate propensity to consume (public and private) was falling. Under these conditions, new outlets for capital formation were wanting. The situation, as Malthus saw it, was one of capital saturation.

Capital Saturation in the Post-Napoleonic Era

During nearly the whole of the war, large additions had been made to Britain's capital facilities. The great wartime expansion had simultaneously increased both "consumption and demand" and also the "powers of production." "To doubt this would be to shut our eyes to the comparative state of the country in 1792 and 1813."[39] So much capital had been invested in plant and equipment that a certain degree of saturation had been reached. Only in the last two years of the war, says Malthus, was the consumption of capital not fully replaced. There was thus no large backlog of demand for capital goods, and the "unusual stagnation of effectual demand" which immediately followed the war made the existing stock of capital redundant. This stopped any further capital formation. Had "effectual demand" been adequate, capital formation could have gone forward. The "stagna-

[39] *Ibid.*, p. 416.

tion itself was much more disastrous in its effects upon the national capital . . . than any previous destruction of stock." [40]

The stagnation so generally felt and complained of after the war appeared to Malthus inexplicable if one were to accept the theory that income will certainly rise if the means of production are increased. At the cessation of the war "more people and more capital were ready to be employed in productive labour; but notwithstanding this obvious increase in the means of production, we hear every where of difficulties and distresses, instead of ease and plenty . . . Altogether the state of the commercial world, since the war, clearly shows that something else is necessary to the continued increase of wealth besides an increase in the means of producing." [41]

It had been alleged, Malthus states, that the trouble was not a general redundancy of capital; that there had "not been time to transfer capital from the employments where it is redundant to those where it is deficient." But where, asked Malthus, are the understocked employments, which, according to this theory, ought to be numerous, and fully capable of absorbing all the "redundant capital, which is confessedly glutting the markets of Europe in so many different branches of trade? It is well known by the owners of floating capital, that none such are now to be found." [42]

Inadequate Effective Demand

The depression, in Malthus' view, was due to the failure of private consumption to offset the decline in government expenditures, thereby causing a general diminution of demand. Taxes had indeed been reduced, but the relief thus granted was going "in part, and probably in no inconsiderable part," into saving, not into increased consumption. "This saving is quite natural and proper, and forms no just argument against the removal of the tax; but still it contributes to explain the cause of the diminished demand for commodities, compared with their supply since the war." [43]

---

40 *Ibid.*
41 *Ibid.*, pp. 419–420.
42 *Ibid.*, p. 420.
43 *Ibid.*, p. 421.

"But when profits are low and uncertain, when capitalists are quite at a loss where they can safely employ their capitals, and when on these accounts capital is flowing out of the country; in short, when all the evidence which the nature of the subject admits, distinctly proves that there is no effective demand for capital at home, is it not contrary to the general principles of political economy, is it not a vain and fruitless opposition to that first, greatest, and most universal of all its principles, the principle of supply and demand, to recommend saving," and to direct an increased flow of income into capital accumulation? [44] If, following the principle laid down by Say, the "society were greatly and generally to slacken their consumption, and add to their capitals, there cannot be the least doubt, on the principle of demand and supply, that the profits of capitalists would soon be greatly reduced." [45]

Capital Backlogs and Prosperity

Malthus noted that those countries which "have suffered the most by the war have suffered the least by the peace," since such countries had an accumulated backlog of capital requirements which helped to sustain postwar demand. But for countries, like England, "where the pressure of the war found great powers of production, and seemed to create greater; where accumulation, instead of being checked, was accelerated," the coming of peace had a very different effect.

Difficulty of Raising the Propensity to Consume

Malthus was not arguing in favor of the maintenance of the wartime level of government expenditures. His whole analysis, as we shall see, was directed toward ways and means of raising the schedule of consumption in relation to income. But this could not, he thought, be accomplished quickly. A rich country, with powers of production greatly increased under the wartime "stimulus of a great effective consumption," might be able to pay "heavy taxes imposed upon it, out of its revenue, and yet find the means

---

[44] *Ibid.*, pp. 417–418.
[45] *Ibid.*, p. 419.

of adequate accumulation."[46] Once the "habits of the people were accommodated to this scale of public and private expenditures,[47] it is scarcely possible to doubt that, at the end of the war, when so large a mass of taxes would at once be restored to the payers of them, the just balance of produce and consumption would be completely destroyed, and a period would ensue, longer or shorter, according to circumstances, in which a very great stagnation would be felt in every branch of productive industry, attended by its usual concomitant general distress. . . . We should constantly keep in mind that the tendency to expenditure in individuals has most formidable antagonists in the love of indolence, and in the desire of saving, in order to better their condition and provide for a family; and that all theories founded upon the assumption that mankind always produce and consume as much as they have the power to produce and consume, are founded upon a want of knowledge of the human character and of the motives by which it is usually influenced."[48]

The Place to Begin: Raise Aggregate Demand

Now if all this is granted, how then can we ever restore prosperity and resume that accumulation of capital which is a necessary condition of progress? It is perfectly true, said Malthus, "that

---

[46] *Ibid.*, p. 423.

[47] Public expenditures, he says, which "would have absolutely crushed the country in 1770, might be little more than what was necessary to call forth its prodigious powers of production in 1816." (Malthus, *op. cit.*, p. 423.)

With respect to the role of public expenditures in the maintenance of aggregate demand, we may revert to Lauderdale, who quotes from Chalmers as follows: "The public expenditure continually distributes this vast revenue among the creditors, or servants of the state, who return it to the original contributors, either for the necessaries or luxuries of life. The exchequer, which thus constantly receives and disperses this immense income, has been aptly compared to the human heart, that increasingly carries on the vital circulation; so invigorating while it flows; so fatal when it stops. *Thus it is that modern taxes, which are never hoarded but always expended,* may even promote the employments and industry, the prosperity and populousness, of an industrious people." (Lauderdale, *op. cit.*, p. 238.) In this quotation, Lauderdale is, of course, not thinking of the tax surplus used to retire debt. That tax money, as he showed, might be saved and hoarded.

[48] Malthus, *op. cit.*, pp. 423–424.

the recovery and increase of our capital can take place in no other way than by accumulation." [49]

To this question, Malthus' answer was identical with that given by Keynes. The place to begin is not to increase saving while income is still low. What is needed is first to raise the level of income. This would tend, on the one hand, to open up investment outlets, and on the other, to lead quite naturally to an increased flow of saving at the higher income level. "What is now wanted in this country," said Malthus, "is an increased national income. . . .[50] When we have attained this . . . we may then begin again to accumulate, and our accumulation will then be effectual." [51]

This is certainly an excellent statement. Moreover, Malthus went on to differentiate between (a) "saving from increased profits" (i.e., moving up *on* the saving schedule) and (b) "saving from diminished expenditure" (i.e., an upward *shift* of the saving schedule). The former—that is, first raising income, which would lead to an increase of both consumption and saving [52]—he favored; the latter—a fall in the consumption function—he argued must of necessity aggravate instead of alleviate distress.[53] He is definitely saying here exactly what we should now express more clearly by using the schedule concept of the functional relation of saving (or consumption) to income. If a country raises its effectual demand, thereby calling forth increased production,[54]

49 *Ibid.*, p. 424.

50 Malthus used the word "revenue," by which he and his contemporaries meant "income," and I have substituted this term above.

51 *Ibid.*, pp. 424–425. Another quite similar statement (*ibid.*, p. 430) is as follows: "And as soon as the capitalists can begin to save from steady and improving profits, instead of from diminished expenditure, that is as soon as the national income . . . begins yearly and steadily to increase, we may then begin safely and effectively to recover our lost capital by the usual process of saving." Again (*ibid.*, p. 365) he says that in consequence of a previous rise in national income, saving may increase "not only without any diminution of demand and consumption, but under an actual increase of demand . . . during every part of the process." This highly interesting statement suggests (however vaguely) the multiplier process.

52 Saving, he says in a footnote (*ibid.*, p. 326), may "take place without any diminution of consumption, if income increases first."

53 *Ibid.*, p. 425.

54 But Malthus did not favor stimulating production by the inflationary process

and saves yearly only that "portion of its income which it could most advantageously add to its capital, expending the rest in consumable commodities and services, it might evidently under such a balance of produce and consumption, be increasing in wealth and population with considerable rapidity."[55]

Thrift Alone Will Not Create Investment Outlets

Saving is a "national benefit, or a national disadvantage, according to the circumstances of the period"; and these circumstances are "best declared by the rate of profits."[56] Thus in the middle of the eighteenth century "there must have been a considerable difficulty in finding employment for capital, or the national creditors would rather have been paid off than have submitted to a reduction of interest from 4 per cent to 3½, and afterwards to 3."[57] This fall in the rate of interest and profits, Malthus argued, "arose from a redundancy of capital and a want of demand for produce . . . Under a more favorable distribution of property, there cannot be a doubt that such a demand for produce, agricultural, manufacturing and mercantile, might have been created, as to have prevented for many, many years the interest on money from falling below 3 per cent."[58]

How to Raise the Propensity to Consume

Malthus' argument proceeds on the assumption that there are severe limits (none too well defined or explained) to the profitable outlets for capital investment. This being so, it was his main concern to show that the propensity to consume is deeply

of "a free issue of paper." His reason is that this would not promote a balanced relation between consumption and capital accumulation, since, through the process of forced saving, it would lead to an abnormal spurt of capital formation which would in the end only create a "still greater glut of commodities than is felt at present" (*ibid.*, pp. 430–431). A monetary inflation has the effect of lowering the consumption function; what is needed is to raise the consumption function.

55 *Ibid.*, p. 419.

56 *Ibid.*, p. 433.

57 This case, also cited by Lauderdale, shows that the government was retiring debt too rapidly. If the investment demand schedule is highly interest-inelastic, and if the heavy taxes seriously depress the consumption function, the net effect of the debt-retirement program is sharply deflationary.

58 Malthus, *op. cit.*, p. 406.

rooted in the structure and habits of the society, and that it is only by changing these institutional arrangements that we can raise the level of "effectual demand." To this end the factors that most deserve our attention are (1) the distribution of income, involving, among other things, the division of landed property and the diffusion of ownership of the public debt, (2) the extension of domestic and foreign commerce as a means of providing a more varied assortment of consumers' goods and so raising the desire to consume, (3) the development of service industries, or what we should now call tertiary employment. These are all ways and means of raising the propensity to consume.

Now the mere mention of these things, says Malthus, indicates that there is no easy solution to the problem of inadequate demand. "If it were true that, in order to employ all that are out of work . . . it is only necessary that a little more should be saved . . . I am fully persuaded that this species of charity would not want contributors, and that a change would soon be wrought in the conditions of the labouring classes. But when we know, both from theory and experience, that this proceeding will not afford the relief sought for . . . . it must be allowed that we may be at a loss with respect to the first steps which it would be advisable to take, in order to accomplish what we wish." Still, it is of the "utmost importance to know the immediate object which ought to be aimed at" so that, even though we may not be able to do much to forward it, "we may not from ignorance do much to retard it." [59]

Income Distribution

If a more equitable distribution of income is one of the main means (as Malthus believed) of *increasing* income, what policy may we adopt? A better division of landed property would help, but Malthus opposed this on broad grounds of social policy. So he looked to other measures. Despite certain evils attendant on a large public debt, it may justly, he felt, become a question whether these are not "more than counterbalanced by the distribution of property and increase of the middle class of society, which it must necessarily create; and whether by saving, in order

[59] *Ibid.*, pp. 425–426.

to pay it off, we are not submitting to a painful sacrifice, which, . . . whatever other good it may effect, will leave us with a much less favorable distribution of wealth." Grievously, he declared, "will those be disappointed who think that, either by greatly reducing or at once destroying it [i.e., the public debt], we can enrich ourselves, and employ all our labouring classes." [60]

Diversity of Products

The second main method of increasing income and "effectual demand" is a broad extension of trade, both domestic and foreign. The better distribution of the produce of the country, the better adaptation of it to the wants and tastes of the consumers, will at once give it a greater market value, and at once increase the national income, the rate of steady profits, and the wages of labor. "One of the greatest benefits which foreign commerce confers, and the reason why it has always appeared an almost necessary ingredient in the progress of wealth, is its tendency to inspire new wants, to form new tastes, and to furnish fresh motives for industry." [61] "No country with a very confined market, internal as well as external, has ever been able to accumulate a large capital, because such a market prevents the formation of those wants and tastes, and that desire to consume, which are absolutely necessary to keep up the market prices of commodities, and prevent the fall of profits." [62]

The Service Industries

The third main method of remedying the "deficiency of effectual demand" is the "employment of individuals in personal services, or the maintenance of an adequate proportion of consumers not directly productive of material objects"; [63] in other words, the development of tertiary employment.

The history of all progressive countries reveals how sound Malthus was in his emphasis on the importance of an expansion of the service industries. As per capita productivity has increased, as standards of living have risen, everywhere, a larger and larger

---

[60] *Ibid.*, pp. 426–427.
[61] *Ibid.*, p. 403.
[62] *Ibid.*, p. 388.
[63] *Ibid.*, p. 398.

proportion of the labor force are employed in the service industries, both public and private. Malthus, to be sure, had a limited conception of the tertiary industries. For the "labouring classes" it was difficult for him to envisage anything but the bare necessities of life. His "personal services" and other service industry activities relate for the most part to the comfort and living standards of the middle and upper classes. But he hoped for a sufficiently wide diffusion of property and income so that this group would be a fairly numerous one.

"What the proportion is between the productive labourers and those engaged in personal services, which affords the greatest encouragement to the continued increase of wealth, it has before been said that the resources of political economy are unequal to determine. It must depend upon a great variety of circumstances, particularly upon the fertility of the soil and the progress of invention in machinery. A fertile soil and an ingenious people can not only support without injury a considerable proportion of consumers not directly productive of material wealth,[64] but may absolutely require such a body of demanders, in order to give effect to the powers of production. . . ."[65]

Malthus referred to those engaged in the service fields as "unproductive consumers." The "productive classes" were those who made *material* goods. In fact, as was later fully recognized, no such distinction can properly be made. The service trades and industries are as productive as those making material objects. A more useful classification is: (1) primary production (including agriculture, forestry, fishing), (2) secondary production (including manufacture, electric power production, mining, construction), and (3) tertiary production (including trade, transportation, and service industries). Broadly speaking, it is the tertiary employments that Malthus wished to develop in order to strengthen "effectual demand."

"On the whole it may be observed," he says, "that the specific use of a body of unproductive consumers, is to give encouragement

[64] "It is also of importance to know that, in our endeavours to assist the working classes in a period like the present, it is desirable to employ them in those kinds of labour, the results of which do not come for sale into the market, such as roads and public works" (*ibid.*, p. 429).

[65] *Ibid.*, p. 64.

to wealth by maintaining such a balance between produce and consumption as will give the greatest exchangeable value to the results of the national industry." And, he added, "we may safely conclude that, among the causes necessary to that distribution, which tends to keep up and increase the exchangeable value of the whole produce, we must place the maintenance of a certain body of consumers who are not themselves engaged in the immediate production of material objects. This body, considered as a stimulus to wealth, should vary in different countries, and at different times, according to the powers of production." [66]

This indeed is exactly what one finds. The higher the productivity the greater the tertiary employment. Colin Clark gives the tertiary employment (in percentage of working population) as 15 for Rumania, 34 for Ireland, and 45 for Canada in 1925–39; while the real output per head was given as 243, 627, and 1337 in international units.[67]

With every increase in productivity, new frontiers of consumption have developed, especially in the area of the service trades and industries. Were this not so, demand would have to be concentrated in a narrower orbit—that of material objects. This would push the marginal utility derived from these objects farther toward satiety. The "propensity to consume" would fall. At any given income level, less would be spent on consumption. All advanced countries would find it difficult to provide full employment if all their productive capacity were to be devoted merely to the production of material things. A varied and rich standard of consumption, involving an expansion of the service trades and industries, has historically gone hand in hand with increasing productivity. This development, in Malthus' view, is a necessary condition for the maintenance of adequate "effectual demand."

JOHN A. HOBSON (1858–1940)

Hobson's *Economics of Unemployment*, published in 1922, is less thorough and penetrating than his *Industrial System*, which

[66] *Ibid.*, pp. 412–413.

[67] Colin Clark, *The Economics of 1960*, Macmillan and Co., Ltd., London, 1942, p. 25.

appeared in 1909 and was revised in 1910. Earlier, with A. F. Mummery, he had first presented his views on oversaving in *The Physiology of Industry* (1889).

Growth in the Economy

After reading Lauderdale and Malthus, one gains relatively little from Hobson's work. Hobson does indeed make clearer than his predecessors the role of growth—changes in technique and increase in population—in opening investment outlets. But he falls short of a definitive analysis of the determinants of investment. And with respect to consumption, his treatment is less penetrating than that of Malthus, and suffers equally by not having the concept of a *schedule* relating consumption to income.

Hobson's best analysis is contained in the chapters on spending and saving and on unemployment in his *Industrial System.*[68] Here he explains how, in a "stationary" economy, in which all the income is spent on consumption goods, there can be no problem of depression and unemployment. The actual industrial system is, however, not stationary, but changing, "and the change is, on the whole, a growth. The structure and working of the actual industrial system must take account of growth of population, a rising standard of consumption and improved economies in the art of production." If provision is to be made for growth, the system must be enabled to set up an increased quantity of the instruments of production. This involves net investment and net saving. The final result is "to add some new forms of capital (buildings, machines, material goods), leaving the productive apparatus of the system larger than before." [69]

Hobson regards hoarding as abnormal in modern industrial societies. He therefore holds that "saving implies demand for creation of more forms of fixed or circulating capital." Saving causes more forms of capital to be produced. Income saved is spent on "productive goods, e.g., new mills, machines, warehouses, raw materials, etc." All this is very much like Malthus: saving means in effect capital accumulation. Saving *is* investment.[70]

---

68 John A. Hobson, *The Industrial System,* New and Revised Edition, Longmans, Green and Co., London, 1910.

69 *Ibid.,* Chapter III.

70 *Ibid.*

Limited Outlets for Investment

"It is sometimes assumed," continues Hobson, "that any proportion of the income of a community can advantageously be saved. But this is not the case." In the modern capitalist society there is indeed an "enormously extended possibility of socially useful saving" in railroads, harbors, mining, afforestations, drainage, and other vast public or private enterprises. "Such investments may swallow up vast masses of new savings." Alterations in the arts of industry, "while greatly extending the limits of saving," still leave some limits. The "amount of saving that can take material shape in new railroads, harbours, and other great capitalist enterprises" is not capable of indefinite expansion.[71]

An industrial community cannot usefully save (and invest) "more than a certain proportion of its income: that proportion is never accurately known, and it is always shifting with changes in the arts of production and consumption. . . . It is only by taking the partial standpoint of an individual or a group of individuals, or some other part of the industrial whole, that it seems plausible to hold that there is no limit to efficacious saving." [72]

The Correct Proportion of Saving to Spending

Hobson is trying here to say that investment outlets are determined by the requirements of growth—namely, changes in technology and increases in population. If now the propensity to consume is such that the amount which would be saved at full employment exceeds these growth requirements, then such a society would suffer from inadequate effective demand.

"There exists at the present moment, a right proportion between saving and spending. . . . Industrial progress, or the economical working of the industrial system, consists largely in the ascertainment of this proportion and the adjustment of industry to it. . . . The right proportion of saving to spending at any given time depends upon the present condition of the arts of production and consumption, and the probabilities of such changes in modes of work or living as shall provide social utility for new

[71] *Ibid.*
[72] *Ibid.*

forms of capital within the near or calculable future." [73] The proportion of its income which "could be saved for conversion into new forms of capital must depend upon the state of the industrial arts upon the one hand, and the standards of consumption upon the other . . . the increased demand for final commodities which a rising consumption of a growing population will create in the calculable future." [74]

Beyond these growth requirements, "saving would defeat its purpose, creating more forms of capital than were wanted and than would actually be used. The test of an extreme hypothesis will make this evident. If some great spiritual or hygienic preacher could impose the gospel of a 'simple life' so effectively upon an entire industrial community as to induce an abandonment of the consumption of all luxuries and comforts, leaving only the use of bare physical necessaries of life, it is obvious that these could be supplied by about one-half of the existing capital and labour of the community, and the other half would remain unemployed." [75]

This quotation is very reminiscent of Malthus. But Hobson is less successful than Malthus in showing why one might not expect every society automatically to adapt its "propensity to consume" so as to provide exactly that amount of saving which the requirements of growth indicate as desirable.

The Propensity to Consume

Hobson does, however, to some extent, discuss this problem. Standards of life are, he says, for most people "more conventional and more stable than the standards of work." The command of "new wealth due to industrial progress passes largely into the hands of a small class." Much of it is "accumulated and applied to industry from sheer inability to make consumption keep pace with rising income. The visible and considerable rise in the luxurious expenditure of all the rich and well-to-do classes is only

---

[73] *Ibid.*
[74] *Ibid.*, Chapter XVIII.
[75] *Ibid.*

an inadequate attempt to keep pace with the modern increased power of production." [76]

A "greater equalization of incomes, either by the successful pressure of the workers for a larger share of wealth or by the taxation of 'surplus' for purposes of public expenditure" would increase demand and employment, and so "validate at least as large an absolute quantity of saving as before, though a smaller proportion of saving to spending"—or, in modern language, an upward shift in the consumption function.[77]

Thus the Hobson analysis, like that of Lauderdale and Malthus, is, properly understood, a saving-investment analysis. Even when he poses the problem in terms of inability to sell all that could be produced at prices that would cover the expenses of production, it is still a saving-investment problem, not the more superficial problem of maintaining a stable price level. In other words, if 85 per cent of a full employment income is all that a given society is prepared to spend on consumers' goods, and if the requirements of growth call for an investment of only 5 per cent of the income, it will not do to attempt to use 95 per cent of the productive power of the society to make consumers' goods. An output of consumers' goods corresponding to 95 per cent of the productive power of the society could not be sold at prices covering costs (namely, 95 per cent of income) if only 85 per cent of the income will be spent on consumers' goods. This, I repeat, is a saving-investment problem, not a problem of selling the products at a stable price level.[78] The latter is a monetary problem (a problem of money wages and money prices) and not a full-employment problem as such. By this I do not mean to say that the problem of money and prices is unimportant, or that it has no bearing on the saving-investment problem. Nevertheless a satisfactory saving-investment adjustment *may* be reached under conditions either of a moderately rising, or of a moderately falling, general price level.

[76] *Ibid.*

[77] *Ibid.*

[78] For the reasons given above, I am inclined to doubt that Hobson's analysis is "a statement of a different, and possibly also a deeper problem" than that raised by Keynes, as suggested by Domar. See *American Economic Review,* March, 1947.

15 · *Confidence and Credit:*
JOHN STUART MILL · JOHN MILLS ALFRED MARSHALL

JOHN STUART MILL (1806–1873)

John Stuart Mill devotes three chapters in his *Principles of Political Economy* (1848) [1] largely to commercial crises, their causes and effects. The discussion is, however, cast on general lines and relates to broader matters—currency, credit, prices, and the rate of interest. The first edition appeared in 1848, and the three chapters in question—"The Influence of Credit and Prices," "The Rate of Interest," and "The Regulation of a Convertible Paper Currency"—were revised and enlarged in the editions of 1857 and 1865.

Crises Are a Commercial Phenomenon

Mill conceived of the crisis as a commercial phenomenon. It had to do with speculation in commodities. It had to do with traders and merchants. In so far as it had to do with investment, it was investment in stocks of commodities, especially for speculative purposes. The fluctuation consisted of a rise and fall in the holdings of commodities, a rise and fall in credit, in prices, and in mercantile or speculative profit.

1 J. S. Mill, *Principles of Political Economy.* I have used the New Edition, edited by W. J. Ashley, Longmans, Green and Co., London, 1909 (reprinted 1920).

"The inclination of the mercantile public to increase their demand for commodities by making use of all or much of their credit as a purchasing power, depends upon their expectation of profit. When there is a general impression that the price of some commodity is likely to rise, from an extra demand, a short crop, obstruction to importation, or any other cause, there is a disposition among dealers to increase their stocks, in order to profit by the expected rise." If the rise is considerable and progressive, other speculators are attracted. Thus a rise of price is often heightened by merely speculative purchases. After a time this begins to be perceived, and holders, thinking it time to take profits, begin to sell. Prices fall, and other holders, to avoid still greater loss, rush into the market, and prices collapse.[2]

There is said to be a commercial crisis when a great number of merchants and traders have a difficulty in meeting their engagements. "The most usual cause of this general embarrassment is the recoil of prices after they have been raised by a spirit of speculation." [3]

Some accident may account for the expectation of rising prices. Thus speculation is set at work. Some holders realize great gains. "In certain states of the public mind, such examples of rapid increase of fortune call forth numerous imitators," [4] and speculation is likely to go far beyond what is justified by the original grounds for expecting a rise of price. At periods of this kind a great extension of credit takes place. An illustration is the "celebrated speculative year 1825." [5]

Irrational Extension of Credit

Errors of judgment play a large role in Mill's conception of the speculative rise and decline. To "rational considerations there is superadded, in extreme cases, a panic as unreasoning as the previous overconfidence." During a commercial revolution general prices fall, he says, as much below the usual level as they had risen above it in the previous period of speculation. The

[2] *Ibid.*, p. 526.
[3] *Ibid.*, p. 527.
[4] This suggests Schumpeter's herd following the innovators.
[5] Mill, *op. cit.*, p. 527.

rise and the fall originate in a "state of credit"; an unusually extended employment of credit in the earlier period is followed by a decline.[6]

In the crisis of 1847, Mill says, there was no extraordinary and irrational extension of credit. "The crisis of 1847 belonged to another class of mercantile phenomena." At this point one might expect Mill to point to the vast fixed capital investment in railroads. But he does not. It is still for him a mercantile crisis. The railroad development did, however, he thinks, play a certain role. The "loan transactions of railway companies, for the purpose of being converted into fixed capital," drew funds from the circulating capital of the country and tightened the loan market. There were also fresh demands for loans, occasioned by a high price of cotton and an unprecedented importation of food. This raised the rate of interest and made it impossible to borrow except on the very best security. A panic was, however, averted by the suspension of the Bank Charter Act of 1844.[7]

Mill, writing in 1848, stated that for nearly "half a century there never has been a commercial crisis which the Bank has not been strenuously accused either of producing or of aggravating." [8] Prices, he argued, "do not depend on money, but on purchases." If merchants have, for whatever reason, expectations of profit, they will use their credit—bank credit, bills of exchange—to purchase. And banks may extend credit via deposits no less than by issuing bank notes. Thus the artificial limitation of the issue of bank notes by the Currency Act of 1844 could not and did not prevent commercial crises.

The Rate of Profit and the Rate of Interest

Apart from accidental factors which arouse expectations of

---

[6] *Ibid.*, p. 528.

[7] *Ibid.*, p. 529. This act restricted the Bank's note-issuing privileges. But the Bank could exceed the limit imposed by permission of the Prime Minister and the Chancellor of the Exchequer, such action constituting "suspension of the Bank Act." The fiduciary portion of the issue was limited to a fixed amount of government debt, £14 million. Note issues by private and joint-stock banks were virtually restricted to the volume then outstanding. Lapses of rights to issue notes by the private and joint-stock banks permitted the Bank of England to increase its fiduciary issue by two-thirds of the lapsed private issue.

[8] Mill, *op. cit.*, p. 648.

profit, loans, according to Mill, may be expanded if the rate of interest, by reason of an excess of competition on the part of lenders, bears a "low proportion to the rate of profit." This may tempt borrowers to ask for a greater amount of loans.

This line of reasoning foreshadows the Wicksellian analysis of the process of expansion in terms of the divergence of the money rate from the natural rate.

The demand for loans is liable to a greater variation than the supply of loans. Accordingly fluctuations in the rate of interest arise mainly from variation in the demand for loans.[9]

The Role of a Low Interest Rate

In the intervals between commercial crises, Mill noted, "there is usually a tendency in the rate of interest to a progressive decline, from the gradual process of accumulation: which process, in the great commercial countries, is sufficiently rapid to account for the almost periodical recurrence of these fits of speculation; since, when a few years have elapsed without a crisis, and no new and tempting channel for investment has been opened in the meantime, there is always found to have occurred in those few years so large an increase of capital seeking investment, as to have lowered considerably the rate of interest . . . and this diminution of interest tempts the possessor to incur hazards in hopes of a more considerable return." [10]

This is the famous analysis to which, as we shall see, Tugan-Baranowsky later referred, and upon which, in a measure, he built his system of cyclical oscillations. Mill argued (as also Tugan) that a part of the funds comes from a "previous accumulation," and is therefore something over and above the amount of "loanable capital" currently being made available.[11]

Mill also believed that, apart from the pressure of a continued rate of accumulation, certain fortuitous events such as gold discoveries might tend to "depress interest relatively to profit." The ordinary rate of interest in proportion to the "common rate

---

[9] *Ibid.*, p. 641.
[10] *Ibid.*, pp. 641–642.
[11] *Ibid.*, p. 644.

of mercantile profit" would be affected by the influx of new gold.[12] "The newly-arrived gold can only get itself invested, in any given state of business, by lowering the rate of interest."[13]

These passages will bear rereading when we come to consider the Wicksellian analysis.

Investment Outlets

"The demand for loans varies much more largely than the supply, and embraces longer cycles of years in its aberrations." Causes for a sustained increased demand for loans may be wars, or the "sudden opening of any new and generally attractive mode of permanent investment," such as the "absorption of capital in the construction of railways."[14] Here, at last, Mill gets close to the modern theory, as exemplified in Tugan-Baranowsky or Wicksell.

Crises and Monetary Reform

We noted above Mill's reference to the popular belief that the issue of bank notes was responsible for commercial crises. With this view he was not in agreement. He therefore devoted a chapter to a consideration of this theory. The recurrence during the last half-century of "the painful series of phenomena called a commercial crisis" had directed the attention, he said, both of economists and of practical politicians to the "contriving of expedients" for averting or mitigating its evils. In particular, those concerned with this problem had fixed their hopes of success of moderating these vicissitudes upon "schemes for the regulation of bank notes." A scheme of this nature was the Peel Bank Act of 1844.[15]

Mill first undertook to state the nature, and examine the grounds, of the theory on which this reform was founded. The issue related in particular to whether banks took the initiative in extending credit, and so caused the speculative advance, or whether the causes of the speculative advance sprang from accidental factors, external to the banking system—factors which raised the prospective rate of mercantile profit. Was bank credit

[12] *Ibid.*, p. 642.
[13] *Ibid.*, p. 647.
[14] *Ibid.*, p. 643.
[15] *Ibid.*, p. 651.

the cause, or merely the facilitating condition, of speculation?

It was believed by many, Mill stated, that banks of issue have the power to throw their notes into circulation, and thereby raise prices. This rise of prices generates a spirit of speculation in commodities, which carries prices still higher and ultimately causes a reaction and recoil, amounting in extreme cases to a commercial crisis. It was generally believed, he said, that every such crisis which has occurred within mercantile memory has either been produced by this cause, or else greatly aggravated by it.[16]

This purely monetary explanation Mill regarded as extravagant. The fixed idea that the currency is the prime agent in the fluctuations of price has made those who hold this view "shut their eyes to the multitude of circumstances which, by influencing the expectation of supply, are the true causes of almost all speculations, and of almost all fluctuations of price." [17] The expansion of bank notes followed and possibly reinforced the speculative movement; it did not precede or cause it. Mill here cites Tooke as follows: "In point of fact, and historically, as far as my researches have gone, in every single instance of a rise or fall of prices, the rise or fall has preceded, and therefore could not be the effect of, an enlargement or contraction of the bank circulation." [18]

Bank Credit and the Role of Expectations

Nevertheless Mill, while reacting strongly against the "extravagance of the currency theorists," did not altogether agree with the "theory of the extreme opposite" as represented by Tooke and Fullarton, who argued that "bank issues, since they cannot be increased in amount unless there be an increased demand, cannot possibly raise prices; cannot encourage speculation, nor occasion a commercial crisis." [19] With this Mill largely agreed, yet

16 *Ibid.*, pp. 651–652.

17 *Ibid.*, p. 652.

18 This needs clarification. Causal relations cannot be determined merely by sequence. A rise in prices may precede expansion of the money supply, if the commodities in question are paid for, say, six months after the date of purchase. See J. A. Schumpeter, *Business Cycles*, McGraw-Hill Book Company, 1939, p. 14.

19 Mill, *op. cit.*, p. 653.

against this "extreme" view he argued that there are two states of the market: the quiescent state and the expectant or speculative state.

In the former state he believed that bankers could not increase the circulating media; that any increase in note issues "either comes back to them, or remains idle in the hands of the public,[20] and no rise takes place in prices." [21]

In the second state of the markets, it is not so obvious, thought Mill, that Tooke and Fullarton's theory is applicable. Special circumstances may arouse favorable expectations. Traders and producers desire to extend their operations. Speculators desire to lay in a stock in order to profit by the expected rise in price, and holders of commodities desire additional advances to enable them to continue holding. "Effects of the same kind may be produced by anything which, exciting more than usual hopes of profit, gives increased briskness to business: for example, a sudden foreign demand. . . . This is a state of business which, when pushed to an extreme length, brings on the revulsion called a commercial crisis; and it is a known fact that such periods of speculation hardly ever pass off without having been attended, during some part of their progress, by a considerable increase of bank notes." [22]

In this second case, Mill argued that when speculation has gone so far as to reach back into production—i.e., when speculative orders given by merchants has had the effect of expanding the operations of manufacturers—then the producers, as well as the merchants, will apply to banks for increased advances, which, if made in notes, are paid away in wages and pass into the various channels of retail trade, where they become directly effective in producing a further rise in prices. Between the "ascending period of speculation" and "the revulsion" the increase in note issue would thus tend to prolong the duration of the speculations. It "enables the speculative prices to be kept up for some time after

---

[20] Mill anticipated Keynes' liquidity preference—L_2—in the following: "Sometimes they [i.e., the public] keep money by them for fear of an emergency, or in expectation of a more advantageous opportunity for expending it." (Mill, *op. cit.*, p. 524.)

[21] *Ibid.*, p. 654.

[22] *Ibid.*, p. 655.

they would otherwise have collapsed; and therefore prolongs and increases the drain of the precious metals for exportation, which is the leading feature of this stage in the progress of the commercial crisis." This drain, however, eventually compels the banks "to contract their credit more suddenly and severely than would have been necessary had they been prevented from propping up speculation by increased advances, after the time when the recoil had become inevitable." To prevent this "retardation of the recoil, and ultimate aggravation of its severity is the object of the scheme for regulating the currency."[23] And Mill adds: "I think myself justified in affirming that the mitigation of commercial revulsions is the real, and only serious, purpose of the Act of 1844."[24]

The Peel Bank Act of 1844

Mill believed that the act was to a certain degree successful in its object of "arresting speculative extensions of credit at an earlier period, with a less drain of gold, and consequently by a milder and more gradual process."[25]

But these advantages are "purchased by still greater disadvantages," since the Act of 1844 restricts advances to the support of solvent firms once the revulsion has come. The invaluable service previously rendered by the Bank of England in making needed advances was "eminently conspicuous in the crisis of 1825–6."[26] The act withholds the very "medicine which the theory of the system prescribes as the appropriate remedy." If the act were not repealed, Mill thought it fairly certain that its provisions would be suspended, as they were in 1847, in every period of great commercial difficulty.[27]

"For these reasons it appears to me, that notwithstanding the beneficial operation of the Act of 1844 in the first stages of one kind of commercial crisis (that produced by over-speculation),

---

[23] *Ibid.*, p. 656.
[24] *Ibid.*, p. 657.
[25] *Ibid.*, p. 659.
[26] *Ibid.*, p. 663.
[27] *Ibid.*, p. 664.

it on the whole materially aggravates the severity of commercial revulsions." [28]

JOHN MILLS (1821–1896)

The paper read by John Mills of Manchester before the Manchester Statistical Society, December 11, 1867, on credit cycles and the origin of commercial panics,[29] appears to have greatly influenced British thinking on trade cycles throughout the last decades of the nineteenth century—and indeed in some measure down to the present day, as revealed in the stress laid on waves of optimism and pessimism.

While John Stuart Mill placed strong emphasis upon external accidental factors which initiated profit expectations, he assigned an important role to errors of optimism and pessimism as factors greatly intensifying the rise and decline. John Mills, however, finds the explanation of his "credit cycle" in a continuing rhythm in the psychology of businessmen.

Crises Are Not Accidents

Mills began his paper by noting that each successive commercial crisis (he notes six—1815, 1825, 1836–39, 1847, 1857, 1866) is promptly followed by a spate of pamphlets which deal only with proximate causes, "each crisis appearing to be the result of its own separate accident." [30] But he asks: "Can we not get beyond this primitive method of dealing with a problem so momentous?" The subject of commercial fluctuations would, he believed, acquire a new dignity if it struck roots far deeper than this level and proved itself "cognate with the sciences of the mind."

He has no doubt whatever about the periodicity of the cycle; [31] the "instances are already too numerous, regular, and persistent, to allow any foothold for a theory of fortuitous coinci-

[28] *Ibid.*, p. 673.

[29] John Mills, "Credit Cycles and the Origin of Commercial Panics," *Transactions of the Manchester Statistical Society*, 1867.

[30] *Ibid.*, p. 11.

[31] Deviations from an exact periodicity—1866 instead of 1867—he explained by accidental factors which cause a "small deflection from the ordinary course of things."

dence. There is no region of scientific enquiry in which the idea of so distinct and prolonged a series occurring *by accident* would not at once be scouted." [32]

Crises Are Not Due to Economic Institutions

This recurring phenomenon cannot, he thinks, be explained by economic institutions. The general conditions under which trade and commerce had been carried on during the preceding six decades exhibited no uniformity whatever. There had been, for example, a regime of inconvertible paper currency, a regime of free issues of convertible paper currency, and finally a regime of regulated issues upon a metallic basis. The laws of banking and mercantile association had been modified in every conceivable way.[33] The "elements which develop commercial crises are too deep and subtle to be conjured out of existence by any legislative manipulation of currencies." [34]

Psychological Factors in the Four-Phase Cycle

Mills divides the credit cycle into four phases: collapse, depression, activity, and excitement; or panic, post-panic, recoil period, and speculative period. He suggests that one must follow the order of the phenomena, and inquire into the nature of the changes they indicate, with a view to detecting the "existence of any corresponding order of things." [35] By patient use of this method, he thinks we shall meet with evidence leading up to the further generalization that the decades interposed between the great commercial crises are *normal* cycles of development of credit. Each phase of the cycle he regards as a necessary development. Each cycle is "composed of well-marked normal stages." And as credit is a thing of "moral" essence, the external character of each stage of its development is traced to a parallel change of mood. Thus he finds the whole subject "embraced under the wider generalisation of a normal tendency of the human mind." [36] In the

32 Mills, *op. cit.*, p. 14.
33 *Ibid.*, pp. 14–15.
34 *Ibid.*, p. 16.
35 *Ibid.*, p. 16.
36 *Ibid.*, p. 17.

course of our investigation, he says, we shall "probably find that the malady of commercial crisis is not, in essence, a matter of the *purse* but of the *mind*." [37] And regret it as we may, it seems as if these rapid mercantile mutations are as "inevitable as the periodical tempests which clear the atmosphere of tropical regions." With respect to any one of these decennial cycles we shall observe that—due allowance being made for incidental disturbances from wars, exceptional harvests, etc.—each stage is, in the main, like the same stages in other cycles.[38]

Broadly defined, panic is the destruction, in the mind, of a bundle of beliefs. The post-panic period is marked by a plethora of unused capital and dormancy of enterprise. "No doubt a new confidence begins to germinate early in this period, but its growth is slow. . . . Time alone can steady the shattered nerves, and form a healthy cicatrice over wounds so deep." [39] If, while matters stand thus, any favorable accident should happen, we find ourselves fairly in what we may call the revival period.[40]

This may be called the healthiest period. It is in this period that new commercial and manufacturing concerns mostly spring into existence. After "two or three years of lucrative trade, there must be a large percentage of new men, to whom the grim story of past panics, and of the nemesis of over-speculation, is a mere myth, or at most a matter of hear-say tradition." [41]

The "great majority of men habitually assume that what *is* is what *will* be; and it is under the influence of this idea that

---

[37] The psychological explanation is a leading thread running through Pigou's thinking on industrial fluctuations. "When expected facts are substituted for accomplished facts as the impulse to action, the way is opened for a second group of causes of industrial fluctuations, namely, psychological causes, which, at the beginning of Chapter IV, I distinguished from the 'real' causes there discussed. These causes consist in variations in the tone of mind of persons where action controls industry, emerging in errors of undue optimism or undue pessimism in their business forecasts." (A. C. Pigou, *Industrial Fluctuations,* Macmillan and Co., Ltd., London, 1927, p. 66).

[38] Mills, *op. cit.,* pp. 17–18.

[39] *Ibid.,* pp. 19, 21, 23–24.

[40] *Ibid.,* p. 24.

[41] *Ibid.,* p. 25. Compare with Schumpeter's view that the "neighborhood of equilibrium" provides a climate favorable for innovation and for the emergence of new men and new methods.

a healthy growth gradually merges into dangerous inflation." From these causes the revival period changes into the speculation period.[42]

With each of these four stages there appears to be a concurrent change in the mental mood of the trading public; and these changes are the same, cycle after cycle, decade after decade. These changes follow in the same relative order.[43]

ALFRED MARSHALL (1842–1924)

In 1879, Alfred Marshall (jointly with his wife) published, as we have already noted, a little book called *Economics of Industry.*[44] It contained two chapters dealing in large part with crises and depressions. While Marshall was not altogether happy in later years with this book, the parts dealing with the trade cycle continued to meet his approval. He made use of these sections in his testimony before the Gold and Silver Commission in 1887–88, and he reproduced the main analysis verbatim in his *Principles of Economics,* published in 1890, and in numerous subsequent editions. His thinking on the trade cycle did not develop over the years. It was cast pretty much in terms of the thinking of John Stuart Mill, and it reinforced John Mills' emphasis on psychological factors. The phenomena remained for him in essence a *commercial* and *financial* crisis, associated with fluctuations in the state of confidence. But there was a slight shift toward a more modern point of view.

Speculation and Credit

"The beginning of a period of rising credit is often a series of good harvests." Less is spent for food, leaving an increased demand for other things. Producers expect rising profits and are prepared to pay good prices. They compete for labor, and wages rise. Employed workers spend more on all kinds of goods. There is a "general rise in the incomes of those who trade." Many specu-

[42] *Ibid.*

[43] *Ibid.,* p. 29.

[44] A. and M. P. Marshall, *Economics of Industry,* Macmillan and Co., London, 1879 (reprinted in 1881, 1883, 1884, 1885, 1886, and 1888).

lators buy on the expectation of a further rise in prices. Often they borrow from bankers and others; and "everyone who thus enters the market as a buyer, adds to the upward tendency of prices."[45]

This movement goes on until at last an enormous amount of trading is being carried on by credit and with borrowed money. Trade is in a dangerous condition. Those who have money are among the first to read the signs of the time. They begin to go about contracting their loans. But this is disturbing to trade. "Trading companies of all kinds have borrowed vast sums with which they have begun to build railways and docks and ironworks and factories." Building costs rise, and this forces these companies to come again into the market to borrow more capital. The demand for more loans raises the rate of interest. It becomes more difficult to borrow. Distrust begins to spread. Some speculators are forced to sell to pay their debts. Other speculators rush in to sell. Some are ruined, and their failures cause others to fail. "As credit by growing makes itself grow, so when distrust has taken the place of confidence, failure and panic breed panic and failure. The commercial storm leaves its path strewn with ruin. When it is over there is a calm, but a dull heavy calm. Those who have saved themselves are in no mood to venture again." New companies cannot be formed. "Coal, iron and other materials for making Fixed capital fall in price." Ironworks and shops are for sale.[46]

After every crisis, in every period of commercial depression, the warehouses are overstocked with goods in almost every important trade. "And it is thought that this state of things is one of general over-production. We shall however find that it really is nothing but a state of commercial disorganization; and that the remedy for it is a revival of confidence."[47]

The Role of Confidence

Marshall then quotes approvingly Mill's classic statement of Say's Law—that the means of payment for commodities is simply

---

[45] *Ibid.*, p. 152.
[46] *Ibid.*, pp. 152–153.
[47] *Ibid.*, p. 154.

commodities; all sellers are buyers; double the supply of commodities and you double the purchasing power.[48] But Marshall does not stop there. He adds that though men have the power to purchase, they may not choose to use it, for when confidence has been shaken, capital cannot be got to start new companies or extend old ones. "Projects for new railroads meet with no favour, ships lie idle, and there are no orders for new ships." There is scarcely any demand for building and the engine-making trades. "In short, there is but little occupation in any of the trades which make Fixed capital." Other trades find a poor market, produce less, and so buy less from still other trades. "Thus commercial disorganization spreads." [49]

"The chief cause of the evil is a want of confidence. The greater part of it could be removed almost in an instant if confidence could return, touch all industries with her magic wand, and make them continue their production, and their demand for the wares of others." The trades making consumers' goods could simply supply one another with the means of earning profits and wages. "The trades which make Fixed capital might have to wait a little longer, but they would get employment when confidence had revived so far that those who had capital to invest had made up their minds how to invest it." Confidence would feed on itself, credit would expand, and prices would recover. And "soon there would be a good demand even for the work of those who make Fixed capital." The "revival of industry comes about through the gradual and often simultaneous growth of confidence among many various trades; it begins as soon as traders think that prices will not continue to fall: and with a revival of industry prices rise."

Neglect of the Saving-Investment Problem

The reader will note that there is here no place for any conception of the possibility of temporary *saturation* in the market for durable or capital goods, whether consumers' durables like

---

[48] J. B. Say, *Traité d'économie politique*, Paris, 1803. An American edition and translation was published in 1857 by J. B. Lippincott and Company, Philadelphia, under the title *A Treatise on Political Economy*.

[49] Marshall, *op. cit.*, p. 154.

homes, or producers' durable equipment. There is no recognition of the declining schedule of the marginal efficiency of capital. There is no discussion of the real factors which underlie the demand for fixed capital. The trouble is conceived to lie exclusively in the *minds* of businessmen. If they *thought* everything was all right, so the argument seems to run, everything would be all right. But Marshall offers little or no analysis of the real factors underlying changing expectations.

In line with his analysis Marshall suggests that the most plausible of all the various proposals to cure the trade cycle is the suggestion that the government, in times of depression, should guarantee each separate industry against risk. Thus each would start to produce and each would buy the other's product. The only trouble Marshall sees with this plan is that it would not distinguish the competent from the incompetent risks, and that the guarantee might hinder that "freedom on which energy and the progress of invention depend." He does not see that, in the absence of new investment opportunities, such a guarantee could not provide full employment, since some part of income would be saved. The Lauderdale-Malthus analysis is overlooked or regarded as invalid. A convincing saving-investment analysis had still to be developed in the future. Marshall's argument might indeed be valid in a society in which *all* the income was spent on consumers' goods.

Reckless Credit the Chief Cause of Economic Malaise

Marshall himself believed that the "only effective remedy for unemployment is a continuous adjustment of means to ends, in such a way that credit can be based on the solid foundation of fairly accurate forecasts; and that reckless inflations of credit—the chief cause of all economic malaise—may be kept within narrower limits." [50]

The Role of Fixed Capital

Marshall noted (and this indicates an advance over the work of J. S. Mill) that the "demand for Fixed capital is liable to more extreme fluctuations than the demand for commodities that are

---

[50] Alfred Marshall, *Principles of Economics,* Macmillan and Co., Ltd., London, 7th ed., p. 710.

wanted for immediate consumption, and the trades which make Fixed capital are more affected than any others by alternations of commercial prosperity and adversity." He shows that the price of pig iron rose "more rapidly than almost any other prices in the years preceding each of the crises of 1837, 1847, 1857 and 1866; and it fell more rapidly than most other prices in the years following each of these crises." Nearly the same may be said of the building trades as of the iron trades.[51]

Marshall explained the great fluctuations in the price of iron partly on the ground that a rise in price does not quickly increase the supply of iron itself or of the equipment needed in its manufacture and partly on the ground that the demand for iron is subject to violent changes, since it is chiefly used in making "machines, railroads, and other forms of Fixed capital." [52] Here Marshall anticipates, in a measure, the stress placed, in the later development of business-cycle theory, upon the role of investment in fixed capital.

Prices are liable to great fluctuations, says Marshall, in trades in which there is a great use of fixed capital. The reason assigned for this is that, since variable costs are relatively a small proportion of total cost, prices can fall very low before output is curtailed. On the other hand, high prices will not tempt new investment in an industry using much fixed capital unless there is reason to expect that the price will be maintained for a long time. "The price of coal may therefore rise far before any attempt is made to increase the supply by opening up new mines; and even after that, a considerable time will elapse before the supplies from the new mines can exert any influence." [53]

Disorganization of Credit and Production

Thus it was in the "organization of production and of credit" that Marshall sought the causes of depression and crisis. "It is true that in times of depression the disorganization of consumption is a contributory cause to the continuance of the disorganization of credit and of production. But the remedy is not to be

---

[51] *Ibid.*, p. 163.
[52] *Ibid.*
[53] *Ibid.*, p. 162. Compare with Aftalion's analysis, Chapter 18 in this book.

got by a study of consumption as has been alleged by some hasty writers." [54]

Marshall agreed that economists had not brought the main study needed—that of the organization of production and credit—to a successful issue, but he thought this due to the "profound obscurity and ever changing form of the problem." Economists, he said, are not indifferent to its supreme importance. "Economics from beginning to end is a study of the mutual adjustments of consumption and production." [55]

There is here only a hint of the saving-investment problem and of the real factors underlying fluctuations in the rate of investment. Accidental disturbances, speculation, and reckless inflation of credit are regarded as mainly responsible for the trade cycle. The "rapidity of invention, the fickleness of fashion, and above all the instability of credit" remained for Marshall the main disturbing factors which account for the shifting expectations of the business community.

In his last book, *Money, Credit and Commerce,* Marshall repeats again what he said in 1879.[56] He never got any farther with the problem. There is no evidence that the new developments, starting with Wicksell and the Continental Investment school,

---

[54] Marshall, *Principles of Economics,* p. 712.

[55] *Ibid.* Marshall calls attention (*Principles,* pp. 687–688) to the considerable unemployment of the medieval artisan and of "those industries of Eastern and Southern Europe in which medieval traditions are strongest." When a modern factory closes down everybody knows it. But few people know "when an independent workman, or even a small employer, gets only a few days' work in a month." There is thus a tendency to exaggerate the notion that unemployment is a problem of large-scale modern industry.

That there was much disguised unemployment prior to the introduction of the modern system of production is certainly true, but when a large factory goes on half time, not only does everybody know it, as Marshall pointed out, but more important is the fact that the unemployment is *concentrated* on those who are dismissed rather than spread over the whole. It was one of the virtues of Sir Hubert Llewellyn Smith's testimony before the Parliamentary Committee on Distress from Want of Employment, that he noted not merely that employment, under the modern organization of industry, is concentrated heavily in the "cyclical trades," but also that *complete* dismissal is concentrated on a *part* of the workers. In medieval towns, whatever distress was suffered was broadly shared by everybody. This aspect of the matter Marshall did not adequately assess.

[56] Alfred Marshall, *Money, Credit and Commerce,* Macmillan and Co., Ltd., London, 1923.

had made any impression on his thinking or that he recognized the significance of their contributions for business-cycle analysis. He refers again in this final volume to "that excessive confidence which causes a violent expansion of credit and rise in prices." Fluctuations in expectations and confidence, together with the induced movements of credit and prices, remained for Marshall the essence of the trade cycle.

Expectations, to be sure, play a highly important role, as we shall see, in the analysis of the investment demand schedule, but it was not in these terms that Marshall envisaged the problem.

16 · *The Role of Investment:*
TUGAN-BARANOWSKY · SPIETHOFF SCHUMPETER · CASSEL · ROBERTSON

MICHEL TUGAN-BARANOWSKY (1865-1919) [1]

We begin first with Tugan-Baranowsky's interesting analysis of the different theories of crises up to the end of the nineteenth century. This will serve not only as an introduction to Tugan-Baranowsky's own theory, but also as a supplement to the preceding three chapters, in which we have surveyed the early conceptions and also the development of business-cycle theory in England from Lauderdale to Marshall. Tugan-Baranowsky's summary is particularly to be welcomed since, except for his treatment of Jevons, his discussion relates to the early continental theories, and not to the early English theories which we have considered in the preceding chapters.

Tugan-Baranowsky classified all theories into three groups: (1) the theories of production (Jevons); (2) the theories of exchange, credit, and monetary circulation (de Laveleye, Juglar); and (3) the theories of distribution of income (Sismondi, Rodbertus). All these are efforts to explain that enigmatic phenomenon —the cycical character of industrial life, the successive phases of

1 In this entire section on Tugan-Baranowsky, I have endeavored to give a precise and carefully paraphrased summary of his *Les Crises industrielles en Angleterre* (1913), especially Part II, Chapters II and III.

upswing and depression. But so far, says Tugan-Baranowsky, economic science has not been able to offer a solution for this difficult problem.

Jevons and the Role of Harvests [2]

Many economists have sought to show that the periodic industrial crises spring from periodic fluctuations of crops. In fact, however, the industrial cycle is regulated, says Tugan-Baranowsky, by its own laws, which are quite independent of harvest movements.

The ingenious theory of Jevons—relating the periodicity of crises to the periodicity of sun spots—is not supported, in Tugan-Baranowsky's view, by the facts. In order to get his neat periodicity figures, Jevons is obliged to resort to forced interpretations. He omits certain crises altogether, and includes doubtful ones. In general, the industrial cycle has, Tugan-Baranowsky believes, no exact periodicity. It varies from seven to eleven years. The industrial cycle is not based on astronomical phenomena subject to a rigorous mathematical periodicity. Instead, industrial fluctuations are tied to characteristics inherent in the nature of the economy itself.

Exchange, Credit, and Monetary Circulation: de Laveleye, Juglar

De Laveleye [3] argues that crises are invariably preceded by an export of gold. Other circumstances vary: this one is invariable. Accordingly he concludes that the loss of gold is the true cause of crises. Immediately the reserves of the Bank of England diminish, credit is restricted, alarm spreads through the country, and commodity prices fall.

But, says Tugan-Baranowsky, the change in the balance of payments is a secondary phenomenon which itself needs to be explained. These movements are symptoms of industrial cycles. Moreover, the loss of gold, while preceding violent crises, did not precede the long periods of stagnation which, toward the end of the nineteenth century, characterized English industry.

---

2 W. S. Jevons, *Investigations in Currency and Finance,* Macmillan & Co., Ltd., London, 1884.

3 E. de Laveleye, *Le Marché monetaire et ses crises depuis cinquante ans,* 1865.

Juglar,[4] says Tugan-Baranowsky, has the distinction of being the first to demonstrate the high periodicity of industrial fluctuations in England, France, and the United States. After studying the accounts of the Bank of England, the Bank of France, and the leading American banks, Juglar came to the following conclusion: Without interposing any theory or hypothesis, observation of the facts suffices to disclose the law of crises and their periodicity. Epochs of activity, prosperity, and high prices always end in crises, and these are followed by some years of depressed activity and low prices.

Wars, droughts, abuse of credit, excessive issues of bank notes—all these are not able to provoke an industrial crisis if the general economic situation does not warrant it. They may hasten the arrival of a crisis, but only when the economic situation is such that a crisis is inevitable. The industrial crisis does not come abruptly; it is always preceded by a high animation of industry and commerce whose symptoms are so characteristic that it is possible to forecast the approach of a crisis.

Whence comes this regular succession of periods of activity and depression? Juglar, says Tugan, can find only one primary cause: the periodic fluctuation in commodity prices. The period of prosperity which precedes the crisis is always characterized by high prices. As prices rise, exports become difficult, the balance of payments becomes less favorable, gold flows out. The crisis approaches when the price movement slows down. In a word, the unique cause of the crisis is the cessation of the price rise.

But Juglar's theory does not resolve, says Tugan-Baranowsky, the problem of crises. If one compares it with de Laveleye's one sees that Juglar has indeed moved a step forward. He has shown that the monetary difficulties which signal the approach of the crisis are only secondary phenomena associated with the price movements. But there is no really satisfactory explanation for the factor which Juglar regarded as at the bottom of the problem of crises: the fluctuation of prices.

Tugan's discussion no doubt underrates the contribution made by Juglar. The vast assemblage of data in Juglar's "great book of facts" laid bare successive phases in a recurring movement. Thus

[4] Clément Juglar, *Des Crises commerciales,* 1st ed., 1860; 2nd ed., 1889.

Juglar was one of the first to see that the problem is not one of *crises* but one of *cycles.* Moreover, he regarded depression as the inevitable result of the maladjustments of the boom phase of the cycle. In this sense prosperity could be regarded as the unique cause of the depression.[5]

Distribution of Income: Sismondi, Rodbertus

The third group of theories finds the explanation of crises in the domain of income distribution. Sismondi's [6] theory of markets is at the same time a theory of crises. The cause of the crisis phenomenon is inadequate consumption, due to the poverty of the masses. The market for industrial products is too restricted, compared with the productive capacity of modern industry.

But, says Tugan-Baranowsky, the history of crises contradicts this doctrine. If one accepted this theory, the prosperity which follows each depression would be absolutely incomprehensible. The crisis, and the stagnation which follows, certainly does not enrich the people; it impoverishes them. How, then, after some years of depression, is a revival of prosperity possible? If this theory were correct, the poverty of the people would prevent any expansion of industry. Industrial stagnation would become chronic. Now in fact one observes something quite different—namely, a rapid growth of production, notwithstanding the interruptions caused by periods of depression.

This simple observation, says Tugan-Baranowsky, shows that the theory which finds the cause of industrial crises in the insufficient consumption of the people must be erroneous. According to this principle we should expect to find chronic stagnation, not a periodic recurrence of the cycle. Put in modern terms, a low propensity to consume might explain continuous underemployment equilibrium, but not cyclical oscillations. Sismondi, as was also true of Lauderdale and Malthus, was trying to explain unemployment and depression, but he offered no explanation of the *cycle.*

To the same group belongs the theory of Rodbertus with his

[5] See J. A. Schumpeter, *Business Cycles,* McGraw-Hill Book Company, 1939, p. 139; also *Quarterly Journal of Economics,* February, 1950, p. 149.

[6] Sismondi, *Nouveaux Principes d'Economie Politique,* 2nd edition, 1827.

iron law of wages. According to this law, wages are always at the minimum of subsistence, while productivity increases with industrial progress. New techniques augment the output of workers, but the worker continues to receive the same low wage. Thus the *relative share* of the worker falls with the progress of technique.

Logically the theory of Rodbertus,[7] says Tugan-Baranowsky, is well constructed. Unlike Sismondi's it does not consider the *absolute* poverty of the workers as causing the crisis, but rather the fact that the workers' *share* diminishes with technical progress. Thus Rodbertus finds the cause of the crisis, not in an excess of production, but rather in a lack of proportionality in the distribution of the product.

The defect in this theory, according to Tugan-Baranowsky, is that it does not accord with the facts. The iron law of wages does not conform to the cyclical movement of wages, since in fact wages rise in the period of prosperity. Moreover, it is those branches of industry which produce capital goods that suffer the most from crises and depressions, not those which produce consumers' goods for the working classes.

Thus Tugan-Baranowsky concludes that none of the theories examined can explain the cycle; it still remains enigmatic and incomprehensible.

A Turning Point in Business-Cycle Theory

We come now to Tugan's own analysis, which represents a violent break with the past. In one sense there is "nothing new under the sun," at least not in economics. It has been said that there is not a new idea in Adam Smith; yet this book turned economic thinking upside down. In some measure, the same can be said about Tugan-Baranowsky with respect to business-cycle theory. He cut his way through the jungle to a new outlook. He began a new way of thinking about the problem.

The history of crises in England, he begins, reveals a recurrent ebb and flow of economic life. The cycle is long or short according to the concrete economic conditions of each historical period. The cycle is not a phenomenon regulated by a mathematical law.

[7] Tugan-Baranowsky's reference to Rodbertus' principal exposition of his theory is to his "Letters" addressed to Kirchmann.

Crises have recurred at intervals of seven to eleven years. The movement is periodic in the sense that there occur successive phases of prosperity and depression which rise and fall like a cycle. The industrial cycle may be conceived of as a law inherent in the very nature of the capitalist economy.

The problem of crises can only be resolved, says Tugan, by leaning on a good theory of markets. Now most representatives of contemporary economic science, he points out, hold at bottom a warped theory of markets, namely, Say's Law. It is therefore no wonder, he thinks, that economists have found no solution of the business cycle.

There follows then a discussion which runs very much along the same lines as that developed by Malthus. As with Malthus, the analysis suffers from the absence of the concept of the consumption function.

Thanks to the money and credit economy, says Tugan-Baranowsky, all the oscillations of the economy acquire a much greater amplitude. But monetary factors only aggravate the cycle. Money is not the primary cause. The industrial cycle has its roots deep in the very nature of the capitalist economy. The inherent characteristics of the modern economy render the cycle inevitable.

That, however, does not explain why the phases of prosperity and depression succeed each other with such amazing regularity. The history of the industrial cycle, however, gives the answer.

The Role of Iron and Instruments of Production

The most characteristic feature of these industrial fluctuations, according to Tugan, is the coincidence of the movements of the *price of iron* with the phases of the cycle. The price of iron is invariably high in prosperity and low in depression. The prices of other products oscillate with much less regularity. This indicates a close relation between the *fluctuation in the demand for iron* and the phases of the cycle. The demand for iron rises in the period of prosperity and falls in the period of depression. Now iron is the material used in making the *instruments* of production. One can estimate the demand for the means of production in general by the demand for iron.[8] The expanding phase of the cycle is then characterized by the augmentation of the demand for the means of production, the descending phase by the decline in this demand.

Now the means of production (iron, coal, timber, etc.) are strongly in demand when large additions are made to the fixed capital of the country—railroads, factories, buildings, houses. The phase of prosperity is the period of very active construction, the creation of new industrial enterprises.

A characteristic of many crises is the speculation in real estate. These are the outgrowth of the expansion of fixed capital, but they are symptoms, not causes, of the industrial cycle.

Fluctuations in the Output of Fixed Capital

The branches of production which disclose the most violent fluctuations are those which produce fixed capital goods. These fluctuations are reflected in a general rise and fall in economic activity throughout industry. The reason for this is the interdependence of the various branches of industry in the whole economy.

The production of fixed capital creates a demand for other goods. In order to create new enterprises, it is necessary to procure the primary materials of production, namely consumption goods for the workers. Expansion of output in one branch increases the demand for the products of other industries. Thus in the period of rapid growth in fixed capital accumulation one observes a general augmentation in the demand for goods.

Here, in a general way, is a description of the multiplier process. But lacking the concept of the marginal propensity to consume, Tugan-Baranowsky was not able to make a precise formulation of the problem.

The Saving-Investment Analysis

But why does not the growth of fixed capital proceed steadily, bit by bit, instead of by violent leaps and bounds? The explana-

8 Cassel's indebtedness to Tugan-Baranowsky is evident here. See discussion of Cassel later in this chapter.

tion, says Tugan-Baranowsky, must be found in the conditions underlying the accumulation of capital in the modern economic order.

The discussion which follows is highly significant for the development of the saving-investment analysis, but there are nonetheless some important gaps which had to be filled by others. Tugan-Baranowsky, however, started a stream of thinking among Continental economists which, fed from another source (namely, Wicksell), finally emerged in the modern theory perfected by Keynes.

Free Capital and Productive Real Capital

In all rich capitalist countries, says Tugan-Baranowsky, free capital, which is not yet embodied as fixed capital in any branch of industry, rapidly accumulates under the prevailing economic conditions. This capital makes its appearance in the market in the form of disposable capital or loanable funds. It is free capital. The banks are reservoirs into which this disposable capital flows and from which it is distributed as loanable funds. Now one must be careful, he says, not to confuse the accumulation of loanable funds with the growth of productive real capital. The growth of loanable funds (free capital) does not per se imply any accumulation of real capital or any increase in fixed-capital formation. The difference between productive capital and loan capital is clearly seen in the case of government loans. Let us assume, he suggests, that the state places loans for unproductive purposes. The creditors of the state are the capitalists who advance the loanable funds, and they remain as creditors after the funds are spent. The increase of government debt does not augment the real productive capital of the country. Nevertheless, government securities are regarded as capital no less than the securities issued by industrial enterprises which represent real capital.

Thus the accumulation of loanable capital is something entirely different from the growth of real productive capital. The loanable funds can accumulate not only when there goes on an expansion of production but even when production declines. In fact, loanable funds do accumulate, says Tugan-Baranowsky, in such conditions.

In the capitalist society, there are several kinds of incomes which depend very little, or not at all, upon the general movement of the national income. The most fluctuating incomes are the profits of enterpreneurs; next are the earnings of workers. These two fluctuate with the cycle. But some incomes are derived from fixed yields that are quite independent of the various phases of the cycle. Thus, for example, the interest payments on bonds and mortgages do not vary with prosperity and depression. Income from real estate is often fixed over long periods. All told, the sum total of incomes which do not fluctuate, or fluctuate very little with the cycle, constitutes a considerable fraction of the national income. And the fixed-income groups, who gain in purchasing power when prices fall, are often able to augment their current savings. Without doubt, the accumulation of loanable cash funds proceeds with more regularity than the formation of fixed capital. Loanable funds accumulate steadily, but their conversion into productive capital proceeds by leaps.

Many times, in the course of his descriptive analysis of each crisis in English history, Tugan-Baranowsky had occasion to call attention to the considerable accumulation of bank reserves immediately after the end of each crisis. At the same moment the savings deposits of individuals in the banks are increased. This indicates the accumulation of disposable cash funds seeking investment outlets. The low rate of discount which follows a crisis and which persists for some years bears testimony to the superabundance of uninvested funds. In general, the prosperity phase is characterized by a considerable investment of capital (via the transformation of free capital into fixed capital); the depression phase is characterized by an accumulation of loanable, free, mobile capital.[9]

This is so evident, says Tugan-Baranowsky, that a number of economists, especially J. S. Mill, have concluded that the immediate cause of the revival is the low rate of interest; this provokes the speculation in the money market which leads to the ensuing collapse. Mill is perfectly right, says Tugan-Baranowsky, in calling attention to the rapid accumulation of loanable capital after the crisis which causes a low rate of interest and favors the

---

[9] Compare this terminology with Cassel's "disposable capital."

development of speculation. But he completely ignores the more profound factors inherent in an economy using capital goods.

The accumulation of loanable cash funds continues, as we have seen, in all phases of the cycle; but the embodiment of this free capital into the form of productive capital, the investment of the loanable funds in industry, encounters an obstacle. The presence of this obstacle is indubitable. During the stagnation years, the market overflows with loanable funds. In order to transform this capital into productive capital, a certain proportionality in the allotment of disposable capital among the different branches of production is needed. Now in arriving at this proportional distribution, one encounters, in view of the anarchy of the individualistic competitive economy, a great difficulty. The following situation develops: The disposable, loanable cash funds accumulate steadily; they energetically seek investment outlets, but none can be found. Uninvested capital earns no interest. But the larger the accumulation of inactive capital, the greater the pressure to find an outlet into productive investment. On the one side industry is saturated with capital, and on the other the new free capital, daily accumulating, endeavors to force itself into industry. A moment finally arrives when the resistance of industry is vanquished; the loanable funds find outlets here and there and begin to be transformed into productive capital. A new period of prosperity begins.

In the transformation of loanable capital into productive capital, the first step alone is difficult. By reason of the mutual interdependence of all industry, expansion in one direction tends to spread over the whole economy. The loanable funds or disposable capital may take the form of idle deposits in banks, thus representing latent purchasing power. This purchasing power, which accumulates in bad years, exercises no influence on the market for goods, since the loanable capital is not invested. But when for one reason or another an investment outlet is found, then latent purchasing power transforms itself into effective purchasing power. A new productive capital is created which increases the demand both for means of production and for objects of consumption. Industry finds a new market, created by the expansion of production itself, by reason of the expenditure of enormous loanable funds which before had remained inactive in the banks. It matters not, so far as industry is concerned, what is the origin of the unexpected growth of demand. What is important is that the demand grows and grows until it absorbs all the accumulated loanable funds. Prices rise and production expands all along the line. The upswing phase is kept up by the continued creation of productive capital goods.

Some years pass by. The accumulated loanable funds are bit by bit exhausted. Without doubt the expansion of production creates a considerable quantity of new free saving. But the market rapidly absorbs it all, since the entrepreneurs are eager to take advantage of the favorable situation. Each one seeks to get all the capital he can for his enterprise. All capital reserves are used. The extraordinary expansion of credit, so characteristic of this phase of the industrial cycle, is indicative of the intensive investment of capital. The high rate of interest which one observes toward the end of this phase of the cycle is a certain proof of the exhaustion of loanable funds.

Let us pause here and take stock. According to Tugan-Baranowsky, prosperity is ushered in via an expansion of investment. This leads (if we apply modern concepts to Tugan's analysis) to the multiplier process via an induced rise in consumption. But it is the increase in investment which generates prosperity.

Now this analysis turns the tables upside down. Tugan's theory is the opposite of Sismondi's, for example. *Investment* is the prime mover. And when it moves forward, it pulls up with it all other branches of the economy, including the consumption goods industries. Income, in Keynesian language, rises by a multiple of the net increment of investment. This is the doctrine expounded by Tugan-Baranowsky.

And the expansion is financed from three sources: (1) idle balances, (2) the growth in current savings generated out of the enlarged income, and (3) expansion of bank credit.

The creation of new productive capital comes to an end when the loanable capital is exhausted. Thus the industrial crisis follows the financial crisis. Depression arrives after the creation of productive capital has suffered a decline.

Tugan-Baranowsky refers to the remarkable article by John

Mills on credit cycles. But he finds it unsatisfactory. Mills tells only one side of the story—the psychological phenomena which accompany the industrial cycle. He neglects completely the objective causes of the cycle. In the end it is cold objective facts that control, not simply psychological moods of optimism and pessimism. The hour of reckoning comes sooner or later.

The Boom and the Upper Turning Point

The period of prosperity is generated, according to Tugan-Baranowsky, out of the expenditure of the accumulated loanable funds. Necessarily this backlog of latent purchasing power is eventually used up. During the period of prosperity new fixed capital is created. Production is directed toward the output of iron, machines, tools, construction materials. Finally the new capital is completed—new factories, new houses, new ships, new railroad lines. The demand for all the materials used in the production of fixed capital suffers a decline. Few new industries are started. But the producers of machines, tools, iron, tile, and lumber are not able to withdraw their capital from their enterprises, and with heavy capital investments in plant and equipment, they are under pressure to continue production. There follows a saturation, an overproduction, of the means of production—capital goods of all kinds. This partial overproduction of the instruments of production, by reason of the interdependence of the different branches of industry, results in a general overproduction. Prices fall. A period of general economic decay ensues.

Lack of Proportionality

It is, moreover, evident, he says, that the general decline in the number of new enterprises necessarily causes a derangement in the proportional distribution of the productive forces. The equilibrium of aggregate demand and aggregate supply is shattered. Since the new enterprises create an enlarged demand not only for producers' goods but also for consumers' goods (the multiplier effect) it follows that, once new enterprises fall off, the branches of industry which furnish consumers' goods also suffer a decline in demand no less than those which furnish the means of production. The "overproduction" becomes general.

In Tugan-Baranowsky's somewhat equivocal language, the explanation of the "overproduction" is to be found in the lack of proportionality between the different branches of production.[10] The productive capacity of society has outrun the power of consumption. In other words, it is a saving-investment problem. Difficulties arising in the domain of money and credit, says Tugan-Baranowsky, are merely secondary phenomena, which result from the fundamental lack of proportionality in the area of saving and investment. This is clearly what Tugan-Baranowsky is driving at when he speaks of the productive forces outrunning the power of consumption.

Quite apart from the repercussions following a decline in new industries, there is another factor which leads to disproportionality in production. In the prosperity phase, some branches enjoy a greater expansion than others. They offer a rich field for speculation. At the end of the ascending phase of the cycle the proportionality of production is accordingly disturbed, and a new balance can only be restored through a destruction of a part of the capital of those branches of industry which have had an excessive expansion.

Thus a general stagnation follows the upswing, and the cycle passes from the phase of prosperity to the phase of depression. During the depressed phase, disposable or free capital (loanable funds) accumulates; then comes a new period of prosperity during which this "free capital" is spent on fixed capital—and the latent purchasing power becomes activated. Eventually comes the crisis, and we start all over again.

The Analogy of the Steam Engine

The working of this mechanism Tugan-Baranowsky compares to the operation of a steam engine. It is the accumulation of loanable capital which plays the role of the steam in the cylinder; when the pressure of the steam against the piston attains a certain force, the piston is set in motion, and is pushed to the end of the cylinder; here the steam escapes and the piston returns to its former position. The accumulated loanable funds operate in the

---

10 Compare with Schumpeter's period of readjustment following a period of rapid innovations. See discussion later in this chapter.

same manner in industry when they reach a certain volume. The funds are set in motion—i.e., expended on fixed capital goods. Once the loanable funds are exhausted, industry returns to its former position. In this manner crises recur periodically.

Consumption and Investment

The capitalist economy is subject to laws inherent in its own inner nature. Common sense is a poor guide toward an understanding of these laws. The capitalist system is highly complex. Each individual member of society is guided by his personal interests. But the collective end result of all these individual volitions, each independent of the other, is something qualitatively different. Here we encounter the logician's "fallacy of composition." What is true for the individual is not necessarily true for the group. The laws of movement of the complex whole are not determined by the volition of individuals, but on the contrary each individual is subject to the laws of the whole. With regard to the cycle, this antinomy arises conspicuously. On the one hand, investment is the only means of satisfying the propensity to save; but on the other hand investment can have no meaning except as the means of supplying the needs of consumers. On a commonsense basis, investment is for the purpose of supplying consumption needs. Yet in reality, in the capitalist economy, the relation between investment and consumption is reversed. In the prosperity phase, it is not an increase in consumption which commands an increase in investment; it is investment which regulates consumption. The phases of the industrial cycle are determined not by the laws of consumption but by the laws of investment.

Thus it is the fluctuations in the rate of investment that dominate and control the cycle; and consumption rises and falls in response to these movements. This is the theory, highly original [11]

---

[11] Keynes, in the *Treatise* (Vol. II, p. 100) says he finds himself in strong sympathy with that school of writers of which Tugan-Baranowsky was "the first and the most original," and especially with the form which the theory takes in the works of Tugan-Baranowsky himself.

Keynes then offers two criticisms (p. 101). The first, which follows Pigou, is, I think, not justified. Contrary to the Pigouvian interpretation, Tugan-Baranowsky's accumulations are purely monetary—idle balances. The second and essentially novel at the time he was writing, advanced by Tugan-Baranowsky.

A Fluctuating Rate of Investment vs. a Steady Rate of Saving

Combined with a fairly steady rate of saving from income, Tugan-Baranowsky sees a rather violent fluctuation in the rate of investment. In the prosperity phase, investment outruns current saving, and the difference between the two is filled by (a) the activation of idle balances (dishoarding) and (b) the expansion of bank credit. In the depression phase, investment falls below current saving, and the difference between them "runs to waste" in idle balances (hoarding) and repayment of debt to banks.[12] This is the nature of the cycle as Tugan-Baranowsky sees it. But his theory of investment demand is inadequate, and his explanation of the turning points is unsatisfactory. What is it, specifically, that starts investment on the upswing, and why does it turn down?

With Tugan-Baranowsky, investment is *pushed* up by the action of lenders eagerly seeking financial investment outlets. But this entirely leaves out of account the "pull" which comes from new technological developments and from *growth* in the economy. This is the most serious defect in Tugan-Baranowsky's analysis, and Spiethoff, as we shall soon find, was quick to see it. With respect to the downturn, Tugan's main explanation is the exhaustion of idle balances, which, together with the limits to bank credit expansion, forces a curtailment of investment. But there is also the suggestion, inadequately stated, of the temporary exhaustion of investment opportunities, the fall in the marginal efficiency of capital.

---

quite rightly touches on a weak link in Tugan-Baranowsky's chain—the role of unequal income distribution in promoting an unsteady rate of expansion.

Not wholly satisfied with Tugan-Baranowsky's treatment, Keynes then points to Schumpeter's important contribution to the theory of fluctuation.

[12] Tugan-Baranowsky's "saving" must be interpreted to mean the same thing as Robertson's saving out of "disposable" (i.e., yesterday's) income. Tugan's theory was the first of those cycle theories (of which Keynes' *Treatise on Money* was a variant) which stress the divergence of investment and saving.

ARTHUR SPIETHOFF (1873-)

The great influence of Tugan-Baranowsky's book on the whole course of business-cycle thinking after the turn of the century is revealed in the literature which rapidly appeared, especially the influential writings of Arthur Spiethoff and Gustav Cassel. Spiethoff's early articles carry on almost every page the imprint of Tugan-Baranowsky's analysis. In the case of Cassel, one can go further, and say that the ideas, and often even the forms of expression, come almost *en masse* from Tugan-Baranowsky. It is often said that Cassel's business-cycle theory was derived largely from Spiethoff, and this is indeed more or less true. There is, however, strong internal evidence that however much he may have drawn from Spiethoff, very much of it flowed directly from Tugan-Baranowsky. It is, of course, true that, in the process of reworking the whole subject matter, both Spiethoff and Cassel left the strong imprint of their own forceful and original thinking in the important contributions which they made. In the meantime, however, the fountainhead of this whole stream of thinking—Tugan-Baranowsky—has unfortunately been somewhat neglected.

Spiethoff himself, however, has warm praise for his predecessor. In his "Die Krisentheorien von M. v. Tugan-Baranowsky und L. Pohle" [13] he refers to Tugan-Baranowsky's work as the first scientific monograph on crises. On December 17, 1901, shortly after Tugan-Baranowsky's *Studien zur Theorie und Geschichte der Handelskrisen in England* had appeared in Germany,[14] Spiethoff delivered an address at a meeting of the Political Science Association in Berlin entitled "Vorbemerkungen zu einer Theorie der Überproduktion." [15] This address shows unmistakably how forcefully this new way of thinking about crises and the industrial cycle had captured the imagination of the young man who rapidly became the leading German specialist on business cycles.[16]

---

13 *Jahrbuch für Gesetzgebung, Verwaltung und Volkswirtschaft,* 1903.

14 Jena, 1901.

15 Published in *Jahrbuch für Gesetzgebung, Verwaltung und Volkswirtschaft,* 1902.

16 Tugan-Baranowsky, in his French edition (p. 277, note), refers to his earlier work as the point of departure for the studies of Spiethoff, Pohle, and others, who, he says, adopted it in whole or in part.

Factors Causing the Upswing

As we have already noted, the weakest part of Tugan-Baranowsky's exposition was his analysis of the causes underlying the fluctuations in investment. Why, asks Spiethoff, is there first a period in which large masses of loan capital are piled up without being invested, followed by a period of "stormy investment"? [17] And it is with respect to this point that Spiethoff made his most significant contribution.

Spiethoff accepted unreservedly Tugan-Baranowsky's view that the essential character of the industrial cycle is the fluctuation in the rate of investment, and also the conception (so radically different from that of the prevailing underconsumptionists) that investment is the dynamic factor, with consumption passively responding as income rises and falls.

With Spiethoff, prosperity begins in especially hopeful branches in which capital expects unusual profits, and from these there is developed a general impetus. First, existing production plants are brought into full use. There follows the second stage, in which new plants are built. These new plants swallow up a large volume of investment capital and constructional raw materials of different kinds. But while this construction is going on there is no counterbalancing output of finished goods. In the third stage of the cycle the new plants begin to turn out finished products. Finally, the "last period is the reverse of the second; a feverishly increased production throws its products on the market without being met by a like consumption." [18]

The upswing is initiated, not in the consumers' goods industries, but in the great industries which furnish the materials required for construction and the manufacture of equipment—iron, steel, lumber, cement, bricks, etc. Great tasks confront these industries, as the expansion gets under way, and when these are completed the "stormy demand" which dominates the boom phase comes to an end. Each upswing springs from exceptional investment opportunities, which provide a powerful impulse toward expansion. The impulse may come from investment in new ma-

---

[17] *Jahrbuch für Gesetzgebung, Verwaltung und Volkswirtschaft,* 1903, p. 696.

[18] Spiethoff, "Vorbemerkungen zu einer Theorie der Überproduktion," *Jahrbuch für Gesetzgebung, Verwaltung und Volkswirtschaft,* 1902, p. 730.

chinery and equipment by reason of new technological developments and inventions. Or it may come from the opening up of new opportunities in relatively undeveloped countries—new markets which require loans and investments from the advanced industrial countries. Whatever the impulse, the important fact is that, at the beginning of each great upswing, industry stands before a "vacuum"—namely, unsatisfied investment opportunities at home and abroad.

Investment Saturation

Eventually, these new requirements are met; industry becomes equipped with new capital facilities and new techniques; both the newly opened territories and the older industrial areas find themselves, to a degree, "saturated" with equipment.[19] But it is not merely a matter of new undertakings: there is also the replacement of old equipment with improved machinery. All this vast demand for new developments and improvements is, after some years of high investment activity, for the most part satisfied; and then a kind of saturation process *(Sättigungsprozess)* sets in. The then prevailing level of technique sets a fairly definite limit to the amount of capital goods—mines, iron and steel works, railroads, transportation equipment, locomotives, factories, machines, electrical apparatus—which can be usefully employed in production. While there is a vast latent demand for consumers' goods as a whole—a demand which is in general highly elastic with respect to both price and income—the demand for capital goods and for the materials needed for the construction of durable goods is highly inelastic and is eventually satisfied. It is then no longer a matter of "filling an empty vessel," but rather of "keeping it full." After the new plant, machinery, and equipment have been erected and installed, one does not build them all over again; there remains only the task of maintenance and replacement.[20] If one

[19] *Ibid.*

[20] "The demand for productive equipment and for durable consumers' goods is not continuous; and when an economy has been fully supplied with such goods, the plant and machines which produced them are thrown out of work. Once the iron industry of a country has produced the necessary railways, mere repair and upkeep are insufficient to keep the industry operating at capacity." Arthur Spiethoff, *Encyclopædia of the Social Sciences,* Vol. XI, pp. 513–517.

misjudges the "filling of the vacuum" and mistakenly considers it a case of "continuing demand," one will overshoot the mark, in view of the inelastic demand for capital goods.[21]

Spiethoff vs. Tugan-Baranowsky

We now see clearly the important new contribution made by Spiethoff. The expansion phase of the cycle—prosperity and boom—does not and cannot come merely from the pressure exerted by loanable funds seeking investment outlets in real capital formation. The period of high investment activity is mainly the result of a "pull," not a "push from behind." Technological developments and the opening up of new territory create a vacuum whose vast "suction power" pulls the economy forward in leaps and bounds. Discoveries and technological advances enlarge the "bucket of capital formation," and there is a crying need to get it filled. This is the period of prosperity; it is ushered in by autonomous investment.

But the need or usefulness of additional capital is rigorously limited. Once the bucket (whose size is fixed by the requirements of technological progress) is full, any additional capital formation rapidly becomes useless; the marginal efficiency of capital falls rapidly toward zero. Thus investment ceases; the period of prosperity comes to a dead stop.

Spiethoff stresses again and again the "saturation process." He who today buys a machine, or builds a factory or a house, has no need, like the man who buys a loaf of bread, to repeat the performance tomorrow or the next day; he must wait until perhaps ten or more years hence.

All this is very different from the explanation offered by Tugan-Baranowsky. Nevertheless, Spiethoff is prepared to support Tugan-Baranowsky's explanations of the boom and of the upper turning point as well as his own. He regards them as complementary, not contradictory. There can be a "push" as well as a "pull" in the upswing period, and at the upper turning point a

[21] Spiethoff, "Vorbemerkungen," p. 731. While Spiethoff's concepts are not sharply defined, it is quite clear from the context that his "inelastic demand for capital" means that once the "bucket is filled," the marginal efficiency of capital would fall rapidly toward zero with every further net addition to the stock of capital goods.

sharp *check* to further expansion, no less than a *petering out* of the forces of expansion. Spiethoff accordingly declared that the period of expansion may be halted not merely by the inelasticity of the demand for capital—the decline in the marginal efficiency of capital—but also by the limited supply of funds seeking investment (disposable capital). Thus there are, he believed, two rather rigorously fixed limits to the process of expansion: (1) from the side of the demand for real capital, and (2) from the side of the supply of disposable capital seeking investment outlets.

On both these grounds, he argued,[22] it is quite impossible that the expansionist movement could go on indefinitely on a balanced or proportional basis. The boom and the collapse may, of course, be artificially intensified by overspeculation and violent price movements. But quite apart from these more superficial factors, the basic fundamental causes are the two factors mentioned above—the inelastic demand for real capital and the limited supply of disposable capital.

Saving and Investment

The production of equipment is conditioned, Spiethoff explains, by an investment of free or disposable capital. At the beginning of a period of prosperity a very large mass of loanable capital, gathered during the depression, is available for investment. This mass is being added to continually, but is nevertheless constantly being absorbed. Eventually the time is reached when production can no longer lean back on the gatherings of depression but must look to the current flow of saving.[23]

At the upper turning point, then, as Spiethoff sees it, the production of fixed capital has grown beyond the prevailing needs and also beyond the available investment-seeking capital. Through these causes the production of fixed capital is undermined.

The influence spreads from the industries affected to other industries; and so general overproduction develops. In the en-

---

[22] Spiethoff, "Vorbemerkungen," p. 732.

[23] *Ibid.*, pp. 730–733; see also "Krisen," *Handwörterbuch der Staatswissenschaften* (1925), VI, p. 74.

suing depression new undertakings are looked upon with suspicion, and the possessors of free capital will rather let their stores lie idle or be satisfied with small interest than take steps toward investment in fixed capital.[24]

With the curtailment of the production of fixed capital there follows an unavoidable pressure on consumers' incomes, for both the profits of the employer and the rewards of labor will decline. With the resulting worsening of incomes, consumption is injured. Underconsumption follows from the fact that certain parts of the productive processes stand still.

The Impact of Fluctuations of Investment on Consumption

The fall in the rate of profit and the low reward of labor reduce consumption, the decreasing consumption lowers prices, the fall in prices reduces production still further, the curtailment in production diminishes again the reward of labor and the rate of profit. There arises a formal vicious circle, and the interdependent effect of the different lines of industry on one another nourishes and increases the tendency to depression.[25]

During depression the chief problem confronting the industrialist is that of reducing costs through increased productivity and labor-saving machinery. But these improvements intensify depression. Many plants lose their value because of the new technique. The labor-saving machinery may either displace workers or press many skilled workers into the ranks of the unskilled.[26]

During prosperity the income distribution does not affect the general expenditure, for even though a part of the income flows into the hands of the people who will not immediately consume it but instead will invest it in fixed capital, still these funds are not abstracted from the income flow. In depression, however, the unequal division of incomes does affect the general expenditure. This is true because that part of the income which is saved *is* likely in such periods to be abstracted from expenditure, since

24 Spiethoff, "Vorbemerkungen," pp. 737–738.
25 *Ibid.*, p. 741.
26 *Ibid.*, pp. 741–742.

it fails to find investment outlets, and is gathered instead into great idle masses of loan capital.[27]

Every limitation of production weakens afresh the buying and consuming power and is therefore a cause of the spread of the "overproduction" into other parts of the economy. It is therefore of the greatest importance that production be kept up as far as possible and not reduced except for the most pressing causes. It may be more profitable for the entrepreneur to sell a smaller quantity for higher prices rather than a greater quantity for lower prices, but depression and unemployment will be increased thereby. This is a case where the individual entrepreneur's interest in special branches is opposed to the general interest and where the cartel contributes to the injury of industry in general.[28]

The Role of Technology and New Territories

With Spiethoff, then, the "real difference between prosperity and depression consists in the increasing or decreasing production of fixed capital and in the decreasing or increasing store of investment-seeking capital."[29]

According to Spiethoff, prosperity is initiated when new territories or new inventions open up new opportunities for investment in fixed capital. The accumulation of idle loan capital during the depression produces after a while a corrective, but that alone is not sufficient. Through the pressure of the mobile loan capital, the rate of interest falls continually lower, and when this tendency coincides with the recovery of the rate of profit in industry a certain condition of equilibrium may be reached. But the entrepreneurs have need for *special* inducements for great investments, and without these a large production of fixed capital will not occur. If unusual opportunities for gain appear, an excessive production of fixed capital will probably ensue. If, on the other hand, great losses have recently been sustained, an exag-

---

27 *Ibid.*, p. 743; see also "Krisen," *Handwörterbuch der Staatswissenschaften* (1925), VI, p. 80.

28 Spiethoff, "Vorbemerkungen," p. 745.

29 *Ibid.*, p. 753.

gerated fear of the risks of investment will prevail. The production of fixed capital is therefore never uniformly progressive, but always proceeds by fits and starts and is followed by reaction and depression. Every false estimate of the future needs, every great technical change, must disturb the equilibrium of prices and the harmony of consumption and production.[30]

If we stand at the beginning of a new period of outstanding inventions, says Spiethoff, then the end of crises is not in sight. Moreover, the territories which are to be added to the European industrial *Kultur* carry similar obstacles and dangers, for every addition of new territory carries with it the tendency to excesses and overproduction. If industry is on the forward march in its extension to peoples who have not yet been made its subjects, then the outlook is not good for the prevention of periodic crises. But we may expect that by the progress of social reform, by a continued adaptation of the capitalistic method of production, the industrial catastrophes will take on a more and more civilized form and finally lose themselves in a milder crossing from prosperity to depression. This development is not a necessary one, but it is worthy, Spiethoff believes, of our earnest labor and effort, and it is also a possible one.[31]

According to Spiethoff, there is no reason to doubt that people will gradually be able to adjust themselves to the capitalistic process of production. The history of crises teaches that its character has largely changed, that we have overcome many "children's diseases" of the capitalistic manner of production.[32]

With respect to these longer-run developments, Spiethoff's analysis was overly optimistic. As outlets for investment declined, once the whole world was equipped with the modern technique, he believed that spurts of investment would subside and so the cycle would tend to die down. But he failed to ask the question whether consumption could *automatically* be expected to rise sufficiently, in relation to income, to fill the gap left by the receding

---

[30] *Ibid.*, pp. 748–749, 754–755.
[31] *Ibid.*, pp. 758–759.
[32] *Ibid.*, pp. 756–758.

tide of investment. No adequate analysis of this problem was made until the appearance of Keynes' *General Theory* in 1936.

Résumé of Tugan-Baranowsky and Spiethoff

In Tugan-Baranowsky's view, the rate of accumulation of free capital or loanable funds goes on steadily. But the accumulations of free capital are "pushed out" into real capital by a jerky process. Once a forward movement is started, expansion proceeds cumulatively because of the interdependence of industries. Any forward thrust spreads throughout the economy. It would keep on expanding more and more were it not for the "reining-in" effect due to the eventual exhaustion of "free capital." Similarly, the cumulative downward movement is sooner or later checked by the increasing pressure of loanable funds seeking real investment outlets. This stops the decline in investment and eventually starts it up again. The higher the propensity to save the greater the amplitude of the fluctuations.

Spiethoff asked why the flow of loanable funds might not move smoothly into investment *at a steady rate.* He offered the explanation that the boom is caused by a suction apparatus, so to speak—the investment vacuum created by technological inventions and the opening of new territories. But why the *fluctuations?* Why not a *steady* suction, and so a steady rate of investment?

Here it becomes necessary to draft into service *initiating* factors on the one side and a *cumulatively responsive mechanism* on the other side. If inventions and discoveries come unevenly like a throw of dice, these *intermittent* shocks may operate upon an economic structure capable of making *cyclical* adjustments. For this case, the Spiethoff analysis is adequate. But suppose these external shocks are distributed *evenly* over time. Suppose there is a steady rate of progress in inventions and discoveries. What then? The answer given by various theorists is that even so the response of the economic structure to these exogenous factors may still produce a cyclical movement. In this case, however, something more is needed than the analyses thus far made. And so we turn to Joseph A. Schumpeter.

JOSEPH A. SCHUMPETER (1883–1950)

The Innovation Process

Schumpeter enters into the argument with his concept of "innovation." *Invention* may indeed proceed at a uniform rate, but *innovation* (given the herdlike characteristic of entrepreneurs) cannot do so in the very nature of the case. Innovation necessarily wells up in a great tidal wave, and then recedes. That is the inherent nature of the process of innovation.[33] Thus the business cycle consists in essence in the ebb and flow of innovation, together with the repercussions resulting therefrom. An economy which experiences innovation, and which is directed by innovators and operated by entrepreneurs having the instincts of the herd, necessarily displays wavelike movements. Innovation involves capital investment, "which accordingly is not distributed evenly in time but appears *en masse* at intervals."

Innovation is an historic and irreversible change in the way of doing things. If instead of varying the quantities of the factors, we vary the form of the production function, we have an innovation. "We will simply define innovation as the setting up of a new production function." [34] This covers not only new techniques, but also the introduction of new commodities, new forms of organization, and the opening up of new markets. Innovation combines factors in a new way. Innovation represents a jump from an old production function to a new production function. The old marginal cost curve is destroyed and a new one put in its place each time there is an innovation. An innovation means a *shift* in the marginal productivity curve.

Major innovations entail the construction of new plant and

---

[33] Schumpeter's theory runs in terms of a process inherent in the inner nature of a dynamic economy in which the impelling factor is the innovating entrepreneur.

See J. Schumpeter, "Über das Wesen der Wirtschaftskrisen," *Zeitschrift für Volkswirtschaft*, 1910, pp. 271–325; *Theorie der wirtschaftlichen Entwicklung*, Duncker & Humblot, Leipzig, 1912; "Die Wellenbewegung des Wirtschaftslebens," *Archiv für Sozialwissenschaft und Sozialpolitik*, 1914, pp. 1–32; *The Theory of Economic Development*, Harvard University Press, Cambridge, 1934; *Business Cycles*, McGraw-Hill Book Company, New York, 1939, Vols. I and II.

[34] Schumpeter, *Business Cycles*, pp. 87–88.

equipment, but not every new plant embodies an innovation. "Add as many mail coaches as you please, you will never get a railroad by so doing." [35] To do something new is very much more difficult than to do something that belongs to the ordinary run of economic routine. The two tasks differ qualitatively. Whenever "the trade beholds the new thing done and its major problems solved, it becomes much easier for other people to do the same thing and even to improve upon it." Thus innovations do not remain isolated events, and are not evenly distributed over time. They tend to "cluster," to come in "bunches," simply because "first some, and then most, firms follow in the wake of successful innovation." [36]

We must distinguish, says Schumpeter, between innovation *possibilities* and the *practical realization* of these possibilities. Prosperity does not arise merely as a result of inventions or discoveries. It waits upon the actual development of *innovations,* which is the driving power of the period of prosperity. Only a few leaders have the intelligence and energy to found new undertakings, to develop new possibilities. While only a few can *lead,* many can *follow.* Once someone has gone ahead, it is not difficult to imitate him. Few are capable of securing financial backing for a new venture of which bankers and investors are skeptical; but once one such new establishment is a going concern, others can easily secure credit and capital for similar undertakings. If a new process is put into successful operation, others can simply copy. If the first one has found the right location, others can simply locate near him. Experiments with workers and customers benefit other entrepreneurs who learn from these experiments.

The problems confronting those who imitate innovations are more difficult than those of the ordinary routine business. But they are not nearly so great as those faced by the leaders who blaze the trail. And whenever a few successful innovators appear, immediately a host of others follow. The appearance of one or a

---

[35] J. A. Schumpeter, *Readings in Business Cycle Theory,* The Blakiston Company, Philadelphia, 1944, p. 7. See also his "The Explanation of the Business Cycle," *Economica,* December, 1927.

[36] Schumpeter, *Business Cycles,* p. 100.

few entrepreneurs facilitates the appearance of others, and these, the appearance of more, in ever-increasing numbers. This is the basis of the "wave movement" of industrial activity.[37]

The Herdlike Movement

Thus the process of expansion is not simply a process of cumulation—the favorable "secondary waves" which flow to interrelated industries from the initial impulse. The expansion proceeds by "rushes" because a forward push by innovators impels a "herdlike" movement of followers who see the tempting profit possibilities opened up. The boom is a phenomenon caused by the herdlike action of entrepreneurs who *en masse* rush into the new openings. Even though inventions were uniformly distributed over time, fluctuations in the rate of investment would still occur, owing to the discontinuity of innovational activity. "Breaking through" the established routine is not something that occurs at a uniform and smooth pace. Innovation is discontinuous. The new combinations are not evenly distributed over time. They appear "discontinuously in groups or swarms." [38]

The "swarm-like appearance of new enterprises" is *intensified* by the cumulative process—the secondary waves which spread all over the business sphere. "Many things float on this 'secondary wave,' without any new or direct impulse from the real driving force." [39] Moreover, errors of optimism may intensify the boom. These are supporting and accentuating circumstances, but not a primary cause of cyclical movements. The central driving force is the appearance of an innovation which sets going the herdlike movement of entrepreneurs.

The End of the Boom

Schumpeter differs from Spiethoff not only in his explanation of the origin of the boom but also in his analysis of the termi-

[37] J. A. Schumpeter, "Die Wellenbewegung des Wirtschaftslebens," *Archiv für Sozialwissenschaft*, 1914, pp. 28–32; also *Theory of Economic Development*, Harvard University Press, 1934, p. 228.

[38] Schumpeter, *Theory of Economic Development*, p. 223.

[39] *Ibid.*, p. 226.

nation of the boom.[40] He accepts Juglar's statement that the "only cause of the depression is prosperity," and this he interprets to mean that "depression is nothing more than the economic system's reaction to the boom, or the adaptation to the situation into which the boom brings the system." [41] The disturbances arising from innovation cannot be currently and smoothly absorbed. These disturbances are "big"; they disrupt the existing system and enforce a distinct process of adaptation.

A railroad through a new country upsets all conditions relating to the location of industry, all cost calculations, all production functions in the area. Hardly any "ways of doing things" remain as before. In the wake of big industrial changes, the various elements of the system do not move in step. Some industries move on, others stay behind. Discrepancies arise. The depression is a process of adaptation to the changed conditions ushered in by the boom.

The Recession: A Period of Readjustment

The process of introducing innovations into the productive system is the essence of the boom. Progress not only proceeds by jerks, but also by one-sided rushes with disruptive consequences. The development is "lopsided, discontinuous, disharmonious." The history of capitalism is "studded with violent bursts and catastrophes." Evolution is a disturbance of existing structures, more like a series of explosions than a gentle transformation.[42] But these new methods cannot become incorporated into the circular flow, cannot become integrated into a new equilibrium system, without an intervening period of readjustment. This process of absorption and liquidation, of incorporating the new things and of adapting the economic system to them is, according to Schumpeter, the essence of the recession.

In the recession period, the economic system is struggling toward a new equilibrium position following the disturbances caused by the boom. The economic nature of depression lies in

---

[40] Schumpeter does say that as a "description of the actual facts" he can accept Spiethoff's explanation as far as it goes (*Theory of Economic Development,* p. 215). But he does not stop here.

[41] Schumpeter, *Theory of Economic Development,* p. 224.

[42] Schumpeter, *Business Cycles,* pp. 101–102.

the diffusion of the achievements of the boom over the whole economic system through the mechanism of the struggle for equilibrium.[43]

Any innovation—be it a new method of production, new goods, the opening up of a new market, any new combination of productive forces—will alter the buying power of consumers, the prices of raw materials, the quantity of sales, etc. These are the basic facts upon which industrial plans are formed. The old plans, formerly correct, no longer fit the facts of the industrial situation. A process of accommodation to the new facts, a fitting of the innovation into the general industrial system, becomes necessary. If the innovations appear simultaneously and in large numbers, then the data change so rapidly that adjustment becomes extremely difficult. Little by little the adjustment is made and a new equilibrium is reached.

We may define the period of depression as one in which there is being completed an accommodation to the new industrial situation created in the preceding period by the appearance of many relatively sudden innovations. A reorganization of the price system, of incomes, of production to fit the new demand situation, is inevitable. This process is the content of the period of depression, and it takes place with losses, resistance, and disillusionment. Thus we come to the conclusion that it is the multiplicity of innovations in the period of prosperity which disturbs the equilibrium and changes the basic industrial data so that a period of readjustment of prices, values, and production necessarily appears.[44]

Neighborhoods of Equilibrium

Cyclical movements are movements away from neighborhoods of equilibrium, and back again. It is the process of innovation which drives the system away from equilibrium into a boom of capital investment. This is the phase of "prosperity," and it is followed by "recession"—the struggle back to equilibrium. But as the depressive forces gather momentum, the system usually outruns also this neighborhood of equilibrium and thus plunges be-

---

43 Schumpeter, *Theory of Economic Development*, p. 251.

44 Schumpeter, "Die Wellenbewegung des Wirtschaftslebens," *Archiv für Sozialwissenschaft*, 1914, pp. 17–20, 23–24.

yond—down into the "depression excursion." From here the recuperative forces of adjustment bit by bit promote "revival" and gradually pull the economy back again toward equilibrium. From here a new swarm of innovations starts the economy on a new cycle. Starting from the neighborhood of equilibrium, the innovational surge drives the economy on into the next phase of "prosperity." Innovators supply the propelling force which generates a new cycle.[45]

Bank Credit and Innovations

Schumpeter stresses not only innovations and economic progress but also the role played by bank credit in economic development. Indeed, bank credit expansion is intimately connected, he believes, with the process of innovation.

"Neutral money" [46] might indeed very probably prove to be the appropriate monetary arrangement in a static equilibrium in which a continuous production process was constantly being maintained—Schumpeter's "*Kreislauf*" or "circular flow." But in a dynamic society in which "development" is going on, a more flexible money system is necessary. "Development," in Schumpeter's sense, is something quite distinct from and foreign to the circular flow. It is spontaneous and discontinuous change in the channels of the circular flow. These changes appear on the side of production, not on the side of consumption. They are technical innovations in the production process. Development means the carrying out of new combinations. And for the carrying out of these combinations, credit is primarily necessary. The detachment of productive means, already employed elsewhere, from the circular flow, and the allotment of them to new combinations—this is the function of credit. These necessary funds are obtained through the

[45] Schumpeter, *Readings in Business Cycle Theory*, pp. 8–11. For a detailed discussion of the four phases in relation to the neighborhoods of equilibrium see pp. 7–9 of this book.

[46] By "neutral money" is meant, in effect, a constant money supply, the idea in the minds of the advocates of such a monetary policy being that money would then be "neutral" in its effect upon the production process. While, as indicated, this might be true under conditions of static equilibrium, the situation in a dynamic economy is quite different.

creation of purchasing power by the banks. With the help of these credit means of payment, innovators who carry out new combinations are able to gain access to the existing factors of production. The banker, therefore, is "essentially a phenomenon of development." It is through the issue of credit that the carrying out of new combinations is made possible. Swarms of innovations have periodically in past history been floated into their places in the new structure of production on the tide of an expanding volume of bank credit.[47]

The essence of economic development, Schumpeter explains, consists in a *different* employment of *existing* productive resources. New combinations require the withdrawal of primary factors from their previous employments, and this "cannot be achieved otherwise than by a disturbance in the relative purchasing power of individuals." [48] It is this function that credit performs. The purchasing power which the entrepreneur—the innovator—needs "does not flow towards him automatically as to the producer in the circular flow, by the sale of what he produced in preceding periods." [49] In the circular flow, there is no need of credit; only for development does it play a fundamental role. The quantity of credit operates as an order on the economic system to accommodate itself to the purpose of the entrepreneur. Credit bridges the gap between products and means of production in the carrying out of new combinations.

Exogenous and Endogenous Factors

Under the impulse of entrepreneurial activity (i.e., innovation) the economic system draws away from the neighborhood of equilibrium. But the farther it moves away from equilibrium, the stronger is the pull back to equilibrium. In the downward readjustment (recession) the economy is likely to "overshoot" and pass through the neighborhood of equilibrium into the depression phase. Again the economy is pulled back toward equilibrium. Once there, it does not come to rest, because it is just in the neigh-

---

[47] Schumpeter, *Theory of Economic Development,* Chapters II and III.

[48] *Ibid.,* p. 96.

[49] *Ibid.,* p. 102.

borhood of equilibrium that the economic climate is favorable for innovations.[50] Thus, in a very fundamental sense Schumpeter's theory runs in terms of an endogenous, self-perpetuating process —a process inherent in the inner nature of a dynamic economy in which the impelling force, which cycle after cycle renews the wavelike movement, is the innovating entrepreneur.

Yet economic development (and the wave movement in economic life) is not merely a product of the innovational process. It is also a product of far-reaching structural changes in technique, within which pattern of change the innovational process occurs. A case in point was the shift to a new technological plateau ushered in by the railroad. In this respect exogenous factors, notably revolutionary inventions, play a highly significant role, especially with respect to secular trends (the Kondratieff long waves), against which background the regular business cycles (Juglar's) unfold.

Economic fluctuations are concerned with "economic changes inherent in the working of the organism itself." [51] Yet we are faced with an economic process which is continually being disturbed by external factors. These external factors "induce a process of adaptation in the system" which will produce wavelike oscillations.[52] The influence of external factors is never absent, and they are often of such a nature that we cannot dispose of them simply according to the "schema of, say, a pendulum continually exposed to numerous small and independent shocks." [53] External factors are always important and sometimes dominant.[54]

GUSTAV CASSEL (1866–1945)

Gustav Cassel's *The Nature and Necessity of Interest,* published in 1903, quickly established itself as a significant landmark in the theory of interest and money. It was some ten years after its publication that Cassel turned to a study of the theory of trade

[50] In his *Economics of Welfare* (1920), Pigou pointed out that inventions become important only when they are applied, and their *time of application* is determined by states of confidence.

[51] Schumpeter, *Business Cycles,* Vol. I, p. 7.

[52] *Ibid.,* p. 11.

[53] *Ibid.,* p. 12.

[54] *Ibid.,* p. 72.

cycles. His *Theory of Social Economy* (Book IV was devoted to trade cycles) was ready for the press in 1914, but, owing to the war, publication (in German) was delayed until 1918. An English translation appeared in 1923. A general revision of the German edition was made in 1931, and from this a new English translation was published in 1932.

Is the Business-Cycle Concept Obsolete?

In this latter edition Cassel raises the question whether the profound changes in economic institutions wrought by the First World War may not have so altered the character of economic development as to make the term "trade cycles" no longer valid. In the first edition he had distinguished sharply the earlier commercial crises (up to 1870) from modern business cycles of the period 1870 to 1914. By 1931, however, he was not sure what significance cycles in this sense still had for economic life. Great monetary disturbances, political insecurity, war debts, nationalistic trade policy, the growth of monopolistic labor organizations, the growing role of the state (maintenance of the unemployed, etc.)—all these had, he found, so profoundly altered the character of economic life after the First World War that the very concept of trade cycles (*Konjunktur*), as that term was applied by him to the period 1870–1914, was perhaps no longer applicable.

This is an interesting reflection, and if valid, would apply even more to the conditions ushered in by the Great Depression and the Second World War.

Historical Developments and the Business Cycle

Cassel has no sympathy for the view that "everything that occurs in economic life is determined by mathematical curves, and that we have only to discover these to be able to learn our predetermined fate." [55] On the contrary, he views economic fluctuations and crises as caused to a great extent by factors which represent passing phenomena of economic history. He is not at all sure that these fluctuations are "necessary concomitants of the modern

---

[55] Gustav Cassel, *Theory of Social Economy* (Harcourt, Brace and Company, 1932), p. 538.

productive and social order." [56] It may be, he suggests, that an explanation must be sought not in the nature of the economic order, but rather in the revolutionary changes in the social and economic system, especially the transition from the old self-sufficing agricultural economy to the modern highly industrialized economy based on division of labor and the system of exchange. Economic fluctuations are due, not to the structural characteristics of the modern economy, but rather to progress, technical change, and transition from a primitive economy to a complex industrialized economy.

The Role of Iron and Fixed Capital

That Cassel was profoundly influenced by the writings of Tugan-Baranowsky and Spiethoff appears plainly evident, though he fails to mention either one in his book. We are reminded of Tugan-Baranowsky when we read that "the movements of the trade cycle are merely expressions of the fluctuations in the production of fixed capital." [57] Both Tugan-Baranowsky and Spiethoff come to mind when we learn that the "production of iron represents the entire production of fixed capital." Cassel defines periods of boom and depression precisely as follows: "A period of boom is one of special increase in the production of fixed capital; a period of decline or a depression is one in which this production falls below the point it had previously reached." [58] He marks off these periods from a chart of world pig-iron production, which reflects, he believes, the world production of fixed capital.[59] The alternation between periods of advance and periods of decline is fundamentally a variation in the production of fixed capital. But the production of consumption goods varies relatively little in relation to the movements of business cycles.[60]

Population Movements and Business Cycles

The demand for workers at the beginning of the period of advance is met by the absorption of the unemployed. In periods

[56] *Ibid.*, p. 537.
[57] *Ibid.*, p. 559.
[58] *Ibid.*, p. 550.
[59] *Ibid.*, p. 594.
[60] *Ibid.*, p. 552.

of intense prosperity additional workers are drawn partly from the increase in population, partly from agriculture. As is well known, there has been a drift of population from agriculture to industry in all the industrial states of Europe (and, we may add, also in America).[61]

The stream, however, has not been steady. The surplus agricultural population has been kept on the land during periods of depression until it could be absorbed by the capital-producing industries in periods of advance. Without these reserves of labor, periods of prosperity could not have assumed the proportions they have hitherto attained.

The migration from agriculture to industry has been due to the revolution in the whole economic organization during the last hundred years. But sooner or later a state of equilibrium between agriculture and industry will be reached. The stream from agriculture to industry will then materially diminish. Here, then, is a factor which in the future will tend to tone down extreme cyclical fluctuations. "If it is clear that the capacity of agriculture to meet this industrial demand for labour will be substantially curtailed at the end of the industrial revolution, we reach the important conclusion that the *trade cycles are, to a very great extent, a phenomenon of the period of transition from the old economic forms to the modern.*"[62]

Growth and Business Cycles

Thus the boom is basically a period of *growth,* of absorption of a growing labor force into industry, and especially into the capital goods industries. The production of consumers' goods grows fairly steadily, but the output of capital goods grows by leaps and bounds.

Yet even in the depression some capital goods are normally produced. Thus the country is typically better equipped with durable means of production at the end of a depression period

[61] Compare Spiethoff, "Krisen," *Handwörterbuch der Staatswissenschaften* (1925), VI, pp. 75, 77.

[62] Cassel, *op. cit.*, p. 573. Cassel points to the fact that cyclical fluctuations have been most violent in the United States, where an almost unlimited labor supply was available through immigration. See also Harry Jerome, *Migration and Business Cycles,* National Bureau of Economic Research, New York, 1926.

than at the beginning. But the great advance is made in the boom. "It is just this significant increase in the production of material means of production above the normal rate which, in particular, creates the trade boom." [63] This statement is particularly worth noting, especially the phrase "above the normal rate." We shall have more to say about this *normal rate of growth* later, particularly in our discussion of Harrod.

The Acceleration Principle

Cassel makes a sharp distinction between those durable means of production which work for the consumer and those employed in the production of "further instruments of production." A fall in the demand of consumers will cause a corresponding idleness of the first group, but possibly *complete* idleness for the second group. This is the acceleration principle. Cassel gives an interesting statistical illustration in a comparison of (a) freightage in millions of tons, and (b) tonnage of ships built. The fluctuation in the demand for shipping "need not be great in order to cause violent fluctuations in the extent of employment in the yards." [64] The "production of durable means of production must be, on the whole, much more sensitive to the fluctuations of the demand of consumers than the production which works directly for the needs of consumers." [65] Accordingly, the prospect of ever attaining completely uniform activity in the "sphere of the capital-producing industries, seems very remote indeed." [66]

The Role of the Rate of Interest

During the last stage of the boom there develops a growing scarcity of capital, says Cassel, which is reflected in a rise in the rate of interest. Even profitable concerns experience a growing difficulty in raising funds.

Consider now more closely those factors which, acting as

---

[63] Cassel, *op. cit.*, p. 585. "We may accept it as a rule that the discarding of antiquated means of production generally takes place during the periods of depression, while, on the other hand, the production of new means of production is carried on more vigorously during expansion of trade" (pp. 586–587).
[64] *Ibid.*, p. 597.
[65] *Ibid.*, p. 596.
[66] *Ibid.*, p. 598.

"driving or restricting forces, determine the movements of the trade cycle." [67] Of these forces the rate of interest occupies the central place. Given certain prospective annual yields or returns on capital goods, the lower the rate of interest, the higher will be the value of such fixed capital. "At a time therefore, when a low rate of interest has been maintained for a long period, prospects for considerable profits await those entrepreneurs who are prepared to undertake building contracts, railway construction, or other works which require a large amount of fixed capital." [68]

These statements come very much to the same thing as the Keynesian proposition that the inducement to invest is strong when the marginal efficiency of capital exceeds the rate of interest —or, in other words, when the *value* of capital goods exceeds their *cost*.

A high rate of interest must reduce the value of fixed capital, and so a prolonged high rate of interest leads to a fall in the production of fixed capital. This is enough, says Cassel, to convert the boom into a depression.[69] During the depression a low rate of interest has a restorative effect upon enterprise; during the boom a high rate acts as a brake. On the other hand, the rate of interest is itself affected by the business cycle. The depression brings a low rate which in turn leads to an end of the slump. The boom raises the rate, and this leads to an end of the boom. Thus there is a reciprocal action between the rate of interest and the cycle.[70] This action operates to cause fluctuations in the *value* of fixed capital.

Cost of Capital Goods and Value of Capital Goods

Also there is reciprocal action and reaction which affects the *cost* of fixed capital. The prices of materials and wages rise in the boom. This raises the *cost* of fixed capital just when the *value* of fixed capital declines by reason of the rise in the rate of interest. Together, "these restricting factors put an end to the abnormally large production of fixed capital, and consequently to the

---

67 *Ibid.*, p. 639.
68 *Ibid.*, p. 639.
69 *Ibid.*, p. 640.
70 *Ibid.*, pp. 640–641.

whole trade boom." Similarly the *cost* of fixed capital falls in the depression period, precisely at the time when the *value* of fixed capital is raised by reason of the fall in the rate of interest. "The cooperation of these forces overcomes the depression and leads to an upward movement in trade." [71]

Cassel rejects the thesis that the extraordinarily increased production of fixed capital during the boom ends up in a saturation (Spiethoff) of capital goods. In his view the investment demand function is highly interest-elastic. There are, he believes, virtually endless investment opportunities. The boom ends, not because of a fall in the prospective annual returns on new capital goods, but because of the rise in the rate of interest. "The typical modern trade boom does not mean over-production or an over-estimate of the demands of the consumers or the needs of the community for the services of fixed capital, but an over-estimate of the supply of capital or of the amount of savings available for taking over the real capital produced." [72]

Growth and Progress

In view of the reciprocal action and reaction of the factors influencing the fluctuation of the *value* of capital in relation to the *cost* of capital, why is there not a leveling-out of the upward and downward movements as a result of these interacting adjustments? To this question Cassel replies that the cycle would indeed gradually die down were it not for the recurrence of events which from time to time cause a renewal of the whole cycle movement. Thus the cycle is not, in Cassel's view, a mere oscillation of in-

[71] *Ibid.*, pp. 641–644. The "length of the trade cycle," says Cassel, "is to some extent connected with the length of the period of production of the undertakings in question" (p. 643).

[72] *Ibid.*, p. 649. Note also the following: "That the crisis really consists in an acute shortage of capital—that is, savings needed for purchasing the real capital produced—is partly shown by the great difficulty of selling the fixed capital already produced, and partly by the very general inability to complete undertakings that have been begun. . . . The increasing scarcity of capital during a boom is hidden in a confusing way from the business world by the usual large increase of bank means of payment at such a time, which are naturally regarded by the business man as capital. Later on, when the banks find it necessary in their own interest to cut down this excessive supply of means of payment, the real scarcity of capital is felt suddenly and acutely" (p. 652).

teracting forces. It is a recurrent phenomenon springing from growth and progress.

Changes in technology may give the cycle a fresh impulse. Thus in the middle nineties the widespread application of various electrical inventions was the cause of enormous demands on fixed capital. This led to a new boom and "started once more the fluctuations of a trade cycle." Electric tramways, electric lighting, power stations, and telephones required a vast production of fixed capital. Thus a cycle "already much attenuated is bound to be restored to full strength by some new technical advance, and will then continue in the form of a fluctuation for some time."[73] Accordingly, anyone who complains of business cycles is really complaining of the advance of our material civilization.[74]

Another event is the exploitation of new countries. The development of new territory requires means of transport, bridges, hydraulic works, lighting installations, houses—in a word, fixed capital. "The pronounced booms since the middle of the nineties have clearly been due to a great extent to the diffusion of Western civilisation." There are still great tasks for the world economy, but "naturally, the stimulation of trade which originates in the exploitation of new countries will tend to disappear altogether when the world is more or less uniformly equipped with the material foundations of Western civilisation."[75]

Thus we note that Cassel accepted Spiethoff's explanation of the cause of the boom—the opening up of richly profitable new investment opportunities by reason of the advance of technique and the development of new territories. With respect to the end of the boom he agreed with Tugan-Baranowsky—the main cause of the downturn is a shortage of loanable (free, disposable) capital.

That Cassel in effect accepted Spiethoff's explanation for the upswing—the process of filling up the "empty bucket"—yet refused to accept the "saturation" argument for the downturn requires some explanation; and it is evident that Cassel himself felt somewhat uneasy about this matter. His explanation is in fact

[73] *Ibid.*, pp. 644–645.
[74] *Ibid.*, pp. 645–646.
[75] *Ibid.*, p. 645.

somewhat lopsided. Technology and growth indeed explain the boom, but the exhaustion of investible funds explains the downturn. Society, he argues, is always confronted with a large number of new opportunities to use fixed capital profitably—the investment demand schedule is highly interest-elastic. Only a limited number of these can be developed, however, in view of the high rate of interest. So far so good. But elsewhere he argues that the development of *still more* investment opportunities provides a fresh impulse to the production of fixed capital and so starts a new boom. At this point one is entitled to ask: If in fact boundless investment opportunities are always present, why then should a new cycle await a fresh burst of new and highly profitable openings? If indeed the rate of interest were the all-important factor, a lowering of the rate of interest should be adequate to start a boom.

Nevertheless, Cassel might perhaps reply that it is all a matter of degree and emphasis; the main stimulus to the boom comes from the side of technological advances, while the main cause of depression comes from a shortage of investment funds. Progress cannot be absolutely uniform. Every development has its specially active periods. Moreover, apart from the spurts coming from the side of technical progress, we must also bear in mind that any unevenness in current consumption will lead to much greater unevenness in the production of capital goods (the acceleration principle). We can hardly conceive of a complete elimination of trade cycles in a progressive economic system. Thus it is "only natural that at the time of the great industrial revolution, when society took the decisive step from the old to the new economic order, there had to be a series of pronounced booms and subsequent depressions." [76]

When we speak of progress, says Cassel, we must also include in this term the growth in population. "Every increase in population necessitates a corresponding increase in the fixed capital of the community." Any increase in fixed capital must afford more room for the play of business cycles. There appears to be a correlation, he suggests, between the growth of population and the violence of business cycles. Apparently, the role of business cycles

[76] *Ibid.*, p. 646.

has been more important in countries like Germany and the United States, with rapidly growing populations, than in France with a relatively stationary population.[77]

Thus the future of business cycles depends essentially upon the future of material progress. The demand for fixed capital has its roots in the desire "to utilise technical discoveries or new lands —the determination of the nation to grow: in a word, the national will to progress. . . . The fluctuations of trade cycles are the result of the struggle of this will to progress against the economic scarcity that it encounters in all points." [78]

DENNIS H. ROBERTSON (1890–)

Dennis H. Robertson begins his *Study of Industrial Fluctuations* [79] with a statement which at once places him among those economists who stress the *real* factors, and particularly those relating to the fluctuations in the rate of investment in fixed capital goods. There are, he says, certain peculiarities inherent in the modern system of large-scale capitalistic industry which may produce an alternation between prosperity and depression. And this is true "even in the absence of any fluctuation in (consumer) demand." The fundamental causes are to be found in the nature of a system of production which uses capital goods.

In his *Banking Policy and the Price Level* [80] he holds "that far more weight must be attached than it is now fashionable to attach to certain *real*, as opposed to monetary or psychological, causes of fluctuations." He then quotes approvingly from Cassel the view that as long as progress necessarily requires a large use of fixed capital, so long must we expect fluctuations akin to the present trade cycles.

---

77 *Ibid.*, pp. 646–647.

78 *Ibid.*, p. 647.

79 D. H. Robertson, *A Study of Industrial Fluctuations*, P. S. King & Son, Ltd., Westminster, 1915.

80 D. H. Robertson, *Banking Policy and the Price Level*, P. S. King & Son, Ltd., Westminster, 1926.

Necessary and Desirable vs. Secondary and Undesirable Fluctuations

This, then, is Robertson's point of departure, from which emerges his most significant contribution—namely, a sharp distinction between (a) *necessary and desirable* fluctuations, which are inherently and inseparably connected with the "explosive forces of industrial progress," and (b) *secondary* or *induced* fluctuations—excessive booms and unhealthy deflation—which serve no useful purpose and which we would do well to eliminate from the cycle if appropriate measures can be found.

There occur, he says, "important fluctuations in industrial output which are relatively desirable, in the sense that . . . those causes are deeply embedded in the technical and legal structure of our actual society; and the remedy, even if practicable, might be worse than the disease." [81]

Secondary Repercussions Due to Error

The unnecessary and undesirable secondary repercussions superimposed upon the necessary and inherently desirable primary fluctuations are basically due to *error*. But the primary fluctuations would remain even though there were no errors of optimism and pessimism. "I do not think it is even nearly true that if all business men always made, and acted upon, true judgments about their own self-interest, industrial fluctuations of a fairly rhythmical character would disappear." [82] Nevertheless Robertson recognizes the "importance of Error, and of the partial Remediability of Error by monetary manipulation." [83]

Progress Comes by Spurts

Past experience indicates that progress has often come by spurts, and these cause dislocations. But they may be worth the price. "I do not feel confident that a policy which, in the pursuit of stability of prices, output and employment, had nipped in the bud the English railway boom of the forties, or the American railway boom of 1869–71, or the German electrical boom of the

[81] *Ibid.*, p. 2.
[82] *Ibid.*, p. 3.
[83] *Ibid.*

nineties, would have been on the balance beneficial to the populations concerned." [84]

Investment Outlets and Temporary Saturation

Robertson stresses the important role of *inventions* in the boom, and of *temporary saturation* in the depression. "The application over a wide field of territory or of industry of an invention such as the railway, electric power, or the Diesel engine, will raise for a more or less prolonged period the intensity of the desire for the constructional implements and materials involved, only to lower it again when the field in question has reached a condition of temporary saturation." [85] With respect to specific cycles he says: "The international boom of 1872 is, in my view, to be particularly connected with railway building; that of 1882 with inventions in the steel trade; those of 1900 and 1907 with electricity; that of 1912 with oil-power." [86]

Appropriate and Inappropriate Fluctuations in Output

There are appropriate and also inappropriate fluctuations in output. The *actual* fluctuations tend to exceed greatly the rational or appropriate fluctuations.

What is appropriate and what is inappropriate is rendered ambiguous by the technical characteristic of modern industry—namely, that it requires very large, expensive, and durable instruments of production. Such instruments are often imperfectly divisible. A railroad must either double its track or not double it. For technical reasons it is not possible to adjust productive capacity neatly to the precise requirements of the desired expansion of output.[87]

The main reason why the actual expansion often exceeds the appropriate expansion of industrial output seems to be the "stress of competition, aggravated by the length of time which is required to adjust production to a changed demand." [88] The

[84] *Ibid.*, p. 22.
[85] *Ibid.*, p. 11.
[86] *Ibid.*, p. 11, footnote.
[87] *Ibid.*, p. 35.
[88] *Ibid.*, p. 37. See the discussion of Aftalion in Chapter 18 of this book.

longer it takes to construct the new instruments the "more scope there is for miscalculation." [89] Other factors fertile in the generation of error are the psychological reactions of businessmen to a "change of tone" in the business community, and illusory inducements to expansion growing out of *price* movements.[90]

Monetary Policy May Prevent Inappropriate Fluctuations

"The aim of monetary policy should surely be not to prevent all fluctuations in the general price-level, but to permit those which are necessary to the establishment of appropriate alterations in output and to repress those which tend to carry the alterations in output beyond the appropriate point." [91]

Whatever the original cause of a recession, after a certain stage is reached it is apt to "degenerate into a purposeless and obscene orgy of destruction." In such circumstances it seems clear that "it is right and reasonable to use the manifold powers of the state to reverse the evil process of cumulation." Under such conditions there is no necessary opposition between "measures helpful to consumption and measures helpful to the formation of capital equipment." [92]

Boom and Glut

Thus the primary cause of boom and depression is the "difficulty of reconciling progress with stability, of ensuring that the provision of the world with increased capital equipment takes place at a steady rate." [93] A higher than average rate of investment in the boom leads to a "glut" of capital goods [94] in the de-

[89] *Ibid.*, p. 38.

[90] *Ibid.*, p. 39. In this connection see his discussion of buffer-stock proposals (*ibid.*, pp. 97–98). Stocks of consumable goods, while not the most important form of capital, have nevertheless played a significant part in the history of trade cycles. Hence considerable interest attaches to suggestions for "large-scale State-dealings in the primary foodstuffs and materials." By regulating the rate of release of these accumulated stocks the state could do something to "promote stability in the estimates formed by the business world."

[91] *Ibid.*, p. 39.

[92] *Essays in Monetary Theory*, P. S. King & Son, Ltd., Westminster, 1940, p. 105.

[93] *Ibid.*, p. 60.

[94] *Ibid.*, p. 60.

pression. Stimulation of the boom by "cheap and abundant money" is likely to lead to "further saturation of already saturated channels of investment." [95] To press on so rapidly with capital formation is a mistake "because it sets before the economic system problems in digestion and readjustment which it cannot possibly solve." [96]

Special circumstances aggravated the Great Depression of the thirties, among them the rapid application of science to agriculture, the decline in the rate of growth of population, and the growing importance of durable consumers' goods. All these developments have contributed to the "glut, whether of capital goods or of raw products." [97]

There are schools of thought which characterize a boom as an *excess* of capital formation relative to saving.[98] Robertson himself thinks that an actual "crisis" may be correctly described as due to a "deficiency of capital" in Cassel's sense.[99] But those who stress this point, he thinks, have given insufficient attention to the possibility that both investment and saving may have been proceeding "at a rate which, having regard to the technique of modern industry and to the nature of men's desires, cannot be continuously sustained without leading to *malaise* and disorder." [100] After some years of high investment, the inevitable result is a glut of capital goods. "For the truth seems to be that the processes of construction of the main modern instruments of production and transport are essentially discontinuous, so that so far as they are concerned it is hard to conceive of 'progress' proceeding continuously rather than by a succession of fits and starts." [101] The phenomena of boom and slump are related to something very deep-seated—namely, "the inevitable discontinuity which attends the efforts of man to achieve material progress." [102]

---

[95] *Ibid.*, p. 61.
[96] *Ibid.*, p. 110.
[97] *Ibid.*, p. 60.
[98] *Ibid.*, p. 100.
[99] *Banking Policy and the Price Level*, p. 90.
[100] *Essays in Monetary Theory*, p. 101.
[101] *Ibid.*, p. 101.
[102] *Ibid.*, p. 126.

Indeed, in terms of the larger problems cast up by the Great Depression, the "trade cycle is properly envisaged not as a passing rash on the fair face of a static equilibrium but as a deep-seated functional disorder of the endocrine glands which control the rate of organic growth." [103] And the problem of the trade cycle is complicated by the fact "that fluctuations in fact occur against a background of secular and structural change, from which they are not always easy to disentangle." [104]

[103] *Ibid.*, p. 103.
[104] *Ibid.*, p. 104.

17 · *The Investment Demand Schedule and the Rate of Interest:*

WICKSELL · FISHER · KEYNES

KNUT WICKSELL (1851–1926)

Wicksell's classic work, *Geldzins und Güterpreise,* appeared in 1898. Later there appeared (in Swedish) his *Lectures on Political Economy*—Volume I, *General Theory,* in 1901, and Volume II, *Money,* in 1906. The Lectures were soon published in German. And long after, in the nineteen-thirties, all three works were translated into English.[1]

Wicksell's writings at once achieved a commanding position on the Continent, and profoundly influenced the development of monetary and business-cycle thinking. Indeed, in terms of cycle *theory* his work is perhaps more important than that of Tugan-Baranowsky or Spiethoff. Yet despite his great influence on Continental thought the Wicksellian type of analysis made relatively little impression in English-speaking countries until the nineteen-twenties. At long last increasing recognition of its importance led

---

[1] *Lectures on Political Economy,* Vol. I, *General Theory,* The Macmillan Company, 1934; Vol. II, *Money,* Macmillan & Co., Ltd., London, 1935. *Interest and Prices,* Macmillan & Co., Ltd., London, 1936.

finally to the translations of the middle thirties referred to above.

Now while the Wicksellian analysis with respect to the investment demand schedule—determined by the real or natural rate in relation to the rate of interest—has become a cornerstone of modern business-cycle theory, it is nonetheless true that Wicksell himself never made any comprehensive study of industrial fluctuations as such. His main contribution has, however, become so much an integral part of current economic thinking that it is difficult to convey any adequate impression of the real significance of his pioneering work.

Real vs. Monetary Factors

In an article on Cassel's *Theory of Social Economy,*[2] Wicksell refers to the extraordinary difficulty of the theory of crises and cycles, and to his own far from adequate comprehension of it; and in his Volume II, *Money,* he speaks of the "puzzling phenomena" of the business cycle. He is not prepared to offer a definitive explanation, but he states flatly that his view agrees closely with that of Spiethoff. Its main feature, he says, is that it ascribes business cycles to *real* causes, and not simply to movements of commodity prices, as Clément Juglar had it. Nevertheless he thinks Juglar may well be right in assigning as the cause of *crises* (as distinct from the cycle in general) the sudden cessation of the rise in commodity prices.[3]

The Determinants of Investment Demand

All now agree, he says, that the outstanding characteristic of good times is the conversion on a large scale of liquid capital into fixed capital. In order to understand why such a conversion occurs—in other words, why real investment expands—it is necessary to analyze the factors controlling the volume of investment in fixed capital.

Wicksell suggests that an expansion of investment in fixed capital goods "will take place when their earnings increase or

---

[2] Reprinted in *Lectures on Political Economy,* Vol. I, The Macmillan Company, New York, 1934, pp. 219–257.

[3] Wicksell, *Lectures on Political Economy,* Vol. II, *Money,* The Macmillan Company, New York, 1935, p. 209.

when the rate of interest falls, so that their capital value now exceeds their cost of reproduction." [4] There will be an inducement to invest when the *value* of capital goods exceeds the *cost* of capital goods. Keynes, as we shall see, accepted this formulation, which comes to much the same thing as the proposition that investment is determined by the relation of the marginal efficiency of capital to the rate of interest. Given the schedule of the marginal efficiency of capital, the volume of investment is determined by the rate of interest.

The Natural Rate and the Money Rate

Wicksell, indeed, employs various concepts to describe the rate of return on capital investment—normal rate, natural rate, real rate, natural real rate, capital rate, real capital rate, natural capital rate. And for the rate of interest actually prevailing in the market, he uses the following terms: loan rate, actual rate, actual loan rate, money rate, bank rate, or simply the rate of interest. That particular loan rate which is a direct expression of the *real rate* he calls the *normal loan rate.* The normal loan rate is the equilibrium rate. Changes in the relation of the real rate to the loan rate underlie, he argues, fluctuations in the rate of investment.

Technological and Growth Factors Raise the Real Rate

The difference between the actual loan rate and the natural rate "arises less frequently because the loan rate changes spontaneously whilst the normal or real rate remains unchanged but on the contrary because the normal rate rises or falls whilst the loan rate remains unchanged or only tardily follows it." [5] Technical discoveries and growth of population he regards as the dynamic factors which tend to raise the real rate above the loan rate. And it is the divergence between these rates which causes the boom.

Expansion may, however, come from factors operating on

[4] Wicksell, *Interest and Prices,* Macmillan and Co., Ltd., London, 1936, p. 134.
[5] Wicksell, *Money,* p. 205. Wicksell cites "increase in population" (p. 206) as a factor raising the demand for fixed capital.

the loan rate, such as increased production of gold or deliberate monetary expansion.[6] A fall in the rate of interest thus brought about would undoubtedly invoke "increasing roundaboutness." The effect of a low rate of interest is greatest in respect of "capital investments of longer duration, such as the building of railways, houses, shops, etc." [7] But historically expansion has typically come from growth and technical progress. These have the effect of raising the real or natural rate above the loan or money rate of interest.

Changes brought about by independent factors affecting the *natural rate of interest on capital* may therefore be regarded as the essential cause of an expanding movement.[8]

Fluctuations in the Rate of Investment

The principal and sufficient cause of cyclical fluctuations should, he says, be sought in the fact that "in its very nature technical or commercial advance cannot maintain the same even progress as does, in our days, the increase in needs—especially owing to the organic phenomenon of increase of population—but is sometimes precipitate, sometimes delayed. It is natural and at the same time economically justifiable that in the former case people seek to exploit the favourable situation as quickly as possible, and since the new discoveries, inventions, and other improvements nearly always require various kinds of preparatory work for their realization, there occurs the conversion of large masses of liquid into fixed capital which is an inevitable preliminary to every boom and indeed is probably the only fully characteristic sign, or at any rate one which cannot conceivably be absent.

"If, again, these technical improvements are already in operation and no others are available, or at any rate none which have been sufficiently tested or promise a profit in excess of the margin of risk attaching to all new enterprises, there will come a period of depression; people will not venture the capital which is now

[6] Wicksell, *Interest and Prices,* p. 167.
[7] Wicksell, *Money,* p. 195.
[8] Wicksell, *Interest and Prices,* p. 167.

being accumulated in such a fixed form, but will retain it as far as possible in a liquid, available form." [9]

"If the prospects of the employment of capital become more promising, demand will increase and will at first exceed supply." An expansion develops when there occurs an increase in the "expected yield on the newly created capital." [10] Fluctuations in the natural rate he regarded as the essence of good and bad times.[11] Again, "good times and a generally hopeful tone in the business world are created by the prospects of gain, and the real foundation is doubtless the gain already obtained in certain enterprises, as a result, for example, of technical or commercial progress." [12]

The Declining Investment Demand Schedule

The "yield of capital in production" is, however, exposed to the law of diminishing marginal productivity. It falls when capital increases, for as it "becomes more and more difficult to find profitable employment for the new capital," competition with the existing capital lowers the rate of return.[13] Wicksell thus agreed with Spiethoff that the investment demand schedule is relatively interest-inelastic. Investment of boom proportions will lead rapidly to saturation. Production is "unable to absorb unlimited quantities of new capital without a reduction in net yield." [14]

Free Capital vs. Fixed Capital

Wicksell regarded the conversion of free capital into fixed capital as the leading characteristic of the boom. Here the influence of Tugan-Baranowsky is evident. And Wicksell's language follows Tugan-Baranowsky's closely. He referred to "mobile capital in its free and uninvested form." The terms he used are free capital, mobile capital, loan capital, and disposable savings.[15] Wicksell agreed with Tugan-Baranowsky that the "demand for

---

[9] Wicksell, *Money*, pp. 211–212.
[10] *Ibid.*, p. 193.
[11] *Ibid.*, p. 208.
[12] *Ibid.*, p. 207.
[13] *Ibid.*, p. 205.
[14] *Ibid.*, p. 199.
[15] *Ibid.*, p. 193.

new capital in an upward swing of the trade cycle is frequently much too great to be satisfied by contemporaneous savings," and on the other hand, "in bad times this demand is practically nil, though saving does not nevertheless entirely cease." [16]

Wicksell's Strong and Weak Points

Wicksell's analysis of the relation of the natural rate to the money rate of interest is an outstanding contribution to the theory of income determination and is basic to the modern theory of business cycles. But his work falls short of an adequate theory of income fluctuations. It relates mainly to one determinant of income—the investment demand schedule. Fluctuations in the natural rate, together with the lagging adjustment of the rate of interest, would indeed cause expansion or contraction of aggregate demand. But the multiplier analysis, based on the consumption function, is missing.

There is, moreover, implicit in some of Wicksell's work, despite his general acceptance of Spiethoff's analysis, a somewhat excessively optimistic view with respect to what can be achieved by monetary policy. He saw only dimly the functional relation of the demand for money to the rate of interest. Even though the investment demand schedule were fairly interest-elastic, the liquidity preference schedule might be such that an increase in the quantity of money would have virtually no effect in lowering the rate of interest. In this situation interest-rate policy would be entirely futile. These matters Wicksell did not clearly understand. Accordingly, he exaggerated (as did also Keynes in the *Treatise*) the power of the banking system to control, by means of interest-rate manipulations, the flow of investment and so of aggregate demand.

Impulse and Propagation in the Cycle

In addition to his analysis of the determinants of investment, Wicksell advanced a highly significant idea as early as 1907,[17] re-

---

16 *Ibid.*, p. 212.

17 Wicksell, "Krisenas Gåta," *Statsøkonomisk Tidsskrift*, Oslo, 1907, pp. 255–286. As we shall see, this idea was later effectively developed by Pigou.

lating to the mechanism by which irregular impulses may be transformed into cycles. Ragnar Frisch has called attention to the importance of this contribution. "Knut Wicksell," says Frisch, "seems to be the first who has been definitely aware of the two types of problems in economic cycles analysis—the propagation problem and the impulse problem—and also the first who has formulated explicitly the theory that the sources of energy which maintain the economic cycles are erratic shocks. He conceived more or less definitely of the economic system as being pushed along irregularly, jerkingly. New innovations and exploitations do not come regularly, he says. But on the other hand, these irregular jerks may cause more or less regular cyclical movements. He illustrates it by one of those perfectly simple and yet profound illustrations: If you hit a wooden rocking-horse with a club, the movement of the horse will be very different from that of the club." [18]

IRVING FISHER (1867–1947)

Fisher's *Rate of Interest* appeared in 1907, and the *Theory of Interest* in 1930. In these volumes Fisher puts forward the divergence between the expected rate of return on investment and the rate of interest as the regulator of expansion and contraction. Investment opportunity requires that the *"rate of return over cost must exceed the rate of interest."* [19] The "rate of return over cost" plays the "central role on the investment opportunity side of interest theory." [20] Now the "rate of return over cost" is precisely the same as Keynes' "marginal efficiency of capital." [21] Fisher puts it as follows: "The rate of return over cost is always that rate which, employed in computing the present worth of all the

[18] Ragnar Frisch, "Propagation Problems and Impulse Problems in Dynamic Economics," *Economic Essays in Honour of Gustav Cassel,* George Allen and Unwin, Ltd., 1933.

[19] Irving Fisher, *Theory of Interest,* The Macmillan Company, New York, 1930, p. 159.

[20] *Ibid.,* p. 155.

[21] See Keynes' *General Theory of Employment, Interest and Money,* Harcourt, Brace and Company, 1936, p. 140.

costs and the present worth of all the returns, will make these two equal." [22]

Technology and the Rate of Return over Cost

If there is a high "rate of return over cost" in relation to the rate of interest, much investment will be made. Fisher refers to John Rae, who "clearly pointed out, in communities where the rate of interest is low, swamps will be more thoroughly improved, roads better made, dwellings more durably built . . . than in a community where the rate of interest is high." [23]

The effect of every important discovery and invention is to raise the "rate of return over cost" and so enlarge the opportunities for investment. "The range of man's investment opportunity widens as his knowledge extends and his utilization of the forces and materials of Nature grows. With each advance in knowledge come new opportunities to invest. The rate of return over cost rises. With the investments come distortions of the investors' income streams." [24]

Fisher, very much in the manner of Schumpeter's analysis of the innovator, explains that those "enterprisers and risk takers who are first to enter the new investment field, opened up by an invention, or, in the slang of business, 'get in on the ground floor' often obtain as a consequence a return on their original investment for greater than the rate of interest. Commodore Vanderbilt, Andrew Carnegie and Henry Ford are examples in point." [25]

Now it is only "so long as the rate of return over cost continues to be high," owing to the effects of invention and discovery, that large investment is made and society is tempted "to distort greatly its income stream in time shape. This period is the period of development and exploitation, during which society is sacrificing or investing present income. . . . Later, however, there will come a time when, *so far at least as the effect of that particular invention is concerned,* the income stream ceases to ascend, when

---

22 Fisher, *Theory of Interest,* p. 168.
23 *Ibid.,* p. 168.
24 *Ibid.,* p. 341.
25 *Ibid.,* pp. 343–344.

most of the necessary investment has been completed, when little further exploitation is possible or advisable, and when it is only necessary to keep up the newly constructed capital at a constant level. . . . Thus, though the railway inventions led to a half century of investment in railways, during which the income stream of society rapidly increased, today the limit of steam railway investment has been nearly reached in some places, and in others the rapidity of investment has precipitately slackened. Railroads have been an outlet for the investment of savings, and have tended to supply for them a good return. As the necessity for new railroads becomes less, this outlet diminishes, and the rates of return as well as the rates of interest in general tend to fall as far as this one influence is effective." [26] The rate of return over cost "rises and falls according as the introduction or the exploitation of inventions is active or inactive." [27]

Borrowers and Lenders

Innovation requires foresight, and it is precisely "superior foresight" which characterizes successful "captains of industry." When discovery and invention raises the rate of return over cost, entrepreneurs are prepared to borrow at an even higher rate of interest than before, but lenders are often willing to loan for the same rate as before. The effect of this disparity is that the rate of interest will not rise as high as if both sides saw the conditions equally well. Thus a spread develops between the rate of return over cost and the rate of interest, and this will cause an increase of loans and investments. But when a reversal occurs caused primarily by "the expectation of small profits," borrowers see that they cannot employ "money" productively except on easier terms, but lenders do not see why the terms should be made easier. "In consequence, 'enterprisers' borrow less, trade languishes, and, though interest falls in consequence of decrease in demand, it does not fall enough to keep the demand from decreasing." Thus "inequality of foresight produces overinvestment during rising prices and relative stagnation during falling prices. In the former case society is trapped into devoting too much investment of productive

[26] *Ibid.*, pp. 345–347.
[27] *Ibid.*, pp. 346–347.

energies for future return, while in the contrary case, underinvestment is the rule." [28]

The Rate of Return over Cost in Relation to the Rate of Interest

"A discrepancy of one or two points between the rate of interest as it is and as it should be [29] is therefore of no trifling importance. Its cumulative effects, although seldom realized, are serious. . . . The truth is that the rate of interest is not a narrow phenomenon applying only to a few business contracts, but permeates all economic relations. It is a link which binds man to the future and by which he makes all his far-reaching decisions." [30]

Expectation of high rates of return over cost, arising from the exploitation of rich natural resources and from inventions and discoveries, is the driving force of expansion leading to rising income streams. "The most striking examples of increasing income-streams are found in new countries. . . . American incomes have been on the increase for two hundred years. It is also true that during this period of rising incomes, the rate of interest has been high. The simplest interpretation of these facts is that Americans, being constantly under the influence of great expectations, have been always ready to promise a relatively large part of their abundant future income for a relatively small addition to their present; just as he who expects soon to come into a fortune wishes to anticipate its realization by contracting a loan." In like manner, "while it is quite true that the exploitation of our natural resources required the construction of railways and other forms of capital, this fact is better and more fully expressed in terms of income. We wanted, not the railways and machinery themselves, but the future enjoyable products to which this apparatus led." [31] Thus it is that "in virgin countries like the United States in the last two centuries, Australia and South Africa, rich in timber, untouched ore, and

---

[28] Irving Fisher, *The Rate of Interest,* The Macmillan Company, New York, 1907, pp. 286–287.

[29] Compare this with Wicksell's "actual rate" and "normal rate."

[30] Fisher, *The Rate of Interest,* p. 336.

[31] *Ibid.,* pp. 304–305.

raw materials generally, the income-stream is of the ascending type and produces a high rate of preference." [32]

The "growth or waning of natural resources" and changes due to "misfortunes and inventions" affect the income stream. "The range of choice in any community is subject to many changes as time goes on, due chiefly to one of three causes. First, a progressive increase or decrease in resources; second, the discovery of new resources or means of developing old ones; and third, change in political conditions. . . . The constant stream of new inventions . . . by making the available income-streams rich in the remote future, tends to make the rate of interest high. This effect, however, is confined to the period of exploitation of the new invention, and is succeeded later by an opposite tendency. During the last half century the exploitation of Stephenson's invention of the locomotive, by presenting the possibility of a relatively large future income at the cost of comparatively little sacrifice in the present, has tended to keep the rate of interest high. As the period of railroad building is drawing to a close, this effect is becoming exhausted, and the tendency of the rate of interest, so far as this influence is concerned, is to fall." [33]

These quotations are peculiarly significant, coming as they do from Fisher, who was in general disposed to emphasize the importance of autonomous or independently determined monetary factors, such as gold production or deliberate control of the money supply. In fact, however, Fisher comes to very much the same conclusion as Wicksell: that the initiating impulses for expansion or contraction have in the past come in large measure from technical progress, discoveries, and inventions, which raise the "rate of return over cost"—Wicksell's natural rate or Keynes' marginal efficiency of capital. Moreover, Fisher, as also Wicksell, appears to agree with Spiethoff that the process of investment, given any achieved level of technique, eventually approaches a point of saturation. Thus the "rate of return over cost" falls, the rate of interest lags behind, and contraction sets in.

Fisher, even more than Wicksell, was thinking of rather long-

---

[32] *Ibid.*, p. 311.

[33] *Ibid.*, pp. 311, 330–331.

run movements, and was not primarily concerned with the problem of industrial fluctuations. He did write an article on the "so-called business cycle" and one book, of a rather popular nature, on *Booms and Depressions* (1932). In the former he argued that there is really no cycle, but only erratic fluctuations in the purchasing power of money—the "dance of the dollar." In the latter he argued that the process of debt creation is the cause of the boom, while the high level of outstanding debt in relation to the falling price level is the leading feature of the depression period. Here he is dealing with surface manifestations, and not with fundamentals. The foundation stones for a theory of business cycles contained in his *Rate of Interest* and in his *Theory of Interest* were neglected.

JOHN MAYNARD KEYNES (1883–1946)

Keynes and the Continental Writers

Keynes' *Treatise on Money* (1930) could perhaps be described as a belated, and in some measure confused, effort to catch up with Continental thinking on the saving-investment problem, the natural rate and the money rate of interest, factors affecting the natural rate, and basic factors underlying fluctuations in the rate of investment.

The *Treatise on Money* [34] does indeed contain a wealth of materials and analyses on a wide range of banking and monetary problems. But the chapters dealing with the problems of the business cycle do not stand up well either in terms of the work of Keynes' predecessors or in terms of his own later work.

Keynes himself says that in writing the *Treatise,* which occupied him several years, he felt like one forcing his way through a confused jungle, and he wound up with ideas widely different from those with which he started. Writing the book was a process of getting rid of old ideas. And this process was still going on when the book was published. Gradually there emerged the *General Theory of Employment, Interest and Money,* [35] a work which has

[34] J. M. Keynes, *A Treatise on Money,* Harcourt, Brace and Company, New York, 1930.

[35] *General Theory of Employment, Interest and Money,* Harcourt, Brace and Company, New York, 1936.

added significantly to our tools of theoretical analysis and has, moreover, given stimulus to statistical studies of the business cycle.

In the *Treatise,* Keynes failed to utilize to the full the best work of his predecessors. Nevertheless, he did sense what was most significant and where the frontiers of useful exploration lay. He recognized Tugan-Baranowsky as the "first and most original" of the school of writers with which he found himself in strong sympathy; he accepted "unreservedly" Schumpeter's theory of innovation; he spoke approvingly of the work of Spiethoff; and he gave high praise to the "outstanding attempt at a systematic treatment, namely, Knut Wicksell's *Geldzins und Güterpreise,* published in German in 1898, a book which deserves more fame and much more attention than it has received from English-speaking economists." The terrain covered by those writers was regarded by Keynes as most fruitful for further study and exploration.

Savings and Investment

In the *Treatise,* the cycle was conceived to be essentially a fluctuation in the rate of investment. A boom was a period in which investment exceeded savings, and a depression a period in which investment fell below savings. Income was thus driven up and down around a normal level, which he designated as E. At E, the normal income level, investment was equal to savings; $I = S$. Savings, S, were defined as that part of *normal* income, E, which is not consumed. Thus savings, S, are not *actual* savings but *normal* savings. At the equilibrium or normal income level $I = S$. Now *actual* income is equal to the price level, π, times the output of final goods and services, O. Thus *actual* income is πO, *normal* income is E, and $(I - S)$ will indicate how far *actual* income, πO, exceeds or falls below the normal income E. Accordingly, we arrive at the following equation: $\pi O = E + (I - S)$.

When I exceeds S we have a boom, investment is above normal, actual income rises above normal income, windfall profits are earned. The excess of I over S is the measure of the boom.

Windfall profits are equal to $\pi O - E$, or what amounts to the same thing, $I - S$. If, however, investment falls below savings, actual income, πO, is driven down below the normal income, E, by the amount that I falls below S. Windfall losses develop, equal to $\pi O - E$, or $I - S$.

Keynes' "S" is not actual savings, but the savings which would be made if the actual income were at normal. S is the savings that society *would* make if income were at the normal level. If investment is just sufficient to offset what people would save, S, at a normal income, then the actual income, πO, will be at normal, E. Income is driven up or down if investment exceeds or falls below this level. It is the fluctuation of I around S that produces the business cycle.

Tugan-Baranowsky, we may recall, believed that *actual* savings from current income were relatively stable, and he conceived the cycle as a fluctuation of investment around this relatively stable level of current savings. In boom periods investment exceeded savings; in depression periods investment fell below the rate of current savings. With Keynes (in the *Treatise*) the boom is a period in which investment is above normal saving (when I is normal it is equal to S) and depression is a period in which investment falls below the normal level of saving.

Defects in the Treatise

The Keynesian analysis in the *Treatise* exaggerated, on the side of policy, the role of central bank manipulation of the rate of interest as a means of controlling the cycle. On the side of theoretical analysis it is defective, among other things, in the respect that when I falls below S, income in fact falls by much more than this amount. The *Treatise* analysis failed to take cognizance of the multiplier. Income will fall not by $I - S$, but by $(I - S)k$, in which k is the multiplier, and S is the rate of saving at full employment. (See Chapter 10 in this book.)

The Business Cycle as Viewed in the General Theory

Keynes' *General Theory* has already been taken account of in Part II of this book, which deals with the modern theory of income determination. Here it is only necessary to consider that part of the *General Theory* which deals specifically with the business cycle.

The general proposition laid down in the *General Theory* is as follows: "The succession of Boom and Slump can be described and analysed in terms of the fluctuations of the marginal efficiency of capital relatively to the rate of interest."[36]

Keynes argues that the trade cycle is mainly due to a cyclical change in the marginal efficiency of capital, though complicated (and often aggravated) by changes, induced by the cycle itself, in the state of liquidity preference and in the propensity to consume. These *associated* changes serve to intensify the swings of the cycle; but the cycle itself is basically occasioned by fluctuations in the marginal efficiency of capital.

Movement down the Schedule vs. Shift in the Schedule

Here it is important to be sure that we know precisely what we are talking about. A change in the marginal efficiency of capital may result from *moving down on the schedule;* or it may result from a *shift* in the schedule. Both play highly significant roles in the cycle.

Let us first consider the matter of the downward movement *on* the schedule. If we assume the schedule of the marginal efficiency of capital as given, every additional increment of investment made during the boom years means a movement *down* on the schedule; the marginal efficiency of capital is pushed lower and lower by the process of investment. If, in the short run, we assume no induced shift in the schedule (such as might be caused by technical progress or growth in population), continued investment would drive the marginal efficiency of capital down lower and lower. Further investment would cease when the marginal efficiency of capital was driven down to the prevailing rate of interest. Or if we make the heroic assumption that the rate of interest is progressively lowered (by monetary management) toward zero, investment could theoretically continue until the marginal efficiency of capital reached zero. This would be the condition described by Keynes as "full investment"—i.e., a condition in which further investment could not reasonably be expected to yield anything above mere replacement cost. The "rate of return over cost" (Fisher) would be zero.

Movement *down* the marginal efficiency of capital schedule during the boom is stated by Keynes in the following, in which

[36] *General Theory,* p. 144.

special reference is made to the United States prior to 1929: "Net investment during the previous five years had been, indeed, on so enormous a scale in the aggregate that the prospective yield of further additions was, coolly considered, falling rapidly." The boom dies a natural death, since the very process of investment progressively lowers the marginal efficiency of capital.

A more dynamic, and also more realistic, interpretation of the statement quoted above would involve combining a sliding down *on the schedule* with a *shift* in the schedule. During the rapidly expanding phase of the boom, the net effect of both movements combined might be a *rise* in the marginal efficiency of capital—the upward shift being more rapid than the movement down the schedule. But if the rate of investment continues at a high level for a considerable period, the movement *down* the schedule will eventually outrun the upward *shift* in the schedule; the net effect then would be a progressive fall in the marginal efficiency of capital. Thus the boom would eventually come to an end.

Volatile Expectations

But Keynes points out that there is another aspect to the matter, involving the very difficult business of distinguishing between (a) a schedule of the marginal efficiency of capital, "coolly considered" in terms of a realistic appraisal of capital requirements judged from the standpoint of long-term considerations of growth; and (b) a schedule of the marginal efficiency of capital, based on highly volatile and illusory expectations of yield—errors of optimism being rapidly replaced by errors of pessimism once doubt enters and begins to spread. It is the latter schedule which controls the rate of investment, however illusory the expectations may be.

The former we may perhaps designate as the *realistic* schedule; the latter, as the *volatile* schedule. In the end the underlying technical facts with respect to capital requirements are bound to control. Errors of optimism or pessimism will sooner or later be dispelled by the cooler judgment of the more far-seeing entrepreneurs, who set the pace for the general herd of followers.

Expectations "play a dominant part in determining the scale on which new investment is deemed advisable," and the basis for such expectations is highly precarious. Expectations rest on shifting and unreliable evidence, and are therefore subject to sudden and violent changes. The typical explanation of the crisis is "not primarily a rise in the rate of interest; but a sudden collapse in the marginal efficiency of capital."[37]

As the boom progresses, two hard facts press increasingly for recognition, namely the growing abundance of capital goods[38] and their rising costs of production. Both of these operate in the direction of reducing the marginal efficiency of capital. Yet the latter stages of the boom are characterized by optimistic expectations as to their future yield sufficiently strong to offset their rising costs, and probably also the rise in the rate of interest. These expectations exceed a "reasonable estimate of the future yield of capital assets."[39] Doubts arise with respect to the "reliability of the prospective yield" as the stock of newly produced durable goods steadily increases. When disillusion falls, it may fall with "sudden and even catastrophic force." The ensuing collapse in the marginal efficiency of capital (violent downward shift in the volatile schedule) causes a sharp increase in liquidity preference. Thus the collapse in the marginal efficiency schedule tends to be associated with a rise in the rate of interest, and this *aggravates* the decline in investment. But the essence of the situation is the fall in the marginal efficiency of capital.

"Later on, a decline in the rate of interest will be a great aid to recovery and, probably, a necessary condition of it. But, for the moment, the collapse in the marginal efficiency of capital may be so complete that no practicable reduction in the rate of interest will be enough." This it is which renders the slump so intractable. It is no easy matter to revive the marginal efficiency of capital, "determined as it is by the uncontrollable and disobedient psychology of the business world." It is the "return of confidence" which is so insusceptible to control.[40]

We may pause here to note that these last sentences sound very much like John Stuart Mill, John Mills, and Alfred Marshall.

---

37 *Ibid.*, p. 315.
38 This relates to the movement *down* the schedule.
39 *General Theory*, p. 316.
40 *Ibid.*, pp. 316–317.

Keynes, indeed, suggested here and there, but never adequately explored, the effect of changes in technology and population growth upon the schedule of the marginal efficiency of capital. Yet there are paragraphs in the "Notes on the Trade Cycle" (Chapter 22) which *seem* to say that the fluctuations in the marginal efficiency of capital are due merely to psychological waves of optimism and pessimism and have no basis in the real factors controlling investment outlets. Nevertheless, taking the *General Theory* as a whole, this conclusion could not be justified.

Longevity of Durable Assets

Indeed, immediately after the paragraph on the "return of confidence," Keynes hastens to add that the time element in the recovery of the marginal efficiency of capital relates to the length of life of durable assets on the one side and to the "normal rate of growth" on the other. At this point, however, one could have wished for a more thorough discussion of the influence of the "normal rate of growth in a given epoch" and of the factors underlying this growth. As it is he merely throws out the suggestion that a shortage of fixed capital goods after an interval of time develops partly through use, decay, and obsolescence, and partly because of the normal rate of growth.[41]

Surplus Inventory Stocks

Another factor influencing the length of the depression is the period required to absorb the surplus stocks of inventories which continue to accumulate in the first phase of the downturn. The carrying costs of surplus stocks force their absorption within a certain period. But the process of absorption means negative investment. During the downswing, moreover, there is also a reduction of working capital (goods in process). Thus the initial decline in fixed capital investment exerts a strong cumulative influence operating through the disinvestment of stocks of goods (inventories) and the disinvestment of working capital.

---

[41] Keynes does not say that the stock of capital actually declines in the depression period. He considers the stock of capital, affected as it is by the rate of depreciation and replacement, *in relation to the rate of growth.* His shortage of fixed capital is a relative, not an absolute, concept.

The Stock Market and the Propensity to Consume

A serious fall in the marginal efficiency of capital affects adversely the propensity to consume, particularly with respect to the class who are actively interested in the stock market. This group's readiness to spend is directly influenced by the rise and decline in the market value of their financial investments. The propensity to consume luxury goods rises and falls with the stock market. Thus the depression, once started, feeds on itself, and cumulates; and similarly with respect to the recovery.

The Problem of Overinvestment

Is it *overinvestment* that brings the boom to an end? Well, that depends upon what is meant by "overinvestment." Keynes suggests that the term is ambiguous.

Using his discussion largely as a basis, I propose to set out the following possible interpretations: (1) "Overinvestment" might mean simply an investment based on "a misguided state of expectation." The marginal efficiency is believed to be higher than it in fact is, viewed "in a correct state of expectation." Too much is invested owing to excess optimism. (2) "Overinvestment" might mean that too much has been invested in view of the prevailing high rate of interest. At a lower rate, established by monetary and fiscal policy, the investment might have been quite justified. (3) "Overinvestment" might mean that the stock of capital goods has been increased to a point at which the last increment of capital added could not earn in the course of its life even its replacement cost. Even at zero rate of interest there would then be overinvestment. If the interest rate were negative, however, there would not be overinvestment. Thus (3) is really a sub-point under (2). (4) "Overinvestment" might simply mean that the stock of capital goods is too large if income should fall below full employment. If full employment could be maintained, however, the stock of capital might not be excessive.

It needs, however, to be stressed (as Keynes does not do) that once the *correct* amount of investment has been made, in view of the prevailing level of technique and population growth, no further investment would, for the time being, be justified. The boom would come to an end, even though there were no errors of judgment, once the "bucket" of capital requirements has been filled. It does not require "overinvestment" to bring a boom to a close.

It is, of course, true that misguided expectations are typically rampant in the boom period. Entrepreneurs are in the usual case carried away by errors of optimism. The system "overshoots." But these errors are not a necessary condition. Sporadic rates of growth of capital formation are all that is needed to produce economic cycles, even if the actual stock of capital never exceeds what is justified. In Spiethoff's language, the bucket is filled, but not "overfilled." Cyclical fluctuations will follow from intermittent surges of growth. And such surges of growth need not be based on errors of judgment, though when such errors of optimism and pessimism, induced by the cycle itself, do arise, the cycle will be intensified.

Errors of Optimism

Errors of optimism are in fact important for Keynes' theory of the boom, as can be seen from the following:

"The boom which is destined to end in a slump is caused, therefore, by the combination of a rate of interest, which in a correct state of expectation would be too high for full employment, with a misguided state of expectation which, so long as it lasts, prevents this rate of interest from being in fact deterrent. A boom is a situation in which over-optimism triumphs over a rate of interest which, in a cooler light, would be seen to be excessive." [42]

Keynes, following English tradition, perhaps overstresses errors of optimism. Even though there were no errors of optimistic expectations, the boom would nonetheless develop and subsequently die away if changes in technology led to intermittent surges of growth in capital formation. Of course, if the progress of technique and population growth were absolutely uniform, it could be said that failure on the part of entrepreneurs to respond to such uniform and continuing growth requirements by a quite stable rate of investment might be regarded as a collective error of judgment by entrepreneurs as a class. But such a stable investment response would involve not only perfect foresight but

[42] *General Theory,* p. 322. Compare this with the views of John Stuart Mill, John Mills, and Alfred Marshall (Chapter 15 in this book).

also a homogeneous group of entrepreneurs. Inertia will, in fact, cause a lagged investment response to the capital requirements of normal growth, which, after a time, under the stimulus of innovating leaders, will result in a "catching-up" process. Such a catching-up process might be perfectly rational, devoid altogether of errors of optimism. The investment might be carried to just the "right point" and no further. The inertia of the less responsive entrepreneurs, and their subsequent herdlike rush to make good the investment deficiency, must certainly be sharply distinguished from "waves of pessimism and optimism." Technical advance, as Wicksell rightly said, is sometimes precipitate and sometimes delayed. And it is "natural and at the same time economically justified," as he put it, that "people seek to exploit the favourable situation as quickly as possible." [43] This kind of thing is not to be confused with misguided expectations.

Underconsumption

Keynes devotes a section to the "important schools of thought" which maintain that the chronic tendency to underemployment is to be traced to underconsumption; that is, to a propensity to consume which is unduly low. In conditions where the volume of investment is subject to the "vagaries of the marginal efficiency of capital" and to a long-term rate of interest "which seldom or never falls below a conventional level," these schools of thought are, he felt, undoubtedly on the right track. Still Keynes differed from them on both practical and theoretical grounds; on practical grounds, because they laid, he thought, too much emphasis on consumption in a situation in which there was still a large need, properly guided and directed, for investment; on theoretical grounds, because they neglected the fact that there are *two* ways to expand output, namely investment and consumption. Keynes was impressed by the "great social advantages of increasing the stock of capital until it ceases to be scarce." [44] Hence he thought the wisest course was to advance on both fronts at once, to promote investment and at the same time to promote consumption. With respect to investment he aimed at a "socially controlled rate

[43] Wicksell, *Lectures on Political Economy*, Volume II, *Money*, pp. 211–212.
[44] Keynes, *General Theory*, p. 325.

of investment with a view to a progressive decline in the marginal efficiency of capital." But even so he thought it unlikely that full employment could be maintained with "the existing propensity to consume." [45]

Interest-Rate Policy

Keynes opposed the view that the way to manage the cycle is to choke off the boom; rather, he would try "to enable the so-called boom to last." To this end he favored a lower rate of interest. Referring to the 1929 boom in the United States, he said that the boom "could not have continued on a sound basis except with a very low long-term rate of interest, and an avoidance of misdirected investment."

If indeed major changes of policy (such as the control of investment and drastic changes in the propensity to consume) are ruled out, he agreed that a "more advantageous average rate of expectation" might result from a banking policy which "nipped in the bud an incipient boom" by a rate of interest high enough to discourage misguided optimists. A fluctuating interest rate policy might possibly be better than no policy at all. But something could be said on both sides, and he regarded the evidence as inconclusive. However this may be, he was at any rate convinced that the outlook which merely aims at flattening out the cycle without raising the average level of employment is "dangerously and unnecessarily defeatist." [46]

Stocks of Raw Materials

Finally there is a very interesting section on the role of stocks of raw materials and inventories in the business cycle. The Jevons explanation, that the trade cycle is "primarily due to fluctuations in the bounty of the harvest," he regarded as extremely plausible at the time when Jevons wrote, but as of relatively little importance in the current highly industrialized world. Keynes fits the Jevons explanation into his own pattern of analysis in a most interesting manner. "When an exceptionally large harvest is gathered in, an important addition is usually made to the quantity carried

[45] *Ibid.*, p. 325.
[46] *Ibid.*, p. 327.

over into later years." [47] This raises the level of investment, and promotes a boom. The investment in these stocks is financed out of savings, the funds being paid out to farmers in current income. But this involves no drain on the income expenditure of other sections of the community. If, however, there is a poor harvest, the carry-over stock is drawn upon while no current income flows to the farmers. There is then no current investment in carry-over stocks, and income payments to farmers therefore decline. In earlier periods, when agriculture was the predominant industry, investment in (and disinvestment of) surplus agricultural stocks must have played a leading role in the fluctuations in the rate of investment. But nowadays agriculture plays a much smaller role, and there has, moreover, developed a world market for most agricultural products which tends to average out the effects of good and bad seasons.

Yet even today changes in the stocks of raw materials, agricultural and mineral, play a considerable part in determining the volume of current investment. In a slump, stocks of raw materials at first accumulate, and they have to be liquidated. This means disinvestment. The reduction of stocks to a normal level is a painful but necessary process. Only when it is completed is the way prepared for substantial recovery. Keynes calls to witness the difficulties on this score in the early phases of the "New Deal" recovery program.

Investment in "inventories" of finished and unfinished goods plays a large role, Keynes thinks, in the minor oscillations of the trade cycle. Manufacturers are likely to make minor miscalculations in planning their output in relation to sales. The "difference of pace between running a little ahead and dropping back again has proved sufficient in its effect on the current rate of investment" to display itself in the minor cycles in the United States.[48]

Effect of a Low Propensity to Consume

Reverting to his discussion of the underconsumptionists, Keynes leaves untouched the question whether a low propensity to consume has simply the effect of causing a low average level of

[47] *Ibid.*, pp. 329–330.
[48] *Ibid.*, p. 332.

employment without affecting the *fluctuation* in investment, income, and employment; or whether, on the other hand, it has the effect of "making room," so to speak, for a wider amplitude of fluctuations. If an upward expansionist movement, once started, tends to cumulate until it is at last "reined in" by a scarcity of current savings, as Tugan-Baranowsky and Cassel had it, or by "hitting the ceiling" of full employment (Hicks), then the effect of a low propensity to consume would be to cause not only a low *average* level of employment, but also a more violent fluctuation commensurate with the spread between consumption and income at full employment.

Wider Aspects of Keynes' General Theory

The Keynesian analysis of income determination, which we have discussed in Part II of this book, extends far beyond, though it relates to, the theory of the business cycle as such. In this chapter we have restricted ourselves to Keynes' own comments on the bearing of his theory on the trade cycle. But this by itself alone would not adequately disclose the importance of the Keynesian analysis.

With respect to both Wicksell and Keynes, it would be a great mistake to think that the influence of each of them on business-cycle theory is limited to the formal discussions which they gave to the problem of cyclical fluctuations. In both cases, the theoretical contributions ramify far and wide beyond matters pertaining directly to the cycle; business-cycle theory nonetheless requires the underpinning of the fundamental theoretical apparatus which each of them developed.

18 · *Impulse and Propagation:* AFTALION · PIGOU · J. M. CLARK

Wicksell, as we have noted in the preceding chapter, had already by 1907 pointed out that, given certain characteristics of the economic system, erratic shocks may initiate wavelike movements. His analogy of the wooden rocking horse struck by a club illustrates vividly the problems of impulse and propagation. Later Pigou showed how industrial fluctuations are caused by the action of initiating impulses operating upon a complex of industrial and monetary conditions. And Aftalion's analysis lends itself peculiarly well, as we shall see, to econometric models in which the economy by its inner nature gathers ever stronger reversing forces the further it overshoots the equilibrium point. In this chapter we turn first to Aftalion's contributions.

ALBERT AFTALION (1874–)

Albert Aftalion presented his theory clearly and succinctly as early as 1909 in a series of articles in the *Revue d'économie politique,* entitled "La Réalité des surproductions générales." [1] These articles were followed by his large two-volume work, *Les Crises périodiques de surproduction,* published in 1913. Volume I

[1] The main lines of his analysis are compactly outlined in the March, 1909, issue, pp. 201–229. In fact, a brief introductory article had already appeared in the October, 1908, issue.

of this work consists largely of empirical studies of prices, wages, interest rates, profits, costs and productivity. The last two chapters are devoted to a brief survey and critique of current theories, especially the views of Tugan-Baranowsky and Spiethoff. Volume II begins with an analysis of the cyclical oscillations in the production of raw materials, industrial products, and consumers' goods; and this is followed by an exposition of the rhythm of demand and price movements. The last 150 pages of the volume are devoted to a restatement of his theory along the lines of the *Revue* articles of 1909.

Aftalion, indeed, was profoundly influenced in his thinking by the new directive which Tugan-Baranowsky and Spiethoff had given to business-cycle theory. He accepted the view that cyclical movements consist essentially of fluctuations in the output of fixed capital goods. But he did not agree that the fluctuations in the rate of investment are mainly controlled by the abundance or scarcity of free or disposable capital—in other words, by the volume of investment-seeking funds.

The Role of Consumer Wants

The cause of fluctuations in the rate of investment must be looked for, he believed, in the dynamics of consumer wants.[1a] Decisions to invest are influenced by expectations which relate in the final analysis to consumer demand. Capital goods derive their value from the value of the consumer goods which they produce.

No invention would lead to the formation of fixed capital did it not point the way toward the greater satisfaction of consumer wants. The end of all production is consumption. Thus, in a very fundamental sense, fluctuations in the demand for capital goods must be explained in terms of factors operating upon the wants of consumers and the demand to which these wants give rise.

More specifically, the boom does not come to an end, Aftalion thought, because of a "shortage of capital," as Tugan-Baranowsky

[1a] Aftalion, "La Réalité des surproductions générales," *Revue d'économie politique,* 1909; and *Les Crises périodiques de surproduction,* Vols. I and II, Marcel Rivière et Cie., Paris, 1913.

(and in a measure also Spiethoff) had it.[1b] Rather the boom ends because the vast output of capital goods eventually saturates consumer demand to a point at which there occurs a decline in the inducement to produce new "means of production." It is the progressive "glutting of wants" that eventually brings to an end the feverish output of fixed capital.

Diminishing Marginal Utilities

The descending order of yields from net additions to the stock of capital goods (which underlies the declining schedule of the marginal efficiency of capital) is due (1) to the diminishing possibilities of substituting capital for the other factors of production as more and more capital is added, and (2) to the diminishing value of consumers' goods, in relation to the cost of capital, as more and more consumers' goods are produced.

Take the case of residential building. In the boom more and more houses (fixed capital) are being produced. As more and more houses are added, the marginal utility of "housing" declines. This results in a lowering of rents. As rents decline, the *value* of houses falls in relation to the *cost* of houses. Thus the demand for new houses declines, and the construction boom is over.

An increased supply of consumers' goods causes a decline in their marginal utilities. This expresses itself in a fall in the prices of consumers' goods (and so in the *value* of the capital goods producing them) in relation to the *cost* of capital goods. The marginal utilities of consumers' goods fall by reason of the relative superabundance of these goods in relation to the prevailing level of wants. New consumers' wants must continually be created in order to open up new outlets for capital investment.

What Aftalion means in effect is this: The schedule of the diminishing yields of capital (as more and more increments are added) is in part to be explained by the "gluttability" of wants, and not solely by the substitutability of capital for other factors of production. Thus it is not merely the supply of capital goods in relation to the supply of other factors of production which plays a role in the determination of investment demand; the diminish-

[1b] Aftalion, *Les Crises périodiques de surproduction,* Vol. I, pp. 297–317.

ing utility of consumer goods, as the market becomes increasingly saturated, is also a significant factor.[1c]

The Rhythm in Business Expectations

Aftalion's theory implies that the expectations of those directing production are alternately too optimistic and too pessimistic. His theory aims to explain this rhythm in the forecasts of businessmen. The rhythm in expectations results from the capitalistic technique of production, i.e., from the fact that the modern system of production uses fixed capital which requires a long time for its construction,[2] and which, moreover, is highly durable. The rhythm is due to the "length of the process of production."

Three Strands in the Analysis

There are three strands in Aftalion's analysis of cyclical fluctuations, but all have to do with the nature of the modern industrial technique, which involves the use of fixed capital.[3]

The three strands referred to above are: (1) the long period required for capital construction and the difficulty resulting therefrom in adjusting the stock of fixed capital to the requirements of a fairly steady growth in final demand; (2) the durability of capital goods, which prolongs the period of depression until eventually the stock is gradually worn out and undercapacity develops, leading to a new boom; (3) the "acceleration principle"—wide fluctuations in derived demand for durable capital goods spring from relatively small fluctuations in the primary demand.

Ludwig Pohle had found the cause of fluctuations in the rate of investment in the failure to adjust the growth in the *stock of fixed*

1c Aftalion, "La Réalité des surproductions générales," *Revue d'économie politique,* 1909, pp. 85–100.

2 In Pigou's *Economics of Welfare* (Macmillan and Co., Ltd., London, 1st ed., 1920) we read: "The kernel of the explanation is that optimistic error and pessimistic error, when discovered, give birth to one another in an endless chain, and that the interval between the successive generations is mainly, but not exclusively, determined by the period of gestation of industrial plant and machinery" (p. 848).

3 See A. Aftalion, "The Theory of Economic Cycles Based on the Capitalistic Technique of Production," *Review of Economic Statistics,* October, 1927.

capital to the fairly steadily growing *needs* of an increasing population.[4]

This method of stating the problem of the fluctuation in the rate of investment suggests the central element in Aftalion's analysis—a feature which represents a brilliant and original contribution to business-cycle theory. A fairly stable growth in consumer demand may not be met by a steady growth (net investment) in the stock of capital goods. And the reason is the adjustment difficulties inherent in the long period required for the production of fixed capital. Aftalion's furnace illustration, discussed below, is designed to show how the time element in the production of capital goods can account for the cycle. This matter relates to the first strand referred to above—the "period of gestation."

Karl Marx, in Volume II, Part II, Chapter IX of *Capital,* had already suggested that the *long life* of fixed capital might be a very important element in the theory of economic cycles. This fact involves the possibility of continued production of the final products without even replacing the existing equipment for a considerable period of time and opens the possibility of widely divergent movements in the rate of production of consumers' goods on the one side, and the output of capital goods on the other. The "longevity" of capital goods plays a role in Aftalion's theory, supplementary to the "period of gestation," which relates to the long period required to *produce* fixed capital.

The statement by Marx with respect to the influence of "longevity" is as follows:

"To the same extent that the volume of the value and the duration of the fixed capital develop with the evolution of the capitalistic mode of production, does the life of industry and of industrial capital develop in each particular investment into one of many years, say of ten years on an average. If the development of fixed capital extends the length of this life on one side, it is on the other side shortened by the continuous revolution of the instruments of production, which likewise increases incessantly with the development of capitalist production. This implies a change

[4] See Ludwig Pohle, *Bevölkerungsbewegung, Kapitalbildung, und periodische Wirtschaftskrisen,* Göttingen, 1902.

in the instruments of production and the necessity of continuous replacement on account of virtual wear and tear, long before they are worn out physically. One may assume that this life cycle, in the essential branches of great industry, now averages ten years. However, it is not a question of any one definite number here. So much at least is evident that this cycle comprising a number of years, through which capital is compelled to pass by its fixed part, furnishes a material basis for the periodical commercial crises in which business goes through successive periods of lassitude, average activity, overspeeding, and crisis. It is true that the periods in which capital is invested are different in time and place. But a crisis is always the starting point of a large amount of new investments. Therefore it also constitutes, from the point of view of society, more or less of a new material basis for the next cycle of turnover." [5]

The suggestion here made by Marx is that the life cycle of fixed capital produces replacement cycles, and these lie at the root of the periodic industrial cycle. This is the second strand in Aftalion's thinking.

Finally, there is the acceleration principle. In a capitalistic society which carries on production by the roundabout process very slight fluctuations in consumer demand may give rise to pronounced fluctuations in the demand for fixed capital. The demand for fixed capital, said Aftalion, is a derived demand, "un besoin *dérivé*."

General Synthesis of Aftalion's Analysis

Aftalion speaks of the persistent difficulty of maintaining economic equilibrium. Observation reveals perpetual oscillations rather than a state of equilibrium. These oscillations are brought about in a regime of capitalistic production—not a juridical regime, but a technical regime making a large use of fixed capital. Once the equilibrium is broken in a capitalistic regime, the alternating series of prosperity and depression will succeed each other, and the economic organism will discover itself caught in a chain,

---

[5] Karl Marx, *Capital,* Charles H. Kerr & Co., Chicago, 1919, Vol. II, Part II, Chapter IX, p. 211.

without end, of action and reaction which constitutes the periodic cycles.[6]

It is the capitalistic, time-consuming process of production that transforms the small oscillations of consumer demand into pronounced periods of prosperity and depression. Instead of applying labor and land directly to satisfy wants, the characteristic feature of the modern technique of production is to make first an elaborate outfit of capital goods, the construction of which requires many months or even years; and by means of these, eventually, to make consumers' goods. This phase of capitalistic production, the period in which capital goods are being created, is the period of prosperity, which springs out of an existing scarcity of consumers' goods. This scarcity would at once be satisfied, and equilibrium quickly restored, were it not for the fact that a long time must elapse before the completion of capital goods makes possible the increase in the output of consumers' goods.[7] It is the capitalistic technique of production which renders inevitable the prolonged disruption of economic equilibrium.

But when the new capital is created, there arrives the second phase of capitalistic production, namely a greatly increased output of consumption goods. The supply of fixed capital is now ample to satisfy the requirements of consumers. New capital formation then ceases. This ushers in the period of depression. Its persistence over a considerable extent of time follows from the longevity of fixed capital, which enables it to function over a long period. Eventually much capital is worn out, and so a new burst of investment occurs. This enlarged stock of capital goods will eventually produce a superabundance of consumers' goods, and this superabundance will manifest itself in a reduced demand for new capital goods.[8] This condition will continue as long as there

[6] Aftalion, "La Realité des surproductions générales," *Revue d'économie politique,* 1909, pp. 201–203.

[7] Bouniatian objects to this argument. He points out that the increased demand for consumption goods calls forth a more intensive use of existing equipment. Hence the revival leads at once to an increased output of consumption goods. Cf. M. Bouniatian, "Ma Théorie des crises et les critiques de M. Aftalion," *Revue d'économie politique,* 1924, pp. 659–660.

[8] An increased supply of goods brings a decline in their marginal utilities, which expresses itself in a fall in prices of consumers' goods in relation to the *cost* of capital goods.

is an ample supply of the capital previously created. Finally, a considerable part of this fixed capital is worn out, and so there emerges a new scarcity of consumers' goods, and with it a new derived demand for fixed capital. Thus the economy tends to "overshoot," first in one direction, then in the other.

Aftalion does not pretend to find an exact correlation between different industries with respect to these two stages and the duration of these two periods of the economic cycle. The period of production of fixed capital varies with each type of commodity. He contends that it is sufficient for his theory if you grant that, looking at the general economic organism, a time comes in the capitalistic production when a scarcity of goods reveals itself; later a moment when, thanks to the production of the required capital, the need begins largely to be satisfied; and finally a moment when, thanks to the wearing out of a part of the capital, the glut of goods disappears. Taking industry as a whole into consideration, prosperity does not terminate when a single category of capital goods is completed and put to use. Not until a great quantity of capital in the majority of industries is set to work turning out additional consumers' goods does the period of high capital formation come to an end. Likewise the period of depression does not last until a scarcity of capital appears in *every* industry. Prosperity and depression are not characterized by the peak and bottom of *all prices,* but by the peak and bottom of *most* prices. We are concerned with the general tendency.

The modern technique of production, which uses a large amount of fixed capital, is, then, in Aftalion's view, the chief characteristic which determines the amplitude of the oscillations around the equilibrium and the duration of prosperity and depression. Nothing more, he thinks, is needed to explain the periodicity of the cycle or the emergence of crises from prosperity, and prosperity from depression. The longer the period required to produce fixed capital, the longer is the duration of prosperity and the greater the overcapitalization which brings on the crisis. Thus the entire periodic cycle is due to the inability of capitalistic production to satisfy *immediately* the social need.[9]

When there is a scarcity of consumption goods, their price

[9] Aftalion, *op. cit.,* pp. 203–211.

rises; the need for consumption goods excites a need for capital goods and elevates their price. An excess or deficiency of consumption goods, though weak and giving rise to moderate fluctuations in price, will cause a greater fluctuation in the value of capital goods.[10] The new capital goods must be produced before we can get more consumption goods than existing machinery can manufacture. The manufacturers of consumption goods, attracted by high profits, desire to expand their plants and to multiply their machines. The makers of machines, factories, raw materials, and semifinished goods buy in turn from other manufacturers. But months and years pass before the new machines and factories are ready to fabricate consumption goods. During this time the need for consumption goods goes unsatisfied. The period of high prices, high profits, and prosperity is prolonged.[11]

A rhythmic movement of incomes, wages and profits results from the capital-using system of production. Expansion in the production of fixed capital raises wage incomes and profits, but the scarcity of consumers' goods continues until the fixed capital is finished. Accordingly, the demand for consumers' goods outruns the supply of consumers' goods during the prosperity phase, and prices rise.

Thus it is through the intermediary of *price* and *profits* that the intensity of social wants gives a powerful impulse to production. Prices and profits control production, but as regulating factors they fail to maintain equilibrium because of the long time which in a capitalistic regime separates the beginning of the productive process from the end.[12] Expectations are likely to be based on current prices and current demand. But current prices and the current state of demand are quite deceitful indicators in an economy which uses fixed capital requiring a long period for its construction.

---

[10] Suppose a differential between costs and selling prices of 5 per cent. Then a 5 per cent increase in selling prices will result in a 100 per cent increase in profits, and therefore in a large increase in the value of capital goods. See T. N. Carver, "A Suggestion for a Theory of Industrial Depressions," *Quarterly Journal of Economics,* May, 1903.

[11] Aftalion, *op. cit.,* pp. 208, 211–215.

[12] Aftalion, *op. cit.,* p. 209.

The Furnace Illustration

If because of low temperature one wishes to revive the fire, it will take some time before one obtains the desired heat. As the cold persists and as the thermometer continues to register it, one is likely, if not guided by experience, to put on still more fuel. When at last the fuel begins to burn briskly, the heat will become unbearable. If one is guided by the present sensation of cold and by the indications of the thermometer, one will greatly overheat the room because of the time required before the fuel ignites and the heat circulates through the room. Misled by the "thermometer and the sensation of cold," one will commit a serious error owing to the long lag between the first steps taken to increase the heat and the time when eventually more heat becomes available.[13]

It is exactly the same in the economic world. The continuing shortage of consumption goods, the continuing high prices and profits in consumer goods industries, lead entrepreneurs to suppose that the scarcity of capital is not being overcome. Thus errors of judgment [14] are caused by the capitalistic, or roundabout, process of production.[15] In the pre-capitalistic civilization, price was indeed a good indicator of social wants. In that age the oscilla-

---

[13] Aftalion, *op. cit.*, pp. 209–210.

[14] Pigou, following Aftalion, lays great stress on errors of judgment, and these he attributes chiefly to the roundabout capitalistic process. He says: "The kernel of the explanation is that optimistic error and pessimistic error, when discovered, give birth to one another in an endless chain, and that the interval between the successive generations is mainly, but not exclusively, determined by the period of gestation of industrial plant and machinery" (*Economics of Welfare,* Macmillan and Co., Ltd., London, 1st ed., 1920, p. 848). The section devoted to business cycles was omitted in the second edition. See also Pigou, *Industrial Fluctuations,* 1st ed., pp. 83–84.

[15] See also Taussig, who says that the causes of the larger oscillations are to be found partly in "the time-using or capitalistic method of production." "When there are heavy investments of capital in new enterprises, then the chances of error are greatest, and at the same time a course of error can be persisted in for the longest time without retribution. The railways, so far-reaching in all their industrial effects, have been of the first significance here also. Many of the crises of the nineteenth century were closely associated with excessive or unprofitable railway building. . . . Not until it (the railway) has been in operation for some years can it be definitely known whether the final increase in enjoyable goods, or human satisfactions, has been such as to justify the large investment" (*Principles of Economics,* The Macmillan Company, New York, 1921, Vol. I, pp. 391–392). See also Spiethoff, "Krisen," *Handwörterbuch der Staatswissenschaften* (1925), VI, p. 77.

tions around the equilibrium proved to be short. Not so in a capitalistic society.

But we must not blame the thermometer—price and profits—too much. Even if these were abolished there would still remain the difficulty of adjusting the capitalistic, or roundabout, process of production to social wants.[16]

The Acceleration Principle

An increase in the demand for consumers' goods gives rise to far greater fluctuations in the demand for fixed capital. Take a purely hypothetical case: An industry requires a hundred thousand looms. The average length of life of these looms is ten years. Then ten thousand looms have to be replaced each year. If, now, the consumers' demand increases 10 per cent, there is an additional need of ten thousand new looms. Thus a 10 per cent increase in consumer demand gives rise to a 100 per cent increase in the demand for fixed capital.[17] This statement of the principle of derived demand appeared, it should be noted, as early as 1909.

The demand for equipment not only fluctuates more violently than the demand for consumption goods but also antedates it, because the demand for net additions to fixed capital depends not upon the level of the demand for consumers' goods but upon the *rate of growth* of this demand. When the *rate of growth* of demand for consumption goods slackens (even though the demand is still rising, but at a lower rate of increase), the demand for *additional* equipment suffers an absolute decline.[18] If the demand for consumption goods should cease to grow (that is, should remain constant) no *additional* equipment will be needed, and the capital-producing industries would have nothing to do except to replace and maintain the existing equipment as it wears out.[19]

16 Aftalion, *op. cit.*, pp. 209, 257–259.

17 *Ibid.*, pp. 218–220.

18 Thus the cause *appears* to follow the effect. See C. F. Bickerdike, "A Non-Monetary Cause of Fluctuations in Employment," *Economic Journal*, September, 1914; J. M. Clark, "Business Acceleration and the Law of Demand," *Journal of Political Economy*, 1917; and A. C. Pigou, *Economics of Welfare*, Macmillan and Co., Ltd., London, 1920.

19 In all advanced industrial countries there is a tendency for a larger and larger proportion of labor to be absorbed in maintaining and increasing the supply of fixed capital. The relative proportion of labor devoted to maintenance and

If there should be a slight decline of, say, 5 per cent in the demand for consumables, it would not even be necessary to replace all the worn-out equipment. If one-tenth of the existing equipment wears out each year, then a 5 per cent decline in the demand for consumption goods would reduce the replacement work for the ensuing year to half its former level. On the other hand, an increase in the demand for consumption goods, from the index number of 100 to 110, for example, would result in an increase of 100 per cent in the demand for new equipment. Ten thousand *additional* looms would be needed to supply the *new* consumer demand. Since 10,000 looms are needed to replace the worn-out portions of the old equipment, a total of 20,000 looms will be required. If, in the ensuing year, consumer demand rises still further *absolutely,* to the index number 118 (the *rate* of increase having, however, fallen), 8,000 more looms will be needed. But only 11,000 looms will be needed to replace the old equipment, and so the total number of looms required will now have fallen to 19,000. Thus, if the *rate of increase* in consumer demand begins to decline, even though consumer demand continues to rise, an absolute decline in the demand for fixed capital will ensue, provided the *expansion* demand declines more than enough to offset the rise in *replacement* demand.

The upward movement in the consumption-goods industries causes the upward movement of the capital industries.[19a] It is true that the expansion of the capital industries exercises a reflex influence upon consumption. When capital is produced, more work-

to new additions to fixed capital is highly significant. C. F. Bickerdike says that if the time ever came when maintenance alone absorbed all the available energy, the fluctuations would cease. "It is the fact that the stocks are large and yet are being increased that results in violent fluctuations in annual construction" (*Economic Journal,* September, 1914). The business cycle is a function of economic progress. From Bickerdike's point of view it is not so much the capitalistic, or roundabout, process of production, but rather the *elongation* of the process that is responsible for the cycle. Compare this with J. M. Clark's statement that it is largely due to the "fact of large fixed capital that business breeds these calamities for itself out of the laws of its own being" (*The Economics of Overhead Costs,* University of Chicago Press, 1923, p. 386).

19a As the shortage of consumers' goods becomes pronounced, merchants begin to increase their orders, and this ramifies back through all the stages of inventory accumulation from retailers through manufacturers to raw material producers. (See Chapter 11 in this book.)

ers are employed. The new workers consume a larger volume of consumption goods. Correspondingly less will be available to the rest of the community unless output can be increased. Wants are inadequately satisfied. Prices rise. During depressions the reverse is true: unemployment in the capital goods industries reduces the purchases of consumption goods, leaving more goods on the market for those who are still employed, and so prices fall. Thus the effect reacts upon the cause and reinforces it. But it cannot be doubted, Aftalion thinks, that the first and decisive impulse comes from changes in the demand for consumption goods.[20]

Factors Affecting Consumer Wants

Now what are the forces that produce changes in social wants?[21] First there is the increase in population, with the attendant increase in social wants and the desire for more goods. This point is mentioned but not stressed by Aftalion.[22] The influence of growth of population upon the business cycle is particularly the work of Pohle.[23] Cassel also gives it considerable weight as a dynamic factor disturbing the economic equilibrium. The growth of population creates a demand for fixed capital. A feeble increase of population would diminish business-cycle fluctuations. A large increase in population would give free play to these movements.

The increase in social wants may also proceed from improve-

20 Aftalion, *op. cit.*, pp. 221–222. This view is precisely the opposite of that expressed by Spiethoff. See *Jahrbuch für Gesetzgebung*, 1903, pp. 692–693; "Krisen," *Handwörterbuch der Staatswissenschaften* (1925), VI, pp. 78–79.

21 Aftalion's answer, in the main, is that these fluctuations are generated out of prior conditions developed in previous stages in the cycle.

22 Aftalion, *op. cit.*, pp. 215–216.

23 Compare also: Jean Lescure, *Des Crises générales et périodiques de surproduction*, Librairie du Recueil Sirey, 1907, pp. 370–371; E. H. Vogel, *Die Theorie des Volkswirtschaftlichen Entwickelungsprozess und das Krisenproblem*, 1917, p. 384; Spiethoff, "Die Krisentheorien von M. v. Tugan-Baranowsky und L. Pohle," *Jahrbuch für Gesetzgebung*, 1903, pp. 704–708. Spiethoff raises the objection to Pohle's theory that the increase in population is too steady a factor to cause pronounced upheavals of prosperity and depression. Moreover, if indeed it could be shown that growth of population exhibits periodicity, the question would remain whether this periodicity coincides with the business cycle, and if so, whether it might not be that the population cycle is result rather than cause. In this connection see M. B. Hexter, *Social Consequences of Business Cycles*, Houghton Mifflin Company, 1925, pp. 174–175.

ments in technique and scientific discoveries. These raise productivity and provide the basis for a rising standard of living.[24] Moreover, new products are placed on the market; new desires demand satisfaction.[25] The inventive spirit of mankind is directed not solely toward devising new and better technical processes of production but also toward devising new products of an endless variety. These have unusual significance; for while old industries only require an addition to their existing plant when demand increases, new industries may require a whole new layout of plant and equipment. Hence new products create an unusual demand for fixed capital. As an example, the automobile industry has given rise to an enormous demand for fixed capital. Once built, it has only to be replaced, in the main, and so when the market is saturated there ensues a great decline in the demand for fixed capital.[26]

Sometimes new products give rise to a shift in demand rather than an increase in demand. Thus it is said that the jewelry industry has suffered a severe decline in demand owing to the rise of the radio industry. Such shifts in demand result in large increases in the demand for fixed capital even though there is no increase in the totality of consumer demand. Assume that the two industries require the same amount of fixed capital. The shift in demand will cut off the replacement demand for fixed capital in the old industry, but it will create a demand for a complete new outlay of fixed capital in the new industry, unless, as is rarely the case, it should be possible to utilize part of the old equipment for the production of the new good. It will thus be seen that *shifts* in demand are often as important as *increases* in demand.

Among the most dynamic forces in economic life are the continued fluctuations and shifts in the demands of consumers. People love variety, change, new fashions, new products, novelties of

---

24 Aftalion, *op. cit.*, p. 216.

25 *Ibid.*, pp. 216–218. It should be noted that Aftalion holds that new wants and technical discoveries are only partial causes, like the disturbances set up by wars and political events.

26 *Ibid.*, pp. 216–217. Similar dislocations are produced by the unequal rate of growth of industries in a progressive society. Cf. E. H. Vogel, *Die Theorie des volkswirtschaftlichen Entwickelungsprozesses und das Krisenproblem*, pp. 343–398.

every description. The ensuing changes and shifts in demand are likely to set up waves of capital expansion which upset the economic equilibrium.

The Inner Nature of the Cycle

With Aftalion it is not the modern juridical regime (as he puts it) nor the existence of private property that accounts for the recurrence of crises. They spring rather from the whole economic regime, the capitalistic technique, the necessity for preliminary manufacture of capital goods in order to satisfy the demands of consumption—in short, the capitalistic or roundabout process of production. Nevertheless, Aftalion does not think that the capitalistic technique makes the crisis an inevitable necessity; rather it makes it quasi-inevitable.[27]

Aftalion's Attack on Say's Law

Aftalion criticized the theory that partial overproduction, by spreading to other areas of the economy, could explain *generalized* overproduction. Instead he advanced boldly his view that general overproduction was not only a possibility but indeed a reality. This, of course, was an attack on Say's law of markets. And the attack was not cast in monetary terms. It ran in terms of the satiability of consumers' wants in general.[27a] An increased supply of consumers' goods would result, he believed, in a general diminution in the marginal intensity of wants. Thus the demand for consumers' goods (in real terms) was thought to be relatively stable. (In Keynesian language this means that the marginal propensity to consume is thought to be less than one.) But economic activity, Aftalion believed, was likely to fluctuate rather violently in a society which employs a productive process involving a large amount of fixed capital. Thus there develops first a superabundance, then an insufficiency, of consumers' goods.

Wicksell had argued that just as there could be an excess of demand in relation to the supply of an individual commodity, so also there could be an excess of aggregate demand in relation to aggregate supply; and it was on these terms that he explained

---

27 Aftalion, *op. cit.*, p. 257.
27a *Ibid.*, pp. 81–117.

general price movements. In a somewhat analogous fashion, Aftalion argued that just as there could be an excess of supply of *one* commodity which would tend toward a condition of satiation owing to the law of diminishing utility, so also there could be a condition of general satiety. His attack on Say's Law was thus founded on the law of diminishing marginal utility of consumers' goods in general. His conception of the cycle, therefore, ran in terms of a rather violent fluctuation of aggregate demand around a relatively stable growth in consumer demand. In the nature of the case, an economy using fixed capital would tend to overshoot first in the direction of overcapacity, then in the direction of undercapacity. The actual rate of investment would tend first to outstrip, then to run behind, the normal rate of investment commensurate with the relatively stable growth of consumer demand.

A. C. PIGOU (1877–)

Nature of Fluctuations

Industrial fluctuations may be measured, says Pigou, either by changes in employment or by changes in production, but the best measure is employment. Successive cycles reveal a rough similarity. Moreover, the wavelike movements of different industries and occupations display a general concordance in timing and direction. The amplitude of fluctuations is relatively large in the construction industries compared with the consumption industries. Finally, industrial fluctuations are international in scope.

Causes of Fluctuations: Impulses and Conditions

In his *Industrial Fluctuations* [28] (1927) Pigou makes a notable contribution to business-cycle analysis by his twofold classification of causation of industrial fluctuations. Wicksell had indeed, as we have seen, already in 1907 called attention to the mechanism of impulse and propagation, but it was Pigou who brought this type of analysis into general use.[29]

[28] A. C. Pigou, *Industrial Fluctuations,* Macmillan and Co., Ltd., London, 1927. A second edition appeared in 1929.

[29] See, however, Ragnar Frisch, in *Economic Essays in Honour of Gustav Cassel,* George Allen & Unwin, Ltd., London, 1933, and his references to the

Causes may be considered on two levels or planes: (a) *impulses* which initiate the movements, (b) *conditions* which determine the manner in which the economy responds to the initial impulses. This way of looking at the problem represents a major forward step.

There are many kinds of *impulses* which may initiate economic movements. And when these impulses come into play they operate upon "a certain complex of industrial and monetary conditions. Given the impulse, these will determine the nature of the effect that it produces, and are in this sense, causes of industrial fluctuations." [30]

Classification of Impulses

The impulses toward expansion and contraction of industry operate mainly through variations in the expectations of profit. The impulses which cause these variations may be autonomous monetary changes, real factors, or psychological factors.

Autonomous monetary changes may arise from the issue of paper money, gold production, or movements in international reserves.

The principal real factors which may initiate fluctuations are harvest variations, inventions, industrial disputes, changes in taste, changes in foreign demand. Expectations based on real causes are true or valid expectations.

"Psychological causes," in Pigou's meaning, refers to errors of judgment, changes that occur in men's attitude of mind apart from changed expectations resulting from changes in the basic facts upon which judgment rests.

Origin of Errors and Their Effects

Errors of optimism and errors of pessimism arise from: (1) the fact that many goods are made in advance of demand or serve an untried market, (2) the division of industry into a number of separate units acting independently of one another, (3) the long period required to make many durable goods, especially

---

independent econometric studies of impulse and propagation by Slutsky and Yule, both published in 1927.

[30] Pigou, *op. cit.*, p. 8.

plant and equipment. Errors in different industries are related, and they tend to reinforce one another.

Once errors of optimism are discovered, a reaction sets in and errors are generated in the opposite direction. Optimistic forecasts are at last brought to the test of fact. When this test is applied to a considerable number of things and found wanting, confidence is shaken. The extent of the revulsion toward pessimistic error depends in part upon the methods by which business is normally financed. If borrowing has been heavily relied on, the number and scale of bankruptcies into which the detected errors explode may be very great. The extent of the revulsion may also be affected by the policy adopted by banks in times of crisis and difficulty.

Instrumental vs. Consumer Industries

Fluctuations are larger in the instrumental industries than in consumption goods industries. Moreover, fluctuations in the former industries often precede those in the latter industries. This is due to the acceleration principle, the principle of derived demand. It follows from this principle that the *lead* and the greater *intensity* of the fluctuations in the instrumental industries do not prove that the origin of cyclical fluctuations must be sought in the capital goods industries. "On some occasions, when, for example, means of making some new important capital instrument, e.g., railways, have been discovered, it may well happen that the initiative comes from the side of the instrumental trades. But on other occasions, perhaps on most, it seems that the first stage towards a boom is an expansion in dealers' forecasts of the public demand for consumption goods, and therefore, in their own orders for them, and that the associated expansion of demand for instrumental goods is an effect of this." [31]

On this point, Pigou's theory underwent some modification between the publication of the first edition of *Economics of Welfare* (1920) and the appearance of the two editions (1927, 1929) of his *Industrial Fluctuations.* In the 1920 volume, the role of autonomous investment was explicitly ruled out in a chapter entitled "A False Scent." The acceleration principle was drawn upon

[31] *Ibid.,* p. 104.

to explain that fluctuations in the capital goods industries are a result of fluctuations in the consumer goods industries.

It is significant that this chapter was entirely omitted in the enlarged version appearing in 1927. In the meantime the English translation of Cassel's *Theory of Social Economy* had appeared. Cassel emphasized strongly the rule of autonomous investment. His volume clearly made a deep impression on Anglo-American thinking, though there is little direct evidence of this in Pigou's writings. At all events, Pigou in the 1927 volume appeared to be somewhat on the defensive, though he still argued that "the origin of industrial fluctuations is not always, or even usually, to be found in the instrumental industries." [32] Earlier he had scouted this view as a false scent.

Finally, in the 1929 edition, he inserted a new paragraph in the chapter on "Instrumental and Consumption Trades," in which he commented on the invalidity of a seemingly plausible argument designed to show that it is impossible for general fluctuations to originate in the instrumental trades. Also in the 1929 edition he incorporated a section derived from Schumpeter's 1927 *Economica* article in which the origin of booms was found in innovations; and innovations were described as consisting "primarily in changes in the methods of production of a new article, or in the opening up of new markets or of new sources of material."

Money and Credit

Monetary and banking arrangements act as a *condition* (apart from the *impulse* effect of autonomous monetary changes) amplifying the effects of non-monetary (real or psychological) factors. The creation of bank credits, in response to the demands of business as influenced by changing profit expectations, enhances the elasticity of the supply of "real floating capital." It does so through the "forced levy operated through credit creation."

As between good and bad times, variations in the amount of credit creation, in the proportion of the real income which people desire to hold in money form, and finally in the productivity of industry, will all affect the general price level. A rise in prices operates as a levy on lenders for the benefit of businessmen. The

[32] *Ibid.*, p. 104.

fact that prices have risen creates an expectation that they will continue to rise. "In this way a cumulative tendency towards expansion is set up, which continues under its own impulse until it encounters some external obstacle."[33] Price movements, besides modifying the *response* made to given expectations on the part of businessmen, also modify the expectations themselves. They do this partly by creating a true expectation of the bounty to businessmen on future loan contracts when prices are rising and of a toll when prices are falling; and partly by modifying the businessmen's psychological attitudes.[34]

Relative Importance of Different Factors

Pigou reaches the conclusion that if the general level of prices were stabilized, "the amplitude of industrial fluctuations would be substantially reduced—it might be cut down to half of what it is at present—but considerable fluctuations would still remain."[35] Similarly, if it were possible to eliminate all errors of optimism and pessimism, the "normal range of industrial fluctuations would be reduced substantially, perhaps to the extent of one-half."[36] If harvest fluctuations were somehow eliminated, he offers the guess that (other things not causally related to crop changes remaining the same) the representative trade cycle might be cut down by something like one-quarter.[37]

Other factors, Pigou believes, contribute relatively little to industrial fluctuations. Industrial disputes are of very little importance. "Big industrial inventions may sometimes be important; but it is the *decision to exploit* inventions that is the active

[33] *Ibid.*, p. 122.

[34] Chapters XVIII and XIX of Pigou's *Industrial Fluctuations* are devoted to a discussion of price and wage rigidities in the cycle. Modern theoretical analysis has profoundly altered the views of economists with respect to these matters since the publication of *Industrial Fluctuations* in 1927. See for example, my own discussion on price rigidities in *Fiscal Policy and Business Cycles,* W. W. Norton & Co., Inc., 1941, Chapter XV; and on wage rigidities in *Monetary Theory and Fiscal Policy,* McGraw-Hill Book Company, 1949, Chapter 8.

[35] *Industrial Fluctuations,* p. 198.

[36] *Ibid.*, p. 199.

[37] Each of these factors must of course be taken separately. It must not be supposed that if all three causes were eliminated the cycle would altogether disappear.

cause of disturbance, and the time and intensity of exploitations are largely determined by the state of business confidence." [38] Big wars produce tremendous effects, but they are not relevant to the ordinary run of industrial cycles.

The Periodicity of the Cycle

The periodicity of the cycle may be explained in two ways. First, impulses which are "sporadic in their nature" may nevertheless *start* wave movements due to the mutual generation of errors of optimism (dependent in part upon the period of time required to produce capital goods) and subsequent errors of pessimism. Wave movements may also relate to the *length of life* of durable goods—the "echo" effect, or replacement cycle. The wave movement may, moreover, relate (once the initial impulse has started it) to the ebb and flow of bank reserves in the process of bank credit expansion and contraction. Second, rhythm or periodicity may be due to a succession of disturbing impulses which are themselves rhythmically recurrent and which therefore impose a corresponding periodicity upon the industrial movements. Harvest variations, some have claimed, would be a case in point. "That there is *some* sort of causal sequence here is suggested by the statistical correlations displayed in Chapter IV. These correlations are, however, very imperfect. . . . To attribute the actual rhythm of industry, such as it is, exclusively to an underlying rhythm of harvests is extravagant; but to recognise that harvest variations, whether or not they are truly 'periodic,' play a significant part is concordant both with the evidence and with *a priori* probability." [39]

The Role of Expectations

Pigou's analysis centers upon the role of expectations of profit from industrial spending (which includes increased activity in consumption industries and is not limited to investment in fixed capital). But he stresses particularly the circumstance that errors of optimism and errors of pessimism largely control these expecta-

[38] *Industrial Fluctuations,* p. 203.
[39] *Ibid.,* p. 212.

tions. Thus he places major emphasis, as did Marshall, upon the role of "excessive confidence" and "excessive distrust." [40] Yet there is this difference. In Pigou's analysis, the waves of optimistic and pessimistic error are generated in a system of production which requires the capitalistic technique. A long period of time is required to make the instruments of production. "So long as these are in process of being created—as we may say, throughout this period of gestation—exceptional activity continues." [41] The period of gestation varies greatly for different things and is especially likely to be long for "elaborate constructional instruments." And if a considerable number of ventures are found wanting, confidence is shaken. Thus it is the time-consuming character of the capitalistic technique of production which affords the opportunity for the cumulation and ultimate dispersal of errors of optimism. Errors of judgment develop within the framework and pattern of the modern technique of production; and forecasts are subjected sooner or later to the imperious requirements imposed by that system.

Thus Pigou's work on fluctuations must be linked closely with that of Aftalion, who had already stressed the rhythm in the expectations and forecasts of businessmen, and who had based this rhythm upon the nature of the capitalistic technique of production. Nevertheless, Pigou might perhaps (so far as the main emphasis is concerned) have been placed in the same chapter with J. S. Mill, John Mills, and Alfred Marshall. Basically he represents their type of thinking. Psychological influences, though molded by the pattern of the modern technique of production, still predominate. And monetary and credit factors play a large *conditioning* (and in part *initiating*) role. It is significant that more than a third of Part I, "On Causation," is devoted to monetary, credit, and price factors.

---

[40] Alfred Marshall, *Money, Credit and Commerce,* Macmillan and Co., Ltd., London, 1923, pp. 260–261.

[41] Pigou, *Industrial Fluctuations,* p. 83.

J. M. CLARK (1884-)

Derived Demand

Clark's *Strategic Factors in Business Cycles* [42] lays great stress on the role of the acceleration principle—the principle of derived demand—in business cycles. Already in the March, 1917, issue of the *Journal of Political Economy,* he had written an article elaborating this principle, entitled "Business Acceleration and the Law of Demand." Aftalion's work on the acceleration principle had appeared, as we have seen, in 1909.

Impulses and Responses

In his *Strategic Factors* Clark follows Pigou's lead in dividing causal factors in the business cycles into (a) originating forces, and (b) responses of the business system. If originating forces (wars, weather, new inventions) produce "the familiar business cycles, or play a part in producing them, it is because they are acting on a particular kind of business system, which reacts to them in particular ways." [43] The responses of the business system are "more important in determining the results than the particular character of the original disturbances." [44]

Clark and Aftalion are in substantial agreement with respect to the general character and pattern of the oscillation. "The responses of the business system seem to form a closely-knit sequence of cause and effect, in which a state of over-contraction appears to set in motion forces leading to over-expansion, and this in turn to over-contraction once more." [45] Also Aftalion's general thesis with respect to the periodicity of the cycle is reflected [46] in the following: "The indicated probability is that the average period of these upward and downward swings is determined by the character of business responses, for example, the time required to

[42] J. M. Clark, *Strategic Factors in Business Cycles,* National Bureau of Economic Research, 1934.

[43] *Ibid.,* p. 18.

[44] *Ibid.,* p. 20.

[45] *Ibid.,* p. 18.

[46] Clark's work has all the earmarks of an independent study and in fact was probably influenced but little by Aftalion

finance capital expansions and to construct new factory units or new apartment buildings." [47]

Self-Interest and Collective Error

Both Aftalion and Pigou conceived of the cycle in terms of a "rhythm of expectations" which are alternately too optimistic and too pessimistic—this rhythm being conditioned by the capitalist technique of production. Clark states the rhythmic movement in terms of "responses of the business system," but unlike Pigou he does not stress psychological errors of judgment. He does on occasion speak of "psychological brainstorms" and the "new era of delusion," [48] but he expressly disassociates himself from the theory "that cycles are due to the mistakes of judgment made by individual business men," stating emphatically that he believes this theory to be, in the main, false. "The trouble seems to be not so much that business men mistake their interests—though that does happen, and aggravates some of the difficulties—as that their actual interests lie in doing the things which bring on the cycle, so long as they are acting as individual business men or representatives of individual business interests." [49] Following their own individual self-interest, individual action may lead to collective error. "It takes time to produce the equipment and durable goods, and meanwhile there is a shortage which sends prices up." Guided by the rising prices rather than by a "statistical canvass of demand and supply, competitive producers launch upon the production of more goods and equipment than necessary to meet the requirements of the original expansion of demand." [50] The derived productive activity (induced by the original growth curve of ultimate demand) "does not at once rise to the full extent required to satisfy the increase in original demand, but lags at first, and then rises even more steeply in the effort to catch up, and finally is pushed beyond immediate requirements by the effects of speculation and of competitive duplication." [51]

[47] Clark, *Strategic Factors in Business Cycles,* p. 20.
[48] *Ibid.,* p. 21.
[49] *Ibid.,* pp. 163–164.
[50] *Ibid.,* p. 177.
[51] *Ibid.,* p. 180.

The Duration of Cycles

The duration of cycles is "governed largely by the time consumed in this process of lagging and subsequent catching-up and overexpansion, and in the subsequent process of clearing the markets and exhausting the excess of durable goods. This time-interval is dependent upon several factors, technical, commercial and psychological." [52]

The time required "to develop the potentialities of a basic idea" also affects the length of the period of expansion. "There may be an initial stage of experimental pioneering, followed by a putting of the method into actual production. . . . If the method proves its economic worth, there may be virtually instant recognition of that fact, and a wave of imitation, sweeping over the entire field as fast as the character of the improvement admits and causing a very considerable demand for new equipment. Schumpeter's analysis of intermittent movements of pioneering followed by waves of imitation is pertinent on this point and is the outstanding theoretical treatment of it." [53]

Leads and Lags

Analysis based on the acceleration principle inherently runs in terms of leads and lags, the curve of derived demand logically reaching a peak a quarter-cycle ahead of the peak in the curve of ultimate demand. Clark finds that the "average cycle pattern for construction contracts awarded shows a clear lead of a quarter-cycle at down-turns and a larger lead at upturns" of the general business cycle.[54] He finds, however, considerable variation in the different sections of the construction industry. Industrial construction is "most nearly synchronous with the general business cycle." Commercial construction "manifests no tendency to lead on the down-turn but shows an average lead of more than a quarter-cycle at the upturn of the three general business cycles in which commercial construction manifests a definite trough." Commercial construction is more irregular than industrial, showing less conformity to the general business cycle. Residential construction

---

[52] *Ibid.*, p. 181.
[53] *Ibid.*, pp. 171–172.
[54] *Ibid.*, p. 27.

(in the five cycles, 1915–31) seems to disclose "a clear tendency to an average lead of a quarter-cycle, though with a considerable dispersion around this average." Residential construction is "mainly responsible for the tendency of total construction to lead general business, and entirely responsible for the tendency to lead at the peak." [55]

The pattern of behavior of the construction industry, in relation to the general business cycle, Clark finds not difficult to rationalize on theoretical grounds. "It is a phase of the general principle of intensified fluctuations of derived demand for durable goods. That is, demand for new supplies of durable goods fluctuates more intensely than demand for the current services these durable goods render." [56] While Clark speaks here of the intensification aspect of the principle of derived demand, it is in fact the lead-and-lag aspect of the principle which is here in question. This indeed is the point stressed a few pages later, when he says that as "partial explanation of the *lead* in construction work, we should note that the demand for construction in excess of replacements is logically the heaviest, not when consumers' incomes are largest, but somewhere near the time when they are *increasing fastest.*" [57]

With respect to capital equipment (in contrast with construction) Clark notes "the phenomenon of intensified fluctuation but not the large lead that characterizes construction work." This he explains on the ground that excess equipment capacity "at the moment when revival begins is likely to have more effect in retarding the revival of the derived demand than in the case of residential construction. Equipment can often produce up-to-date goods even though it is not itself completely up-to-date, or can do so with minor changes." [58]

Clark finds that the "production and sales of passenger automobiles show not only fluctuations decidedly more intense than the average, but also a decided lead as compared with the general business cycle. . . . The principle of derived demand dependent on the *rate of growth* of the primary demand applies here as in

[55] *Ibid.*, p. 28.
[56] *Ibid.*, p. 33.
[57] *Ibid.*, p. 41.
[58] *Ibid.*, p. 42.

housing, though to a less extent, since the stabilizing element of need for replacements is a larger part of the picture. Automobiles, being shorter-lived than houses, come that much nearer the type of currently consumed goods, and the elements of lead, and of intensification of fluctuations, would therefore both logically be less marked." [59]

The Process of Intensification

"Fluctuations in the rate of growth are sufficient to start the process of intensification. . . . Thus this principle is of peculiar strategic importance in explaining how alternate rises and falls can be generated out of tendencies whose original form and character need not contain any positive shift from upward to downward movements. It may also be of some help in explaining the duration of the swings, in view of the time required for equipment to catch up with growing demand, or for demand to catch up with equipment." [60]

Agriculture and the Cycle

With respect to agricultural production in the cycle, Clark's position is very similar to that of Pigou. "Agriculture appears to have its own cycles, whose timing has no clear or regular relation to the cycles of general business. This is true whether we consider physical production, prices at the farm, or the product of the two, which may be taken to measure the total purchasing power which agriculture generates and has to offer in the general market." [61] But while agriculture is not a regularly acting force, this does not mean that it has no effect on the cycle. It is one of the "random forces" to which the economy responds. "The cycle as we know it is the resultant of the combination of random disturbances and an economic system which transmits their effects cumulatively. . . . The random forces are not to be disregarded merely because there is no discernible correlation between their timing and that of the business cycle itself." [62]

---

[59] *Ibid.*, pp. 46–47.
[60] *Ibid.*, p. 43.
[61] *Ibid.*, p. 61.
[62] *Ibid.*, p. 63.

Agricultural fluctuations may affect the general course of business through the stimulus to activity which plentiful and cheap raw materials afford. Clark believes, however, that this influence is in fact very slight. Agricultural fluctuations may also affect general business by means of the greater or less purchasing power that they throw into the market. Increases in farmers' purchasing power may, however, be partly at the expense of other groups. Still, agricultural prosperity is likely "to increase the power of farmers to buy equipment on credit without subtracting an equal amount from the corresponding power of other groups." [63]

Elasticity of the Credit System

Prices and wage rates, Clark finds, tend to lag behind production and employment. The latter rise relatively more in the early phases of expansion, the former in the later phases; and similarly with the downturn. Bank rates "are acted upon more than acting," and the "volume of credit seems to respond in the main to the demands of the volume of trade. It is an important enabling cause or condition, but hardly an initiating one in the typical case." [64] Yet the elasticity of the credit system is the "essential link in the chain of causes bringing about cyclical expansions and contractions of general business." The elasticity of the credit system makes possible "increased expenditures for producers' goods without correspondingly limited outlays for consumption—in short, an increase in total expenditures not limited to income derived from previous production." [65]

Consumption and Income

Expenditures for consumption fluctuate less than income, rising less than total income in the expansion and falling less rapidly in the downturn. This fact represents one of "the forces setting limits on the cumulative effects of disturbances." [66] But the "actual expansions and contractions of consumers' purchases are largely results of changes in productive activity." [67] Here we come to

[63] *Ibid.*, p. 65.
[64] *Ibid.*, p. 72.
[65] *Ibid.*, p. 79.
[66] *Ibid.*, pp. 78, 84.
[67] *Ibid.*, p. 72.

grips with the problem of "the dependence of consumers' demand on incomes and the dependence of incomes on the rate of production." [68]

The Rate of Growth

Fluctuations in income relate to changes in the rate of growth. Business cycles in their very nature are "departures from balance." The boom is a concentration in the growth of capital equipment—a rate of growth greater than can be permanently maintained.[69]

Impulses leading to an upturn of business may come from changes in technical methods of production, the development of new goods, the need for replacement which has been temporarily postponed, increased optimism, or a shift in consumers' demand. "An upward inflection in the course of 'original demand' has its most substantial result in the shape of an intensified upward swing in the output of means of production and of durable goods." [70] After a while having caught up with the requirements, the production of equipment and durable goods slackens. Thus we have a "cycle of expansion and contraction, interrupting the normal growth curve." [71]

Consider a community with a growing population and rising per capita income. "The 'growth' in excess of this trend represents the process by which a new good or a new process makes its way to a fairly stable place relative to others, in an expanding economic system." If it is an absolutely new good, the growth curve may start from zero, reach a maximum rate of expansion, and then taper off to a saturation point. "If it is a case of a change enlarging the normal place held by an existing good, the growth-curve may be superimposed on a secular upward trend, or different growth-curves with different periods may be superimposed on each other." [72]

The normal growth curves may have to do with the "development of new goods and of the conscious and active desire for them,

---

[68] *Ibid.,* p. 202. This statement foreshadows Keynes' consumption function.
[69] *Ibid.,* pp. 104, 128.
[70] *Ibid.,* pp. 174–176.
[71] *Ibid.,* p. 178.
[72] *Ibid.,* pp. 169–170.

or with new processes of production calling for increased investment in productive equipment." [73] In boom times too much is spent "on capital and on durable goods in general to maintain the rate permanently, technical methods and knowledge being what they are." At the height of a boom we are "diverting more of our productive power to capital goods than we can permanently use. . . . If we were to produce capital equipment steadily at a rate we could absorb, and devoted all the rest of our productive energy to goods for consumption, our consuming power would be increased, possibly five per cent." [74]

But how to achieve this is no easy matter. If wages were raised in the boom more would be consumed, but "would this mean a reduction of the unduly concentrated production of capital goods" or would it stimulate this concentrated production still further? "The latter result seems more than probable. And this points toward the conclusion that changes in the distribution of incomes are not alone sufficient; they can be effective only in connection with direct stabilization of these branches of production in which undue fluctuations are concentrated." [75]

Clark's discussion at this point is highly pertinent to cycle policy, and we shall revert to it again in Part IV of this book. The relation of boom-time investment to maintainable rates of growth, and how to deal with this problem, are currently of crucial importance; and much attention has been devoted to the question in the President's Economic Reports. Should the problem be attacked directly via a better balance between wages and profits, or is this relationship basically a reflection, rather than a cause, of the disproportionate volume of investment at the height of the boom? If stabilization could first be achieved, by the use of more indirect methods, a better wage-profit balance (and so a better balance between consumption and investment under conditions of full employment) might follow. Yet this result could in turn become a powerful factor reinforcing and sustaining full employment stability.

---

[73] *Ibid.*, p. 170.
[74] *Ibid.*, pp. 152–153.
[75] *Ibid.*, p. 154.

19 · *Monetary Disequilibrium:*
HAWTREY · HAYEK

R. G. HAWTREY (1879–)

In Hawtrey's analysis the important variables are: (1) consumers' income, (2) consumers' outlays, and (3) cash balances[1] (currency and deposits).

Cash Balances and Income

The people find it convenient to hold cash balances which have a "fairly constant average" relation to income. If we designate Hawtrey's cash balances as "M," income as "Y," and this average relation as "k," we get the Marshallian equation $M = kY$. There are, to be sure, "casual variations" in k, but these variations, Hawtrey thinks, usually do not exceed certain limits, so that a fairly constant average relation holds between income and cash balances.

If traders borrow at banks for the purpose of financing addi-

1 Hawtrey uses an unnecessarily confusing terminology. The national income he calls "consumers' income," which simply means income at factor cost. "The consumers' income of a *nation* is simply the national income reckoned in terms of money" (*The Gold Standard in Theory and Practice,* Longmans, Green and Co., New York, 1947—first edition published in 1927—pp. 10–11). The total demand for goods (including capital goods) and services he calls "consumers' outlay," but he excludes the "expenditure of traders on buying or producing goods to sell again" (*Readings in Business Cycle Theory,* The Blakiston Company, 1944, p. 332). Cash balances he calls the "unspent margin."

tional goods in process of production, or to add to their inventory stocks, new money is created. An expansion of credit is started through the "sensitiveness of merchants to the rate of interest. Merchants are tempted by cheap money to hasten their purchases." [2]

The Unspent Margin

The new money flows into the hands of the public, who now hold an undue proportion of cash balances. Momentarily income has outrun outlays, and there is an increased "unspent margin." This leads to increased outlays, and so a part of the cash flows back to the traders. But a part of the new money is retained by the public in order to maintain a due proportion between cash balances and the enlarged income. The traders now find that the increased "consumer outlays" have the effect of reducing their stocks of goods below the level they had wished, and so they will tend to use the returned cash in further purchases in an effort to rebuild their stocks. Moreover, since sales have increased, they may wish to build their stocks still higher, and this would entail still more borrowing and so a further extension of bank credit.

The total of bank deposits may be compared to a reservoir. "The flow through the reservoir is increased by the additional lending and borrowing, and this stream in the course of its passage takes the form of an addition to the consumers' income. In the same way the banks, by restricting the amount they lend, can diminish the flow through the reservoir, and curtail the consumers' income." [3]

The Lag in the Flow of Cash

Hawtrey takes the position that there is an inherent tendency toward fluctuations in the money economy, with its existing banking institutions and practices.[4] So long as credit is regulated with reference to reserve proportions, the trade cycle is bound to recur.

[2] Hawtrey, *Readings in Business Cycle Theory,* p. 346.

[3] *The Gold Standard in Theory and Practice,* 1947, pp. 13–14.

[4] R. G. Hawtrey, *Good and Bad Trade,* Constable Company, Limited, 1913, p. 199; also *Currency and Credit,* Longmans, Green & Co., 1919, *Monetary Reconstruction,* Longmans, Green & Co., 1923, and *The Economic Problem,* Longmans, Green & Co., 1925.

The flow of legal-tender money into circulation and back is one of the very tardiest consequences of a credit expansion or contraction. If the central bank waits for this flow to affect bank reserves, and sits passively looking on at an expansion or contraction gathering impetus before it takes any decisive action, we cannot escape from the alternations of feverish activity with depression and unemployment.[5]

The periodicity of expansion and contraction of credit which has long attracted the attention of economists is, Hawtrey tells us, the natural result of the slow response of people's cash holdings to credit movements. Credit expansion is not immediately accompanied by a proportionate increase in the earnings of the working classes or in their power to "absorb" cash. When earnings do increase, they go to a great extent not into cash holdings, but into increased expenditure. In so far as the money paid out on one pay day comes back through the shops to the banks by the next, no additional strain is put upon bank reserves. But as earnings rise, there begins a gradual accretion of people's cash holdings, which will continue until these holdings are in due proportion to the increased earnings. But this process takes a considerable time. The increase in holdings lags behind the increase in earnings. Credit increases, then earnings, and finally the cash holdings of people. When earnings reach the maximum, the currency portion of the "unspent margin" is still short of the level corresponding to this maximum. "The wage-earners are still absorbing more money than they spend." This creates a drain on the bank reserves. Finally the current is reversed, and currency returns to the banks. But the depletion of people's cash reserves is gradual, and bank reserves continue to increase long after the banks have ceased to contract credit. Thus there accumulates an excess of reserves in the banks, which provides opportunity for a renewed credit exapnsion.[6]

It is this lag of currency in circulation in the hands of the people which automatically swings the pendulum and keeps the industrial mechanism constantly oscillating up and down.[7] An

[5] Hawtrey, *Monetary Reconstruction*, p. 145.

[6] Hawtrey, *Currency and Credit*, Longmans, Green & Co., pp. 125–126.

[7] If an "increase or decrease of credit money promptly brought with it a proportionate increase or decrease in the demand for cash, the banks would no

overaccumulation of bank reserves induces bankers to lower the rate of discount, and this encourages traders to borrow. Prices rise, then wages, but a period of time elapses before an appropriate amount of cash is drawn out into hand-to-hand circulation. Bankers do not realize that they have overexpanded until this drain of cash from the banks severely reduces bank reserves. At this point bankers conclude that the amount of credit money in existence is more than they think prudent, having regard to their holdings of cash, and so they raise the rate of discount. Dealers accordingly reduce their stocks by giving fewer orders to producers. Prices fall, but wages lag behind, and people's cash holdings lag still more. When cash finally does begin to flow back to the banks in large volume, it is found (too late) that the credit contraction has been excessive, since there now develops an overaccumulation of cash reserves. The banks must get rid of this excess. They lower the discount rate, traders are induced to increase their stocks, and so another period of expansion ensues. Were it not for the *lag of cash holdings* and the consequent alternating excess and deficiency of bank reserves, a stable equilibrium might be reached.[8] "The too ready acceptance of reserve proportions as the guide to credit policy was the real cause of the trade cycle before the war." [9]

If, on the other hand, the central banks would watch, not the reserve proportions but the flow of purchasing power, early action could then be taken.

It is the *flow* of purchasing power that is important, not the

---

longer either drift into a state of inflation or be led to carry the corresponding process of contraction unnecessarily far" (Hawtrey, *Good and Bad Trade,* p. 266).

[8] Hawtrey, *Good and Bad Trade,* pp. 267–272.

[9] Cf. *Economic Journal,* June, 1926, p. 330. In this connection it should also be noted that even if trade were temporarily stable a lowering of the discount rate would cause, according to Hawtrey, an increased demand for loans. This would increase purchasing power, and so prices would rise, which would raise profit expectations. Thus equilibrium is essentially unstable in the sense that any expansion will tend to grow greater and greater until steps are taken to correct it. "This of itself shows that the money market must be subject to fluctuations" (*Good and Bad Trade,* p. 76). Credit is "by nature unruly. It is always straining at its tether, or rather, it is perpetually starting to run away, and then is being pulled up with a jerk when the limit of inflation consistent with the maintenance of the metallic standard is reached" (*Currency and Credit,* p. 127).

outstanding aggregate of money units.[10] The "unspent margin," in terms of money units, is made up of the money in circulation and the bank credits outstanding.[11] The unspent margin of real purchasing power equates to the command over wealth which the people hold in reserve.[12]

Under the conditions of uncontrolled banking institutions the discount rate is regulated by the cash reserves of the banks, and so it acts too tardily to check the inflation and deflation. Hawtrey would raise and lower the discount rate earlier and so stabilize the flow of purchasing power and the price level. Pigou

10 Hawtrey, *Monetary Reconstruction*, pp. 120, 145. "Stagnant cash balances are a characteristic of periods of trade depression. When trade is profitable dealers cannot afford to let money lie idle, but when every transaction threatens, under the stress of falling markets, to end in a loss, idle balances are allowed to mount up" (p. 119).

11 Hawtrey, *Currency and Credit*, p. 35.

12 Hawtrey, *Currency and Credit*, Longmans, Green and Co., London, 1919, p. 39. Hawtrey's "command over wealth which the people hold in reserve" appears superficially similar to the Cambridge (England) cash-balance approach to the theory of money and prices. With Hawtrey, however, the volume of spending is closely related to the volume of cash balances, an increase in cash leading to increased spending. With Marshall, and others of the Cambridge school, it was rather changes in "k" (the fraction of real income which people wish to hold command over in the form of cash) which controlled the volume of spending. Thus Keynes (*Economic Journal*, March, 1924; and *Monetary Reform*, Harcourt, Brace and Company, 1924) argued that the volume of real balances may fluctuate violently even though there is little change in the volume of cash or in the reserve policy of the banks.

"The characteristic of the credit cycle (as the alternation of boom and depression is now described) consists in a tendency of k and k′ to diminish during the boom and increase during the depression irrespective of changes in n and r, these movements representing respectively a diminution and an increase of 'real' balances (that is, balances, in hand or at the bank, measured in terms of purchasing power); so that we might call this phenomenon deflations and inflations of real balances. . . . Cyclical fluctuations are characterized, not primarily by changes in n or r, but by changes in k and k′." (*Monetary Reform*, Harcourt, Brace and Company, 1924, pp. 91, 95).

$k =$ the number of consumption units, the monetary equivalent of which the public find it convenient to keep in "cash"; $k' =$ the number of consumption units, the monetary equivalent of which the public find it convenient to keep in bank balances; $p =$ the price of each consumption unit, or the index number of prices; $n =$ the number of units of "cash" in circulation; $r =$ the proportion of their potential liabilities to the public which the banks keep in "cash." Thus $n = p(k + rk')$. See *Economic Journal*, March, 1924, p. 65; and *Monetary Reform*, Harcourt, Brace and Company, 1924, pp. 84–85. See also Alvin H. Hansen, *Monetary Theory and Fiscal Policy*, McGraw-Hill Book Company, 1949, Chapter 3.

has pointed out that such a discount policy would differ from past practice "not in the fact that the discount rate would be moved up in booms (and correspondingly down in depressions), but only in respect of the *time at* which, and the *extent to* which, the rate of discount would be changed." [13]

The Discount Rate and Inventory Stocks

But, it may be asked, is the discount rate really a sufficiently powerful regulator of the price cycle? Hawtrey contends that it is. How can a slight change of 1 or 2 per cent in the rate of interest on temporary loans have such far-reaching results? The explanation is in part to be found in the immediate reaction on merchants, and these, in Hawtrey's view, occupy a strategic place in the business mechanism. It is perfectly true, says Hawtrey, that the producer is not much troubled by the rate of interest he has to pay his banker.[14] But that is not so in the case of the merchant or dealer, who is constantly carrying stocks of goods large in proportion to his own capital, and who makes very nice calculations as to his margin of profit and the cost of borrowing. A moderate rise in the cost of borrowing will make the carrying of stocks appreciably less attractive to him. He will buy less and sell more, and so a fall in prices is started.[15] The problem of regulating prices is reduced to the problem of regulating trade borrowing, and the volume of trade borrowing can be controlled by the discount rate.[16]

But suppose prices are rising rapidly. How can a relatively slight rise in the discount rate check the tendency to buy with a view to the advance in prices? Hawtrey's answer is that it is not the *past* rise in prices, but the *future* rise that has to be counteracted. It is a psychological problem. "To the trader the high rate of interest presents itself in the first instance as an expense to be subtracted from his profits, but behind this initial loss looms the far more serious menace of a difficulty in borrowing, which will affect not merely himself but those to whom he hopes to sell." [17] The

[13] Pigou in *Is Unemployment Inevitable?* The Macmillan Company, p. 115.
[14] Compare with Snyder, *American Economic Review,* December, 1925, and W. F. Mitchell, *American Economic Review,* June, 1926.
[15] *Monetary Reconstruction,* p. 140; *Currency and Credit,* p. 124.
[16] *Monetary Reconstruction,* pp. 139, 143.
[17] *Currency and Credit,* p. 128.

rise in the discount rate discourages buying and encourages selling. Once deflation is started, the holding of commodities in stock means an actual loss. The fall of prices reinforces the original process. Once the high discount rate has become deterrent at all, it tends to grow more and more deterrent. Thus mighty changes can be wrought by relatively slight changes in the discount rate.[18]

The discount rate, then, influences particularly the actions of dealers, and fluctuations in dealers' purchases are, Hawtrey believes, at the center of business fluctuations. When dealers proceed to reduce their stocks and give fewer orders to producers, production is curtailed, unemployment ensues, earnings decline, and purchases are reduced. The movement thus spreads from the dealers to the rest of the community and back again, and so reinforces itself.[19]

Hawtrey's analysis is far from being convincing. Inventory fluctuations are very much influenced by expectations with respect to sales and price movements. If sales expectations are favorable, the discount rate is not likely to determine significantly the volume of inventory investment.

Prices, Profits, and Wages

Thus, in Hawtrey's view the unregulated money and banking mechanism produces in an unceasing round the alternating rise and decline in prices and consequently prosperity and depression.[20] A fall in prices forces the producer either to reduce output or to reduce the cost of production. If he chooses the first horn of the dilemma, unemployment ensues, and so business depression; if he chooses the second, wages, salaries, interest, rents, or profits must be lowered. Interest on borrowed funds is a fixed charge, and it cannot be reduced unless the business actually becomes insolvent. Profits will likely first be encroached upon. But if the margin of profit is narrow, there is no recourse except to lower wages or dismiss some of the employees. If wages are lowered suf-

---

[18] *Monetary Reconstruction,* pp. 108, 111.

[19] Hawtrey, *Good and Bad Trade,* pp. 267–268.

[20] Cf. Irving Fisher, "Our Unstable Dollar and the So-called Business Cycle," *Journal of the American Statistical Association,* June, 1925.

ficiently,[21] production might (Hawtrey thinks) be maintained, but the consequent redistribution of the national income would at least entail a necessary shift in production.[22] However, wages cannot in point of fact be lowered except by the pressure of distress. Thus, unemployment being the inevitable whip by which labor is forced to accept lower wages, the readjustment to a lower price level cannot be accomplished except by passing through a period of depression. Nor can the fixed charges be reduced except by the pressure of insolvency. If the habits of the people could be adapted without delay to the change, the production of wealth might continue unabated in spite of a fall in prices. But customary wages, rents, interest, and profits exert such a profound influence upon men's minds that the readjustment can in point of fact not be made except under the pressure of such distress as is experienced in periods of depression.[23]

FREDERICK HAYEK (1899–)

Real and Monetary Factors

Real as opposed to *monetary* phenomena do not adequately account for business cycles in a money and price system. The impact of technical change upon a capitalistic economy is magnified,

---

[21] In all this type of argument, there is a tendency to forget that lower wages reduce not only *costs* but also *demand.* Wage reduction is double-edged. See the chapter on "Wages and Prices" in Alvin H. Hansen, *Monetary Theory and Fiscal Policy*, pp. 115–130.

[22] Hawtrey, *op. cit.*, pp. 40–41.

[23] This argument reminds one of Veblen's statement that depression is a "malady of the affections." "The discrepancy which discourages business men is a discrepancy between that nominal capitalization which they have set their hearts upon through habituation in the immediate past and that actual capitalizable value of their property which its current earning capacity will warrant. But where the preconceptions of the business men engaged have, as commonly happens, in great part, been fixed and legalized in the form of interest-bearing securities, this malady of the affections becomes extremely difficult to remedy" (*The Theory of Business Enterprise*, Charles Scribner's Sons, 1915, pp. 237–238). Mill expresses a somewhat similar view as follows: ". . . there is hardly any amount of business which may not be done, if people will be content to do it on small profits' (*Principles of Political Economy*, Longmans, Green & Co., 1909, pp. 561–562).

in its disrupting effect, by passing through the money transformer. It is important to keep this general fact in mind as background against which to appraise Hayek's theory.

Summary Statement of Hayek's Theses

In order to facilitate discussion, let us state Hayek's theses in a series of propositions as follows: [24]

Thesis No. 1. That depression is brought about by a shrinkage in the structure of production (i.e., a shortening of the roundabout, capitalistic process of production. In Hayek's view, the phenomenon of depression *is* a shrinkage in the structure of production.

Thesis No. 2. The leading cause which ultimately brings about a shortening in the process of production is the phenomenon of *forced* saving.

Thesis No. 3. An elongation of the process of production caused by *voluntary* saving tends to remain intact; or, at least, there is no inherent reason why such an elongation must necessarily be followed by a shrinkage in the structure of production. An increase in voluntary saving would cause an enlarged demand for producers' goods in relation to consumers' goods, and this would make possible a permanent elongation of the process of production.

Thesis No. 4. A lengthening of the process of production caused by forced saving (the money supply not having been held neutral) cannot possibly be permanently maintained, but must necessarily be followed by a shortening in the process of production. An increase in money supply (bank credit) made available to entrepreneurs would cause an increase in the demand for producers' goods in relation to consumers' goods. The consequent elongation of the process of production could not, however, be maintained, because a reversal in the price relationship of producers'

[24] These propositions are our own formulations of the doctrines advanced by Hayek in his *Prices and Production*, George Routledge & Sons, Ltd., London, 1931. See the article by Alvin H. Hansen and Herbert Tout, "Investment and Saving in Business-Cycle Theory," *Econometrica*, April, 1933; also Hayek's reply in *Econometrica*, April, 1934, reprinted in the second edition of *Prices and Production*, 1935.

goods and consumers' goods would appear as soon as the money supply ceased to increase. Thus a shrinkage in the artificially elongated process of production would inevitably occur.

Thesis No. 5. That an increase in consumer demand inevitably brings about a shortening in the process of production, and so causes depression. An increase in the purchasing power made available directly to consumers would cause an increase in the demand for consumers' goods in relation to producers' goods, more would be consumed and less would be saved, and this would inevitably bring about a shortening in the process of production.

Thesis No. 6. That increased public expenditures, by increasing the ratio of spending to savings, will force a shortening in the process of production and so cause depression. An increase in spending would cause an increased demand for consumers' goods in relation to producers' goods. The effect is to bring about a shortening of the process of production.

Thesis No. 7. That the supply of money should be kept constant, except for such increases and decreases as may be necessary (a) to offset changes in the velocity of circulation, (b) to counteract such changes in the coefficient of money transactions as are occasioned by the amalgamation of firms and the like, and (c) to provide for any changes in non-monetary means of payment, such as book credit, that may be taking place. A distinction is thus made between a "constant" money supply and a "neutral" money supply.

Thesis No. 8. That any change in the money supply (other than that necessary to hold money neutral) is harmful because it necessarily brings about, eventually, a shortening in the process of production: (a) If the increased money supply goes to entrepreneurs, the process of production is first elongated, but, subsequently, necessarily shortened, returning to its previous status, or to a still shorter process; (b) if the increased money goes first to consumers, the shortening of the process of production takes place at once, and the process remains shortened until the money flow ceases.

Thesis No. 9. That an increase in production and trade forms no justification for an increase in bank credit.

Thesis No. 10. That a period of depression should not be

counteracted by any inflation of the money supply, though, in theory, there is the possibility that during the acute stage of the crisis, while the capitalistic structure is tending to shrink more than will ultimately prove necessary, a nicely regulated increase might prove beneficial.

Hayek's Theses Criticized

Thesis No. 1, if taken literally, would mean that depression is synonomous with a *shrinkage* in the stock of capital goods. But this is not correct. In most depressions there is considerable net investment (and therefore some growth in the total capital stock), though far below that of boom levels. Depression begins when the rate of net investment starts to decline (which in turn induces a decline in consumption). Only rarely have depressions been so serious that net investment has fallen to zero.

Theses No. 2 and 4 are commented on in connection with Nos. 7 to 10 inclusive, below.

Thesis No. 3 implies that if the investment which is undertaken yields a rate of return equal to the rate of interest on voluntary saving, *disinvestment* will not follow; hence no shrinkage in the structure of production, and so no depression. But the mere maintenance of an achieved structure of production will not prevent a depression. The capital stock must continue to grow; investment outlays must be adequate to absorb the flow of potential current saving at full employment.

Theses No. 5 and 6. In both cases, so the argument runs, the injection of funds into the hands of consumers will raise consumer demand and consumers' prices. If indeed there occurs, as Hayek assumes, an increase in the prices of consumers' goods in relation to those of producers' goods, this would mean a higher rate of return over cost [25] (Fisher), or in other words a higher marginal efficiency of capital (Keynes). This would stimulate investment, not retard it.

Hayek here assumes that capital formation must be curtailed whenever there occurs an increase in consumption. But this need not be the case in a society that has unused resources. As income

25 What Hayek calls a higher rate of interest is really a higher rate of return on investment.

rises, both saving and consumption would rise. Thus the increase in consumer demand can *induce* an increase in investment; and this increase in investment, via the multiplier process, can raise income until voluntary saving equals the new high level of investment.

To be sure, it *may* be that this induced level of investment is not maintainable in view of the long-run capital requirements (determined by population growth and changes in technology). But this problem arises whenever any advance is made from depressed conditions. From this there is no escape, unless one is prepared to give up the problem altogether and resign oneself to perpetual depression. But the impossibility of maintaining the level of investment *induced by the rise in income* results from any rise in income, no matter how brought about. The problems connected with a maintainable rate of investment are indeed real, but they are not restricted to the particular method of advance suggested in the thesis here under discussion.

In this connection we may compare Hayek's maintainable rate of investment with that of Harrod.[26] With Hayek it is the volume of voluntary savings which fixes the *maintainable* rate of investment. With Harrod the maintainable rate of investment is determined by the capital requirements springing from population growth and changes in technology. In Harrod's view, however, the capital requirements so determined may involve a rate of investment considerably less than the rate of saving at full employment. Thus it is investment *opportunities,* not the rate of saving, which determine the level of investment which can be maintained over the long run.

Theses 2, 4, and 7–10 inclusive relate to the central hypothesis underlying Hayek's analysis. This may be restated and summarized as follows: An artificial stimulus is given to fixed capital investment by the injection of new money (bank credit expansion) or idle balances into the stream of "money-capital." The boom represents an abnormal volume of capital formation wrung out of an economy through the process of "forced saving"—that is, through the process of monetary expansion. The boom represents

[26] R. F. Harrod, *Towards a Dynamic Economics,* Macmillan & Co., Ltd., London, 1948.

a rate of capital formation in excess of the sustainable rate of capital formation. The sustainable rate of capital formation is determined, in Hayek's view, by the rate of voluntary saving. Monetary expansion drives the volume of capital formation to a level which exceeds this rate. And this produces the condition which we call a boom.

The boom *must* be followed by depression because the volume of capital formation cannot continue to be fed from an increase of bank credit. The limitation of bank reserves calls a halt to credit expansion. And if no restraints were imposed by the monetary authorities in a paper monetary system, continued monetary expansion would produce inflation. To avoid inflation, the credit expansion must be stopped, and when this happens, depression, according to Hayek, inevitably ensues. In the boom period, investment (fed by bank credit expansion) exceeds current voluntary savings. At the end of the boom there is an *excess* stock of capital in the sense that capital formation has been pushed (under the stimulus of an abnormally low money rate of interest) to a point at which the rate of return on invested capital falls below the normal rate of interest on current voluntary savings.

The reader will readily see certain points of affinity between this analysis and that of Tugan-Baranowsky and Wicksell. Wicksell, however, in agreement with Spiethoff, stressed the real factors (technology, etc.) which raise the prospective rate of return on investment and so cause a spurt in capital formation. With Wicksell it is "changes, brought about by independent factors, in the *natural rate of interest on capital* that are regarded as the essential cause of such movements. . . . Abundance or scarcity of money . . . is now imbued with a merely secondary importance." [27] Monetary factors, he says, may be "regarded as consequences" following from the increased inducement to invest springing from real factors.

Now this is fundamentally different from Hayek. The real factors stressed by Wicksell are not the ones stressed by Hayek. With Hayek the investment boom is due to monetary factors operating on the money rate of interest, not to real factors operating

[27] Wicksell, *Interest and Prices,* p. 167.

on the natural rate of interest. Moreover, the boom comes to an end, as Hayek sees it, not because investment opportunities, given the prevailing state of technique, have temporarily been exhausted (Spiethoff, Robertson); rather, it comes to an end because current voluntary savings are inadequate to sustain the boom level of investment once bank credit has run out.

In Hayek's view any monetary expansion *must* produce an investment boom that is not maintainable. Monetary expansion necessarily produces booms and depressions. There can therefore be but one solution to the problem: "neutral money."

Hayek's analysis not only overlooks the *real* factors which cause spurts in capital formation, but it also overplays, to a degree that is not defensible, monetary causes of disturbance. It is not true that monetary expansion *must* produce a rate of capital formation in excess of a maintainable rate. Let us assume that the long-term capital requirements (determined by population growth and changes in technology) justify an annual rate of capital formation equal to 10 per cent of income. Assume that the propensity to save is such that *in the absence of the income-redistributional effect of monetary expansion* only 8 per cent is saved. Monetary expansion (bank credit extended to entrepreneurs) would, however, in fact redistribute income to the advantage of business profits so that, say, 10 per cent of current income is saved. Assume the rate of monetary expansion is equal to, say, 3 per cent per annum; assume also a rate of increase in total output of 3 per cent per annum. Thus the total money supply would rise at the same rate as real income. Now this *percentage* rate of increase could continue indefinitely without producing an inflation.[28] The rate of investment, under the assumptions given, would not be excessive or non-maintainable over the long run. Of the 10 per cent of income expended on investment goods, 8 per cent would be financed from "voluntary current savings" in the Hayekian sense, and 2 per cent from expansion of bank credit ("forced

[28] A constant *percentage* rate of increase of money means, of course, an ever-growing *absolute* rate of increase. This constantly increasing *absolute* rate appears alarming to Hayek only because he forgets that output (assuming a constant percentage increase of 3 per cent or so) is also growing at a constantly increasing *absolute* rate.

saving"). There is no reason why this situation should produce an excessive (non-maintainable) investment boom and a subsequent depression. "Forced saving," in Hayek's sense, is therefore not necessarily inconsistent with continued stability.

Consumer Demand and the Capital Coefficient

Returning to Theses 5 and 6, we find them presented in a new garb in *Profits, Interest and Investment*[29] and in a *Fortune Magazine* article in 1945.[30] Here again, as in the earlier *Prices and Production,* the paradoxical argument is advanced that increasing the purchasing power of consumers will inevitably result in a decline in investment and so cause a depression. This new formulation makes use of the acceleration principle.

Hayek here advances the argument that the volume of induced investment, resulting from the principle of derived demand, will depend upon (a) the increase in final demand, and (b) the capital coefficient, or in other words the amount of capital required in relation to final product. If the capital coefficient declines as the boom advances, the total volume of investment may fall even though the rate of increase in final demand is rising. In other words, the fall in the capital coefficient may more than offset the rise in the rate of increase in final demand. This is certainly possible. Here, however, we are concerned with the reasons assigned by Hayek for the possible decline in the capital coefficient as the boom advances.

The reason for the decline in the capital coefficient, Hayek tells us, is precisely the increase in consumer demand. If this is granted, it then appears that it is the rise of consumer demand itself which may call a halt to the rising tide of prosperity. There is too much consumption, too little saving. All policies designed to raise consumption inevitably bring on the depression. This is the argument.

---

29 Frederick Hayek, *Profits, Interest and Investment,* George Routledge and Sons, Ltd., London, 1939.

30 A review of Sir William Beveridge's *Full Employment in a Free Society,* in *Fortune Magazine,* March, 1945.

The Ricardo Effect

The explanation given by Hayek for the decline in the capital coeffiicent is that as the boom advances it becomes increasingly profitable to substitute labor for machinery—in other words to resort to less roundabout processes of production. This substitution effect (the "Ricardo effect") follows, it is argued, from the decline in real wage rates in the upswing period. When real wage rates decline, says Hayek, labor will be substituted for machinery. And real wage rates will decline because as the boom advances consumer demand outruns the supply of consumers' goods. Consumers' goods prices will rise more than money wage rates; real wage rates will fall. The rise in prices and the fall in real wage rates "usually occurs in the latter stages of the boom," beginning about halfway through a cyclical upswing. At this point, "any further rise in demand for consumers' goods will lead to a rise in their prices and a fall in real wages," since the "excess stocks of consumers' goods have been absorbed, and employment in the consumers' goods industries is high." [31] And the fall in real wages will encourage capitalists to substitute labor for machinery—the "Ricardo effect."

There are several things in this analysis which on closer scrutiny appear more than doubtful. It is not clearly established that real wages do in fact typically fall in the last half of the boom. Pigou holds, indeed, the contrary view—namely, "that the upper halves of trade cycles have, on the whole, been associated with higher rates of real wages than the lower halves"; [32] and Dunlop and Tarshis have presented data [33] which indicate a rise in real wage rates in the upswing phase of the cycle. Moreover, it is not the relations of the money wage rate to the index of cost of living (real wage rate) which determines the substitution of machinery for labor, or vice versa; rather it is the money wage rate in relation to the price of machinery, assuming no change in technology or the personal efficiency of the worker. If the prices of machinery and other capital goods rise relatively less than money wage rates, such a condition would tend to induce entrepreneurs to substitute

[31] *Profits, Interest and Investment,* p. 11.

[32] Pigou, *Industrial Fluctuations,* p. 217.

[33] *Economic Journal,* September, 1938, and March, 1939.

machinery for labor. Processes of production would tend to become more capitalistic, and so the capital coefficient (ratio of capital to output) would tend to rise. This is precisely the opposite of the tendency alleged by Hayek. I am not aware, however, of any adequate statistical data which definitively establish the facts with respect to machinery prices and wage rates in past cycles. Moreover, the relative movements of machinery prices and wage rates might change considerably under varying conditions of collective bargaining on the one hand, and varying degrees of monopoly or monopolistic competition in the capital goods industries on the other.

As far as I am aware there is no satisfactory statistical evidence to show what is the cyclical behavior of the capital coefficient. Changes in the capital coefficient may indeed occur both in the short run and in the long run, as a result of technological developments, but such changes could be in either direction. Changes of this character are not likely to be sufficient to play an important role in the explanation of the drastic decline in investment which typically ushers in a depression. The explanation must rather be sought for the most part in the declining marginal efficiency of capital (as represented, first, in the movement *down* the curve as more and more capital goods are added to the stock, and second, in the downward *shift* of the curve as expectations turn gloomy). In short, the reason why the boom rate of investment is not maintainable is that it tends to exceed the long-term capital requirements as determined by population growth and changes in technology. This, however, does not rule out the possibility that other factors (for example, the rate of interest) *may* in greater or smaller measure, varying from cycle to cycle, play a role.

20 · *Sequences, Leads, and Lags:* WESLEY MITCHELL

WESLEY MITCHELL (1874–1948)

The early researches of Wesley Mitchell (beginning with *A History of Greenbacks* [1]) ended in the publication of the 1913 volume on *Business Cycles.*[2] The early researches started with the explosive upheaval of the Civil War with its massive tidal waves of inflation and deflation. But this upheaval was followed by a long period of rather moderate undulating waves which at times, to be sure, shot up to pretty high peaks and fell into deep troughs. No sooner were these early researches, covering half a century of American history, ended than the First World War broke out. Throughout the remainder of Mitchell's lifetime, fairly stable conditions prevailed for less than one decade—the good years of the twenties. For the rest there was a world depression of unprecedented severity and duration, followed by a second world-engulfing war which dealt smashing blows (the effects of which we cannot yet appraise) upon the economic structures and institutions of western Europe, and in less but still impressive measure upon the United States.

Mitchell had trained himself to study *an economy in motion.* But he had increasingly come to regard its dynamic quality in

1 W. C. Mitchell, *A History of Greenbacks,* University of Chicago Press, 1903.
2 W. C. Mitchell, *Business Cycles,* University of California Press, 1913.

terms of relatively *moderate* wavelike movements. The term "business cycle" became a popular and agreeable concept. Businessmen found it no reproach to describe the system of free enterprise as moving in continuing and self-generating cycles. Rather they regarded these oscillations as the "heart-throb" of a lively, dynamic system. The business cycle became a fad with the business community; forecasting became a national sport, for a time even more interesting than the game of national politics.

World War and Depression

The thirty-five years of Mitchell's life from 1913 (the publication date of *Business Cycles*) to the time of his death in 1948 may be divided into two equal parts. The first seventeen or eighteen years repeated (if we may be permitted a very rough comparison) the Greenback episode and its aftermath. First came the war upheaval of prices, the short postwar restocking boom, a short but sharp depression, and then a plateau of high prosperity and employment with mild oscillations. These were exciting developments; and Mitchell, more than any other living economist, had prepared himself to understand them. Eagerly he plunged into the adventures in economic explorations and public policy to which this flow of events forcefully directed attention. First came his studies on index numbers and prices during the war years, and then, beginning in 1920, the vast program of empirical research by the National Bureau of Economic Research of which he became Director. The second period (1930–48) brought the Great Depression and the Second World War.

The Process of Cumulative Change

Advances in technology, with intermittent surges of innovations and capital formation, never played an important role in Mitchell's concept of the business cycle. Moreover, it is not easy to fit into his scheme the titanic upheavals of two great wars and the devastating collapse of the Great Depression. For him business cycles were essentially *oscillations* or fluctuations. The recurrent phases of economic activity "grow out of and grow into each other." In his 1913 volume he declared that a theory of business cycles must be a "descriptive analysis of the cumulative changes by which one set of business conditions transforms itself into another set." The inner processes of business are quite competent to develop from one phase of the cycle into another without the adventitious help of any "disturbing circumstance." Mitchell thus conceived it to be the essential task of business-cycle analysis to look for the regular sequences, to discover the leads and lags of the significant economic variables, to trace the "processes of cumulative change."

The thesis that each phase of the cycle is generated out of the preceding stage, that it is not dependent upon exogenous factors external to the system of business itself, such as the intermittent, or perhaps steady, progress of technology, the growth of population, wars, harvests, autonomous monetary developments, or other outside impulses, is a hypothesis which Mitchell advanced, but which he found it no simple matter to prove by his empirical data. The cumulative self-generating process can easily be made to satisfy the test in the periods of expansion and contraction. Difficulties are, however, encountered (and Mitchell struggled with them) at the turning points. Exogenous factors he did in fact call to aid—for example, new products, new processes, and the increase in population at the lower turning point. But it is especially with respect to the upper turning point (as a careful reading of *Business Cycles* will disclose) that the self-perpetuating process stood in need of more explanation than was offered by a recital of the sequence of events. Skeptical of such abstract theorizing as that involved in rigorous endogenous explanations of the upper turning point, Mitchell contented himself with a descriptive analysis.

Mitchell's Conception of the Cycle

Nevertheless the conception of the cycle as a self-generating movement growing out of the quiet inner processes of the business system itself was an interesting and fruitful hypothesis; and it had a profound effect upon economic thinking all over the world. The conception was forcefully and skillfully stated; it was woven into the description of the sequence of events with endless variation; and it was driven home by constant reiteration. No one ever thought of depression and prosperity in quite the same way again, it is safe to say, after reading Mitchell's *Business Cycles.*

The 1913 volume took business cycles out of the ivory tower and made them the "stock in trade" of every financial writer and businessman. It was phrased in the language of the market place. The man of affairs at once recognized that here at last was a competent account of what goes on in actual economic life. And for the professional economist all discussion of "crises" became at long last obsolete. The concept of the cycle had indeed been advanced long before by many, but it was nonetheless Mitchell who put it over. Henceforth the phenomenon to be studied was the *cycle,* an unfolding integrated movement which had to be looked at as a whole.

Favorable or unfavorable events, says Mitchell, *may* play a role. But typically they do no more than to hasten or retard a process of expansion or contraction already under way. Happy accidents deserve no more credence as explanations of business revival than the "abandoned theory that crises are 'pathological' phenomena due to some 'abnormal' cause." The inner processes of business are quite competent to develop from one phase of the cycle into another "without the adventitious help of any disturbing circumstance." [3]

The Quest for Profits

The quest for profits, in Mitchell's view, is the central factor controlling economic activity. Accordingly, the whole discussion must center, he says, about the prospects of profits.[4]

Thus whatever factors affect profits come within the sweep of the analysis. The factors of chief significance are: (1) the prices which constitute business receipts, (2) the prices which constitute business expenses, (3) volume of sales, (4) currency to make payments, (5) availability of bank credit. We must know what fluctuations these factors undergo, and we must follow their interactions to see how they affect the prospects of profits.[5]

---

[3] *Ibid.,* p. 453.
[4] *Ibid.,* p. 450.
[5] *Ibid.,* p. 451.

The Revival Phase

A summary statement of the sequence of events as described by Mitchell follows: We begin with the upswing phase of the cycle. The "very conditions of business depression beget a revival of activity." The revival can be ascribed to processes necessarily unfolding in the period of depression, which breed favorable conditions. Among the favorable effects of a period of hard times are the following: (1) a reduction of costs, both prime and supplementary, (2) reduction in inventory stocks, (3) low rates of interest, (4) strong lending position of banks, (5) growth of investment-seeking funds. These conditions develop out of the depression, and each contributes to an environment favorable to revival.

Once disinvestment of inventories ceases, current purchases of retailers and wholesalers increase even though there may be no change in current consumer purchasers. Dealers no longer sell from stocks. Orders to manufacturers are therefore increased. Similarly families' stocks of clothing and furnishings are gradually worn out and discarded. It becomes necessary to buy new articles if money can be found for the purpose. The continued growth of population tends to influence the aggregate volume of consumers' demand. The "development of new tastes among consumers, the appearance of new materials, and the introduction of new processes do not come to a stand-still even in times of depression." New men seeking business openings can for a time buy into old enterprises on favorable terms (owing to bankruptcies and reorganizations caused by the depression) but after a while these opportunities become less favorable. Thereafter new enterprising men seeking business adventure build for themselves. The demand for new construction and new equipment is encouraged by the low rate of interest, the availability of investment-seeking funds, and the low cost of construction. During the depression new construction and new installations of equipment are checked, but the "accumulation of technical improvements continues." There develops, accordingly, an increasing "inducement to invest in new equipment." [6]

Under the combined pressures of these various forces there

[6] *Ibid.*, pp. 565–567.

occurs a marked increase in consumers' and producers' demand. This expansion in demand raises the physical volume of business. The reduction in prime costs and fixed charges combined with this increase in physical volume raises current and prospective profits.

Let us pause a moment and take stock. Apart from the favorable conditions (monetary situation, costs, etc.), two factors, it is suggested, account for giving the economy an upward push. They are: (1) the cessation of disinvestment of stocks of goods by dealers and consumers, (2) technical progress [7] as revealed in new products and new processes of production. Now the former does indeed grow out of the internal process of the cycle itself; but technological developments do not unfold automatically from the cyclical sequence. Technological change is for the most part an exogenous factor, an outside impulse to which the economy responds. In short, the process of "cumulative change" involves, after all, more than the sequence of variables endogenous to the cycle itself.

The first indication of revival, according to Mitchell, is the increase in the physical volume of business. Then, with a lag, comes the rise in prices. And this spreads and cumulates. Different parts in the price structure (wholesale, retail, consumers' goods, producers' goods, raw materials, wages, interest rates) respond with varying degrees of promptness. A shift thus occurs in the internal structure of prices as the cycle proceeds from depression to the peak of prosperity.[8]

The interrelation of costs and selling prices unfolds in a manner to widen the profit margin. This process, combined with the greater physical volume, increases profits. And since the "quest of profits is the driving force of the money economy" the cumulative process is reinforced.

Accumulation of Stresses

"The more vividly this cumulative growth of prosperity is appreciated, the more difficult becomes the problem why prosper-

[7] To this may be added the factor of population growth, another important exogenous factor.

[8] *Business Cycles,* pp. 452–468.

ity does not continue indefinitely." Unfavorable events may and often do occur. But for such misfortunes the superabounding prosperity is more than a match, and "over many such rocks the accumulated momentum of good times may run without serious mishap." Misfortunes do not explain the ending of prosperity. Indeed, many periods of "intense prosperity have ended in years of plenty, peace, and good fortune. The waning, like the waxing of prosperity, therefore, must be due, not to the influence of 'disturbing causes' from outside, but to processes which run regularly within the world of business itself." [9] Stresses accumulate within the system of business itself "until they finally disrupt its equilibrium." [10]

Among the threatening stresses which gradually accumulate during seasons of high prosperity is the slow but sure increase in costs. Fixed charges (interest rates, rentals, and depreciation charges) rise. Antiquated equipment is brought back into use in view of unfilled orders and heavy demand. Wage rates rise, less efficient labor is employed, and over-all labor efficiency declines in periods of prosperity. The cost of materials rises. Rising interest on short-term loans is a matter of some importance, especially to the mercantile classes. Business management itself is overburdened and loses its grip on economic administration. All these increasing costs threaten to encroach upon profits.

The rapid extension of industrial equipment breeds other stresses. The construction of new plants and the launching of new projects swell the volume of business and lift prices. "But at the same time, the bidding of these trades for labor and materials aids in drawing up the costs of doing business in all the various ways described in the preceding section." When sections of the new equipment are finished and put into active use, the enterprises owning them compete for operatives and raw materials, and on the other side pour their products upon the market. "This activity serves both to strengthen the forces which are already raising the costs of doing business and to obstruct the advance of selling prices." But since the construction of equipment takes

[9] *Ibid.*, p. 473.
[10] *Ibid.*, p. 474.

time, prosperity may have "neared its high tide before the new equipment begins to aggravate seriously the encroachments of costs upon profits." [11]

Stringency develops in the market for investment funds. Complaint begins to be heard of a "scarcity of capital." The supply of funds is no longer equal to the demand at the old rate of interest. "The terms exacted for long loans become onerous." [12] Borrowers raise "more capital on stocks and less on bonds," and they "take up one-, two-, or three-year notes at a high rate of discount instead of selling long-term bonds."

The "volume of public applications for capital usually suffers a heavy decline in the year preceding a crisis." This decline does not mean, so Mitchell asserts, "that the desire on the part of business enterprises to secure funds has shrunk, but that the men in control are unwilling to saddle their companies for a long series of years with the heavy fixed charges which would result from borrowing under the prevailing conditions. They prefer to defer the execution of their plans until funds can be procured on better terms." [13]

No recognition is here given to the possibility that investment in plant and equipment, houses, office buildings, hotels, etc., may have reached a temporary saturation point, as suggested by Spiethoff, Robertson, and others.

The explanation offered by Mitchell for the ending of prosperity is the rise in costs engendered by prosperity itself. This increase in costs threatens to diminish profits. "But, granted so much, there still remains a problem to be faced. Why cannot business men defend their margins of profits against the threatened encroachments of costs by marking up their selling prices sufficiently?" [14] A surface answer, Mitchell suggests, would be:

[11] *Ibid.*, p. 485.
[12] *Ibid.*, p. 486.
[13] *Ibid.*, p. 487.
[14] One may also ask: If profit margins are being encroached upon, why is not the competitive bidding for labor and materials lessened so as to stabilize costs at a satisfactory profit margin? Indeed, Mitchell did, as noted above, raise some such question, but he failed to give it a satisfactory answer. And the reason for this failure is mainly that he neglected the factors causing a decline in the rate of real investment.

"inadequacy of the quantity of money." With limited reserves, bank credit cannot be expanded indefinitely.

But Mitchell thinks this answer has only a "certain academic interest." Other causes check the rise in prices "before the banks have allowed themselves to be jeopardized in this fashion." Indeed, it is not enough to show that the rise in the general level of prices must come to an end. The real problem is to show what "prevents business enterprises from maintaining a profitable adjustment between the advance of two sets of prices, those which constitute costs and those which constitute returns." What must be explained is the "accumulation of stresses between these two parts of the system of prices."[15]

The Upper Turning Point

Having posed the problem in this manner, it would be logical to consider the possibility of the adjustment of costs to the stabilized level of selling prices so as to maintain a satisfactory profit margin. Why might not this lead to perpetual prosperity? If the problem is only one of balance between costs and prices, market forces should be able to take care of that. But Mitchell does not, in fact, tackle this problem, though he himself, as we have seen, raised it. Instead he goes on to explain why selling prices cannot continue to rise. The assumption seems to be that there is no possibility of stopping the continued rise in costs, even after profit margins begin to be squeezed. There is therefore no way out except to continue to raise selling prices. Hence Mitchell, instead of seeking a means of balancing costs and prices, seeks to explain why (apart from hypothetical limits imposed by the money supply) a continued rise in prices is not possible.

First, some prices are fixed by public regulation (public utilities), by long-term contracts, or by custom. Next, errors of optimism "lead in every period of prosperity to an overstocking of certain markets." Furthermore, when rising interest rates and rising construction costs begin to restrict orders for materials and supplies, "the decline of demand threatens to stop the rise of prices in other industries, if not to cause a decline."[16] (To this

[15] *Business Cycles,* p. 496.
[16] *Ibid.,* p. 499.

it might be objected that this development should be favorable to the maintenance of prosperity, since it serves to slow down the rising costs of labor and materials for other industries). Finally, Mitchell raises the problem whether the increase of selling prices is not precluded by the lag of consumers' demand—the under-consumption theory. But he argues that this is not plausible, since the prices of consumers' goods fall later than the prices of producers' goods. Mitchell here overlooks the possibility that, according to the acceleration principle, a slowing down in the rate of increase of consumer demand might explain the prior absolute decline in the demand for, and prices of, producers' goods. "Until the under-consumption theories have been shored up by more convincing evidence than has yet been adduced in their favor, therefore, the view must prevail that the difficulty of warding off encroachments upon profits by advancing costs comes to a head earlier in other lines of business than those concerned with consumers' goods." [17] Mitchell's confidence that the study of leads and lags could settle the question of causation is here disclosed. That the confidence was misplaced, however, was conclusively proved by means of the theory of derived demand—the acceleration principle.

Mitchell thus concludes that there are three reasons why prices fail to continue to advance: (1) the relative fixity of certain prices, (2) the curtailment of construction and equipment investment due to high construction costs and high interest rates, (3) excess production and excess capacity in certain lines due to errors of optimism. A "reduction in the rate of profits must therefore infallibly occur." [18] Nowhere has it been shown, however, why costs might not cease advancing, once selling prices stop rising.

Moreover, this analysis does not correspond to Mitchell's own data (admittedly meager) on profits. The German figures used indicate that profits "continued to rise without interruption through the revival of activity and the period of prosperity to a climax in 1899." [19] The "net income from operation" of American railways, and also "net income" (which includes income from

---

[17] *Ibid.*, p. 502.
[18] *Ibid.*, p. 503.
[19] *Ibid.*, p. 503.

other sources) continues to rise right up through the entire boom period.[20] Meade's figures for twenty-nine industrial trusts quoted by Mitchell show profits reaching high point in the last year of the boom.[21] "Many, probably the majority, are making more money than at any previous stage of the business cycle." [22] But an important minority, says Mitchell, face the prospect of declining profits before that decline has become general.[23]

Highly pertinent, I suggest, are the data recently published by the National Bureau of Economic Research on corporate profits. These data show that the index of total net corporate profits is synchronous with the index of industrial production and with the general reference cycle. The profits index continues to rise right up to the very peak of the boom. Their studies also disclose, however, that the *percentage of companies* undergoing cyclical expansion of net profits reaches high point roughly around the halfway mark in the expansion phase of the cycle. This indicates that many companies reach the peak of their *own* profits cycle rather early in the general business upswing and continue at high (but not peak) profits levels until the end of the boom. Other companies continue to advance in their own profits cycle right up to the boom peak. Aggregate net profits continue to rise so long as the *majority* of companies are still advancing on their own profits cycle. When the peak of the general business boom has been passed, less than 50 per cent of the companies are still advancing toward their own profits peak.[24]

No convincing case can be made for the thesis that the turning point from prosperity to depression is *caused* by declining profits, as Mitchell seems to suggest. We are perhaps nearer the truth if we regard profits as the *result* of the cycle movement, not the cause of the cycle.

It is highly important to differentiate average profits currently being made from the *prospective* rate of return on the *next increment* of real investment—the marginal efficiency of cap-

---

20 *Ibid.*, pp. 424–426.
21 *Ibid.*, p. 431.
22 *Ibid.*, p. 575.
23 *Ibid.*, p. 503.
24 For a further discussion of the relation of net corporate profits to the general cycle, see Chapter 29 in this book.

ital. The latter may be low, even zero, while the former is still running at a high rate. Thus an automobile company may currently be making very good profits, but it may see no prospect that *additional* equipment can earn a satisfactory rate of return. The newest equipment may already have been installed, and existing plant and equipment may be fully adequate for the prospective volume of sales. Thus *new* investment is not a function of the current average rate of profits; it is a function of the *prospective rate of return over cost of an additional increment* of investment. Net investment is induced by either advancing sales or cost-reducing inventions—the widening and deepening aspects of the investment process.

Depressions Inevitably Follow Booms

Once the downswing has started, the cumulative process drives the economy, Mitchell believed, from crisis into depression. But the question may be asked: Is there really any good reason why the depression phase might not be skipped? The crisis, some argue, arises from impaired confidence. If confidence could be restored, they maintain, no real reason would remain why business should not be resumed on the scale prevailing before the panic. Let businessmen talk prosperity instead of hard times and all would be well.[25]

This point of view, we recall, was indeed advanced by Alfred Marshall. But Mitchell placed no faith in these "sunshine movements." Hard experience, in 1893 and again in 1907, proved in a few weeks the futility of an artificially inspired revival. Are there not elements in the business situation following a boom and crisis which make "a period of depression inevitable—elements beyond the control of sentiment?" [26]

If the real investment boom has temporarily exhausted investment opportunities, if the marginal efficiency of capital has been pushed by the process of large investment in fixed capital to a low figure, then indeed the depression is inevitable in a society which has evolved no powerful anti-cyclical policy. Moreover, the unfavorable expectations would cause a cumulative downward

[25] *Business Cycles,* p. 554.
[26] *Ibid.,* p. 554.

movement. These are the root causes of the depression, according to Spiethoff, Wicksell, and Robertson.

But this is not the explanation offered by Mitchell. There is resort instead to a general description of what happens. Workmen are discharged, with a resulting decline in consumers' demand. Merchants sell from left-over stocks. While existing factories stand idle there is little inducement to install new equipment. The prospect of a further fall in prices induces the postponement of new projects. These processes are cumulative in effect. Each reduction in employment and in consumers' demand causes further decline.

Under the pressure of hard times, costs are reduced, money becomes redundant, accumulated stocks are gradually used up, new products and new processes are developed, and so depression prepares the way once again for revival.[27]

This, then, is the story as Mitchell saw it in 1913. He described a sequence of events, leads and lags in different variables, a process of price-cost adjustment. But this sequence of events, these leads and lags, are but the *manner* in which the cycle development unfolds. They themselves explain nothing. The driving force back of the cycle, Mitchell believed, was the quest for profits. What was needed was a deeper analysis than he offered of the *factors causing a fluctuation in the rate of real investment.*

Business Cycles as Seen in 1927

The next landmark in Mitchell's work is *Business Cycles, the Problem and Its Setting.*[28] Here the theoretical, historical, and statistical literature is comprehensively canvassed. Sixty pages are devoted to a survey of theoretical works. There is some recognition of the Continental development (especially Tugan-Baranowsky), but one carries away strongly the feeling that the basic contributions of this group of thinkers never fully registered on Mitchell's mind. At any rate, there is no penetrating exposition of *investment analysis,*[29] together with a rigorous discussion leading to

[27] *Ibid.*, pp. 562–569.

[28] W. C. Mitchell, *Business Cycles, the Problem and Its Setting,* National Bureau of Economic Research, 1927.

[29] Note should, however, be taken of the reference to a stock of man-made equipment, the maintenance and extension of which need not be kept nearly so uniform as the output of consumers' goods. Accordingly, modern industrial

acceptance or rejection of the bold and impressive formulations of the Investment school. Mitchell's panoramic survey of business-cycle theory, as of the year 1927, gives one the impression that here is a vast, disorganized workshop in which many workers have thrown their tools about. The reader is unhappily not instructed which tools, if any, are of workmanlike quality. Working hypotheses are indeed needed, he tells us, to guide our selection of data and to suggest ways of analyzing and combining them, and for this purpose he seems to suggest that the different theories, if they appear at all plausible, serve almost equally well.

The Inner Tendency Toward Cyclical Behavior

His survey of statistical findings and of business annals discloses that the "normal" condition is a state of change, incessant fluctuation. The fluctuations differ from cycle to cycle, but there is no reason for doubting that these cycles constitute a valid species of phenomena. In a world in which powerful and sporadic disturbances—wars, harvest variations, epidemics, floods, and earthquakes—come and go at irregular intervals, the "tendency toward alternations of prosperity and depression must have considerable constancy and energy to stamp its pattern upon economic history." Similarly there is the widest variation in random events from nation to nation. Yet the "quiet business forces working toward uniformity of fortunes must be powerful indeed to impress a common pattern upon the course of business cycles in many countries." [30]

The conclusion to Mitchell's 1927 volume suggests further working plans for the future. These include an effort to find "what features have been characteristic of all or most cycles." More must be learned about the workings of the interrelated processes. After this is done "it will be time to see what the question about the cause of business cycles means, and in what sense it can be answered." Once again there is the confident faith that the way

methods and modern business organization in combination "open the door to wide cyclical fluctuations in at least one important field of economic activity," namely, the equipment-producing industries. (*Business Cycles, the Problem and Its Setting*, p. 182.)

30 Mitchell, *Business Cycles, the Problem and Its Setting*, p. 450.

to study cycles is to study sequences, leads and lags, interrelations between different variables with respect to timing, amplitude, deviations from a critical range, etc. The conception of the problem remains as in 1913. The data accumulated and analyzed in the intervening fourteen years had not altered this basic concept. And the time was not yet ripe, he thought, to uncover the cause or causes of the phenomenon. The 1927 volume adds further to our detailed knowledge of the sequence of events as the cycle unfolds, but we do not yet know its innermost nature.

Ten years later (1937) there appeared a notable publication of the National Bureau of Economic Research—*National Income and Capital Formation, 1919–1935,* by Simon Kuznets. Here was rich grist for Mitchell's mill as he worked at the problem of causation. But one misses in anything he wrote an adequate appreciation of the significance for business-cycle analysis of Kuznets' data on income and capital formation. Kuznets' aggregates are, to be sure, subjected (in Mitchell's posthumous *What Happens during Business Cycles*) to the Bureau's standard measurements with respect to amplitude, leads and lags, etc. But many would question whether this represents all that could be learned from Kuznets' rich empirical study.

Measuring Business Cycles

Long years of further research produced the massive *Measuring Business Cycles,* by Burns and Mitchell. The volume is mainly devoted to statistical methodology, but it also contains a vast amount of data on the sequence of different time series in the cycle. The title indicates that the "command" given in the 1927 volume had been faithfully obeyed. The objective was not explanation but measurement of the cycle behavior. Deviation of movement, timing of peaks and troughs, duration of phases, amplitudes, and rates of change are noted. "These measures together with those showing the sequence in which different activities turn up at business-cycle revivals and turn down at business-cycle recessions are essential in tracing causal relations." [31]

The crux of the investigation involves passing from the specific

---

[31] A. F. Burns and W. C. Mitchell, *Measuring Business Cycles,* National Bureau of Economic Research, New York, 1946, p. 12.

cycles of individual time series to business cycles. Thus a table of "reference dates" was drawn up "that purport to mark off the troughs and peaks of successive business cycles, and to measure the leads or lags of specific-cycle troughs and peaks from these benchmarks." [32]

Once a set of fairly well tested reference dates is obtained "we can show in detail how different activities behave during business cycles: how the cyclical turns of different series are related to one another, and how their movements compare in magnitude and direction from stage to stage of business cycles." [33]

The authors conclude the volume holding fast to the thesis (fundamentally similar to the view held in the 1927 volume) that a central core of stable features runs through successive cycles. There is "little evidence that secular, structural, or cyclical changes have impressed their influence strongly on the cyclical behavior of single activities or business as a whole." [34] Successive cycles of the same series are found to bear a family resemblance. When we strike averages for groups of specific or reference cycles, the story is almost always the same: "The idiosyncrasies of individual cycles tend to vanish, the average patterns of the same series look much alike in different samples of cycles, the patterns of different series become sharply differentiated, and the relations among the series persist with great regularity from one sample of cycles to the next. This tendency of individual series to behave similarly in regard to one another in successive business cycles would not be found if the forces that produce business cycles had slight regularity." [35]

Two conclusions emerge from the analysis: (1) business cycles consist of roughly concurrent fluctuations in many activities; (2)

---

32 *Ibid.*, p. 12.

33 *Ibid.*, p. 13. The measures of business cycles represented by the Burns-Mitchell 1946 volume are only a part of the whole program of research. Numerous separate monographs have been initiated on the cyclical behavior of different areas of economic life such as agriculture, manufacturing, construction, money and banking, etc. Others are contemplated on public finances, savings and investment, securities markets, etc., together with a series of historical studies. A final volume is intended giving a theoretical account of how business cycles run their course, of which a "preview" by Mitchell was partially completed at the time of his death.

34 Burns and Mitchell, *Measuring Business Cycles*, p. 480.

35 *Ibid.*, p. 480.

there is a pronounced tendency toward repetition *in the relations* among the movements of different activities in successive business cycles.

Finally in his paper, "The Role of Research in Economic Progress," [36] Mitchell refers to the widely different responses that a general business expansion evokes from the different industries ranging all the way from coal mining to farming. These different responses cannot be ascribed to chance, since they recur, cycle after cycle, with the same regularity as the general tides of business. Again he suggests that leads and lags, differences in amplitude, the "relative importance of leaders and laggers that fluctuate little or much" are the all-important problems for anyone "trying to understand how business cycles come about." And the posthumous "progress report" entitled *What Happens during Business Cycles* is a comprehensive study worked out along these lines.

Thus to the end Mitchell continued to be interested primarily in the *sequence of events.* This sequence doubtless displays a certain regularity from cycle to cycle, given fundamentally similar economic institutions. The sequence of events can indeed throw illumination on, but cannot of itself explain, the "forces" that "cause" the cycle.

[36] *The Conditions of Industrial Progress,* University of Pennsylvania, 1947.

21 · *Exogenous and Endogenous Theories*

Business-cycle theories have sometimes been classified into (a) theories explaining fluctuations in terms of exogenous factors and (b) theories explaining fluctuations in terms of endogenous factors.

Many "literary" (or non-mathematical) theories draw heavily upon exogenous factors for an explanation of both the cumulative process and the turning points. Econometric theories, on the other hand, have stressed endogenous movements.

The mathematical treatment provides an insight into the "types of movements that economic systems may perform." [1] Econometric theories lay stress on the systematic movements which spring from the internal nature of the economic structure. This structure can be described in terms of a system of relations between various economic variables. Econometric analysis shows that "constant relationships can produce a fluctuating process," once an initial shock has disrupted equilibrium.[2] The econometric approach stresses the effect of the economic structure on cyclical fluctuations; or, more precisely, it seeks to explain how cyclical movements result from the response of the economic structure to random shocks. Econometric models disclose the kinds of move-

---

[1] J. Tinbergen, "Econometric Business Cycle Research," Chapter 4 in *Readings in Business Cycle Theory,* The Blakiston Company, 1944, p. 73.

[2] J. Tinbergen and J. J. Polak, *The Dynamics of Business Cycles,* University of Chicago Press, 1950, p. 255.

ments which the economic system would develop (if later left undisturbed) in response to a certain initial disturbance.

A rigidly exogenous theory regards economic fluctuations as "nothing but a purely arbitrary and random succession of changes." [3] Fluctuations in the "data" or exogenous variables would produce corresponding fluctuations in the economy as a whole if the system responded *immediately* to changes in the data. But this, in fact, is not the case. The economic structure adapts itself more or less slowly to external disturbances. And as soon as *lags* are introduced we are at once involved with endogenous factors in cyclical behavior. But it must also be stressed that an endogenous theory cannot leave out of account the external disturbance to which the economic system responds in a manner which sets going cyclical movements.

Exogenous movements may be random or periodic. If external factors—crops or inventions—themselves fluctuated in a periodic manner, and if the system responded with no time lag, we should then have a truly exogenous theory explaining periodic cyclical movements. If, however, the exogenous factors were quite *random* in character (and the system responded with no time lag), we should have purely random fluctuations revealing no cyclical behavior.

When the system exhibits a *lagging response,* random disturbances may produce a cumulative unilateral movement upward or downward; or they may produce cyclical movements, owing to the peculiar internal nature of the economic structure. In either case such movements would be endogenous.

Exogenous theories place primary emphasis upon changes in the data; endogenous theories upon the lagged reactions of the economic structure (with constant internal relationships) to such changes.

Exogenous theories explain the turning points in the cycle by reference to some external factor. Endogenous theories explain the turning points by reference to the internal functioning of the system itself.

The system of internal relationships may, however, be such that the endogenous movements are of a unilateral character, con-

[3] *Ibid.*, p. 253.

sisting simply of a cumulative process upward or downward. If nonetheless a cyclical movement occurs, the turning points must then be explained by exogenous factors. In this case we have a mixed theory.

In general, there is perhaps a tendency in business-cycle literature to stress the role of exogenous factors at the lower turning points, and to stress the role of endogenous factors at the upper turning points. The endogenous forces that lead to recovery are at any rate often regarded as weaker than those that terminate a boom.[4]

Fully endogenous theories rely upon internal forces at both turning points, each phase of the cycle leading into the next. Semi-endogenous theories rely upon endogenous factors only to explain crises and depressions. In this case each cycle movement comes to a halt, until exogenous factors eventually start a new recovery. Each cycle is thus regarded as a separate entity.

The recent emphasis on endogenous movements in business-cycle analysis stems from Aftalion. It was he who first stressed the lagged response of entrepreneurs in their continuing effort to adjust fixed capital capacity to demand. The rhythm in investment, he explained, was due to the fact that it requires a long time to construct fixed capital. The alternating excess and deficiency of capacity is due, he explained, to the time lag between the decision to increase the capital stock and the completion of the new capital goods. The time element in the modern system of production, in his view, is responsible for the lagged and imperfect adjustment of capacity to output.

High prices can induce increased output only after a long lapse of time, owing to the modern roundabout method of production. There is a lag between the price and the related production. Small supplies are at once reflected in high prices; but high prices lead to larger quantities only after the lapse of a given time period. Here, then, the stage is set for a continuing cyclical movement: alternating overproduction and underproduction, overcapacity and undercapacity, with consequent fluctuations in investment, and so in income and employment.

Econometric models of endogenous movements may for the

[4] *Ibid.*, p. 257.

most part be classified into the following three main groupings with subtypes:

I. Output-lag models: Aftalion's furnace analogy.

A. The lagging adjustment of *actual* current supply available in the market to the *desired* supply. A typical example is the hog cycle of about three to three and one-half years. Supply cannot instantly adjust itself to price. There is a production lag. This lag is (1) partly a *decision* lag due to the time required for farmers to respond in their planning to price changes; and (2) partly an *execution* lag, due (a) to the natural period of gestation, and (b) to the "growing and feeding" period. The lagged adjustment of output to prices will produce cycles of output and prices, inversely correlated. From one price peak to the next trough (and similarly from one output trough to the next peak) the period will be equal to the lag, and the full cycle will be twice the lag.

B. The lagging adjustment of actual capacity of fixed capital to the desired capacity. This case involves fluctuations in the total accumulated stock of capital goods. Net investment represents net additions to capital stock, or gross investment minus capital consumption. Net disinvestment represents net reductions from the total capital stock. But disinvestment can never exceed capital consumption.

The lagged adjustment of actual *capacity* to desired capacity is even more difficult than that of adjusting the current *supply* of a consumer's good to the desired supply (Case I, A above). The reason for this is that the stock of a highly durable capital good is very great, and even large current additions (net investment) can increase the accumulated stock relatively little. Examples are houses, the gold stock, railway equipment, steel-manufacturing plant and equipment, etc. It may thus take a long time to bring actual stock up to the desired stock. Moreover, the interval between the moment when the need for more capacity is recognized and the moment when deliveries of fixed capital goods come on the market is a long one. Investment will likely continue to be planned so long as actual capacity is below desired capacity. But in view of the production lag, deliveries are likely to be made for a considerable period *after* actual capacity has caught up with desired capacity. Thus there is likely to develop a recurring cycle of excess capacity followed later by undercapacity. (See the discussion of the cobweb theorem in Chapter 22 of this book.)

In the case of residential construction, a sixteen- to eighteen-year cycle appears, as we have noted in Chapter 3, in American experience. This is a good example of the "time period of production" giving rise to a cycle of overcapacity and undercapacity. The cycle is due to a lag in construction. Once a deficiency in houses appears, new completed construction does not appear at once, but only after a lag. First, it takes some time before rent contracts reflect the house shortage. Secondly, the abnormal level of rents must prevail for a period before contractors and real estate owners decide to build. Finally, a considerable time must elapse before the new construction is finished and put on the market. These three lags—the rent-contract lag, the decision lag, and the construction lag—may well, under ordinary peacetime conditions, add up to around four years, as suggested by Tinbergen and Polak.[5] Thus a deficiency of houses, once started, would continue to grow, up to the fifth year, before any new construction appeared. Moreover, the new construction is likely to match the deficiency only gradually. Thus the total deficiency which has accumulated by the fifth year may not be made up until, say, the ninth year. But the construction then in process, based on deficiencies apparent four years earlier, will go on for a while, leading to an excess supply of houses by, say, the thirteenth year. And this excess may finally be worked off by, say, the seventeenth or eighteenth year—and so the cycle is completed. This, at least, is a reasonably plausible hypothesis.

II. The acceleration principle: The demand for final output (quantity demanded) may fluctuate in a systematic manner owing to prior movements in income, started by some initial disturbance away from equilibrium. Any systematic fluctuation in expenditures will cause fluctuations in investment (the principle of derived

[5] *Ibid.*, pp. 242–243.

demand). The interaction of fluctuations in *final* demand and fluctuations in *derived* demand, once equilibrium is broken, will perpetuate the cycle. The oscillation is an endogenous movement based on the internal relationship of final demand to derived demand.

III. The interaction of the multiplier and the accelerator: Econometric models of endogenous movements achieved the widest applicability for business-cycle analysis following the integration of the Aftalion acceleration principle with the Kahn-Keynes multiplier.[6] These two principles are natural twins, and together constitute powerful tools for analyzing the laws of motion of an economy using large quantities of fixed capital. Given investment, the multiplier tells us how income will evolve. Given the evolution of income, the accelerator tells us how investment behaves. Taken together, they are self-determining, and we have a complete dynamic theory. They constitute an essential structure or skeleton of any econometric theory of the cycle. Moreover, this analysis serves to integrate the exogenous factor—autonomous investment—with the endogenous factors—the multiplier and the accelerator.

A more detailed account of the development of econometric methods of analysis is given in the next chapter.

---

[6] See Paul Samuelson, "Interactions between the Multiplier and the Principle of Acceleration," *Review of Economic Statistics,* May, 1939; and Alvin H. Hansen, *Fiscal Policy and Business Cycles* (W. W. Norton & Company, Inc., 1941), Chapter 12.

22 · *Econometrics in Business-Cycle Analysis*

By RICHARD M. GOODWIN

A. ECONOMETRIC METHODS

No better statement of the meaning and significance of this new type of cycle investigation can be given than that made by Ragnar Frisch in an editorial of the first issue of *Econometrica* in January, 1933: "Thus, econometrics is by no means the same as economic statistics. Nor is it identical with what we call general economic theory, although a considerable portion of this theory has a definitely quantitative character. Nor should econometrics be taken as synonymous with the application of mathematics to economics. Experience has shown that each of these three view-points, that of statistics, economic theory, and mathematics, is a necessary, but not by itself a sufficient, condition for a real understanding of the quantitative relations in modern economic life. It is the *unification* of all three that is powerful. And it is this unification that constitutes econometrics."

Econometric business-cycle research is extremely ambitious in its aims, and if successful would completely outmode all other analysis. This is, however, a long-run ideal, for so bold a program cannot be successfully carried out directly in view of the difficulty of the problem and the unsatisfactory character of the available statistics. If the results achieved thus far are somewhat disappointing, it should be remembered that the work has proceeded for barely twenty years, which is short compared with the life span of general economics. To this may be added the consideration that the errors and shortcomings of econometrics appear more glaring by virtue of the fact that all vagueness or indefiniteness is consistently eschewed.

Operational Hypotheses

In the present state, at least, of statistical technique it is not possible to extract from raw data the correct hypothesis about economic reality; these must be supplied by the economist. Unfortunately the matter does not end there. Often the economists' hypotheses are vague if not actually confused, or, worse still, they may be of a type which cannot possibly be tested: in the language of modern science, they are non-operational, and hence their truth or falsity cannot, even under ideal conditions, be established. Also a great deal of economic theory is operational but nonetheless useless because it is too complicated either to analyze or to test. Concretely, most micro-analysis (theory of the individual firm and of the individual household) has to be violently simplified into aggregative or macro-analysis before it is simple enough to be usable in practice.

Once a theory is in satisfactory form, the econometrician may proceed to statistical testing if the required data are available. He may be able to prove the theory wrong, but he can never prove it conclusively right; he can only show that it is in conformity with observed fact. However, under favorable circumstances, the econometrician aims to do more than this; in fact, he hopes to achieve a substantive addition to economic theory. It is vital to know not only that X influences Y but by how much it does so. Only when we have some *numbers* telling us quantitatively the amount of influence of the various factors on one another can we tell whether our set of hypotheses will give rise to oscillations, or to smooth transition from one equilibrium to another, or to unstable, explosive behavior. Also in modern economics almost everything influences everything else, but it is necessary to find out quantitatively which relations are weak enough to be neglected so that we may be enabled to simplify our theories down to manageable form.

We may allow ourselves great flexibility in the mathematical statement of the problem. Thus our aim may be the very modest one of trying to explain the variations in some one variable such as the output of automobiles, or of a whole group of such goods as consumer durables. A familiar example is the attempt to explain the behavior of aggregate consumption. This may involve such quantities as national income, the price level, and population, as well as a number of other factors. Here these other variables are treated as *exogenous*—that is, they must be taken as given and unexplained by the one relation being investigated. We may extend our system by taking account of the definition of national income as the sum of consumption and investment, this being a definition and hence requiring no statistical test. Hence two of our variables, consumption and income, are *endogenous* (explained by our system) and three, investment, prices, and population, are exogenous and are to be explained "outside" the system. But this division is arbitrary. If we can, for example, find a relation between income and investment, then we may extend the range of our system so as to reduce the number of exogenous variables to two. By further complications we might hope to include the price level among the endogenous variables, but population, containing non-economic influences, would require a much more complete theory of the whole of social forces.

Exogenous and Endogenous Theories

Business-cycle theories may be classified in many ways, but one essential way is according to the principle by which the swinging motion is kept alive. At once the oldest and the simplest are the exogenous theories in which the cycle is maintained by perpetually alternating "outside" disturbances. The most famous of these is the sunspot theory, which bases cycles on the effect of the cycle of sunspots on crops and hence on the rest of the economy. The economy may be completely devoid of dynamic elements (i.e., time lags or time rates of change in the structural relationships), and yet oscillate. Whether or not the economy has dynamic elements, it will oscillate with the same period (duration of cycle) as the exogenous disturbance. Schumpeter's theory of the cycle partly fits into this category, since the occurrence of innovation cannot be explained except in terms of the whole social development of technology and entrepreneurial boldness and freedom of action.[1] Yet the tendency for these to bunch at somewhat regular intervals has, in part at least, an economic explanation.

By contrast there are the endogenous or self-generating theories that create, by virtue of their own structure, the alternations of expansion and contraction. This type must be dynamic in that some of the variables must depend on lagged values of the others, or on their rates of change. One of the most fruitful ways of regarding econometric models is to look for the essential dynamic elements which give rise to the oscillation.

The Pendulum Model

Probably the most basic distinction between various endogenous systems is again the question of how the cycle is maintained. Most econometric models are linear in the sense that the variables are proportional to the other variables and their lagged values or their time derivatives. If oscillatory, such a system can give rise, depending on the values of the proportions (the constants or parameters) in the equations, to any one of three types of behavior: (a) its amplitude of fluctuation may grow ceaselessly, thus being unstable; (b) it may be stable, with an ever-decreasing amplitude; (c) its behavior may lie exactly in between the other two, so that it neither grows nor decreases in violence. The third category must be rejected as improbable[2] and the first as in contradiction to experience, leaving us with (b) as the only realistic case. Yet there remains the problem of how the cycle persists if it is always dying away. One very plausible kind of answer has been given by Frisch following a suggestion of Wicksell.[3] The

---

[1] Cf. J. A. Schumpeter, *The Theory of Economic Development,* Harvard University Press, Cambridge, 1936, Chapter VI.

[2] Kalecki's model was originally of this type, but Frisch's criticisms (in *Econometrica,* 1935) must be held to have rendered the hypothesis untenable. Kalecki subsequently modified his formulation.

[3] Cf. Ragnar Frisch, "Propagation Problems and Impulse Problems in Dynamic Economics" in *Economic Essays in Honour of Gustav Cassel,* George Allen and Unwin, Ltd., London, 1933.

pendulum of a clock would gradually stop swinging if it were not for the escapement, which delivers a push to it once each way and thus keeps it going. Schumpeter's theory is perhaps best considered as an example of this: innovational investment gives a shock to the economy once a cycle, although, unlike a clock, the violence of the shock is different every time, and depends on the "unexplained" historical evolution of technology.[4] Indeed, Frisch has shown that the shocks need not have any regularity in timing or violence in order to explain the maintenance of the oscillation. This type of hypothesis is particularly important for another reason: it can explain the well-established fact that no two cycles are alike and that therefore there is no strict periodicity in economic time series. In fact, some economists have been led to deny that there is any cycle-generating mechanism at all. Although the Frisch hypothesis cannot be proved, it does seem the only acceptable one, for we must explain both the tendency to regularity and the tendency to irregularity; the two elements must be included in any model.

The Billiard-Table Model

The second general type of self-generating cycle is that in which the equations are not all linear. There exist in economics a number of well-known saturation effects, technical barriers like full employment, and thresholds such as no investment until capacity is reached, all of which point to non-linearities. In such a system the expansion may proceed uninhibited until it reaches some barrier, such as full employment or the limits to credit expansion, and then, its regime violently broken, it will move downward to the other limit. As a mechanical analogy, one may picture a ball which rolls on a polished table until it hits a wall, where it reverses and moves backward until it hits a second wall, and so on. By contrast the pendulum, as in all linear theories, gradually accumulates increasing reversing forces the farther it proceeds away from its equilibrium point. The non-linear system is the general oscillation type of which the linear one is to be considered a very special case. It comprehends all possible

[4] Cf. Richard Goodwin, "Innovations and the Irregularity of Economic Cycles," *The Review of Economic Statistics,* 1946.

types of oscillation shapes, whereas the linear one is restricted to sine waves. Also it may, and indeed commonly does, give rise to oscillations which neither die away nor expand but rather maintain themselves at a determinate level, even in the absence of "outside" disturbances. An example of such a system is worked out in detail in Section B of this chapter.

Difference Equations

There are two mathematically distinct kinds of cycle models, those based on difference (lag) equations and those based on differential (rates of change) equations, as well as mixed varieties involving both. Thus the simple Robertsonian lag produces the following difference equation multiplier:

$$Y_t = C_t + I_t$$
$$C_t = C(Y_{t-1}) \text{ and hence,}$$
$$Y_t = C(Y_{t-1}) + I_t$$

Differential Equations

If we consider induced investment only, according to the acceleration principle, we have

$$K = aY$$

where K is capital stock and "a" is the acceleration coefficient. Since I_t, net investment, is the rate of growth of capital,

$$I = \frac{dK}{dt} = a\frac{dY}{dt}$$

and, ignoring the time lag in consumption,

$$Y = C(Y) + a\frac{dY}{dt}$$

which is the simplest differential equation one can have.

Mixed Difference-differential Equations

Taking account of the fact that the rate of growth of income may determine decisions to invest, but that the corresponding outlays will be lagged by some considerable time, we get the following mixed difference-differential equation:

$$I_{t+e} = a\frac{dY}{dt}$$

$$Y_{t+e} = C(Y_{t+e}) + a\frac{dY}{dt}\text{, or}$$

$$\frac{dY}{dt} = \frac{1}{a}\left[Y_{t+e} - C(Y_{t+e})\right]$$

Difference equations have been more frequently used in economics, in sharp contrast to the natural sciences, where no major theory makes use of difference equations. Difference equations are attractive because it is possible to make simple numerical calculations with them and to see the nature of the solutions as they evolve. Thus if we have, as a representation of an economic system:

$$Y_t = 80 - 1.3Y_{t-1} - 0.80Y_{t-2}$$

and if we are given (historically) the values of Y at time $t-2$ and $t-1$, then we may very simply multiply the first by .8 and the second by 1.3 and subtract them both from 80 to get the value of Y at time t. Then, we can take Y_{t-1} and Y_t to compute Y_{t+1} and thus extrapolate our results forward (or backward, for that matter) as long as nothing changes. Such calculations are conveniently arranged, as in Table XXII, where the "initial" values 30 and 25 are given. Thus to get Y_2 we multiply 25 by -1.3 (giving -32) and 30 by $-.80$ (giving -24) and then subtract these from 80 to get $Y_2 = 24$.

TABLE XXII

(1)	(2)	(3)	(4)	(5)
t	80	$-1.3Y_{t-1}$	$-0.80Y_{t-2}$	(2) + (3) + (4) Y_t
0				30
1				25
2	80	−32	−24	24
3	80	−31	−20	29
4	80	38	−19	23
5	80	−30	−23	27
6	80	−35	−18	27
7	80	−35	−22	23
8	80	−30	−22	28
9	80	−36	−18	26
10	80	−34	−22	24
11	80	−31	−21	28
12	80	−36	−19	25

As a result we get the time series of Y_t plotted in Figure 62. The reader is urged to carry out the calculations for at least one example in order to see the genesis of an endogenous cycle. To save effort, it is permissible to drop the constant term (here 80) from the calculations. The results are then in the form of deviations from equilibrium, which is all we care to know if our interest lies primarily in dynamics. The complete solution is then obtained by adding the equilibrium quantity to all the deviations.

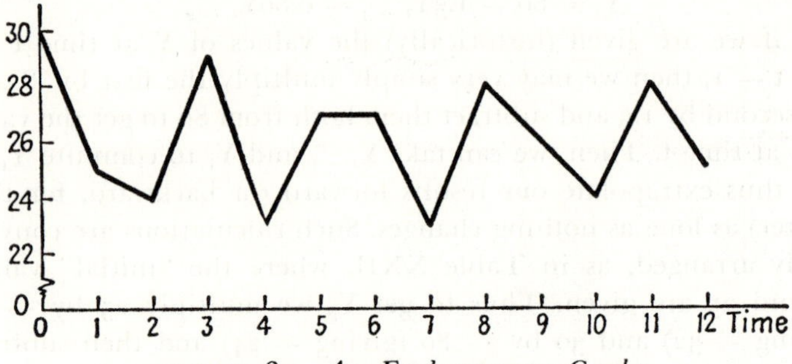

FIGURE 62. *An Endogenous Cycle*

Economists are often not clear as to precisely what kind of reality they wish to represent by difference equations. One interpretation is that time is discontinuous and only takes on the values $-1, 0, +1, +2$, and so on, as in the case of a market which meets only once a month. As such it represents a crude approximation to what is in most cases a rather continuous process. On the other hand, it is sometimes held to refer to ordinary time series which represent sums of goods traded, or transactions and the like, over a period such as a month or a quarter year. Finally it may mean—and this is the most legitimate interpretation—a true lag, in which what happens at any one time influences something else a constant time later; e.g., production commenced now becomes output a few weeks or months later.

Although apparently quite distinct, differential equations have rather similar solutions, for which the student may consult any standard mathematics book.

Tinbergen's Cobweb Theorem

Econometric business-cycle research may be said to have begun with Professor Tinbergen's brilliant analysis of the cobweb theorem.[5] Although this was not the business cycle, it charted the future course of development by making a dynamic and mathematical closed-system analysis of a well-observed phenomenon, the hog cycle. With straight-line supply and demand curves, we get the simplest of lag cycles, because of the fact that the quantity supplied depends on the price one lag unit ago, whereas the demand depends on the price now. As is easily seen from Figure 63, the cycle is stable if the demand curve is less steep than the supply curve, and unstable if the converse holds. If it takes Θ months to breed and bring to market a pig (or in general to produce anything), then the quantity sold *now* is a function of price Θ months ago. The cycle is necessarily of $2\ \Theta$ months' duration regardless of the shape of the curves.

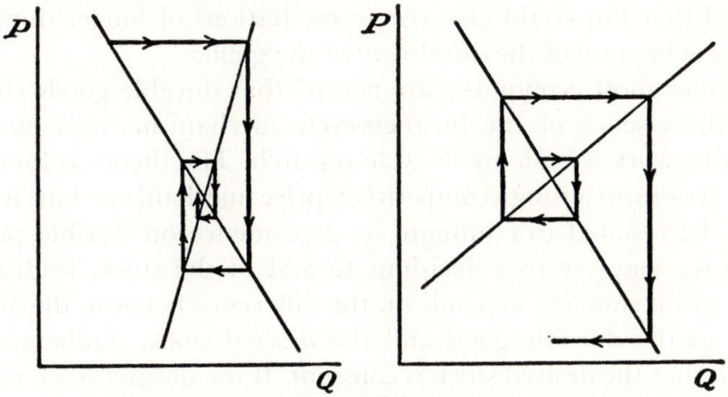

FIGURE 63. *The Cobweb Theorem*

Tinbergen saw clearly the tremendous implications of this type of analysis and soon extended it to apply to *durable* goods in which there is a significant lag between decisions to produce

[5] "Bestimmung und Deutung von Angebotskurven, Ein Beispiel," *Zeitschrift für Nationalökonomie,* 1930. A good account in English may be found in Mordecai Ezekial, "The Cob-Web Theorem," *Quarterly Journal of Economics,* 1938, reprinted as Chapter 21 in *Readings in Business Cycle Theory,* The Blakiston Co., 1944.

and actual deliveries of goods.[6] Perishable goods (hog products, for example) are consumed in one go, and hence total supply is purely the result of price prevailing Θ months ago; but durable goods do not disappear, and hence the previous price determines not supply but rather the additions to total stock. Therefore Q in the cobweb theorem is replaced by the *rate of increase* of stock K at time t, or $\frac{dK}{dt}$. Consequently the rate of increase of the stock depends on the total stock some time ago. Tinbergen demonstrated that this could give rise to oscillations of longer duration than $2\,\Theta$ because of the durability of the good.

Since most economists are agreed that durable goods constitute the essence of the business-cycle mechanism, it is obvious that this work is basic to all cycle research. The theory is founded on a free-functioning, competitive price mechanism, but it can easily be restated to eliminate its dependence on flexible prices. Thus we may say that decisions to add to the stock, leading to production starting, depends on the difference between the *actual* stock of the durable good and the *desired* stock. Tinbergen assumed that the desired stock is constant. If the desired stock varies, we have then introduced an outside disturbance or shock which will maintain the oscillation.

Frisch and Kalecki

With the publication in 1933 of his "Propagation Problems and Impulse Problems," [7] Professor Frisch injected at least two fundamental principles into the discussion. The first was the analysis of the role of "outside" shocks in maintaining the swings of an otherwise stable system; the second was the pure theory of what determines the rate of production (and hence also the rate of payments) in a firm with a variable rate of orders or production startings. This problem is more familiar to most economists in the form of the sausage-grinder analogy of D. H. Robertson.[8] There arises as a result of the time required for fabrication a kind

[6] "Ein Schiffbauzyklus?," *Weltwirtschaftliches Archiv,* 1931.

[7] See footnote 3.

[8] *Money,* Harcourt, Brace and Company, New York, 1929, p. 112. Robertson, however, is concerned with the quantity of working capital rather than with the dynamic implications of the implied lags.

of average lag between the starting of production and the actual disbursing of funds. This Frisch sausage-grinder function is a basic dynamic characteristic of all capitalistic production and has a central position in many econometric cycle models. This fact, along with a form of the acceleration principle, constitutes the essential dynamic element in the Frisch model. The accelerator introduces a rate of change, and the sausage machine a lag, with the result that this system also is of a mixed difference-differential form.

In the same year, 1933, Michal Kalecki published a paper giving an econometric model.[9] The essential dynamic features of his system were (a) the Frisch sausage-grinder mechanism applied to the aggregate investment goods trades, and (b) an investment function based on the functional relation of I (investment) to K (capital stock) and Y (income); thus $I = f(Y, K)$.

Present national income, Kalecki assumes, is determined by investment decisions in the preceding period; and current investment decisions are determined partly by current income and partly by the stock of capital equipment. Income will rise if present investment decisions exceed past investment decisions.

If investment decisions are rising, this will cause both an increase in income and an increase in capital stock. The higher income will raise investment decisions, but the increasing capital stock will tend to lower them. Eventually the latter factor will predominate, and so the upper turning point is reached. Investment decisions will fall, and this will drive income down. As income declines, investment decisions will fall, but this tendency is increasingly offset by the fact that the capital stock is shrinking. Eventually this latter factor takes the upper hand. Thus the interaction of the income effect on investment and the capital stock effect creates an automatic business cycle.[10]

[9] An English version was published as "A Macrodynamic Theory of Business Cycles," *Econometrica,* 1935. See also his *Essays in the Theory of Economic Fluctuations,* Farrar & Rinehart, Inc., New York, 1939; and *Studies in Economic Dynamics,* Farrar & Rinehart, Inc., New York, 1944. For a related theory see N. Kaldor, "A Model of the Trade Cycle," *Economic Journal,* March, 1940.

[10] See M. Kalecki, *Essays in the Theory of Economic Fluctuations,* Chapter 6, especially pp. 137–149.

Tinbergen's Survey of Econometric Cycle Research

In his famous article "Suggestions on Quantitative Business Cycle Theory,"[11] Tinbergen made what is still today the best statement of the whole range of the problems of econometric cycle research. He gave a penetrating review and critique of all the work, including some of his own, not otherwise available in English, done up to that time. Beyond that, he stated the central problems of theory, choice of variables, structure of dynamic systems and analysis of their behavior, methods of statistical testing, and implications for public policy. In its rich interplay between theoretical and empirical investigation, this monograph is extraordinarily original and stimulating. Tinbergen took up the various basic elements in the functioning of an economy—profits, wages, consumption, and the corresponding markets for capital, machinery, labor, consumers' goods, and raw materials—and considered in each case what kind of theory best agreed with the known facts.

Some of his novel conclusions, based on a careful sifting of empirical data, have been strikingly borne out by subsequent work. "The chief reasons for this fact (the quantitative unimportance of interest rates) may perhaps be expressed as follows: the total amount of short term interest included in costs of production is small, whereas the variations in the amount of long term interest are small."[12] Or consider his assessment of the importance of monetary factors: "Whether a higher sales volume is completed with more money or with money circulating more rapidly seems of only secondary interest to the business cycle theorist."[13] Finally, he found that most of the evidence did not fit the simple acceleration principle.

In line with most modern practice, he formulated various complete models and subjected them to the test of comparison as a whole with observed facts. In several different models the constants were determined from the statistical data for the United States, for England, and for Germany. He then checked the re-

---

[11] J. Tinbergen, "Suggestions on Quantitative Business Cycle Theory," *Econometrica,* July, 1935.
[12] *Ibid.,* p. 247.
[13] *Ibid.,* p. 264.

sults by the criteria of the length of cycle produced and the implied lag patterns. Some of the models proved to be possible explanations of actual cycles and some did not. He discussed the two vitally different possible methods for statistical determination of the constants, the structural and the historical. "This [one of the constants in the system] might, therefore, be determined from a cost distribution function, in any case from a timeless structural datum. It might, however, also be determined in the usual statistical way of determining supply curves from historical data on prices and production figures considered to correspond to these prices." [14]

Lag Systems: Lundberg, Metzler, Samuelson, Klein

In 1937, the appearance of Lundberg's *Economic Expansion* [15] provided a good introduction to the general problem of economic dynamics, incorporating Tinbergen lag systems as well as much modern Scandinavian thought on these problems. This line of thought has been developed and applied to cycles in inventories by Metzler.[16] He incorporates the Keynesian multiplier into a Frisch-type production lag, actuated by an inventory accelerator, and shows that cycles may easily arise. Earlier, the Hansen-Samuelson analysis of the interaction of the multiplier and the accelerator utilized a Robertsonian lag between income and consumption expenditure.[17] The most ambitious recent econometric cycle analysis is Klein's "The Use of Econometric Models as a Guide to Economic Policy" in *Econometrica,* April, 1947.

Tinbergen's Multiple Correlation Studies

By far the most impressive single effort in econometric cycle research is the pair of monographs executed by Tinbergen for

---

14 *Ibid.,* p. 282.

15 E. Lundberg, *Economic Expansion,* P. S. King, London, 1937.

16 L. Metzler, "The Nature and Stability of Inventory Cycles," *The Review of Economic Statistics,* 1941, and "Factors Governing the Length of Inventory Cycles" in the same journal, 1947.

17 Paul Samuelson, "Interaction between the Multiplier Analysis and the Principle of Acceleration," *The Review of Economic Statistics,* May, 1939; Alvin H. Hansen, *Fiscal Policy and Business Cycles,* Chapter 12.

This multiplier-accelerator econometric model is discussed in some detail in Chapter 11 of this book.

the Economic Intelligence Service of the League of Nations.[18] The source of the cycle theories to be tested was Haberler's *Prosperity and Depression,* prepared as a part of the same project. On the basis of widespread agreement among economists, Tinbergen selected investment as the crucial cycle variable to be explained. In his first volume he sets forth a vivid and simple account of multiple correlation analysis and its difficulties as applied to time series. Then he proceeds to apply the technique to a wide variety of investment series and countries.

"In the early phases of *statistical business cycle research,* attention was paid to somewhat superficial phenomena, such as the length of cycles, the degree of simple correlation between series and the relative amplitudes of their movements, the decomposition of series into trend, seasonal components, etc. . . . For the purpose of applying more searching tests, however, it is necessary to dig deeper. . . .

"The part which the statistician can play in this process must not be misunderstood. The theories which he submits to examination are handed over to him by the economist, and with the economist the responsibility for them must remain; for no statistical test can prove a theory to be correct. It can, indeed, prove that theory to be incorrect, or at least incomplete, by showing that it does not cover a particular set of facts: but, even if one theory appears to be in accordance with the facts, it is still possible that there is another theory, also in accordance with the facts, which is the 'true' one, as may be shown by new facts or further theoretical investigations. . . .

"On the other hand, the role of the statistician is not confined to 'verification.' As the above example illustrates, the direct causal relations of which we are in search are generally relations, not between two series only—one cause and one effect—but between one dependent series and several causes. And what we want to discover is, not merely what causes are operative, but also *with what strength each of them operates:* otherwise it is impossible

---

[18] *Statistical Testing of Business-Cycle Theories:* Volume I, *A Method and Its Application to Investment Activity,* and Volume II, *Business Cycles in the United States of America, 1919–1932,* Geneva, 1939.

to find out the nature of the combined effect of causes working in opposite directions."[19]

As an example of his method, we may take his results for the explanation of the consumption of iron and steel as representing investment activity in the United Kingdom, 1920–36.[20] If we take:

x_1—physical volume of iron and steel consumption in percentage deviations from average;

x_2—profits, all industries, percentage deviations from average;

x_3—bond yield, deviations from average in hundredths of 1 per cent;

x_4—iron prices, percentage deviations from average;

x_5—time in years;

then he finds that

$$x_1 = 1.17x_2 - 0.08x_3 - 0.24x_4 + 2.39x_5$$

This may usefully be represented graphically as in Figure 64.

His conclusions, based on the analysis of a considerable body of evidence from the United States, the United Kingdom, France, and Germany, are that "the factors short-term interest rate, price of iron, rate of increase in production and in prices, and profit margin are, in the main, far less important than profits and share yields. In particular cases some of them seem to be important, but a general indication is lacking."[21]

In his second volume Tinbergen systematically investigated an enormous volume of statistics relating to the cycle in the United States from 1919 to 1932. To describe the developments he found it necessary to include a large number of variables and equations, which makes the system somewhat unwieldy. In any short space it is impossible to describe the structure of his model, and the interested student is referred to the original monograph.

As Tinbergen himself has pointed out, no absolute confidence can be placed in any particular result. The most penetrating criticism of his results has been given by Keynes. "In plain terms,

19 *Ibid.*, Volume I, p. 12.

20 *Ibid.*, Volume I, pp. 26–27.

21 *Ibid.*, Volume I, p. 55. He gave further statistical evidence against the influence of rate of increase in production in his "Statistical Evidence on the Acceleration Principle," *Economica*, 1938.

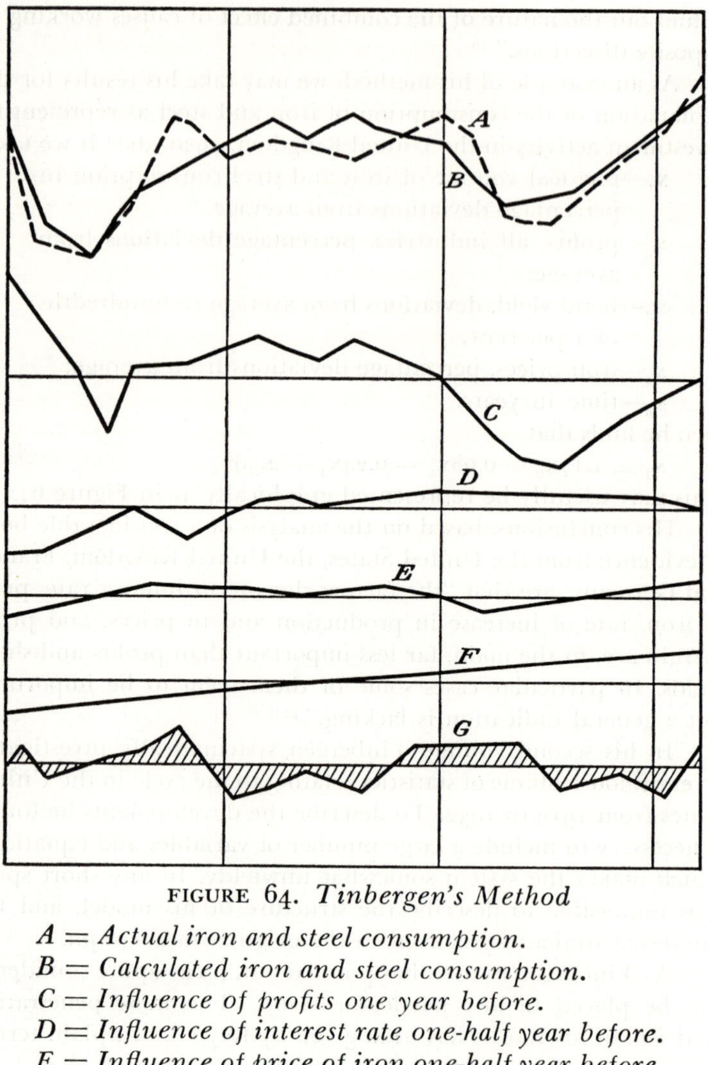

FIGURE 64. *Tinbergen's Method*

A = Actual iron and steel consumption.
B = Calculated iron and steel consumption.
C = Influence of profits one year before.
D = Influence of interest rate one-half year before.
E = Influence of price of iron one-half year before.
F = Influence of time.
G = Residuals, i.e., A − B.

Source: J. Tinbergen, *A Method and Its Application to Investment Activity,* League of Nations, Economic Intelligence Section, Geneva, 1939.

it is evident that if what is really the same factor is appearing in several places under various disguises, a free choice of regression coefficients can lead to strange results. It becomes like those puzzles for children where you write down your age, multiply, add this and that, subtract something else, and eventually end up with the number of the 'Beast of Revelation.'"[22] Thus if we reverse the direction of causality and say that investment determines profits through the multiplier and income, we rob one of Tinbergen's chief results of much of its significance. In general in the cycle most things go up and down together, and hence the danger of "spurious" correlation is very great. This criticism was anticipated by Tinbergen, although how successfully it was answered remains an open question. Also it should be remembered that this is not limited to Tinbergen's work but is a central difficulty with all time series analysis. "The danger threatening the accuracy of our results is especially that of multicollinearity. The simplest form of multicollinearity consists of a high degree of parallelism between two of the explanatory series. . . . If such a situation occurs, the separate regression coefficients cannot be determined. . . . The opinion is often expressed that these cases must be frequent in business-cycle research, since all relevant variables show more or less parallel cycles. In the United States, in the period studied here, this was not the case."[23]

Statistical Testing of Cycle Theories

The attack by Keynes produced two exceptionally clear and readable restatements of the method: Tinbergen stated the nature and methods of analysis of simple lag systems;[24] T. Koopmans elaborated carefully the assumptions and problems involved in the statistical testing of cycle theories with time series.[25] Since

---

[22] J. M. Keynes, "Professor Tinbergen's Method," *Economic Journal,* 1939, p. 562. In the same article Keynes makes a number of other valid criticisms as well as a few quite invalid ones, as was pointed out by Tinbergen in his reply in a later issue (1940).

[23] J. Tinbergen, *Business Cycles in the United States of America, 1919–1932,* League of Nations, Geneva, 1939, p. 12.

[24] "Econometric Business Cycle Research," reprinted as Chapter 4 in *Readings in Business Cycle Theories,* The Blakiston Company, 1944.

[25] "The Logic of Econometric Business-Cycle Research," *The Journal of Political Economy,* 1941.

Tinbergen's pioneer work, a very rapid and technically involved elaboration of statistical methodology (with particular emphasis on explicit probability hypotheses) has been proceeding. The mathematical complications exclude any discussion of these developments here, but the interested reader can find a good, nontechnical account, as well as references to the literature, in Professor Leontief's chapter on econometrics in *A Survey of Contemporary Economics.*[26] His conclusion is that "one could say that in its present conditions the further progress of quantitative economic analysis will depend upon successful, essentially nonstatistical search for promising analytical insights, as much as upon the final statistical sifting of the empirical 'pay dust.'"[27]

B. THE CONSTRUCTION OF AN ECONOMETRIC MODEL

It is not difficult to construct a model of the business cycle. By inserting any of a large number of plausible lags or derivations, one gets a system which will oscillate if the values of the parameters lie within easily determinable limits. Embarrassment arises not from the difficulty of finding such a result but rather from the fact that there are many different hypotheses which will do much the same thing. Therefore, the choice between hypotheses becomes a crucial step. As we have seen in Section A of this chapter, statistical work is still effectively limited to testing the hypotheses already selected and cannot be used to find the one correct hypothesis or set of hypotheses. Also if we determine the parameters of an oscillatory system from cyclical data of a single cycle we will obviously get a pretty good "explanation" of the cycle from which we took the data.

The Problem of Selecting Hypotheses

Therefore we must lay great emphasis on the question of selecting hypotheses, and it seems wise to preserve considerable skepticism about any one theory. In sifting hypotheses we can get help from reflection on the essential nature of cycles and why

[26] *A Survey of Contemporary Economics,* H. E. Ellis, editor, The Blakiston Company, 1948, p. 393.
[27] *Ibid.,* p. 393.

they arise and why they persist. For aid we may turn to the natural sciences. Here oscillations play a dominating role, and as a result scientists have evolved a more or less complete theory of the nature of oscillations in general. In the last eighty years especially, enormous progress has been made in analyzing the general nature of cycles, apart from particular types. Again and again new oscillation problems have been successfully formulated and solved by a careful study of how the analogous situation has been faced in relation to quite different phenomena. Routine transfer of analogies from physical science to economics can give (and has given) useless or even misleading results. But this is not to say that we cannot gain vital insights into the nature of the problem and its solution by considering how scientists and mathematicians have dealt with similar problems. By the mere abstract statement of how an oscillation arises and persists, we begin to see what sort of theories are likely to be important and what ones may be discarded or kept only as complications to the more fundamental ones. In any case it is highly desirable to construct in some detail an example of a cycle model in order to see what considerations enter into the choice of central hypotheses, what the difficulties are, and how satisfactorily such a model may be used as a rough explanation of the actual, observed fluctuations.

The Theory of Aftalion

As an illuminating point of departure, it is stimulating to take the theory of Aftalion, both because it is essentially quantitative and econometric in its point of view and because of the great role which this type of theory has played in all business-cycle research, theoretical and statistical. As in almost all cycle theories, he found that investment is the essence of the matter. "My principal thesis is that the chief responsibility for cyclical fluctuations should be assigned to one of the characteristics of modern industrial techniques, namely, the long period required for the production of fixed capital." [28] This theory has been used in

---

[28] "The Theory of Economic Cycles Based on the Capitalistic Technique of Production," *Review of Economic Statistics,* October, 1927, p. 165. This article contains a compressed statement of his theories which are stated more completely in *Les Crises périodiques de surproduction,* Paris, 1913.

almost all econometric cycle research. Tinbergen stated it precisely and completely for shipbuilding and investigated it both theoretically and statistically in his epoch-making article on the shipbuilding cycle.[29] It is interesting to note that Aftalion mentioned shipbuilding as one of the examples corroborating his argument. The Tinbergen study (and his allied work on the cobweb theorem) was the first work in econometric cycle research, and in a certain sense it was the archetype of all subsequent work in this field. The same lag was central to Frisch's analysis of the cycle [30] and also to Kalecki's.[31] In the form of the acceleration theory Aftalion's work has, of course, been fundamental to modern cycle theory.

One reason for the profound influence of this capital theory is that it is already in a more or less carefully thought out, *quantitative* form. There is perhaps no better statement of it than in the famous analogy given by Aftalion. "If one rekindles the fire in the hearth in order to warm up a room, one has to wait a while before one has the desired temperature. As the cold continues, and the thermometer continues to record it, one might be led, if one had not the lessons of experience, to throw more coal on the fire. One would continue to throw coal, even though the quantity already in the grate is such as will give off an intolerable heat, when once it is all alight. To allow oneself to be guided by the present sense of cold and the indications of the thermometer to that effect is fatally to overheat the room." [32] It is evident that the analogy is quantitative and has a clear causal structure and an evident parallelism with capital theory. Nothing is proved, but a fruitful line of attack is vividly suggested.

A Feedback System

If we accept the analogy as valid and useful, then implicitly we have narrowed somewhat the class of oscillations of which

---

[29] J. Tinbergen, "Ein Schiffbauzyklus?," *Weltwirtschaftliches Archiv,* 1931.

[30] Ragnar Frisch, "Propagation Problems and Impulse Problems in Dynamic Economics," in *Economic Essays in Honor of Gustav Cassel,* George Allen and Unwin, Ltd., London, 1933.

[31] Michal Kalecki, *Essays in the Theory of Economic Fluctuations,* Farrar and Rinehart, Inc., New York, 1939.

[32] Quoted by Professor Haberler in *Prosperity and Depression,* third edition, League of Nations, New York, 1946, p. 135.

business fluctuations are one kind. This type of system, which has been the subject of much research in the last twenty years, is now commonly called a servomechanism or, more broadly, a feedback system. "A mechanical or electrical system with feedback is one in which the output of some part of the system is used as an input to the system at a point where this can affect its own value. A servo system is a feedback system in which the actual output is compared with the input, which is the *desired* output, and the driving element is activated by the difference of these quantities." [33] Thus a furnace's own output in the form of heating is fed back to it in order to reach the desired house temperature. Here a human being is the essential feedback device, and it is in this form that we find the oldest and most common servo systems. The steering of ships and vehicles, manual aiming of guns, indeed possibly all human motor activity may be regarded from this point of view. Perhaps the most hopeful line of development in the study of the brain and nervous system is that of regarding it as a feedback device.[34]

But the human being is rapidly being replaced as a control device by electromechanical contrivances. A furnace may be turned on and off by thermostatic control devices whenever the temperature passes certain threshold levels, thereby yielding a completely automatic servomechanism. The temperature will not only oscillate between, say, 68° and 70°, but it will tend to "overshoot" at both limits because of the time lag between switching on and off and the actual delivery of a higher or lower temperature to the room. Both human beings and machines tend to overshoot, and the degree to which they do (their "stability" of behavior) is of vital importance, which explains the connection between servo and oscillation theory. An ideal servo system would not oscillate, but rather would always deliver the desired performance; but in practice this is almost never realizable. If the

---

33 *Theory of Servomechanisms,* M.I.T. Radiation Laboratory Series, ed. by H. M. James, N. B. Nichols, R. S. Phillips, courtesy of McGraw-Hill Book Co., New York, 1947, p. 62.

34 For this, and other profoundly stimulating, more general points of view regarding servo systems, consult N. Wiener, *Cybernetics,* or *Control and Communication in the Animal and the Machine,* John Wiley and Sons, New York, 1948.

person is unskilled or the feedback mechanism badly designed, the system may "hunt" its desired output or target but never find it. In the course of the analysis of hunting, modern scientists have developed a much richer, more complete oscillation theory—one which explains the various types and why they may persist instead of dying away or becoming so excessive as to wreck the machine. This may happen even if the desired output of the mechanism is never changed, as was the case with badly designed governors for steam engines, which hunted even in the absence of changes in load or desired speed. The situation is made worse and the size of oscillation increased if there are changes in the data (load or desired output) which are supplied to the machine.

In principle one should make a sharp distinction between (a) a system which hunts a particular quarry but never finds it, and (b) a system which would find a single unmoving objective but in practice is always hunting because its quarry is always shifting its position. In the example to follow we will rely mainly on type (a) to explain the persistence of business cycles. This possibility has been universally ignored in economics in favor of type (b), i.e., oscillations maintained by random or erratic exogenous disturbances.

Thus even if the servo system is stable, it may be kept oscillating by changes in desired output, as in the case of an automatically steered ship in heavy seas, or of a radar device for tracking an airplane which is trying to evade the resultant anti-aircraft fire. Since business cycles never die out and since they exhibit ever-changing characteristics, one or both of these hunting tendencies must be present in any model. The feedback control or servo character of our economy must be more definitely specified.

We have the "command" or *desired* level for our system, and we have its *actual* output or achieved level. Then we have an error-sensitive device which takes the difference between the command and the output, and this or some function of it becomes the input to the system which in turn gives its response, which is the actual output.

Call $K_0(t)$ the *desired* capital. This is given by the real national output and the state of technology. Call the *actual* capital $K(t)$. Now the difference between the two, $K - K_0$, is the error, and this is fed back to the system. If the feedback is negative—i.e., if $K > K_0$ ($K - K_0$ representing excess capital)—we get negative net investment and a return to equilibrium. If $K < K_0$ ($K - K_0$ being negative), we get positive net investment $\frac{dK}{dt}$ or $\dot{K}$) and an approach to equilibrium.

Making no more complicated assumption than this, we may give a representation of a crude Schumpeterian innovation theory by taking as historically given the fact that K_0 shifts upward in irregular jumps, sometimes weakly, sometimes strongly, at more or less regular intervals. The varying command, $K_0(t)$, is represented in Figure 65 by the solid line, and the broken line represents the "output" of the system, which in this case is the actual capital accumulated, $K(t)$.

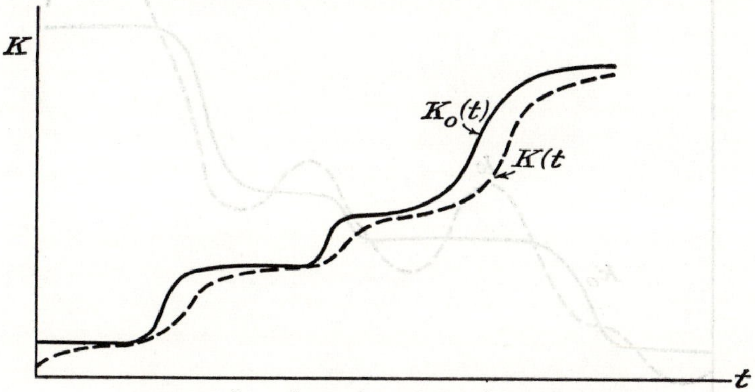

FIGURE 65. *Actual and Desired Capital*

It is a fact that most such servo systems tend to overshoot, and this is clearly also the case with the economic system. They may overshoot very little and quickly approximate the desired level, but it is also a fact that they may overshoot seriously, even so seriously that instead of getting closer to the desired level on each swing, they may get still farther from it. Actually, when the oscillations get too large (in all easily observable cases, which are those that do not disintegrate), the previous laws of behavior cease to hold (i.e., we have a non-linearity) and something ceases to function as before. There is a saturation point of some kind, and the oscillation settles down to a steady level until a new "command" is given. Or it may be stable in its behavior so that it tends always to diminish its overshoot, as is suggested by Figure 66. This gives rise to the phenomenon of the "hunting" of servo systems —it is this that we are dealing with in Aftalion's fire controller. The furnace firer is the error-sensitive device. The varying temperature outside continually disrupts any tendency to steady routine

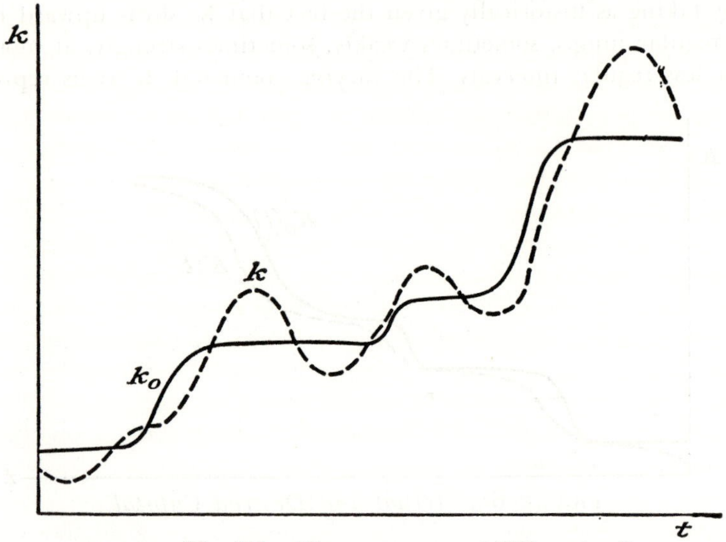

FIGURE 66. *The Phenomenon of "Hunting"*

and hence makes it difficult to develop anticipatory skill which might lead to the gradual elimination of the cycle.

What causes the overshoot in the economy? The lag in the construction of capital will explain it, and this is what Aftalion correctly cites, as do Tinbergen, Frisch, and Kalecki. Ships, for example, continue to be started so long as freight rates are such as to give a present value of ships greater than their cost of construction. But for many months after no new ones are laid down, ships that were in construction continue to come down the ways, with the result that rates will be driven below the level which justified their construction. As ships are not replaced, rates will eventually rise and make it profitable to begin building, but again many months will elapse before the new ships are actually carrying freight. Meanwhile ships continue to wear out and freight rates go on rising. In this way the industry, and (taking account of other similar industries) the economy, may easily overshoot in both directions, thus generating a cycle.

For reasons to be explained presently, it is preferable, however, to assign the crucial role of explaining the overshoot to another element, the *multiplier* with its effect on national income and hence (via the accelerator) on the desired amount of capital. The economy overshoots because in reaching its new desired level of capital, there is of necessity net investment. Yet this raises national income by the multiplier value of the net investment, which leads to still more desired capital, and so on. Intuitively it is fairly clear that this is a distinctly unstable factor. It is inherently unstable because the feedback is positive: a deficiency of capital leads to investment, but this leads to a greater deficiency instead of to its elimination. When we have reached the desired level—and it will be reached eventually because of the strict limits to the amount of real capital (limits set by the requirements of growth fixed by technological change and population increase)—investment ceases because no more capital is needed. Such a situation cannot be maintained, since by reason of the cessation of net investment, national income is forced down so that less capital is desired and we have thus (in a curious way) overshot. Our error-sensitive devices, the entrepreneurs, report an error, and command a decrease of capital. Although such a servo system is essentially unstable, the limitational factors keep it from completely breaking down.

Aftalion's model—the furnace analogy—does indeed provide, as we have seen, an explanation of the overshoot. But it leaves out of account a highly significant fact which, it is now widely believed, mainly accounts for the overshoot, and which was lacking in Aftalion's model, as well as in that of the other writers mentioned above. This fact is the consumption function and the associated multiplication process; ". . . business-cycle and other theorists from Malthus to Wicksell, Spiethoff, and Aftalion, did not have at hand this powerful tool (the multiplier)." [35]

It is worth noting that there is *apparent* circularity of reasoning here. Income controls investment; investment controls income. Yet it is not so if we have two independent, distinct relationships. Thus the one is the multiplier, the other the accelerator or some form of investment determinant. The circularity merely means that we have as many equations as we have unknowns; and hence we have a definite, determinate result. It is, in fact, a central feature of feedback systems that the system controls itself, and thus its circularity lies in its automatic quality, which constitutes its peculiar character. In all this we see clearly one important feature of econometrics. It does more than take theories full-blown from the heads of the theorists; it suggests to us new and important ways of formulating the theories.

Capital Accumulation

The nature of capital accumulation is to be the center of our model. But before we can construct definite hypotheses, we must dispose of one difficulty. By the very fact that they are durable, all capital goods yield their revenues in the future. Hence we are placed in the middle of the thorny question of expectations. It is doubtful whether any theory can deal adequately with it, and certainly no theory simple enough for business-cycle analysis will be adequate to do so. I shall therefore assume the simplest and perhaps most plausible hypothesis—that businessmen act as if they expected the current situation to continue indefinitely. In defense of such a drastic simplification, it may be argued that businessmen have no basis for a rational calculation of the future and yet must make decisions. Therefore they may tend to fall back on what they do know, the present.

Assuming that the future is known, or at least that it is thought to be known, on the basis of current experience, we may construct a demand curve for capital goods in the traditional manner. Given a rate of interest, we may discount to the present the expected future yields for all different types of capital goods,

---

35 Alvin H. Hansen in *The New Economics*, ed. by S. E. Harris, Alfred A. Knopf, Inc., New York, 1947, p. 135.

and thus get their present values. Then we may arrange them in descending order of present values to form a demand curve.[36]

There are four points to note about this curve: first, it consists largely of the possibilities of substituting capital for the other factors of production; second, it must include the effects of a reduction of price with increased output, although this may in practice be difficult to distinguish from the first; third, it assumes some given general level of output and hence of demand; and fourth, an increase in the rate of interest will shift the curve to the left and a decrease will shift it to the right.[37]

The capital market (including all durable goods) is inherently and inescapably dynamic. Although most discussions tend to obscure this fact, it becomes evident when we observe that there is no supply curve corresponding to the demand curve. Instead we have (a) the existing stock of capital, (b) the rate of disappearance from wear, obsolescence, etc., (c) the rate of additions to capital stock from new production. These are the essential dynamic features of modern economics and are not open to question, as in the case of particular lags, anticipations, speculative behavior, etc.

If we make any definite assumptions about the supply curve of new capital and the disappearance rate (i.e., the capital consumption rate), we may then describe the dynamic process of capital accumulation. Throughout we shall assume that the disappearance or capital consumption rate is constant, which seems as good an approximation to reality as any other simple hypothesis. In Figure 67 this disappearance rate is represented by the distance from O′ to O.[38] The output (supply) of new capital is gross;

[36] Or we may arrange them in a descending order of rates of return over cost (Fisher) or rates of marginal efficiency of capital (Keynes in *General Theory*), but this comes to the same thing. In the case of the diminishing marginal efficiency of capital schedule, an increase in the cost of the capital goods will shift the schedule to the left; a decrease in cost of the capital goods will shift the schedule up and to the right. See Chapter 9 in this book.

[37] A fall in the rate of interest means that the yields (at different amounts of investment) will have a higher capitalized value, since they are now discounted at a lower rate. Thus the *schedule* of value of successive increments of investments will shift up or to the right.

[38] The magnitude of disappearance is of great importance to cycle theory, and depends on the durability. Thus if a good lasts ten years, it will be at a rate of 10 per cent per annum; if 100, 1 per cent—and so on. For aggregative

being gross, it cannot be negative. It is assumed to become quite inelastic beyond a certain point. Net additions to capital (i.e., net investment) are gross output of capital goods less disappearance, and hence must be measured from O, which is henceforward considered to be the origin. In Figure 67 net additions to capital are labeled $\dot{K}$, which stands for $\frac{dK}{dt}$, where K is capital stock.

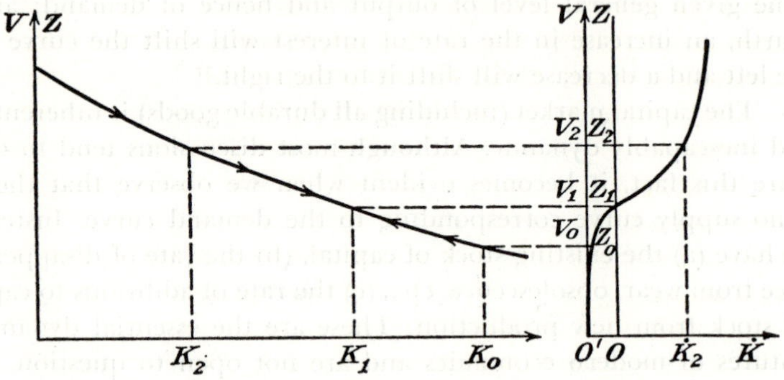

FIGURE 67. *The Traditional Theory of Capital Accumulation*

Figure 67 represents the traditional theory of capital accumulation, although it is not often made explicitly dynamic. It is also the Keynesian theory (Chapter 11 of the *General Theory*), although Keynes stated it in a curious way, so that it can easily be misunderstood as static. All units of capital, K, will be purchased whose present value, V, is greater than or equal to the supply price of new capital, Z. But for each Z there exists a definite rate of creation of new capital, $\dot{K}$, and hence the system is completely determinate. Thus if the given amount of capital is K_2, the present value is V_2 (which is equal to Z_2, the supply price) and the rate of growth is $\dot{K}_2$. As the supply price falls to Z_1, capital will accumulate and move toward K_1, the equilibrium or desired amount. It will approach this point with decreasing speed as the price falls and

models it represents some kind of average rate. Also it should obviously depend on the amount of capital and the rate of output, but these modifications, though desirable, are not too important.

gross output of new capital slowly decreases until just equal to wastage. At this point, K_1, we have stable, dynamic equilibrium with a constant amount of capital and no tendency for it to increase or decrease, since actual capital equals desired capital.

Should there be too much capital, K_0, the present value, V_0, would be so low as to induce no replacement investment, with the result that there will be a steady decrease (of maximum amount O′O) at an eventually decreasing rate toward K_1. This system will always move toward any given equilibrium point, K_1.[39] It will, moreover, fluctuate about its equilibrium point if we introduce the Aftalion lag in the output of new capital goods. Thus when K_1 is reached, no new capital will be ordered, but all the orders for the last year and a half, say, will still be in production and will mature in the coming year and a half. Thus the economy will overshoot, present value will go too low, new production will not equal wastage, and there will be gradual attrition of the excess capital. Similarly it will overshoot on the other side, since for many months after orders are placed wastage will still be in excess of gross capital formation. While this lag exists and should be taken account of, Aftalion was perhaps wrong to make it the explanation of the major business cycle—rather it should serve to explain shorter fluctuations. At least it is worth remembering that as we get closer to equilibrium, gross capital formation is little greater than wastage, and that therefore the last months' net contribution will be quite small and hence the overshoot and undershoot are not likely to be large. Consequently the cycle would have a relatively short duration and be quite mild. If our economy functioned according to these criteria, it would be a tolerably good servo system and have a much better chance of escaping a drastic redesigning. But, as I shall attempt to show below, both Aftalion, excusably, and Keynes, inexcusably, left out of account a much more violent, positive, and hence unstable, feedback through the multiplier.

Unfortunately for the simplicity of the theory, the shifts in the capital demand curve are perhaps more important than movements along it. Technological advance uncovers capital outlets

39 Keynes sometimes seems to imply that it will, by itself, explain a cycle. Cf. *General Theory*, Chapter 18.

with a present value greater than the equilibrium value, and hence the system never tends to remain there. This may be roughly visualized as an irregular shifting of the curve to the right, but strictly it is only the unexplored portion of the curve which is shifted in order to insert the new, profitable outlets for capital.

It is possible to account for cycles in our system if we assume with Schumpeter that this innovational investment comes in swarms.[40] The schedule is deformed to the right in a burst which begins slowly, then gathers speed, and finally ceases. Consequently, investment rises slowly and declines as all the possibilities are exhausted and the new products come on the market, forcing down prices and lowering the present values of the remaining possibilities. This process repeats itself with only a rough regularity and with a varying violence, depending on the historically given course of technological change. These facts must be incorporated in any cycle theory, and they are vital because in this way we may explain how, given a relatively unchanging economic structure and hence mechanism of response, each cycle is a historical individual, very unlike either its predecessors or its successors. It should be noted, however, that the essential explanation of the cycle, for this simple model, lies outside the model—in the Schumpeterian theory of the bunching of investment outlays—and that this theory is difficult to formulate in econometric terms.

In one respect the mechanism represented by Figure 67 has an unreal air. It assumes that when there is too little capital, its supply price rises so as to choke off demand to the existing supply. And conversely when there is too much capital, its price falls so as to keep it all in use. In some capital markets there may still be substantially a competitive clearing of the market through flexible prices. For example, there may be some approximation to it in housing, without rent control. But for the most part, and above all in capital goods, this has an unrealistic ring in the twentieth century. Prices are rigid (indeed in much machinery there is really no market), and capital is most of the time either in excess (idle) or in short supply; i.e., entrepreneurs would like to have more of it or less of it than they do have.

From this point of view we may make an alternative and more

---

[40] Cf. Schumpeter's *The Theory of Economic Development,* Harvard University Press, Cambridge, 1934, Chapter VI, pp. 223 ff.

realistic interpretation of our mechanism. In all markets we may have either a variable price which provides a "flexible" link between demand and supply, or we may have a rigid price and simply a gap between demand and supply price. Thus we may say that price is rigid and that it is the gap between value and price which determines the additions to total stock or the failure to replace. Another, and in some ways more suggestive, way to say the same thing is to call the intersection of the rigid price with the demand curve the desire for capital. Then we may say, calling K_0 desired capital, that new investment depends on the difference between actual capital and desired capital and that some function of this "error" is fed back to the system in the form of the rate of change of capital stock.[41] It is in this form that we see most clearly the "servo" character of the economy. Thus the same formulation may be interpreted in either or both of two ways, depending on the realities. The important fact is that the behavior will be the same in both cases.

At one central point Keynes failed to see the consequences of his own theory. The demand curve for capital must assume a given level of aggregate demand. In the traditional theory this was not a serious qualification because full employment, along with the corresponding effective demand, was assumed throughout. But it was precisely this that Keynes attacked, and hence it becomes necessary to take account of effective demand, or what comes to the same thing, national income, Y. Thus, with a given national income, an increase in capital must mean either less of other factors, or more output and lower price, or both. But with an increase in income along with employment, there can be an increase in capital without any necessity to lower its present value through substitution or lower price of product. A somewhat crude version of this fact is familiar to students of the business cycle in the form of the acceleration principle. It is also familiar as the distinction between the widening and the deepening of capital or extensive and intensive investment.[42]

---

[41] Cf. my remarks on this subject in *Income, Employment, and Public Policy, Essays in Honor of Alvin H. Hansen*, W. W. Norton and Company, New York, 1948, pp. 118–121.

[42] Cf. Alvin H. Hansen, *Fiscal Policy and Business Cycles*, W. W. Norton & Company, Inc.. New York, 1941, pp. 44–46 and 349–365.

Consequently any given capital demand, as in Figure 67, corresponds to a particular national income; the larger the income, the farther the curve is shifted to the right. Or to take a more complete view of the matter, we may say that present value of capital, V, depends positively on Y and negatively on K, as shown in Figure 68 and represented by:

$$V = \phi_1(K) + \phi_2(Y).$$

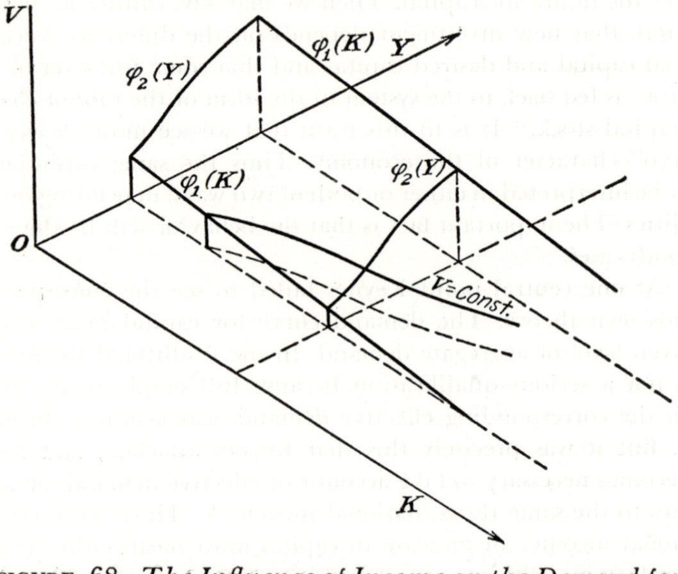

FIGURE 68. *The Influence of Income on the Demand for Capital*

In this equation the two effects are assumed, for simplicity of analysis, to be independent of one another and therefore merely additive. V is represented by a surface, which may be sliced in three ways. If we hold Y constant we get $\phi_1(K)$, which is the curve of Figure 67, representing the deepening of capital,[43] and motion along it is intensive investment. By our assumption of additivity, its shape will be the same for all values of Y, the effect of Y being

[43] Deepening in the Hawtrey sense, i.e., more capital per unit of output.

confined to raising or lowering its height. If we take a section holding K constant, we get $\phi_2(Y)$. This eventuality occurs so rarely (possibly in wartime), that it seems to have escaped the attention of economists. Finally, by holding V constant, we get the acceleration principle or the widening of capital, and motion along it is extensive investment.

The reason why the influence of income on the demand for capital is so important is that it is a second and nefarious channel of feedback. Thus the difference between the actual stock of capital and desired capital is fed back to the stock of capital through net additions to capital, whereas the same difference is fed back to income via net investment by virtue of the multiplier, and hence to the desired amount of capital. The first type of feedback is stable; i.e., a difference or "error" leads to change which diminishes the difference. By contrast the second type feeds the difference back in such a way as to increase the difference between desired capital and actual capital. Therefore the introduction of the multiplier-income effect increases the instability of the system. Indeed, it may make it so unstable as to lead to "hunting" for the equilibrium without ever finding it. This result may be characterized as bad design in a servomechanism. It hunts its equilibrium but can never settle down there. It is the multiplier-income effect that explains why there is such a serious overshoot as to create a major cycle. While capital accumulation is proceeding we need a great deal of capital, just because of the high demand resulting from this net investment. When finally enough capital has been accumulated, the system cannot rest there, because net investment must cease, but then there is too much capital and the process of elimination begins. When the amount of capital has finally been reduced enough, gross investment must be increased to equal wastage; but this raises income, and so the desired amount of capital has increased, and so there is a deficiency of capital. Such a system can never settle down, and it will maintain its fluctuations even without disturbances from "outside."

Now we have the difficult task of modifying Figure 67 to take account of the multiplier-income effect as suggested by Figure 68. This we may do by drawing, in the familiar manner, a number of different $\phi_1(K)$ curves and labeling each according to the various values of Y, as is done in Figure 69. Calling the multiplier k, for each different rate of investment $\dot{K}$, there will be a corresponding deviation from the break-even [44] income, which we shall here call Y. Thus $Y = k\dot{K}$. From this we get the appropriate demand curve, $\phi_1(K)_y$, for capital, since

$$V = \phi_1(K) + \phi_2(k\dot{K}).$$

In Figure 69, ϕ_1 is drawn for eight different levels of investment and income. There is the lowest attainable level (maximum disinvestment) $\dot{K}_C$ and hence Y_C. The curve $\phi_2{}^*(k\dot{K})$, drawn on the right in Figure 69, shows us by how much the curve $\phi_1(K)_Y$ (starting with zero net investment, $\dot{K}_0$) must be shifted up (or down) so as to correspond to the actual rate of investment.[45] Thus a high level of investment, $\dot{K}_3$, gives a high demand curve, $\phi_1(K)_Y$, for $Y_3 = k\dot{K}_3$; and a medium level, $\dot{K}_2$, means an intermediate level of $\phi_1(K)_Y$ for $Y_2 = k\dot{K}_2$. For each quantity of capital, K, its demand price, V, must equal the supply price of new capital, $Z = \phi_3(\dot{K})$. Thus a stock of capital, K_C, is greatly excessive, leading to a low capital value, V_C, and maximum disinvestment, $\dot{K}_C$. Therefore the capital stock is slowly reduced, as indicated by the arrows, to K_D, with a gradual rise in its value.

As the value increases at M (with K_M of capital), some replacement investment commences, since eventually the *value* of capital, V, will rise above the minimum supply price of capital, Z_M. Thus $\dot{K}$ rises slightly above $\dot{K}_C$ until we reach the point at which the slope of $\phi_2{}^*(k\dot{K})$ is equal to that of $\phi_3(\dot{K})$ (i.e., at the points D and $\dot{K}_D$). Here the expansive effect of the slowly rising income outweighs the depressing effect of the rising cost of new capital, with the result that the economy moves rapidly to the boom condition of a high income at A, where $\dot{K} = \dot{K}_A$ and $Y = Y_A$.

That the economy must go to A can be seen by considering why it cannot establish some more moderate level, such as $Y_3 =$

---

[44] By "break-even income" we mean the income at the point at which net investment is zero.

[45] It should be noted that we are assuming no lag in income's response to any change in investment. That there is a lag is not open to question, but there is some doubt as to whether it is large enough to be significant for the major cycle.

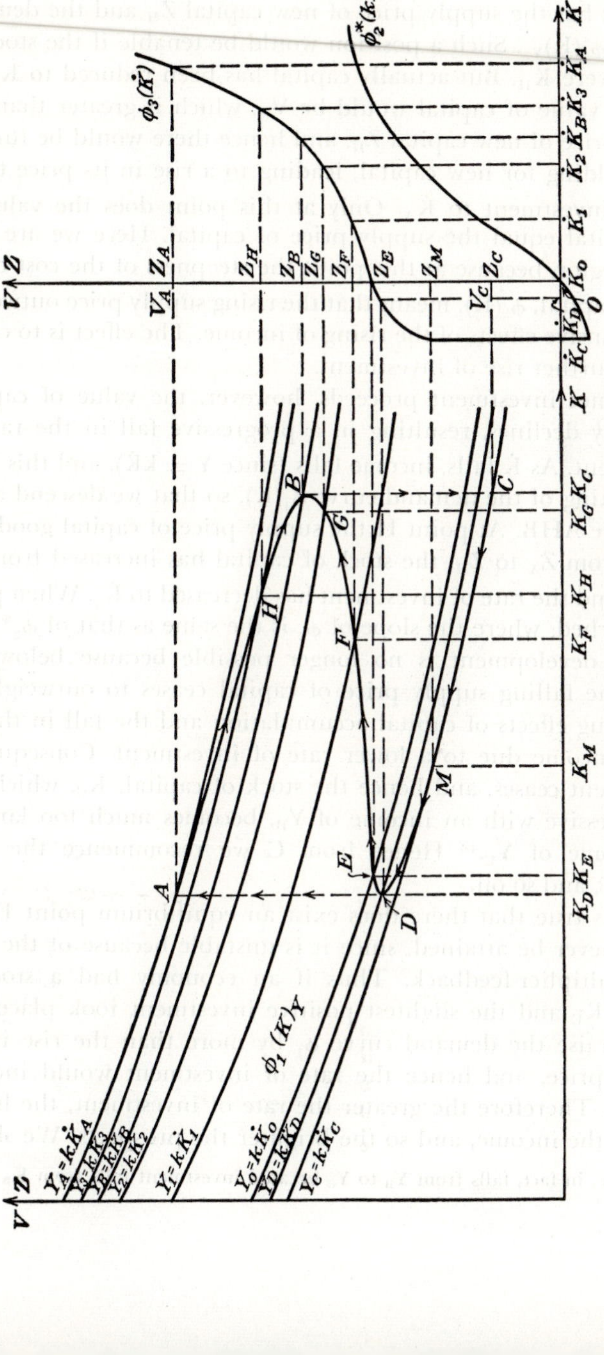

FIGURE 69. *The Multiplier-Income Effect*

$k\dot{K}_3$. This corresponds to the rate of investment $\dot{K}_3$. Now $\dot{K}_3$ investment has the supply price of new capital Z_H and the demand curve is $\phi_1(K)_{Y_3}$. Such a position would be tenable if the stock of capital were K_H. But actually capital has been reduced to K_D, so that the value of capital would be V_A, which is greater than the supply price of new capital Z_H, and hence there would be further brisk bidding for new capital, leading to a rise in its price to Z_A and in investment to $\dot{K}_A$. Only at this point does the value of new capital equal the supply price of capital. Here we are in a stable region because at this point the steepness of the cost curve of new capital, $\phi_3(\dot{K})$, means that the rising supply price outweighs the expansive effects of the rising of income. The effect is to choke off any further rise of investment.

As net investment proceeds, however, the value of capital, V, slowly declines, resulting in a progressive fall in the rate of investment. As $\dot{K}$ falls, income falls (since $Y = k\dot{K}$), and this leads to a sinking of the demand curve $\phi_1(K)$, so that we descend along the curve AHB. At point H the supply price of capital goods has fallen from Z_A to Z_H, the stock of capital has increased from K_D to K_H, and the rate of investment has decreased to $\dot{K}_3$. When point B is reached, where the slope of ϕ_3 is the same as that of $\phi_2{}^*$, this smooth development is no longer possible because below this point the falling supply price of capital ceases to outweigh the depressing effects of capital accumulation and the fall in the national income due to a lower rate of investment. Consequently investment ceases, and hence the stock of capital, K_C, which was not excessive with an income of Y_B, becomes much too large at an income of Y_C.[46] Hence from C we recommence the cycle CDABC, and so on.

It is true that there does exist an equilibrium point E, but it can never be attained, since it is unstable because of the positive multiplier-feedback. Thus if an economy had a stock of capital K_E and the slightest positive investment took place, this would raise the demand curve ϕ_1 by more than the rise in the supply price, and hence the rate of investment would increase further. Therefore the greater the rate of investment, the higher will be the income, and so the brighter the prospects. We should

46 Income, in fact, falls from Y_B to Y_C because investment falls from $\dot{K}_B$ to $\dot{K}_C$.

therefore proceed in the direction of the arrows along the path EFG. At point B the expansion becomes untenable because the depressive effect of rising capital cost (supply price) outweighs the expansive effect of rising income, and hence there is a catastrophic collapse to point C and thereafter the cycle is repeated. The stretch DEFGB represents the unstable behavior of a multiplier-accelerator system, and the violent impasse at B (as indicated by the direction of the arrows approaching it from the two sides) demonstrates the untenability of a high-level employment equilibrium with such a system.

It is worth repeating that it is only a matter of convenience to describe all this in the somewhat unrealistic terms of a flexible market price for capital goods. As has been pointed out above, the whole process can be translated into terms of investment resulting from a discrepancy between desired and actual capital stock (with a rigid supply price for new capital goods throughout). Whenever there is too little capital, a backlog of orders or plans accumulates, which is then worked off at capacity production; and the opposite occurs when there is too much capital. Also it should be noted that we are abstracting from secular progress, and hence we have a "pure" cycle which always returns to its previous low. This is a useful abstraction but implies nothing about reality, nor is it an essential property of the model.

This model is a crude and oversimplified representation of the business cycle, but it has a number of points to recommend it. It does not oscillate because of some lagged response; it oscillates because of its inherent dynamic contradictions. The only assumptions made are broad, qualitative ones which are acceptable to a very large part of all cycle theorists. It meets the fundamental criticism of the acceleration principle (that the assumption of a perfect adjustment of capital to output is false) by behaving in such a way that the economy almost never has the desired amount of capital. It is a complete and self-contained theory in that it will maintain its oscillation even in the absence of disturbances from without the system. No matter how it begins or how it is disturbed by wars and technological progress, it will always tend toward a certain definite type of oscillation. It does not rest on any errors by entrepreneurs or irrational alternations of optimism and pessimism.[47] All such elements may, however, be introduced as secondary modifications of the essential structure.

There is one rather special assumption which is vital to the structure of the theory—the severe inelasticity of the supply of capital. It is essential because the introduction of the acceleration principle renders the system unstable, and it would explode except for the fact that investment cannot increase materially beyond a certain point. This assumption may be based on the evident reluctance of the capital goods trades to expand capacity. But even if this were not true, there exists another and inevitable upper limit to the expansion. As income increases with rising investment, the desired capital is thereby increased; but this cannot go on indefinitely with a given labor force. When full employment is reached, essentially no further increase in real income is possible, and this puts an upper limit on the expansion of the demand curve for capital in exactly the same way as the inelasticity of the supply curve of new capital. In this case it is not necessary to rely on the inelasticity of the supply curve of new capital. At that rate of investment corresponding to full employment, real income ceases to rise and hence the $\phi_2^*(k\dot{K})$ curve becomes horizontal; i.e., the acceleration-induced investment ceases to operate through the multiplier feedback. Consequently the source of instability is removed and the $\phi_3 - \phi_2^*$ curve changes from a negative to a positive slope. The relevant portions of Figure 69 would appear as drawn in Figure 70. The arrows indicate the required paths of motion, and by the use of the $\phi_3 - \phi_2^*$ curve we may avoid use of all but one of the $\phi_1(K)$ curves, namely the one for $Y_0 = k\dot{K}_0$. Thus

$$\phi_3(\dot{K}) = Z = V = \phi_1(K)_{Y_0} + \phi_2^*(k\dot{K}),$$

or

$$\phi_3(\dot{K}) - \phi_2^*(k\dot{K}) = \phi_1(K)_{Y_0}.$$

Therefore we may say that the unstable expansion is checked either by the capacity of the investment goods trades or by full

[47] It is interesting to note that a violent and catastrophic collapse occurs at the peak of the boom without the necessity of introducing an irrational and herdlike collapse of expectations as suggested by Keynes.

employment, whichever is reached first.[48] The full employment upper limit depends both on the available labor supply and on the accumulated capital. In fact, it is only reasonable to suppose that these two upper limits are reached at about the same point,

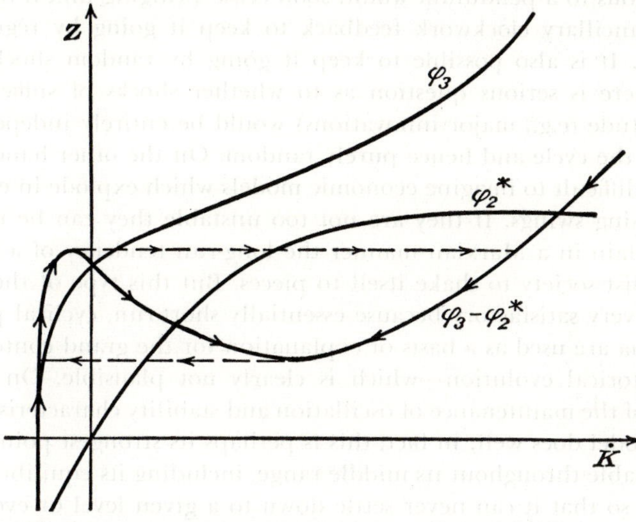

FIGURE 70. *The Check to Expansion*

since it is difficult, expensive, and risky for the capital goods trades to expand beyond this point by bidding factors away from the consumers' goods industries.[49]

---

[48] In his admirable book, *The Trade Cycle* (Oxford University Press, 1950), which appeared while this chapter was undergoing its final revision, Professor Hicks develops a model which is strikingly similar to this one. The reader will find it illuminating to compare the two. It is interesting to note that he reverses the order followed here, by placing primary emphasis on general full employment and only secondary emphasis on full employment in the capital goods trades.

[49] I ignore the Wicksellian cumulative process, which allows for an increase beyond this point by means of inflation. Throughout I am assuming no monetary inflation or deflation. It is also to be noted that secular progress can be inserted easily into our system. Thus as capital is accumulated secularly, the full employment limit is continually increased, even without population growth. The course of population, or rather available labor force, makes a vital difference to the dependence of full-employment income on capital.

Testing the Models

There are many tests to apply to models short of actually trying to determine the structural constants. One is stability: they must be stable, but not too stable, else they die away. All models analogous to a pendulum would soon cease swinging unless there is an ancillary clockwork feedback to keep it going by regular shocks. It is also possible to keep it going by random shocks,[50] but there is serious question as to whether shocks of sufficient magnitude (e.g., major innovations) would be entirely independent of the cycle and hence purely random. On the other hand, it is not difficult to imagine economic models which explode in ever-increasing swings. If they are not too unstable they can be used to explain in a Marxian manner the long-run tendency of a free capitalist society to shake itself to pieces. But this type of theory is not very satisfactory because essentially short-run, cyclical phenomena are used as a basis of explanation for the grand contours of historical evolution—which is clearly not plausible. On the score of the maintenance of oscillation and stability characteristics, our model does well; in fact, this is perhaps its strongest point. It is unstable throughout its middle range, including its equilibrium point, so that it can never settle down to a given level or even a steady trend. Yet it is extremely stable at its upper and lower limits; this explains very well why, once started down, it does not proceed to universal unemployment and collapse, or why, once launched on expansion, it does not proceed invariably to perpetual inflation.

The other central test to apply to any model is the following: Can it explain cycles of eight to ten years in duration? Many models give the possibility of such long cycles, but upon closer inspection this proves to be rather illusory. For example, the simple producers' goods cycle with production lag (Aftalion's theory) but without multiplier-income feedback can yield cycles of any duration, given the proper values for structural parameters; but this involves such great stability that the cycle has substantially disap-

There are severe limits to the expansibility of income with a constant labor force. The available labor force is largely a given, outside factor and can be taken account of by a shift in the full employment limit to real income.

[50] Cf. Frisch, "Propagation Problems" (footnote 3).

peared before one full swing is completed. There is an embarrassing multiplicity of lags in our modern economy, but these are all so short that it is difficult to construct a plausible model which will persist for five or six years and then reverse, all because of lags of less than one year's duration, although many capital goods provide longer lags than this. Again our model stands this test well. Taking the data for the United States in the 1920's, we find that real annual gross national product rose from 1920 to 1929 by about 30 billions of dollars. This should lead to an increase in desired capital of one or two times that amount.[51] Net capital formation proceeded at a fairly constant rate of about 9 to 10 billion dollars per year, but since some of this was innovational investment, we might estimate induced investment at 5 to 6 billions per year. Therefore, to accumulate about 50 billion dollars of capital would require eight to nine years, so that our result is of the right order of magnitude. It is important to remember that this is not validation of our hypotheses but rather only a demonstration that they are not obviously absurd and useless to explain the major business cycle.

When, however, we come to the downswing, our model is not at all satisfactory as it stands. The problem is to remove all the capital accumulated during the previous boom. This can only be done by physical wastage, which, for the thirties, is put at about 7 or 8 billion dollars per year for the United States economy, and at the low point in the Great Depression the maximum achieved rate of wastage was only 6 billion dollars. Therefore, eight or more years would be required to create the conditions for a new expansion, and this is *not* of the right order of magnitude, since downswings are definitely of shorter duration than upswings. The reason for this unsatisfactory result is not difficult to find. In fact, the secular trend of capitalism has been strikingly

---

[51] Strictly it should lead to an increase of about three times that amount, since tangible capital is usually estimated at about three times national product. But Tinbergen's studies indicate that where producers react specifically to increased output, they tend to increase capital stock by only about one-half the average ratio of capital to output. The aggregative character of these figures serves to point out the violent simplification involved in dealing with simple aggregates. Some industries would need only a fraction of a year's output; others, like railways, many years' output.

upward, so that we do not return to the previous low level of capital before starting up again. With this model we cannot abstract from trend without getting absurd results.

The analysis of technological progress is difficult—and particularly so with our simplified aggregative model, because this hides the specific differences within apparently homogeneous wholes. Thus, while much capital is still in excess, new possibilities are worked out which are feasible even though some older types of capital are still unemployed. Therefore, gross investment may recommence (indeed, it never quite ceases) before all the undesired capital disappears. When this happens income goes up and the capital demand curve is shifted to the right, although there will be no induced investment until all the excess capital—*according to the new curve*—is gone.[52] Consequently we may represent technological progress by a shift to the right in the capital demand curve $\phi_1(K)$ in Figure 69, although this does not tell the whole story. The consequences of steady technological progress are shown in Figure 71. Capital stock contracts from K_1 to K_3 only, instead of to K_2, as would be the case for an unprogressive society. Therefore the depression phase is made much shorter. On the other hand, the boom phase is lengthened because K must grow from K_3 to K_5 instead of to K_4.

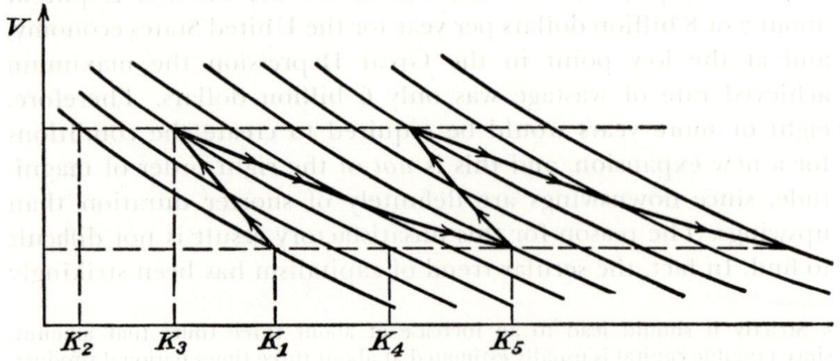

FIGURE 71. *Technological Progress*

[52] Here again a shortcoming of aggregative analysis appears, because excess capacity in some industries will have ended while it persists in others. Therefore, it is in reality not necessary for all the excess capacity to vanish before induced investment begins.

There is no reason to assume a steady occurrence of innovations, except for simplicity of representation. At times there may be few inventions, or they may require little capital. Then the depression will last longer and the boom will be shorter. At other times there may be innovations which require enormous amounts of capital, as with the railroads, which then shorten the depression and prolong the prosperity. In such a manner we may make our model meet one of the most obvious and difficult empirical requirements—that each cycle is very different from the others. From an econometric point of view, however, the price paid for this concession is great, since we cannot separate, statistically, autonomous or innovational investment from induced. Nor can we make any hypothesis about its behavior, since its very nature is that it is historically, not economically, determined and hence obeys complicated laws of its own which we cannot hope to explain even though, no doubt, they are explicable.

Until now we have not given serious consideration to the question of time lags in the economy, although almost all cycle models depend on them in an essential way. The basis for this somewhat unorthodox treatment is the guess that the long period of the cycle and its maintenance are best explained without lags. In our model we have explained the overshoot by means of feedback through the multiplier. Ordinarily the overshoot is explained as a kind of error resulting from lagging responses. That these lags exist cannot be doubted. And hence in order to approach closer to reality, they must be taken account of. It is a matter of judgment whether it is better to assume that lags are the primary explanation of cycles or that they are secondary complications giving a better approximation to reality. The proper way to decide, and finally the only conclusive way, is to test the various hypotheses statistically. But for any test to be final, we must have hypotheses that are simple enough and realistic enough to be definitively established or rejected by existing statistics. These conditions are unlikely to be fulfilled for some time, and therefore we must proceed more cautiously, weighing various hypotheses in a more qualitative fashion.

Three Types of Lag

There are at least three types of lag which should be taken account of in our model. In the first place, it is generally agreed that the multiplier process takes some time to have its full effect. Therefore, even if investment jumps rapidly from a very low value to a very high value (or vice versa) it will take some time for income to rise (or to fall). The effect then is to round off the corners of the model's turning points. Also it lessens the rapidity of the jump in the investment, because this depends on the acceleration effect of the income change. Both of these facts will tend to lengthen the cycle, since the mechanism is slower in getting at its work, but has no less work to do.

Second, between an investment decision and the actual money outlays there intervenes considerable time, which introduces a further sluggishness. Actually the situation is a little more complicated still. The whole investment is not made in one burst of expenditure, but rather is spread over a period of time in some complicated way. Therefore, as investment decisions are made, there is a gradual accumulation of spendings proceeding on different projects. And after no more investment decisions are made, there will be the gradual termination of the spending resulting from previously undertaken projects.

Third, an essential part of our model is the depressing effect of the appearance in the productive machine of the newly produced capital goods. This may either result from the flooding of the market by the increased output, or merely from the fact that producers who previously had too little capital goods now have enough or more nearly enough. But there elapses some time, often quite a considerable time, between the ordering and the installation of capital equipment and houses. Aftalion and others after him have made important investigations of these lags. Again the result is an overshooting and resultant error, which increases the magnitude and the length of the cycle and softens the rapidity of shift from boom to depression and vice versa.

A Model Based on Lags

The addition of lags to our previous model makes analysis rather awkward, although it remains possible. We may, however, state our model in terms of lags throughout, and this is what most model builders have done. Every variable must be dated, which is most conveniently done by a subscript, in terms of its lead or lag compared with some other variable. These lags are assumed to be constant throughout, and hence time, t, is not specified, all the variables being stated at any time, t, plus or minus a given and constant number of time units.

In line with our previous assumptions, we take the value of capital made up of two effects, the one, V_1, being negatively proportional ($-\mu$) to the stock of capital, and the other, V_2, positively proportional (ν) to the level of income. For a constant value of capital, we have an implied relation of proportionality (ν/μ) between capital, K, and income, Y, and this proportionality coefficient is the acceleration coefficient.[53] The rate of output of new capital (i.e., investment) may be taken to be positively proportional (ρ) to its value, this relation representing the supply curve of new capital, with the critical proviso that it cannot be uncreated (negative output) at greater than some given rate. Income is proportional (k, the multiplier) to the rate of outlay on new capital goods.

The first type of lag mentioned above, the lag between the rate of outlay and the multiplier value of income, we shall assume to be short enough to be ignored. The lag between a decision to invest and the corresponding outlay we shall take to be one time unit. The lag between a decision to invest and the completion of the capital good we shall take to be two time units. Total capital, K, will be measured throughout in deviations from its equilibrium value.

Making these assumptions, it is not difficult to derive the difference equation governing the operation of an economy obeying these rules. It is

$$K_t = (\nu k/\rho + 1)K_{t-1} - (\nu k/\rho + \mu/\rho)K_{t-2}.$$

To illustrate its functioning, we may assign the following plausible values: given a multiplier of 2, (k = 2); given an ac-

[53] See Figure 68, p. 447 of this book, where the acceleration relation is represented by the line "V = const." The slope of this line is the acceleration coefficient, namely, the ratio between an increment of capital and an increment of income. If the curves are all straight lines, this slope is the ratio of ν to μ.

celeration coefficient of 2 (which means $\nu/\mu = 2$); taking $\nu/\rho = \frac{1}{2}$, we get, by dividing ν/ρ by ν/μ, $\mu/\rho = \frac{1}{4}$. We can then fill in the numerical values in our equation, giving:

$$K_t = 2K_{t-1} - 1.25K_{t-2},$$

so that by our assumptions K is proportional to its own magnitude in the two previous periods. In addition we must assume that capital cannot wear out at greater than some realistic rate, which we shall take to be 4 per time unit. If our equation decrees a greater decrease than this, it must be superseded by the steady rate of 4, which simply means that entrepreneurs have more capital than they desire or than would constitute an optimum economic adjustment.

The operation of such a dynamic system is shown in Table XXIII, starting from two arbitrary initial quantities of capital (in deviations from equilibrium). To find K at time $t = 2$ we multiply the coefficient of K_{t-1} (i.e., 2) by 2.0 (the value of K at time $t = 1$); and from this we subtract 1.25 times K_0 (i.e., 1.0), which yields 2.75. Then to get K_3, we multiply K_2 (i.e., 2.75) by 2 and substract from it 1.25 times K_1 (i.e., 2.0), and so forth.

Evidently it is an unstable system giving rise to cycles of increasing violence. After a time, however, it is checked by the physical limits on the wastage of capital. The periods for which the equation is superseded by a steady decline of 4 per period are indicated by asterisks. That this moderating factor does actually check the explosive violence of the cycle is demonstrated by the fact that, after it has once encountered the maximum rate, it settles down to a steady cyclical routine. It is not too difficult to prove that it must be so, and that this is a particular example of a general phenomenon known as a limit cycle. Other examples are bells and buzzers, vacuum tube oscillators, string and wind instruments, steam engines, and clocks. Once started, they build up to a certain range of oscillation beyond which they do not expand. The peculiarity of our mechanism is that, by itself, it would explode and hence has to be held down, whereas all the others would, by themselves, tend to die away but have some device (like the escapement of a clock) for renewing their vigor.

TABLE XXIII

Where $\dot{K} = -4$, an asterisk (*) indicates this limitation acting.

t	$-1.25K_{t-2}$	$2K_{t-1}$	K_t
0			1.0
1			2.0
2	− 1.25	4.0	2.75
3	− 2.5	5.4	2.9
4	− 3.4	5.8	2.4
5	− 3.6	4.8	1.2
6	− 3.0	2.4	− .6
7	− 1.5	− 1.2	− 2.7
8	.8	− 5.4	− 4.6
9	3.4	− 9.2	− 5.8
10	5.7	−11.6	− 5.9
11	7.2	−11.8	− 4.6
12	7.4	− 9.2	− 1.8
13	5.7	− 3.6	2.1
14	2.2	4.2	6.4
15	− 2.6	12.8	10.2
16	− 8.0	20.4	12.4
17	−12.7	24.8	12.1
18	−15.5	24.2	8.7
19	−15.1	17.4	4.7*
20	−10.9	9.4	0.7*
21	− 5.9	1.4	− 3.3*
22	− .9	− 6.6	− 7.3*
23	4.1	−14.6	−10.5
24	9.1	−21.0	−11.9
25	13.1	−23.8	−10.7
26	14.9	−21.4	− 6.5
27	13.4	−13.0	.4
28	8.1	.8	8.9
29	− .5	17.8	17.3
30	−11.9	35.6	23.7
31	−21.6	47.4	25.8

t	$-1.25K_{t-2}$	$2K_{t-1}$	K_t
32	−29.6	51.6	22.0
33	−32.2	44.0	18.0*
34	−27.4	36.0	14.0*
35	−22.5	28.0	10.0*
36	−17.4	20.0	6.0*
37	−12.5	12.0	2.0*
38	− 7.5	4.0	− 2.0*
39	− 2.5	− 4.0	− 6.0*
40	2.5	−12.0	− 9.5
41	7.5	−19.0	−11.5
42	11.9	−23.0	−11.1
43	14.4	−22.2	− 7.8
44	13.9	−15.6	− 1.7
45	9.7	− 3.4	6.3
46	2.1	12.6	14.7
47	− 7.9	29.4	21.5
48	−18.4	43.0	24.6
49	−26.9	49.2	22.3
50	−30.8	44.6	18.3*
51	−27.9	36.6	14.3*
52	−22.8	28.6	10.3*
53	−17.9	20.6	6.3*
54	−12.9	12.6	2.3*
55	− 7.9	4.6	− 2.3*
56	− 2.9	− 4.6	− 6.3*
57	2.9	−12.6	− 9.7
58	7.9	−19.4	−11.5
59	12.1	−23.0	−10.9
60	14.4	−21.8	− 7.4
61	13.6	−14.8	− 1.2

The cycles maintain themselves until stopped or altered from outside.

There is the important question of how long the cycle lasts. In the arithmetical example, our model has a period of 13 units of time before it hits the limitational element. The "floor" under disinvestment lengthens the period to 17. One may ask how long this is in clock time. Our unit of time is one-half the length of time required to produce a unit (average) of capital goods. There is, of course, no such thing as an average piece of capital, and hence we cannot be very definite about the size of our time unit. If the gestation period of capital goods is taken to be one year, so that our time unit is one-half year, then the cycle is 8½ years long, which is about right.

The Nature and Problems of Cycle Policy

In conclusion, we should consider the nature and problems of cycle policy in the light of econometric models.[54] As the matter stands now, we cannot place enough confidence in any one model as a representation of complex reality to base a positive, quantitative policy on it. Yet it is stimulating and useful to consider how we would go about such problems if, as ultimately we must hope will be the case, our model were adequate to the task.

In constructing a theory one's ultimate aim is to lay the foundations of an intelligent course of action. The Marxian theory, although seriously incomplete, leads—or perhaps jumps—to the conclusion that nothing can be done, and this must be accounted as a policy. The Keynesian analysis prescribes a positive range of possible courses of action to bring the cycle to an end, or at least to ameliorate it.

The Keynesian program has one great strength; it does not rest on any detailed cycle theory. Rather it simply prescribes more spending and/or less taxing whenever full employment is not attained. It is significant that no one has proposed a simple policy for bringing the economy to full employment and holding it there. This problem is more intractable than is generally realized. On the simplest level, if a government has economic advisers, they may study the state of the economy and recommend appropriate increases in the government deficit or surplus. But if the government refuses to delegate to this body the power to tax and spend—and this has always been held to be the core of state authority and to be in its essence *political, not technical*—then a

[54] The basic treatment of this question is to be found in Tinbergen's *Les Fondements mathématiques de la stabilisation du mouvement des affaires*, Hermann & Cie., Paris, 1938.

considerable lag will ensue between the observing of the deviation from full employment and the taking hold of the corrective measures.[55] Without working out a detailed mathematical analysis, our intuition based on servomechanism analogies is helpful. The relationship of the Council of Advisers to the President, and of the President to the Congress, constitutes a clear example of a feedback mechanism, and one that can easily function badly. The Council of Advisers is an "error-detecting device" and reports on the deviation between desired course and actual course. The Congress amplifies this signal into some large-scale input of the creation or destruction of purchasing power. Such a "servo" system will overshoot, as we have seen, and, depending on its structure, may take to "hunting" its course without ever finding it. In the case of the steering of ships we have some of the oldest "servo" systems, sometimes with and sometimes without a human link. A rudder is set according to the deviation of the actual course from the changing desired course. If the course is not altered too frequently or too violently and if the mechanism is properly designed, the feedback will produce a good result. "On the other hand, under certain conditions of delay, etc., a feed-back that is too brusque will make the rudder overshoot, and will be followed by a feed-back in the other direction which makes the rudder overshoot still more, until the steering-mechanism goes into a wild oscillation or *hunting,* and breaks down completely." [56] The discovery of hunting almost a hundred years ago has led to extensive study of how to avoid it; and the great progress made in the last twenty-five years may be the source of helpful hints, though scarcely more than that, to the economist and statesman. "It is important to note that this instability is closely related to the time lags in the system. The probability of getting into an unstable situation becomes materially reduced as the reaction time of the rudder to small errors in heading becomes extremely short.

[55] On this point, consult the illuminating discussion by Arthur Smithies, "Federal Budgeting and Fiscal Policy," in Ellis, *A Survey of Contemporary Economics.*

[56] Reprinted from Norbert Wiener, *Cybernetics,* published by The Technology Press of the Massachusetts Institute of Technology, John Wiley & Sons, Inc., and Hermann & Cie., 1948, p. 14. A more quantitative discussion of the general nature of the problem is given in Chapter IV.

The stability can also be increased and errors reduced if the rudder displacement is made proportional to the heading error (proportional control). The behavior of the system can be improved even further by anticipation control. Anticipation in this application implies that in the setting of the rudder, use is made of the fact that the gyro-compass error is decreasing or increasing; it may go as far as to take into account the actual rate at which the error is increasing or decreasing." [57]

It might be maintained that the problem may easily be solved by a government counter-cyclical policy which was equal but opposite in timing to private investment. Then, it seems, total spending would be constant and the economy would be kept at full employment. In general this is a difficult question to answer, but *if* we have a linear system like the last one, mathematical cycle theory enables us to answer immediately that it is not so. Rigid adherence to a simple cyclically varying government deficit would lead not to the erasure of the cycle but rather to its intensification. In this case we have a driven cycle, analogous to the sunspot hypothesis, and the cycle would follow the spending instead of opposing it, and we would get an exaggerated cycle —indeed, in the case of some cycle models, a cycle of perpetually increasing violence. No doubt the advocates of this policy have in mind a flexible spending adjusted to the actual course of events, but then we are back to the problem of a "servo" system and it must be analyzed as such.

The engineer, observing a machine which functions badly, will set about redesigning its structure in such a way as to alter its behavior for the better. In the case of unwanted oscillations, this means changing the constants, or even the nature, of the system so that the stability is increased. In our model the stability depends on constants describing the behavior of consumers and producers—e.g., the slope of supply and demand curves for capital, the marginal propensity to consume, and the acceleration coefficient. If we could alter these behavior constants in the right way, we could ameliorate the cycle, and if we could alter them

[57] I. A. Getting, "Servo Systems," p. 3 in the *Theory of Servomechanisms*, M.I.T. Radiation Laboratory Series, ed. by H. M. James, N. B. Nichols, R. S. Phillips, courtesy of McGraw-Hill Book Co., New York. 1947.

at will we could make the economy respond so quickly and smoothly to changes that the cycle would cease to be of any interest. There seems, however, little hope that we can have much effect on the behavior of people in a free, capitalistic economy, the essence of which is the freedom of people to do whatever they think best for themselves. In socialist or mixed-type economies the situation becomes quite different. The public servant managers may be told to follow some other rules of action. For this policy to be successful in doing away with the cycle, we must have a reasonably complete, quantitative model of the economy; otherwise we shall not be able to calculate the effect of a given change of decision structure. Here again servomechanism theory is suggestive. For almost the first time, scientists have been faced with the problem of designing a complicated mechanism which will yield a given desirable performance. This process of *synthesis* is to be contrasted with the classical one of the *analysis* of a given mechanism. Instead of proceeding by trial and error until some acceptable result is achieved, a real start has been made in the problem of saying what the mechanism *must* be, *given* the aims. Econometrics has been concerned mostly with analysis, but in fiscal policy and other methods an approach is being made which really requires the methods of synthesis.

23 · *Oscillation and Growth*

Oscillation: Hawtrey's Model

The business cycle is often viewed simply in terms of oscillation. A good illustration of this point of view is the theory presented by Hawtrey. The oscillations described by him could occur just as well in a society in which there was no growth in the stock of capital goods from one cycle to the next, no changes in technique, no growth of population, no increase in real income, no progress. Hawtrey's system does indeed involve the accumulation and de-accumulation of inventories in different phases of the cycle. But there need be no secular growth either in inventory stocks or in the stock of fixed capital. The cycle, in his view, has no relation to technical progress, capital accumulation, or population growth. The cycle is not a by-product of growth; it is purely and simply an oscillation. The society may, of course, in fact be experiencing growth. But that is not regarded as an essential or necessary factor in the business cycle.

Oscillation: Aftalion's Model

It is possible to abstract from Aftalion's analysis certain elements and conclude that his also is purely a theory of oscillation. Aftalion's work taken as a whole involves in fact more than that. Nevertheless, let us for the moment consider it from this more restricted point of view. In the case of Aftalion it is at any rate necessary to assume an economy that has already accumulated a large stock of fixed capital. Once this is granted, cyclical fluctuations will occur, in Aftalion's view, in a society which uses the capitalistic technique of production. Once the equilibrium between the appropriate stock of fixed capital goods and consumer demand is broken, an oscillatory movement is set up. Since it takes time to produce fixed capital goods, the effort to make good any temporary deficiency will tend to overshoot the equilibrium point. Too large a stock of fixed capital goods will therefore be produced. This *excess* will in turn lead to a diminution of capital replacement; and since it takes a long time for the capital to wear out, the process of disinvestment, in turn, will tend to overshoot the mark and usher in a period of fixed capital deficiency. Over the cycle, however, the volume of *net investment* will tend to be balanced by a corresponding volume of *disinvestment.* Thus the capital stock need not necessarily grow secularly. There is oscillation, but not necessarily growth.

In the absence of growth factors, such oscillations as are likely to occur will gradually die down. But Aftalion does not exclude the possibility of dynamic impulses which serve to reinvigorate the cycle movement.

Intermittent Surges of Growth

Those economists who have particularly emphasized the role of investment in fixed capital—Wicksell, Tugan-Baranowsky, Schumpeter, Cassel, Robertson, Keynes—have at the same time, in varying degree, stressed the point that capital formation proceeds, not uniformly, but in intermittent surges. It is the tendency to grow by leaps and bounds, by spurts, that characterizes the modern economy. Cyclical fluctuations are thus seen to be a byproduct of *growth.*

We have cited Hawtrey's analysis as representative of the pure oscillation theory. In general, theories built around inventory movements fall naturally into this class. Moreover, econometric models, as we have seen in Chapter 22, usually run in terms of oscillatory movements.

An Inventory Model

A good example of an oscillation theory is the inventory model developed by Lloyd Metzler.[1] The theoretical model which we develop below, while differing in various respects from Metzler's model, was, however, largely inspired by his work.

Two assumptions underlie this theoretical model: (a) businessmen tend to hold inventories in some fairly stable relation to sales; (b) businessmen's expectations with respect to sales typically conform to the condition of unity elasticity (i.e., sales are expected to continue to move in the same direction and at the same rate of change as in the recent past).

Let us suppose that aggregate demand is increased, perhaps by an increase (autonomously determined) in fixed capital investment. In consequence of the rise in aggregate demand, sales increase. Businessmen accordingly find themselves with smaller stocks of inventories (in view of the unexpected increase in sales) at the very moment when an increase in inventory stocks (in view of the rising sales volume) is indicated as desirable. Businessmen therefore plan to make larger purchases, partly to replenish their stocks, and partly to meet the requirements of increasing sales volume.

Now an expansion of sales, in real terms, from a depressed level to a level appropriate to the new income flow, as determined by the volume of autonomous investment and the propensity to consume, necessarily assumes the familiar S-shaped curve. At first the absolute increments of sales, from period to period, grow until the point of inflection is reached. Then the *increments* begin to taper off until they dwindle to zero at the point at which "sales" reach peak volume. Thereafter sales decline, the *decrements* becoming larger and larger until the point of inflection on the downswing is reached. Beyond this point the fall in sales volume slows down until finally "sales" reach bottom, at which point the decrement becomes zero.

---

1 Lloyd Metzler, "The Nature and Stability of Inventory Cycles," *Review of Economic Statistics*, August, 1941; "Business Cycles and the Modern Theory of Employment," *American Economic Review*, June, 1946; and "Factors Governing the Length of Inventory Cycles," *Review of Economic Statistics*, February, 1947.

Assume the sales volume to fluctuate as indicated in Figure 72. Up to the point of inflection at A (reached in time period T_{10}) the sales volume in each successive period (between T_0 and T_{10}) exceeds that of the immediately preceding period. Accordingly

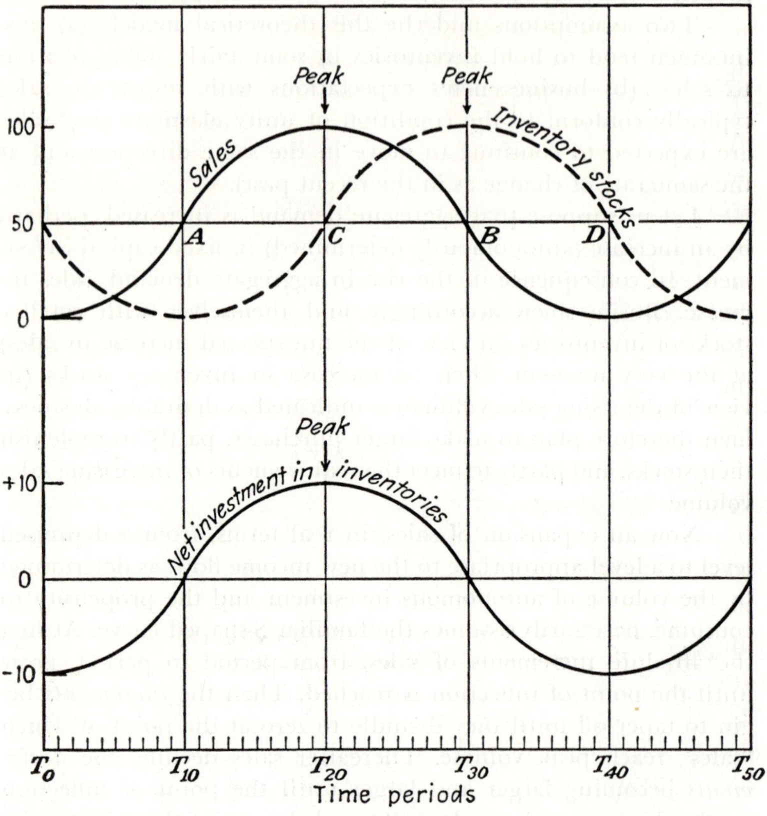

FIGURE 72. *Sales, Inventory Investment, and Inventory Stocks*

inventory stocks tend to be depleted just at the moment when businessmen desire to increase their holdings of inventories in order to maintain a constant ratio of stocks to sales volume. In each succeeding period up to point A, businessmen will plan their purchases on a scale adequate, first, to rebuild their depleted stocks, and second, to raise the level of their stocks in view of the expected higher sales volume (normal ratio level). But in each successive period (up to point A) the sales in fact turn out to be higher than had been expected.[2] Accordingly, inventory stocks continue to be depleted up to period T_{10}. Inventory stocks (see broken line in Figure 72) will therefore fall until period T_{10}, at which time the point of inflection A is reached in the sales curve.

Once the point of inflection A is passed, the *increments* of sales become smaller and smaller. Accordingly, in each succeeding period, from T_{10} to T_{20}, the increments (sales increases) turn out to be less than businessmen had anticipated. This is true since we assume that they will always expect the sales increase of tomorrow to be equal to today's increase. Inventory stocks now begin to accumulate, since businessmen's purchases are based on sales expectations that exceed the realized sales.

This state of affairs will continue, not only until the peak of sales is reached (at period T_{20}) but even to the second point of inflection at B. This is true because, in each succeeding period from T_{10} to T_{30}, actual sales will always fall short of anticipated sales. After the sales peak is reached, businessmen will indeed expect a *falling* off of sales, but they will always expect tomorrow's decline to be the same as today's. In fact, however, the decrements, from period T_{20} to T_{30}, get larger and larger until they eventually reach the point of inflection at B. Since actual sales in fact decline, in each period, by an amount in excess of that planned for, inventory stocks will continue to grow until period T_{30} is reached.

Now if inventory *stocks* fluctuate as indicated in Figure 72, it follows that *net investment* in inventories will fluctuate as shown at the bottom of the chart. "Net investment" in inventories means the *net additions* to inventory stocks. Now the net additions must keep rising until the point of inflection "C" in inventory stocks is reached. From this point on, any net additions to stocks become successively smaller until the peak of inventory stock accumulation is reached at period T_{30}. At this point net inventory investment will have fallen to zero (see bottom curve in chart). Since *stocks* keep falling from period T_{30} to

2 An increase is indeed expected, but only equal to the last period's increase. Up to point "A" however, the *increments* keep rising. Hence actual sales always exceed the expected increases.

period T_{50}, net inventory investment will be running below zero (i.e., there is disinvestment). From period T_{40} to period T_{50}, however, the decrements in inventory stocks become progressively smaller and smaller and finally (at period T_{50}) become zero. Thus from period T_{40} on, disinvestment is gradually vanishing; the net inventory investment curve rises and reaches zero at period T_{50}, beyond which disinvestment ceases. Net investment again becomes a positive quantity.

From the theoretical model illustrated in Figure 72 it is evident that inventory stocks tend to *lag* about one-quarter cycle behind sales. On the other hand, net investment is *synchronous* with sales.

Empirical Data

The empirical data presented in Figures 29 and 30 (Chapter 5 in this book) are broadly in agreement with the relationships disclosed in the theoretical model of Figure 72. Change in business inventories (i.e., net investment) fluctuated synchronously with the *minor* cycles of business activity from 1919 to 1932, net inventory investment reaching high points in the peak business years. It follows from this that inventory stocks must have lagged considerably behind general business activity. From 1932 to 1941, however, net investment in business inventories appeared to *lead* general business activity, both in the upturn of 1933 and in the downturn of 1937. This would indicate for the period in question a somewhat shorter lag of inventory stocks behind general business activity.

In general it is reasonable to suppose that inventory stocks will lag behind the general cycle of business. Such a lag is indicative of a failure to adjust output rigorously and instantly to sales. In our theoretical model, we have assumed that this failure was due to the inability to forecast sales accurately. If output could rigorously and instantly be adjusted to sales, we should find net inventory investment *preceding* total sales (general business activity) by about a quarter-cycle. Such a movement would conform exactly to what we should expect from the acceleration principle. Under these circumstances inventory stocks would be timed perfectly with sales, while net investment in inventories would correlate with rates of change in sales. In fact we find, however, that net inventory investment is not perfectly adjusted to rates of change in sales, and so stocks tend to lag behind sales.

The failure to adjust net inventory investment perfectly to rates of change in sales is due, under actual conditions, not merely to imperfect forecasts of sales (as in our theoretical model) but also to certain practical considerations confronting businessmen. Often, as sales decline, it is deemed inadvisable to cut output at once, partly because of the difficulty of discharging large numbers of workers and reassembling them later, and partly because businessmen dislike spreading overhead costs over a smaller volume of output.[3] Accordingly, the stocks of finished goods will continue to accumulate for a time after sales have declined. Moreover, with respect to the purchase of agricultural raw materials it may be necessary, as in the case of crude rubber, to continue to purchase the supply coming off the plantations after sales of automobile tires fall. Thus inventory stocks continue to grow after sales have dropped off.

Inventory stocks consist, on the one hand, of raw materials (or partly finished goods) and, on the other, of finished products.[4] With respect to raw materials the possibility of adjusting inventory stocks to sales differs with the character of raw materials (agricultural or non-agricultural, etc.) and with the conditions under which they are produced. With respect to finished products, the possibility of adjustment of inventory stocks to sales depends in part upon the character of the market, whether "made to order" or "made to stock," etc.

Similarly with respect to wholesalers and retailers, inventory stocks tend to lag considerably behind sales. Here again there are great differences in the ability of merchants in different trades to adjust stocks to sales. In some lines conditions are such as to

[3] See Moses Abramovitz, *The Role of Inventories in Business Cycles*, National Bureau of Economic Research, Occasional Paper 26, 1948.

[4] In a broader classification one could also include "goods in process." Goods already in the process of production belong to a quite different category from genuine inventory stocks of raw materials awaiting production or finished goods awaiting sale. Goods in process necessarily correlate with output. See Abramovitz, *op. cit.* If we exclude goods in process, about half of manufacturers' inventory stocks consist of raw materials and about half of finished goods.

produce a long lag of stocks behind sales, in others less so. No simple, general explanation is possible.

We have noted that theories of business cycles which emphasize the role of inventories are likely to run in terms of oscillations. Those which emphasize the role of fixed capital investment tend to run in terms of intermittent surges of growth. We turn now to the "growth" theories.

Growth and Continuing Rates of Change

Those who emphasize growth and progress are likely to be impressed with the precarious nature of the boom. The primary expansion, due to innovational investment, is blown up to boom dimensions by reason of the induced secondary expansion. Each dollar of primary (autonomous or spontaneous) investment induces a magnified rise in real income (output)—the multiplier process. But there is also a secondary investment called forth by the rising tide of income—the process of acceleration.

These two investments—the primary and the secondary—combined will cause an increase in the stock of capital goods. And the growth in capital stock is related to the long-term growth requirements associated with changes in technology and increases in population. Output can only grow as per worker productivity rises and the labor force increases. And capital *must* grow if output rises in a growing economy. But the volume of boomtime investment (both autonomous and induced) may overshoot the mark and exceed the maintainable rate of new capital formation.

R. F. Harrod, in a brilliant article in the March, 1939, issue of the *Economic Journal*,[5] and more recently in *Towards a Dynamic Economics*, has centered attention on the problems of a *growing* economy, in particular those associated with the process of saving and capital formation. Harrod's dynamics has to do with "continuing changes generated by the special nature of a growing economy." [6] The growth trend may itself generate forces making for oscillation.

[5] R. F. Harrod, "Essay in Dynamic Theory," *Economic Journal*, 1939.

[6] R. F. Harrod, *Towards a Dynamic Economics*, Macmillan & Co., Ltd., London, 1948, p. 11. See also the brilliantly suggestive articles by Evsey Domar, *Econometrica*, April, 1946, and *American Economic Review*, March, 1947.

With respect to one detail Domar's alleged discrepancy between the

Harrod on Dynamics

Thus Harrod goes back to the classicals prior to Marshall. The "classical economics contains in roughly equal proportions what I define as static and dynamic elements." Saving is rightly treated by Ricardo as a dynamic concept. So long as there is any positive saving the shape of society is progressively altering. Dynamics must concern itself with "the necessary relations between the rates of growth of the different elements in a growing economy." [7]

The potential growth in output is compounded of two factors —increases in per worker productivity and increases in the labor force. The rate of growth of real income in the United States was around 3½ per cent per annum in the forty-year period from 1889 to 1929,[8] though somewhat higher from 1920 to 1929. From 1929 to 1950 the rate of growth appears to have been around 3 per cent. This decline in the rate of growth is due in part to the slower percentage rate of growth of the labor force.[9] Of this 3 per cent rate of growth, more than half was due to increases in productivity and somewhat less than half to increases in the labor force.

Associated with the growth in output is the growth in the capital stock.[10] A part of the growth is necessary in order to ef-

---

"demand side" ($\frac{\Delta I}{I}$) and the "supply side" ($\alpha\sigma$) is wholly due to the fact that he uses Robertsonian definitions (period analysis) for the left side of his equation and Keynesian definitions (continuing functions) for the right side of his equation. Once this is corrected, and Keynesian definitions are applied throughout, we get a constant percentage rate of increase of investment corresponding to the constant percentage rate of growth which Domar assumed to be determined by the propensity to save and the capital coefficient.

7 Harrod, *op. cit.*, pp. 15, 16, 19.

8 See Kuznets, *National Income: A Summary of Findings*, National Bureau of Economic Research, 1946, p. 63; and Senate Committee Print No. 4, 79th Congress, 1st Session. *Basic Facts on Employment and Production*, p. 11.

9 See *The Economic Report of the President*, January, 1950, p. 162; also Chapter 2 in this book.

10 We may usefully divide capital growth, I would suggest, into two categories: (a) widening of capital, and (b) deepening of capital (meaning more capital per worker, *not* more capital per unit of output, as with Hawtrey). "Widening" of capital means in these terms simply equipping the net additions to the labor force with standard capital equipment. This requires no change in technique, only a growth of population. "Deepening" of capital means to

fectuate technological change; a part is needed to provide capital equipment for a growing labor force.

The Capital Coefficient

Let K represent the capital stock and Y the income, both in real terms (money values being corrected for price changes). The ratio $\frac{K}{Y}$ is then the average "capital coefficient," while the ratio of an *increment* of capital to an *increment* of income, $\frac{\Delta K}{\Delta Y}$, is the *marginal* "capital coefficient." This latter ratio we shall designate as "ϵ."

Now if output grows per annum by a certain rate, g, and if the marginal capital coefficient is ϵ, then $g\epsilon$ must equal the ratio of investment to income, or the proportion of output which can be invested in net capital formation. Thus $g\epsilon = \frac{I}{Y}$. If g and ϵ are given we know what is the potential growth of capital facilities. Thus $g\epsilon$ represents that fraction of income which the rate of growth and the prevailing marginal capital coefficient make it possible to invest on a maintainable basis. Similarly $g\epsilon$ indicates the optimum ratio of saving to income at full employment. If $\frac{S}{Y}$ (ratio of saving to income) at full employment exceeds $g\epsilon$, then income and employment must fall until $\frac{S}{Y}$ is brought into equilibrium with $g\epsilon$.

Harrod's analysis is particularly applicable to secular problems relating to long-term rates of growth, while Hicks' analysis (which is discussed below) relates to the trade cycle. Harrod is concerned with (1) the long-term rate of growth of output (real income) and (2) the required growth of the capital stock associated with this growth in output. He is therefore dealing fundamentally with the problem of long-term underemployment equilibrium, or

equip each worker with more capital. This requires a change in technique, if we assume the rate of interest to be constant. Inventions have throughout the modern period right down to the present had the effect of increasing capital per worker; but since around 1880, the ratio of capital to income (both in real terms) remained fairly constant until about 1920; since then this ratio has, perhaps, declined. No great reliance can, however, be placed on the available statistical evidence.

secular stagnation, taking account of investment opportunities on the one hand and the propensity to save on the other. Harrod finds that growth in output is compounded of two factors: (a) change in production methods which cause an increase in per worker productivity, and (b) increase in labor force (i.e., population growth). Given the growth in output as determined by these factors, the capital coefficient states the necessary increase in the capital stock (i.e., investment) which is required by the prevailing state of technique. Putting this bundle of relationships all together, it means that investment outlets are determined by (a) changes in per worker productivity, (b) population growth, and (c) technological developments which control the capital coefficient. The capital coefficient, for example, will fall if inventions tend to become "capital-saving" in the sense that less capital is needed to produce the same output.[11]

Table XXIV gives estimates (in 1929 prices) of the capital stock, and the real national income (output) for certain years covering the last half-century. Included in the table are also the average capital coefficients. At the mid-point of the decade 1899–1908 the value of the capital stock (1929 prices) was $100,700,000,000, while the national income (also in 1929 prices) was $32,400,000,000. Accordingly, the ratio of capital to income was 3.1. By 1919–28 the capital stock (1929 prices) had risen to $194,500,000,000, while national income (1929 prices) had risen to $68,600,000,000. The ratio of capital stock to income had thus fallen, it would appear, to 2.9.

The Rate of Growth and the Capital Coefficient

The annual rate of growth of output or real income, g, for the period 1889–1928 was under 4 per cent per annum (see Table XXIV), while the marginal capital coefficient was apparently around 3. Applying these values in the equation $g_\epsilon = \frac{I}{Y}$, we get $.04 \times 3 = .12$. Thus the net investment (public and private) in this period averaged about 12 per cent of income. The figures are

---

11 In connection with Harrod's analysis see my own discussion of these problems in *Fiscal Policy and Business Cycles,* W. W. Norton & Company, Inc., 1941.

rough approximations and are used here for illustrative purposes only.

TABLE XXIV [12]

Year	Capital Stock (in 1929 prices) K	Average Yearly Income or Output (in 1929 prices) Y	$\frac{K}{Y}$
	In billions of dollars	In billions of dollars	
1889–1898 (At mid-point)	64.5	21.2	3.0
1899–1908 (At mid-point)	100.7	32.4	3.1
1909–1918 (At mid-point)	147.2	45.0	3.3
1919–1928 (At mid-point)	197.1	68.6	2.9
1950	375.0	150.0	2.5

During the last quarter-century the rate of growth appears to have slowed down to around 3 per cent per annum, and the capital coefficient may possibly also have fallen. But this period has been profoundly disturbed, first by the Great Depression and then by the gigantic war upheaval. In the meantime great changes

[12] Fellner, in his *Monetary Policies and Full Employment* (University of California Press, 1946), has estimated K, the stock of capital, at $184,000,000,000 for the year 1922. Using the Federal Trade Commission estimate of national wealth for 1922, he deducted the value of land and of goods in the hands of consumers and the value of the stock of monetary metals. Using this 1922 figure as a bench mark, he calculated, from Kuznets' data, changes in the capital stock. The figures for 1889 to 1928 in Table XXIV are taken from his work, p. 80. See also Kuznets, *National Income and Its Composition, 1919–1938,* Volume I, National Bureau of Economic Research, 1941, p. 269. The figures for 1950 are rough estimates based on the Commerce Department data on national income, gross private investment (account being taken of capital consumption), and public construction. Correction was made for the price changes by using an average of the indexes of wholesale and consumers' prices. The result is very rough, and I have rounded out the figures at $375 billion for capital stock and $150 billion for national income, both at 1929 prices.

have occurred in the economic structure, and these have all affected both the rate of growth and the capital coefficient.

Real income, we estimate, increased from $68.6 billion in 1919–28 to around $150 billion in 1950 (at 1929 prices), at an annual compound rate of increase of about 3 per cent per annum. For this second quarter of the twentieth century the marginal capital coefficient, ϵ, was apparently less than in the first quarter of the century. The accounting figures, however, probably do not tell the true story. The actual net additions to the capital stock (in the thirties especially) were probably considerably in excess of that indicated by the bookkeeping figures on net investment. Replacement investment was in fact more than mere replacement and was adding substantially to the capital stock.

We reached the high level of output of 1950 by a great, indeed unprecedented, bound in the decades of the forties, after being stagnant and depressed during the thirties. Had we maintained something approaching full employment throughout this period, we should have reached the 1950 level of output gradually, instead of first developing an unused potential capacity in the thirties, which capacity was suddenly expanded and put to work in the forties. If we had had fuller employment throughout these two decades, we might well have reached a higher level of output by 1950 than that actually achieved. A higher level of employment might well have stimulated technical progress, but this is not altogether certain; the birth rate would probably have been higher in the thirties but perhaps lower in the forties; and finally, under more prosperous conditions, a fuller utilization of the achieved level of technique might have been reached than was actually realized. Accordingly, both the "g" and the "ϵ" might well have been higher.[13] But the prodigious increase in output from 1929 to 1950 appears to have been won by a relatively small

[13] With respect to "g," it is necessary to distinguish year-to-year changes in productivity from long-run trends. The short-run increases in per worker productivity have come unevenly and intermittently; but decade by decade the progress made has been rather steady. Productivity per worker reveals until now no tendency to decline. Thus it is the second component of the rate of growth—increases in the labor force—which accounts mainly for a moderate slowing down in "g" during the last quarter-century.

increase (judged by earlier experience) in the capital stock. The statistical data are, however, far from being conclusive.

Autonomous Investment and the Super-Multiplier

Of special importance for a study of the business cycle is an analysis of the conditions under which the full growth potential can be reached; and conversely, the conditions under which the economy will fall short of its growth potential. This is both a cyclical and a long-run problem—a problem of oscillation and a problem of growth.

The factors to be considered are: (1) the autonomous investment which we denote as I_A, (2) the multiplier, k, (3) the accelerator, α, and finally the ratio of saving to income, $\frac{S}{Y}$, at full employment.

A distinction must be made between the accelerator, α, and the marginal capital coefficient, ϵ. The accelerator is smaller than the marginal capital coefficient because the autonomous investment provides part of the additional capital stock which is required. Autonomous investment, when completed, contributes to output no less than induced investment. If the three factors (I_A, k, and α) are large, a powerful boom will develop, driving the economy up to full employment (unless, indeed, $\frac{S}{Y}$ is very large) and perhaps even into an inflationary situation. If one or more of them are weak the boom may peter out before full employment is reached. If all three are weak, recoveries will be stillborn and the economy may settle down to a stagnant and depressed situation. But if $\frac{S}{Y}$ is very high, the recovery may not reach full employment even though I_A, k, and α are relatively large.

The volume of autonomous investment basically depends upon the growth impulses inherent in technological developments. If inventions, new industries, the opening of new territory, and the development of new products open rich investment opportunities, autonomous investment may be so large that even with a weak multiplier and a weak accelerator the economy may still be driven on to full employment. Failing this, a moderate volume of autonomous investment may still do the trick, provided only the multiplier and the accelerator are large enough to play a strong expansionist role. The multiplier, k, and the accelerator, α, form together a super-multiplier.

If I_A is weak, the boom will quickly peter out for lack of a strong initial impulse; if k is weak, even a considerable I_A will not drive income up very high; and if α does not reinforce k sufficiently, the super-multiplier, k*, may not drive income up to the full employment ceiling. In all these cases the boom will die a natural death before a full recovery is reached.

Hicks on Free and Constrained Cycles

Hicks, in his *Trade Cycle*,[14] distinguishes between "free" and "constrained" cycles. A "free cycle" will die of its own accord because of a low autonomous investment, a weak multiplier, or a weak accelerator. A "constrained cycle," driven by powerful expansionist forces, will hit the ceiling of full capacity output; and since this necessarily has the effect of retarding the increases in output, the accelerator acts to reduce investment, and this then causes a downward movement in the economy as a whole. Constrained booms are killed by hitting the ceiling. Instead of going through the ceiling, the accelerator quickly drives the economy into a tailspin. And the downward cumulative movement might depress the economy until gross investment became zero.

At this point all investment, even replacement investment, ceases; and therefore all connection between changes in income and investment is severed. Thus the accelerator loses all force; its downward pressure ceases. At this point the continuous process of growth will no longer be offset by the accelerator working in reverse. An upward push now comes from the continuing rise in productivity, and the economy is started on the road to a new recovery.

Students of the interaction of the multiplier and the accelerator have usually been impressed with the great apparent potency of the super-multiplier. The system has therefore seemed

---

14 J. R. Hicks, *Trade Cycle*, Oxford University Press, 1950. See also the excellent review article, "Hicks on the Trade Cycle," by James S. Duesenberry, *Quarterly Journal of Economics*, August, 1950.

to be explosive. But in fact it is saved from this fate by the cessation of the rise in output as the economy hits the ceiling of full use of resources, since then the accelerator goes quickly into reverse.[15]

A Weak Accelerator

The tendency to regard the system as explosive is partly due to an exaggerated belief in the size of the capital coefficient, ϵ. As we have seen (Table XXIV), ϵ appears to have been somewhat smaller since around 1920 than was formerly the case. Moreover, as we have seen, the accelerator, a, is necessarily smaller than the marginal capital coefficient, ϵ. But quite apart from this, the accelerator appears in fact to be relatively weak during much of the expansionist phase of the cycle. This is true because all through the depression and the first stage of the recovery, depreciation allowances have been expended on constantly improving and more productive equipment. Thus when output recovers to the level of the previous peak, there is likely to be a very considerable amount of excess capacity. Output can therefore increase considerably beyond the previous peak level without any large *net* additions to the capital stock. This means a relatively weak accelerator. As likely as not, therefore, the boom will die *before* the ceiling of full use of resources is reached. In fact, experience appears to show that the "free cycle" hypothesis often offers a better explanation of the upper turning point than does the "constrained cycle" hypothesis.[16]

---

15 The point that the accelerator goes into reverse, owing to the decline in the rate of increase in output as the full employment ceiling is approached, is used by Frisch in his article "The Interrelation between Capital Production and Consumer-Taking," *Journal of Political Economy,* October, 1931. Harrod also referred to it in his *Trade Cycle,* Clarendon Press, Oxford, 1936. See Alvin H. Hansen, *Full Recovery or Stagnation,* W. W. Norton & Company, Inc., 1938, pp. 48–49. This point is especially stressed by Hicks in his *Trade Cycle.*

16 See my discussion (*Monetary Theory and Fiscal Policy,* 1949, pp. 148–150) of three self-limiting factors, within the dynamic process of expansion: (1) the exhaustion of autonomous investment, (2) the fading out of the boom as the *rate of increase* of physical output tapers off when full employment of factors is approached, and (3) the slope of the consumption function.

The Growth Phase of the Cycle

The various phases of the cycle have typically been conceived purely in terms of oscillation. Having regard to *growth* in the cycle, let us break it up into three phases, starting from one peak and ending with the next peak. These phases are designated as I, II, and III in Figure 73.

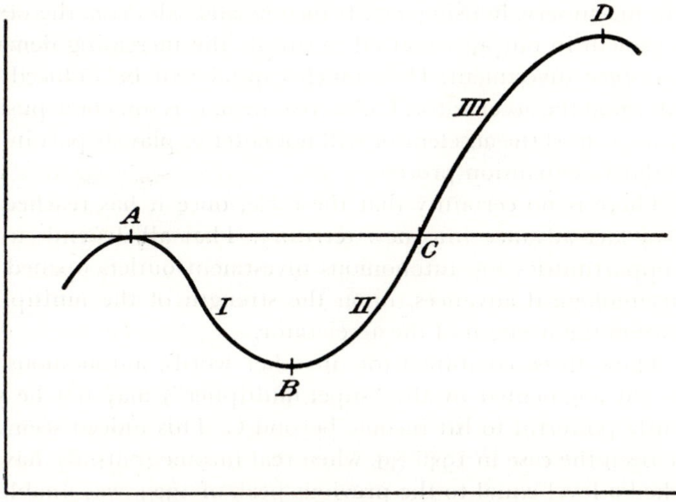

FIGURE 73. *Oscillation and Growth*

The cycle movement, presented in Figure 73, represents both oscillation and growth. Phase I (from A to B) is the downswing from peak to bottom; phase II is the recovery up to C, representing a level of output equal to that at A; phase III represents growth—the upward push into new high levels of output reaching a peak at D.

Phase III is in many ways, especially for the analysis of this chapter, the most interesting. The gain in output from C to D is due to two factors: (a) increased productivity (per worker), and (b) growth in the labor force. Increased productivity (due to inventions, improved machinery, more capital per worker) will have occurred throughout phases I and II. The investment associated with this increase in productivity is autonomous investment. By the time C is reached (the same level of output as that of the previous peak A) many workers will have been displaced by improvements in technology. These displaced workers, together with the net addition to the growing labor force, could, if employed, lift output to D. But the employment of these workers (the displaced workers plus the new workers) will require the equipping of each with standard capital facilities in terms of plant, machinery, housing, etc. If income and sales rise, the necessary growth in output required to supply the increasing demand will *induce* investment. How much capital will be induced depends upon the accelerator. Unless real income is somehow pushed up from C to D the accelerator will not enter to play its part in the cumulative expansion process.

There is no certainty that the cycle, once it has reached C, will in fact advance into new territory. That all depends upon the opportunities for autonomous investment outlets opened up by technological advances, upon the strength of the multiplier, and upon the strength of the accelerator.

These three combined (or, in other words, autonomous investment augmented by the "super-multiplier") may not be sufficiently powerful to lift income beyond C. This indeed seems to have been the case in 1936–39, when real income (output), having reached a level equal to the previous peak of 1929, was unable to rise higher. Continued improvements in productive methods, replacement investments, and some new investments in advanced techniques, had lifted output back again to the 1929 level by processes requiring two million workers less than were needed to produce the same output in 1929. In the meantime, six million new workers had come on the labor market. If, somehow, income could have been raised, this in itself would have *induced* the investment required for the efficient employment of these eight million workers. But induced investment *follows* an increase in income; only autonomous investment can lead the way.[17]

Given the prevailing multiplier and accelerator, had autonomous investment been much larger, income would have

[17] The significance of the capital coefficient and the role of the acceleration process in a growing economy is stressed in the articles by Evsey Domar referred to in footnote 6.

risen above C, and this in turn would have produced a further rise via induced investment—the acceleration process. The combined effect of a larger autonomous investment plus the induced rise in consumption (the multiplier) plus the induced increase in investment (the accelerator) could together have pushed the output up to D. But the expansionist forces inherent in I_A, k, and a, were not adequate to produce this result. Thus the economy remained stagnant and semi-depressed at the 1936–39 level—the level of output corresponding to the previous peak. The forces making for expansion were not adequate to provide a boom of sufficient magnitude to take care of the growth potential in the economy.

In the case of this particular episode it was the war expenditures which gave the economy the necessary push to achieve its new productive potential. Once this new plateau was reached, significant adjustments were made to fit the requirements of the new high level of income. The capital stock had to be raised to a point commensurate with the new level of output. Consumption standards were adjusted upward to correspond to a higher income level. So long as the national real income remained, as in 1936–39, at a level no higher than that of 1929, it was not possible to move up quickly into substantially higher consumption terrain such as that reached in 1947–49. In the absence of an adequate investment boom, it required government action to raise income to the level of the (g_ϵ) growth ceiling.

Possibly the mere passage of time and the continued development of new products tends in a measure to induce people to spend a higher proportion of a given income.[18] This of itself tends to lift income by a magnified amount. The multiplier applies to an upward shift of the consumption function no less than to an increase of investment. But this process is a slow one. What was urgently needed in 1939 was a powerful upward surge of autonomous investment reinforced by the multiplier and the accelerator. In the absence of this, an all-out government program was necessary. The peacetime needs of society in many areas—

[18] This tendency may, however, be offset in whole or in part if new products merely have the effect of supplanting old products—the radio supplanting the piano, etc.

housing, resource development, public improvement projects, education, health—would have amply justified such an all-out effort. In the process we would have created real wealth and income for the entire population. Politically, it did not prove possible to do so; finally the necessities of war forced the expansion.

The new high level of income having been achieved, consumption standards have been adjusted upward. Once won, these new consumption standards will be held tenaciously against any impending recession. This fact represents a great gain—a new plateau from which to oppose an oncoming depression. There is no danger of a return to the income level of 1939. But there is the danger that we may not achieve, on a sustained basis, our growth potential.

"The economy can absorb increases in productivity provided that a boom of sufficient magnitude occurs periodically. A burst of innovations or a war is capable of doing this." [19]

Finally, over against the growth potential (g_ϵ) must be set the savings coefficient, $\frac{S}{Y}$, at full employment. "When the savings coefficient is low it is not very likely that the boom will be weak." [20] The power of the expansionist factors—I_A, k, and α—to achieve periodically a boom commensurate with the requirements of growth must be judged in terms of how high or low the savings coefficient is. The growth factors, g_ϵ, can stand in an equilibrium relation with $\frac{S}{Y}$ only if $\frac{S}{Y}$ at full employment does not exceed the capital requirements of growth. In a full employment equilibrium position, g_ϵ will equal $\frac{S}{Y}$.

[19] James S. Duesenberry, *Income, Saving and the Theory of Consumer Behavior,* Harvard University Press, 1949, p. 116.
[20] J. R. Hicks, *Trade Cycle,* Oxford University Press, 1950, p. 112.

24 · *Modern Cycle Theory:* A SUMMARY STATEMENT

An Unsolved Riddle?

Throughout the development of the literature on business cycles, it has been suggested time and again by various economists that the phenomenon of cyclical fluctuations remains an unsolved riddle. Tugan-Baranowsky, in the preface to his *Les Crises industrielles en Angleterre* (1913), refers to the industrial cycle as the most enigmatic phenomenon in modern economic life and one which economic science has not yet solved. Dr. Adolph Lowe (formerly of Kiel University, Germany), writing in 1926,[1] expressed doubt that the wealth of statistical materials poured out during the preceding fifteen years or so had made any significant contribution toward the theoretical analysis of cyclical fluctuations. The fundamental opposing theories still stood, he thought, unreconciled over against each other. Finally, Gustav Cassel, in the preface to the second English translation of his *Theory of Social Economy*,[2] referring to the postwar economic difficulties, voiced the opinion that the "attempts which are continually being made to bring the analysis of the economic history of this period under the old scheme of regular trade cycles are, in my view, a grave mistake, preventing us from seeing clearly the essential

[1] "Wie ist Konjuncturtheorie überhaupt möglich?," Weltwirtschaftliches Archiv, October, 1926.

[2] Gustav Cassel, *Theory of Social Economy,* Harcourt, Brace & Co., 1932 (preface dated September, 1931).

features of the great economic revolutions taking place in our time."

Opposing Theories

Lowe suggested that the fundamental opposing theories, as of the time he was writing (1926) could be classified into three main systems. On the one side cyclical fluctuations were to be explained by *monetary* factors, and on the other by *real* factors; and if by real factors, the analysis proceeded either from influences operating on *investment* or from influences operating on *consumption.* He suggested also that these theories might be differentiated according to countries, the *monetary* theory being the ruling doctrine in Anglo-Saxon economics, whereas the Continental conception continued to direct its analysis preponderantly to the *real* phenomena. By way of illustration, one could cite the monetary theory of Hawtrey (indeed, money and credit factors loomed large in English thinking from Thornton and Ricardo to Marshall and Pigou); the role of investment in the theory of Wicksell and Spiethoff; and the role of consumption in the theory of Aftalion. These leading and seemingly unreconciled theories were already represented, as we have seen, by an impressive literature as early as 1913.

D. H. Robertson, writing in 1915,[3] contended that "in the deathless words of the Dodo, everybody has won and all must have prizes, in the sense that almost all writers who have made any serious contribution to the study of the matter appear to have had a considerable measure of right on their side." And he offered the opinion that the "most important work which remains to be done lies in the direction of developing and synthesizing the various and often conflicting opinions which have been already expressed."

Foundation Stones

The really essential elements—the foundation stones—in the modern theory of business cycles and the authors of these major contributions can succinctly be stated as follows:

---

[3] *A Study of Industrial Fluctuations,* P. S. King & Son, Ltd., Westminster, 1915.

1. The role of fluctuations in the rate of investment (Tugan-Baranowsky, Spiethoff, Cassel, Robertson).

2. The analysis of the determinants of investment: the natural rate in relation to the money rate—in current terminology, the schedule of the marginal efficiency of investment in relation to the rate of interest (Wicksell, Keynes).

3. The role of dynamic factors—technology, resources, territorial expansion, and population growth—as determinants of investment (Spiethoff, Harrod).

4. The bunching of investment due to the herdlike movement induced by innovational activity (Schumpeter).

5. The capitalistic technique of production (the time element in the construction of fixed capital, the longevity of fixed capital), and the principle of acceleration (Aftalion, Pigou, Clark).

6. Initiating impulses and the propagation of cyclical movements conditioned by the structure of the economy (Wicksell, Pigou).

7. The investment multiplier and the consumption function (Kahn-Keynes).

8. The interrelationships of economic variables—econometric models (Tinbergen, Frisch, Samuelson, Hicks, Klein, etc).

This, to be sure, is a bare skeleton outline which could be filled in and supplemented in various directions from the work of many writers. But it will serve, at least, as a useful framework against which to assess the current status of business-cycle theory.

An Integrated Synthesis

It is above all the analytical tools forged by Wicksell, Aftalion, and Keynes which enable us at long last to formulate an integrated theory—a theory which at one stroke takes cognizance of the role of money, the role of investment, and the role of consumption.

An analysis of the factors determining the marginal efficiency of investment (Wicksell's "natural rate" and Fisher's "rate of return over cost") discloses how this piece of theoretical apparatus serves to unify, synthesize, and integrate the seemingly unreconciled explanations offered by various theorists, particularly with respect to the turning points.

Consider the upper turning point, for example. Keynes, following the general stream of thinking developed by the investment school (and especially the point of view represented by Wicksell), takes the position in the *General Theory* that the essential character of the trade cycle must be sought in the fluctuations in the marginal efficiency of capital. Now the inducement to invest depends upon the schedule of the marginal efficiency of investment (rate of return over cost) in relation to the rate of interest. Three factors—the expected returns on a new capital good, the cost of the new capital good, and the rate of interest—together determine the fluctuations in the inducement to invest. Thus the Wicksellian analysis (reformulated by Fisher and Keynes) represents a portmanteau which subsumes a number of significant factors emphasized by various writers as playing a major role in the cycle. With respect to the upper turning point, the rising cost of equipment and building structures, the rising rate of interest (money and capital market factors), and the diminishing expected yields or returns on new investment (waves of optimism and pessimism, law of proportionality of factors, diminishing marginal utility)—all play a role in causing fluctuations in the inducement to invest.

The Wicksellian analysis thus represents a synthesis or integration of the role of *costs, expected returns,* and *rate of interest* in the cycle. All these elements, instead of being viewed in isolation, each playing a prima donna role as many cycle theorists had it, are integrated by the Wicksellian (Fisher, Keynes) formulation and forged into a powerful theoretical apparatus. This is the first major stepping stone toward the modern theory of cyclical fluctuations.

The second stepping stone—the multiplier analysis—logically comes next, though chronologically it came last. That fluctuations in investment (determined by the marginal efficiency schedule in relation to the rate of interest) could induce fluctuations in consumption, and thus cause income to expand and contract by a magnified amount was, as we have seen, long ago recognized by various writers who contributed significantly to the development of the investment theory of the cycle. But not until Keynes developed the theory of the investment multiplier, based on the concept of the consumption function,[4] was it possible to formulate clear-cut principles with respect to the relation of fluctuations in investment to fluctuations in income. Anyone who will take the trouble to reread the earlier literature (prior to 1936), keeping in mind the multiplier and consumption function concepts, and supplying the missing analysis where needed, cannot fail, I believe, to see how many dark corners are illuminated once the searchlight of these new instruments is put to use. The investment theory of income fluctuations was able to tell only half the story so long as the consumption function concept and the multiplier analysis were missing. This is the area in which Keynes made his greatest contribution, not only to the general theory of income determination, but also to business-cycle analysis.

And now we come to the third stepping stone, though chronologically it came second. It was early recognized by writers on investment theory not only that autonomous investment is a determinant of income (the growth of investment being the essence of the boom) but also that changes in income affect the inducement to invest. This, for example, was well recognized by Tugan-Baranowsky, Spiethoff, and Wicksell. But the precise character of this relationship awaited the formulation of the acceleration principle, of which the first precise statement was made by Aftalion in 1909.[5]

Three Strands in the Modern Analysis

There are, then, three strands to the modern analysis of fluctuations in income: (1) the marginal efficiency schedule in relation to the rate of interest, (2) the effect of changes in income upon the rate of investment (the principle of acceleration) and

---

4 Kahn's employment multiplier, 1931, the size of which depended on the leakages in successive spendings, was the forerunner of Keynes' investment multiplier.

5 See Aftalion's articles entitled "La Réalité des surproductions générales," *Revue d'économie politique,* 1909; also his *Les Crises périodiques de Surproduction,* Marcel Rivière et Cie., Paris, 1913. In an article in the *Quarterly Journal of Economics,* May, 1903, T. N. Carver discussed the magnified effect on profits (and so on the value of capital goods) of relatively small fluctuations in the prices of consumers' goods.

finally (3) the role of the investment multiplier (based on the consumption function) in relation to income formation. These are the basic interrelationships which comprise the "mechanics" of expansion and contraction.

Now it is a distinctive feature of the modern theory of fluctuations that it provides an explanation of why an expansion does not move on and on in a self-reinforcing manner. According to the older view a movement once started, whether up or down, tended to propagate itself in a continuing, cumulative, self-perpetuating process.

The theory of a self-reinforcing, cumulative process can be stated as follows: Any flow of income will tend to perpetuate itself into the future if the elasticity of expectations is unity. Rising sales volume will induce businessmen to enlarge their production plans and to compete among themselves for the factors of production. Output, prices, wages, and money incomes tend to rise. All income earned, it was assumed, will tend to be spent, whether on investment goods or consumers' goods. Moreover, the income stream will continually be fed from the spring of rising expectations. Thus an expansionist process "was believed to be reinforced by optimistic expectations . . . and since Say's Law (supply creates its own demand) was generally accepted, it was difficult to see how producers' expectations, in the aggregate, could be disappointed. . . . The cumulative movement of income and prices was thus regarded as an obvious process; the real difficulty lay in an explanation of the turning points." [6]

In terms of the older analysis, it was necessary to introduce external limiting factors to explain why any cumulative movement was cut short. Most commonly, resort was had to the limits imposed by the gold standard. Limited gold reserves, so ran the argument, finally checked any self-perpetuating expansion which was being fed by an increasing volume of bank credit. This was the explanation offered by the quantity theory and the currency school from Ricardo on. Limited reserves called an inevitable halt to easy terms of lending. If banks "charge less than the market

[6] Lloyd Metzler, "Business Cycles and the Modern Theory of Employment," *American Economic Review*, June, 1946.

rate of interest,"[7] says Ricardo, "there is no amount of money which they might not lend."

The "reining-in" effect from limited bank reserves was generally used to explain the upper turning point not only by monetary theorists, but also by the earlier contributors to the investment theory of the cycle. Tugan-Baranowsky explained the exhaustion of the investment boom by the "scarcity of capital" which made its appearance at the point when "loan capital" could no longer be fed from bank credit expansion. Heavy reliance was also placed upon this factor by Cassel. Hayek argued (in *Prices and Production*) that the boom was fed from "forced saving," wrung from the community through bank credit expansion; and once this "forced saving" ceased, owing to limited bank reserves, the loan rate would rise above the expected rate of return on new investment. Thus a halt would be called by the cessation of monetary expansion causing a "shortening of the process of production." With Hawtrey (representing the purely monetary point of view) it was the flow of currency into active circulation, and the ensuing depletion of bank reserves, that "reined in" what would otherwise turn out to be a self-reinforcing, cumulative process of expansion. Similarly with Léon Walras, it was the rigidity of the monetary system, imposed by the limitation of gold supply, that created the *tension* which finally counteracted further expansion—the "reining-in effect of the *encaisse désirée*."[8]

In contrast to this analysis, with its emphasis on the need for external limiting factors to stop the cumulative process, the modern theory holds that there are three *self-limiting* factors which come into play: (1) the falling marginal efficiency of capital, partly due to a movement *down* the schedule as more and more investment is undertaken, and partly owing to a *shift* in the schedule;

---

[7] Ricardo explains that the "market rate of interest" is regulated by "the rate of profit which can be made by the employment of capital." In view of Wicksellian terminology, Ricardo's "market rate" is likely to be misunderstood. He used "market rate" to mean the same as Wicksell's "natural rate." See David Ricardo, *Political Economy* and *Taxation* (Everyman's Library), p. 246.

[8] See Ragnar Frisch, "Propagation Problems and Impulse Problems in Dynamic Economics," in *Economic Essays in Honour of Gustav Cassel,* George Allen and Unwin, Ltd., London, 1933.

(2) the acceleration principle, under which induced investment necessarily fades out as the *rate of increase* in output tapers off when full employment of resources is approached; and (3) the slope of the consumption function, under which a widening gap of saving must be filled by investment offsets if a reversal is to be avoided.

Consider how these three factors, taken together, explain the upper turning point. Let us take them in reverse order. The slope of the consumption function tends to place an upper limit upon the expansion. As full employment is approached, the gap between consumption and investment tends to widen; though in a prolonged boom, as in the 1920's, the spread between them, while widening absolutely, may remain proportionally fairly constant with continuing high levels of investment filling the gap.

This situation, the longer its lasts, becomes more and more precarious. In the first place, the *rate of increase* in output, during the first phase of the expansion when employment is rapidly rising, necessarily begins to flatten out as full employment of resources is approached. Thus the acceleration principle comes into play; induced investment begins to fall off. The perpetuation of any achieved level of induced investment rests on a highly precarious basis—namely, the continued maintenance of past rates of increase in final real demand. In the second place, the available *autonomous* investment becomes progressively exhausted the longer the boom lasts. The new investment opportunities (opened up by advances in technique and other dynamic factors) tend to be exploited at a pace that exceeds the normal rate of growth. Innovation (progress) proceeds by spurts, by intermittent surges (Spiethoff, Schumpeter, Cassel, Robertson). While this lasts, the backlog of *autonomous* investment plus the investment *induced* by rapid expansion may be adequate to fill the consumption-income gap. Once the backlog is exhausted, however, and once the *rate of increase* in output begins to taper off, then both the autonomous and the induced investment will tend to die down. Thus the boom "dies a natural death." Investment has caught up with the requirements of growth and technical progress. Net investment falls off, and income recedes by a magnified amount.

These factors similarly explain why, once a depression is under way, the system does not fall continuously in a cumulative downward movement. The slope of the consumption function is such that, as real income falls, consumption falls less than income. Thus the forces making for contraction weaken. Moreover, as the *rate of decline* eases off more and more, the principle of derived demand operates to lessen the forces making for decline. Finally, continued technical progress opens up new investment opportunities.

There are, accordingly, self-limiting factors inherent in the nature of the economy which explain the oscillatory process of expansion and decline. The system does not *progressively* feed on itself; it does not move on indefinitely in a cumulative fashion. On the contrary, there are self-limiting factors within the structure of the system itself which limit both expansion and contraction. And the explanation is to be sought (a) in the marginal efficiency schedule, (b) in the principle of acceleration, and (c) in the slope of the consumption function.

Thus the consumption function, together with the autonomous and induced investment functions (the marginal efficiency schedule and the accelerator), explains the process of expansion, recession, contraction, and revival. And the system is so constituted that wavelike movements tend to fall between fairly well defined upper and lower limits. These relationships are rigorously disclosed in the econometric models.

The Cycle in a Dynamic Society

The modern analysis reveals that, so long as the economy remains dynamic, so long as the requirements of growth and progress call for large investment outlays, powerful forces will be at work to produce cyclical fluctuations. One cannot, therefore, regard the cycle as a pathological condition. It is inherent in the nature of the modern dynamic economy. "Built-in" institutional arrangements can indeed narrow the limits of oscillation. But only in a measure. A positive counter-cyclical program is necessary.

Thus we turn to Part IV, where we consider (a) "built-in" automatic regulators, (b) a managed compensatory cycle policy, and (c) long-run structural reforms and programs without which any short-run cycle policy would, so to speak, be suspended in mid-air, or (to change the metaphor) cut off from its "base of supplies," from which it draws its strength and nourishment.

PART FOUR

Business Cycles and Public Policy

25 · *Is Cycle Policy Obsolete?*

The Persistence of Business Cycles

In an article[1] appearing in the Dutch *De Economist* in 1926, Hawtrey stated emphatically the view that "since the war there has been no trade cycle." While the output of literature on the subject had increased beyond precedent, writers "have not always noticed that for the time being there *is* no trade cycle." In a somewhat similar vein, Gustav Cassel, in the preface (written in 1931) to the second English edition of his *Theory of Social Economy,* expressed his belief that trade-cycle theory could not fruitfully be applied to the period of economic history following the First World War.

As we look back over it now, we must, I think, conclude that these were hasty and unwarranted judgments. Every period is indeed characterized by more or less unique conditions. The boom of the twenties and the depression of the thirties were certainly affected by conditions peculiar to those periods. But special conditions were also strikingly present in the eighteen-seventies and the nineties.

Again following the Second World War one hears it said that the concept of the cycle is obsolete, that we are passing through a period for which business-cycle theory has no relevance. Among other things the vast peacetime military outlays, together with

1 Reprinted in *Readings in Business Cycle Theory,* The Blakiston Company, 1944.

the foreign aid program, it is suggested, play so large a role that market forces have little effect on income formation.

That governmental fiscal operations exerted in 1947–50 a much larger influence than in any earlier peacetime period cannot be questioned. This indeed represents a major structural change in the economy. Moreover, in other directions—collective bargaining, social security, farm programs, financial, banking, and stock market reforms—the American economy has undergone a far-reaching and fundamental remodeling of its institutional framework. But the process of structural change is not new. Other developments, also revolutionary for their time, occurred in the nineteenth century, notably the emergence of the modern giant corporation, the growth of commercial banking, and finally the beginnings of governmental regulation and control.

The Boom Following the Second World War

Despite all the unique features which have characterized the economic conditions following the Second World War, the years 1947–50 nevertheless exhibited familiar boom characteristics. These years disclosed the same distortions common to all boom periods. They were not years, as was sometimes alleged, in which the economy had reached a maintainable balance. True, the price level flattened out by 1948, but an economy may be violently distorted even when the price level is substantially stable.

That this is true is apparent when we consider the good years of the nineteen-twenties. A common mistake then made was to confuse "balance" in the economy with mere price stability. This, perhaps more than anything else, accounts for the quite unwarranted complacence of the twenties.

Every Boom Is a Distortion

Every boom represents a distortion away from an equilibrium or balanced condition. This distortion consists essentially of an unmaintainable rate of capital formation.

Private gross domestic investment averaged 16.3 per cent of the gross national product for seven consecutive years, from 1923 to 1929. In no year did it fall below 15.1 per cent, and it reached

17.5 per cent in the peak year. Now 16 per cent of gross national product is more than can profitably be laid out on private income-producing capital year in and year out. Experience in the twenty-year period 1921–40 indicates that it was probably not possible to invest profitably more than, say, 12 per cent of the gross national product in capital facilities.[2]

It is indeed quite possible that the $104 billion poured into new construction, producers' equipment, and inventory accumulation (the latter amounted to only $6.5 billion) in the seven years 1923–29 might have been reasonably justified if a full employment income could somehow have been maintained from 1929 on. It is not just a question of *mistaken* investment. It is simply a question of the "bucket of capital formation" (determined by the requirements of technique and population growth) being filled to the brim. By 1929 we had "caught up" with our then prevailing capital requirements and needs. We could not continue to pour around $15 billion a year into office buildings, apartment houses, business plant and equipment, and other private investment projects. We had temporarily reached, more or less, a point of saturation.

This is the dilemma confronting any economy that has not developed an adequate anti-cyclical program. Boom levels of private investment outlays are not maintainable over the long run. Without an anti-cyclical program the inevitable collapse in investment will induce a magnified fall in income, and this in turn will induce a further fall in investment in a cumulative fashion until eventually the internal stabilizing factors come into play.

Unmaintainable Spurt in Capital Formation

Precisely as in the twenties, the high volume of private investment outlays in 1947–50 represented an unmaintainable spurt

---

2 For the twenty-year period 1921–40 the proportion of gross national product expended on private domestic investment was 12 per cent. In the January, 1949, *Annual Economic Review of the Council of Economic Advisers,* it is suggested that a sustainable long-run pattern may require a level of private capital expenditures of about 11 or 12 per cent of the gross national product.

in capital formation. The war left accumulated arrears in commercial structures, houses, and producers' equipment. These "deferred demands" largely account for the wave of investment which carried gross private domestic capital formation up to $45 billion in 1948.

Starting from 1946, the first full peacetime year following the Second World War, the United States has experienced a great postwar restocking boom. In some respects this boom resembles that of 1919–20, but there are a great many dissimilarities. Comparison might also be made with the prolonged boom of the twenties, but here again we would find a number of striking differences.

Table XXV gives data on gross national product, production, and prices for the year 1946–50, inclusive. A considerable

TABLE XXV

Year	*Gross National Product* (in billions)	*Total Production* (1935–39 = 100)	*Wholesale Prices* (1926 = 100)	*Consumer Prices* (1935–39 = 100)
1946	$211.1	161	121.1	139.3
1947	233.3	174	152.1	159.2
1948	259.1	183	165.1	171.2
1949	255.6	174	155.0	169.1
1950 (1st half)	265.3	—	153.8	167.8

price rise occurred in the eighteen months from July, 1946, to January, 1948, after which prices substantially flattened out. Total production rose significantly from 1946 to 1948, owing mainly to the progressive elimination of bottlenecks and the filling of "pipe lines" in areas in which materials were in short supply. The substantial rise in gross national product was compounded partly of increases in total production, but much more largely of price increases.

The component parts of the gross national product for 1946–50 are shown in Table XXVI.

TABLE XXVI

Year	Gross National Product	Gross Investment (including net foreign investment)	Government Outlays on Goods and Services	Private Consumption
1946	$211.1	$33.3	$30.9	$146.9
1947	233.3	39.1	28.6	165.6
1948	259.1	45.0	36.6	177.4
1949	255.6	33.4	43.3	178.8
1950 (1st half)	265.3	40.3	41.5	183.5

In order to make significant comparisons with the booms culminating in 1920 and in 1929, it will be useful to compare the relative importance of these components in the gross national product for each of the three years 1920, 1929, and 1948. These data are presented in Table XXVII.

TABLE XXVII

	Percentage of Gross National Product in Given Year		
Year	Gross Investment (including net foreign investment)	Government Outlays on Goods and Services	Private Consumption
1920	21.5	9.3	69.3
1929	16.0	8.2	75.9
1948	17.4	14.1	68.5

Three Booms Compared

The 1920 boom was characterized by an extraordinary spurt of investment, considerably greater, relative to gross national product, than the investment of either 1929 or 1948. In order to obtain a clearer picture of the role of investment in each of the three booms, let us break up investment into its component parts —construction, equipment, inventories, net foreign investment— for each of the three periods. Table XXVIII gives the percentage of gross national product expended on each of these investment categories. The percentage of gross national product spent on consumers' durables for each period is also added.

TABLE XXVIII

Percentage of Gross National Product in Given Year

Year	*Construction* (private)	*Producers' Equipment*	*Inventories*	*Net Foreign Investment*	*Consumers' Durables*
1920	5.5	7.8	5.7	2.6	8.0
1929	7.5	6.2	1.5	0.7	9.0
1948	7.1	7.5	2.1	0.7	8.8

The years 1929 and 1948 are strikingly similar, except that somewhat more, relatively, was spent on producers' equipment and inventories in 1948. The relative amounts spent on total fixed capital (construction plus equipment) were very similar for the two years. Also the role of consumers' durables was nearly the same in 1948 as in 1929.

Following the First World War (1920) the proportion of the gross national product going into private construction was somewhat less than that in 1948, while in the case of producers' equipment the proportions were very similar for the two years. But with respect to inventory accumulation and net foreign investment the year 1920 presents a strikingly different picture from that of 1929 and 1948. Both these items were fantastically large in 1920, and it is here that one must find the reason for the phenomenally large proportion of gross national product going into investment in this postwar spurt. The 1920 boom did not present a disproportionate investment in fixed capital compared with other high boom years; but it did present a quite abnormal investment in inventories, and a remarkably large net foreign investment.

The slump of 1921–22 was mainly due to the collapse in inventory investment and net foreign investment. Investment in inventories fell practically to zero in 1921, and by 1922 net foreign investment had shrunk to less than a quarter of the 1920 level. Construction, on the other hand, declined scarcely at all from 1920 to 1921 and had already risen substantially by 1922. Outlays on producers' equipment fell by 45 per cent from the 1920 level, while expenditures on consumers' durables fell by about

20 per cent. The depression of 1921–22 was due in great part to the inventory situation and the adverse change in the net foreign balance.

The depression of 1929 was clearly fundamentally different from that of 1920. The drastic decline, following the boom twenties, was mainly due to a severe drop in the investment in fixed capital. Private construction fell off from $7.8 billion in 1929 to $1.7 billion in 1932, while outlays on producers' equipment fell from $6.4 to $1.8 billion. There followed, to be sure, a heavy disinvestment in inventories *induced* in large measure by the severe decline in sales volume. But the depression did not begin with any such overextended inventory situation as prevailed in 1920. In 1929 it was investment in fixed capital that had been overextended, and it was in this area that the primary collapse occurred.

As in the 1923–29 boom, particular attention was paid in the pre-Korean years to prospects for capital outlays on construction and on producers' equipment. With respect to (a) the world agricultural situation and the outlook for American agricultural exports, and (b) the foreign aid program, conditions resembling those following the First World War prevailed. Then the foreign aid program consisted largely of loans (which, however, were largely defaulted), whereas after the Second World War it consisted heavily of government grants.

Prior to the Korean crisis, four main areas could be regarded as precarious from the standpoint of the maintenance of sustained high levels of income and employment: (a) fixed capital outlays, (b) expenditures on consumers' durables (such as automobiles and electrical appliances), (c) agricultural surpluses, (d) the possible tapering off of the European aid program.

The crumbling of all four areas together, combined with the induced secondary effects, could certainly have produced a very severe depression if no effective counter-action were taken. But the outlook was completely changed by the outbreak of the Korean war and the prospect of continued large military expenditures for years to come.

The remarkable thing about the period from the end of the Second World War to the Korean crisis is the fact that, notwithstanding the large backlog of deferred demand for plant, equipment, houses, and consumers' durables, and despite the vast military and foreign aid programs, the American economy, after a catching-up period of only a couple of years, proved fully equal to the task. This was a tremendous demonstration of how vast a volume of aggregate demand is necessary to keep the highly productive American economy fully employed.

Cushioning and Offsetting Policies

Fluctuations, even violent fluctuations, in the rate of investment can be expected under peacetime conditions in private enterprise economies. We are indeed in process of developing institutional arrangements that serve to lessen the secondary, induced effects of these primary fluctuations in the volume of investment. Programs of this sort may be called "cushioning" cycle policies. But "offsetting" cycle policies are also necessary. Business-cycle theory, from Tugan-Baranowsky and Spiethoff to Schumpeter and Robertson, has taught us that the fluctuation in private capital expenditures is an unruly characteristic of the modern economy. It is not a pathological behavior pattern. It is a basic characteristic of a technologically dynamic and growing economy. It is a characteristic which can only be understood by examining the factors underlying the intermittent surges of private investment. If, indeed, it turns out that investment comes more and more under the direct control of the state, the cycle phenomena can be expected to change. This latter program represents a "direct control" cycle policy. But in a private economy, where the basic freedom to invest would not be directly interfered with, cycle policies must assume the form of the "cushioning" or "offsetting" varieties. These matters will be discussed more fully in the chapters which follow.

In the event that we should be confronted in the next decade or more with quasi-war conditions involving very large military expenditures, the pressing problem will be the control of inflation. And if total war breaks out, rigorous over-all controls will inevitably become necessary. But these are war problems, not business-cycle problems as such.

26 · *Changing Views on Cycle Policy*

The Old and the New

Students of economics nowadays are sometimes surprised to discover a large literature on counter-cyclical policies published in the decade of the twenties, prior to the Great Depression and prior to the Keynesian and related thinking dealing with the grave problems of the depressed thirties. Anyone who delves into economic literature, whether theoretical or applied, will soon discover that, in a sense, there is "nothing new under the sun." Yet this statement is only half true. It is indeed true that modern thinking on cycle policy is related to, and is in a great measure the outgrowth of, past thinking. Yet something could also be said for the thesis that modern cycle policy represents a new approach to the problem. The truth lies somewhere between.

There is perhaps no single cycle policy commanding currently wide support which does not have its counterpart in the literature of the twenties. In a measure the difference between the modern point of view and that of the twenties is not so much in the specific proposals as in the horizon or scope of the thinking in the two contrasted periods.

Policies Dominant in the Twenties

In a number of respects rather fundamental changes have, however, occurred. In the twenties emphasis was placed upon central bank policy, interest rate adjustments, and price stabilization; wage reductions as a means of overcoming unemployment played a large role in depression policy; finally, fiscal policy, while recognized as useful, was relegated to the very moderate job of transferring a part of the regular government capital outlays (public works) from good times to bad. With respect to each of these points, modern cycle policy differs substantially from that typically advocated in the twenties. Illustrative of this change in thinking is the important document on postwar economic stability issued by the League of Nations in 1945.[1]

It would be difficult to find more representative accounts of the thinking of the twenties than those given by Wesley Mitchell in *The Stabilization of Business*[2] and by Pigou in Part II of his *Industrial Fluctuations.*

Credit Policy and Price Stabilization

One-third of Pigou's section on remedies is devoted to credit policy and price stabilization. While critical of the purely monetary theory of the cycle, nevertheless Pigou believed that if a policy of price stabilization were successfully carried through, the amplitude of industrial fluctuations might be cut down to one-half. Similarly Mitchell gives great weight to discount policy.

In line with the prevalent thinking of the twenties, it was believed that bank credit policy could be used to regulate prices by applying brakes and stimulants. Pigou discusses two types of mechanisms—credit rationing and discount control. Both methods were regarded as competent to restrict credits in good times, but were thought to be rather inefficient as means to expand credits in bad times. It was, however, thought that effective restriction in good times (restraining the boom) would of itself tend to mitigate the severity of the depression.

Credit rationing was generally regarded as inferior to discount policy, partly because it would be difficult to distribute loans fairly among rival claimants, and partly because it required

---

1 *Economic Stability in the Post-War World,* Report of the Delegation on Economic Depressions, Part II, League of Nations, Geneva, 1945.

2 *The Stabilization of Business,* Lionel D. Edie, ed., The Macmillan Company, New York, 1923.

a high degree of co-operation among independent bankers. Especially in a country like the United States, with thousands of independent bankers, credit rationing was not regarded as a practical proposal. On the contrary, discount policy was a relatively simple matter, since it could be carried out by the central bank.

In the United States, open market operations of the Federal Reserve System were mainly relied upon as the means of implementing monetary and credit policy. By means of open market operations, the Reserve System could raise or lower the reserves of the member banks, thereby expanding or restricting their capacity to lend. These operations could, moreover, be backed up by raising or lowering the discount rate of the Federal Reserve Banks. Thus when reserves were tightened by open market operations, member banks could be deterred more or less, by a high discount rate, from rebuilding their reserves. Open market operations and discount rate manipulation could thus be used to influence the availability of credit and the terms of lending.

A central issue much discussed during this period related to the appropriate time to raise and lower the discount rate. With respect to the 1920 boom, for example, Governor Benjamin Strong of the New York Federal Reserve Bank expressed the view that the rate should have been raised early in 1919, before the boom began. An advance in the discount rates, it was widely believed, would have moderated the 1920 boom and reduced the severity of the 1921 depression.

Various views were expressed with respect to appropriate signals to be relied upon in timing discount rate adjustments. Historically the Bank of England had varied its discount rate largely with a view to protecting its reserves. But this meant tardy action, and in Hawtrey's view, as we have seen in Chapter 19, this delayed action was the essential cause of industrial fluctuations. "The flow of legal tender money into circulation and back is one of the very tardiest consequences of credit expansion or contraction." Thus the principle of watching the reserves brought effective action too late. Hawtrey suggested that the central bank should be guided, not by reserve proportions, but by "the aberrations of the flow of purchasing power (as measured by prices subject to the necessary allowances) from a perfectly even course." [3] In the United States, in lieu of the traditional reserve-ratio as the guide to credit policy, it was suggested that index numbers of physical production be used. When this index began to flatten out, indicating that full employment of productive resources had approximately been reached and that further credit expansion would only have the effect of raising prices without adding appreciably to output, the time had come, it was suggested, to raise discount rates. "Our aim, accordingly, should be," said Wesley Mitchell, "to check the rise of prices when the index numbers of physical output indicate that the limit of existing capacity is being approached. At that point it would be desirable to raise discount rates—even though reserve ratios might still be high." [4]

Whatever the appropriate signals for action, the general aim widely acclaimed in the twenties was price stabilization. A vigorous and voluminous literature urged (1) the stabilization of prices as the proper *aim* of central bank policy, and (2) open-market operations and changes in discount rates as the suitable *means* to that end. This, it was believed, would go far toward avoiding unnecessary and undesirable industrial fluctuations.

It was natural, following the price upheaval of 1916–21, including both the war boom and the deflation following, that attention should be concentrated upon the relation of *price* fluctuations to fluctuations in *production* and *employment*. Moreover, as we have seen, traditional economic thinking, both in England and in America, had stressed the role of money and credit as an important controlling factor in the cycle. Currency reform had always loomed large in British thinking on remedies for commercial crises. High hopes had been entertained for the Peel Bank Act of 1844. And while disillusionment quickly followed this experiment, nevertheless credit policy continued to

---

[3] R. G. Hawtrey, *Monetary Reconstuction,* Longmans, Green, Ltd., London, 1923, pp. 144–145. Pigou, however, was not convinced that prices would be a better guide than "reserve-ratios." He gives data to show that in fact reserve changes generally precede price changes. Pigou suggested that a suitable signal might perhaps be found in the prices of speculative stocks. See Pigou, *Industrial Fluctuations,* p. 260.

[4] Wesley C. Mitchell, in Edie's *The Stabilization of Business,* p. 43. The suggestion, stated by Mitchell, had been proposed by Professor O. M. W. Sprague.

be regarded as the major weapon with which to attack the trade cycle.

In the United States, the crisis of 1907 had called attention to the urgency of banking and currency reforms. The ensuing discussion, in and out of Congress, led to the establishment of the Federal Reserve System in 1914. As in the case of the Peel Bank Act of 1844, it was confidently expected that this monetary reform would serve to mitigate industrial fluctuations.

For a time, this optimism appeared to be justified. Once the sharp but brief postwar readjustment was over, the country enjoyed high and stable prosperity from 1923 to 1929. During this period the Federal Reserve System was learning to use open-market operations and discount control as means to influence the credit situation. In the famous Report of 1923, it was urged that open-market operations should be used to influence the general credit situation. Open-market sales of securities, with the consequent reduction of Federal Reserve credit and the tightening of member bank reserves, appeared to be successful in checking an undue rise in prices and an impending excessive inventory boom in 1923. In fact, however, it is doubtful that the moderate action taken had any appreciable effect. Nevertheless, this episode led many to believe that relatively stable prices and the avoidance of speculative inventory accumulations would ensure permanent prosperity. There was no adequate recognition of the fact that the rate of *fixed* capital investment throughout 1923–29 exceeded the long-run maintainable rate. There was lacking in the prevalent thinking of the twenties an adequate appreciation of the role of real investment and the theory of investment demand.

The Stock Market

Despite the stability of commodity prices, the stock market surged up and up to unprecedented levels. This phenomenon did indeed occasion much concern. Speculative uses of credit, it was felt, should be discouraged. Brokers' loans rose to extravagant proportions. The Federal Reserve Board wished, while providing ample credit for production, to check speculation. But for this purpose its powers were inadequate. General control over credit, by means of open-market operations and discount policy, could not segregate the flow of credit moving into productive use on the one side and into the speculative market on the other. A mere tightening of the general money market could only mean that the more stable run of industries would be checked, while the highly speculative parts of the economy would continue to forge ahead—lured on by the prospect of profits far in excess of the cost of borrowing. Thus the conviction grew that more direct controls were necessary (such as the control of margin requirements on security purchases) if the speculative sector were to be brought under control.

Undoubtedly, the ease with which new security issues could be floated, in the highly inflated stock market of the twenties, carried the investment boom into unwise and economically unjustifiable ventures. Errors of optimism were generated by the stock market inflation. Investment was accordingly pushed to a higher degree of saturation than would otherwise have occurred. The failure to control speculation was an important factor in the extravagant boom of the twenties. General recognition of this fact led to the establishment of the Securities Exchange Commission; the passage of several acts, including the Securities Act of 1933, the Securities Exchange Act of 1934, and the Public Utility Holding Company Act of 1935; and finally the control of margin requirements by the Federal Reserve Board.

An important section of expert opinion remained undisturbed by the stock market inflationary developments. The continuing stability of commodity prices seemed to indicate a secure and balanced condition in the economy. It is therefore not surprising that the collapse, beginning in 1929, completely mystified those who pinned their faith on credit and price stabilization policies.

Monetary Policy in the Depression

Once the onslaught of the Great Depression struck with full force, attention was directed toward monetary means of checking the deflation. To this end, the discount rates of the Federal Reserve Banks were sharply reduced, while at the same time open-market purchases of government securities were increased. All this availed but little, since, under the process of liquidation and general contraction, banks strove to reduce their borrowings at the Reserve Banks. Federal Reserve credit actually declined from $1.6 billion in 1929 to less than $1 billion by July, 1931. This contraction occurred despite the fact that the sharp reduction in bills discounted was offset in considerable measure by open-market purchases of securities by the Reserve System.

After the passage of the Glass-Steagall Act of February, 1932, had freed the gold formerly held to secure the Federal Reserve notes, the Federal Reserve System was able to extend greatly its open-market operations. Federal Reserve holdings of United States securities rapidly rose from $0.7 billion in February, 1932, to $1.9 billion by December, 1932. Total Federal Reserve credit was increased from less than $1 billion in July, 1931, to $2.2 billion in December, 1932, thus creating for the first time a large volume of excess member bank reserves. This action helped the banks to weather for some time the successive liquidation crises. Eventually, however, the terrific decline in security and real estate values, the increasing burden of frozen loans, together with the continued withdrawals of deposits, forced the temporary closing of all the banks and the liquidation or reorganization of the weaker members.

By the end of 1933 the banks had repaid most of their borrowings at the Reserve Banks. Federal Reserve holdings of government securities were now increased to nearly $2.5 billion. In consequence of these open-market purchases, member bank excess reserves increased to nearly $1 billion. Beginning with 1934, the excess reserves were progressively augmented by gold imports, until at the beginning of 1936 they amounted to about $3 billion. And the accelerated gold inflow after the Munich crisis raised excess reserves to $6 billion by the middle of 1940.

This unprecedented development was mainly the result of gold imports into the United States. While deliberate central bank action would doubtless never have pushed an easy money policy to the extremes actually experienced, the outcome, more or less accidental, has given us a striking laboratory experiment. We have been privileged to observe what contribution can be made by the utmost limit of central bank action toward economic recovery.

The result is very illuminating. The money rates charged customers by banks in New York City fell from 6 per cent in 1929 to 1.7 per cent in 1936, and in other northern and eastern cities from 6 per cent to 3 per cent. Commercial paper rates fell from 6 per cent to ¾ of one per cent in the same period. United States Government long-term rates fell from 4 per cent in 1929 to 2½ per cent in 1939 and just over 2 per cent in 1940. High-grade corporate bonds fell from 4¾ per cent in 1929 to 3 per cent in 1939.

The areas in the interest-rate structure that can be reached by central bank policy are the short-term rates and the gilt-edged long-term rates. But they constitute only a part of the complex structure of interest rates, and very probably not the most important ones. Low interest rates in these areas do indeed "spill over," in a measure, into other areas, but not very effectively. The flooding of the banking system with excess reserves did indeed bring the rates down in the areas enumerated above, but it had little effect on real-estate mortgage rates or on commercial and personal loans in the smaller cities and rural communities. "In 1938 about one-fifth of all member banks received on the average more than 7 per cent on their loans, and the proportion must be larger for non-member banks." [5] For residential building, for intermediate and small-scale business, for the more risky ventures, and for small cities and interior communities, fantastically high excess reserves and a high degree of bank liquidity proved to be of relatively little avail.

Lending and Guaranteeing Agencies

The inadequacy of central bank action in these important areas forced the development of other types of institutions designed to cope directly with the problem. To this end, several types of governmental corporations were organized. These include the various lending agencies. The R.F.C., from February, 1932, to December, 1939, poured altogether $4,075,000,000 into the banking system, including loans to open and closed banks. To railroads with weakened credit it made loans aggregating $1,372,-

[5] Woodlief Thomas, "The Banks and Idle Money," *Federal Reserve Bulletin,* March, 1940, p. 197. See also E. A. Goldenweiser, "Cheap Money and the Federal Reserve System," *Federal Reserve Bulletin,* May, 1940.

000,000. In addition $2,443,000,000 was advanced for the benefit of agriculture, including commodity loans and loans to agricultural and livestock credit corporations. The Federal Farm Mortgage Corporation and the Federal Land Banks refinanced about two billion dollars of farm mortgages. In a similar manner, the Home Owners' Loan Corporation refinanced about three billion dollars of frozen urban mortgages. All these salvaging operations had to be completed before it was possible to start again a flow of expenditures on the current production of consumption or investment goods.

In addition, certain lending agencies, such as the Rural Electrification Administration, made funds available directly for new investment. Further, the Federal Housing Administration, by insuring and in effect guaranteeing loans on residential construction, encouraged banks, insurance companies, and other financial companies to enter a field where, without insurance and guarantee, they would not venture except on terms so prohibitive as to preclude willingness to borrow.

We have seen how central bank action alone was not adequate to check unsound speculative tendencies in the boom twenties, and how more direct measures of control had to be devised. Similarly, central bank action was not adequate to cope with the depression. A high degree of bank liquidity was indeed essential. To be effective, however, the cheap money policy had to be implemented by direct measures involving the establishing of lending and guaranteeing agencies such as the Rural Electrification Administration and the Federal Housing Administration. These agencies supplemented the easy-money policies of the Reserve System in ways that made the money effectively available at low rates of interest. It is one thing to provide the banking system with the means to lend; it is another thing to make the funds available on terms and conditions suitable to the requirements of special areas—for example, home mortgages. Cheap money alone is not adequate. Central bank action alone is not sufficient. Effective monetary policy involves much more than open-market operations and discount control.

Thus modern monetary policy is more complex and extends into areas not contemplated in the twenties. This is one important difference. In addition we see more clearly, in part by reason of the experience of the thirties and in part because of the progress of theoretical analysis, what monetary policy can, and cannot, be expected to do. Monetary policy is a necessary part of an anti-cyclical program, but it is not by itself a sufficient cycle policy. This, indeed, was already recognized by the more cautious writers such as Mitchell and Pigou. It is safe to say, however, that general economic opinion has shifted heavily in the direction of placing less reliance than formerly upon purely monetary policy. At the same time, there is a growing awareness that neglect of monetary policy would be fatal. A wrong monetary policy can seriously damage and even destroy the effectiveness of fiscal policy. Monetary policy and fiscal policy, each reinforcing and supplementing the other, are both essential elements in the development of an adequate cycle program.

Wage Policy

A major difference between the thinking current in the twenties and modern cycle theory has to do with wage policy. This can be strikingly illustrated in Pigou's thinking. In 1927 Pigou had no doubt that wage reductions, if drastically applied, could effectively be used to counter (and indeed cure) a depression. On broad social grounds, indeed, he favored only a very moderate use of a flexible wage policy. But on purely theoretical grounds he had no doubt of its efficacy.

In suggesting, as a means of lessening the amplitude of industrial fluctuations, that "real wage rates should be made somewhat more plastic in the face of changes in demand than they now are," he did not intend "that they should be made more plastic only in a downward sense." [6] He suggested that employers should raise wage rates "sooner and more largely" in good times to offset "earlier and larger reductions" in depression.

"If we can bring ourselves to tolerate the conception of nega-

[6] A. C. Pigou, *Industrial Fluctuations,* Macmillan & Co., Limited, London, 1927, p. 282. I cite Pigou as the most eminent (and withal one of the most socially minded) representative of thinking generally current among economists in the twenties; innumerable references from a host of economists (including paragraphs from my own earlier writings) could easily be added by anyone who will take the trouble to do so.

tive wages, it is possible to imagine a wage policy that would ensure full employment in all industries continuously, whatever changes demand might undergo." [7] He concluded his chapter on wage policy with the statement that if wage rates are "rendered less rigid, the amplitude of industrial fluctuations associated with given variations in demand will be *pro tanto* reduced." [8]

The fallacy in this reasoning lay in its neglect of the effect of wages rates on aggregate demand. We cannot assume demand as given, irrespective of the wage rate. The wage rate, the aggregate income flow, and the share of total income going to labor are a complex which must be considered as a whole, as Pigou has himself pointed out [9]—one of many instances in his later writings which reveal how profoundly his thinking has been changed as a result of the vigorous theoretical discussions stemming from Keynes' *General Theory*. In a memoir on Keynes, prepared by direction of the Council of King's College, Cambridge University, Pigou gives it as his opinion that a major contribution of Keynes was "to bring into the centre of the picture and illuminate with strong light, aspects of economic analysis whose vital significance for practice had not been seen before. Thus, while nobody could ever have formally argued that, because reduction in money wages in a particular industry usually increases employment there, *therefore* a reduction all around would usually increase employment all around, nevertheless the possible indirect effects of wage cuts upon prices and incomes had certainly not received adequate attention. Keynes brought this central and very important matter to the forefront of discussion." [10]

Aggregate demand, wage rates, and employment do indeed stand in a certain relation to each other. This no one denies. Given the wage rate, employment will be uniquely determined by the volume of aggregate demand. The important question for cycle policy, however, is: Where do we break into this circle? Shall we manipulate wage rates, or shall we manipulate aggregate demand?

7 *Ibid.*, p. 284.

8 *Ibid.*, p. 288.

9 A. C. Pigou, "Employment Policy and Sir William Beveridge," *Agenda*, August, 1944.

10 Pigou, in *John Maynard Keynes*, Printed for King's College, Cambridge, 1949, p. 22.

The older policy was to manipulate wage rates, it being assumed that demand was given.

Now it is the modern view, strongly advanced by Keynes, that the way to increase employment is to raise aggregate demand while holding money wage rates substantially stable. Aggregate demand could, Keynes believed, be increased by fiscal and monetary policy, with prices and wage rates remaining relatively stable. About this there is now substantial agreement. Pigou has recently said quite plainly that he does not favor "attacking the problem of unemployment by manipulating wages rather than by manipulating demand." [11]

This represents a major change in cycle policy. During the decade of the twenties, it was generally believed that a flexible wage policy during both the boom and the depression was appropriate. The modern view is that if money wages are raised in the boom faster than increases in labor productivity, the effect is inflationary; and similarly that general wage reductions in the depression period accelerate the deflation.[12]

Fiscal Policy

Finally, we consider the marked change in attitude with respect to monetary and fiscal policy. In the twenties, it was generally believed that fiscal policy was subject to very rigid limits. The scope and magnitude of public intervention was severely limited by the tenets of so-called "sound finance." State action on a sufficiently large scale to cope with a serious depression could not, it was believed, be undertaken without destroying the workability and sound functioning of the monetary and financial structure. Hence only a very moderate cyclical policy was believed possible.

[11] *Lapses from Full Employment,* Macmillan & Co., Ltd., London, 1945.

[12] See *Economic Stability in the Post-War World,* Report of the Delegation on Economic Depressions, Part II, League of Nations, 1945, in which the general conclusion is reached "that a general wage cut would intensify domestic deflation" (p. 129). Also note this statement: "We believe that it would be unwise to attempt either a general increase or a uniform reduction of wage rates during a depression . . ." (p. 128). Adjustment of wage rates as between different trades and industries might of course lead to a better balance in the whole wage structure (see pp. 128–129).

Ironing Out the Cycle

This attitude, moreover, reinforced the view that cycle policy should consist simply of ironing out relatively moderate oscillations, such as the inventory recessions of 1924 and 1927. Now in deep depression periods, fixed capital expenditures and inventory investment both decline. The total effect of this fall in investment can only be assessed by taking account also of the induced decline in private consumption expenditures. To prevent this induced decline in private consumer expenditures would require that some *offset* be found to compensate fully for the decline in private capital expenditures. But in 1932 private capital outlays were $15.5 billion smaller than in 1929. This left a gap in income formation equal to more than five times the entire federal budget of 1929.[13] The gap to be filled was stupendous, though the figure of $15 billion certainly overstates the case, since correction must be made for the secondary induced decline in investment caused by the cumulative collapse itself. There was nowhere in the cycle-policy thinking of the twenties any preparation for a depressional onslaught anywhere near approaching the violence of the 1929–32 crash. We were perhaps prepared in our thinking on counter-cyclical policy to fight (if we may pose the problem in military terms) an invading army of one million, but not an army of fifteen million.

The volume of aggregate demand created by market forces (private consumption plus private capital expenditures) was not adequate to maintain full employment. Given the prevailing consumption function, the gap to be filled exceeded by a considerable margin the maintainable rate of private investment. The gap was indeed filled in boom years. But the boom-time excess of investment over the maintainable rate only prepared the way for a serious deficiency in total outlays in subsequent years. Accordingly, if cycle policy was not prepared to cope with the fundamental problem of aggregate demand, nothing could be done except perhaps to moderate somewhat the swings of the cycle.

The task confronting the makers of cycle policy was very much underestimated in the decade of the twenties. It was underestimated because it was not recognized how far the capital out-

[13] The federal budget in 1929 was $2,958,000,000.

lays in the good years outran the long-run maintainable rate. So long as it was believed that investment could be maintained indefinitely, it was easy to be optimistic about the feasibility of ironing out relatively moderate oscillations. Indeed, the oscillations of the period 1922–29 (*vide* the mild recessions of 1924 and 1927) were of such a gentle character that people began to scout the danger of another serious depression.

The Transfer of Expenditure from Good to Bad Times

In this climate of opinion it was to be expected that fiscal policy should be conceived in narrow and restricted terms. In fact, nothing was proposed except the transfer of some part of the regular public works from good times to bad. A. L. Bowley, conceiving of the typical cycle in terms of unemployment ranging from 2½ per cent to 7½ per cent, estimated the scale of adjustment needed to iron out the cycle. According to his estimates a very moderate transfer of expenditure from good to bad years could iron out the cycle.[14] In the United States Otto T. Mallery was a pioneer in the long-range planning of public works, and under his leadership legislation looking modestly in this direction was passed in Pennsylvania in 1917, and copied in California in 1921. Said Wesley Mitchell in 1923: "Clearly the average annual volume of construction work now undertaken by various public bodies runs high in the hundreds of millions, and a considerable fraction of this imposing total can be allocated on the basis of the business cycle without detriment to social welfare. Further, it is quite possible that in addition to construction work, public purchases of many standard supplies might advantageously be planned on this basis."[15]

The New Horizon

No one in the twenties could have been expected to foresee the magnitude and the intractable character of the collapse of 1929–32. The magnitude of the depression can be judged in

14 See *Is Unemployment Inevitable?*, The Macmillan Company, 1924, pp. 367–368.

15 Wesley Mitchell, "The Problem of Controlling Business Cycles," in Edie's *The Stabilization of Business*, The Macmillan Company, New York, 1923.

terms of the decline of capital expenditures, and the intractability of the depression is traceable to the high saturation reached after seven years of continuous high rates of capital formation. For a depression of this extent the then current ideas regarding fiscal policy—mainly a moderate transfer of standard public works—were hopelessly inadequate. Thus all countries were caught quite unprepared. And it was not possible to orient thinking to the vastness of the task until the stark realities of the Great Depression forced wide open the narrow horizon within which cycle policy had theretofore moved. Even so, it was simply not possible to conceive the dimensions of the problem until the war shattered the inadequate yardsticks which habitual thinking had regarded as adequate guides for policy.

The deficiency of capital and consumption expenditures in the years 1930–40 inclusive, below the 1929 level, is presented in Table XXIX. The aggregate figure is $300 billion—an accumulated total consisting of $100 billion of capital expenditures and $200 billion of consumer expenditures.

TABLE XXIX

Year	*Gross Private Domestic Investment Deficiency below the 1929 Level*	*Private Consumption Deficiency below the 1929 Level*
1930	$ 5.6	$ 8.0
1931	10.4	17.6
1932	15.0	29.6
1933	14.5	32.5
1934	13.0	26.9
1935	9.7	22.6
1936	7.5	16.3
1937	4.4	11.7
1938	9.5	14.3
1939	6.8	11.3
1940	2.8	6.8
Total, 1930–40:	$99.2	$197.6

These data give a measure of the kind of problem that is presented when a high degree of capital saturation is reached and capital outlays shrink to low levels, inducing a further decline in expenditures all around, both for investment and for consumption goods. The mere transfer of even a sizable proportion of public capital expenditures from good times to bad times could plainly have made only a negligible impression. Something quite different was required—namely, the creation of new demand to take the place of the declining capital outlays. Had the decline in capital expenditures been offset by a fully compensating fiscal program, we can be sure that private consumption expenditures would not have declined. Moreover, had a vigorous compensatory program been instituted, the *secondary* or *induced* decline in investment outlays would not have occurred. To assert that it would be necessary to fill the entire gap of $100 billion capital-outlay deficiency would be a gross exaggeration. Indeed, had the deficiency of the first three years, amounting to $30 billion, been fully and boldly met, the terrific *secondary* depression which was induced by the collapse itself might well have been in large part avoided.

This is the kind of situation that has to be faced, and which we are likely, sooner or later, to be confronted with again. A moderate transfer of expenditures would serve if it were only a question of mild oscillations. It does not meet the situation presented by the onslaught of a great depression.

Employment Policy in Democratic Countries

The current status of modern cycle policy can best be judged in terms of the pronouncements of leading democratic countries, beginning with the epoch-making White Paper on Employment Policy issued by the United Kingdom Government in May, 1944,[16] and followed shortly by somewhat similar pronouncements in a number of other countries including Canada, Australia, Sweden, and the United States.[17] These declarations may perhaps best be taken as indicative of the new trend in political thinking with

16 The Employment Policy Paper was issued by the Churchill Government. The victory of the Labor Party in July, 1945, made it evident that the country had in some respects moved considerably beyond the White Paper of 1944.

17 See Alvin H. Hansen, *Economic Policy and Full Employment*, McGraw-Hill Book Co., 1947, Chapters V–X, for a full discussion of the various governmental programs, including the Employment Act of 1946 in the United States.

respect to cycle policy. They represent hopes and plans; there is still the job of developing the institutional machinery and administrative experience needed for an effective cycle policy. In fact, in the first postwar years the problems related to the control of inflation. The test with respect to depression policy still lies ahead.

It is fully recognized in the White Paper that the task of postwar reconstruction would ensure full employment and even overfull employment for a considerable period. And the paper directs considerable attention to these problems. But in the light of past experience the danger, sooner or later, of unemployment and depression is envisaged. The government accordingly announced its acceptance of responsibility for the maintenance of a "high and stable level of employment." Such a pronouncement was definitely something new in government cycle policy.

The first step in such a policy "must be to prevent total expenditures from falling away." The total demand for goods and services must be maintained at a high level. Variations in private expenditure on capital equipment and fluctuations in the foreign balance are recognized as key trouble areas; yet it must be admitted that the programs suggested in the White Paper for moderating these fluctuations are not highly convincing. In practice, under the Labour Government, resort has thus far been had mainly to direct controls both of investment and of the foreign balances. Public investment, it is urged in the White Paper, should be planned ahead to offset, as far as possible, fluctuations in private investment, and the government should be prepared to check and reverse the decline in consumer expenditures which normally follows as a secondary response to the falling off in private capital outlays.

In this paper the government expresses the belief that the power of public expenditures to check the onset of a depression has been underestimated in the past. The crucial moment for public intervention is at the very beginning of the decline. It is then, says the White Paper, that it is necessary to press forward quickly with public expenditures. This requires a new outlook—the view "that periods of trade recession provide an opportunity to improve the permanent equipment of society by the provision of better housing, public buildings, means of communication, power and water supplies, etc." [18] The government announced that it was "prepared to accept in the future the responsibility for taking action at the earliest stage to arrest a threatened slump." [19]

With respect to ways and means to stabilize consumption, a scheme was suggested for varying the social insurance contributions so that as unemployment rose, the contributions rate would be cut. Additional money would thus be left in the hands of millions of employed workers, and this would help to maintain the demand for consumers' goods. Consideration was also given (without recommendation) to (a) varying the income tax rate, and (b) a system of deferred credits under which (tax rates remaining unaltered over the cycle) a part of the tax collected in good times would be treated as a credit repayable to taxpayers in bad times.[20]

Vigorous action to arrest a slump would almost inevitably require deficit financing. On this matter the British White Paper is not altogether clear. On the one hand there is discussion about balancing the budget *over the cycle,* and on the other it is suggested that a *secular* growth in debt may be permitted in view of the expected growth (under a policy of expansion) in the national income.

The Canadian Paper on Employment and Income and the government's declaration in the Dominion-Provincial Conference on Reconstruction in August, 1945, is definite and outspoken with respect to deficit financing and depression policy. It was proposed that in periods of declining business activity public expenditures should be boldly expanded, while at the same time tax rates should be reduced. This of course would result in large deficits. "The Government is not only prepared to accept these but will deliberately plan them in periods of threatened depression in order to give the economy a stimulus and relieve unemployment." [21]

---

[18] Cmd. 6527, p. 22.
[19] *Ibid.*, p. 16.
[20] For a full discussion of the White Paper involving a variety of proposals see Hansen, *Economic Policy and Full Employment,* Chapter V.
[21] Dominion Provincial Conference, August, 1945, p. 60.

The government planned enlarged public expenditures in a variety of directions, including resource development projects, housing and urban redevelopment, social security programs, and farm programs. "The modern governmental budget must be a balance wheel of the economy; its very size today is such that if it were allowed to fluctuate up and down *with* the rest of the economy instead of deliberately *counter* to the business swings it would so exaggerate booms and depressions as to be disastrous." [22]

With respect to the public debt, the Canadian Paper on Employment and Income noted that, despite the growth in the national debt during the war, "the steady reduction in the rate of interest, acquisition of revenue producing assets, and the rise in the national income have served to keep the cost of carrying the debt down to about the same relative weight it had in 1939." As the national income grows (in the United States the national income in constant-value dollars has historically doubled every twenty to twenty-five years) the debt may also grow without raising the *ratio* of debt to income.

Thus the Canadian government considered the postwar debt problem quite manageable, and indeed in a forthright manner announced its deliberate intention "to incur deficits and increases in the national debt resulting from its employment and income policy, whether that policy in the circumstances is best applied through increased expenditures or reduced taxation." [23] In periods of buoyant employment and income, the government would plan for surpluses. These were in fact achieved (as was also true for some years in the United States) in the highly prosperous postwar years. Indeed, a policy of deficit financing as a means of coping with a serious depression can only be carried out successfully by a country which has acquired a high degree of financial responsibility, involving the capacity to tax heavily and to run budgetary surpluses whenever inflationary pressures appear.

It must not be supposed that England, Canada, or any of the other countries making postwar pronouncements on employment policy relied exclusively on the fiscal operations of the central government as means of promoting adequate aggregate

---

22 *Ibid.*

23 Paper on *Employment and Income,* presented to Parliament, 1945, p. 21.

demand. The Papers, in fact, cover a wide range of policies, of which a considerable part has to do with long-range programs involving the development of a vigorous, dynamic, and expanding economy operating mainly in terms of a system of private enterprise. Indeed, the Canadian government expressly stated that it did *not* look to the expansion of government enterprise to provide, to any large degree, additional employment.[24]

[24] *Employment and Income,* p. 5.

27 · *The President's Economic Reports*

Machinery for Cycle Policy

The Employment Act of 1946 requires the President to transmit to the Congress, at the beginning of each regular session, a new type of message—the *Economic Report of the President to the Congress.* It serves as map and chart from which one can more clearly see where the American economy stands and where it is going. It is no exaggeration to say that the President's Economic Report is the most important economic document of our times. All over the world it is read with anxiety and close attention, since the American economy represents so large a part of world production that fluctuations in it transmit powerful impulses throughout the trading world. The stability and prosperity of the United States have become a matter of general concern for all Western nations.

The Employment Act was designed "to maintain employment, production, and purchasing power." The Congress declared in this act the "continuing policy and responsibility of the Federal Government . . . to coordinate and utilize all its plans, functions, and resources" to achieve this goal. The President's Economic Report must set forth "a review of the economic program of the Federal Government and a review of economic conditions affecting employment in the United States," together with a "program for carrying out the policy" declared in the act.

The act established in the Executive Office of the President a Council of Economic Advisers to assist and advise the President in the preparation of the Economic Report, to gather timely and authoritative information concerning economic developments and economic trends, to appraise the various programs and activities of the federal government in the light of the policy declared in the act, to develop and recommend to the President national economic policies designed "to avoid economic fluctuations or to diminish the effects thereof, and to maintain employment, production, and purchasing power."

The act, moreover, established a Joint Committee on the Economic Report, to be composed of seven members of the Senate and seven members of the House of Representatives. It is the function of this Joint Committee to make a continuing study of matters relating to the Economic Report, and, as a guide to the various committees of Congress, to file a report with the Senate and the House of Representatives containing its findings and recommendations with respect to each of the main recommendations made by the President in the Economic Report.

This is the machinery which has been set up in the United States to implement public policy with respect to economic stability and economic expansion. In the Economic Reports of the President one can find an authoritative statement of the program of the federal government with respect to the control of cyclical fluctuations and the maintenance of high levels of employment.

Cycle Policy in Action

Thus in the Economic Report of 1949 the President had very much to say about cycle policy. He thrust aside the thesis that continued prosperity could be left to the chance play of market forces. "Courageous and positive action" is required, he said, "to combat the remaining dangers of post-war inflation," to build "strong bulwarks against deflation and depression," and to move forward to "new levels of sustained prosperity."

Consider the fiscal and monetary policy employed by the government since the passage of the Employment Act of 1946. This relates, on the one hand, to policies actually pursued and to programs urged by the President to fight the postwar inflation; and on the other to programs and plans designed to check depression and deflation.

Inflationary pressures were let loose when Congress terminated general price controls in July, 1946. Wholesale prices moved up rapidly for nine months, slowed down in the next nine months, and flattened out thereafter. From June, 1946, to March, 1947, wholesale prices increased 32.9 per cent and consumers' prices increased 17.3 per cent; from March, 1947, to December, 1947, wholesale prices increased 8.8 per cent and consumers' prices 6.8 per cent.[1] In eighteen months, the main inflationary forces had spent themselves, bottlenecks had largely been eliminated, the supply "pipe lines" were again generally full, total physical production had substantially increased; a marked improvement had occurred in agricultural and food supplies; the more pressing pent-up demands had been satisfied; total demand was moving into balance for the time being with total supply.

The sharp break in grain prices early in 1948 signaled the turn of prices. Concern was felt lest this break might "set off a train of consequences similar to those which, following World War I, had turned the boom into a deflation of unusual depth and rapidity in 1920–22." [2] That this episode had not been repeated, the President argued, was not just sheer luck. "Affirmative national policies and greater caution in the business community combined with other developments to make the economy more shock-resistant." Among these developments he referred to the farm price support program, which tended to prevent "a chain reaction of price breaks in other markets," the stronger financial and banking structure (deposit insurance, margin requirements, securities exchange regulations, etc.), the accumulated savings, and the social security programs.[3] Finally, he asserted that the "Government had so employed a large budget surplus as to pre-

1 Note that these are not *points* in the index numbers, but actual *percentage* increases over the base months indicated.

2 *Economic Report of the President to the Congress,* January, 1949, p. 2.

3 "In general, large Government budgets make an economy more resistant to shock, and on the revenue side the progressive income tax increases flexibility." *The Annual Economic Review,* Council of Economic Advisers, January, 1949, p. 74.

vent the inflation from becoming as hectic as it otherwise would have been; and such policies served to moderate the extent of the reaction." [4]

In 1949, there developed an inventory recession. Inventory accumulation declined from a rate of 9 billion dollars (annual rate) in the last quarter of 1948 to a liquidation of inventories at the rate of 1.5 billion dollars in the fourth quarter of 1949—a total decline of 10.5 billion dollars. In addition, there was in the same period a decline of approximately 3 billion dollars in the investment in producers' durable equipment. This 13.5 billion dollars' decline in private business investment mainly accounted for the recession. Consumption expenditures declined by only 3 billion dollars. This relatively small drop in consumption partly reflected the well-known consumption-expenditure lag (in very short-run movements) and partly the "built-in" cushions against depression. Thus unemployment benefits payments increased from 80 million dollars per month in December, 1948, to 170 million dollars in December, 1949.

Fiscal policy played an important role in cushioning the 1949 recession. Government cash payments increased 7 billion dollars from 1948 to 1949, and tax receipts substantially declined. Thus a cash surplus of 7 billion dollars in 1948 was converted into a cash deficit of 3 billion dollars in 1949. This shift-over of 10 billion dollars helped to sustain private spending and played a major role in preventing the recession from turning into a more serious depression.

Here we see fiscal policy in action, in the rough-and-tumble of political forces. It is not the ideal cycle policy of the theorist; but it is nonetheless profoundly influenced by theory.

Anti-Inflation Program: 1947–48

Stripped of its general price control powers, the government was nevertheless far from helpless in its struggle to control inflation. First and foremost was the large excess of federal cash revenues over expenditures, running at the rate of $6 billion in 1947 and $8 billion in 1948. This was the main bulwark of the government's anti-inflationary policy.

[4] *Economic Report of the President to the Congress,* January, 1949, p. 2.

Second, there was the management of the public debt and monetary policy. The budget surplus was used to retire bonds held by the banks, especially the Federal Reserve Banks. This tended to reduce bank reserves and thereby to restrain credit expansion, since it put banks under pressure to obtain additional reserves. Reserves could, to be sure, be recouped through member-bank sale of U.S. securities to the Federal Reserve Banks. The government policy to support the bond market thus made it impossible to exercise any tight control over bank reserves. The government was confronted with a very complex situation in which it found it necessary to pursue the "dual objective of maintaining a stable and orderly market for Government securities and at the same time attempting to prevent an excessive credit expansion." [5] Achievement of the first objective necessarily limited the scope of the second. The President voiced the view—widely supported by competent economic and financial opinion—that the maintenance of stability in the government bond market was important for the stability of the economy. Said the Council of Economic Advisers: "The stability of the Government bond market has been a significant element in the smooth post-war reconversion. This stability has contributed to the underlying strength of the financial structure of the country. It would be a serious error to introduce new elements of uncertainty and possible financial disturbances which would follow a change of the policy with respect to the support of bond prices." [6] Indeed, "it is entirely conceivable that, in some circumstances, the unsettling of financial markets following complete removal of the peg would contribute to a serious business downturn." [7]

Other aspects of monetary policy related to (a) raising the rate on government short-term securities, the increase in the discount rate, and the rise in short-term rates generally, (b) raising the reserve requirements under the authority granted by Congress in August, 1948, and (c) the regulation of consumer installment credit. But when all is said and done, by far the most important weapon in the fiscal-monetary arsenal was: first, the expenditure-

[5] *The Annual Economic Review*, Council of Economic Advisers, January, 1949, p. 41.

[6] *Ibid.*, p. 43.

[7] *Ibid.*, p. 42.

restraining effect, or *income* effect, of a large budgetary surplus; and second, the *monetary* effect of using this surplus to retire bank-held debt. Supplementing this was the promotion of sales of savings bonds by the Treasury, with the co-operation of banks and business firms throughout the country.

A Possible Downturn

The prosperity of the postwar years, said the President, rested in considerable part on somewhat temporary factors which were the aftermath of the war. "The momentum of war-created demand and war-created purchasing power has waned, and we must now rely more fully on currently generated purchasing power to absorb a full output of goods and services. We must be more than ever on the alert to make sure that withdrawal or lessening of temporary demand factors is not accompanied by a reduction of productive activity and the mounting of unemployment to which this would lead." [8] The leaders of our enterprise economy, said the President, "should draw sustaining confidence from the fact that it is the policy of the Government under the Employment Act of 1946 to use all its resources to avoid depression and to maintain continuous prosperity." [9]

The President recognized that effective action involves a highly flexible policy. It is essential, he said, "to have available a range of governmental measures which can be applied as brake or as accelerator according to the need." Economic stability will not be realized automatically; it depends upon our capacity and willingness to adopt the salutary policies which are required by changing circumstances and to put them into effect.

"The vigorous commitment by the Government to an anti-inflation policy should not obscure the fact that the Government is equally committed to an anti-depression policy . . . And in times like the present, when the economic situation has mixed elements, the Government needs both anti-inflationary weapons and anti-deflationary weapons so that it will be ready for either contingency." [10]

---

[8] *The Economic Report of the President to the Congress,* January, 1949, p. 3.
[9] *Ibid.,* p. 3.
[10] *Ibid.*

"The national tax policy should be flexible and should be promptly adjusted to the changing needs of business and consumers in the course of evolving economic events. The same dictates of prudent policy which call for higher taxes in a period of inflation would call for tax adjustments designed to counteract any serious recessionary movement."[11] It is essential, said the Council in its 1949 *Annual Economic Review,* "to permit fiscal policy to be reversed if recessionary trends should later develop which might call both for tax reductions to stimulate business and markets and for additional public expenditures."[12]

The Problems of Overfull Employment

As we have seen in earlier chapters in this book, very often in the past, booms have presented no serious inflationary pressures. Investment was, indeed, often in excess of the long-run maintainable rate, but it was not in excess of the current flow of saving. Aggregate demand did not outrun aggregate supply. There was no excess draft on productive resources. In the period following the Second World War, however, this was not the case. On top of the postwar capital requirements there were other very large unavoidable programs—national defense and international reconstruction. There were, moreover, the demands for better housing, urban redevelopment, regional resource development, a greatly expanded public health program, improved educational facilities, and extended social security coverage, together with higher benefits. Our productive resources were clearly inadequate for an early fulfillment of all these needs.

Now this is the kind of situation that is likely to confront, even in ordinary peacetimes, a society that goes all out for the security and welfare of the people. The result will be overfull employment. The productive resources will not be adequate to meet the pressing needs of the community as a whole.

In circumstances such as these, government outlays, investment outlays, and consumption outlays are in sharp competition with one another. There is not enough production to go around, even at full employment. Something must be curtailed. The in-

[11] *Ibid.,* pp. 9, 10.
[12] *Annual Economic Review,* 1949, p. 38.

flationary process itself is a method of curtailment, usually having the effect of suppressing consumption. If inflation is to be avoided, either private spending (on investment and consumption) or government spending must be reduced; and if it is not deemed possible or desirable to reduce the government outlays, then private spending must be cut either by an increase in taxation or by direct controls.

Under the circumstances confronting the country in the early postwar years the President did indeed favor the curtailment of the less essential government outlays. Federal public works were held to a low level—a total of $1.3 billion in 1948, roughly the same value as in 1940 despite a doubling of construction costs and accumulated needs. But there were some areas in which he believed it necessary to continue to develop our resources for healthy growth—programs of high priority needed to conserve and increase the strength of our nation. "We must fulfil the requirements of our essential programs—national defense, international reconstruction, and domestic improvements and welfare—even if doing so may require the temporary exercise of selective controls in our economy. We want the greatest amount of economic freedom that is consistent with the security and welfare of the people; but we do not want to sacrifice that security and welfare because of narrow and selfish concepts as to the acceptable limits of government action. If we could have the amount of national defense that we need, make the contributions to international reconstruction to which we are committed, and at the same time maintain and expand our standards of living now and in the future without any kind of selective controls over our economy, that would be most highly desirable. And it is possible that we may not, in fact, be forced to use such controls. But we would rather have these relatively unpleasant restrictions on our freedom of action for a while than imperil our security or allow our human and material resources to deteriorate." [13]

Inadequate productive resources prevent the pursuit of "affirmative programs for housing and health, for education and resource development . . . with the speed and on the scale that

[13] *Economic Report of the President to the Congress,* January, 1949, p. 9.

would otherwise be desirable." [14] To reconcile these objectives, the President sought to strike the safest balance. That balance involved (a) a controlled program of government spending regarded as necessary and essential, (b) a heavy program of taxation, and finally, (c) authority to impose, if necessary, certain selective controls. These controls included allocation powers, selective price and related wage controls, and export controls.

The President asked, in the event of the recurrence of inflationary pressures, for authority to employ mandatory controls over key materials in short supply. The problems of acute shortage could not, he thought, be adequately met by voluntary allocation agreements. These mandatory allocation powers, while authorized, would be employed on a selective basis only when and where they proved to be needed.

Similarly, he asked that selective price control authority be made available to the government. The President did not ask for general or over-all price control. All that was needed, he believed, was the authority to introduce, if conditions so warranted, control over the prices of certain critical materials. "Legislation to authorize selective price control should encourage voluntary adjustments without the actual imposition of price control. It is in this spirit that I would administer the authority. But I am firmly convinced that such voluntary efforts, which have been tried with partial but insufficient results since the middle of 1946, cannot meet the problem unless the Government possesses the authority to act firmly. With such authority available, however, its actual application might not be required. It should be supplemented with the provision permitting the Government to order the withholding of price advances for a reasonable period while public inquiry into their justification is being made." [15]

Reaffirming his belief in "wage increases based upon productivity," the President asked that the government be granted authority to limit wage adjustments which would force a break through the price ceiling.[16]

---

14 *Ibid.*, p. 8.
15 *Ibid.*, p. 13.
16 *Ibid.*, p. 13.

Finally, the large volume of exports under the foreign aid program made it essential, he felt, that the existing powers of control over exports be extended.[17]

This is where the President came out, confronted as he was with the cold realities of a given political and economic situation. One might view the problem differently in an abstract discussion of monetary and fiscal policy where one could comfortably set aside awkward and inconvenient facts. And it is precisely for this reason that I have chosen the method adopted in this chapter in order to set out vividly the difficult, and often conflicting, practical issues involved. I have not attempted here to resolve these issues.[18] In the final analysis, the conclusion which anyone will reach will depend heavily upon his evaluation of factors that lie far beyond the scope of economics, involving broad aspects of social and political philosophy. To a considerable measure Congress did not agree with the President. In part, this was due to a different appraisal of the circumstances; and with respect to a large section of the Congress it was due to a different economic philosophy. The issues remain to be thrashed out on the political battlefields of the future.

Long-Run Programs for Growth and Expansion

According to the so-called "sound finance" view, it is only in periods of prosperity that governments can "afford" to go forward with needed improvement projects. In depression periods, tax revenues fall off and so the country is "too poor" to undertake such programs. But this is looking at a monetary mirage and not at realities. What we "can afford" must in the final analysis be determined in terms of the optimum uses to which our productive resources can be put. It is in periods of high prosperity that we cannot afford to do many things that are urgently needed, for the very good reason that there is not sufficient productive capacity of labor, capital, and other resources to do everything which may justifiably be desired. This was notably the case, for example, in 1947–48. It is in periods of slackening private capital outlays that

---

[17] *Ibid.*, p. 14.

[18] In this connection see Hansen, *Economic Policy and Full Employment* (1947) and *Monetary Theory and Fiscal Policy* (1949).

we can best "afford" the public improvement and welfare projects of which the community is in need.

In the *Annual Economic Review* (January, 1949) the Council of Economic Advisers presented a substantial section on "balanced economic growth." It called attention to the tremendous underuse of productive resources in the thirties, and the fears, expressed by many, of a return to underemployment conditions after the postwar restocking boom. The large national defense and foreign aid programs did indeed considerably modify this prospect.

The Council stated its conviction that continuing high and stable levels of employment will not just come automatically, and it recognized that "decisions affecting the whole economy which we make from year to year will be more intelligent if we take a longer look ahead." [19] It examined the investment potentialities in manufacturing, electric utilities, mining facilities, railroads, agriculture, forests, housing, and commercial construction. It was suggested that the long-run investment needs might require private capital outlays equal to 11 or 12 per cent of the gross national product. This was considerably less than the proportion of the nation's economic budget (about 17 per cent) which had gone into private domestic investment in 1948. Moreover, it was expected and hoped that national defense and foreign aid programs would decline as general world conditions improved. Accordingly, some offsets would be needed. For one thing, the consumption function might have to be raised, permitting a consumption of, say, 75 per cent of gross national product (instead of 70 per cent, as in 1948). Again, government outlays on public improvement and welfare projects might have to be increased in order to take the place of the decline in defense and foreign reconstruction expenditures; or if the consumption function could not be raised sufficiently, public investment and welfare outlays would need to be still further increased. One way to raise the consumption function would be to cut taxes.

The heavy postwar demands for national security and foreign

---

[19] *Annual Economic Review,* January, 1949, p. 50. This review was signed by Edwin G. Nourse, generally regarded as a highly conservative economist, and by Leon H. Keyserling and John D. Clark, often referred to as New Deal economists.

aid had required some reduction and deferment of essential programs relating to the conservation and development of natural resources. "Yet the requirements of a high-level economy for agricultural and forest products, oil, minerals, electric power, and other basic materials can be met only by early action." [20]

Water resources and power represent important areas for expanded public investment programs. These include irrigation, navigation, flood control, hydroelectric power, the construction of transmission lines, and industrial and municipal uses of water. The conservation and efficient use of our land resources involves public outlays for the control of erosion, for soil conservation, for drainage and irrigation, and for the production of concentrated fertilizer. Our depleted forest resources call, on the one hand, for the regulation of privately owned forest properties in order to develop a sustained yield—the timber cut still far exceeds annual growth—and, on the other hand, for an expanded public investment program in forest resources. The development of a "unified program for the development of water, agriculture, forests, and other resources" suggests an extension of the "successful experiment in the Tennessee Valley." Experience has shown that an authority of this type can co-ordinate effectively a variety of programs and co-operate with states and localities and with private individuals and groups. Whether or not precisely the same methods are applicable to other river valleys, the "programs in the Missouri River and Columbia River and other river basins should be examined in order to perfect coordinated development plans." [21]

A vast field for useful public investment (precluded from adequate fulfillment by the grim military expenditures now in prospect) is that of urban redevelopment and housing. A million or more new dwelling units in urban areas need to be built each year for a ten-year period.[22]

In July, 1949, Congress enacted a comprehensive housing measure—the Housing Act of 1949. It is one of the most far-

---

[20] *Ibid.*, p. 67.

[21] *Ibid.*, p. 69.

[22] *Economic Report of the President to the Congress,* January, 1949, p. 16.

reaching planning measures thus far enacted into law in the United States. It made available, over a five-year period, one billion dollars in loans to assist local communities in eliminating their slums and blighted areas, and 500 million dollars in capital grants to local public agencies to enable them to make land in project areas available for redevelopment at fair values for the uses specified in the redevelopment plans. Provision was in addition made in this act for federal annual contributions to local public housing agencies. These subsidies, together with reasonable rental charges from low-income families, would permit projects amounting to 810,000 dwelling units to be constructed in a six-year period.

A notable feature of the act was its flexible provisions. The President is empowered, within limits, to expand or contract the loans and grants, and to increase or decrease the construction "starts" within any one year if such action is indicated as helpful to promote economic stability.

Equally important are the needs with respect to the improvement of our human resources, particularly programs relating to education and health. In his Economic Report for January, 1948, the President called attention to the inadequacy of our educational plant. "State school officials report minimum needs for 7.5 billion dollars of capital outlays for elementary and secondary schools —twice as great as total construction expenditures for all levels of education during the decade of the twenties." He referred to the maldistribution of educational opportunities. "Federal aid to elementary and secondary education should contribute to that equalization of opportunity in various parts of the country which will fit our youth for living and working in the kind of economy that we shall have when they are grown." [23] Health "affords another example of the connection between the economic objective of maximum production and the humanitarian objective of improved well-being." [24] On these grounds the President urged the Congress to enact a comprehensive national health program.

23 *Economic Report of the President to the Congress,* January, 1948, p. 70.
24 *Ibid.,* p. 72.

The Korean war and the military expenditures required for international security indicate that we shall in the years ahead be confronted with pressing problems of overemployment and inflation, not problems of unemployment and inadequate demand. The imperious necessities of national security and defense will perforce curtail much-needed governmental programs. "In schools, housing, health and community facilities, resource development and conservation, transportation and other fields, there are enormous discrepancies between the work now being done and the needs of a growing economy." [25]

The Current Status of Cycle Policy in the United States

The Council's discussion with respect to long-run aspects of cycle policy must be viewed as relating largely to proposals and suggestions. Thoroughly worked out long-range programs sufficiently developed to be integrated into an effective cycle policy are largely lacking. Yesterday we were confronted with recession, today with inflation. We are still pretty much on a "twenty-four-hour" basis, improvising when necessity compels action.

The President did indeed, as we have seen in his 1949 Report, utter brave words about being prepared to adjust promptly to changing needs in the course of evolving economic events. But he flatly pronounced in favor of a four-billion-dollar increase in taxes at a time when a "watch and wait" policy was more appropriate, and he stuck to his plan, in the face of changing conditions, to a degree that indicated too great adherence to the principle of rigid "consistency" rather than the flexibility needed in a workable cycle-policy program. Later, in his Mid-year Report, July, 1949, when the 1949 recession was plainly in progress, he withdrew his request for a major increase in taxes. Finally, the Korean crisis in 1950 led to a swift change in tax policy.

Admittedly there are serious difficulties in an administered or managed compensatory cycle program. They relate partly to the overwhelming difficulty of forecasting, of judging accurately where the economy is currently trending; and partly to the stubbornness and inflexibility of the individuals in charge. Confronted

[25] *Annual Economic Review,* January, 1949, p. 77.

with these awkward facts, many have felt it necessary to turn away from conscious management, and to develop instead an automatic scheme of adjustment. An intermediate program is also possible—one in which managed intervention operates within a quasi-automatic pattern. Plans of this character are considered in Chapter 28.

28 · *Current Fiscal and Monetary Proposals*

Recent thinking with respect to cycle policy can best be discussed in terms of concrete proposals made by responsible organizations or groups of experts. I propose in this chapter to discuss three such proposals. The first is the series of pronouncements on monetary and fiscal policy made by the Committee for Economic Development; [1] the second is the policy statement issued by a group of sixteen economists under the auspices of the National Planning Association; [2] and the third is the report by a group of experts appointed by the Secretary-General of the United Nations.[3]

Three Types of Compensatory Programs

All of these reports deal with compensatory measures designed to promote stability. Altogether three types of programs are discussed: (1) built-in flexibility, (2) automatic compensatory counter-measures, and (3) a managed compensatory program.

Built-in flexibility is an automatic system which serves to

1 *Taxes and the Budget,* November, 1947; and *Monetary and Fiscal Policy for Greater Economic Stability,* December, 1948.

2 *Federal Expenditure and Revenue Policies,* Hearing before the Joint Committee on the Economic Report, September 23, 1949, Government Printing Office, Washington, 1949.

3 *National and International Measures for Full Employment,* Department of Economic Affairs, United Nations, December, 1949.

dampen the fluctuations, but which is powerless to promote a positive recovery from a depressed level. The system is so set up that it automatically responds to changed economic conditions. It requires no conscious management. A steeply progressive income tax is one element in such a program. With a fixed system of rates, tax revenues will rise sharply as income increases, and fall sharply as income recedes. Thus a boom tends to develop budgetary surpluses, and depressions budgetary deficits. This is as it should be. Likewise, an unemployment insurance system acts automatically in a compensatory manner. In prosperous periods, with few unemployed, total benefit payments fall, while pay-roll social security tax receipts rise; in depressed periods, with extensive unemployment, total benefit payments rise, while pay-roll tax receipts decline. Social security taxes exceed benefit payments in prosperity, and this acts to restrain the boom; benefit payments (at least in a balanced or "pay-as-you-go" system) exceed social security taxes in depression, and this acts to cushion the decline. Similarly, farm price supports operate to cushion the decline in farmers' income when agricultural prices are falling. A variant from the usual type of price-support program is the proposal under which farmers sell at market price but receive compensatory payments from the government for any gap between the market price and the support price.[4] All these are illustrations of "built-in flexibility" operating on the side of either taxes or expenditures.

While the system of "built-in stabilizers" can dampen the amplitude of fluctuations by cushioning the decline and in some measure braking the boom, it cannot bring about an actual *rise* in income and employment. For this, more positive measures are necessary. But positive counter-measures can also be implemented in an automatic manner. Such an automatic scheme provides for counter-cyclical variations in tax rates, on the one hand, and in government expenditures on the other, with these variations automatically going into effect when certain designated indices rise or fall to specified levels. Thus the specified variations in taxes and expenditures might go into effect when the unemployment index rises or falls above or below a specified range.

---

[4] See T. W. Schultz, *Agriculture in an Unstable Economy*, McGraw-Hill Book Co., 1945, pp. 220–235.

The third type—a managed compensatory program—involves deliberate judgment by the Executive and the Congress as to the timing and execution of a counter-cyclical program. The range of action might be fixed in advance by the Congress, while the responsibility for execution is left with the Executive or with a designated administrator.

A quasi-automatic program, involving a partial approach toward automaticity, could be established as follows: Congress might set up "signposts" to serve as guides for the Executive or administrator. Thus when unemployment reached a certain percentage of the labor force, action by the Executive, while not mandatory, is indicated. Thus within limits established by Congress, the President, directed by market indices as specifically set out in the law, might be guided to "step up," by some multiple, the increases or decreases which are automatically determined. For example, the President might be empowered, within limits fixed by Congress, to alter the basic (first bracket) income tax rates.[5] But this would be an act of judgment and would not involve the mandatory execution of an automatic program. The President would, however, be required to make a quarterly report to Congress on why he had or had not exercised his power to modify, within the established range, the increases or decreases automatically indicated by the series of signposts set up by the plan. Another means of introducing management into an otherwise automatic system might involve the acquiescence of the Joint Committee on the President's Economic Report whenever the President deemed it wise to act within the indicated range.

The CED Program

The Research and Policy Committee of the Committee for Economic Development issued two documents[6] in which they placed at the center of their program, for greater economic stability, compensatory cycle policy. They did not favor a year-by-year balanced budget; instead they favored what they called a

---

[5] See Alvin H. Hansen, *Monetary Theory and Fiscal Policy*, McGraw-Hill Book Co., New York, 1949, Chapter 13.

[6] *Taxes and the Budget*, November, 1947; and *Monetary and Fiscal Policy for Greater Economic Stability*, December, 1948.

"stabilizing budget policy." This involved a scheme which provided automatically for a budgetary surplus in boom years and a budgetary deficit in depressed years. The scale of public expenditures, determined on the basis of social needs, would remain fixed over the cycle, requiring therefore no conscious management. Similarly, the tax rates would remain fixed over the cycle. But a fixed tax rate structure would produce fluctuating revenues if national income fluctuated; indeed, a progressive income tax would produce revenues increasing much more rapidly than income in good years, and falling much more rapidly than income in declining years. The rates, so the CED urged, should be fixed at a level adequate to balance expenditures when employment equals 93 per cent of the labor force, and to provide a surplus of three billion dollars when employment is "full" (defined as equal to 96 per cent of the labor force); if employment should fall below 93 per cent, a deficit would develop. "Set tax rates to balance the budget and provide a surplus for debt retirement at an agreed high level of employment and national income. Having set these rates, leave them alone unless there is some major change in national policy or condition of national life." This scheme would provide an automatic system of compensation which would tend to restrain the boom and cushion the depression. Federal surpluses would be called for in boom years and federal deficit expenditures would be welcomed in depressed years.

The CED wished, however, to supplement this automatic fiscal policy device with related monetary measures designed to strengthen the stabilizing program. In periods of inflation these measures were intended to restrain the rise of total expenditures in the economy. They included: (1) the use of the government surplus to retire debt held by the banking system; (2) the refunding of maturing debt so as to reduce the holdings of the banking system; (3) tightening the reserve position of the banks by Federal Reserve sales of government securities in the open market, by increase of rediscount rates, and/or by increase of reserve requirements; (4) reducing the volume of federal government loans and guarantees of loans. In periods of depression, a reverse set of measures was called for, involving (1) the financing of the government deficit in a way that would induce the banking system to acquire government securities, with such Federal Reserve action in providing additional bank reserves as might be necessary for this purpose; (2) the refinancing of maturing federal debt in part by borrowing from the banking system, including the Federal Reserve Banks; (3) expansion of the money supply and increase of bank reserves by Federal Reserve open-market purchasing of government securities, easing reserve requirements, and reducing rediscount rates; and (4) expanding the volume of federal government loans and guarantees of loans.

Finally, the CED recognized that extreme conditions might require temporary modification of their normal budgetary policy. This was made explicit in the following statement:

"The recommendations of this report are presented in the belief that, if they are combined with appropriate measures in other fields, economic fluctuations can be confined to moderate departures from a high level. Yet it would be foolhardy to ignore the possibility that we may again confront an economic crisis of great magnitude—either severe depression or major inflation. Some extraordinary action must and will be taken if such a crisis appears. An emergency Congressional reduction or increase in tax rates (perhaps with a fixed, automatic termination date) would then be one of the most effective and least dangerous of the available courses." [7]

The NPA Conference

The conference of sixteen economists,[8] held under the auspices of the National Planning Association in September, 1949, made two reports—one dealing with general stabilization policies and procedures, and the other with the immediate or near future situation.[9]

---

[7] *Taxes and the Budget,* Committee for Economic Development, Research and Policy Committee, New York, November, 1947, p. 25.

[8] H. R. Bowen, (Illinois), H. S. Ellis (California), J. K. Galbraith (Harvard), J. K. Hall (Seattle, Washington), A. G. Hart (Columbia), Clarence Heer (North Carolina), E. A. Kincaid (Virginia), S. E. Leland (Northwestern), Paul Samuelson (M.I.T.), L. H. Seltzer (Wayne Univ., Detroit), Sumner Slichter (Harvard), Arthur Smithies (Harvard), Tipton R. Snavely (Virginia), H. Christian Sonne (NPA), Jacob Viner (Princeton), D. H. Wallace (Princeton).

[9] The second report was not signed by Slichter.

In the main report, stress was laid on the impact of government expenditures (federal, state, and local outlays being around \$60,000,000,000) and taxation upon the economy. Both expenditures and taxes affect the state of business. Expenditures tend to expand the market for business, increase employment, and raise prices; tax collections, taken by themselves, tend to shrink the market, contract employment, and lower prices.

Inflation may thus be a sign of a weak government which is too eager to spend and unwilling to tax; and conversely, deflation and depression may indicate too high taxation in relation to the rate of expenditure.[10]

The traditional goal of fiscal policy was to secure a balanced budget every single year. This, indeed, would be appropriate if private investment and saving were in balance. But if in fact the private sector fluctuates more or less violently, a balanced budget would violate the canon of economic stability. When private expenditures and incomes fall, tax rates would have to be increased (or government expenditures reduced) in order to balance the budget. But this would accelerate the decline in the private sector. The opposite is true in inflationary periods.

When the economy is prosperous and stable, with no expectation of change in either direction, the objective of policy should be to "adapt the budget to changes in the government's requirements but to leave its economic impact on total employment and purchasing power unchanged." This could approximately be achieved by matching increases or decreases in expenditures by increases or decreases in tax receipts.[11] In a stable full-employment situation, "taxes should grow or shrink" according to desired changes in expenditures.

If, however, the near future outlook indicated a decline in expenditures in the private sector of the economy (for example, a fall in investment outlays), budgetary changes should be made

---

[10] Inflation may of course also be due to an excess of private investment over savings; and conversely, deflation may be due to a deficiency of private investment in relation to saving.

[11] Even so, the increase (or decrease) in a balanced budget would probably have some expansionist (or contractionist) effect. The word "approximately" suggests that the authors had this in mind. See the discussion of the effect on income of a tax-financed budget in Chapter 12 of this book.

to offset this. New taxes intended to match new expenditure programs should be deferred. If the evidence pointed to inflation, new government programs might be deferred (but new taxes at once imposed, anticipating later revenue needs) and current programs reduced. "Tax reductions that would normally be in order should be deferred."

These adjustments might be sufficient for moderate fluctuations. If, however, a serious recession or inflation was in prospect, more strenuous measures would be required, involving emergency fiscal action.

Emergency fiscal action should include provision for employment projects that can be started and ended quickly. "There can be no social or economic justification for allowing mass unemployment to persist for extended periods at a time when there is abundant need for roads, schools, hospitals, and other useful objects of public expenditures." Such projects would tend to stimulate the demand for the products of private industry, though an overambitious and ill-timed government program might dislocate resources and delay needed price adjustments.

The above discussion relates to legislative action aiming at fiscal adjustment to changing economic developments. But the legislative process is necessarily too slow-moving to make "delicately timed adjustments in fiscal policy." Consideration should therefore be given to two devices looking toward speedy adjustments: (a) automatic flexibility, and (b) formula flexibility.

Automatic flexibility has already in a measure been incorporated into our economic structure. Under the unemployment compensation system, as unemployment increases, total pay-roll taxes decline while benefit payments increase. Also the progressive rate structure in the personal income tax has the effect that tax receipts rise sharply as income and employment rise, and fall sharply in a period of recession. The economists expressed the view that "the existing automatic flexibility makes an important contribution to economic stability, which should not be frittered away." But it is only a "first line of defense." More must be done to cope with serious inflation or depression.

The next step *(formula flexibility)* in the development of fiscal policy should be the enactment by Congress of rules under which tax rates, and perhaps certain expenditure programs, would shift, in accordance with a prearranged schedule, with specified changes in unemployment or prices. These shifts might apply, for example, to the withholding income tax rate and to the length of the period during which unemployed workers could draw benefits. Thus the tax rate might be stepped up by predetermined amounts, in inflationary periods, if the index of *retail prices* rose by a certain figure in the preceding six months; and conversely, the rate might be cut by specified amounts if *production* and *employment* dropped below stated levels or trends.

The conference called attention to the question of granting wider authority to the Executive to initiate changes in the timing and extent of the fiscal program. (Reference might here have been made to the discretionary flexibility actually implemented in the Housing Act of 1949.) [12]

In the second report of the conference, reference was made to the possible need of prearranged legislation to become effective if activity should decline to a specified level. If unemployment should reach the level of 5,000,000, the prearranged temporary emergency measures should be put into effect. These measures included (besides the once-for-all repeal of the wartime excise taxes) the temporary abatement of the first bracket rate (or increase in the exemptions) of the personal income tax, the lengthening of the period of unemployment benefits, the execution of stand-by, ready-to-start public works projects prearranged for this specific purpose. These emergency measures should automatically be terminated when activity again reached a satisfactory level.

A final recommendation stressed the importance of continued preparedness by Congress to make prompt alterations in the policies adopted in any fiscal year in accordance with changed circumstances.

The Report of the U.N. Group of Experts

In the report of the experts appointed by the United Nations, three methods of stabilizing the aggregate demand were suggested: (1) stabilizing the level of private investment, (2) countercyclical variations in public investment outlays to compensate in

[12] See Chapter 27 in this book.

whole or in part for fluctuations in private investment, and (3) counter-cyclical variations in consumer expenditures to compensate for any fluctuations in total investment, public and private combined.

In order to implement counter-cyclical variations in consumer expenditures—the third point referred to above—two types of governmental programs are suggested. On the one hand private consumer expenditures could be raised or lowered by increasing or decreasing consumers' subsidies or family allowances or payments to the unemployed. On the other hand private consumption could be raised or lowered by changing the personal income tax rates, or by lowering or raising the social security contributions and even *reversing* the social security taxes in periods of unemployment so that taxes (contributions) are replaced by "payments to both employers and employees on a pre-determined basis."

Most significant are those portions of the experts' report relating to (a) the fixing of a full employment "target," (b) continuing policies designed to promote stability and expansion, and (c) the automatic system for varying taxes and governmental expenditures.

The report, made as it was for the United Nations, suggested that each country, according to its own particular circumstances, should set a target "expressed in terms of the smallest percentage of unemployment of wage-earners which the country in question can reasonably hope to maintain." This target may be defined as a range rather than as a precise figure. It is suggested that for some countries the range might be 2 to 4 per cent, and for others, 3 to 5 per cent. Any growth of unemployment beyond the limit of the range set as a target could be regarded as evidence of inadequate aggregate demand. It should be the policy of each government to direct its stabilization policy toward "maintaining effective demand at the level necessary to keep unemployment within the target." [13]

---

[13] *National and International Measures for Full Employment, Report by a Group of Experts Appointed by the Secretary-General,* United Nations, Lake Success, New York, December, 1949, p. 74. The economists comprising the group were J. M. Clark, Arthur Smithies, N. Kaldor, Pierre Uri, and E. R. Walker.

The committee recommended the following continuing policies designed to promote stability and growth:

1. "Deliberate and continued action by governments to maintain effective demand at full employment levels." [14] This would involve continued revision from year to year of the entire budgetary program of the government, with respect to both expenditures and taxation. In some countries—where there are serious deficiencies in programs of social security, education, health, housing, and resource development—this might involve increased expenditures. In countries where governmental expenditure programs are adequate it might involve reduction in taxation. Apart from fiscal and budgetary measures, the continuing activity of governments might involve control of monopoly prices and profit margins in order to effect a more equitable distribution of income and to increase private consumption.

2. "Built-in" flexibility such as is provided in the progressive income tax, and in a social security program under which total contributions would rise in good times while total benefit payments would rise in bad times, even though no changes were made in the contribution rates or in the benefit rates. Such a continuing program, while automatic, must be sharply distinguished from the positive counter-cyclical automatic measures involving changes in expenditure and tax rates.

3. Control of the volume of private investment. This would include special credit facilities (e.g., RFC loans to new and small businesses), lending institutions such as the Rural Electrification Administration, insurance and guarantee of private loans (e.g., Federal Housing Administration),[15] and special tax inducements to private investors. To restrain an excessive investment boom it might be desirable to institute control over capital issues, to restrict construction permits, and in some cases to allocate raw materials. It might also be feasible for some countries to co-operate with private industries, such as railroads and the steel industry, in planning long-range investment programs.

4. Planning public investment. For some countries public

---

[14] *Ibid.*, p. 77.

[15] These particular illustrations are not given in the report, but they represent the types of activities suggested.

utilities, transport, and housing lie wholly or in large part within the public sector; accordingly, investment in these areas could largely be planned in a co-ordinated public investment program. Such a program, together with public works construction, could in a measure be used to offset fluctuations in private investment.

5. Stabilization of the agricultural income by means of price support or guaranteed price programs, production payments to support farm income, and international commodity stabilization schemes, such as the International Wheat Agreement.

Finally, we come to what is perhaps the most interesting part of the suggestions made in the experts' report, at least so far as the domestic program is concerned.[16] This relates to the automatic counter-cyclical measures which involve changes in taxation and expenditure rates according to a prearranged announced formula.

It was suggested that legislation be enacted providing that, when unemployment exceeds the range defined in the full-employment target for *three consecutive months,* a specific schedule of changes in rates of taxation and expenditure should automatically become mandatory. This would involve: (a) variations in the income tax rates or, alternatively, variations in the levels of exemption, therefore raising at once the disposable income (income after taxes) of individuals, (b) variations in social security contributions and benefit payments, (c) variations in general sales taxes (applicable to countries with less developed systems of income taxation and social security systems), (d) release of compulsory savings (applicable to countries which have employed this device to fight wartime inflation), (e) introduction of cash payments such as bonuses or subsidies,[17] (f) incorporation of a counter-cyclical public works program into an automatic compensatory scheme.

Legislation authorizing such an automatic system should make it mandatory upon governments to put the measures *automatically* into effect at once when the specified guideposts indicate action. The executive branch of the government should, however, be granted the power to waive the obligations with respect to the

---

16 The international program is discussed in Chapter 31 in this book.

17 In the United States the payment of a veterans' cash bonus in the first half of 1950 contributed greatly to recovery after the 1949 recession.

automatic measures if there is clear evidence that the increase in unemployment is due to causes *other* than a fall in effective demand. In such cases other kinds of measures would be needed, and this rule would prevent blindly carrying out an automatic prescription which might not cure the malady. In the usual case, however, the difficulty is likely to be inadequate aggregate demand.

The Tax-Reduction Multiplier

All these three proposals have referred to tax reduction (leaving governmental expenditures unchanged) as a means of raising demand. In this connection, note should be made of the fact that a given amount of tax reduction would have a magnified effect on aggregate spending, depending upon the size of the "tax-reduction multiplier." [18]

Let us assume that the tax reduction applies to personal incomes alone, not to corporations. Let T stand for the total amount of tax reduction. Now the *initial* increase in spending due to tax remission would depend upon the *marginal propensity to consume out of disposable income* (i.e., personal income after taxes), which we may call "c′." Assume T is \$5 billion and c′ is .8, then the initial increase in spending is c′T, or \$4 billion.

But this increase in spending will raise income by more than \$4 billion. The relevant multiplier, k, is determined by the *marginal propensity to consume out of net national product,* which we may call "c." Thus $k = \frac{1}{1 - c}$. Assume that the marginal propensity to consume out of net national product is .6; then $k = 2.5$. Thus if the initial increase in spending is \$4 billion, the total increase in aggregate demand would be \$10 billion. But the tax reduction was assumed to be \$5 billion. Hence the "tax-reduction multiplier" in this case would be 2.

The "tax-reduction multiplier" is equal to c′ (the marginal propensity to consume out of disposable income) times k (the

---

[18] See Paul Samuelson in *Income, Employment and Public Policy,* W. W. Norton & Co., Inc., 1948, Part I, Chapter VI; also Robert L. Bishop, *ibid.,* Part III, Chapter V; and T. C. Schelling, "Income Determination: A Graphic Solution," *Review of Economics and Statistics,* August, 1948.

multiplier based on the marginal propensity to consume out of net national product). Let k′ stand for the "tax-reduction multiplier." Thus $k' = c'k$. Inserting the values for c′ and k assumed above, $k' = .8 \times 2.5 = 2$. Thus Tk′ equals the total increase in aggregate spending resulting from a personal income tax reduction of the amount T.

29 · *Wage-Price-Profit Policy*

In a highly fluctuating society certain characteristics are necessarily present; and it is always a difficult matter to determine how far these characteristics are responsible for, and how far they merely reflect, the expansion and contraction of economic activity.

The fact that fluctuations occur indicates imbalance and disequilibrium. Outstanding among these evidences of imbalance is the disproportionate volume of investment in the boom phase of the cycle.

Investment and Consumption

Investment and consumption together might, indeed, in some booms be just adequate to provide full employment without inflation. But the boomtime volume of investment, as we have noted again and again in preceding chapters, regularly exceeds (even though there are no inflationary pressures) the long-run maintainable rate.

From this, one might hastily conclude that an appropriate stabilizing policy would be to raise wages, at the expense of profits, in the boom period. As a first approximation, it would appear that this policy would have the effect of reducing the volume of business saving, thereby making less funds available for investment. Investment might thereby be reduced to a level consistent with the long-run requirements of growth. Higher wages, on the other hand, would raise consumption, since wage earners have a high propensity to consume. Thus, it would seem, a balanced ratio of investment to consumption might be achieved on a sustained basis.

In fact, however, the effect might turn out to be very different, for the situation is far more complex than here indicated.

Wages and Aggregate Demand

The problem of the appropriate relation of wages to profits, and of consumption to investment, has to be viewed from both the short-run and the long-run standpoint. And wage rates need to be considered in relation to aggregate demand.

Under fairly normal conditions, wage increases (corrected for productivity changes) may be regarded as more or less neutral so far as employment is concerned, since such increases raise aggregate demand on the one hand and costs on the other. The main effect is therefore a price effect.[1] But under the buoyant psychology which prevails in boom periods, it is reasonable to suppose that the cost-raising effect of wage increases would dampen optimism but little, while the demand-increasing effect would be fully operative. Thus the wage increases, and the consequent rise in consumption outlays, might not supplant investment outlays; indeed, they might stimulate them all the more. Total outlays, fed by wage increases, might thus raise aggregate demand to inflationary levels.

For example, with respect to the nineteen-twenties, it was often said that wages lagged in a period when profits were unduly large. Had wages been raised, however, the probable effect might very likely not have been to check the advance in profits. A round of wage increases might have raised aggregate demand still more and so induced a further rise in investment and profits. Under full-employment conditions and an inflationary boom psychology, an imbalance between wages and profits is not easily remedied by what on the surface appears to be a fairly plausible and obvious method of attack.

Wage-Profit Imbalance

The wage-profit imbalance may in fact be regarded more as a result of cyclical fluctuations than as a cause of it. If this is true,

[1] For a general discussion of modern wage theory, see Alvin H. Hansen, *Monetary Theory and Fiscal Policy* (1949), Chapter 8.

to cure the imbalance it would be necessary first to iron out the cycle at a sustained high level of employment. Once this is done, an attack could then be made on the wage-profit imbalance.

There are two possible methods of attack on the cycle. One is to stabilize the volume of investment directly. The other is to offset fluctuations in private investment by fiscal and monetary policy.

Stabilizing Investment

The first method is perhaps feasible and within the range of practical politics in countries like England and Sweden, in which the state plays so large a role in total investment. First, there is the large area of state-owned enterprises. Second, residential construction is largely, directly or indirectly, under state control. Finally, direct methods of control of private investment (licensing, allocations, etc.) appear to be politically feasible in these countries.

In a country like the United States, private investment is largely outside the range of state intervention. With respect to residential contruction the government does indeed play a growing and an important role. But in other areas state intervention is unimportant, and in peacetime direct controls are, in the American political climate, scarcely feasible.

Offsetting Investment Fluctuations

There remains, however, the method of offsetting fluctuations in private investment by fiscal and monetary policy. Various proposals with respect to this type of policy were discussed in the preceding chapter.

Let us assume that this policy proved reasonably successful. What consequences would be likely to flow from a condition approaching stable and continuing full employment? What would probably be the effect on wage-profit relations, on income distribution, and on the growth of business and labor monopolies in special areas? Could a better balance be reached under these conditions in the cost-price structure and in the consumption-investment ratio than has proved feasible under conditions of rather violent cyclical fluctuations in the past?

Fluctuating Profits

Corporate profits are the most volatile component in the national income, fluctuating from $10.2 billion in 1919 to $1.0 billion in 1921, back to $9.8 in 1929, down to aggregate net *losses* of $3.0 billion in 1932, up to $9.3 profits in 1940 and finally to $34.8 billion in 1948. Table XXX gives data on net profits from 1919 to 1950.[2]

TABLE XXX

Corporate Profits
(in billions)

Year	*Profits before Tax*	*Profits after Tax*
Average, 1919–28	$ 5.8	$ —
1929	9.8	8.4
1930	3.3	2.5
1931	−0.8 (deficit)	−1.3 (deficit)
1932	−3.0 (deficit)	−3.4 (deficit)
1933	0.2	−0.4 (deficit)
1934	1.7	1.0
1935	3.2	2.3
1936	5.7	4.3
1937	6.2	4.7
1938	3.3	2.3
1939	6.5	5.0
1940	9.3	6.4
1941	17.2	9.4
1942	21.1	9.4
1943	25.1	10.6
1944	24.3	10.8
1945	19.7	8.5
1946	23.5	13.9
1947	30.5	18.5
1948	33.9	20.9
1949	27.6	17.0
1950 (1st half)	30.1	18.4

[2] *Report to the Committee on Banking and Currency,* Senate Committee Print No. 4, 79th Congress, 1st Session; and the *Economic Report of the President to the Congress,* January, 1950, p. 177.

A more meaningful picture of the position of profits in the economy can be obtained by relating profits to gross national product. These data are given in Table XXXI [3] for 1919–50, the war years 1941–45 being omitted.

TABLE XXXI

Ratio of Profits to G.N.P.

Year	*Profits before Income Taxes as Per Cent of Gross National Product*	*Profits after Income Taxes as Per Cent of Gross National Product*
Average 1919–28	6.7%	—%
1929	9.4	8.1
1930	3.6	2.8
1931	−0.1 (deficit)	−1.7 (deficit)
1932	−5.1 (deficit)	−5.8 (deficit)
1933	0.4	−0.7 (deficit)
1934	2.6	1.5
1935	4.4	3.2
1936	6.9	5.2
1937	6.9	5.2
1938	3.9	2.7
1939	7.1	5.5
1940	9.2	6.3
1946	11.1	6.5
1947	13.4	8.1
1948	13.3	8.1
1949	10.7	6.5
1950 (1st half)	11.7	6.9

Profits are closely correlated with fluctuations in industrial production, and appear to be largely a function of volume of sales. At high income levels they become inordinately large and at low income levels inordinately small. Neither extreme is for long maintainable. Business could not continue to operate at the low levels reached in 1931–34; and the economy cannot con-

[3] *Ibid.*

tinue to function well with an income distribution distorted by boomtime profits.

In the ten-year period 1919–28 profits amounted to 6.7 per cent of the gross national product, and this level was regained (6.8 per cent) in the five-year period 1936–40. In high boom years profits exceeded this figure by a considerable margin. Thus they were 9.4 per cent in 1929 and 13.3 per cent in 1948. Profits after taxes stood at the same level in relation to gross national product in 1947–48 as in the great boom of 1929. The ratio of profits of all manufacturing corporations (before federal taxes) to stockholders' equity in 1948 was 25.6 per cent; after deducting federal taxes, the ratio was 16.1 per cent.

Diversity in Profits Experience

Not all firms continue to enjoy advancing profits right up to the peak of business activity. In general the smaller corporations appear to reach the high point in profits earlier than the giant corporations. Thus in the period 1947–49, the aggregate profits of each of the three corporate groups with assets from 250 to 999 thousand, 1 to 5 million, and 5 to 100 million dollars reached the peak in the first quarter of 1947,[4] while the aggregate profits of all large corporations with assets of over 100 million dollars reached, as a group, the peak in the fourth quarter of 1948 (see Table XXXII).

An interesting recent study by the National Bureau of Economic Research[5] discloses the high diversity in the fortunes of industrial corporations over the cycle. Some corporations reach the peak of their profits very early in the expansion phase of the cycle, while many reach their profits peak considerably in advance of the peak of the cycle of general business activity, and some even enjoy advancing profits considerably after the recession has started. Indeed, some corporations, for various reasons, have high and even advancing profits throughout the depression

[4] The smallest corporations, with assets under 250 thousand dollars, reached the peak of profits, as a group, in the third quarter of 1947.

It should also be noted that the profits of small corporations as a class fluctuate much more violently over the cycle than those of large corporations as a group. There are, of course, many individual exceptions to the rule.

[5] Occasional Paper 32.

TABLE XXXII

Ratio of Corporate Profits before Federal Taxes to Stockholders' Equity

(Manufacturing corporations grouped according to size)

Year	*Quarter*	(1) *Assets:* 1–249 (thousands of dollars)	(2) *Assets:* 250–299 (thousands of dollars)	(3) *Assets:* 1–5 (millions of dollars)	(4) *Assets:* 5–100 (millions of dollars)	(5) *Assets:* Over 100 (millions of dollars)
		%	%	%	%	%
1947	1st quarter	26.8	35.2	38.8	31.2	20.8
	2nd quarter	28.4	30.8	32.4	28.4	19.6
	3rd quarter	30.0	30.0	28.4	26.0	19.6
	4th quarter	10.0	22.4	25.2	27.6	24.0
1948	1st quarter	14.4	28.0	28.0	27.2	26.8
	2nd quarter	21.6	27.6	26.4	26.8	23.6
	3rd quarter	23.2	23.2	25.2	25.6	26.4
	4th quarter	2.8	16.4	19.6	26.0	27.6
1949	1st quarter	14.4	17.2	17.2	20.0	22.4
	2nd quarter	10.4	12.8	15.2	16.0	18.8
	3rd quarter	14.0	16.0	16.0	17.2	30.8

Sources: Federal Trade Commission and Securities and Exchange Commission.

phase. But despite this wide diversity, aggregate corporate profits correlate almost perfectly with the cycle of general business activity.

It is of special interest to note that many corporations reach the bottom of their profits cycle very early in the contraction phase of the cycle. Indeed, at the trough of the business cycle, when general business starts to move upward, about 50 per cent of all corporations included in the study [6] had already turned the corner and were enjoying advancing profits. About halfway up the general business cycle, around 80 per cent of corporations were enjoying expanding profits, but thereafter the percentage began to decline.

The fact that a company has reached the peak of its own profits cycle does not necessarily mean any significant deterioration in its profits position. Profits may continue at a high level for months and even years after the peak has been reached. Thus, as shown in Table XXXII,[7] while the decline of aggregate profits for three of the groups represented (columns 2, 3 and 4) came at the first quarter of 1947, the drastic decline did not come until the third and fourth quarters of 1948. Indeed, until then profits continued at the very high rate of over 25 per cent of the stockholders' equity. And the aggregate profits for all corporations reached their peak in the third quarter of 1948, despite the fact that many corporations had reached their own peak much earlier.

The study of corporate profits by the National Bureau of Economic Research discloses (1) that aggregate corporate profits correlate closely with general business activity, reaching troughs and peaks corresponding to the troughs and peaks of the business cycle, and (2) that a curve showing the *proportion* of all corporations enjoying advancing profits leads, by approximately a quarter-cycle, the curve for aggregate profits. A bare majority (50 per cent) of corporations have turned the corner by the time business activity reaches the trough, and they are joined by many others as the upswing progresses. But there is never a point in the

---

[6] The number ranges from 17 companies in the early twenties to 185 companies in the period 1929–33, and 244 corporations from 1923 to 1938.

[7] See *Economic Reports of the President to the Congress,* July, 1948, January, 1949, and January, 1950.

cycle, not even in the period of high prosperity when all companies enjoy expanding profits. The highest proportion, around 80 per cent, is reached when the upswing in general business activity is *advancing at the most rapid rate,* i.e., around the middle of the expansion phase of the cycle, or in other words at the point of inflection. As the rate of advance begins to slow down, though aggregate profits are still rising, more and more corporations have already reached their profits peak. By the time the peak of the cycle is reached, only around 50 per cent of corporations are still enjoying expanding profits. Yet profits in general remain high, even for those that have already reached their maximum, and indeed the peak of *aggregate* profits of all corporations combined coincides with the peak of the business cycle.

Leaders and Laggers

Figure 74 represents a model showing a hypothetical distribution of corporations with declining and expanding profits at four points in the general business cycle.[8] Point I is the point of inflection on the downswing; Point II is the trough; Point III is the point of inflection on the upswing; and Point IV is the peak of the cycle. Now the National Bureau's study shows that at Point I about 80 per cent are having declining profits, while about 20 per cent are enjoying expanding profits; [9] at Point III the reverse is the case, around 20 per cent having declining profits and 80 per cent expanding profits; at Points II and IV about 50 per cent have expanding and 50 per cent declining profits.

It would, however, be a mistake to assume that all companies (about 80 per cent of the total) with declining profits at Point I, for example, are in the same boat. Some are, in fact, laggers behind the general cycle movement, having only recently passed their upper profits turning point. Others, far down on their profits curve, are rapidly approaching their lower profits turning point and are about ready to move forward ahead of the general

[8] I have devised this model purely for purposes of illustration. The figures used are hypothetical and are designed merely to indicate the general character of the changes that must occur in the position of companies in various phases of the cycle.

[9] In mild depressions such as those of 1923 and 1926, the proportion enjoying expanding profits at Point I in the cycle was as high as 40 to 45 per cent.

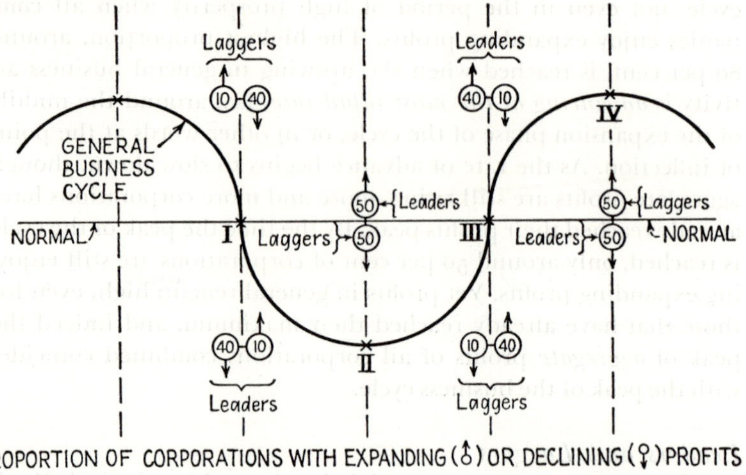

FIGURE 74. *The hypothetical figures in the circles represent percentages of all corporations. At each point (Points I, II, III, and IV) the sum of the figures equals 100. The arrows indicate whether the group has expanding profits (arrow pointing up) or declining profits (arrow pointing down). The position of the circles above or below the "normal line" indicates whether the group is near its peak profits or near the profits trough. Circles above the normal line indicate that corporations are advancing toward (or receding from) their peak; circles below the normal line indicate the companies are falling toward (or moving up from) their profits trough.*

upturn of business. The former group are laggers and the latter are leaders in relation to the general business cycle; yet both are experiencing declining profits.

Similarly, among the 20 per cent or so with expanding profits at Point I, some are leaders and some laggers. The laggers are still approaching their peak of profits even though general business passed its peak a quarter-cycle back. The leaders, on the other hand, have just recently reached bottom in their own profits cycle and have already started up ahead of the general business cycle.

In like manner, at Point II, about 50 per cent are experiencing expanding profits and the other 50 per cent declining profits. This could be interpreted to mean that the 50 per cent with rising profits are ahead of the cycle movement, since their profit situation is already on the upgrade while business is just turning the corner. The 50 per cent with declining profits might be regarded as laggers, still going down, while general business is just rounding the lower turning point.

At Point III, around 80 per cent have rising profits, and of those perhaps half are leaders, being just near the point of their profits maximum while general business still has a quarter-cycle to go to reach its peak. The other half, say, are laggers, moving up from near the bottom of their profits cycle, though business began to turn up a quarter-cycle back. Again, of the 20 per cent with declining profits, some are leaders, having just reached their profits peak, though business activity in general still has a quarter-cycle to go before it reaches its peak. The remaining corporations having declining profits are laggers, having not yet reached the bottom of their profits cycle, though business has long since passed the trough and is already halfway up the ladder toward the next peak.

Thus we see that the *proportion* of corporations with advancing profits tends to correlate with the *rate of change* of business activity. The proportion is lowest when business activity is falling at the most rapid rate and highest at the point of most rapid advance. Accordingly the curve showing the proportion of firms with advancing profits leads the curve of general business activity by roughly a quarter-cycle.

This development is inherent in the very process of the cycle movement. The curve representing the rate of change necessarily anticipates that of the general business cycle. But this does not mean that this, or any other series representing rates of change, is in any sense the "cause" of the cycle. Such series are reflections of the cycle movement, not causes. Thus with respect to profits, it may well be that profit fluctuations are a result of the cycle movement, not the cause of it. Nevertheless the interrelationships of the various component parts of the cycle, as our econometric models have taught us, in a sense cause the cycle. These interrelations, with their lagged adjustments, mean that "causes" produce "effects" and these "effects" in turn become "causes." It is not a simple matter of cause and effect; it is a matter of interrelated movement of action and interaction.

Boom Profits and Average Profits

Profits, as a result of the cycle movement, continually move away from, and back toward, a balanced equilibrium relation to income. In depression they are abnormally low; in boom, abnormally high. Associated and connected with this fluctuation is a distortion of income distribution. This imbalance is bound to continue so long as cyclical fluctuations occur. It can only be corrected by the stabilization of the cycle itself. A steadily growing income at full employment would give us a better balance in the ratio of profits to income than is possible in a society with violent cyclical fluctuations. In the former case abnormal boom profits would tend to disappear. Yet the ratio of profits to income might be as high as the average ratio which we have experienced in a highly fluctuating society in the past.

A society experiencing wide cyclical fluctuations is presented with a wage-profit dilemma. Depression losses must be offset by high profits in good years. Yet the large profits of boom years distort the long-run balance between consumption and investment. After some years of boom investment (exceeding the long-run maintainable rate), it is discovered that profitable investment outlets can no longer be found for the large savings from profits (whether corporate savings or the savings of dividend recipients). Thus an economy geared to high profits in boom years inevitably drives headlong into depression. The aggregate savings function is too high, given the long-run maintainable rate of investment.

Thus a serious dilemma presents itself. The modern economy operates in a vicious circle. Low profits must be balanced by prosperity profits. From this there is no escape. But prosperity profits are not compatible with the high-consumption (high-wage, low-profit) economy required for sustained full employment. And unless a high-consumption economy is achieved, the scale of compensatory fiscal action by government may need to be so great that it encounters serious difficulties, both economic and political.

Fortunately, any progress toward stability lessens the task to be done.

Wages-Profits Ratio

A sustained full-employment society would tend to raise the ratio of wages to profits. Profits of the magnitude reached in a few high boom years, in a fluctuating society, could not long be maintained in a stabilized (but growing) society. Profits of this volume would soon be eaten into, partly by competitive price decreases benefiting consumers, and partly by the pressure for higher wages which invariably occurs in industries making large profits. Either development would tend toward a more equal distribution of income than has prevailed in high boom years in the past. Nevertheless the ratio of profits to gross national product might continue as high as the *average* ratio experienced in the past in a fluctuating society.

Probably something like this average ratio is necessary in a well-functioning private enterprise economy. There are limits to wage increases or price decreases which, if transcended, will lead to unfavorable economic repercussions upsetting a balanced cost-price structure. Wage increases or price reductions are likely to cut across all firms in an industry, whether they are marginal- or high-profit firms; and wage increases are likely to spread over all industries, even those that are not very profitable. Thus the process of encroachment upon profits by wage increases and price reduction, if carried too far, may disrupt the appropriate balance in the cost-price system.

Primary versus Secondary Distribution of Income

Those economists who believe that price adjustments alone can solve the problem of adequate aggregate demand (in short, the savings-investment problem) fail to face up squarely to this dilemma. Indeed, they forget the lessons of economic theory (generally accepted by both the Keynesians and the classical schools) with respect to the price-determining factors that govern the distribution of the product between the factors of production. There are severe limits to a program aiming to change the primary distribution of income. Much more can be accomplished by means of a secondary distribution of income via taxation. Redistribution of income through corporate and personal income taxation is less disruptive of the cost-price structure for the reason that such taxes apply only where profits and income actually emerge. They do not enter into cost, though they may, if carried to extremes, lessen incentive.

A substantial wage and price adjustment favorable to income distribution can, however, be made, as we have seen, in a sustained full-employment society without lowering the historical average ratio (from decade to decade) of profits to gross national product. In a sustained full-employment economy it is not necessary to price products so high that the company can "break even" at low capacity output. That policy is doubtless necessary in a highly fluctuating society, but it is not necessary in a fairly stable full-employment society. Thus a pricing and wage policy more favorable to a wide distribution of income is feasible under sustained full employment without interfering with an appropriate balance between wages, prices, and profits.

Over and above this adjustment, a wider distribution of income can and should be achieved via social security and welfare measures combined with a progressive tax structure. The stability and progress of the economy as a whole would be promoted by the widest participation of all groups in the general prosperity which full employment makes possible. Moreover, such participation gives strength and stability to the social structure and to democratic political institutions. It was considerations such as these that the Congressional Subcommittee on Low-Income Families had in mind when it referred to the importance of "bringing the majority of these low-income groups within our system of high employment, production, distribution and consumption." [10]

How important this problem is in the United States can be seen from Table XXXIII.[11] Nearly half of the income is received by the upper 20 per cent. America is a country of great wealth

[10] *Report of the Subcommittee on Low-Income Families of the Joint Committee on the Economic Report,* Senate Document No. 146, 81st Congress, 2nd Session.

[11] *Economic Report of the President to the Congress,* January, 1950, pp. 145–46.

TABLE XXXIII

Income Distribution in the United States
Year, 1948

Families Ranked by Size of Income	*Distribution of Income, Income after Taxes, Taxes, and Saving* (per cent)				*Median Income of Each Group*	*Average Income of Each Group*
	Per Cent of Total Money Income before Taxes	*Per Cent of Total Money Income after Taxes*	*Per Cent of Total Federal Personal Income Tax*	*Per Cent of Total Net Saving by Families*		
Lowest Fifth	4	5	1	−24	$ 860	$ 893
Second Fifth	11	12	5	− 3	2,000	2,232
Median Fifth	16	17	9	7	2,840	3,410
Fourth Fifth	22	22	16	21	3,750	4,711
Highest Fifth	47	44	70	99	6,000	9,911
All Groups	100	100	100	100	2,840	4,231

but also of serious poverty in large sections of the community. Some 25 to 30 per cent of all families have money incomes of less than $2,000. Low incomes, poor education, bad housing, slum neighborhoods, malnutrition, disease, and crime go together. It is a vicious circle which cannot be successfully attacked except by general community action.

The most basic solution is to raise the level of education, health, and efficiency of the low-income groups. "Such investment in the basic productive capacities of our people will safeguard their free and independent status as citizens, and will help to knit together and strengthen the social and economic fabric of our Nation." [12] This program involves expansion and improvement of social security, health services, national school lunch program, minimum wage legislation, federal aid to education, low-cost public housing, slum clearance, and urban redevelopment. These measures, in conjunction with a progressive system of income taxation, mean a redistribution of income. But they would also lead to a more equal primary distribution of income, because these measures would tend to promote greater equality of opportunity.

Greater equality in the distribution of "earned" income could thus be achieved. Moreover, greater equality in the distribution of property income could be attained by a steeper progressive rate and lower exemptions in inheritance taxes, and by a wide distribution of ownership of government bonds, savings accounts, life insurance, and home ownership in the lower and middle income groups.

Inequality in the distribution of income tends to lower the consumption function. To the extent that a higher proportion of the national income flows to the lower income families (those spending a high proportion of their income) the total outlays on private consumption at a given income level would rise.[13]

---

[12] *Report of the Subcommittee on Low-Income Families,* p. 2.

[13] Strictly speaking, it is the higher marginal propensity to consume of the lower income groups which counts. This also is considerably higher for lower income families, though the *marginal* difference in spending between low and high income groups is not as great as the difference between the *average* propensities. See Hansen, *Economic Policy and Full Employment,* pp. 47–48.

Social security and social welfare measures, tax programs, and other measures affecting the distribution of income are important and cannot be neglected. Nevertheless, in a dynamic society, income distribution would quickly and seriously deteriorate unless the fruits of progress were continuously passed on to the general community in the form of higher wages and lower prices. The fruits of progress first flow into profits, but in a dynamic society they are quickly dispersed via lower prices to consumers under the pressure of competition, or via higher wages under the pressure of collective bargaining and the competitive bidding for labor. Otherwise a serious imbalance would quickly develop in the wage-profit ratio.

Wages and Prices

Wages in general should rise in accordance with *average* over-all gains in productivity. Unfortunately, these gains are not evenly distributed among all industries. Some industries (partly by reason of unusually favorable technological possibilities) can make exceptional gains, while others, through no fault of their own, cannot. If only the efficient industries granted wage increases, we should soon reach a seriously distorted wage structure.

Wages in general should be raised in accordance with general, over-all increases in productivity in the economy as a whole. This means that industries making exceptionally large gains in productivity, after making wage increases equal to (or perhaps slightly in excess of) the average over-all gains in productivity, should pass the remainder on to the general consuming public in lower prices. Industries unable to make any technical progress, being compelled to raise wages (in line roughly with the average advance), would have to raise their prices. Intermediate industries making average gains in productivity could raise wages by the average figure without any increase in prices. Thus, in the over-all picture, wages (and other active incomes) would rise in accordance with general increases in productivity, while the general price level (some individual prices being reduced, some raised, and others remaining fixed) would be roughly stable. Thus the gains of progress would be passed on in higher money incomes while the *general level* of prices remained stable. But the *structure* of prices would change in accordance with changing technological conditions varying from industry to industry.[14]

Continuous wage and price adjustments are accordingly necessary in a dynamic society with widely diverse technological developments going on in different industries. Such a process presupposes that wages and prices are not frozen by monopolistic arrangements. A well-intentioned expansionist program could easily be dissipated in higher prices, higher costs, and monopolistic restrictions on employment and production. Monopolistic price and output policies (by both management and labor) work counter to a full-employment program and could defeat it. Thus a full-employment program must also include an attack on monopolistic and restrictive practices affecting prices, costs, output, and employment.

Several years ago I proposed [15] the establishment of an Office of Price Research designed to report to the President and Congress on proposed price increases. Under this plan no industry would be permitted to increase administered prices (steel, automobiles, household equipment, etc.) for, say, ninety days, until a full investigation had been made. Publicity, not coercion, would be relied upon for enforcement of a rational price policy—one which would promote, on the one hand, general price stability and, on the other, continuous adjustment of the price structure in accordance with technological developments. A suggestion along these lines has since been made by the Joint Economic Committee on the Economic Report with special reference to the steel industry.[16]

Wage and price adjustments are continuously necessary to promote a balanced wage-profit, cost-price structure in a dynamic society. Some economists would stop here, and insist that nothing further is needed. Unfortunately, however, there is no assurance whatever that even a perfectly balanced wage-price-profit rela-

[14] See Hansen, *Economic Policy and Full Employment*, pp. 240–247.

[15] Alvin H. Hansen, "Stability and Expansion," in *Financing American Prosperity*, Twentieth Century Fund, 1945, p. 260.

[16] See *Report of the Joint Economic Committee on the Economic Report*, Senate Report No. 1843, 81st Congress, 2nd Session, 1950.

tionship would necessarily provide a balance between saving and investment. In a well-balanced wage-price society, it could still be true that the propensity to save was too high in relation to the investment opportunities continually being opened by growth and technological progress. Despite a balanced wage-price structure, there might still be an imbalance between saving and investment.[17] And it is for this reason that we have considered in this chapter not merely wage-price relationships, but also more general measures affecting the distribution of income and the propensity to consume. But the effects of all these measures come into full operation very slowly and gradually, and the magnitude of the changes effected is at best uncertain.

Saving and Investment

When all is said and done, therefore, there is no assurance that a balance will indeed be reached between investment and saving. But only if investment does equal the saving society would wish to make at full employment will it be desirable to balance the government's budget. If investment falls below full-employment saving, government loan expenditures sufficient to fill the gap would need to be made to provide full employment. Equilibrium at full employment cannot be reached on a balanced budget [18] unless saving and investment are equal.

Fiscal Policy and Monopoly

Some economists fear that too heavy reliance on fiscal policy to sustain full employment may tend to defeat itself by worsening cost-price relationship and thus promoting an imbalance between saving and investment. They fear that under the cover of easy prosperity spending, monopolistic and restrictive practices would flourish. They would indeed use fiscal policy, but sparingly, believing as they do that at the worst a tolerable amount of unemployment provides a better opportunity for continuing adjust-

---

[17] Saving is here used in the Robertsonian and Wicksellian sense. See pp. 160–163 in this book.

[18] The budget here referred to is the government *cash* budget, not the conventional budget. See Chapter 7 in this book.

ments so that the economy can reasonably well function without large governmental intervention.[19]

The decision hinges partly on how well grounded is the fear that full employment tends to promote monopolistic price and restrictive policies, and partly on what is a tolerable amount of unemployment.

With respect to the former, no conclusive answer is possible. Much of the literature on monopoly supports the view that monopolistic tendencies are fostered more by depression than by conditions of full employment. Cartels and trusts have tended to break up under the influence of a sellers' market, and trade union restrictive practices appear to be less serious in good times. Whether this is true or not, it appears doubtful that we should forgo the advantages of full employment until there is more evidence than we now have that monopoly practices, in a full em ployment environment, cannot be controlled with at least as much success as in the past. Monopoly is a problem we have always had to contend with, and we cannot afford to neglect it, with or without full employment.

The Choice of Risks

With respect to the latter question—the degree of unemployment which is tolerable—it is interesting (and highly pertinent in view of present world conditions) to consider the reflections by J. M. Clark in his separate concurring statement to the report on *National and International Measures for Full Employment.* He refers to the importance of the wage-price structure but believes that the competent study of this area is still in its infancy, and that no finding with respect to policy matters which is at once positive and simple can be made. A thorough knowledge of what constitutes a truly balanced wage-price structure might provide an "understanding of what is required to give us a type of economy which may spontaneously tend to maintain a high average rate of operation, and thus minimize the burden imposed on the devices of fiscal policy. The two are co-ordinate and com-

---

[19] See in this connection the thoughtful and stimulating discussions of these problems by J. M. Clark and J. H. Williams in Chapters 3 and 7 in *Financing American Prosperity,* Twentieth Century Fund, New York, 1945.

plementary, and it is possible that fiscal policy may succeed or fail, according as the economy, and its constituent parts, work with it or against it." [20] Clark goes on to discuss the problems of monopoly prices, the danger that profits may absorb so large a part of the national income that adequate demand may require an "investment component too large to be enduringly maintained," and the danger that the wage-price structure may place obstacles in the way of stable full employment.

He concludes that we are probably taking some chances if we try to do too much with fiscal policy, but that we are also taking chances if we do too little to stabilize income and employment at a high level. The United States, by itself alone, might, he thinks, be inclined to accept moderate fluctuations, relying on social security to provide for the resulting unemployment. But the impact of our fluctuations upon the world is decisive, and the world situation is such, says Clark, as to demand a higher performance than we might be inclined to attempt on domestic considerations alone. The world situation warns us, he says, to take very seriously "the risks of doing too little, as against the risks of using imperfectly tested fiscal devices."

Apart from the international situation, it is possible that Clark may be somewhat too complacent with respect to a tolerable level of unemployment from the purely domestic standpoint. One thing is certain: as the labor movement grows stronger it will not and cannot tolerate any unavoidable unemployment. There are indeed problems—some of them new problems—that will confront any country practicing a policy of sustained full employment. But there appears to be no convincing evidence that they are less soluble than the problems we should have to face under conditions involving considerable unemployment. Modern democratic societies have to learn how to make a full employment society work. It requires self-discipline and self-control. Perfection we shall not reach. A workable economic society in the modern highly industrialized and urbanized community presents grave difficulties indeed for economic and political statesmanship.

Professor Clark, writing his memorandum before the Korean

[20] *National and International Measures for Full Employment,* Department of Economic Affairs, United Nations, December, 1949.

war, had in mind the danger of an impending recession. The aftermath of the Korean war, with its continuing vast military expenditures, confronts us with the problems of overemployment and inflation involving a serious distortion in wage-price-profits relationships. To meet these problems, high wartime taxation and rigorous controls (involving allocation, price, and wage controls) are indicated.

In an inflationary situation, collective bargaining contracts which tie wage rates to the cost of living index intensify the inflationary pressures. Under such contracts, the wage lag (which otherwise acts as a brake on inflation) is eliminated; and this tends to create an explosive situation once prices start to rise at all rapidly. If such contracts became general, it would become urgently necessary to prevent price rises from occurring in the first place. This would require rigorous controls and strong fiscal measures.

30 · *Statistical Indicators and Business Forecasting*

In the nineteen-twenties there developed an enormous interest and undue faith in business forecasting. Widely advertised agencies with a national clientele of thousands of subscribers flourished in that decade. Five of the leading services had combined subscription lists of around 35,000. In addition, scores of the larger corporations established statistical research departments designed to aid business planning in the ups and downs of general economic activity.[1]

Three main methods of forecasting were developed, which I shall designate as follows: (1) the "overshoot" method, (2) the "lead and lag" method, and (3) the method of "weighing opposing factors." These labels, it should be noted, are introduced here as descriptive aids; they are not the terms used by the forecasting services themselves.

The "Overshoot" Method

When a group of statistical series (which exhibit cyclical fluctuations conforming in general to the business cycle) are plotted, the idea will readily occur to anyone that forecasting must to some degree be feasible. The very simple idea will at once be suggested

[1] See Hardy and Cox, *Forecasting Business Conditions,* The Macmillan Company, 1927.

that it should not be too difficult to know when economic activity is above or below normal. Thus, looking at the past record of prices of industrial common stocks, one is likely to reflect that here is a wonderful system by which one can surely get rich: simply buy when the market is below normal and sell when it is above normal. Looking at historical curves of stock prices one is likely to get the impression that it is not even necessary to achieve any very high degree of accuracy in forecasting, since if one bought somewhere near the bottom and sold somewhere near the top, one could not fail to win. Looking back over past developments, it all seems deceptively simple.

It was thus inevitable that the "overshoot" method of forecasting should be developed. In its simplest form this method is based on the proposition that whenever business activity rises above normal, one may expect a reaction to set in sooner or later. And similarly, when business falls below normal, one may sooner or later expect a backswing. And the farther the departure from normal—in other words, the greater the "overshoot"—the greater the reaction which is bound to follow.

From this point of view, then, an important area for statistical research is to study past fluctuations with a view to determining what is *normal* and to devise ways and means of continually projecting this normal trend so as to keep it up to date. If this could be done with reasonable assurance, one could then always determine the extent to which the economy had "overshot" either above or below normal. And if one were doubtful about the precise accuracy of the estimated normal, one could take a somewhat less exacting position and merely seek to ascertain whether business was considerably above normal, at *supernormal* levels, or at more or less seriously *subnormal* levels.[2]

In the decade of the twenties, the Babson Economic Service relied in considerable measure upon the device of locating the position of the economy at, above, or below normal.[3] Emphasis

---

[2] Supernormal and subnormal levels were employed (among other methods) by the Brookmire Service; this service currently presents a chart giving deviations of business from normal.

[3] This method was, however, supplemented by other procedures and types of analysis.

was placed not only on the *amplitude* of departure from normal, but also on the *duration* of the departure. Thus the entire *area* in a chart (on which time is measured on the horizontal axis) above or below the normal trend line, and not merely the divergence from normal, was regarded as important. Indeed, under the law of action and reaction, it was assumed that any depression area could normally be expected to balance in size the preceding prosperity area.

In a somewhat more flexible manner, the "overshoot" method was also used extensively by Moody's Service. A barometer was constructed consisting of fourteen series representing production, trade, transportation, prices, interest rates, the stock market, and business failures. A secular trend of the actual barometer figures was estimated, together with an index of seasonal variations. On the basis of these estimates of long-run trend and seasonal variations, the normal figure for each month was computed.[4] The "normal" figures column was then compared with the "actual" figures column, and in the third column were presented the percentage deviations of actual from normal. The forecast was then based on an analysis of these deviations, supplemented by other available information, including among other things the prospective profit margins of leading industries and the movements of operating costs in relation to receipts.

The "Lead and Lag" Method

The "lead and lag" method was developed very thoroughly by the Harvard Economic Service and was also used extensively by the Brookmire Service. This also is a method that readily suggests itself to anyone who looks at the cyclical movements of statistical series relating to the securities market, prices, production, and money rates. In the usual case, certain of these series are leaders, and as we look back over past fluctuations, these "anticipators" appear to afford an easy and sure basis upon which to predict the turning points in the cycle. But experience shows that, however simple the problem appears aided by hindsight,

---

[4] The Alexander Hamilton Institute currently uses a Market Trend Indicator; also the United Business Service presents a chart showing deviations of general business volume from normal.

once one turns toward the future no easy or certain road is opened for accurate prediction. The difficulty is that when an "anticipator" begins to turn either down or up, one never knows whether it is just a minor irregularity or the real thing. Only after the event can one know for sure that the downturn was in fact definitive. In addition, the "anticipators" have a way of getting out of step just when one begins to use them. Many a forecaster, after working out a beautiful sequence which could be shown to have functioned admirably over a period of several cycles, has found to his sorrow that the moment he began to apply it to forecast the next turn, it failed.

The Harvard Economic Service classified various statistical series into three categories: (1) speculation, (2) business, and (3) money. The series included in Curve A, Speculation, were: (a) the prices of industrial stocks, and (b) New York City bank debits. In the B Curve, Business, were included: (a) bank debits outside of New York City, and (b) commodity prices. In Curve C, Banking, were included commercial paper rates. Generally Curve A was found to anticipate Curve B by from four to ten months, while Curve B preceded Curve C by from two to eight months.

The selection of these three curves was based on a study of the sequence of cyclical fluctuations of a much larger number of series covering the period from January, 1903, to July, 1914. Twenty-one series were classified into five groups. Group I consisted of three series of bond yields and stock prices. Group II consisted of three series including building permits, New York bank clearings, and shares trades. Group III was composed of five series including production of pig iron, bank clearings outside of New York, imports, unfilled orders of the U.S. Steel Corporation, and business failures (inverted). Group IV included two wholesale price series, gross earnings of railroads, and reserves of New York banks. Group V comprised dividend payments of industrial corporations, loans and deposits of New York Clearing House banks (inverted), and rates on 60- to 90-day paper and on 4- to 6-month paper. The time relationship of these five groups was found to be as follows:

Group I preceded Group II by from 2 to 4 months;

Group II preceded Group III by from 2 to 4 months;

Group III preceded Group IV by from 2 to 4 months;
Group IV preceded Group V by from 4 to 6 months.

The Standard Trade and Securities Service also made use of leads and lags in their forecasting work. Among other devices this service used a credit supply curve as a barometer of the major stock market and business movements. When the credit supply curve crossed normal on the rise, a major revival of stock prices, and later of business, was forecast. When the credit supply curve crossed normal going down, a major decline of stock prices was indicated, followed three to nine months later by a major decline in general business.

Weighing Opposing Factors

The method of "weighing opposing factors" consisted simply of listing, identifying, and measuring as far as possible the forces making for expansion on the one side and for depression on the other. An effort was made to appraise the relative strength of the opposing forces. Since the weight to be given to the various factors was a matter of judgment, no definitive quantitative conclusions could be reached. This method was at times used as a supplement to other methods even by services, such as Babson's and the Harvard Service, which in general relied mainly upon rigorously mechanical statistical procedures.

Disillusionment

It is easy to see how fascinating were these calculations of normal trends, deviations from normal, leads and lags, together with special studies of expanding, contracting, and limiting factors. And they captivated the business community. But the measure of success achieved was very disappointing.

The two most comprehensive studies on the success or failure of efforts to forecast business and the stock market are Garfield V. Cox's *An Appraisal of American Forecasts* [5] and the survey by the Cowles Commission for Research in Economics (by Alfred Cowles, 3rd).[6]

Cox analyzed the forecasting record of six services: Standard Statistics, Babson, Harvard, Brookmire, Moody, and National

[5] University of Chicago Press, 1929.
[6] "Can Stock Market Forecasters Forecast?" *Econometrica,* July, 1933.

City Bank. The conclusion gave qualified support to the thesis that forecasting could, as of the year 1929, show some measure of success. The results, he said, do not justify anyone in placing implicit faith in any given forecast, but they do support the "expectation that the services will be right considerably oftener than they will be wrong." Summarizing the record of all services studied in relation to each major turn in the cycle, he concluded that the predictions were helpful in thirteen cases, slightly helpful in eighteen, neutral in five, and slightly or wholly misleading in four.

But this experience related to 1918–28. The great crash came in 1929. In that devastating experience forecasting received a body blow. In the hour of urgent need it failed.

Cowles' study deals with (1) the attempts of sixteen financial services in the period from January, 1928, to July, 1932, to forecast which *specific* securities would prove most profitable, (2) the effort of twenty fire insurance companies in the period 1928 to 1931 to select common stocks, (3) the experience of eighteen professional financial services and six financial weeklies or letters in forecasting the course of the stock market from January, 1928, to June, 1932, and (4) the twenty-six-year forecasting record of W. P. Hamilton, former editor of the *Wall Street Journal,* the principal sponsor of the Dow theory.

The conclusions are disillusioning:

1. The sixteen financial services made some 7,500 recommendations with respect to the purchase of *specific* common stock. The average record shows that if an investor had followed their advice, his selection of stocks would have netted a return worse by 1.43 per cent annually than if he had simply held across the board an average of all stocks listed. Six out of the sixteen services did indeed show a better than average (of all stocks) record. But statistical tests failed to demonstrate that this was due to skill, and pointed to the conclusion that it was probably the result of chance. On a chance basis, some of the sixteen would of course do better than others.

2. The twenty fire insurance companies similarly disclosed a "record 1.20 per cent annually worse than that of the general run of stocks." Again the best companies failed to exhibit in any convincing way the existence of skill.

3. The twenty-four financial publications, in forecasting the market for January, 1928, to June, 1932, failed as a group "by 4 per cent per annum to achieve a result as good as the average of all purely random performances." Again, statistical tests indicated that the "most successful records are little, if any, better than what might be expected to result from pure chance."

4. The twenty-six-year forecasts of the stock market based on the Dow theory, 1904 to 1929, did achieve a result better than what is regarded as an ordinary normal investment return, but it was nevertheless a poorer return than an investor would have got in this period if, instead of buying and selling according to the forecasts made, he had simply continuously held a list of representative common stocks throughout the period. Over the twenty-six years, changes in market outlook were announced by the forecast on ninety occasions. Of these, forty-five predictions were correct and forty-five wrong. This study of the Dow theory, it should be noted, ended in 1929.

The Dow Theory and Formula Timing Plans

The central proposition of the Dow theory[7] seems to be especially applicable in a major cycle of stock prices such as we had in 1929–37. The downswing, beginning in 1929 and reaching bottom in 1932, was, indeed, not a steady downward movement. Intermediate movements occurred, based on technical conditions in the market involving a succession of rallies each of which occurred whenever the market had oversold itself. These rallies, however, rather quickly suffered reversals under the pressure of the fundamental depressional factors from 1929 to 1932. Accordingly, each successive high was lower than the previous high. Not until a high was reached (as in 1933) which *exceeded* the previous high, could it be considered, according to the Dow theory, that a new bull market was under way. Once the market moves above the previous high, the chances are, according to the theory, that it will continue to move up. A new high indicates that strong underlying factors have been able to overcome caution and

[7] Robert Rhea, *The Dow Theory*, Simon & Schuster, 1938; Elmer C. Bratt, *Business Cycles and Forecasting*, 3rd edition, Richard D. Irwin, Inc., 1948, Chapter XIX.

hesitation. A new high is thought to be the signal that a business cycle upswing is under way. Having pierced the ceiling, the market is regarded as likely to move still higher, though there will be intermediate reactions and rallies as the economy climbs by fits and starts up the ladder toward prosperity.

By the time the first ceiling is pierced, however, the market may already be far above the depression low, so that the forecast, even though dependable, comes rather late. Moreover, the market level reached when the first ceiling for railroad stocks was pierced in 1933 was not well maintained, since prices below this level ruled during the last half of 1934 and virtually all of 1935. Finally, there is the difficulty that it is not always easy to know with certainty, in view of the many "technical," intermediate movements, what is the relevant "previous high." After the event, it is always easy to locate it, but one is far from sure when still in the midst of the rapidly moving and oscillating flow of current events.

A special use of the Dow theory is reflected in certain "formula timing" plans currently employed by individual investors and also by some educational and other investing institutions. There are a variety of plans, but common characteristics involve the following principles: (a) The account is started with a definite proportion between the defensive section (bonds and cash) and the aggressive section (stocks), determined by a specific formula based partly on the *level* of the market and partly on the *direction* in which the market moved into its present range. (b) This proportion is periodically adjusted by fixed rules designed to sell stocks and to increase the defensive part of the account as the market moves up into new highs, and to sell bonds and increase the aggressive portion as the market moves to the historically low ranges. The market range may be divided into several zones. In the top zone the fixed defensive (bonds) proportion might be 90 per cent of the investors' total holdings, and in the bottom zone, 10 per cent. Intermediate zones, with intermediate percentages, lie in between.[8]

If, at the time of rebalancing or periodic adjustment, the

[8] See *An Investment Program for Capital Growth,* the Keystone Company, Boston, 1950.

market is below the middle zone, the account may be adjusted so as to bring the aggressive (stocks) proportion up to the level of the proportion set for the lowest zone reached since last crossing the center zone. This is on the theory that new ceilings have been pierced since the last low, and so a cyclical upswing is presumed to be in prospect. If, at the time of rebalancing, the market is above the middle zone, precisely the opposite procedure is adopted.

Thus the movements of the market itself fix the points at which switches are made from stocks to bonds and vice versa, and also the proportions which are held of each. The formula and the market together decide the course of action. This tends to give the investor a sense of security, but it does not necessarily provide a "sure-fire" investment program. That, in an uncertain world, would be to ask the impossible.

Current Developments

Despite many disillusioning past performances, forecasting, in the nature of the case, must go on. Decisions have to be made, and that means that one must peer as best one can into the future. The general failure of highly technical or mechanical methods has led in recent years to a wider use of the more flexible and "commonsense" method of weighing the opposing forces, supplemented by industry studies of new orders, unfilled orders, production, sales, shipments, inventories, costs, and profits.

Scores of business and investment research agencies,[9] some of them large national concerns, operate currently in leading metropolitan centers. Numerous investment trusts have been organized, many of them since 1932. As an illustration of this growth, it may be noted that the total net assets of open-end investment funds alone increased from $400,000,000 in 1940 to $2,120,000,000 in 1950.

There is, moreover, currently a revival of interest in more technical forecasting methods. These involve in part a renewal of work along old lines, and in part new procedures. There are,

9 Among leading currently operating forecasting agencies one may mention Standard & Poor's Corporation, Babson's Business Service, Alexander Hamilton Institute, Moody's Investors Service, Securities Research Corporation, Brookmire Economic Service, and United Business Service.

in particular, three lines of attack currently being pursued by research agencies, private and public, along the following lines: (a) more careful work on "anticipators"—the old lead and lag method; (b) fuller and more up-to-date information on strategic areas; and (c) the GNP "pattern of relationship" method.

STATISTICAL INDICATORS

The first of these approaches is well illustrated in a recent study of the National Bureau of Economic Research on statistical indicators.[10] It is a continuation of an earlier study by Mitchell and Burns.[11] In that study out of about 500 monthly or quarterly series, 71 were selected which promised some degree of reliability as indicators of revival, and a closer screening of these in turn yielded 21 series that were deemed most trustworthy.

Seven of the 21 series in the earlier study are now thrown out, and seven new ones added. These 21 series are classified into three groups as follows:

A. LEADING GROUP

1. Business failures (liabilities, industrial and commercial), $1879\text{–}1938_w$[12]
2. Industrial common stock price index, 1899–1938
3. New orders of durable goods, 1919–38
4. Residential building contracts, 1919–38
5. Commercial and industrial building contracts, 1919–38
6. Average hours worked per week in manufacturing, 1921–38
7. New incorporations, 1860–1938
8. Wholesale prices of 28 basic commodities, $1893\text{–}1937_w$

B. ROUGHLY COINCIDENT GROUP

1. Employment in non-agricultural establishments, 1890–1938

---

10 Geoffrey H. Moore, *Statistical Indicators of Cyclical Revivals and Recessions,* Occasional Paper 31, National Bureau of Economic Research, 1950.

11 Wesley Mitchell and Arthur F. Burns, *Statistical Indicators of Cyclical Revivals,* Bulletin 69, National Bureau of Economic Research, 1938.

12 The figures after each series give the historical period for which each series relative to the reference cycle has been studied. The "w" indicates that the war years are omitted.

2. Unemployment (monthly data, Census Bureau, beginning 1940)
3. Corporate profits, quarterly, 1920–38_w
4. Bank debits outside New York City, 1879–1938_w
5. Freight car loadings, 1918–38
6. Industrial production index, 1919–38
7. Gross national product (quarterly data beginning 1939)
8. Wholesale price index (excluding farm products and foods) 1914–38_w

C. LAGGING GROUP

1. Personal income, 1921–38
2. Sales by retail stores, 1919–38
3. Consumer installment debt, 1929–38
4. Bank rate on business loans, 1919–38
5. Manufacturers' inventories, in current prices, 1929–38

Of the eight leaders, however, there is not a single series in which the lead has been consistent, either at the peak or at the trough of the cycle, throughout the period studied. Each of the eight series, in the order named above, failed to lead at the peak one or more times. Thus the first series failed 3 out of 14 times; the second, 3 out of 11; the third, 4 out of 25; the fourth, 1 out of 5; the fifth, 1 out of 5; the sixth, 1 out of 4; the seventh, 8 out of 20; and the eighth, 4 out of 11. At the trough the corresponding figures indicating failure are: 2 out of 16; 3 out of 11; 6 out of 30; 1 out of 6; 2 out of 6; 2 out of 5; 5 out of 20; 3 out of 11. This is far from a dependable record.

A second method of attack on this problem suggested by the National Bureau is to construct a series consisting of the proportion of all cyclically well-conforming series (ranging from 83 in 1890 to 330 in 1940) which, at each point in the cycle, were experiencing expansion.

Such a curve tends to fluctuate about a quarter-cycle ahead of the general business cycle—or, in other words, to correlate synchronously with the rate of expansion and contraction of general business activity.

Again the behavior of this curve is far from being dependable.

In the sixteen cycles from 1885 to 1938, in many cases the curve declined in terms of amplitude relatively little in advance of the peak of the reference cycle, and only in a few cases was the *lead* early enough and the *amplitude of decline* sufficient to give any strong indication of an impending turning point. A fairly sharp decline typically occurred in the months preceding the peak of the reference cycle. Similarly around the trough of the cycle, the curve typically rose sharply, but in only about half of the cases was the lead considerable.

Short leads in the curve here in question often look fairly impressive in the historical record, but they are likely to be of little value in current forecasting. This is true partly because, even if the statistical data are highly current, it is not yet known whether any change in direction will not prove abortive; and partly because this type of data is peculiarly difficult to maintain on a reasonably current basis, since on a current basis it is difficult to know whether a series is still moving up to its own cyclical maximum. Month-to-month changes are usually very erratic, and it is only by some method of moving averages that one can determine whether a series is still advancing. Thus on top of the necessary lag in obtaining data, a further lag in constructing the series is inescapable. These practical difficulties lessen the predictive value of this particular device. Along with other methods, however, it may be of some help in recognizing the turn of events fairly early after the peak or trough has been passed.

STRATEGIC AREAS

The second current method relates to a continuing survey of the developments in strategic areas. These areas, as we have emphasized throughout this book, are the various categories of investment and consumers' durables. Specifically the strategic areas include: (1) automobiles, (2) household equipment and electrical appliances, (3) inventories of manufacturers, wholesalers, and retailers, (4) machinery and business equipment, (5) business plant, (6) residential construction. In the government sphere the strategic areas to note are: (1) public construction and development projects, and (2) the expansion or contraction in the relation of payments to receipts in the federal cash budget.

An excellent illustration of this type of forecasting can be found in the June, 1950, issue of the *Survey of Current Business,* made by the Office of Business Economics of the U.S. Department of Commerce. Charts and statistical information are presented dealing with various components of private investment and consumers' durables.

A notable feature of this survey is the quarterly study made jointly by the Office of Business Economics and the Securities and Exchange Commission of reports on projected investment outlays on new plant and equipment planned by business over the next three months. Thus in the June issue referred to above, figures are presented, based on reports made by business in April and May, on planned outlays on investment in the third quarter (July–September) of 1950. As it turns out, actual outlays often vary considerably from those anticipated three months earlier, and this is especially true if exceptionally favorable or unfavorable expectations develop in the meantime. Nevertheless these estimates, projected three months in advance, mark an important forward step in efforts at forecasting.

Other features of the June, 1950, issue include a chart showing the development of residential construction during the current quarter and each of the preceding five quarters, together with an analysis of building materials price movements. Charts and tables are presented on changes in business sales and inventories. These are broken down to show the considerable variation in the inventory positions of individual industries. An analysis is made of the inventory-sales ratios of all retail establishments; and separate ones are made for the automotive group, the home-furnishings group, other durables, and the nondurable goods group.

A special section is devoted to an analysis of the demand for automobiles. Variables affecting the demand for new cars include the age distribution of cars, the average age of cars scrapped, the ratio of automobile prices to the consumer price index, disposable income in the current year and in the immediately preceding year, movements of farm income, and population movements to suburban areas. More or less similar analyses are made of the demand for electric refrigerators, vacuum cleaners, electric washing machines and electric ranges. Charts showing the *actual* sales are compared with a "calculated" curve, presented for each of these markets.

THE PATTERN OF RELATIONSHIPS

Finally, there is the "pattern of relationship" method relating particularly to the components of the gross national product.[13] Among the relationships or functions relevant to the problem are (1) consumer expenditures in relation to disposable income, (2) gross (and net) business and individual savings in relation to gross (and net) national product, (3) inventory stocks in relation to sales, (4) fixed-capital business investment in relation to stock of capital, (5) fixed-capital business investment in relation to population growth, (6) fixed-capital business investment in relation to measurable changes in technological efficiency, (7) residential construction in relation to growth in number of families, (8) residential construction in relation to geographical shifts of population, (9) residential construction in relation to building costs, (10) residential construction in relation to vacancies, (11) residential construction in relation to income distribution, (12) consumption expenditures in relation to changes in the tax structure.

A feature of this type of analysis[14] is to estimate each component part of the GNP separately and then revise the estimates

---

[13] See Eric Schiff, "Employment during the Transition Period, in Prospect and Retrospect," *Review of Economic Statistics,* November, 1946; L. R. Klein, "A Post-Mortem on Transition Predictions of National Product," *Journal of Political Economy,* August, 1946; A. G. Hart, "Model Building and Fiscal Policy," *American Economic Review,* September, 1945; J. Mosak, "National Budgets and National Policies," *American Economic Review,* March, 1946, and September, 1946; E. E. Hagen, "The Reconversion Period: Reflections of a Forecaster," *Review of Economic Statistics,* May, 1947.

[14] Criticisms of postwar efforts at forecasting based on GNP pattern relationship were justified to the extent that prewar relationships were relied upon to measure the quite abnormal postwar conditions, and partly because the secular upward drift in the consumption function, after the country had moved into much higher income areas, was often not adequately recognized. On occasion, however, the criticisms seemed to suggest that the failure of the forecast proved the unreliability of the prewar relationships. This, however, would be like arguing that measurements of the tides are invalid since such measurements do not fit post-hurricane conditions.

by cross-checking for consistency when the parts are added together to make up the whole. This procedure compels the investigator to go back of the estimates and to make a new interpretation and analysis of the underlying factors in the situation. As events unfold, each separate forecast can be checked against the actual data, errors can be detected, and continuous adjustments can be made.[15] Short-run abnormalities in relationships as they actually unfold can be detected against the background of the standard relationships. One should, moreover, be continually on guard to discover secular shifts in these relationships and to uncover factors which may account for them.

In the nature of the case, as long as the free-price system is dominant and as long as investment is largely a function of market expectations, forecasting will continue to prove in large measure unreliable. Businessmen and government must, however, continue to attempt forecasting, and at the very least an alert and up-to-date statistical appraisal may help to identify "reversals in the direction of total activity" more promptly.[16]

Forecasting and Government Policy

It is the function of the Council of Economic Advisers to appraise the trends and tendencies in economic development and to suggest programs and policies to promote high and stable levels of income and employment. The annual and mid-year economic reviews which the Council issues serve as a focal point around which public discussions and criticisms can be crystallized. This procedure has already proved its worth. Above all, the Council should remain highly flexible, continually prepared to reverse its judgment and to recommend measures counter to those previously proposed if events indicate them to be wrong. A stubborn determination to be consistent is the greatest danger in a world of rapid change and above all in a world not amenable to accurate forecasting.

15 E. D. Bratt, *Business Cycles and Forecasting,* Richard D. Irwin, Inc., 1948, Chapter XVIII.

16 Arthur F. Burns, *New Facts on Business Cycles,* 30th Annual Report of the National Bureau of Economic Research, Inc., p. 27.

31 · *International Aspects*

Synchronization of Cycle Movements

Major booms and major depressions tend to spread all over the world. Notwithstanding a good deal of variation in the timing and intensity of cyclical fluctuations from country to country, the grand sweeps are in greater or less degree transmitted throughout the trading world. Even in the period between the two world wars, when many countries, especially in Europe, were confronted with monetary and reconstruction problems peculiar to themselves, the great waves of expansion and contraction were felt everywhere. Thus industrial production, despite considerable irregularities, displayed a general upward sweep from 1924 to 1929, downward to 1932, and upward to 1937, in the United States, Canada, United Kingdom, Germany, France, Italy, Sweden, and Japan.[1]

How Cycles Spread

For advanced industrial countries like the United States, the dynamic factor which sways the movements of income and employment is typically domestic or home investment; for the undeveloped countries, such as many Latin American countries, the value of exports usually calls the turn in the cycle. For some countries, like Canada, Australia, and Sweden, which are in an intermediate position, home investment and exports are both vitally important, but the predominant influence is likely to be exports.

Expansion in the rate of investment in the large industrial

---

[1] *Economic Stability in the Post-War World,* Report of the Delegation on Economic Depressions, Part II, League of Nations, 1945, p. 89.

countries first has the effect of raising income within these countries. This increase in income in turn tends to raise the volume of imports from abroad. Industrial expansion requires more imported raw materials, and higher incomes stimulate the importation of consumers' goods of all kinds. Countries producing raw materials feel the effects of the expansion rather quickly, and somewhat later countries producing specialty and luxury goods begin to experience them. Exports from these countries start to rise. This in turn has a magnified effect on the national income of these countries, and soon they begin to import manufactured goods of all kinds in considerable volume. These products—automobiles, electrical appliances, agricultural and industrial machinery, road-building equipment, electrical power equipment, equipment for the construction of transportation and communication facilities, and finished consumers' goods—are imported mainly from the advanced industrial countries. Thus the circle is complete: Impulses leading to expansion have been transmitted and re-transmitted from country to country via the international market mechanism.

Similarly, contracting impulses spread out from the advanced industrial countries and return to reinforce the originating decline. Falling income and employment in the large industrial countries means a collapse of the export markets of the primary producing countries. The money value of their exports declines, causing a serious contraction of their national incomes. This forces a sharp curtailment of their imports from the advanced industrial countries. Thus the depressional influences are finally transmitted back to the countries initiating the cycle movement.

The influence which one particular country exerts upon the prosperity of other countries depends upon its share of world trade and the violence of the fluctuations in its imports. In both respects, the United States occupies a unique and hitherto disturbing position. Its share in total world industrial production ranged from one-third before the Second World War to nearly one-half in 1949. Its import requirements are peculiarly sensitive to fluctuations in consumption and national income. From 1929 to 1932, the United States national income fell by 52 per cent and United States purchases of foreign goods and services fell 68 per cent. From 1937 to 1938, national income fell by about 10 per cent and the dollar value of commodity imports fell by 35 per cent. From the fourth quarter of 1948 to the second quarter of 1949, the United States national income fell by 5 per cent and the value of imports fell by 15 per cent.[2]

Accordingly, the United States plays a dominant role in the propagation of business-cycle movements throughout the world.

International Cycle Policy

International anti-depression policy consists basically of programs of collaboration between countries designed (a) to maintain high and stable levels of employment in the large industrial countries, (b) to stabilize the prices of primary products in order to protect the export values of the primary producing countries, (c) to promote a high and stable level of international investment designed to raise the productivity of the underdeveloped countries, and (d) to help countries meet their balance of payments problems.

From the analysis given above, it is evident that the success of any international program depends in no small degree upon the United States. Continued prosperity in the United States is a basic prerequisite to world economic security, for the impact of the United States upon world trade and world economic conditions is great. Unemployment and a low level of output in our mass-production industries have a seriously depressing effect upon world prices. Depression here reduces American imports and American tourist expenditures in foreign countries, with repercussions back upon ourselves. Foreign countries have every reason to fear the economic impact of this country upon world affairs if we continue to have violent economic fluctuations or chronic unemployment.

But unless there is effective international co-operation, the United States will encounter difficulties in maintaining domestic economic stability. Inflationary or deflationary developments anywhere in the world create problems for other countries. Divergent price movements are particularly disturbing. If every country could succeed reasonably well in maintaining a substantial stability in the general level of prices, this would greatly contribute to

[2] See *National and International Measures for Full Employment,* Department of Economic Affairs, United Nations, December, 1949.

international stability. The policy of price stability requires that each country must continually adjust its money wages to changes in productivity. Thus a country enjoying rapid technical progress should adjust wages upward at a correspondingly rapid rate so as to hold labor costs in industry in general about constant. On the other hand, a country experiencing only small increases in productivity should raise wages slowly, thereby also keeping labor costs approximately stable. If money incomes were adjusted to changes in productivity, no important divergent tendencies would occur with respect to price levels. Under these circumstances no country would be priced out of world markets. Countries might indeed find themselves at an increasing comparative disadvantage in special lines, but no country would be priced out of all markets as would be the case were it experiencing a general all-around increase in costs in relation to other countries. Thus general price stability all around would tend to promote international balance.

A Co-ordinated Program

An Economic and Social Council has been established in the United Nations, whose function it is, among other things, to promote and co-ordinate international anti-cyclical policies. The urgent need of such a co-ordinating body is evident from the experience of the interwar period. In that period there was virtually no co-operation between governments in their efforts to cope with the problems of the Great Depression. Each country seized upon opportunistic measures to alleviate the situation. There was no regard for the effects of these unilateral policies upon other countries. Often the measures used were detrimental to other countries and called forth retaliatory action. Thus the unilateral policies pursued often made matters worse instead of better. There was no effort to fight a common foe together.

Accordingly it is important that countries move along together in a co-ordinated manner in their anti-depression policies. In reality, what is above all needed to secure effective results is concerted action by the larger industrial nations, since it is so largely from the major advanced countries that the initiating impulses come.

This does not mean that each country must be strait-jacketed into a uniform pattern to which all must conform. There may well be large and important differences in the anti-cyclical policies employed by various countries. What is important is timing and direction. If co-ordinated action is taken, then the program of each country will be reinforced and strengthened by the general all-around effort to check inflationary tendencies on the one hand and to fight the onslaught of a general world depression on the other.

International economic co-operation is at best extraordinarily difficult, and certainly quite impossible without established international institutions persistently at work on the problem. This involves a continuous program of research on international economic relations and continuous consultation and discussion, both at the high official level and also at the technical or expert level. Fortunately such international institutions have been established under the auspices of the United Nations, and there is therefore the prospect that, at the very least, the serious dislocations caused by such utter lack of co-operation and even outright economic conflict as was witnessed in the interwar years may in some measure be avoided.

Foremost among the international institutions concerned with economic co-operation are the International Bank for Reconstruction and Development, the International Monetary Fund, the Food and Agricultural Organization, and the International Trade Organization. The activities of these organizations seek to secure an adequate flow of international investment designed to raise the productivity of countries in need of reconstruction or development; to promote a balanced structure of exchange rates throughout the world and to provide short-term lending facilities designed to strengthen a country's position with respect to its international monetary reserves; to improve the diet of people everywhere and increase the volume of food production, while at the same time avoiding undesirable surpluses in certain areas; to promote the optimum international division of labor based upon the maximum development of resources throughout the world, while at the same time dealing in a realistic and co-operative manner with the imperative necessity of countries having to face up with shorter-run or longer-run balance of payments problems.

With respect to the immediate problems of postwar reconstruction, the European Recovery Program is the most far-reaching example of international co-operation which the world has ever seen, and the longer-run repercussions flowing from it are likely to affect the pattern of international economic co-operation for decades to come.

The Problem of Internal Stability in a Depressed World

It cannot be denied, however, that countries heavily dependent for their own internal prosperity upon export markets are very much concerned over the constant danger of inflationary or deflationary influences coming from abroad. Even for the United States this is a matter of no small importance, and for many countries it is the all-important, overriding concern. The freedom enjoyed by the United States to pursue a domestic policy designed to maintain high and stable levels of income and employment, regardless of impulses coming from the outside, is unique in modern history. The size of our internal market, the diversity of our resources and productive facilities, the relatively small dependence on international trade in terms of the total gross national product, the vast gold reserves and persistent strength of our trade position—all these afford a freedom to carry out, despite adverse influences from abroad, a domestic program of internal stability and full employment. But the matter is far from easy for many other countries, which hold a weaker and less sheltered international position.

Confronted with a general world depression, a country like Canada, for example, will be presented with grave problems if it seeks, despite adverse foreign factors, to maintain a high level of income and employment. Let us suppose that a strong compensatory program is undertaken to prevent any substantial decline in national income, despite the fall in exports. The effect will be to sustain the demand for imports, since income has not fallen. At the same time exports are declining because of the collapse in foreign markets; and this decline will now be reinforced by the fact that the maintenance of income prevents a deflation of costs in the export industries. Canada will therefore experience balance of payments difficulties. If the prospects are for a brief world depression, the gap in the balance of payments could probably be filled by boldly throwing in the accumulated reserve of gold and foreign exchange assets held at the inception of the depression. But in a long depression these international monetary reserves would become exhausted. Another course of action thus becomes imperative.

In these circumstances, action to protect its balance of payments position is likely to involve ways and means of controlling imports. This, to be sure, is unfortunate, both for Canada and for the countries from which she imports. But once the foreign exchange reserves approach the minimum below which it is not deemed prudent to go, there is no escape. Even if it were decided to abandon the program of internal stability and deflate in concert with the rest of the world, such a course would also have the effect of cutting down on imports. Canada's enforced policy of cutting imports is, in the circumstances assumed, no fault of hers; the fault lies with the foreign countries which have failed to maintain adequate aggregate demand. Whichever way she turns, imports must be curtailed. Only by a concerted program of international expansion would it be possible to restore world trade.

There are broadly two means of reducing imports: (a) exchange depreciation, and (b) direct controls such as import quotas and exchange control.

In the circumstances here discussed the term "exchange adjustment" might well be preferred to that of "exchange depreciation," since deflation abroad, combined with income maintenance in Canada, has the effect of making Canada a high-cost country with an overvalued currency. A change of the exchange rate to compensate for the discrepancy in price levels would only serve to re-establish balance. Such an adjustment would in no sense mean competitive exchange depreciation. Canada would not be undercutting her neighbors.

A variant form of exchange depreciation is the plan proposed by Robert Triffin, which may be termed alternatively either "partial exchange depreciation" or "selective exchange control." Under this system imports are classified in two or more lists as essential and nonessential. Importers of goods on the preferred or essential list can purchase foreign exchange at the official rate. These limited imports presumably will not exhaust the whole current supply of foreign exchange. The excess amount of exchange is then sold in an auction market to the importers of commodities that are on the nonessential list. Since there is not enough foreign exchange to go around, the limited amount of exchange offered in the auction market will be in great demand. There will be sharp competition for it; in other words, the local currency will depreciate in value in relation to foreign currencies.

Thus the auction rate will be a depreciated rate. But all "necessary" imports and all exports will be traded in terms of the official exchange rate. As soon as the emergency is over and sufficient exchange again becomes available to meet all requirements, the auction rate would tend to move toward the official rate and might eventually disappear altogether.[3]

The Triffin plan is intermediate between complete exchange depreciation on the one side and complete exchange control on the other. It is peculiarly suitable for a country which, in a depressed world, is struggling, by means of internal expansionist policies, to maintain a high level of income and employment. Under these circumstances, outright exchange depreciation is hardly justified, since the cause of the balance of payments difficulties is not a fundamental disequilibrium. From the long-run standpoint costs are not out of line with those of foreign countries. Nor is there a fundamental disequilibrium from the long-run standpoint between the structure of its imports and that of its exports in relation to world demand conditions. On the contrary, the difficulties arise wholly from the depression abroad. Outright depreciation is likely to involve distortions in the economy not justified by the long-run conditions, and not easily rectified when the emergency is over. Partial depreciation, with a flexible auction market, not only helps to meet the emergency but also minimizes the distortions incident to depreciation, and thereby facilitates the return to more normal conditions.

[3] See Alvin H. Hansen, *Monetary Theory and Fiscal Policy,* McGraw-Hill Book Company, Inc., New York, 1949, Chapter 15.

International Buffer Stocks

Apart from the general program of international collaboration aiming at the co-ordinated timing and direction of domestic measures, a specific area for co-operation relates to the stabilization of the prices of primary products. A leading suggestion, which has received widespread attention, relates to a "plan for the constitution and financing of an international buffer stock agency with the function of purchasing certain crude products when prices tend to fall and selling them when prices tend to rise. . . . Such an agency would effect its stabilizing influence by offering to buy at some predetermined minimum price and sell at some predetermined maximum price. Price fluctuations would thus be confined within the limits set by these minima and maxima so long, at any rate, as sufficient stocks remained at the disposition of the agency. Should a tendency for stocks to accumulate or to disappear altogether manifest itself, the agency would modify its prices; but its purpose should be to modify its prices only to the extent necessary to adjust production to demand over, for instance, the period of the trade cycle."[4] In addition to its initial capital, the agency should be empowered to raise funds in the most favorable capital markets.

International Investment

A second specific area for international co-operation relates to the functions of the International Bank for Reconstruction and Development. The central purpose of this institution is to promote and finance those basic development projects which underlie and are prerequisite to the agricultural and industrial progress of any country. Such projects relate particularly to the development of natural (including agricultural) resources and the construction of transportation and power-generating facilities. These development programs not only serve to raise the productivity and standard of living of the people, but may also help to change the structure of the country's imports and exports so as to facilitate equilibrium in its balance of payments. Finally an interna-

[4] *Economic Stability in the Post-War World,* Report of the Delegation on Economic Depressions, Part II, League of Nations, 1945, pp. 313–314.

tional program of capital investment could, among other measures, be used in a counter-cyclical manner so as to minimize inflationary pressures and offset depressional declines in private capital outlays. Large-scale international projects should be pushed on an expanded scale whenever an increasing volume of unemployment in the advanced countries releases productive resources for export to the undeveloped countries. While development programs must in large measure be undertaken on a continuing basis, they can be stepped up or reduced as circumstances require, so as to promote world-wide stability of income and employment.

In his inaugural address, January, 1949, President Truman aroused world-wide interest in a proposal, rather vaguely advanced, to raise the level of technique throughout the world. Emphasis was placed upon the spread of technical knowledge, but it was widely believed that the proposal involved also ways and means of accelerating the export of capital goods, financed in large measure by private investment, with government co-operation and support.

International Monetary Collaboration

Finally, there is the special area of international monetary collaboration involving the problems confronting the International Monetary Fund. These relate mainly to a continuous program of adjustment looking toward a balanced structure of exchange rates, to continuing programs of collaboration with respect to monetary aspects of inflationary or deflationary developments, and finally to the provision of financial aid to help countries over emergency balance of payments difficulties.

Under the old gold standard, deflation was the remedy for disequilibrium in the balance of payments. If imports were excessive in relation to exports, a fall in income and employment quickly had the effect of cutting down imports. Deflation could be depended upon to restore balance.

The experiences of the interwar years have pointed the way toward a different monetary policy. Everywhere countries demand freedom to pursue a program of internal stability and full employment. The pursuit of this goal may well involve countries in balance of payments difficulties. Yet, unwilling to follow the painful deflationary process of adjustment, they are determined that the balance of payments shall no longer control their internal monetary policy.

But independent monetary management is likely to lead to disequilibrium in the balance of payments unless the various countries, and especially the leading countries, keep in step with respect to their internal programs of stability and full employment. Even though only partial success is achieved, the matter can indeed, in considerable measure, be managed if the International Monetary Fund assumes a flexible attitude with respect to adjustment of exchange rates. But obviously this is only possible within reasonable limits. If violent disparities in international cost- and price-level relationship continually occur, no process of exchange adjustment can satisfactorily compensate for such disturbances. Thus there is no escape from the basic need for responsible action by individual countries with respect, first, to an internal anti-cyclical program and, second, to collaboration with other countries.

Proposals by a Group of U.N. Experts

Two interesting proposals looking toward stabilizing international fluctuations were made by a group of United Nations economic experts. One relates to stabilizing the flow of purchases from abroad; the other, to a scheme to stabilize the flow of long-term international investment.[5]

The first proposal is that each government should accept the responsibility of offsetting any depletion of the international monetary reserves of foreign countries caused by a fall in its demand for imported goods and services, in so far as this fall is due to a general decline in its internal effective demand. Each country should make a deposit in its own currency with the International Monetary Fund of an amount equal to the fall in its imports less the fall in its exports *in the given year as compared to the reference year.*[6]

[5] United Nations, *National and International Measures for Full Employment,* Lake Success, N.Y., December, 1949.

[6] The International Monetary Fund should be empowered to waive the deposit requirement in the event that the country concerned could show to the satis-

According to the second proposal, each lending country should fix annual targets for long-term international investment for five-year periods. The lending countries should then put at the disposal of the International Bank, at half-yearly intervals, an amount equal to the total foreign investment planned, less the amount expected to be made through private investors or national agencies, including the International Bank's own issues on national capital markets. If it still turned out that the total amounts fell short of the target set, the amounts placed at the disposal of the Bank in the subsequent period should be adjusted so as to stabilize as far as possible the total amount of lending at the target level.

In connection with this plan, the International Bank should be empowered to borrow from governments, on the one hand, and to lend to governments, on the other hand, for general developmental purposes. A new department for this purpose should be set up in the Bank. This new department should operate without recourse to the Bank's capital and should rely entirely on funds borrowed from lending governments.

These proposals have the great virtue that they implement an automatic and mandatory prearranged program. The effect is, within limits, to remove uncertainty or fear of drastic decline, which so often in the past has turned even a moderate fall into a rapidly cumulating movement.

---

faction of the Fund that the fall in its external currency disbursements was not due to a fall in its internal effective demand.

PART FIVE

Prosperity and Recession since the Second World War

32 · The Four Postwar Cycles

The Cycle New and Old

Following the First World War, several leading economists voiced the belief that the business cycle had vanished for good. And after the Second World War some expressed the view that continued and sustained prosperity was here to stay. By now, however, experience has demonstrated beyond doubt that the cycle of production, income, and employment is still with us.

The cycle is indeed in some ways a new kind of phenomenon. The basic interactions are the same, yet something new has obviously been built into the economic structure. The "rocking chair" doesn't rock in quite the old familiar way.

Some things are much the same. For one thing, investment in inventory stocks continues to play a very important role. Fluctuations in investment in fixed capital (new construction and producers' equipment) have toned down. In consequence, we have had no truly *major* cycle in the postwar period. But a new actor in the cycle drama, or at least one that has by now assumed a leading role, is the federal budget.

A Changing Capitalism

If, however, one turns one's attention away from the minutiae of cyclical interactions to the great tidal waves of historical changes and their impact on the economy, and so upon the nature of business cycles, one cannot fail to note that we are indeed living in a new world. The last three decades of the nineteenth century were a period of great territorial expansion, massive immigration, transformation of a rural society into an industrial society, the growth of huge corporations and vast fortunes. It was not a stable society. Price upheavals, boom, bursts of prosperity, unemployment, bankruptcies, deflations, "now prince, now pauper"—these were the order of the day; millionaires and slums—vast wealth, squalor and poverty. Still, Americans for the most part retained a middle-class status; they operated small family farms and small family businesses. But growing industrialization pressed more and more illiterate immigrants into ever-growing cities. A labor class (foreign to American tradition) and a labor movement developed, still largely outside the pale of the law. An unbridled capitalism flourished.

A progressive income tax and a Federal Reserve System had been built into the economic structure just in time to help finance the First World War. Collective bargaining was weak; and while efforts were made to strengthen the competitive system and hold back the growing power of trusts, combinations, and monopolies, for ten years after the First World War unbridled private capitalism held sway, virtually unchallenged by either labor or the government. The untrammeled excesses that ensued ended in the great stock market crash of 1929 which ushered in the devastating depression of the nineteen-thirties.

That depression changed the face of America. Railroads, banks, state and local governments went broke. Homeowners, farmers, and small businesses became bankrupt. The federal government was compelled to bail them out. New Deal reforms were introduced—the Securities and Exchange Commission, guarantee of bank deposits, social security for the aged, unemployment insurance, minimum wage laws. A vast salvaging operation was undertaken, together with expansionist measures involving housing, rural electrification, and public works. Eventually, recovery got under way. But it was a superhuman task and many mistakes were made. There were still 9.5 million unemployed when the Second World War broke out in Europe.

War and Postwar Developments

The European war boosted United States exports, and soon the nation itself became involved. Before the Second World War was over, nearly half our productive resources had been drawn into the struggle. Unemployment vanished. The country came out of the war rich in monetary assets and monetary savings and desperately short of consumers' durables, houses, business plant and equipment. This laid the groundwork for a vast postwar prosperity which continued (with two short interruptions) until 1957. In the meantime, the Korean war added still more fuel to the burst of prosperity.

After 1957, progress continued, but at a slower pace. The whole fifteen-year period 1948–63, however, shows a degree of stability and growth rarely, if ever, matched at any time in our history. The standard of living rose steadily. Per capita consumer expenditures, after correcting for price changes, increased 30 per cent from 1948 to 1963, or 2 per cent a year. The "social dividend" (private consumption plus government civilian outlays) increased every year, including the recession years. Compared to the turbulent history of the nineteenth century and the disastrous nineteen-thirties, the period 1948–63 must be regarded as one of high stability and growth. But gradually, high-level prosperity was slipping. The unemployment rate was rising. Recoveries were becoming short-lived. The cycle was running down.

A broad general picture of economic fluctuations and trends in the last fifteen years can be obtained from Figure 75. The curve here presented—gross national product in real terms—discloses fluctuations with peaks in 1948, 1953, 1957, 1960 and troughs in 1949, 1954, 1958, and 1961. A careful inspection will reveal a sharp upward trend from 1948 to 1956, and a marked slowing down in this rate of growth from 1956 to 1963. This matter will be discussed in some detail.

Troughs, Peaks, and Time Spans in Four Cycles

The peaks and troughs of each of the four cycles are as follows:

	Pre-recession Peaks	*Troughs*	*Recovery Peaks*
First cycle	November, 1948	October, 1949	July, 1953
Second cycle	July, 1953	August, 1954	July, 1957
Third cycle	July, 1957	April, 1958	May, 1960
Fourth cycle	May, 1960	February, 1961	?

In this chapter, each cycle is labeled by its recession trough. Thus the first cycle is referred to as the 1949 cycle; the second, as the 1954 cycle; the third, as the 1958 cycle; and the fourth, as the 1961 cycle.

From the table, the time span of each cycle, from its pre-recession peak to the subsequent recovery peak can readily be calculated. The 1949 cycle, from peak to peak, ran for 4 years and 8

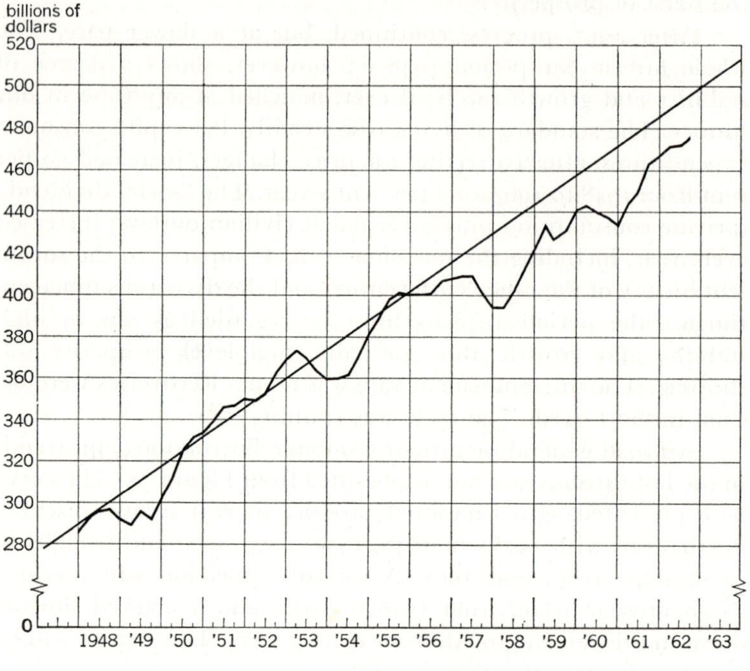

FIGURE 75. *Gross National Product (at 1954 prices)*

months; the 1954 cycle ran exactly 4 years; the 1958 cycle 2 years and 10 months (an abnormally short cycle), whereas the 1961 cycle bids fair to run a more normal length.

The time span of the recession phase was approximately similar for all the four cycles—11 months, 13 months, 9 months, and 9 months, respectively. The expansion phase, however, varied greatly. The 1949 recovery ran for 45 months; the 1954 recovery,

35 months; the 1958 recovery, only 25 months; and the 1961 recovery, it is hoped, will run a more normal period. Indeed, perhaps for the first time, a strong effort is being made, months in advance, to forestall a recession altogether. Many, perhaps most, professional economists believe that this could be achieved. But Congress is reluctant to act before the recession has actually occurred. Some Congressmen have said they would favor a tax cut *after* a recession is clearly already upon us, but not in advance of a downturn.

Each cycle is characterized by circumstances peculiar to itself. The 1949 cycle was prolonged and buoyed up by the Korean war, and its termination in 1953 was closely associated with the cessation of hostilities. The 1954 cycle, in the recovery phase, was swayed by a burst of business investment and consumer acquisitions of durables (cars, household electrical appliances, and furniture). In part these outlays represented advances in technology; in part, catching up on accumulated shortages. The 1958 cycle was peculiar in that it had two jagged peaks caused by abnormal inventory developments incident to a strike by steelworkers in 1959. The recovery phase of this cycle, moreover, was cut short by a sharp curtailment in federal budget expenditures from $80.3 billion to $76.5 billion. Finally, the incomplete character of the 1958 recovery may have contributed to the mildness of the downturn that followed, beginning in May, 1960.

Relative Severity of the Four Recessions

Among the various criteria of severity, employment and production indexes probably give the clearest answer. We have two over-all measures of production: (a) the index of industrial production and (b) the GNP in real terms (i.e., at constant prices). Both point to the 1958 recession as the most severe. The GNP in real terms declined by $22.1 billion; the index of industrial production fell by 14 per cent. The unemployment rate rose from 3.6 per cent of the labor force to 7.5 per cent (seasonally corrected).

Why was the 1958 recession so severe? The preceding investment spurt was clearly overdone. Investment in producers' plant and equipment rose by 40 per cent from a level which was already high. Consumers' durables jumped nearly 25 per cent in one year, automobiles 37 per cent. These rates were not maintainable. Offsets to the subsequent decline were nowhere in evidence. Accumulated shortages, emerging from the two wars and from delayed technological advances, had, for the most part, been filled. The time was ripe for a pretty sharp drop ($9.6 billion) in producers' investment in plant and equipment.

In the 1954 recession, the GNP in real terms fell by $13.7 billion. The index of industrial production fell 10 per cent, and unemployment rose from an average of 2.9 per cent for 1953 to a quarterly high of 6 per cent in 1954.

The 1949 recession was on balance not very different. The industrial production index fell by 9 per cent and the GNP in real terms by $7 billion. Unemployment rose from a 1948 yearly average of 3.8 to a quarterly high of 7 per cent in 1949.

Both the 1949 and the 1954 recessions were followed by long and buoyant recoveries. The 1949 recovery was, of course, fed by the Korean war; the 1954 recovery, by a burst of private investment.

In contrast, both the 1958 and the 1961 recoveries enjoyed nothing that could remotely be called a boom. The recoveries were incomplete and fell far short of reaching full employment. Whereas the first two cycles registered, at their pre-recession peaks, unemployment rates around 3.5 per cent (or less in the best quarters), the last two cycles displayed unemployment rates of around 5 to 5.5 per cent at their pre-recession peaks.

In one important respect, the last two cycles were very different. Although the 1958 decline was the most severe of all four cycles, the 1961 decline was the mildest. The index of industrial production in the 1961 cycle fell by only 6 per cent, and the GNP declined by only 2 per cent. Unemployment however increased by 2.1 percentage points. But although the decline was mild in terms of product, the 1961 cycle started the downswing from a low performance peak. The unemployment rate at the pre-recession peak was nearly 5 per cent and the GNP in real terms was running some $30 billion or more below our historically determined potential growth trend.

Both the 1958 and the 1961 recoveries turned out to be anemic —equally unable to reduce unemployment to an acceptable level. The unemployment rate for the entire peak year 1960 was 5.6 per cent, and again 5.6 per cent for 1963.

Under favorable employment opportunities, the labor force tends currently to grow at the rate of 1.3 per cent per year, and the potential increase in productivity per worker is estimated by the Council of Economic Advisers as 2.7 per cent per year.[1] This would put our potential rate of growth at 4 per cent per annum. Indeed a line on a ratio chart drawn through the GNP (in real terms) for 1948 and 1956 (both years of good employment, but not over-employment, rates) discloses a 4 per cent (compounded) growth rate. On this basis, the GNP record in the last two cycles has run some $50 billion below the full-employment level. Thus although the 1961 recession was mild, as measured from the pre-recession peak, the bottom of the recession was low, as measured from the potential growth trend.

Expansion vs. Semistagnation

The weakness of the last two recoveries becomes painfully evident when we compare the last six years (1957–63) with the preceding eight years (1948–56). Table XXXIV presents the data on output; Table XXXV on employment, income, and profits. It is evident that the growth rates in terms of output were far stronger in the period 1948–56 than in the period 1957–63.

These tables show how dynamic the period 1948 to 1956 was, and how stagnant the period from 1957 to 1963. Cyclical com-

TABLE XXXIV

Percentage Increases in Output

Period	*GNP* (in constant dollars)	*Industrial Production Index*	*Durable Goods Output* (in constant dollars)	*Industrial Production Index of Durable Manufactures*
1948–56	38.0	46.0	50.0	55.0
Increase per year	4.7	5.7	6.2	6.9
1956–62	18.0	6.0	9.0	13.0
Increase per year	3.0	1.0	1.5	2.2

[1] *President's Economic Report*, 1962, p. 113.

parisons alone fail to bring out this important point. In the period of the last two cycles, employment, income, and output had dropped substantially below the economy's potential. The gap between actual performances and the potential growth trend was widening.

TABLE XXXV

Increases in Employment and Income

Percentage Increases

Period	*Total Employment*	*Personal Disposable Income* (in constant dollars)	*Corporate Profits before Taxes*	*Unemployment Rate* (average per period)
1948–56	9.5	37.0	36.0	4.3
Per year	1.2	4.6	4.5	
1956–62	3.5	18.0	14.0	5.6
Per year	0.6	3.0	2.3	

Counter-cyclical Policy

The first two recessions were cushioned by substantial reductions in federal tax rates. Specifically, a tax cut, amounting to about $4.7 billion [2] was made in 1948, retroactive to January of that year. This involved large refunds in mid-1949. This tax relief no doubt helped to soften the downturn, and the economy began to turn upward in November, 1949.

Similarly, fairly large tax cuts were introduced in the 1954 recession. Effective January 1, 1954, the excess profit tax (designed to help finance the Korean war) was repealed. Personal income tax cuts were made, and excise taxes reduced in April, 1954. Altogether, the individual and corporate tax cuts amounted to about $7.4 billion.[3] This was, however, partly offset by increases amounting to $1.4 billion, in social security taxes.[4]

---

[2] A comparable figure (in terms of the magnitude of 1963 GNP) would be about $10 billion.

[3] In terms of 1963 magnitudes, this would be about $11.5 billion.

[4] *Economic Report of the President*, 1963, pp. 69–70.

In the recovery phase of each of the first two postwar cycles, substantial increases in federal spending began early in the upswing and continued on through into the period of extended expansion. Thus, in the 1949 recovery, the administrative budget expenditures rose from fiscal 1948 to fiscal 1949 by $6.5 billion and (by reason of the Korean war) averaged a per annum increase of $8.6 billion from 1949 to 1953. In the 1954 expansion, budget expenditures rose by $4.6 billion from fiscal 1955 to fiscal 1957, and cash payments to the public rose by $9.5 billion.

Early in 1957, these latter expenditure increases gave rise to heated discussion about the impending 1958 budget. Treasury Secretary Humphrey openly attacked the President's budget, and the President in turn ordered the Budget Director to resurvey the proposed expenditures. Senator Byrd urged a $5 billion cut, and leading business organizations asked for cuts ranging from $5 billion to $8 billion. Defense contracts were in fact restrained, and by September, business analysts were pointing to defense cutbacks as responsible for the unfavorable turn in the business outlook.[5]

But the policy quickly shifted from restraint to methods of coping with the recession which began in July, 1957. This new turn of affairs called for expansionist measures. More powerful still in causing a policy turnabout was the impact on defense spending occasioned by the spectacular Russian achievement in orbiting Sputnik. These events weakened the powerful political pressures demanding fiscal restraint. Budget expenditures increased by $2.4 billion from fiscal 1957 to fiscal 1958.[6]

Nevertheless, the deflationary forces which had been gathering proved to be overpowering. The heavy inventory decline (already overdue) was reinforced by a severe drop in fixed capital outlays together with a decline in consumers' durables. The 1958 downswing came on with full force. Tax receipts fell off sharply and this, together with the increased spending (the fiscal 1959 budget ran $9.0 billion above 1958), produced a deficit in fiscal 1959 of $12.4 billion—an unprecedented peacetime figure.

These budgetary developments stirred up a strong political

[5] Wilfred Lervis, Jr., *Federal Fiscal Policy in the Postwar Recessions,* p. 195.
[6] The increase was $4.2 billion from calendar 1957 to calendar 1958.

movement by fiscal conservatives to reverse the spending and deficit trend. A determined effort was made to balance the budget in fiscal 1960. Fiscal restraint was energetically applied, and this time the administrative budget was actually cut back from $80.3 billion in fiscal 1959 to $76.5 in fiscal 1960. This sharp reversal no doubt played a major role in cutting short the brief recovery which reached a peak in May, 1960, after only 25 months of expansion from the trough of April, 1958.

The Kennedy recovery from the February, 1961, trough did no better in its first two years than the previous recovery. Private housing starts, after 24 months of recovery, stood no higher relative to the trough low than in a corresponding period of the 1958 recovery. Employment and the index of industrial production and personal income had risen even somewhat less; and the rise in the GNP in real terms was about the same. The unemployment rate, after falling to 5.3 in July, 1962, stood at 6.1 in February, 1963, and at 5.9 per cent in May, 1963.

With this two-year record of poor recovery behind it, the Kennedy Administration early in 1963 offered a new program—a program designed not only to move the economy on toward full employment and its long-term growth potential, but also to forestall a threatening new recession. Two years before, upon first assuming office, the new Administration had pinned its hopes on a strong recovery based on an upward surge of private investment. This was to be sparked by an investment tax credit and by new Treasury guidelines permitting faster depreciation rates on fixed capital assets. A critical Congress delayed passage of the tax credit until late in 1962, so that two years had gone by before these investment incentives could begin to operate. How effective they would prove to be remained problematical. At any rate, by early 1963 it appeared evident that something more was needed. The Administration then proposed a drastic tax cut of $13.5 billion, applicable to both individuals and corporations, and spread out over two or three years. The tax-cut plan, however, included reforms looking toward a broadening of the tax base (accomplished primarily by restrictions on deduction allowances). These reforms, if enacted, would have brought in an estimated $3.5 billion of new revenue, leaving a net tax cut of about $10 billion.

The Built-in Stabilizers

Thus far, we have been discussing various discretionary, deliberate, or contrived fiscal programs, such as tax cuts and increased expenditures. But these have not always been introduced with a view to stabilizing the cycle though, on occasion (as in the case of the 1948 tax reduction), they have helped by accident to achieve that result. Quite apart from discretionary action is the automatic stabilizing effect of new institutions built into the social structure—new mechanisms tending to promote stability. The built-in stabilizers can operate with force only because of the enormously increased role of government expenditures and tax revenues. While total governmental cash payments to the public—federal, state, and local—amounted in 1929 to only $10 billion in an economy producing $100 billion of goods and services, in 1962, governmental cash payments (including the trust funds) amounted to $160 billion in an economy of $555 billion.

These increased expenditures have been more or less offset by increased tax receipts. But the ratio of expenditures to receipts varies greatly over the cycle, and the changes in this ratio can be very significant when the aggregates are as large as they have become in the postwar period. Indeed it is the change in the ratio of expenditures and receipts that constitutes in essence the so-called built-in stabilizers. In the recession phase, tax receipts fall off, while expenditures, such as unemployment compensation, relief, etc., rise. In the recovery phase, revenues rise rapidly, indeed more rapidly than GNP, owing partly to the progressivity of the individual income tax and especially to the sharp cyclical fluctuations in corporate profits. A cushion is thus placed under a recession and restraint is imposed on the upward movement. The economy is more or less stabilized.

In earlier periods of our history, the swings were more violent. Recessions were deeper, but the forces making for recovery were unrestrained. Now the "stabilizers" choke off both the recession and the boom. This may leave us on the average over the entire cycle as far from full employment as formerly. But at least greater stability has been achieved. There still remains the problem of full employment and a growth rate equal to our potential. The built-in stabilizers will not by themselves ensure full employment.

It is indeed quite possible that we could drift further and further away from our potential growth trend from cycle to cycle. The problem of adequate growth has not been solved. A solution awaits more effective *discretionary* action and long-range development planning.

Aggregate Shifts in Expenditures and Receipts

The *actual* shifts in expenditures and receipts are partly the result of the automatic built-in stabilizers and partly the outcome of deliberate policy decisions with respect to expenditures and tax rates. The accompanying table shows the actual shifts (built-in and deliberate) in expenditures and receipts (quarterly data) in the four postwar cycles: (a) from the previous peak to the trough, (b) from the trough to the succeeding peak.

Changes in Federal Expenditures and Receipts
(in billions: national income accounts)

	Expenditure Changes		*Changes in Receipts*	
Period	Downswing: Peak to Trough	Upswing: Trough to Peak	Downswing: Peak to Trough	Upswing: Trough to Peak
1949 cycle	$+ 3.4	$(+37.2)	$−6.5	$(+33.8)
1954 cycle	(−11.6)	+12.3	(−9.1)	+19.3
1958 cycle	+10.6	+ 0.7	−6.9	+23.3
1961 cycle	+ 9.8	+13.5	−6.2	+16.2
Average (excluding figures in parenthesis)	+ 7.9	+ 8.8	−6.5	+19.6

Excluded from the *average* figures given at the bottom of the table are the shifts in expenditures and receipts due to the Korean war and its termination. The "average" figures thus represent shifts occuring under more or less normal conditions.

Excluding the cut in expenditures in 1954 owing to the cessation of the Korean war, we note that in all the other downswings expenditures rose. In both the 1958 and 1961 cycles, the increase was about $10 billion from peak to trough. This expansionist effect was *reinforced* by a decline in receipts of around $6.5 billion in each downturn (omitting the special case of the cut in taxes in 1954). Thus the cushioning or sustaining effects of expenditure changes and shifts in receipts amounted to about $16.5 billion in the case of the last two cycles and to about $14.5 billion when the 1949 cycle downturn is included. These cushions prevented the cumulative downturn which characterized "pre-New Deal" depressions.

In the recovery phase of the cycle deliberate increases in expenditures contributed substantially to the upswings following the 1954 and the 1961 troughs. But this expansionary impact was more than offset by the automatic increases in receipts. Thus the actual fiscal program (built-in and deliberate combined) exercised a restraining influence upon the recovery movements. Cyclically, the swings in receipts play a tremendous role.

In the downswing, both tax and expenditure changes cushion the recession. But in the upswing, they offset each other: taxes restrict and expenditures expand. Taking account of both taxes and expenditures, the cushioning effect on the downswings has been more powerful than the net restraining effect on the upswings.

Social Priorities, the Level of Spending, and the Level of Tax Rates

Broadly speaking, over-all fiscal policy involves two types of decisions. One has to do with the goal of full employment; the other, with social priorities.

The second policy decision has to do with the problem of allocation of our productive resources. How much shall be employed to fill the needs of the public sector? Shall we use more of our resources for education, retraining programs, schools, hospitals, urban renewal, mass transit systems, slum clearance and public housing, etc. The amount of expenditures in any society will, of course, be guided by the prevailing social values. Decision-making with respect to social priorities constitutes the first step in a fiscal policy program. In our democratic society, the final decision is necessarily made by Congress and the President, but what they will do will be guided by the cultural and educational standards of the entire nation. Historically, we know that government expenditures have pursued a fairly steady upward trend in a growing and increasingly urbanized society.

The expenditures being determined, it then becomes the function of fiscal policy to regulate the flow of private spending so as to achieve full employment of labor and capital resources. This is the function of the tax structure. Tax rates should be adjusted, cyclically and trendwise, in such a manner that aggregate spending, public and private, will match the potential aggregate supply of goods and services which the nation is able to produce. Tax rates should be high enough to prevent inflation and low enough to permit full employment.

But is this not precisely what the monetary authorities are supposed to do: to regulate the money supply and the rate of interest so as to prevent inflation on the one hand and to promote full employment on the other? That is indeed the case. Unfortunately, we have found that monetary policy is not sufficiently powerful to do the job. Monetary policy is a necessary tool, but not a sufficient tool. Happily we have at last come to take for granted a system under which the Federal Reserve Board is given complete power over our money supply. Formerly, the delegation of such vast powers to a monetary authority was regarded as unthinkable. Similarly most people would regard it as unthinkable to entrust the regulation of the tax rate to a Fiscal Authority. The time will come, however, when we shall likewise take this for granted. Such an Authority, precisely as in the case of the Federal Reserve Board, would operate within the pattern of the democratic process.

Tax-rate adjustment has long been advocated by economists. In 1962, however, this proposal at last made its appearance on the stage of practical politics. President Kennedy in his 1962 budget message asked for legislation enabling the President, within limits imposed by Congress and subject to congressional veto, to adjust tax rates so as to promote full employment and price stability. Alternatively, this power could be delegated to a Fiscal Authority similar to the Federal Reserve Board.

Congress might legislate the administrative framework within which the Fiscal Authority would act so as to provide a semiautomatic system of tax-rate adjustment guided within limits by agreed-upon criteria of employment, industrial production, and prices. The basic rate would be fixed by Congress; the Fiscal Authority would regulate (within the established limits) the deviations from this rate. As an accepted policy instrument, such deviations should cause no surprise; indeed they should be expected as routine performance precisely as is now the case with Federal Reserve interest-rate adjustments. Perhaps these tax-rate adjustments should be restricted to the first income tax bracket where they can readily be tied in directly to our system of collection at the source.

Monetary Policy in the Postwar Cycles

Monetary policy has played a role, though a modest one, in all four postwar cycles. In the usual case, the Federal Reserve System has sought to provide monetary ease in recession periods and monetary restraint in the later stages of expansion. Reserve ratios were cut in the 1949 recession and were raised to check undue expansion in 1951. Again in 1953, at the very beginning of the downturn, reserve ratios were lowered. In the 1958 downturn, open-market purchases of United States government securities lifted the outstanding volume of Federal Reserve Bank credit, thereby enlarging the monetary base (member bank reserves) which regulates our money supply. Similarly in the 1961 downturn, monetary ease was effected by means of open-market purchases.

Monetary ease appears to have been particularly helpful in the 1954 recession and in the subsequent first phase of the recovery. Monetary restraint appears to have been applied too rigorously in the 1959–60 recovery. This, together with the fiscal restraint of the sharply reduced 1960 budget, no doubt partly explains the short-lived and incomplete expansion of this cycle. From 1958 to 1960 there was no increase at all in the money supply. Both the fiscal and the monetary restraints were in large part inspired by an exaggerated fear of inflation and by a genuine balance-of-payments crisis.

In the 1961 recovery, a strong effort was made to employ

monetary policy to help boost the recovery. Inflationary pressures were no longer imminent, and a new monetary approach was introduced to help meet the balance-of-payments problem while at the same time promoting economic expansion. An open-market and debt-management program was designed to keep the short-term rate relatively high (at least 2¾ per cent) and the long-term rate relatively low. This result was in some measure achieved by means of (1) open-market purchases by the Federal Reserve of longer-term securities in order to raise the price of such securities and thereby lower the long-term rate while, on the other side, it sold short-term securities in order to lower their price and so raise the short-term rate; and (2) Treasury issues of short-terms instead of long-terms, the effect being to lower the price (and so raise the rate) of short-terms, thereby helping to prevent the exchange into gold of dollar holdings by foreign central banks and treasuries.

The effort of the monetary authorities to influence the fluctuations and trends of the economy can be indicated in a fairly meaningful way by the following signposts of monetary ease and restraint:

1. Changes in the money supply (currency and demand deposits)
2. Changes in velocity, i.e., GNP ÷ M
3. Changes in the rate of interest
4. Open-market purchases
5. Changes in reserve requirements

For five years following the Second World War, the money supply remained nearly constant. War-financing had overdosed the economy with money, and with general price and wage controls in effect, the velocity of circulation had fallen. As GNP rose in the first postwar years, the economy was growing up to its expanded money supply. With the burst of activity associated with the Korean war and the 1951–53 expansion, the money supply again began to rise along with a moderate increase in velocity.

Up to the end of the Korean war, the economy suffered no monetary shortage. The quantity of currency and demand deposits increased by 15.8 per cent from 1949 to 1953, or 3.9 per cent per annum. In the same period, the GNP in real terms increased by 27 per cent, or 6.8 per cent per year. But the money supply, used somewhat more intensively, was on balance adequate. Interest rates (AAA bonds) rose only moderately from 2.7 per cent to 3.2 per cent.

The period of semistagnation from the mid-fifties on witnessed, however, a fairly drastic slowdown in the rate of increase of the money supply. From 1955 to 1962, the money supply grew by only 9.4 per cent, or 1.3 per cent per year. In a society with a growth potential of 3.5 to 4.0 per cent per year, the money supply could be expected to grow at more or less (though within rather wide limits) the same rate, and if one may judge by past history, even a greater rate. An increase of 1.3 per cent per year suggests an unduly tight monetary restraint. Even from 1960 to 1962, the rate of increase was only 2.3 per cent per year. The rate of interest on high-grade bonds rose from 3.1 per cent in 1955 to 4.3 per cent in 1962. The rate of discount of the New York Federal Reserve Bank rose from 1¾ per cent in August, 1955, to 3 per cent in 1962.

Defining the income velocity of money as the ratio of GNP to currency and demand deposits $\left(\frac{GNP}{M} = V\right)$, we find the following changes in the intensity of utilization of money over the last three decades. This table pretty much tells its own story.

Year	$\frac{GNP}{M} = V$
1929	3.9
1940	2.4
1948	2.3
1956	3.1
1962	3.8

A Theoretical Note: The Consumption Function and the Postwar Cycles

In a theoretical discussion of the secular and cyclical consumption functions, the author has prepared a chart that discloses the long-run secular relation of consumption to income, and also the short-run cyclical relation.[7] It is repeated here as Figure 76a.

[7] See p. 165.

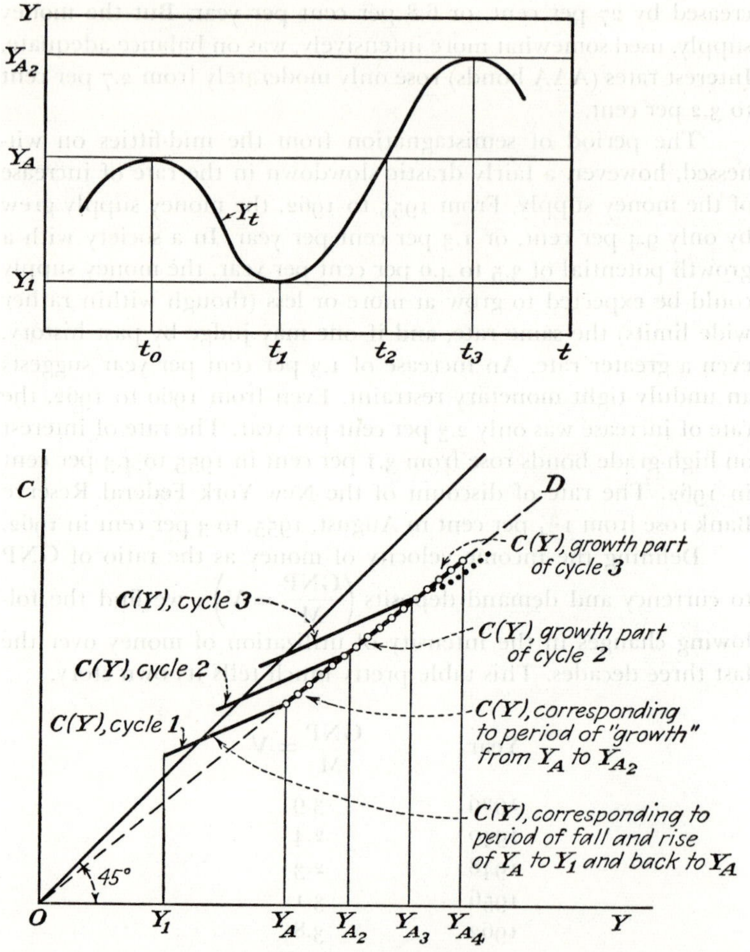

FIGURE 76a. *Secular and Cyclical Consumption Functions*

The secular curve is drawn through the peaks of three successive cycles. Cyclically, as income falls after the peak is reached, consumption falls also, but not back to its former position in relation to income. A new standard of consumption once achieved resists the downward pressure caused by the fall in income. Thus the cyclical consumption function is relatively flat. As income gradually moves back to its former level, consumption responds slowly. Thus in the recovery phase, $\frac{C}{Y}$ is relatively large compared with the smaller peak $\frac{C}{Y}$. Once the former income level is again achieved and the growing economy moves forward to new high levels of income, the secular ratio of C to Y is progressively restored. During the downswing, saving was cut into in order to maintain as nearly as possible the former consumption standard. Now when recovery has at last restored the former high income level, the habitual ratio of saving to income again becomes possible of realization. From there on out, as income reaches up to new levels, the habitual or secular ratio of C to Y is restored.

The theoretical analysis just referred to was presented without giving it any empirical backing. But now let us get a picture of the actual behavior cyclically and secularly, of the relation of C to Y in the post-Korean period. Figure 76b presents a highly interesting empirical confirmation of the earlier theoretical model. When we draw a line through the peak points we see that it is

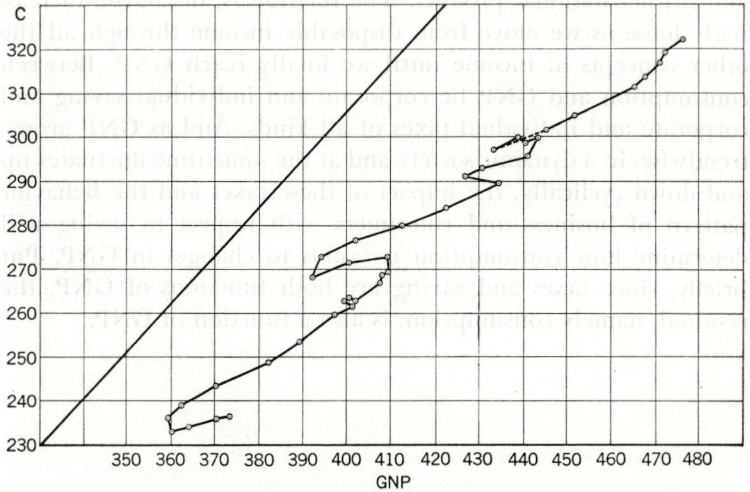

FIGURE 76b. *Secular and Cyclical Consumption Functions: The Post-Korean Period*

substantially straight, starting (if extended) at the point of origin. This line gives us the slope of the secular consumption function; given the parameters of the system as we find them in the post-Korean period. The ratio $\frac{C}{Y}$ is approximately 67/100.

A curve drawn to fit the points from the first recovery quarter to the peak represents the cyclical consumption function for each cycle. This curve is much flatter than the secular consumption function curve. But it becomes progressively steeper as it approaches the next cycle peak. The built-in stabilizers have no doubt exerted a flattening impact upon the consumption function compared with earlier periods in our history. Particularly, note that as shown in the chart, the consumption function is even flatter in the downswing phase of the cycle than in the first phase of the recovery, and much flatter than in the second recovery phase.

In this chart, GNP is used to represent income, and we have accordingly defined the consumption function as the relation of C to GNP. But it could also be defined as the relation of C to (a) disposable income, (b) personal income, (c) national income, and (d) net national product. The relation is, of course, increasingly loose as we move from disposable income through all the other concepts of income until we finally reach GNP. Between consumption and GNP lie corporate and individual saving and corporate and individual taxes of all kinds. And as GNP grows, trendwise, in a dynamic society and at the same time fluctuates up and down cyclically, the impact of these taxes and the behavior pattern of business and consumers with respect to saving will determine how consumption responds to changes in GNP. Put briefly, since taxes and saving are both functions of GNP, the residual, namely consumption, is also a function of GNP.

33 · *Spontaneous Factors and Deliberate Policy*

1948–56 vs. 1956–63

In Chapter 32, we employed the device of dividing the postwar years into two periods: (a) the period of rapid expansion, 1948–56, (b) the period of slack demand, 1956–63. In the first period, powerful spontaneous forces were at work *automatically* generating a high level of aggregate demand. These forces were weaker in the second period. In the first period, prosperity just happened; in the second it had to be contrived. This, for the most part, we failed to do. Unemployment averaged only 4 per cent in the first period; 6 per cent in the second. The growth rate was 4¼ per cent per year in the first period; 2¾ per cent per annum in the second.

The autonomous developments of the first period included (1) the backlog of construction; producers' durable equipment and consumers' durables left from the Second World War and not fully made up until around the middle fifties; (2) the Korean war and the cold war which followed; (3) the population increase, growth of large cities, new products and techniques representing years of technological advance which the Second World War, and to a degree also the Korean war, had pushed aside for later development.

The force of these expansionist factors in 1948–56 and their decline in 1956–63 can be measured by (a) gross private domestic investment, (b) purchases of consumers' durables, and (c) defense expenditures.

All three are "spontaneous" in the sense that they are not the product of heated partisan debate and political discussion. The first two are determined by market forces, the third essentially by external international forces which only military experts can even pretend to evaluate. The prolonged and difficult process of decision-making or deliberate policy is therefore scarcely involved to any appreciable degree in any of these three cases.

The data for these "spontaneous" factors for the years 1948, 1956, 1962, and 1963 (I) are as follows—all in billions of dollars (1962 prices):

Year	*Gross Private Domestic Investment*	*Consumers' Durables*	*Defense*	*Total*
1948	$59.5	$25.9	$16.8	$102.2
1956	74.5	40.1	46.8	161.4
1962	76.2	47.6	53.0	176.8
1963 (I)	76.8	50.0	56.6	183.4

The percentage increases per annum for each of these three "spontaneous" factors are as follows (data in 1962 prices):

Factor	*Percentage Increases per Annum* 1948–56	1956–63
Gross Private Domestic Investment	3.1	0.4
Consumers' Durables	6.8	3.4
Defense Expenditures	22.4	2.9
Total	7.3	1.9

Private investment moved forward at a fairly satisfactory rate (3.1 per cent) in the first period but dwindled in the second. Consumers' durables made a tremendous advance in the first period—100,000,000 household electrical appliances were installed. But the rate of growth dropped to one-half in the second period. Defense naturally receded after Korea and the rate of increase declined to the moderate rate of 2.2 per cent per year in the second period.

Was not general consumption (durables excluded) also a prime determinant of the relative rates of expansion in the two periods? Broadly speaking, the answer is "No." Consumption remained throughout closely tied to disposable income. There was indeed a moderate downward shift in the consumption function from 1948 to 1956. Far from making the first period expansionist, the shift put a moderate brake upon the general buoyancy. The function rapidly shifted up again, settling down at its historical normal position. These shifts—first down, then up—conformed to the expected adjustments induced by the aftermath of war. But the shifts were relatively small. Although durables (in reality goods of capital type) played an important role in the expansion of the first period and in the slowdown of the second period, the consumption of non-durables and services remained throughout closely dependent upon changes in disposable income. To this, one must make one important qualification: moderate *cyclical* fluctuations occur in consumer debt. Consumer borrowings flatten out in the recession phase and begin to rise again fairly early in the recovery phase.

So much for the "spontaneous factors" in autonomous developments. Now how about the discretionary or contrived factors, in other words, deliberate policy? These include federal civilian expenditures and transfer payments, and state and local expenditures of funds raised by themselves (excluding expenditures financed out of federal aid).

The distinction between "spontaneous factors" and deliberate policy measures is of the highest importance. In the United States, the Employment Act of 1946 places responsibility upon the federal government to promote maximum production, employment, and purchasing power. In essence, as far as full employment and optimum use of productive capacity is concerned, the federal government has been made the "lender of last resort," so to speak. If market forces provide full employment, good and well. The government then has little to do with respect to the problem of full employment, though there remain other problems, such as social insurance for old age and health, problems relating to distribution of income and to urgent public needs. But the full-employment goal as such would have been met automatically without deliberate governmental policy. If the market forces (spontaneous factors) do not provide full employment, then the government, according to the 1946 act, should step in. The problem for the government becomes very difficult, however, if the "natural" or autonomous factors making for prosperity are weak. Governmental policies in a democratic society are made by the President and the Congress. Congress represents a wide variety of opinion. Debate, conflict, and finally compromise eventually emerge. Whether or not a given period will prove to be expansionist or stagnationist will depend very much upon the potency of the spontaneous factors. Only if a government has reached a viable consensus on an appropriate fiscal and monetary policy, and perhaps also on planning programs, can one expect a high score of performance. It requires a good deal of doing in terms of deliberate policy to achieve satisfactory goals if the spontaneous forces or autonomous developments for expansion and growth are weak.

Government Civilian Expenditures

Federal civilian expenditures, as here used (total administrative budget outlays excluding defense and interest), include a wide range of public services, such as education, health, welfare, veterans, housing and community development, grants-in-aid to state and local governments, space research and technology, natural resources and agriculture, transportation and commerce, subsidies to the Post Office and other government enterprises, and general government. It is astonishing, considering the broad range of areas covered, how relatively small the aggregate figure for civilian expenditures is.

The absolute figures are as follows, in billions of dollars, 1962 prices:

Year	Federal Civilian Expenditures (defense and interest excluded)	State and Local Government Expenditures (from their own funds)	Total: Federal, State, and Local Governments
1948	$18.0	$21.5	$39.5
1956	18.0	34.6	52.6
1962	28.4	47.7	76.1

The percentage rates of increase per annum, are as follows:

Type of Expenditure	1948–56	1956–62
Federal Civilian Expenditures	0.0%	9.7%
State and Local Expenditures (own funds)	7.6	6.3
Aggregate: All Governments	4.1	7.4

Adding together the three spontaneous factors and the two discretionary or deliberate factors we get the accompanying tables, in billions of dollars, 1962 prices:

Year	Spontaneous Factors	Discretionary Factors
1948	$102.2	$39.5
1956	161.4	52.6
1962	176.8	76.1

Percentage Rates of Increase per Annum

Factors	1948–56	1956–62
Spontaneous Factors	7.3%	1.6%
Discretionary Factors	4.1	7.4
Weighted Aggregate	6.4	3.0

The spontaneous factors (strong in the first period and extremely weak in the second) were indeed partially offset by the discretionary factors. Still, as the weighted aggregate figures show, the combined effect of both sectors was more than twice as expansionist in the first period as in the second. The spontaneous factors, being three times as large in absolute terms as the discretionary factors, dominated. The weakness of the large spontaneous sector left a job too big for the discretionary factors, at least for a country not firmly committed to full utilization of deliberate policy to ensure full employment. The net effect was a sluggish economy for the second period.

The Role of Government Outlays

In absolute figures, private investment and consumers' durables each gave the economy a forward push of $15 billion in the first period, and defense stood $30 billion higher in 1956 than in 1948. In the second period, expansion slowed down to a $2 billion increase for private investment, $7.5 billion for consumers' durables, and $6 billion for defense. In both periods, defense played twice as powerful an expansionist role as private investment. In the discretionary sector, state and local governments outdid the federal government. The federal government, in its civilian outlays, provided no expansionist impact whatever in the first period and only $10 billion in the second. State and local governments pushed ahead with $13 billion in each of the two periods. These figures, it should be remembered, are all in *real terms*. The state and local figures include only expenditures financed from their own funds, the federal grants-in-aid being included in the federal civilian outlays.

The state and local governments' postwar record of expenditures is often cited on the optimistic side of the balance sheet when an attempt is made to assay future expansionist factors. Considering the constitutional restrictions and other limitations confronting local governments, the record is a pretty good one, considerably better than one might have expected. The increases in public school attendance and the increased enrollments in state-supported higher institutions of learning, the doubling of motor vehicle registration from 1948 to 1962—these are indicative of the pressures upon reluctant governments to meet urgent public needs. In 1960, two-thirds of all state and local expenditures went into education and highways. Moreover, the Great Depression and the Second World War accounted for a large backlog of deficiencies to be met in sewage disposal plants, water supply, streets, government office buildings, mental hospitals, reformatories, etc. Considering the accumulated backlog of urgent needs, a minimal part of which could no longer be deferred, the state and local increases in expenditures become easily understandable. And the pressures will continue for years to come because of the rapid growth of urban populations.

The sharp increases in taxes and borrowing, such as have in fact come since 1948, have given a severe jolt to many citizens. Sudden increases are not easily absorbed into the habitual pattern of family budgets. All through this period, average incomes were also rapidly rising. Nevertheless, a rising percentage of income was being taken by state and local taxes.

Property, sales, and income taxes collected by state and local governments rose from 5.3 per cent of personal income in 1948 to 6.6 per cent in 1956 and to 8.0 per cent in 1962. In the meantime, federal personal income taxes took 9.1 per cent of personal income in 1948, 9.7 per cent in 1956, and 10.4 per cent in 1962.

The *percentage* of income left after taxes did indeed decline, but not as much as most people might suppose. The good side of the picture—the absolute rise in income—is always less impressive than the bad side, namely, the increase in taxes. But after deducting all taxes, federal, state, and local, and after correcting for price changes and for the increase in population, we find that the *per capita* private consumption *in real terms* increased 30 per cent from 1948 to 1962, an increase of 2 per cent per year. This represents a gain in the standard of living, measured by per capita consumption in real terms, which is quite in line with our best long-term records in the past. We have achieved this average gain in the last fifteen years despite the very large diversion of our productive resources to defense and despite an average unemployment rate of 5 per cent for the entire fifteen-year period.

The foregoing discussion, however, is not quite fair. It seemed to assume that the standard of living can properly be judged entirely in terms of private consumption. But public services also contribute to the standard of living. Tax money is not just money poured down the drain. It purchased education, highways, streets, hospitals, national defense, etc., etc.

Taking an over-all view of the economy as a whole, government—federal, state, and local—absorbed in round numbers 10 per cent of GNP in 1929, 20 per cent in 1948, and around 25 per cent in 1962. But military expenditures (including expenditures directly related to war, such as outlays for veterans and interest on war debt) account for most of the increase. Military expenditures (as just defined) took 1 per cent of GNP in 1929, 10 per cent in 1948, and 12.5 per cent in 1962. Civilian expenditures took 9 per cent in 1929, 10 per cent in 1948, and 12.5 per cent in 1962—no great change, be it noted, between 1929 and 1962.

It is a striking fact that one-half of all civilian expenditures in 1962 by federal, state, and local governments went into education and highways. The remainder was expended in a long list of public services, such as those previously outlined. Clearly, no civilized community can exist without these outlays. Show me a country with a low level of public outlays and I will show you a low-standard country. We have sad examples of this in some of our low-standard states.

Per capita personal income increased sufficiently from 1948 to 1962 not only to pay increased taxes and permit a 30 per cent rise in per capita private consumption in real terms but also to permit a continuing high rate of personal saving. Consumers have saved, year in and year out, around 7 per cent of personal income after taxes. In 1962, this represented an annual saving of $26 billion. These savings went into private life insurance, private health insurance, savings deposits, building and loan associations, etc. In addition, $25 billion was paid into publicly administered social insurance trust funds. In 1962, Americans poured $50 billion dollars into what the Life Insurance Institute termed "personal protection programs"—a billion dollars each week.[1]

The Role of State and Local Governments

Many of the rich northern states, hard pressed to increase expenditures on education, hospitals, public welfare, state parks

[1] *Life Insurance Bulletin,* February, 1963.

and recreational facilities, complain that they cannot find the money to supply widely recognized public needs. A little inquiry into the facts will disclose, however, that things are not quite that desperate, at least as far as the richer states are concerned. In many of our poorer states, the problem is indeed a serious one, and federal aid is urgently needed. There remains a wide spread in per capita personal income between the rich and the poor states, but this spread is happily narrowing. In 1938–40, the average per capita income in Mississippi, Arkansas, Alabama, North and South Carolina was $249, exactly *one-third* of the average per capita income ($748) in the five rich states, New York, California, Illinois, Connecticut, and New Jersey. By 1959, the five poor states had risen to an average per capita income of $1,346, or *one-half* of the $2,664 income of the five rich states. The poor states are gaining but they have a long way to go.

In the case of some of the richer northern states, tax revenues as a percentage of aggregate personal income are relatively low compared with the national average. And so also, unfortunately but understandably, are their standards of public service.

Fifteen or so of our poorer states offer, as could be expected, low standards of public service, basically because of low fiscal capacities. Even though a heavy tax burden may be imposed, the amount that can be collected is too small to provide adequate public services. In many of these states, the tax take per thousand dollars of personal income is a heavy one. Yet though a high *proportion* of aggregate income is taken in taxes, nevertheless, the taxpayers get little for their money. This is true because the whole state is poor. The result is poor schools and a generally low standard of public services despite the high tax take as a per cent of aggregate personal income.

Some northern states fall considerably below their northern neighboring states in public-service standards, and this is typically due to a relatively low ratio of tax revenues to aggregate personal income. Their fiscal problems arise not because they are poor but because their tax levels are low by northern standards. This is notably true for example of a tier of large industrial states—Illinois, Indiana, Ohio, and Pennsylvania. In terms of per capita expenditures (state and local) Illinois ranks thirtieth, Ohio, thirty-first, Indiana, thirty-third, and Pennsylvania, thirty-seventh [2]—in other words at the very bottom of the list of some thirty-five of the richer states of the Union. In terms of tax effort measured as ratio of revenues per thousand dollars of personal income, Pennsylvania ranks thirty-ninth among all the states of the Union; Indiana, fortieth; Illinois, forty-third; and Ohio, forty-seventh. Obviously these states are not excessively hard pressed by tax burdens relative to the country as a whole.

Basically, the question of the weight of the tax burden reduces to the matter of social values. Do we prize good public schools more than expensive "tail fins"? Recently Detroit, Michigan, held an election in which the citizens of this fifth largest city in the United States voted on a millage tax and a bond issue to provide funds for school expansion commensurate with a rapidly growing school population. All leaders in the community—business, labor, the churches, parent-teachers associations, the League of Women Voters, the newspapers—supported the tax increase and the proposed bond issue. Still, the tax and the bond issue were heavily voted down. Yet the average citizen may well have spent as much or more on his luxury automobile (amortization of the purchase price, interest, insurance, repairs, and operating expenses) as his aggregate state and local taxes. Indeed it is estimated that Americans spend more per year on automobiles than all state and local taxes put together.

Not only is the *average* tax burden relatively light in these four large industrial states; it is also regressive. None of these rich industrial states have an income tax. And so far as the country as a whole is concerned, although well over half of the states do have an income tax, still as an over-all average, state and local taxes, including all kinds of taxes, appear to be seriously regressive, as the accompanying table discloses. It may be added that, even at the federal level, the tax structure, including all federal taxes, does not really begin to become progressive until we reach the $15,000 income level.

---

[2] See James A. Maxwell, *Tax Credits and Intergovernmental Fiscal Relations.* Also see *A Staff Report, Measures of State and Local Fiscal Capacity and Tax Effort,* The Advisory Commission on Intergovernmental Relations, October, 1962.

Industry, so it is argued, tends to locate in states with low tax rates. The fear of competition tends to make legislatures reluctant to raise taxes. But as we have seen, low tax rates also yield low standards of public services. Families will find little inducement to locate in states where schools, hospitals, and municipal services of all kinds are below generally prevailing standards.

Estimated Tax Rates by Income Levels, 1958[3]

Income	*State and Local Taxes*	*Federal Taxes*
Under $2,000	12.6%	15.7%
2,000–3,999	10.4	15.9
4,000–5,999	9.5	16.4
6,000–7,999	8.5	17.2
8,000–9,999	7.8	16.2
10,000–14,999	6.9	17.2
15,000 and over	6.1	29.8
All Classes	8.2	19.2

From the standpoint of industrial competition, however, we may be moving into a new era. Industry may increasingly be more interested in high standards of public services, in high standards of education, etc., than in low tax rates. One observes a growing number of advertisements by state development offices in which it is not the low tax rate that is played up; rather it is the alleged high quality of public education, municipal services, housing, hospital facilities, etc. Today, industry wants high school and college graduates, engineers, skilled technicians, and highly trained scientists. The U.S. Chamber of Commerce has alerted its local membership to do what they can to help reduce the percentage of ninth graders who drop out of school. We may well be moving into a period in which the high standards of public services argument may more and more take precedence over the low tax rate argument as far as state competition for industry is concerned.

Local governments often vote down bond issues for schools, sewage disposal, hospitals, and other urgently needed capital

[3] George A. Bishop, "The Tax Burden by Income Class, 1958," *National Tax Journal*, March, 1961.

facilities. Heated political arguments are concerned with the legitimacy of financing such improvements on the "pay-as-you-use" principle. Sometimes local governments are confronted with legal restraints. Often there is public apathy or fear of debt. Some local governments may indeed be confronted with real limits, not simply imaginary ones. Yet most readers will probably be surprised to learn that the ratio of local debt to gross national product was 9 per cent in 1880, again in 1902, 10.9 per cent in 1913, and only 10.2 per cent in 1960.[4] On a "pay-as-you-use" basis there is far more room for sorely needed state and local expenditures than current practice permits.

Of all our five "dynamic" factors making for an expanding economy—three spontaneous and two discretionary—state and local outlays have in fact ranked high during the last fifteen years. Indeed, this is the only factor that has given the economy an equally strong push in both 1948–56 and again in 1956–63. In the latter period, state and local outlays performed the best of all, exceeding by $3 billion the federal contribution. As far as *increases* in outlays are concerned, state and local governments outdistance private investment increases by sixfold. There is reason to believe that state and local governments will continue to perform reasonably well within the severe limits of operation, but it is scarcely plausible to assume that the record will outdo past performance. If we are going to pull out of our semistagnation, we shall have to look elsewhere.

Future Prospects

As far as can be learned, nobody believes that consumers' durables can play the preponderant role which they did in 1948–56. The volume of sales will remain high and it will grow, but the *growth* will be a relatively modest one. Merely to hold its own at a $50 billion per year level is no small achievement in a market already well supplied. Henceforth, replacement will necessarily be by far the major outlet.

With respect to defense, we must continue to hope that the international situation will permit a cutback in defense expendi-

[4] *State Constitutional and Statutory Restrictions on Local Government Debt,* Advisory Commission in International Relations, September, 1961, p. 18.

tures. Where would this leave us? A big tax cut—bigger than the cut in defense outlay—would be needed, as we know from the "balanced-budget theorem." We should need a drastic tax cut, or a large increase in civilian expenditures, or both.

This would put us severely to the test. Are we prepared to push forward with a full-employment program? Whether we take the increased civilian government expenditure route or the drastic tax cut, or both, large deficits will be incurred. This is true, at least unless a new technical revolution involving a vast release of "spontaneous" expansionist forces should suddenly loom up over the horizon.

Has Fiscal Policy Proved Itself Ineffective?

Critics of fiscal policy often say that postwar experience shows that it is relatively ineffective. Look at the huge postwar budgets, and yet we have semistagnation! What is wrong? To this there are at least two answers. The first has to do with the tax structure and with saving and investment. We have immunized the economy against the effectiveness of large budgets by a tax-rate structure so high that over-all cash budget surpluses begin to choke off recovery long before full employment is reached. Such restraint would indeed be fine if private investment were strong enough to swallow up the flow of both public and private saving generated at full employment.

This country is demonstrably a high-savings economy. As has been mentioned earlier, it generates an enormous volume of saving at high levels of employment—depreciation allowances, corporate retained earnings, pension funds, life and health insurance reserves, savings deposits, mutual funds, and large latent federal surpluses. No society can maintain its *current* achieved level of income unless all these savings funds can find borrowers—business borrowers, consumer borrowers, and government borrowers. If borrowers cannot be found, the potential savings go to waste and income declines. More than that, in a growing society, borrowing must exceed the funds offered by lenders; investment must exceed saving, or the economy cannot grow. To buy the larger product that will be produced "tomorrow" requires the spending not merely of the whole of today's income (including finding sufficient borrowers to take up all current savings). Credit expansion and new debt obligations also are needed to supplement current income sufficiently to take up tomorrow's *enlarged* output.

Viewed from the standpoint of the size of our GNP and our growth requirements, we need in this country a scale of borrowing considerably in excess of that recently experienced. Business, particularly since 1957, has borrowed too little, partly because of its own huge internal sources of funds, partly because for more than a decade, we have been building up a gigantic capacity of plant and equipment, partly because consumer demand has been shifting into services (an area in which the capital-output ratio is comparatively low), and partly because consumer demand has not been growing fast enough (the vicious circle) to induce a growing rate of investment. Consumers and state and local governments are perhaps borrowing as much as can be expected. So we are left with the federal government. The federal government has borrowed only a negligible amount in the postwar period. The federal debt in relation to GNP has fallen to half of the 1947 level. In the only terms that can have any real meaning, namely, the relation of debt to the size of the economy, the federal debt has been shrinking at a rapid—too rapid—rate. This was quite all right so long as business plus state and local governments were taking up the savings flow, as was roughly the case until 1957. And should technology open up vast new private investment outlets in the future, the "debt shrinking process" could be resumed. But when this is not the case, federal government borrowing is not only in order, but becomes a necessary condition for growth and expansion.

And now we give the second answer to the allegation that fiscal policy has not been able to turn the trick. The point that needs to be pressed home is this: growth and expansion cannot be achieved merely by maintaining current high levels of government expenditures (no matter how high) plus business outlays in investment. Growth requires *increases* of expenditures. Consumers, we know, will respond as far as their personal incomes grow together with some moderate trend growth in consumer credit. But the primary forward push must come from business investment and government outlays. So long as the business forward thrust was strong, as in the period 1948–56, so long as the international situation (defense) supplied a spontaneous outlet—just so long was there no great need for much deliberate or discretionary action. From 1957 on, the situation changed. The "spontaneous forces," though weaker, are by no means inconsiderable. They remain the basis for continued "high-level" stagnation with moderate growth. We continue to move forward to so-called record levels, but unemployment is rising and our rates of growth are too low. Deliberate policy has not been strong enough to get us back onto our normal growth trend.

Those who despair of deliberate policy are looking for some renewal of spontaneous forces. Some eagerly look forward to the household upsurge that is expected in the late sixties. We should not underestimate its importance, but we need a good empirical study of its probable impact. It has been suggested that any significant increase in spending will come some five years after the formation of new households. Two adults may continue to live on a restricted level saving up for the future. As the family grows, more space will eventually be needed. A secure job backed by some years' savings will justify some consumer debt for household equipment and a house. If this delayed spending theory is correct, the happy emergence of a new spontaneous factor will be pushed forward into the seventies.

Space. This will no doubt help to spur government spending, perhaps without much acrimonious debate. Space has all the allurements. As pure sport, it vastly exceeds horse racing or professional football. And it surely offers large possibilities for scientific research and technology. Space can be counted on the plus side, not indeed in terms of our serious public needs, but in terms of sheer expansion.

One can, however, see a grand long-range urban renewal program as the one big hope. Here is something that should appeal to the pocketbook. It is said that, for every dollar of federal money, private investment outlets of five to seven dollars can confidently be expected. We are learning about so-called French-type planning—business and government both committed to a well-developed, dependable, long-range program.[5] Urban renewal could be a gold mine for business. It could probably be sold to the Congress. We shall indeed do something for education, hospitals, and other urgent public needs. But large-scale commitments in these areas are scarcely probable. Urban renewal, with its pocketbook appeal, presents really big expansionist possibilities.

We hear much about business "confidence." Often the term is barren of real content. A development program budget, with prior congressional sanctions and commitments, could spark a large volume of private investment. This could put real meaning into the word "confidence." Business could budget ahead based on commitments to carry through an orderly long-range program.

There is growing evidence that fiscal policy will fail to operate at maximum effectiveness unless geared to planned development programs. Public spending and tax cuts, let loose on their own, can indeed, via the multiplier and the accelerator, substantially raise the national income. But the process is indirect and may involve serious lags and leakages. Hitched to a planned program the induced effects can quickly take hold. Business can know rather exactly what its investment outlets will be over a term of years. It can plan ahead. A planned development program is not just a "shot in the arm." In such an undertaking, both the spontaneous and the discretionary factors are marshaled together in a joint government-business undertaking. We may perhaps safely predict that this kind of planning will more and more become the leading characteristic of modern capitalism as we move into the last decades of the twentieth century.

There remains the dreadful prospect that we shall not tackle at all adequately the gigantic task of rehabilitating the deteriorating segment of our society—the delinquent and unemployed teenagers, the workers displaced by automation, the racial groups suffering from discrimination, the 8.3 million adult functional illiterates, the 7.7 million recipients of relief.

In Victorian England, Disraeli once said: "England consists of two nations—the rich and the poor." So in America two nations

---

[5] For an excellent discussion of the role of spontaneous forces vs. deliberate policy in the United States, in contrast with Europe, see Edward S. Mason, "Presidential Address," *American Economic Review,* March, 1963.

are developing—affluent America and deteriorating America. The difference is this: In Disraeli's time, the rich constituted a very small per cent of the population; the poor, the great masses. With us, affluent America is a vast majority—perhaps 85 per cent; deteriorating America is only some 15 per cent, but the proportion is apparently growing.

This problem cannot be solved by mere expansion of the economy. Expansion toward full employment is indeed a necessary condition; but it is not a sufficient condition to cure this distressing problem. The deteriorating segment of our society can never be rehabilitated except by a gigantic program involving very large federal expenditures over many years. Minor efforts will be swamped by the cumulative deteriorating forces already at work. Dr. Conant's great book on *Slums and Suburbs* presents the magnitude of the problem—social dynamite in the midst of our complacent, affluent society.

Abraham Lincoln, who had strong convictions about the role of government, has often been misquoted as saying that "government should do for the people only what they cannot do for themselves." But this is not what he said. Instead his statement suggests a positive, active role of government. The correct quotation is as follows: "The legitimate object of government is to do for the people what needs to be done, but which they can not, by individual effort, do at all, or do so well for themselves." [6]

[6] See Roy P. Basler, ed., *The Collected Works of Abraham Lincoln.*

34 · *The Full-Employment Surplus and the Tax Cut*

The Latent Surplus

In view of the fact that more often than not we have been running deficits rather than surpluses in the conventional administrative budget, the reader may think it strange to open this chapter with a section on budget surpluses. At 92 per cent full employment we have typically been running deficits of around three billion dollars or so. Why then talk about surpluses?

The answer to this conundrum is as follows. Given a certain level of expenditures, and given a certain structure of tax rates, revenues will rise if perchance the economy should move into higher gear in response to some powerful spontaneous factor (new products, for example, which could inaugurate a burst of investment in plant and equipment). Public expenditures not having increased, it follows that the increased tax receipts will rapidly bring the budget into balance and eventually produce a surplus. If the tax rates are so high that a near balance is achieved at low employment levels, it follows that such a tax structure would produce an overflow of receipts if high employment levels were reached. It follows also that if spontaneous forces should drive the economy upward, the increasing tax bite would act as a restraint on the expansion.

There can be no question about the great educational value of the "Full Employment Surplus" analysis which the Council of

Economic Advisers presented in January, 1962.[1] It has contributed in no small measure to a better public understanding of the role of fiscal policy. The fiscal-program curve, and its relative stability over recent years, has helped to drive home the point that, in the absence of a yearly increase in expenditures, or alternatively, a yearly reduction in tax rates, our tax structure acts continuously as a brake upon the economy.[2] This brake could completely have stopped all growth had it not in fact been eased by an approximately $5–6 billion yearly increase in federal expenditures (national income accounts) from 1956 to 1963.

This formulation of the impact of a given fiscal program upon expansion or restraint tells, of course, only a part of the story. There is, moreover, the danger, as is almost necessarily true of any proposition in so complicated a field of inquiry as economics, that quite erroneous conclusions may flow, seemingly inexorably, from the analysis. The formulation seems to suggest that if the "hurdle" of the restraint imposed by the latent full-employment surplus were removed by expenditure and tax policies, this in and of itself would ensure full employment. The analysis could indeed suggest that the concept of a "balanced budget" *per se* remains as an appropriate goal of national economic policy.[3] In short, it seems to suggest that a fiscal program which would produce a balanced budget at full employment would more or less *automatically* ensure a full-employment GNP.

I propose to incorporate the full-employment surplus within the broader pattern of the saving-investment problem. As a first step in this direction, Figure 77 includes, along with the latent budget surplus, the induced increments of private saving which emerge as full employment is approached. The full-employment surplus schedule by itself *alone* contributes little toward an understanding of the factors that determine whether the GNP is high or low. Within the framework of the saving-investment analysis, however, it supplies an important element, namely the contribu-

[1] *Economic Report of the President*, pp. 78–81.

[2] This general approach has for many years been the central thesis of the Committee for Economic Development.

[3] Similarly, those who advocate the adoption of a capital budget (desirable in itself as good accounting procedure) appear at times to suggest that it be made the basis for fiscal policy decisions.

tion of the federal government (tax rates and expenditures being given) to aggregate gross saving.[4]

Figure 77 shows the increments of (a) federal government saving and (b) private saving above (or below) the point at which

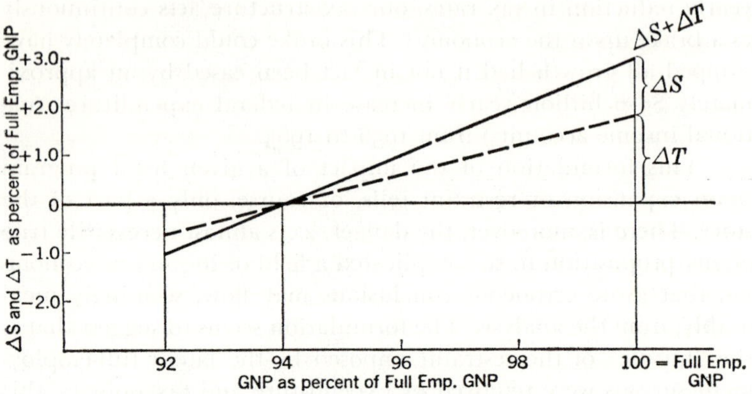

FIGURE 77. *The Latent Budget Surplus*

federal government net saving is *zero,* i.e., the budget is in balance, i.e., T = G.[5] Let us call this point the "zero" point. The govern-

[4] Gross saving equals (a) gross *private* saving, plus (b) government net saving (or dissaving). Gross saving (public and private), *ex post,* will always equal gross private investment. It follows that gross *private* saving will not equal gross private investment except in the special case when government net saving is zero (i.e., when the budget is in balance). See the precise definitions given below.

[5] The reader should note carefully the somewhat arbitrary definitions here used for the different symbols. "G" stands for federal government expenditures (national income accounts, which include transfer payments). "I" stands for gross private investment, including net exports of goods and services. "S" stands for gross *private* saving, including, be it noted, the net saving (or dissaving) of state and local governments but *not* including the net saving (or dissaving) of the federal government. "T" stands for the tax and other receipts (national income accounts) of the federal government, including the trust funds. (T − G) = federal net saving.

It should be noted that, in line with these definitions, GNP − (I + G) is *not* equal to private consumption. Rather GNP − (I + G), as here used is equal to private consumption, plus state and local expenditures (i.e., community consumption), less federal transfers to the public and to state and local bodies. In short, GNP − (I + G) is equal to "self-financed personal consumption plus self-financed state and local expenditures."

ment surplus plus the private saving differential will tell us how much gross private investment must rise above the "zero" point level in order to reach full employment via the route of an investment boom. Similarly, at the left of the "zero" point, one sees how far investment must fall to drive the GNP down sufficiently to produce the indicated government deficit and the negative private saving differential.

Figure 77, although schematic and not intended to be accurate, does fairly well disclose the *average* situation for the four semistagnant years 1958–61, and it fits almost exactly the actual data for the year 1961. For the four-year period as a whole, the economy *averaged* about 8 per cent below full employment. At this level of GNP, the average federal deficit (national income accounts) was about \$3 billion, and the negative private saving differential was about \$2 billion. Had full employment been reached, however, an average federal surplus of \$9 would have appeared, together with a positive private saving differential of about \$6 billion. From the low point to the high point, the aggregate *increase* in saving (public and private) would have been about \$20 billion; hence, to reach full employment via the investment route would have required an *increase* in gross private investment of around \$20 billion.

The full-employment surplus (when supplemented by the private saving differentials) does indeed provide one of the basic factors needed for income determination. Still this incremental type of analysis is not quite adequate. A clearer picture will emerge if we consider the role of the G and T schedules as aggregates in relation to the I and S schedules.

The (S + T) Schedule

The relation of the (S + T) schedule to GNP is shown in Figure 78. Also, the T schedule is shown separately, and the S schedule is represented by the area between the (S + T) curve and the T curve. The nine observations cover the period 1954–62—a period in which tax *rates* remained for the most part fairly stable. The regression lines fitted to these observations disclose a stable relation, year after year. For any given increase in GNP, private

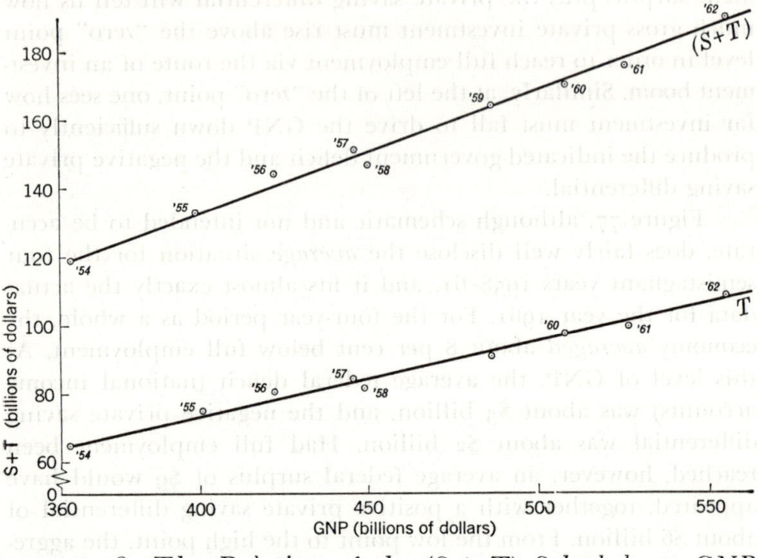

FIGURE 78. *The Relation of the (S + T) Schedule to GNP*

saving and federal receipts rose, as indicated, in a fairly dependable manner as revealed by the slope of the curves. The slope of the T schedule $\left(\frac{\Delta T}{\Delta GNP}\right)$ was 0.23; that of the (S + T) schedule $\left[\frac{\Delta(S + T)}{\Delta GNP}\right]$ was 0.38, which gives the S schedule slope a value of 0.15.

For convenience, in what follows, let us use round figures (nine observations are in any event not enough to justify too great refinements). Thus we shall assume that the slope for the T schedule was 0.25, and for the (S + T) schedule 0.40. The slope for the T schedule tells us that, for every $100 increase in GNP, approximately $25 was captured by the federal government in the national income account receipts. Only a part of this, however, would show up in the administrative budget receipts, the rest going to the trust funds. The slope of the (S + T) schedule tells us that we might normally assume a multiplier (k) of approximately 2.5.

The slope of the T schedule for the period covered was tilted up somewhat (upward shifts in the schedule) by reason of the built-in increases in social security tax rates. This development was, however, offset more or less by opposite tendencies that tended to flatten the slope of the T schedule. Corporate profits ran pretty much on a flat plateau, owing partly to the slow rate of growth of the economy, and partly to the exceptionally rapid rise in depreciation allowances from $11.8 billion in 1953 to $26.2 billion in 1961. These factors had the effect of narrowing the profit margin and so tended to hold back normal increases in corporate income taxes.

Given the T and S schedule, the actual level of GNP will depend upon the level of gross private investment and government outlays. Without embarking upon the difficult problem of interdependence, we shall here assume that I and G are in large measure autonomously determined. Investment outlays and government expenditures are the result of decisions made by men of affairs—businessmen and government officials—based on innumerable and highly complicated matters, among which exogenous factors play a major but not exclusive role.

Figure 79 shows the intersection of the (I + G) schedule with

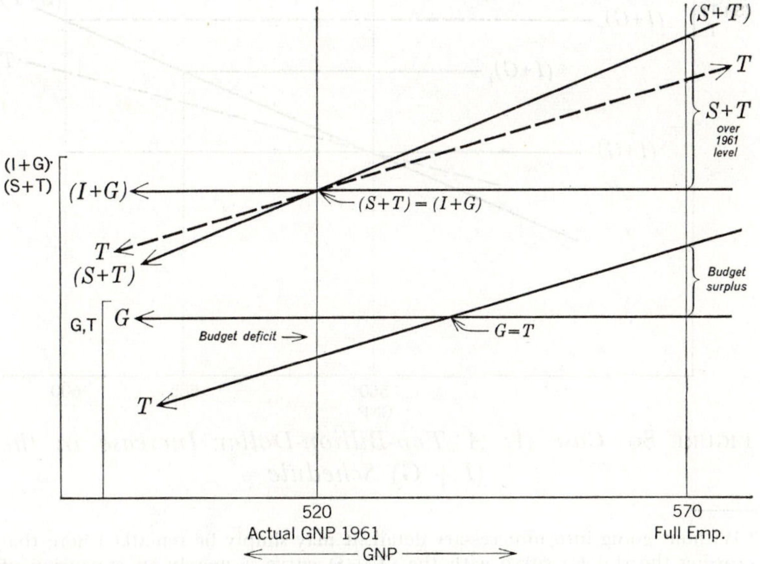

FIGURE 79. *The Intersection of the (I + G) Schedule with the (S + T) Schedule*

the (S + T) schedule.[6] The data are derived from the calendar year 1961. The equilibrium level of GNP settled at $520 billion. Broadly speaking, the chart presents substantially the same picture as Figure 77. Here, however the G and T schedules are placed against the background of the over-all savings-investment problem.

By shifting any one (or more) of the four schedules, we can readily trace the impact upon the GNP and upon government deficits and surpluses. In particular let us experiment a bit with fiscal policy shifts designed to achieve fuller employment. We shall consider two approaches to this problem: Case A, a $10 billion increase in federal outlays, and Case B, a $10 billion cut in taxes. The results are shown in Figures 80 and 81. In view of past relationships, based, however, on an inadequate number of observations, these results may perhaps be regarded as reasonably plausible, though certainly a long way from being dependable or predictable.

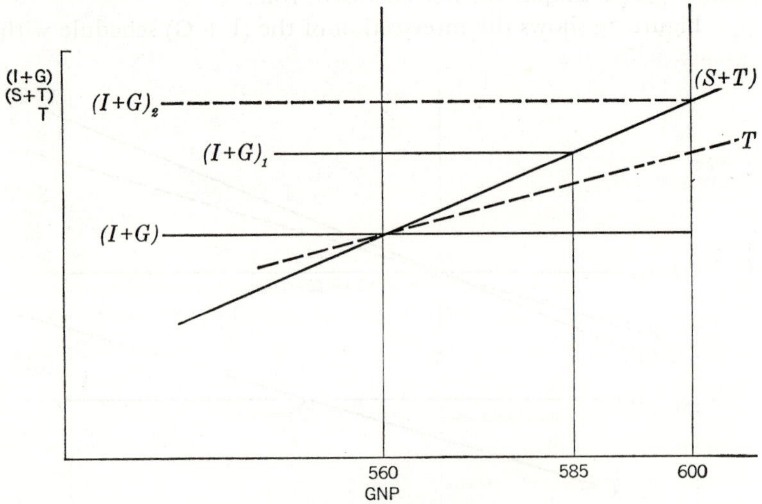

FIGURE 80. *Case A: A Ten-Billion-Dollar Increase in the (I + G) Schedule*

[6] Without going into unnecessary detail, it may simply be remarked here that crossing the (I + G) curve with the (T + S) curve is merely an expansion of the familiar crossing of the I and S curves to determine the level of GNP.

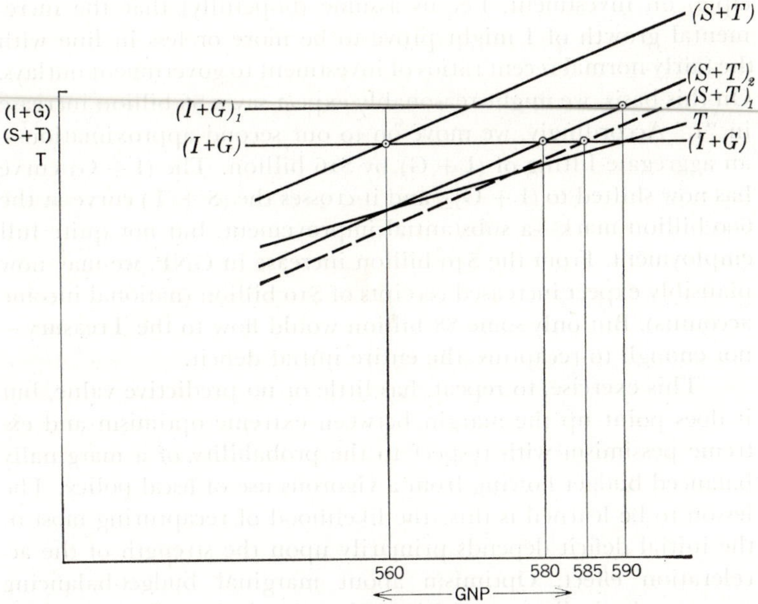

FIGURE 81. *Case B: A Ten-Billion-Dollar Reduction in the (S + T) Schedule*

A Ten-billion Increase in Expenditures

Case A: Starting from a GNP of $560 billion (approximately that of 1962), we introduce an increase in government expenditures. As a first approximation, we shift the (I + G) schedule up by $10 billion to become $(I + G)_1$. The $(I + G)_1$ curve now crosses the (S + T) curve at the $585 billion GNP level, an increase of $25 billion (the multiplier, as we have seen, being 2.5). In accordance with the slope of the T schedule, such an increase in GNP should raise the national income accounts receipts by $6.25 billion. Of this, only some 80 per cent would flow into the Treasury, the rest going into the trust funds. Thus the Treasury might recapture only $5 billion of the $10 billion deficit initially created by the increased expenditures.

An increase of $25 billion in GNP, however, could certainly be expected to have some induced effect (the acceleration principle) on investment. Let us assume (hopefully) that the incremental growth of I might prove to be more or less in line with the fairly normal recent ratios of investment to government outlays. On this basis, we might reasonably expect say a $6 billion increase in "I." Accordingly, we move on to our second approximation—an aggregate lifting of (I + G) by $16 billion. The (I + G) curve has now shifted to $(I + G)_2$, and it crosses the (S + T) curve at the 600 billion mark—a substantial improvement, but not quite full employment. From the $40 billion increase in GNP, we may now plausibly expect increased receipts of $10 billion (national income accounts). But only some $8 billion would flow to the Treasury—not enough to recapture the entire initial deficit.

This exercise, to repeat, has little or no predictive value, but it does point up the margin between extreme optimism and extreme pessimism with respect to the probability of a marginally balanced budget flowing from a vigorous use of fiscal policy. The lesson to be learned is this: the likelihood of recapturing most of the initial deficit depends primarily upon the strength of the acceleration effect. Optimism about marginal budget-balancing must rest basically upon faith in the stimulating effect of expansionist fiscal policy upon the inducement to invest.

A Ten-billion Cut in Taxes

Consider next Case B—a tax cut—as shown in Figure 81. As a first approximation, we assume a downward shift in the (S + T) schedule to $(S + T)_1$. This implies an increase in GNP of $25 billion to $585 billion. But this first approximation is clearly not defensible because not all of the tax relief will be spent—a part will be saved, possibly $2 billion. This shifts the (S + T) curve up, as a second approximation, to $(S + T)_2$ and the GNP now shrinks from $585 billion to $580 billion. So far we have assumed no acceleration effect. Since the tax cut boost has now been cut down to $8 billion (after taking account of the induced increase in saving), we can expect a somewhat smaller acceleration effect than that assumed in Case A, say, perhaps a $4 billion increase in I. The (I + G) curve now shifts, as a third approximation to $(I + G)_1$ and crosses the $(S + T)_2$ curve at the $590 billion GNP level. In the final analysis, then, GNP is lifted by $30 billion, and the "super-multiplier" applied to the $10 billion tax cut turns out to be only 3. A $30 billion increase in GNP suggests recovery of $7.5 billion in receipts of which some $6 billion would flow to the Treasury. This would leave a net marginal deficit of some $4 billion.

Transitory vs. Permanent Deficits

It has often been suggested that a tax cut might well induce so large an increase in GNP that the recaptured revenues could eventually more than offset the initial deficit. Thus President Kennedy, in his speech to the New York Economic Club on December 14, 1962, alluded to a "temporary deficit of transition, resulting from a tax cut designed to boost the economy, increase tax revenue and achieve a future budget surplus."

This eventuality is certainly not impossible. The foregoing analysis, however, helps us to keep our feet on the ground. In the case of a tax cut, even a marginally balanced budget (let alone a surplus) could scarcely be expected from a *normally* strong acceleration effect. But, if latent *autonomous* forces (advances in technology, etc.) have been accumulating—lying dormant and not yet having found corporeal expression in new investment—then the stimulus of a tax cut might well open the door to the full force of these exogenous expansionist factors. The increased spending, directly flowing from the tax cut, plus the normal acceleration effect, plus the release of latent autonomous forces, could indeed, under a combination of favorable circumstances, raise the GNP to the point suggested by the President.[7] More probably, in the usual case, we should have to settle for a continuing deficit equal to, say, a quarter or a third of the initial tax cut.

The events of the last fifteen years, including, it should be noted, the eight years of the Eisenhower Administration, reaffirm the long-standing lesson of history that growth requires an increase in money, credit, and debt. And in the public-private economy of today, a well-balanced growth suggests an increase of debt at all levels—business debt, consumer debt, state and local debt,

[7] Especially in the first year or two of a vigorous upturn, revenues might rise sharply. Thus the spurt from 1954 to 1955 boosted the budget receipts of fiscal 1956 mainly as a result of the temporary sharp rise in corporate profits.

and federal debt. History shows that aggregate debt tends to rise more or less in direct proportion to increases in GNP, or in other words, the ratio of aggregate debt to GNP tends to remain fairly constant. Past relationships indicate that a growth in GNP of $25 billion per year requires approximately an increase in aggregate debt of about $40 billion to $45 billion per year. Since the federal government contributes about 20 per cent of the aggregate flow of GNP, it is not unreasonable to suppose that the government might assume about $8 billion to $10 billion of the per annum aggregate increase in debt. A major cause of the sluggish rise in GNP in recent years is our failure to permit a balanced expansion in the federal debt via either tax cuts or greater increases in federal expenditures.

Booming investment outlets could indeed swallow up budget surpluses and marginal increases in private saving and thereby produce both full employment and a balanced or even an overbalanced budget. Private investment and private debt, if large enough, could conceivably carry the load. So the question arises why in fact this has not occurred in the post-Korean years. One might indeed well have expected overflowing private investment, stimulated as it has been by the huge cold war military contracts and the rapid growth of population. Military hardware requires heavy investment in plant and equipment. And urbanization, in contrast with rural living, requires a vast investment overhead. Still private investment has languished. Why?

The Problem of Investment Outlets

Many reasons have been assigned for the recent poor investment record in the United States. Among other things, it has been suggested that the growth of oligopoly is one reason for the tendency of investment to lag under modern conditions. Oligopolies, it is said, confronted with a downward-sloping demand curve, tend to limit their investment within the bounds of a restricted market, whereas a single competitor among many in a competitive situation is confronted with a horizontal demand curve, and therefore (for him) a limitless market and, as he sees it, unbounded investment opportunities.[8] As a long-run trend this contention may have

[8] See P. Sylos-Labini, *Oligopoly and Technical Progress*, Harvard University Press, 1962.

merit. But in the period since 1957 what seems most impressive in comparing the sluggishness of investment in the United States with the buoyancy of investment in western Europe is the fact that, with us, the demand for consumers' durables has remained on a stagnant plateau, whereas in Europe, with their rapidly rising standard of living, the market in consumers' durables is only now opening up in a big way. With respect to durables, Europe is currently very much where we were back in the booming twenties. This difference in our respective situations accounts in no small measure for the sluggish investment here and the booming investment there.

In the United States, the biggest growth sector is "services." But we have already noted a difficulty: services require less capital investment per dollar unit of output than consumers' durables. The capital-output ratio is lower. Moreover, the service area, fast-growing as it is, is not growing fast enough to absorb the unemployed. Adequate growth in the service area requires large government outlays. If education, schools, hospitals, medical schools, nursing schools, nursing homes, technical training and retraining centers, urban mass transit systems, water resources, river antipollution projects, parks, open sites for recreation, civic cultural centers, and even such traditional functions as police protection and well-paved streets were given sufficient support to bring the public sector up to the best standards of the private sector—if these things were done, the service area would grow by leaps and bounds and these public outlays would in turn provide a wide range of outlays for private investment. A growing demand for education will induce no private investment unless school bonds are voted to provide schools. In contrast, a growing demand for consumers' durables *automatically* opens up private investment outlays.

Our modern scarcities are not in consumers' durables; they are in the area of services associated with (a) the conglomeration of vast populations in urban communities, (b) the skills required by an advanced technology, (c) the cultural needs and aspirations of high community living standards.

Private investment outlets have, of course, not dried up by any means. From 1957 to 1962 inclusive, gross private investment amounted in the aggregate to around $425 billion or about $70 billion per year. This is not a bad record but it is not good enough.

The current tax-cut proposal is essentially an effort to end our high-level stagnation by lifting private investment to higher levels. This can be done, it is hoped, by easing the tax burdens on corporations and by the impact of higher consumer demand (the acceleration effect) on private investment. Yet without the stimulus of substantially larger government expenditures, an adequate increase in investment may not occur. A tax cut will help, but it does not meet squarely the urgent needs imposed by the service-oriented economy of a highly urbanized society.

Nevertheless, there can be no doubt that our tax structure is repressive and a tax cut is desirable.[9] But alone, it will not do the job, nor does it measure up to the social-priorities test of the best allocation of resources. A tax cut, however, is clearly in line with current social values, and this cannot be overlooked in a political democracy. Indeed, it is doubtful whether the public-sector approach can ever be fully accepted until we have employed to the limit the "market" approach, namely, pushing private expenditures to a far deeper saturation point than has so far been reached. The disparity between the marginal utility of the pay-envelope dollar and the marginal utility of the public-expenditure dollar has to be widened a good deal more before it becomes crystal clear that our modern scarcities lie in the public sector. In the meantime, the pressure of ever-present public wants will push us year by year, both at the state and federal level, into increased, though seriously inadequate, public expenditures.[10]

To sum up, the whole thing can be put in a nutshell: In the United States the (S + T) schedule is too high and the (I + G) schedule is too low.

One final brief comment about the first horn of our dilemma –the (S + T) function. In the previous section, the main emphasis

---

[9] See the author's letter to *The New York Times,* May 27, 1962, and Alvin H. Hansen, "A Permanent Tax Cut Now," *Challenge,* October, 1962.

[10] Europe, especially on the Continent, presents not only a more favorable situation with respect to private investment as just indicated, but also a more favorable climate, from the standpoint of social psychology and social values, for making the necessary adjustments to the demands of a "service" economy This is true because there government has traditionally been accepted as the natural instrument to foster the needs of an advanced society in its effort to meet the demands of highly urbanized and culturally rich communities.

has been placed on the T schedule. What about the S schedule? A difficult question. It is rather easy to agree on tax policy. It is not so easy to agree on policy with respect to saving. Is the saving schedule too high or too low? On this there will be wide differences of opinion. In my analysis of secular stagnation made a generation ago, I invariably concentrated on inadequate investment outlets. It was not argued that the propensity to save had been rising secularly; on the contrary, it was held that the propensity to save had remained approximately stable. The analysis ran in terms of investment, not in terms of saving. One may suspect that again today our trouble is inadequate investment, not too high a propensity to save. Growth demands a high rate of investment public and private, and this necessarily implies a high rate of saving.

It is, however, quite possible that recent institutional changes are working in the direction of pushing the S schedule upward. In this connection, note may be taken of the growth of pension funds, of mutual investment funds, of building and loan associations, of time and savings deposits, of accelerated depreciation allowances, of low break-even points in oligopolistic industries, and finally the upward-tilting impact on the S schedule of the built-in stabilizers. Whether the S schedule has, on balance, in recent times been trending up or down is by no means altogether clear. Gross private saving amounted to 15.0 per cent of GNP in the high-employment year 1929. It *averaged* 15.3 per cent of GNP in the five relatively low-employment years 1957–61 inclusive.[11] This occurred although the tax take was far higher in 1957–61 than in 1929. In a sluggish economy, we might have expected the realized private savings to have fallen even though the saving-schedule may have risen. Empirical research into *ex post* saving, considered by itself alone, can mislead us.

Savings-Investment 1956–63

Throughout this period, the latent federal surplus, plus the potential increase in private saving which a full-employment in-

[11] Given the same propensity to save, it is clear that a smaller amount (a smaller ratio of saving to GNP) will be saved in low-employment years. Since in fact a slightly larger proportion was saved in the low-income years than in the highly prosperous year 1929, it appears that the saving function may have shifted slightly upward.

come would produce, amounted on the average to around $20 billion. This means that it would have required a sharp increase in private investment to reach full employment via the investment route. With large excess capacity following the postwar investment spurt of 1955–56, this was not attainable.

But what about federal expenditures? Throughout the 1956–63 period (1960 omitted) the administrative budget expenditures increased by $14.1 billion (1956–59) under Eisenhower and by $12.8 billion (1961–63) under Kennedy. Cash payments (1960 omitted) increased by around $7.5 billion per year (Eisenhower) to about $8.5 per year (Kennedy).

These expenditure increases were just about enough to offset the potential increase in revenue automatically induced by growth. This left the saving-investment problem unchanged. The economy throughout the period hovered at 92 per cent of full employment. A society with a rapidly growing population and large increases in productivity must run fast to remain in the same place.

In fiscal 1960, President Eisenhower made a desperate effort to balance the budget. Instead of the average per annum $5 billion increase in the administrative budget expenditures, the 1960 budget was cut back by nearly $4 billion. This action contributed to cutting short a recovery after only 25 months of advance.

In a somewhat comparable stage in the recovery movement, President Kennedy proposed for fiscal 1964 an increase in the administrative budget of $4.5 billion, which, however, was perhaps about $1.5 billion short of the figure needed merely to offset automatic revenue increases. Private investment, an equally potent offset, was, however, beginning to respond to the 1962 investment tax credit and to the new depreciation guidelines. There was, moreover, the prospect of a proposed tax cut to be spread over two or three years. Business prospects seemed to offer the hope that the periodically recurring recession due in 1963–64 might be avoided. Indeed, one might propose a question for business-cycle analysts to speculate about: how far a dependable per annum increase in federal expenditures of, say, $6 billion [12]

[12] An increase of this magnitude in the years immediately ahead would not fully meet the growing needs in the public sector.

(plus the recently experienced per annum increase of about $4 billion in state and local expenditures) might prevent recessions altogether. Of course the absolute expenditure increase would need to be adjusted upward, as time goes on, to the requirements of growth. This, of course, would not imply a *uniform* rate of growth in GNP each year, but only the prevention of a downturn. This tentative (and optimistic) conclusion would of course become more plausible if a steadily rising expenditure policy were supported by effective *counter-cyclical* tax and monetary policies.

Some reader may feel that my accelerator, as used in this chapter, is too small. One must bear in mind, however, that the accelerator is much smaller than the marginal capital-output ratio. The net addition to capital stock in any period consists partly of autonomous investment and partly of induced investment. The accelerator measures the ratio of *induced* investment to the increment of output.

There is moreover the additional fact that the accelerator will be small whenever there is large unused capacity.

35 · *Growth Trends and the Business Cycle*

In the postwar period too much attention has been devoted merely to the *range* of fluctuations without paying attention to the potential growth trend. The range of the fluctuation of the cycle may be quite narrow while at the same time the spread between the *actual* output (GNP in real terms) and the potential growth trend may be large and perhaps increasing. Much has been said about the mildness of a recession (a few percentage points below the previous peak), and subsequently about recovery "records" even though these so-called "records" were moving farther and farther away from the growth trend that a dynamic society could be expected to achieve.

Some economists, however, have sought to show that the dynamic forces at work producing the recovery phase of the cycle are precisely the growth factors, and that moreover the limits of the potential growth trend may play an important restraining effect on the boom.

Hicks on Growth and the Cycle

In his article, "Mr. Harrod's Dynamic Theory" (*Economics,* May, 1949) and in *The Trade Cycle,* Hicks develops a cycle theory based on the combination of a continuing growth (with occasional spurts) of autonomous investment together with the multiplier and acceleration effect of such movements upon aggregate investment, and through investment in turn upon aggregate output.

The analysis can perhaps best be followed by reference to Figure 82.

I_A represents a steady growth of autonomous investment in a dynamic society continuously making progress in technology. kaI_A represents the magnified investment resulting from the ever-growing autonomous investment. The fact that autonomous in-

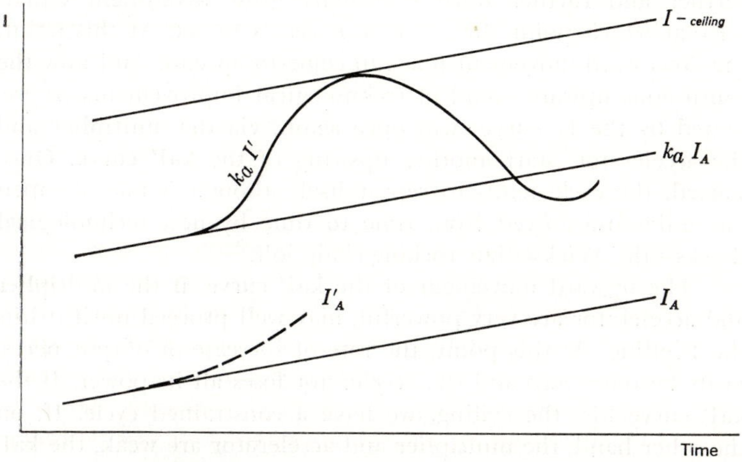

FIGURE 82. *Hicks' Theory of the Cycle*

vestment is growing causes, via the multiplier, an increase in consumption outlays, and this in turn, via the accelerator, causes a rise in aggregate investment represented by the curve kaI_A. Associated with this investment curve is a level of national income (not shown on the chart) commensurate with the level of aggregate investment represented by kaI_A.

I'_A represents a spurt of autonomous investment, such as might develop from the introduction of an exceptionally important new technique. It is the Wicksellian push to the rocking chair. Indeed Hicks' theory is a combination of Wicksell's rocking chair plus the continuous *growth* of autonomous investment. The autonomous investment *spurt* will swerve the curve off its trend course, driving it up toward the I-ceiling. The I-ceiling represents the full-capacity utilization of the industries producing capital goods. Associated with this full-capacity investment ceiling, we assume a full-employment aggregate output (also not shown on the chart). As the kaI′ curve moves toward the I-ceiling, the rate of *increase* of output will begin to decline. As soon as this happens, the accelerator begins to go into reverse, forcing a downward movement of the kaI′ curve. The interaction of the accelerator and the multiplier will drive the kaI′ curve down further and further until eventually gross investment equals zero, at which point the accelerator ceases to act. At this point, the downward movement tends to come to an end. And now the continuous upward trend of technological improvements (represented by the I_A curve) will once again, via the multiplier and the accelerator, start another upswing of the kaI′ curve. Once started, the cycle tends to repeat itself, though it may dampen out unless reinforced from time to time by new technological shocks—the Wicksellian rocking-chair jolt.

The upward movement of the kaI′ curve, if the multiplier and accelerator are very powerful, may well proceed until it hits the I-ceiling. At this point, the rate of increase of output necessarily becomes zero and the accelerator loses all its power. If the kaI′ curve hits the ceiling, we have a constrained cycle. If, on the other hand, the multiplier and accelerator are weak, the kaI′ curve will flatten out before the I-ceiling is reached. It flattens out because the *rate of increase* of output is weakened by reason of ever-growing bottlenecks—scarcities of production factors—long before the I-ceiling is reached. This Hicks calls the "free cycle." A powerful multiplier or accelerator, or both, may, however, despite bottlenecks, be sufficiently strong to drive the kaI′ curve fully up to the I-ceiling. In either case, the slowing down of the rate of increase will throw the accelerator into reverse and start the downward movement.

Capital-output Ratio, Income-investment Ratio, and Autonomous Net Investment

$\frac{K}{O}$, or the "capital-output ratio," represents the average relation of the aggregate stock of capital (plant, equipment, and inventories) to output per annum. $\frac{\Delta K}{\Delta O}$ represents the "marginal capital-output ratio."

Given the state of technology, a certain stock of capital is optimally necessary to produce a given volume of output. If sales increase, entrepreneurs will need to expand their plant and equipment; or conversely, if expectations of sales justify expansion, a net addition to the stock of capital will make possible an increase in output. Bold entrepreneurs may push ahead and increase output capacity, step up their marketing drive, and sell the enlarged output. Thus the capital stock may grow *because* more plant and equipment are required to match the anticipated growing demand with a growing output. Here, the growing O induces an increase in K. Or again, a boldly expanded K will produce a large O. Whichever takes the lead, a capital-output adjustment process is always going on. This is the essence of the "capital adjustment theory" of the business cycle.

Historically, the capital-output ratio, $\frac{K}{O}$, has been remarkably stable—around 3/1. From about the eighteen-eighties to around 1920, the capital-output ratio was apparently rising somewhat; after 1920, we note a falling tendency. This doubtless reflects a change in technology. Inventions may be capital-saving, meaning relatively less capital per unit of output. Or an invention may be capital-using, meaning more capital per unit of output. But we should not forget that, barring a fall in the rate of interest, inventions must always be *labor-saving,* whether they are capital-saving or capital-using inventions. The progress of technology, broadly stated, means less labor per unit of output, taking the entire productive process into consideration. $\frac{K}{O}$ may remain constant, or the ratio may rise or fall, but however that may be, the stock of capital in relation to labor, $\frac{K}{L}$, has always risen historically, and so also has $\frac{O}{L}$. Were this not so, new investment in plant and equipment would not have been made.

Entrepreneurs will always be busily engaged making the appropriate adjustment of capital stock to output. In Figure 83, we represent this relationship in the curves labeled K and O. The two curves are tied together by the capital-output ratio, which we shall call "c." Thus $c = \frac{K}{O}$, or marginally, $c = \frac{\Delta K}{\Delta O}$.

The K and O have already been taken care of in what has been said earlier. Below the aggregate output line, O, we see a line labeled (I + G). This represents gross private domestic investment and federal government expenditures (national income accounts). In 1962, I was $75 billion, and G was $110 billion. For 1962, $\frac{GNP}{I + G}$ was equal to 3, and this ratio held, broadly speaking, with more or less variation, over the recent past. Gross private investment and federal outlays are the result of decision-making largely of an autonomous character. Given a set of institutions and behavior patterns of business firms and individuals, the volume of gross private saving can be regarded as a function

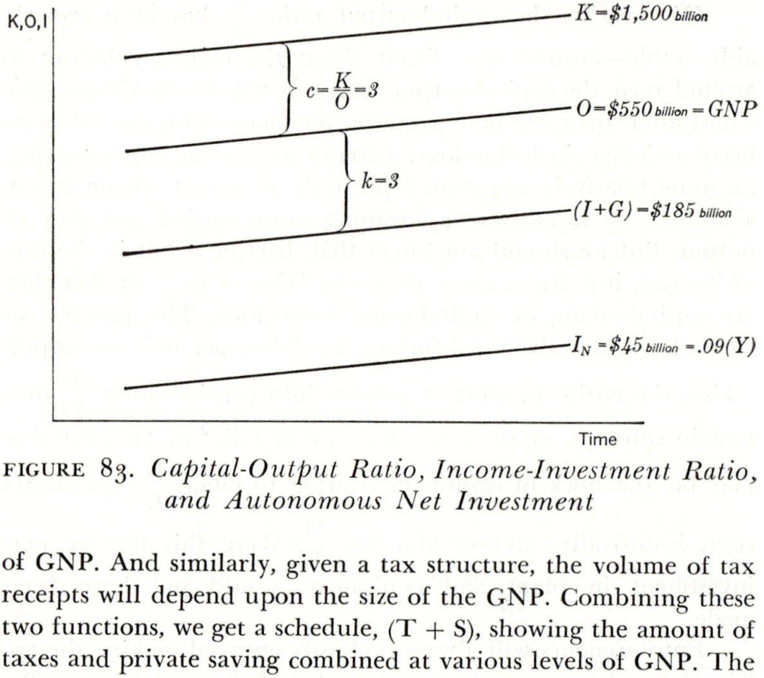

FIGURE 83. *Capital-Output Ratio, Income-Investment Ratio, and Autonomous Net Investment*

of GNP. And similarly, given a tax structure, the volume of tax receipts will depend upon the size of the GNP. Combining these two functions, we get a schedule, (T + S), showing the amount of taxes and private saving combined at various levels of GNP. The shape of this curve will give us the multiplier relation of (I + G) to GNP, i.e., k(I + G) = GNP.

The multiplier appears to be roughly around 2.5, as shown in Figure 78.

Finally we come to *net* investment, I_N. This, in recent years, has normally amounted to approximately 9 per cent of GNP, or recently around $45 billion. Now 9 per cent of GNP is about 3 per cent of the capital stock K. And if the capital stock grows by about 3 per cent per year, we can expect, from the relationship just indicated, that output, GNP, in real terms, will grow at about the same percentage rate. This at least would tend to hold so long as the ratio of $\frac{K}{O}$ remains about the same. It must be remembered, however, that $\frac{\Delta K}{\Delta O}$ will vary considerably over the cycle. Thus the growth of GNP from 1961 to 1962 was 5 per cent, not 3 per cent.

The Harrod-Domar Growth Equation

The Harrod-Domar equation for growth is $g = \frac{s}{c}$. "g" is the rate of growth; "s" is the ratio of net saving to aggregate income; and "c" is the capital-output ratio. A large s makes *possible* a high rate of investment and thus (if in fact the investment is made) a high rate of growth. A small c means that a relatively large output can be obtained from a given net addition to the capital stock. Thus the rate of growth is directly proportional to s and inversely proportional to c.

The actual figures for the United States, under normal conditions, are approximately as follows: $s = 0.09$, $c = 3$, and so $g = 0.03$, i.e., a 3 per cent rate of growth.

This simple equation raises more questions than it answers. First we must know whether the s ratio is a marginal or an average ratio of saving to income. If the marginal s is larger than the average s, then within the range of this marginal curve, aggregate saving, S, in relation to aggregate income, Y (i.e., $\frac{S}{Y}$) will be an increasing function of income. It follows from our equation ($gc = s$) that the rate of growth (g) will then also be an increasing function of income. From this, we conclude that, in these circumstances, a full-employment income will yield not only a *higher level* of income, but also a *higher rate of growth.*

This, however, would not be true in the event that the marginal s were always equal to the average s. For in this case the $\frac{S}{Y}$ would be a constant at all levels of income.[1] And if $\frac{S}{Y}$ were a constant at all levels of income, the same rate of growth would hold whether the economy were running along at full employment or considerably below full employment. It is of course theoretically possible that an economy utilizing 80 per cent of capacity could *grow* at exactly the same percentage *rate* as an economy utilizing 100 per cent of capacity. At any rate, we know that, in a cyclically fluctuating economy, $\frac{S}{Y}$ is lower in depression years than in full-employment years, and therefore a stable full-employment economy can experience a higher rate of growth than an economy which fluctuates.

In the case of a stable underemployment economy, the matter is not so clear. Perhaps here a favorable verdict, as far as the growth *rate* is concerned, would have to rely on faith that a full-employment economy tends to encourage not only a higher ratio of $\frac{S}{Y}$ but also offers a more favorable climate for technological progress.

This leads us to consider the role of c in the *rate* of growth. Here again c can be defined either in terms of a long-run average ratio of capital to output, $\frac{K}{O}$, or as a short-run marginal ratio, $\frac{\Delta K}{\Delta O}$. Over the long run, c apparently has remained fairly constant at around 3/1. The marginal c can, however, vary considerably up and down over the short run, especially in various phases of the business cycle. Now it could be possible that a full employment economy might show a different marginal c than an underemployment economy. Would the marginal c be higher or lower under conditions of full employment? Presumably it

---

[1] We assume that the $\frac{S}{Y}$ curve starts at point of origin.

would be lower. This would appear probable because, under the pressure of high employment, the capital stock would be used more intensively than at lower levels of employment. Thus as we move from low to high employment, the marginal c would tend to fall. On the other hand, it could be argued that the growing scarcity of labor, together with the concomitant rise in wage rates would tend to induce the substitution of machinery for labor; hence the marginal c might tend to rise.

If now the marginal c is high, the rate of growth will tend to be lower than would otherwise be the case; and conversely, if the marginal c is low, the rate of growth will tend to be greater. In some industries, the tendencies making for a high marginal c, as full employment is approached, may predominate over those making for a low marginal c, whereas in others the reverse may be the case. Theoretical analyses cannot give a clean-cut answer, and empirical research is as yet inconclusive. Taking account of both s and c, however, it is perhaps plausible to conclude that a full-employment economy is likely to experience not only the obvious advantage of a higher *level* of income, but also the less obvious probable achievement of a higher *rate of growth* than a slack economy. Yet it is theoretically conceivable that a less than full-employment society, although offering a lower current standard of living, might promise a higher growth rate. More likely, however, the opposite will be the case.

If marginal s is larger than average s, it follows that $\frac{S}{Y}$ is an increasing function of income. In this event, our growth equation cannot tell us what the rate of growth will be unless we already know what the income will be. But is there perhaps something inherent in the capital-output ratio which determines the level of income? This idea cannot altogether be dismissed, since the marginal capital-output ratio is certainly a function of changing technology. And a changing technology is a determinant of real income. An improving technique and a growing population open up investment outlets; and investment, via the multiplier and the accelerator, determines the level of output.

Changing techniques may be either capital-saving, thereby tending to reduce c, or they may be capital-using, thereby tending to increase the value of c. If c falls, the effect will be one thing in the short run and another thing in the long run. Or more precisely, the effect is one thing on the level of current aggregate demand and another on the productive power of a full-employment economy. On the level of current aggregate demand, a lower c is unfavorable, since a lower c opens up smaller investment outlets than a higher c. A lower c means a smaller acceleration effect. But a lower c also means a more efficient society and therefore a larger real income, provided always that full employment can somehow be achieved despite the diminished investment outlets. A lower c tends in the short run to make it more difficult, if reliance is placed upon spontaneous forces (and less on deliberate policy) to reach a full-employment aggregate demand. But it makes for a larger output potential if, indeed, full employment can be achieved.

It appears therefore evident that our growth equation, $g = \frac{s}{c}$, cannot tell us what the level of income will be. Instead we must look to the theory of income determination to find the level of income. And we need to know the level of income before we can know the value of s. Only then can the rate of growth be derived from our equation.

The theory of income determination is based on the following tools of analysis: (a) the marginal efficiency of capital schedule, (b) the consumption function, (c) the liquidity preference schedule, (d) the money supply.[2] In a dynamic society, the marginal efficiency schedule will always be in process of shifting up or to the right. This shift is primarily a function of technological innovations and growth in the labor force. Technology and growth of population (in terms both of quantity and quality) are the prime determinants of growth.

The Harrod-Domar growth equation can be a useful tool of analysis, but it can easily be misused. It has, in fact, been employed in planning programs for the development of economically backward countries in a far more rigid manner than is justified. The

---

[2] See also Alvin H. Hansen, *Guide to Keynes,* and, of course, Keynes, *General Theory of Employment, Interest and Money,* Harcourt, Brace, and World, 1936.

capital-output ratio varies from industry to industry, from country to country, and from one stage of economic development to another. It will be one thing if the planned program for development emphasizes heavy industry (steel, etc.) and quite a different thing if the planned program emphasizes education, agriculture, and population control. The capital-output ratio analysis tends almost inevitably to overemphasize brick and mortar and to underemphasize investment in human resources. In fact, the standard statistical measurements of capital-output ratios are based entirely on estimates of the accumulated stock of material capital goods. Yet fully as important, if indeed not more important, is the stock of human capital—knowledge, skill of all kinds.[3] Why was the Marshall aid program so effective whereas the Alliance for Progress encounters almost insuperable difficulties? The answer is clear: Europe had knowledgeable entrepreneurs, skilled workers, an educated citizenry, a body of technical know-how. Well-equipped with rich human capital resources, it was no difficult matter to fill the deficiency in the stock of material capital. Even in the United States, it is estimated that $100 put into education will induce a higher growth in productivity than $100 put into plant and equipment.

In addition to the Harrod-Domar growth equation, reference may perhaps usefully be made to a growth equation based on expectations of a rising income. The basis for such expectations lies of course in the continuous growth over time of autonomous investment (Hicks). Rising expectations rest upon an ever-improving technology, a growing and a better-educated labor force. Given such expectations, transcending the shorter waves of optimism and pessimism of the cycle, we can say that today's income is a function of yesterday's income. The expectational trend will determine at what rate today's income will exceed yesterday's income. The equation is as follows: $\frac{Y_1}{Y_0} = \frac{c + s}{c}$. Y_1 is today's income, Y_0 yesterday's income. Starting from the Harrod-Domar equation, $g = \frac{s}{c}$, we assume that $s = 0.12$, $c = 3$, and so the rate of growth is 0.04.

[3] See Theodore W. Schultz *et al.*, "Investment in Human Beings," *The Journal of Political Economy,* October, 1962.

Applying the same figures to our expectational equation, we get

$$\frac{Y_1}{Y_0} = \frac{c + s}{c} = \frac{3 + 0.12}{3} = 1.04.^4$$

The rate of growth is therefore 4 per cent. The larger the s, the greater is the rate of growth.

Summary Statement on the Role of c and s

At the risk of repetition, a summary view of the growth problem may perhaps be in order. First of all, let us keep in mind that, in dealing with c and s, we are involved in the multiplier-accelerator analysis. This is true because the strength of the accelerator depends upon the capital-output ratio, and the multiplier is the reciprocal of the marginal propensity to save, i.e., $k = \frac{1}{s}$. But although any equation which uses c and s necessarily encounters the problem of demand creation (i.e., the multiplier-accelerator interaction), its primary usefulness relates not to the level of income but to the growth of income.

From the standpoint of generating adequate aggregate demand, the larger the c and the smaller the s, the more expansionist will be the spontaneous forces—forces which are exogenous to the system but whose impact upon the system will be determined (given the strength of the initial jolt) by the endogenous or internal structure of the system itself (namely the multiplier-accelerator interaction). A small s means a powerful multiplier, and a large c a buoyant accelerator. A small s and a large c will *tend* to give us a full-employment economy.

But from the standpoint of growth, the matter is entirely different—the larger the s and the smaller the c, the higher the potential rate of growth. But this growth cannot be achieved without a strong deliberate policy of full employment. If we must rely primarily upon spontaneous forces, we will be better off with a small s and a large c and be content with a low rate of growth. If we can count on strong deliberate policy, we would be better

[4] See R. C. O. Matthews, *The Business Cycle*, Cambridge Economic Handbooks, The University of Chicago Press, 1959. Matthews makes his expectational growth equation $\frac{c}{c - s}$. This is approximately right but not quite. Using the figures just given, from his equation, we get the answer 1.0417, not 1.04.

off with a large s and a small c which, under contrived full employment, would promise a high rate of growth.

Is there perhaps something here which has a bearing on the low rate of growth in the United States and the high rate of growth in Europe?

A high s means a large flow of saving if full-employment levels can be reached. And if c is small, this large flow of saving can finance a highly productive (high-output) stock of capital. The smaller the capital-output ratio, the more potent is a given amount of saving; in other words, the further a given amount of capital will go. A large c and a small s are ideal for demand creation but unfavorable from the standpoint of growth.

The Circular-flow Economy vs. a Growing Economy

In a circular-flow economy (Schumpeter) there is no net investment and so no growth. There is indeed a stock of capital, but no additions to this stock are being made. As old capital wears out, it is replaced by new capital. Thus the whole income is spent on consumers' goods. The income received by the factors of production today in return for their productive effort is spent tomorrow on tomorrow's output. And since there is no growth, tomorrow's output is equal to today's output, which in turn is equal to today's income. Income equals expenditures, and expenditures equal income. $Y_0 = E_1 = Y_1$.

In a growing society, however, net investment must be made. If this net investment is stable (no increase), the output will rise, but at a declining rate. If the investment is stable, however, then income will remain fixed. Out of each year's income a certain amount is saved, an amount equal to investment. Thus all the income received today is expended tomorrow, partly on investment and the rest on consumers' goods. The savings of today are expended on investment tomorrow. $I = S$. Income remains constant. But since output is rising (owing to the continuous process of new investment), demand is insufficient to buy the growing output. Thus such a society suffers the depressing effect of deflation or falling prices. Demand and supply are not in equilibrium.

To have growth there must be net investment. And to maintain equilibrium in a growing society, a constant rate of investment will not do. Investment must grow; investment made tomorrow must exceed the saving out of today's income. I_1 must exceed S_0. The difference must be financed out of the activation of idle hoards or out of the creation of new money. Growth must be financed from credit or net increases in debt.

In all modern dynamic societies, debt (public and private) is an increasing function of growth. Aggregate debt (public and private combined) has remained from 1929 to the present at approximately a constant ratio of GNP. The relevant data decade by decade are as follows:

Aggregate Debt and GNP
(in billions)

Year	*Aggregate Net Debt —Public and Private*	*Debt as a Multiple of GNP*	*Individual Debt*	*Corporate Debt*	*State and Local Debt*	*Federal Government Debt*	*GNP*
1929	$ 191	1.83	$ 72	$ 89	13	16	$104
1940	190	1.89	53	76	16	45	101
1950	490	1.72	109	142	21	219	285
1963	1,000	1.81	341	331	72	257	554

36 · *Inflation and the Balance of Payments*

In recent years, the United States has been bedeviled by two problems that limit our freedom of action: the fear of inflation and our international balance of payments. Undoubtedly, they are serious problems which must be dealt with effectively. Unfortunately, however, it is also true that irresponsible groups have exploited these problems for propaganda. Expansionist and social welfare programs have had to encounter not only the opposition of rigid conservatism against progressive measures as such, but also the argument that, even though justified on their own merits, these programs cannot be implemented under existing circumstances without endangering domestic price stability and, internationally, the soundness of the dollar.

The remedies proffered to prevent inflation and to safeguard the dollar have too often assumed that the only effective cure is the continued maintenance of semistagnation. Admittedly, a depressed economy need have no fear of inflation, but is this defeatist policy the only solution? And can continual semistagnation really make the American economy competitive in world markets?

What does history tell us about American experience with inflation? One must say first that, throughout our entire history, this country has never suffered any price increases that remotely deserve the name of inflation except in wartime or in the immediate aftermath of war. And this also holds for our recent postwar experience.

Immediately following the war—1946 and much of 1947—we did indeed have sharp increases in the general price level. Wholesale prices rose by 50 per cent from 1945 to 1948. This price rise was a consequence of the war. At the end of the war, cupboards and closets were empty, retailers' shelves were bare, business firms were short on inventory stocks; there was a terrific shortage of houses (young couples had to double up with their parents), automobile production had been cut almost to zero. During the war, monetary savings had accumulated in the hands of both consumers and business firms. Once price control was removed, prices inevitably rose. The surprising thing was not that prices rose. The surprising thing was rather that, after nine months, the main inflationary upsurge rapidly subsided. Many an economist who had looked for dire inflation was astonished to discover how quickly it had dwindled away. By the end of 1947, it was all over. But people needed some considerable time to find that out, so firmly had the notion become ingrained that inflation was the new order of the day. In fact, however, the last month of 1948 gave us a price level slightly below that of January, 1948. And two years later, the average index of wholesale prices for the year 1950 stood 1 per cent lower than the average for the year 1948.

In midsummer 1950, the Korean war broke out. The whole world was shocked. All over western Europe and in the United States prices rose in nine months by about 15 per cent. Consumers rushed out to buy electrical appliances, cars, etc. Business firms hastily stocked up with inventories. Once again, the surprising thing was how rapidly the inflationary fever vanished. By February, 1951, it was all over, and prices began to recede. The wholesale price index for 1952 stood 3 per cent below that of 1951, and there was a further decline of 1½ per cent by 1953.

And what has been our peacetime record since Korea? Except for the investment boom of 1955–57, wholesale prices have held stable. Wholesale prices did indeed rise an average of 2.2 per cent per year from 1954 to 1957. Historically, we have typically experienced moderate price increases of this order of magnitude in the expansionist phase of the business cycle. Indeed in the nine cycles from 1894 to 1913, and from 1921 to 1929, the average increase in wholesale prices per year of expansion was 3.5 per cent. Moreover the 1955–57 episode was a special case. The price increases were restricted mainly to the capital goods sector—metals, machinery, construction. In the economy as a whole there was no inflation.

This investment boom did, however, leave its imprint on the wholesale price level. From 1957 to 1963, the index remained stable but on this new high plateau. Even so, in 1963, the wholesale price index stood only 6 per cent above the 1952 index—an increase for the eleven years of only one-half of 1 per cent per year. Everyone must agree that this represents not only "reasonable" price stability, but stability of a very high order. Compare this record with the price increase of 2.5 per cent per year from 1897 to 1915—the good old peacetime days! Of course there was the Spanish-American War, but its role was minor and short-lived compared with the sweep of economic factors which brought about the worldwide upward price trend.

But this is the record of wholesale prices. How about consumer prices? Here we come closer to a real problem. The consumer price index has not done so well. Yet the record is far better than the inflation-alarmists would have us believe. Consumer prices were pushed up along with wholesale prices by the shock of Korea. And from 1952 to 1963, the increase has aggregated 15 per cent.

Why this greater rise in consumer prices? The explanation can mainly be found in the "service" sector. From 1957 to 1963, the price of services rose by 14 per cent while the commodity sector rose by only 5 per cent. And in the service area by far the greatest increases have come in medical care—a 20 per cent increase since 1957.

In general, the price index for services can be expected to rise even though the commodity sector is stabilized. This will occur because productivity increases in the commodity sector permit price stability even though money wages rise in line with productivity increases. That is not true in the case of services. Here productivity gains are meager, yet wages must rise more or less in line with general nationwide increases. Accordingly, the price index for services is pushed up out of line with the commodity price index.

Not much can be done about this, even though the special case of medical and hospital services deserves attention. This problem, however, lies beyond the scope of this chapter. For our purposes here, the important question to ask is this: Given the unquestioned fact that the consumer price index tends to outstrip the wholesale price index, which index should we try to stabilize?

Assume that we successfully stabilized the consumer price index. This implies a downward trend in wholesale prices. Is this desirable from the standpoint of the economy? The answer is "No." The wholesale price index is a matter of deep concern for business and for farmers. Continuous wholesale price deflation would put a squeeze, probably an intolerable squeeze, upon the entrepreneurial class.[1] The conclusion is that we should plump for stability of wholesale prices. But this means that we must expect a continuous upward trend in the consumer price index. An increase in the consumer price index of 1 to 2 per cent per year, such as we have had since 1957, is tolerable and perhaps more or less inevitable. Even the more rigid stabilizers have come to regard increases of this magnitude as "reasonable stability."

The record has therefore on the whole been good since the end of the Korean conflict, except for the years 1955–57. But here we encounter an alarming fact. These were just the years when the unemployment rate fell close to the Kennedy goal of 4 per cent. In all other post-Korean years, the unemployment rate has averaged from 5.6 to 6.8 per cent, and in no year did it fall below 5.5 per cent. Does this mean that we can buy price stability only at the cost of 5.6 per cent unemployment?

No conclusive answer can be given, but the following comments may be pertinent. The 1955–57 episode represented a sharp spurt in the durable-goods sector. Admittedly, this is typically the

---

[1] Of course, if we could assume perfect mobility of factors, perfect competition, and perfect fluidity of all prices and costs, a continuous fall in prices would make no great difference. But this is not the kind of world we live in; indeed, it is a world that never existed except in the minds of highly speculative economists.

case in the boom phase of the cycle. Yet this appears to have been an extreme case. The exceptional spurt in auto sales and other consumers' durables, the spurt in the capital goods industries was the result of pent-up demand accumulations occasioned by the war and by rapid postwar technological developments. Normally, we could expect a more balanced recovery. Moreover, we could do a better job of stabilizing private spending both for investment goods and consumers' durables than we have thus far attempted. This matter has already been discussed in Chapters 32 and 33. Discretionary adjustment of tax rates to stabilize the cycle could go a long way toward shifting the so-called modified Phillips curve [2] downward. Similarly the removal or lessening of structural bottlenecks via educational and retraining programs could also help to shift the Phillips curve downward or to the left.

Finally, price stability involves statesman-like collective bargaining. On the average, money wage rates can rise no faster than productivity increases permit. These matters were explored with some care in the writer's *Economic Policy and Full Employment,* published in 1946.[3] Broadly speaking we can very roughly divide industries into three classes: (1) those making average increases in per worker productivity, (2) those making exceptionally large increases in productivity, and (3) those making very small increases in productivity. The first group can raise wages equal to productivity increases while holding prices stable. The second can raise wages equal to, or perhaps somewhat above, the general average productivity increases, while lowering prices to consumers. The third group is compelled to raise wages more or less in line with the national average, and is therefore compelled also to raise prices sufficiently to cover wage costs. In a dynamic society, some prices will fall and some will rise, while others remain stable. If money

[2] On the vertical scale put a schedule of price increases ranging from 0 to 8. On the horizontal scale put a schedule of unemployment rates ranging from 0 to 6. Draw a line through the point 8 in the price scale and point 5.5 on the unemployment scale. This line will show a price increase of 1.5 per cent at 4.5 per cent unemployment, and a price rise of 2.2 per cent at a 4 per cent unemployment rate. The Phillips curve purports to show that price increases are a function of the rate of unemployment.

[3] The guidelines for wage increases were extensively discussed in the Report of the Council of Economic Advisers in the *President's Economic Report,* January, 1962.

wages and money increases generally rise in line with productivity, the general price level can remain stable. "Productivity-wages" constitute the backbone of the price level.

Historically, the aggregate share of labor and capital in the final product has remained about equal. Assuming a constant capital-output ratio, a 10 per cent increase in output per worker will mean also a 10 per cent increase per worker in the capital stock. Assume that the yield on capital remains the same. It follows that a 10 per cent increase in output will permit a 10 per cent increase in the income of capitalists. Assume that wages rise percentage-wise as much as output, namely 10 per cent. It follows then that labor's income will have increased 10 per cent per worker. In other words Kr ("K" being the capital invested and "r" the yield per dollar invested) would rise by 10 per cent. Similarly Lw ("L" being the number of workers, and "w" the money wage rate) would also rise by 10 per cent. Thus capital's share would remain constant and labor's share would also remain constant. Broadly speaking, this is what history shows to have been the fact.

In the event that the capital-output ratio should decline, this might result in some drop in capital's share in the growing output. This in fact appears to have been the case to a small degree in the last two or three decades.

Why should the yield on capital (the "r") tend to remain stable while wages (the "w" in our equation) rise along with productivity? The answer is that so long as the stock of capital, K, tends to rise as fast as output per worker, K is obviously becoming plentiful in relation to labor. Under the law of factoral substitution, this means that a unit of capital is becoming cheap while a unit of labor is becoming dear. Thus wages per worker rise in line with productivity whereas the yield on a unit of capital remains constant. But since the stock of capital, K, rises in line with output, capital's share of the growing product continues to hold its own against labor's share.

The Balance-of-Payments Problem

The second roadblock to freedom to pursue full-employment policies is the international position of the dollar. Briefly the story is as follows: For four years following the war (1946–49), we averaged an over-all surplus in our international accounts of $1.75 billion per year. Government grants and credits to foreign countries, averaging around $5.5 billion per year, were more than offset by a gigantic excess of exports over imports [4] of goods and services—an excess of $8.5 billion per year. This huge excess was, of course, to be expected in the immediate postwar period when Europe was still economically speaking flat on its back. But by 1950 things began to change.

For the seven years 1950–56 inclusive, the net excess of exports fell to $4.4 billion per year. Europe was again exporting in volume. Offsetting this surplus were three items: (a) military expenditures abroad ($2.2 billion); (b) United States grants and credits ($2.5 billion); (c) private capital outflows ($1.4 billion). This left an average over-all deficit in our international accounts for these seven years of $1.4 billion per year.

Our gold losses, however, averaged only $0.36 billion per year; hence the adverse balance was accepted without causing any great concern. And in 1957, owing to special factors, particularly the favorable impact of the Suez crisis upon our trade balance, our over-all international account was in surplus by over $0.5 billion.

Thus everything moved satisfactorily until 1958. Then came the crash. Our trade balance ($5.6 billion), although well below the 1957 exceptional year, was $1.2 billion above the previous five years. Nothing wrong there. United States grants and credits abroad held at the seven-year average of $2.5 billion. Military expenditures abroad ($3.4 billion) did exceed the seven-year average by about $1.2 billion. But this was exactly covered by the larger trade surplus. There remain the private capital outflows of $3.0 billion, or $1.6 billion in excess of the 1950–56 average.

The largest increase came in the private capital outflows. Long-term investment, both direct and portfolio, took a big leap forward in 1958. Europe was rapidly expanding. American firms, in line with the buoyant European prosperity, were enlarging their investment outlays on plant and equipment. Europeans needing capital floated a large volume of securities in New York, by far the most favorable capital market in the world. The prospect of early

[4] For our present purposes, we place military expenditures abroad in a special category and therefore exclude this item from the import column.

convertibility of European currencies (achieved by late 1958) was also a factor favoring American investment abroad. All in all, our over-all deficit in 1958 was $3.5 billion.

The 1959 deficit of $3.7 billion only slightly exceeded the 1958 deficit. But the composition of the deficit had changed. Private capital outflows declined by $1.0 billion; government grants and credits by $0.5 billion. These were offset by a corresponding reduction in our trade surplus.

The 1960 deficit rose to $3.9 billion. A spectacular recovery in our trade surplus was offset by renewed capital outflows, this time consisting heavily of speculative short-term funds—the so-called hot money.

A determined effort was made to reduce the deficit in 1961, and with a moderate degree of success. The deficit fell to $2.5 billion. A variety of measures was employed—none of outstanding significance but all contributing something. These involved:

1. The assurance that we would use *all* our gold resources if necessary to meet foreign demands.

2. Higher short-term money rates to remove unfavorable interest rate differentials between the United States and Europe.

3. Cutting the tourist allowance for tariff-free purchases from $500 to $100.

4. Tieing our loans to underdeveloped countries to American exports.

5. Efforts to induce Europe to assume more of the foreign-aid burden.

6. Inducing European governments to purchase military equipment in the United States.

7. Federal promotion programs to aid American exports.

These policies, together with advance repayments of loans, brought the 1961 deficit down to $2.5 billion and the 1962 deficit to $1.9 billion. Confidence in the dollar was restored; gold outflows dropped from $2.3 billion in 1958 to $0.9 billion in 1962. In no year has there been an over-all "run" on the dollar. In each year, gold withdrawals have been more than offset by increases in foreign holdings of United States short-term dollar assets—deposits in banks, United States government securities, etc. One cannot talk about a "run on a bank" if fresh deposits considerably exceed currency withdrawals.

Our balance-of-payments deficit is not due to an "unfavorable" trade balance. Our combined net receipts on merchandise and service account have been running at $7.6 billion per year [5] in 1960–62—up about $3 billion above the level of the early fifties. Our problem is rather that the international political situation requires military expenditures abroad amounting to about $3 billion per year, together with net foreign aid of about $3 billion. Add to this an outflow of private long-term and short-term capital of around $3.5 billion. These three items (military expenditures abroad, foreign aid, and capital outflows) tell us that we are supplying foreigners with around $9.5 billion dollars a year outside of the normal channels of trade. Our favorable trade surplus of goods and services of $7.6 billion is not enough to offset the $9.5 billion outflow of dollars. Hence the deficit. It does not mean that United States products are being priced out of world markets.

The balance-of-payments problem is not only a headache for the United States. It almost perennially concerns Great Britain. It is chronically a concern for the underdeveloped countries, and potentially a cause of concern for all countries. The free world should somehow learn to manage its international monetary relations far better than it has so far succeeded in doing. What if anything can be done about it?

Two quite distinct problems confront us: One relates to liquidity; that problem is how to provide an *amount* of international monetary reserves adequate to meet the requirements of international payments. The other problem has to do with maintaining a balanced structure of foreign exchange rates and keeping it continually in balance.

With respect to the first problem, international monetary reserves consist of gold holdings and liquid asset holdings (deposits and short-term securities) of key currencies—mainly the United States dollar and the British pound. Other currencies—the Ger-

[5] Remember that United States military expenditures abroad are not included in the "import" category. Logically, that item deserves a separate classification along with foreign aid, etc.

man mark, the Swiss franc, etc.—are beginning to play the same role. Holding liquid assets of gold and key currencies (generally accepted all over the world) enables a country to pay its foreign bills. The problem of adequate international liquidity involves an adequate gold supply plus an adequate volume of key currency holdings. Gold and key currency holdings can, however, be supplemented by borrowings, especially borrowings from the International Monetary Fund.

The aggregate volume of International Monetary reserves is equal to about $60 billion. World trade increases at about a 5 per cent rate per year. This means that around $3 billion new "international money" is needed each year in a growing, dynamic world. Where will this come from? About $1 billion can come from new gold production. The rest must come from (a) an increase in the holdings of key currencies, (b) increased potential borrowings from the International Monetary Fund, or (c) an increase in the price of gold. Any other source must await drastic monetary innovations.

The growing volume of dollar holdings by foreigners has contributed greatly to international liquidity. In 1950, we held a disproportionate share of the world's gold. We still held in 1963 about $16 billion out of a total of $41 billion of free world gold stocks. As a result of new gold production and the United States deficits, foreign countries have steadily increased their holdings of gold and dollars until by 1963 their aggregate holdings of monetary reserves amounted to $42 billion.

Some economists hold that gold production, key currencies, and an expanding role of the International Monetary Fund as an international lender will not be sufficient to provide adequate liquidity. Two widely advocated solutions are offered. Sir Roy Harrod favors a drastic increase in the price of gold. If this were done worldwide, say, through the auspices of the International Monetary Fund as permitted in its charter, it would in no way disturb the structure of exchange rates. The only effect would be an increase in the monetary value of gold. A doubling of the price of gold would simply mean that current world gold stocks, instead of being worth $41 billion in money terms would be worth $82 billion.

A second method of increasing international liquidity would require a shift from the current key currency type of international monetary reserves to a strictly international kind of money. Keynes called his proposed new international money the "bancor." Whatever the name, this new international monetary unit would supplant the key currencies. It would be issued by a truly international central bank. This bank would not simply be a lending agency like a savings bank—lending out funds deposited with it—as is now true of the International Monetary Fund. The new truly international bank would have the power to *create* new international money precisely as our own Federal Reserve System can do with respect to domestic currency. The Federal Reserve can and does create new dollars. It does so by buying United States securities in the open market and paying for them by checks drawn on itself which, if so desired, can be cashed into new Federal Reserve notes. The money supply has thus been increased. If the bonds were purchased from a comercial bank, this bank would be credited for the amount of the purchase with a deposit at the Federal Reserve Bank. In this way, member bank balances with the Federal Reserve Banks would rise, and thereby make possible a multiple expansion of the money supply. In precisely the same manner, an international central bank could create "bancor" by buying the government securities of any member country.

A mere increase in liquidity will not, however, solve the balance-of-payments problem. For this relates, at least in the long run, not to a country's supply of international monetary reserves, but to disequilibrium forces which are continuously at work causing a drain on its reserves. Larger reserves can, of course, tide a country over a period of *temporary* disequilibrium, but cannot cure a *fundamental* disequilibrium.

International equilibrium can be maintained in two ways. One involves unilateral action by each country to keep its cost and price level in line with those of other countries, to broaden if possible the range of its exports, to develop its own industries so as to minimize its need for imports, etc. Moreover, international collaboration on simultaneous expansionist policies can help to keep each country in step. Self-discipline and international cooperation are both involved.

The other method of maintaining equilibrium involves continuous adjustment of the exchange rate structure so as to maintain the value of each country's currency in terms of world markets and internationally traded financial assets. The exchange rate of the dollar, for example, would fluctuate according to changes in the world demand for dollars. In other words, the exchange rate would vary so as to maintain the purchasing power of the dollar in the world commodity and securities market.

This ideal cannot be reached all at once, but we are moving in this direction. The problem is building up the institutional machinery needed for a managed international monetary system. In fact, in many of the advanced countries there is being built up what, in effect, amounts to national stabilization funds equipped with the power to buy and sell their own currencies against other currencies. This means controlling, through sales and purchases, the exchange value of currencies within the limits of the selling and buying gold points. The current range within which exchange rates fluctuate is 1½ percentage points. This could bit by bit be widened to say five or more percentage points, within which a managed exchange rate could be allowed to fluctuate. In time, international cooperation between the national stabilization funds could dispense altogether with gold, just as all modern domestic currencies are no longer dependent upon gold.

Our money supply, and so the value of money, is no longer determined by a gold standard. Our money supply is completely controlled by the Governors of the Federal Reserve Board without any regard to gold. At long last, we have achieved management of our domestic monetary system. We must achieve international monetary management. Increasing cooperation between the central banks of advanced countries and a growing role for the International Monetary Fund point the way toward eventual international management comparable to domestic monetary management.

Many of the current schemes of international monetary reform are simply plans to support the glutted currencies of the deficit countries, notably the United States and Great Britain. At best, such schemes serve only to tide a country over a temporary difficulty without doing much if anything to promote equilibrium.

What is needed is an orderly management of exchange rates so that the various currencies will represent *true* values in goods, services, and assets. Not until this is done will a country be wholly free to tackle effectively the problem of keeping its economy continuously close to full employment without periodic lapses from its full growth potential.

Appendix · The Robertsonian and Swedish Systems of Period Analysis

I

In the current literature comparison continues to be made between the Robertsonian [1] and Swedish conceptions [2] of sequence analysis and of saving and investment. These conceptions appear to be in some manner similar, yet different; but just what the difference is seems to be a somewhat baffling question.

To guide the reader, I propose to state certain propositions at the outset. They are as follows:

1. The Robertsonian formulation may consist merely of a set of definitions, as presented in his 1933 *Economic Journal* article on "Saving and Hoarding" (and it is this formulation which Keynes comments upon in the *General Theory*); second, his period analysis may be presented as a definite formulation of the multiplier sequence over time,[3] as is done in his *Quarterly Journal*

[1] Dennis H. Robertson, *Essays in Monetary Theory,* P. S. King & Son, Ltd., London, 1940.

[2] Gunnar Myrdal, *Monetary Equilibrium,* W. Hodge & Co., Ltd., London, 1939; Eric R. Lindahl, *Studies in the Theory of Money and Capital,* George Allen & Unwin, Ltd., London, 1939; and Bertil G. Ohlin, *Readings in Business Cycle Theory,* The Blakiston Company, Philadelphia, 1944, Chapter V. See also N. Kaldor, "A Model of the Trade Cycle," *The Economic Journal,* March, 1940, pp. 78–79.

[3] The multiplier process over time had earlier been formulated by R. F. Kahn

of Economics review of Keynes' *General Theory*.[4] The second formulation makes use of the earlier terminology, but it does not stop with mere definitions; it suggests a definite empirical hypothesis.[5] Throughout the following I shall be considering chiefly the second formulation.

2. The second Robertsonian formulation is not, as is commonly supposed, a mere tautology. The view that it is such overlooks the third equation referred to below.

3. The Swedish analysis, based on the divergence of planned saving and planned investment, as originally interpreted, does not appear to offer a satisfactory theory of income expansion or contraction.

4. Useful analyses can, however, be made in terms of the discrepancy between certain magnitudes, such as the divergence between desired consumption and actual consumption (expenditure lag) and the divergence between intended investment and actual investment (output lag). These formulations are often stated in terms which bear some resemblance to, though in fact they are different from, the original Swedish formulation. The expenditure lag is an integral part of the Robertsonian formulation. And the output lag[6] (divergence of output from sales) has been employed by Lundberg and Metzler. Both formulations play a significant role in the explanation of the cumulative process. In each case expansion or contraction will follow as a result of the unsatisfied conditions.

---

in "The Relation of Home Investment to Employment," *The Economic Journal,* June, 1931, and by J. M. Clark, *Economics of Planning Public Works,* National Planning Board, Federal Emergency Administration of Public Works, 1935.

[4] *Quarterly Journal of Economics,* November, 1936.

[5] Robertson used this formulation merely as a means of expounding the multiplier sequence over time, and it should not be assumed that he himself is sympathetic to this or any other formulation of the multiplier analysis.

[6] The output lag is, of course, not necessarily excluded from the Robertsonian system. Ordinarily his investment may be taken to mean *actual* investment. No difficulty is involved, however, in complicating his system by introducing the possible divergence between "intended investment" and "actual investment." I am indebted to William Fellner and Fritz Machlup for this and other helpful suggestions.

II

The second Robertsonian formulation [7] can be represented by the following equations: [8]

$$(1)\ Y_0 = C_1 + S_1$$
$$(2)\ Y_1 = C_1 + I_1$$
$$(3)\ C_1 = f(Y_0)$$

in which Y_0 is yesterday's income, Y_1 today's income, C_1, S_1, and I_1 today's consumption, saving, and investment, respectively.

The Robertsonian definitions are specific and unambiguous. Income, consumption, saving, and investment are so defined that it is possible to relate one period to the next. But the two equations $Y_0 = C_1 + S_1$ and $Y_1 = C_1 + I_1$ are, taken by themselves alone, mere identities. They are truistic statements about Y_0 and Y_1.[9] As such they have no operational value in analyzing income changes. It is the third equation which saves the system from being a mere truism. The third equation is not an identity; it is a real function and as such makes the system as a whole operational. The third equation states a hypothesis which can be verified or disproved as a pattern of economic behavior. Thus the three equations taken together can contribute to an understanding of the process of income change.

In the Robertsonian model, it is assumed, today's consumption depends upon yesterday's income, tomorrow's consumption on today's income. C_1 is related to Y_0, C_2 to Y_1, etc. Consumption, it is assumed, is functionally related to *prior* income. An "expenditure lag" is postulated. Consumers are expected to increase their consumption outlays when income rises, but not at once. There is a lagged adjustment of consumption to income. A functional relation between consumption and income is, however, as-

7 See the models (based on the Robertsonian definitions) in D. H. Robertson, *Quarterly Journal of Economics,* November, 1936, p. 173 (reprinted in *Essays in Monetary Theory,* p. 119); F. Machlup, *Quarterly Journal of Economics,* November, 1939, p. 18; and Alvin H. Hansen, *Fiscal Policy and Business Cycles,* 1941, p. 272. Also contrast J. M. Keynes, *Means to Prosperity,* Macmillan & Company, Ltd., London, 1933, with his *General Theory.*

8 This method of presentation was suggested by Fritz Machlup.

9 Keynes, in the *General Theory* (p. 78), discusses the first Robertsonian formulation and regards it as merely truistic. The functional relation of consumption to *prior* income (C_1 to Y_0) was not explicitly stated by Robertson until the November, 1936, *Quarterly Journal* article.

sumed. When this is the case, the Robertsonian concepts acquire operational and analytical value.

If income rises (owing, let us say, to an increase in investment) consumption will respond gradually in the specific manner set out in the models. Precisely how the lagged adjustment of consumption to income will develop will depend upon two things—the length of the expenditure lag and the marginal propensity to consume. Thus when investment increases, income rises by the increment of investment plus a lagged rise in consumption. When the process is complete, income will have risen by $k \Delta I$.

Both the Robertsonian "expenditure-lag model" and the Keynesian "instantaneous multiplier" are based on the concept of a "normal" consumption function. Both are operational concepts, since the analysis assumes that consumption is not fortuitous or capricious, but instead is mainly determined by income, past or current. Both models are based on the consumption function, a schedule of economic behavior.

It is not yet entirely clear how far empirical data support (1) the view that consumption is related to current income with no significant expenditure lag (the Keynesian instantaneous multiplier) or (2) the view that consumption is related to past income (the Robertsonian model with an expenditure lag).[10] Lloyd Metzler [11] presents data which tend to support the former (no expenditure lag) view. It should be recognized that Keynes himself, while presenting the instantaneous multiplier concept as a useful tool for pure theory, believed nevertheless that a *short* expenditure lag could reasonably be assumed.[12]

Suppose, however, that consumption were regarded as more or less fortuitous or autonomous. It could be argued, for example, that consumption was determined more or less by expectations.

---

[10] If there is no expenditure lag, then the Robertsonian system becomes transmuted into the Keynesian "logical theory of the multiplier, which holds good continuously without time-lag" (*General Theory,* p. 122).

[11] In *Income, Employment and Public Policy,* W. W. Norton & Company, Inc., 1948, Chapter I.

[12] See Alvin H. Hansen, "Note on Saving and Investment," *Review of Economics and Statistics,* February, 1948; reprinted as Appendix B in Hansen, *Monetary Theory and Fiscal Policy.*

But consumers' expectations may usually be regarded as related closely to current and past trends. If this were not so, expectations, together with expenditure plans based on them, would have to be regarded as exogenous, unrelated to the variables which are endogenous to the system itself. Exogenous expectations (based on inventions, etc.) certainly play an important role with respect to *investment* decisions. It is, however, a reasonable assumption that *consumers'* expenditures are determined mainly by income earned currently (Keynes) or in the recent past (Robertson), and only to a very limited degree by exogenous expectations not based on present and past experience.

In his *Quarterly Journal* article,[13] Robertson developed a model based on the assumption (as also in the Machlup-Hansen models) that today's consumption is determined by yesterday's income, tomorrow's consumption by today's income,[14] etc. If today's consumption is in fact not related functionally to yesterday's income, but instead behaves capriciously or depends mainly upon some other variables, then the Robertsonian concepts lose all operational or analytical value. The definitions still hold—that is, $S_1 = Y_0 - C_1$ and $Y_1 = I_1 + C_1$—but if consumption is unrelated functionally to income, then any autonomous increase in C_1 will by definition mean a decrease in S_1. In this case (Robertson's first formulation), the equations become purely tautological. An excess of I_1 over S_1 by *definition* means simply an excess of Y_1 over Y_0, and vice versa. If, however, C_1 *is functionally related* to Y_0 (second formulation), then the equations become determinate; the analysis, running in terms of the relation of saving to investment as defined by Robertson, then acquires operational value.

The Robertsonian formal identity, $I_1 - S_1 = Y_1 - Y_0$, springs to life only when there is added to it the living verifiable hypothesis that the left-hand side of the equation is a known quantity, depending (once the autonomous pattern of investment is given)

[13] In his *Essays on Monetary Theory* (p. 7), however, he suggests that current consumption may be influenced by expectations regarding future income.

[14] This lagged adjustment reveals a divergence between "desired" saving and "actual" saving, not a difference between planned investment and planned saving in the Swedish sense.

upon previous income through the assumption that today's consumption is a determinate function of yesterday's income. But even when we make this empirical assumption and consider the simplest case of a new permanent plateau of investment, we will not find it very informative to say that the cause of the growth of income is the excess of investment over saving,[15] since this statement applies only to *each step* in the process. The complete multiplier process involves, however, a succession of steps, and finally approaches a limiting asymptote. $(I_1 - S_1) + (I_2 - S_2) + \ldots\ldots (I_n - S_n) = k\triangle I$. But the value of k is determined by the marginal propensity to consume, derived from the consumption function, which is a schedule of economic behavior. $Y = k\triangle I$ is not a mere identity equation; it is a determinate equation based on a verifiable pattern of behavior.

III

This brings us to the Swedish concepts. Can the process of income expansion or contraction be analyzed in terms of the divergence between planned saving and planned investment as these terms are usually defined in the Swedish literature?

The Swedish analysis does not relate "today" to "tomorrow" or "yesterday" to "today." Instead it considers the relation of tomorrow's "planned investment" to tomorrow's "planned saving," [16] and these in turn are regarded as related to tomorrow's "expected income." But realized income may diverge from expected income.

Tomorrow's "expected income" may, however, mean either of two quite different things, and this fact is the source of much confusion. First, it may refer to the total sales (of both investment and consumption goods) expected by *entrepreneurs.* Second, it may refer to the income expected by consumers. If consumers expect a certain income, they will plan to consume a part of it and to save a part, according to the propensity-to-consume schedule.

---

15 Robertson's excess of investment over saving is fundamentally similar to the analysis of Tugan-Baranowsky and Wicksell with respect to the divergencies of investment from saving. See Chapters 16 and 17 in this book.

16 "Planned consumption" (or "planned saving") is a function of the "expected income" of consumers.

Similarly, tomorrow's "realized income" is also ambiguous. It may be used to mean actual sales. Or again it may be used to mean actual output. The question involved is whether unintended inventory accumulation is or is not to be counted as a part of "realized income."

We may, then, differentiate the following concepts:

1. Tomorrow's "expected income," an ambiguous term, may be used to mean either of the following:
   (a) The income expected by consumers.
   (b) The sales expected by entrepreneurs.
2. Tomorrow's "realized income," also an ambiguous term, may be used to mean either of the following:
   (a) Actual output (the result of production plans carried out by entrepreneurs).
   (b) Actual sales (the result of purchase plans, i.e., investment plans plus consumption plans).

We must assume that plans—whether purchase plans or production plans—are carried out, else they would have no meaning. Ohlin says so specifically: "Investment plans, like consumption plans, are realised as far as purchases go." [17] Plans that are not executed have no significance. But production plans (including the production of both investment and consumption goods) may differ from the purchase plans. Thus total planned production may not equal planned investment plus planned consumption. If the production plans exceed the purchase plans, there will be unintended inventory accumulation. "Realized investment" thus exceeds "planned investment." The production plans are based on *expected* sales; but since the actual sales may differ from the expected sales, unintended changes may occur in the inventory stocks. Ohlin puts this very clearly when he says that "investment is influenced also by sales from stock of goods, and these sales may differ from expectations." [18] All this relates to the output lag—the divergence of output from sales; it cannot be stated in terms of the looser concept of the divergence between planned investment and planned saving.

It is the sales expected by entrepreneurs which determine

---

17 *Readings in Business Cycle Theory,* footnote p. 127.

18 *Ibid.*

production plans, and these, when carried out, determine what tomorrow's realized output will be. But how are *purchase* plans (investment and consumption) determined? Investment purchase plans are only in part determined by expected sales, being in large measure determined by autonomous factors, including inventions and cost-reducing improvements. Now the expectations of entrepreneurs are one thing and the expectations of consumers are another. And particularly with respect to the latter, the theory of expectations has very little to go on.

Ohlin is himself aware that nothing can be learned about income changes from one period to another by comparing planned investment with planned saving. In one place [19] he says categorically that planned investment and planned saving may be equal, yet income may still rise. Income will, in fact, rise if investment and consumption purchases rise from period to period. In each period, however, planned saving and planned investment may well be equal. In another place,[20] after first stating that "the discrepancy between planned savings and planned investment can be regarded as the cause of the expansion (or contraction) process," he adds that this is only "one side of the story." "Even if planned savings and planned investment should happen to be equal, a process of expansion is possible."

As already noted, Ohlin recognizes that the planned-saving, planned-investment approach cannot be relied upon to explain income changes. What then? Apart from lapses into a type of analysis fundamentally similar to the Robertsonian, resort is had to a succession of expectations which cause total expenditures (income) to rise or fall. Says Ohlin: "The cumulative process—meaning a continuing rise in total purchases relative to the normal development—goes on so long as *expectations are such* that the investment purchases and the consumption purchases involve a relative rise in total purchases. This rather meaningless conclusion is not without importance, as it shows clearly that the 'cumula-

19 *Ibid.*, p. 127.

20 *Ibid.*, p. 103. See also Ohlin, *The Problem of Employment Stabilization*, Columbia University Press, 1949, p. 119, where he says (referring to the possibility that people may expect higher incomes and therefore increase their consumption outlays): "If so, there will be a process of expansion, even if planned saving equals planned investment—which is quite possible."

tive' character of the process depends on the fact that certain kinds of expectations are set up." [21] Total expenditures then rise or fall according to a sequence of expectations which determine successive investment and consumption plans.[22] The analysis of the expansion and contraction process in terms of a divergence of saving and investment is therefore in effect abandoned.

The level of income is indeed determined by decisions to invest and decisions to consume. The investment demand schedule is based on entrepreneurial expectations. But there are strong reasons for believing that consumption decisions are mainly determined by the level of current (and recent) income.

IV

A basic postulate of the second Robertsonian formulation is the dependence of consumption on the income of the recent past. When an increase or decrease in income occurs, induced changes in consumption expenditures occur. But consumption expenditures lag behind. Thus there develops, in consequence of a change in income, a divergence between desired (normal or equilibrium) consumption and actual consumption. By "desired consumption" I mean that (steady) rate of consumption which would be compatible with the actual present level of income *maintained indefinitely over time at a steady rate*. Suppose, however, that expenditures do not stand in the normal or desired relation to current income. Accordingly, expenditures are changed in the succeeding period, and thus further changes in income will occur until an equilibrium position is eventually reached. At this point desired consumption equals actual consumption. This amounts to the same thing as saying that desired saving and realized saving are equal.

The output lag,[23] on the other hand, is due to a divergence between planned output (which is related to expected sales) and realized sales. By reason of this divergence, unintentional invest-

---

21 *Readings in Business Cycle Theory,* p. 110.

22 Investment and consumption plans in *successive* periods, not the divergence of planned investment and planned saving in the same period.

23 The inventory models developed by Metzler (*Review of Economic Statistics,* August, 1941, and February, 1947) illustrate the output lag. See also Lundberg, *Economic Expansion,* P. S. King & Son, Ltd., London, 1937.

ment (or disinvestment) in inventories occurs. Entrepreneurs, accordingly, find their inventory stocks too high (or too low). In consequence, investment outlays in the succeeding period are altered and so further changes in income are brought about. At equilibrium, "intended" investment equals actual investment. Unintended investment thus plays a role in the oscillations of income.

In the recent revised edition (1948) of Robertson's *Money,* a chapter is appended in which "intended investment" and "designed saving" are used in a sense corresponding to my "intended (desired) investment" and "desired saving." Robertson here explains that intended investment and designed saving will be equal at the point of equilibrium, while actual investment and actual saving (being mere identities) are always equal. "So it is equality of *designed* or *intended* 'investment,' not of actual 'investment,' with designed saving that can be regarded as a condition of equilibrium." [24]

At equilibrium, as we have indicated above, "intended investment" equals actual investment, and "desired saving" equals actual saving. But since *actual* investment and *actual* saving are always equal, it follows that *at equilibrium* "intended investment" must equal "desired saving." Nevertheless, taken by itself alone, this statement is not fully adequate.

While the equality of intended investment and designed (desired) saving is a *necessary* condition of equilibrium, it is not a *sufficient* condition for equilibrium. Suppose the existing level of income (today) is 100, while the intended investment (for tomorrow) is 10 and intended or designed saving is also 10, intended consumption being 90. New entrepreneurs may nonetheless expect consumption to be 100 and so plan an output of 110. In this event there will be an unintended inventory accumulation of 10. This is not an equilibrium position. Actual investment is in excess of intended investment and actual saving is in excess of designed saving; yet intended investment is equal to designed saving. The condition of equilibrium requires *both* that intended investment shall be equal to designed saving *and* that actual in-

---

24 Dennis H. Robertson, *Money,* Second Revised Edition, Isaac Pitman and Sons, 1948, p. 210.

vestment shall be equal to intended investment. Or what comes to the same thing, the condition of equilibrium requires *both* that intended investment shall be equal to actual investment and *also* that desired (or designed) saving shall be equal to actual saving.

A dynamics of income development has scarcely been formalized as yet. Economists have long had the notion that the system is driven upward or downward by the "discrepancy" between certain magnitudes, just as the furnace of a house is driven by the discrepancy between the "intended" temperature set into the thermostat and the actual room temperature. But it is the upshot of the previous discussion that business-cycle writers have been confused with respect to the definitions and significance of the various quantities whose discrepancies are given such an important role. To an electrical engineer, the magnitudes involved in the thermostat case are perfectly clear; but in the economic literature there is too often an ambiguity in the concepts used and a confusion with respect to their formal and observable relations to each other.

The above reflections suggest the following conclusions:

1. The discrepancy between investment and saving (second Robertsonian formulation) is a useful way of analyzing fluctuations in income. The *primary* inflationary gap, for example, can conveniently be stated in terms of a divergence between the prospective *actual* investment, I_2, in the next quarter and the saving (S_2) from the income (Y_1) of the current quarter. $I_2 - S_2$ gives the primary inflationary gap. The full inflationary gap, primary and secondary, involves the multiplier effect in addition to the initial impulse; it is equal to $(I_2 - S_2)k$.

2. The discrepancy between "intended investment" and "actual investment" means unintended inventory change. The resulting undesired condition brings about expansion or contraction. This output-lag analysis is useful for the study of oscillations.

3. The discrepancy between actual consumption and desired consumption (actual saving vs. desired saving) is a useful way of stating the multiplier process over time.

Bibliography

Abramovitz, Moses: *Inventories and Business Cycles,* National Bureau of Economic Research, New York, 1950.

———: *The Role of Inventories in Business Cycles,* Occasional Paper 26, National Bureau of Economic Research, New York, 1948.

Aftalion, Albert: "La Réalité des surproductions générales. Essai d'une théorie des crises générales et périodiques," *Revue d'économie politique,* 1909.

———: *Les Crises périodiques de surproduction,* Vols. I and II, Marcel Rivière et Cie., Paris, 1913.

———: "The Theory of Economic Cycles Based on the Capitalistic Technique of Production," *Review of Economic Statistics,* October, 1927.

Åkerman, Johan: *Economic Progress and Economic Crises,* Macmillan & Co., Ltd., London, 1932.

American Economic Association, Committee of: *Readings in Business Cycle Theory,* Blakiston, Philadelphia, 1944.

———: *Readings in Monetary Theory,* Blakiston, Philadelphia, 1951.

Angell, James W.: *Investment and Business Cycles,* McGraw-Hill Book Co., New York, 1941.

Barger, H.: *Outlay and Income in the United States,* National Bureau of Economic Research, New York, 1942.

Beveridge, W. H.: *Full Employment in a Free Society,* W. W. Norton & Co., New York, 1945.

Bickerdike, C. F.: "A Non-Monetary Cause of Fluctuations in Employment," *Economic Journal,* September, 1914.

Bishop, G. A.: "The Tax Burden by Income Class, 1958," *National Tax Journal,* March, 1961.

Bratt, E. D.: *Business Cycles and Forecasting,* Irwin, Homewood, Illinois, 5th ed., 1961.

Brookings Institution: *America's Capacity to Consume,* Washington, 1934.

———: *America's Capacity to Produce,* 1934.

———: *The Formation of Capital,* 1935.

———: *The Recovery Problem in the United States,* 1936.

Burns, Arthur: *Economic Research and the Keynesian Thinking of Our Times,* National Bureau of Economic Research, New York, 1946.

———: "Keynesian Economics Once Again," *Review of Economic Statistics,* November, 1947.

———: *New Facts on Business Cycles,* 30th Annual Report of the National Bureau of Economic Research, Inc., New York, 1950.

———: *The Frontiers of Economic Knowledge,* Princeton University Press for National Bureau of Economic Research, Princeton, 1954.

Burns, Arthur (Ed.): *Wesley Clair Mitchell, the Economic Scientist,* National Bureau of Economic Research, New York, 1952.

Burns, A. F., and Mitchell, W. C.: *Measuring Business Cycles,* National Bureau of Economic Research, New York, 1946.

Carver, T. N.: "A Suggestion for a Theory of Industrial Depressions," *Quarterly Journal of Economics,* May, 1903.

Cassel, Gustav: *Theory of Social Economy,* Harcourt, Brace & Co., New York, 1932.

Clark, Colin: *The Conditions of Economic Progress,* Macmillan & Co., Ltd., London, 1940.

———: *The Economics of 1960,* Macmillan & Co., Ltd., London, 1942.

Clark, J. M.: "Business Acceleration and the Law of Demand," *Journal of Political Economy,* 1917.

———: *The Economics of Overhead Costs,* University of Chicago Press, Chicago, 1923.

———: "Capital Production and Consumer Taking—A Reply," *Journal of Political Economy,* December, 1931.

———: *Strategic Factors in Business Cycles,* National Bureau of Economic Research, New York, 1934.

———: *Economics of Planning Public Works: A Study Made for the National Planning Board,* Government Printing Office, Washington, 1935.

———: *Social Control of Business,* rev. ed., University of Chicago Press, Chicago, 1939.

———: "Financing High-Level Employment," *Financing American Prosperity,* Twentieth Century Fund, New York, 1945.

Clemence, R. V. and Doody, F. S.: *The Schumpeterian System,* Augustus Kelly, New York, 1962.

Cole, A. H.: *Wholesale Commodity Prices in the United States, 1700–1861,* Harvard University Press, Cambridge, 1938.

Columbia University Commission: *Economic Reconstruction,* Columbia University Press, New York, 1934.

Committee for Economic Development: *Taxes and the Budget,* November, 1947, and other policy statements.

Copeland, M. A.: *A Study of Money Flows in the United States,* National Bureau of Economic Research, New York, 1952.

Cowles, Alfred, 3d: "Can Stock Market Forecasters Forecast?" *Econometrica,* July, 1933.

Cox, G. V.: *An Appraisal of American Business Forecasts,* University of Chicago Press, Chicago, 1930.

Creamer, D.: *Personal Income During Business Cycles,* Princeton University Press for National Bureau of Economic Research, Princeton, 1956.

de Laveleye, Emile: *Le Marché monétaire et ses crises depuis cinquante ans,* Guillaumin, Paris, 1865.

Dewey, D. R.: *Financial History of the United States,* 12th ed., Longmans, Green & Co., New York, 1934.

Dewey, E. R., and Dakin, E. F.: *Cycles, the Science of Prediction,* Henry Holt & Co., New York, 1947.

Dillard, Dudley: *The Economics of John Maynard Keynes,* Prentice-Hall, New York, 1948.
Domar, E. D.: "Expansion and Employment," *American Economic Review,* March, 1947; "The Problem of Capital Accumulation," *American Economic Review,* December, 1948.
Douglas, Paul: *Controlling Depressions,* W. W. Norton & Co., New York, 1935.
Duesenberry, James: *Income, Saving and the Theory of Consumer Behavior,* Harvard University Press, Cambridge, 1949.
———: *Business Cycles and Economic Growth,* McGraw-Hill Book Co., New York, 1958.
Economic Essays In Honor of Gustav Cassel, George Allen & Unwin, Ltd., London, 1933.
Economic Essays In Honor of Wesley Clair Mitchell, Columbia University Press, New York, 1935.
Economic Report of the President, together with the Annual Economic Review of the Council of Economic Advisers, Washington, D.C., 1948 and since.
Edie, Lionel D.: *The Stabilization of Business,* The Macmillan Co., New York, 1923.
Einarsen, Johan: *Reinvestment Cycles and Their Manifestation in the Norwegian Shipping Industry,* University Institute of Economics, Oslo, 1938.
Ellis, H. S. (Ed.): *Survey of Contemporary Economics,* The Blakiston Co., Philadelphia, 1948.
———: *German Monetary Theory,* Harvard University Press, Cambridge, 1934.
England, M. T.: "Analysis of the Crises Cycle," *Journal of Political Economy,* October, 1913.
———: "Promotion as the Cause of Crises," *Quarterly Journal of Economics,* August, 1915.
Ezekial, Mordecai: "The Cob-Web Theorem," *Quarterly Journal of Economics,* February, 1938.
Fellner, William: *Monetary Policies and Full Employment,* University of California Press, Berkeley, 1946. "Employment Theory and Business Cycles," Chapter 2 in *A Survey of Contemporary Economics,* The Blakiston Co., Philadelphia, 1948.
———: "The Robertsonian Evolution," *American Economic Review,* June, 1952.
———: *Trends and Cycles in Economic Activity,* Henry Holt & Co., New York, 1956.
Fels, R.: *American Business Cycles 1865–1897,* University of North Carolina Press, Chapel Hill, 1959.
Firestone, J. M.: *Federal Receipts and Expenditures During Business Cycles, 1897–1958,* Princeton University Press for National Bureau of Economic Research, Princeton, 1960.
Fisher, Irving: *Rate of Interest,* The Macmillan Company, New York, 1907.
———: "Our Unstable Dollar and the So-Called Business Cycle," *Journal of the American Statistical Association,* June, 1925.
———: *Theory of Interest,* The Macmillan Company, New York, 1930.
———: *Booms and Depressions,* Adelphi Co., New York, 1932.
Foster, W. T., and Catchings, W.: *Profits,* Houghton Mifflin Co., Pollak Foundation, Boston, 1925.
Frickey, Edwin: *Economic Fluctuations in the United States,* Harvard Univer-

sity Press, Cambridge, 1942.
———: *Production in the United States 1860–1914,* Harvard University Press, Cambridge, 1947.
Friedman, M.: *A Theory of the Consumption Function,* Princeton University Press for National Bureau of Economic Research, Princeton, 1957.
Frisch, Ragnar: "The Interrelation between Capital Formation and Consumer-Taking," *Journal of Political Economy,* October, 1931, and April, 1932.
———: "Propagation Problems and Impulse Problems in Dynamic Economics," in *Economic Essays in Honor of Gustav Cassel,* George Allen & Unwin, Ltd., London, 1933.
Galbraith, J. K.: "The Disequilibrium System," *American Economic Review,* June, 1947.
Gayer, A. D. (Ed.): *The Lessons of Monetary Experience: Essays in Honor of Irving Fisher,* Farrar & Rinehart, Inc., New York, 1937.
Goodwin, R. M.: "Innovations and Irregularity of Economic Cycles," *Review of Economic Statistics,* May, 1946.
———: "A Non-linear Theory of the Cycle," *The Review of Economics and Statistics,* November, 1950.
Gordon, R. A.: "A Selected Bibliography of the Literature on Economic Fluctuations, 1930–36," *Review of Economic Statistics,* February, 1937.
———: "A Selected Bibliography of the Literature on Economic Fluctuations, 1936–37," *Review of Economic Statistics,* August, 1938.
———: *Business Fluctuations,* Harper & Brothers, New York, 2nd ed., 1961.
Haberler, Gottfried: *Prosperity and Depression,* League of Nations, Geneva, and Columbia University Press, New York, 1941. 4th ed., Harvard University Press, Cambridge, 1958.
Hansen, Alvin H.: *Cycles of Prosperity and Depression in the United States, Great Britain and Germany: A Study of Monthly Data, 1902–08,* University of Wisconsin, 1921.
———: *Business-Cycle Theory,* Ginn & Co., Boston, 1927.
———: *Economic Stabilization in an Unbalanced World,* Harcourt, Brace, New York, 1932.
———: *Full Recovery or Stagnation?* W. W. Norton & Co., New York, 1938.
———: *Fiscal Policy and Business Cycles,* W. W. Norton & Co., New York, 1941.
———: *Economic Policy and Full Employment,* McGraw-Hill Book Co., New York, 1947.
———: *Monetary Theory and Fiscal Policy,* McGraw-Hill Book Co., New York, 1949.
———: *A Guide to Keynes,* McGraw-Hill Book Co., New York, 1953.
———: *The American Economy,* McGraw-Hill Book Co., New York, 1957.
———: *Economic Issues of the 1960's,* McGraw-Hill Book Co., New York, 1960.
———: *Letter to The New York Times,* May 27, 1962.
———: "A Permanent Tax Cut Now," *Challenge,* October, 1962.
Hansen, Alvin H., and Clemence, Richard V.: *Readings in Business Cycles and National Income,* W. W. Norton & Co., New York, 1953.
Hansen, Alvin H., and Tout, Herbert: "Investment and Saving in Business-Cycle Theory," *Econometrica,* April, 1933.
Hardy and Cox: *Forecasting Business Conditions,* The Macmillan Company, New York, 1927.
Harris, Seymour E.: *Inflation and the American Economy,* McGraw-Hill Book Co., New York, 1945.

———(Ed.): *Postwar Economic Problems,* McGraw-Hill Book Co., New York, 1943.
———(Ed.): *New Economics,* A. Knopf, New York, 1947.
———(Ed.): *Schumpeter, Social Scientist,* Harvard University Press, Cambridge, 1951.
Harrod, Roy F.: *The Trade Cycle,* Clarendon Press, Oxford, England, 1936.
———: *Towards a Dynamic Economics,* Macmillan & Co., Ltd., London, 1948.
———: *The Life of John Maynard Keynes,* Macmillan & Co., Ltd., London, 1951.
Hart, Albert G.: *Money, Debt, and Economic Activity,* Prentice-Hall, New York, 1948.
Hawtrey, R. G.: *Good and Bad Trade,* Constable Co., Ltd., London, 1913.
———: *Currency and Credit,* Longmans, Green & Co., New York, 1919.
———: *Monetary Reconstruction,* Longmans, Green & Co., New York, 1923.
———: *The Economic Problem,* Longmans, Green & Co., New York, 1925.
———: *Capital and Employment,* Longmans, Green & Co. New York, 1937.
———: *The Gold Standard in Theory and Practice,* Longmans, Green & Co., New York, 1947 (first edition in 1927).
Hayek, Frederick: *Prices and Production,* George Routledge & Sons, Ltd., London, 1931.
———: *Monetary Theory and the Trade Cycle,* Harcourt, Brace & World, New York, 1932.
———: *Profits, Interest and Investment,* George Routledge & Sons, Ltd., London, 1939.
Hexter, M. B.: *Social Consequences of the Business Cycle,* Houghton Mifflin Co., Boston, 1925.
Hicks, J. R.: *Value and Capital,* Oxford University Press, Oxford, England, 1939.
———: *A Contribution to the Theory of the Trade Cycle,* Oxford University Press, Oxford, England, 1950.
Higgins, Benjamin: *Public Investment and Full Employment,* International Labour Office, Montreal, 1946.
———: *Trade Cycle,* Oxford University Press, London, 1950.
Hobson, John A.: *The Industrial System* (new and revised edition), Longmans, Green & Co., London, 1910.
———: *The Economics of Unemployment,* George Allen & Unwin, Ltd., London, 1922.
Hobson, J. A., and Mummery, A. F.: *Physiology of Industry,* London, 1889.
Homan, P. T., and Machlup, F. (Eds.): *Financing American Prosperity,* Twentieth Century Fund, New York, 1945.
Hull, G. H.: *Industrial Depressions,* Frederick A. Stokes Co., New York, 1911.
Hultgren, Thor: *Cyclical Diversities in the Fortunes of Industrial Corporations,* Occasional Paper 32, National Bureau of Economic Research, New York, 1950.
Income, Employment and Public Policy, W. W. Norton & Co., New York, 1948.
Isard, W.: "Transport Development and Building Cycles," *Quarterly Journal of Economics,* November, 1942.
———: "A Neglected Cycle: The Transport-Building Cycle," *Review of Economic Statistics,* November, 1942.
James, H. M. (Ed.): *Theories of Servomechanisms,* M.I.T. Radiation Laboratory Series, McGraw-Hill Book Co., New York, 1947.

Jerome, Harry: *Migration and Business Cycles,* National Bureau of Economic Research, New York, 1926.
Jevons, W. S.: *Investigations in Currency and Finance,* Macmillan & Co., Ltd., London, 1884.
Johannsen, N.: *A Neglected Point in Connection with Crises,* Bankers Publishing Co., New York, 1908.
———: *Business Depressions, Their Cause* (pamphlet), Stapleton Press, New York, 1925.
Juglar, Clément: *Des Crises Commerciales* (first edition, 1860, second edition, 1889), Guillaumin, Paris.
Kahn, R. F.: "The Relation of Home Investment to Employment," *Economic Journal,* June, 1931.
Kaldor, N.: "Stability and Full Employment," *Economic Journal,* December, 1938.
———: "A Model of the Trade Cycle," *Economic Journal,* March, 1940.
Kalecki, Mr.: "A Macrodynamic Theory of Economic Fluctuations," *Econometrica,* July, 1935.
———: *Essays in the Theory of Economic Fluctuations,* Farrar & Rinehart, New York, 1939.
———: *Economics of Full Employment,* Blackwell, Oxford, England, 1944.
———: *Studies in Economic Dynamics,* Farrar & Rinehart, Inc., New York, 1944.
Keynes, J. M.: *Monetary Reform,* Harcourt, Brace & Co., New York, 1924.
———: *Treatise on Money,* Harcourt, Brace & Co., New York, 1930.
———: *Means to Prosperity,* Macmillan & Co., Ltd., London, 1933.
———: *General Theory of Employment, Interest and Money,* Harcourt, Brace & Co., New York, 1936.
Kitchin, Joseph: *First Interim Report of the Gold Delegation,* League of Nations, Geneva, 1930.
Klein, Lawrence R.: *The Keynesian Revolution,* The Macmillan Company, New York, 1947.
———: *Economic Fluctuations in the United States,* John Wiley & Sons, Inc., New York, 1950.
Koopmans, T.: "The Logic of Econometric Business Cycle Research," *Journal of Political Economy,* April, 1941.
Kondratieff, N. D.: "The Long Waves in Economic Life," *Review of Economic Studies,* November, 1935.
Kuznets, Simon: *Cyclical Fluctuations,* Adelphi Co., New York, 1926.
———: *Secular Movements of Production and Prices,* Houghton Mifflin Co., Boston, 1930.
———: *National Income and Capital Formation, 1919–1935,* National Bureau of Economic Research, New York, 1937.
———: *National Income and Its Composition,* Vol. I, National Bureau of Economic Research, New York, 1941.
———: *National Income, A Summary of Findings,* National Bureau of Economic Research, New York, 1946.
———: *Economic Change: Selected essays in business cycles, national income, and economic growth,* W. W. Norton & Co., New York, 1953.
———: *Capital in the American Economy, Its Formation and Financing,* Princeton University Press for National Bureau of Economic Research, Princeton, 1961.

Lauderdale, Lord: *An Inquiry into the Nature and Origin of Public Wealth and into the Means and Causes of Its Increase,* Archibald Constable & Co., Edinburgh, 1819 (2nd ed.).

League of Nations: *The Course and Phases of the World Economic Depression,* rev. ed., World Peace Foundation, Boston, 1931.

———: *Economic Stability in the Post-War World,* Report of the Delegation on Economic Depressions, Part II, Geneva, 1945.

Lerner, A. P.: *Economics of Control,* The Macmillan Company, New York, 1944.

———: *Economics of Employment,* McGraw-Hill Book Co., New York, 1951.

Lerner, A. P., and Graham, F. D.: *Planning and Paying for Full Employment,* Princeton University Press, Princeton, 1946.

Lescure, Jean: *Des Crises générales et périodiques de surproduction,* Librairie du Recueil Sirey, 1907.

Lester, Richard A.: *Monetary Experiments,* Princeton University Press, Princeton, 1939.

Lewis, Wilfred, Jr.: *Federal Fiscal Policy in the Postwar Recession,* The Brookings Institution, Washington, D.C., 1962.

Lindahl, Eric: *Studies in the Theory of Money and Capital,* George Allen & Unwin, Ltd., London, 1939.

Long, Clarence D., Jr.: *Building Cycles and the Theory of Investment,* Princeton University Press, Princeton, 1940.

Lundberg, Erik: *Studies in the Theory of Economic Expansion,* P. S. King, London, 1937.

———(Ed.): *The Business Cycle in the Post-War World,* St. Martin's Press, New York, 1955.

Malthus, T. R.: *Principles of Political Economy,* William Pickering, London, 1836.

Marshall, Alfred: *Principles of Economics,* Macmillan & Co., Ltd., London, 7th edition (1st edition 1890).

———: *Money, Credit and Commerce,* Macmillan & Co., Ltd., London, 1923.

Marshall, Alfred, and Marshall, Mary: *Economics of Industry,* Macmillan & Co., Ltd., London, 1879 (reprinted in 1881, 1883, 1884, 1885, 1886 1888).

Marx, Karl: *Das Kapital,* Vol. I, 1867, Vol. II, 1885, Vol. III, 1894, Charles Kerr & Co. edition, 1907.

Marx, Karl and Engels, Friedrich: *Communist Manifesto,* 1848.

Mason, E. S.: *Controlling World Trade,* McGraw-Hill Book Co., New York, 1946.

———: "Presidential Address," *American Economic Review,* March, 1963.

Matthews, R. C. O.: *The Business Cycle,* University of Chicago Press, Chicago, 1962.

Maxwell, J. A.: *Tax Credits and Intergovernmental Fiscal Relations,* The Brookings Institution, Washington, D.C., 1962.

Metzler, Lloyd: "The Nature and Stability of Inventory Cycles," *Review of Economic Statistics,* August, 1941.

———: "Business Cycles and the Modern Theory of Employment," *American Economic Review,* June, 1946.

———: "Factors Governing the Length of Inventory Cycles," *Review of Economic Statistics,* February, 1947.

Mill, John Stuart: *Principles of Political Economy* (1st edition, 1848); new edition edited by W. J. Ashley, Longmans, Green and Co., New York, 1909 (reprinted in 1920).

Mills, John: "Credit Cycles and the Origin of Commercial Panics," *Transactions of the Manchester Society*, Manchester, 1867.

Mitchell, Wesley: *History of Greenbacks*, University of Chicago Press, Chicago, 1903.

———: *Business Cycles*, University of California Press, Berkeley, 1913.

———: "Interest Cost and the Business Cycle," *American Economic Review*, June, 1926.

———: *Business Cycles, the Problem and Its Setting*, National Bureau of Economic Research, New York, 1927.

———: "The Role of Research in Economic Progress," *The Conditions of Industrial Research*, University of Pennsylvania, Philadelphia, 1947.

———: *What Happens During Business Cycles—A Progress Report*, National Bureau of Economic Research, New York, 1951.

Monetary, Credit and Fiscal Policies (Douglas Report), Senate Document No. 129, 81st Congress, 2nd Session, Washington, D.C., 1950.

Money, Trade, and Economic Growth, The Macmillan Company, New York, 1951.

Moore, Geoffrey H.: *Statistical Indicators of Cyclical Revivals and Recessions*, Occasional Paper 31, National Bureau of Economic Research, New York, 1950.

———(Ed.): *Business Cycle Indicators*, 2 Vols., Princeton University Press for National Bureau of Economic Research, Princeton, 1961.

Moore, H. L.: *Economic Cycles: Their Law and Cause*, The Macmillan Company, New York, 1914.

———: *Generating Economic Cycles*, The Macmillan Company, New York, 1923.

Morgenstern, O.: *International Financial Transactions and Business Cycles*, Princeton University Press for National Bureau of Economic Research, Princeton, 1959.

Musgrave, Richard A.: *Public Finance and Full Employment*, Postwar Economic Studies, Board of Governors, Federal Reserve System, Washington, 1945.

Myrdal, Gunnar: *Monetary Equilibrium*, W. Hodge & Co., Ltd., London, 1939.

Newman, W. H.: *The Building Industry and Business Cycles*, University of Chicago Press, Chicago, 1935.

Ohlin, Bertil: "Some Notes on the Stockholm Theory of Savings and Investment," *Economic Journal*, March, 1937.

———: *The Problem of Employment Stabilization*, Columbia University Press, New York, 1949.

Oxford University, Institute of Statistics: *The Economics of Full Employment: Six Studies in Applied Economics*, Blackwell, Oxford, England, 1944.

Persons, W. M.: *Forecasting Business Cycles*, John Wiley & Sons, New York, 1931.

Phillips, A. W.: "The Relation Between Unemployment and the Rate of Change Of Money Wage Rates in the United Kingdom, 1861–1957," *Economica*, November, 1958.

Phinney, J. T.: "Gold Production and the Price Level: The Cassel Three Per Cent Estimate," *Quarterly Journal of Economics*, August, 1933.

Pierson, J. H. G.: *Full Employment*, Yale University Press, New Haven, 1941.

Pigou, A. C.: *Economics of Welfare*, Macmillan & Co., Ltd., London, 1920.

———: *Is Unemployment Inevitable?* Macmillan & Co., Ltd., London, 1924.

———: *Industrial Fluctuations,* Macmillan & Co., Ltd., London, 1927.

———: *Employment and Equilibrium,* Macmillan & Co., Ltd., London, 1941, 1949.

———: "Employment Policy and Sir William Beveridge," *Agenda,* August, 1944.

———: *John Maynard Keynes,* Printed for King's College, Cambridge, England, 1949.

———: *Keynes's "General Theory,"* Macmillan, London and New York, 1950.

Pohle, Ludwig: *Bevölkerungsbewegung, Kapitalbildung, und Periodische Wirtschaftskrisen,* Göttingen, 1902.

Ricardo, David: *Works and Correspondence of David Ricardo* (Ed. Sraffa), Cambridge University Press, Cambridge, England, 10 vols., 1955.

Riefler, Winfield W.: *Money Rates and Money Markets in the United States,* Harper & Bros., New York, 1930.

Robbins, Lionel: *The Great Depression,* The Macmillan Company, New York, 1934.

Robertson, D. H.: *A Study of Industrial Fluctuations,* P. S. King & Son, Ltd., Westminster, 1915.

———: *Banking Policy and the Price Level,* P. S. King & Son, Ltd., Westminster, 1926.

———: *Essays in Monetary Theory,* P. S. King & Son, Ltd., Westminster, 1940.

———: *Money* (Cambridge Economic Handbooks), Nisbet, London, 1948.

Robinson, Joan: *Essays in the Theory of Employment,* The Macmillan Company, New York, 1937.

———: *The Rate of Interest and Other Essays,* Macmillan & Co., Ltd., London, 1952.

Roos, C. F.: *Dynamic Economics,* Principia Press, Bloomington, Ind., 1934.

Röpke, Wilhelm: *Crises and Cycles,* William Hodge & Co., Ltd., London, 1936.

Rostow, W. W.: *British Economy of the Nineteenth Century,* Oxford University Press, 1948.

Ruggles, Richard: *National Income and Income Analysis,* McGraw-Hill Book Co., New York, 1949.

Samuelson, Paul A.: "Interaction between the Multiplier Analysis and the Principle of Acceleration," *Review of Economic Statistics,* May, 1939.

———: "Full Employment After the War," Chapter II in *Post-War Economic Problems,* McGraw-Hill Book Co., New York, 1943.

———: *Foundations of Economic Analysis,* Harvard University Press, Cambridge, 1947.

———: "Alvin Hansen and the Interactions Between the Multiplier and the Principle of Acceleration," *Review of Economics and Statistics,* May, 1959.

Schultz, Henry: *The Theory and Measurement of Demand,* University of Chicago Press, Chicago, 1938.

Schultz, T. W.: *Agriculture in an Unstable Economy,* McGraw-Hill Book Co., New York, 1945.

Schultz, T. W. et al.: "Investment in Human Beings," *Journal of Political Economy,* October, 1962.

Schumpeter, J. A.: *Theory of Economic Development,* Harvard University Press, Cambridge, 1934.

———: *Business Cycles,* McGraw-Hill Book Co., New York, 1939.

———: *Capitalism, Socialism, and Democracy,* Harper & Bros., New York, 1942.

———: *Essays* (Ed. R. V. Clemence), Addison-Wesley, Cambridge, 1951.
———: *Ten Great Economists—from Marx to Keynes,* Oxford University Press, New York, 1951.
———: *History of Economic Analysis,* Oxford University Press, New York, 1954.
———: "Über das Wesen der Wirtschaftskrisen," *Zeitschrift für Volkswirtschaft,* 1910.
———: "Die Wellenbewegung des Wirtschaftslebens," *Archiv für Sozialwissenschaft und Sozialpolitik.*
Shackle, G. L. S.: *Expectations, Investment, and Income,* Oxford University Press, New York, 1938.
Shaw, Edward S.: *Money, Income, and Monetary Policy,* Richard D. Irwin, Inc., Chicago, 1950.
Shoup, Carl S.: *Principles of National Income Analysis,* Houghton Mifflin Co., Boston, 1947.
Silberling, N. A.: *The Dynamics of Business,* McGraw-Hill Book Co., New York, 1943.
Simons, Henry: *Economic Policy for a Free Society,* University of Chicago Press, Chicago, 1948.
Sismondi, Jean C. L.: *Nouveaux Principes d'Economie Politique,* 2nd ed., Delaunay, Paris, 1827.
Slichter, S. H.: *Towards Stability,* Henry Holt & Co., New York, 1934.
———: *The American Economy,* Alfred A. Knopf, New York, 1948.
Slutzky, Eugen: "The Summation of Random Causes as the Source of Cyclic Processes," *Econometrica,* April, 1937.
Smith, Sir Hubert Llewellyn: *Report on Distress from Want of Employment,* Commission of Labor, Labor Department of the Board of Trade, Great Britain, 1895.
Smith, W. B., and Cole, A. H.: *Fluctuations in American Business, 1790–1860,* Harvard University Press, Cambridge, 1935.
Smithies, Arthur: "Process Analysis and Equilibrium Analysis," *Econometrica,* January, 1942.
———: "Full Employment in a Free Society," *American Economic Review,* June, 1945.
Snyder, Carl: "Influence of Interest Rate on the Business Cycle," *American Economic Review,* December, 1925.
———: *Business Cycles and Business Measurements,* The Macmillan Co., New York, 1927.
———: *Capitalism, the Creator,* The Macmillan Co., New York, 1940.
Somers, H. M.: *Public Finance and National Income,* The Blakiston Co., Philadelphia, 1949.
Spiethoff, Arthur: *Encyclopaedia of the Social Sciences,* Vol XI, The Macmillan Co., New York.
———: "Vorbemerkungen zu einer Theorie der Überproduktion," *Jahrbuch für Gesetzgebung, Verwaltung und Volkswirtschaft,* 1902.
———: "Die Krisentheorien von M. von Tugan-Baranowsky und L. Pohle," *Jahrbuch für Gesetzgebung, Verwaltung und Volkswirtschaft,* 1903.
———: "Krisen," *Handwörterbuch der Staatswissenschaften,* 1925. English translation in *International Economic Papers,* No. 3, Macmillan, London and New York, 1953.
———: *Festschrift für Arthur Spiethoff,* Duncker & Humblot, Munich, 1933.

———: *Die Wietschaftlichen Wechsellagen,* 2 vols., Mohr, Tübingen, 1955.

Sprague, O. M. W.: *History of Crises under the National Banking System,* Publications of the National Monetary Commission, Senate Document No. 538 (61st Cong., 2nd Sess.), 1909.

———: "Discount Policy of Federal Reserve Bank," *American Economic Review,* March, 1921.

Stanback, T. M.: *Postwar Cycles in Manufacturers' Inventories,* Princeton University Press for National Bureau of Economic Research, Princeton, 1962.

Temporary National Economic Committee: *Recovery Plans,* Monograph No. 25, Government Printing Office, Washington, D.C., 1940.

Terborgh, George: *The Bogey of Economic Maturity,* Machinery and Allied Products Institute, Chicago, 1945.

Thomas, Brinley: "The Monetary Doctrines of Professor Davidson," *Economic Journal,* March, 1935.

———: *Monetary Policy and Crises,* George Routledge & Sons, Ltd., London, 1936.

Thorp, W. L., and Mitchell, W. C.: *Business Annals,* National Bureau of Economic Research, New York, 1926.

Tinbergen, J.: "Bestimmung und Deutung von Angebotskurven, Ein Beispiel," *Zeitschrift für Nationalökonomie,* 1930.

———: "Annual Survey: Suggestions on Quantitative Business Cycle Theory," *Econometrica,* July, 1935.

———: *An Econometric Approach to Business-Cycle Problems,* Hermann et Cie., Paris, 1937.

———: *Les Fondements Mathématiques de la Stabilisation du Mouvement des Affaires,* Paris, 1938.

———: *Statistical Testing of Business Cycle Theories,* Vol. I, *A Method and Its Application to Investment Activity,* Vol. II, *Business Cycles in the United States of America, 1919–32,* League of Nations, Geneva, 1939.

Tinbergen, J., and Polak, J. J.: *The Dynamics of Business Cycles,* University of Chicago Press, Chicago, 1950.

Tugan-Baranowsky, Michel: *Studien zur Theorie und Geschichte der Handelskrisen in England,* Jena, 1901; French edition, *Les Crises industrielles en Angleterre,* 1913.

United Nations: *National and International Measures for Full Employment,* Department of Economic Affairs, December, 1949.

Veblen, Thorstein: *The Theory of Business Enterprise,* Charles Scribner's Sons, New York, 1904.

Wagemann, Ernst: *Economic Rhythm: A Theory of Business Cycles,* McGraw-Hill Book Co., New York, 1930.

Warren, G. F., and Pearson, F. A.: *Prices,* John Wiley & Sons, New York, 1933.

———: *World Prices and the Building Industry,* John Wiley & Sons, New York, 1937.

Wicksell, Knut: *Geldzins und Güterpreise,* Gustav Fischer, Jena, 1898.

———: *Lectures on Political Economy,* Vol. I, *General Theory,* 1934, Vol. II, *Money,* 1935, Macmillan & Co., Ltd., London.

———: *Interest and Prices,* Macmillan & Co., Ltd., London, 1936.

Wiener, N.: *Cybernetics,* published by Technology Press of M.I.T., John Wiley & Sons, Inc., New York, and Hermann & Cie., Paris, 1948.

Williams, J. H.: "Free Enterprise and Full Employment," *Financing American Prosperity,* Twentieth Century Fund, New York, 1945.

———: *Post-War Monetary Plans,* Blackwell, Oxford, 1949.
Williams, J. H.: *Economic Stability in a Changing World—Essays in Economic Theory and Policy,* Oxford University Press, New York, 1953.
Wilson, T.: *Fluctuations in Income and Employment,* Pitman, New York, 1948.
Wright, D. M.: *The Creation of Purchasing Power,* Harvard University Press, Cambridge, 1942.
———: *The Economics of Disturbance,* The Macmillan Company, New York, 1947.

Index